BUSINESS FINANCE FOR THE MULTINATIONAL CORPORATION

Taken from:

Multinational Business Finance, Eleventh Edition
by David K. Eiteman, Arthur I. Stonehill, and Michael H. Moffett

Corporate Financial Management, Third Edition
by Douglas R. Emery, John D. Finnerty, and John D. Stowe

Custom Publishing

New York   Boston   San Francisco
London   Toronto   Sydney   Tokyo   Singapore   Madrid
Mexico City   Munich   Paris   Cape Town   Hong Kong   Montreal

Taken from:

Multinational Business Finance, Eleventh Edition
by David K. Eiteman, Arthur I. Stonehill, and Michael H. Moffett
Copyright © 2007 by Pearson Education, Inc.
Published by Addison Wesley, Inc.
Boston, Massachusetts 02116

Corporate Financial Management, Third Edition
by Douglas R. Emery, John D. Finnerty, and John D. Stowe
Copyright © 2007, 2004, 1997 by Pearson Education, Inc.
Published by Prentice-Hall, Inc.
Upper Saddle River, New Jersey 07458

All rights reserved. No part of this book may be reproduced, in any form or by any means, without permission in writing from the publisher.

This special edition published in cooperation with Pearson Custom Publishing.

All trademarks, service marks, registered trademarks, and registered service marks are the property of their respective owners and are used herein for identification purposes only.

Printed in the United States of America

10 9 8 7 6 5

ISBN 0-536-39498-9

2007160113

EM

Please visit our web site at *www.pearsoncustom.com*

**Pearson
Custom Publishing**
is a division of

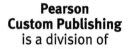

www.pearsonhighered.com

ISBN 10: 0-536-39498-9
ISBN 13: 978-0-536-39498-9

CONTENTS

COMPARATIVE CORPORATE GOVERNANCE AND FINANCIAL GOALS

1

This book is about international financial management with special emphasis on the *multinational enterprise.* The multinational enterprise (MNE) is defined as one that has operating subsidiaries, branches, or affiliates located in foreign countries. It also includes firms in service activities such as consulting, accounting, construction, legal, advertising, entertainment, banking, telecommunications, and lodging.

MNEs are headquartered all over the world. Many of them are owned by a combination of domestic and foreign shareholders. The ownership of some firms is so dispersed internationally that they are known as transnational corporations. The transnationals are usually managed from a global perspective rather than from the perspective of any single country.

Although *Multinational Business Finance* (MBF) emphasizes MNEs, purely domestic firms also often have significant international activities. These include the import and export of products, components, and services. Domestic firms can also license foreign firms to conduct their foreign business. They have exposure to foreign competition in their domestic market. They also have indirect exposure to international risks through their relationships with customers and suppliers. Therefore, domestic firm managers need to understand international financial risk, especially those related to foreign exchange rates and the credit risks related to trade payments.

1.1 WHAT IS DIFFERENT ABOUT GLOBAL FINANCIAL MANAGEMENT?

Table 1-1 describes in detail some of the main differences between international and domestic financial management. These differences include institutions, foreign exchange and political risks, and the modifications required to financial theory and financial instruments.

International financial management requires an understanding of cultural, historical, and institutional differences with a potential effect on corporate governance. Although both domestic firms and MNEs are exposed to foreign exchange risks, MNEs alone face certain unique risks that are not normally a threat to domestic operations, such as political risks.

MNEs also face other tasks that can be classified as extensions of domestic finance theory. For example, the normal domestic approaches to the cost of capital, sourcing debt and equity, capital budgeting, working capital management, taxation, and credit analysis need to be modified to accommodate foreign complexities. Moreover, a number of financial instruments that are used in domestic financial management have been modified for use in international financial management. Examples are foreign currency options and futures, interest rate and currency swaps, and letters of credit.

The rest of this chapter examines how cultural, historical, legal, political, and institutional differences affect a firm's choice of financial goals and corporate governance.

1.2 SEPARATION OF OWNERSHIP FROM MANAGEMENT

The U.S. and U.K. stock markets are characterized by widespread ownership of shares. Management owns only a small proportion of stock in their own firms. In contrast, in the rest of the world, ownership is usually characterized by controlling shareholders. Typical controlling shareholders are:

1. Government (such as privatized utilities)
2. Institutions (such as banks in Germany)

TABLE 1-1   What Is Different About International Financial Management?

CONCEPT	INTERNATIONAL	DOMESTIC
Culture, history and institutions	Each foreign country is unique and not always understood by MNE management	Each country has a known base case
Corporate governance	Foreign countries' regulations and institutional practices are all uniquely different	Regulations and institutions are well known
Foreign exchange risk	MNEs face foreign exchange risks due to their subsidiaries, as well as import/export and foreign competitors	Foreign exchange risks from import/export and foreign competition (no subsidiaries)
Political risk	MNEs face political risks because of their foreign subsidiaries and high profile	Negligible political risks
Modification of domestic finance theories	MNEs must modify finance theories like capital budgeting and cost of capital because of foreign complexities	Traditional financial theory applies
Modification of domestic financial instruments	MNEs utilize modified financial instruments such as options, futures, swaps, and letters of credit	Limited use of financial instruments and derivatives because of fewer foreign exchange and political risks

3. Family (such as are common in France and Asia)
4. Consortiums (such as *keiretsus* in Japan and *chaebols* in South Korea).

Control is enhanced by ownership of shares with dual voting rights, interlocking directorates, staggered election of the board of directors, takeover safeguards, and other techniques not used in the Anglo-American markets.

1.3   WHAT IS THE GOAL OF MANAGEMENT?

The introductory course in finance is usually taught within the framework of maximizing shareholders' wealth as *the goal of management*. This perspective is dominant not only in the Anglo-American-based courses, but also to some extent in basic finance courses taught in the rest of the world. One has only to observe that the same textbooks, or translated versions, are used worldwide. Even when local authors write basic finance textbooks for their own national markets, they still often adopt the same prescriptive model that is used in the Anglo-American markets.

Although the goal of maximizing shareholder wealth is probably realistic both in theory and in practice in the Anglo-American markets, it is not always exclusive elsewhere. Some basic differences in corporate and investor philosophies exist between the Anglo-American markets and those in the rest of the world. Therefore, one must realize that the so-called "universal truths" taught in basic finance courses are actually "culturally determined norms."

Shareholder Wealth Maximization Model

The Anglo-American markets have a philosophy that a firm's objective should follow the *shareholder wealth maximization* (SWM) model. More specifically, the firm should strive to maximize the return to shareholders, as measured by the sum of capital gains and dividends, for a given level of risk. Alternatively, the firm should minimize the risk to shareholders for a given rate of return.

The SWM model assumes as a universal truth that the stock market is *efficient*. This description means that the share price is always correct because it captures all the expectations of return and risk as perceived by investors. It quickly incorporates new information into the share price. Share prices, in turn, are deemed the best allocators of capital in the macro economy.

The SWM model also treats its definition of risk as a universal truth. Risk is defined as the added risk that the firm's shares bring to a diversified portfolio. The total operational risk of the firm can be eliminated through portfolio diversification by the investors. Therefore, this *unsystematic risk*, the risk of the individual security, should not be a prime concern for management unless it increases the prospect of bankruptcy. *Systematic risk*, the risk of the market in general, cannot be eliminated. This concept reflects risk that the share price will be a function of the stock market.

AGENCY THEORY   The field of *agency theory* is the study of how shareholders can motivate management to accept the prescriptions of the SWM model.[1] For example, liberal use of stock options should encourage management to think like shareholders. Whether these inducements succeed is open to debate. However, if management deviates too much from SWM objectives of working to maximize the returns to the shareholders, the board of directors should replace them. In cases where the board is too weak or ingrown to take this action, the discipline of the equity markets could do it through a takeover. This discipline is made possible by the one-share-one-vote rule that exists in most Anglo-American markets.

---

[1]Michael Jensen and W. Meckling, "Theory of the Firm: Managerial Behavior, Agency Costs, and Ownership Structure," *Journal of Financial Economics*, No. 3, 1976, and Michael C. Jensen, "Agency Cost of Free Cash Flow, Corporate Finance and Takeovers, *American Economic Review*, 76, 1986, pp. 323–329.

LONG-TERM VERSUS SHORT-TERM VALUE MAXIMIZATION   During the 1990s, the economic boom and rising stock prices in the United States and abroad exposed a flaw in the SWM model, especially in the United States. Instead of seeking long-term value maximization, several large U.S. corporations sought short-term value maximization (e.g., the continuing debate about meeting the market's expected quarterly earnings). This strategy was partly motivated by the overly generous use of stock options to motivate top management. In order to maximize growth in short-term earnings and to meet inflated expectations by investors, firms such as Enron, Global Crossing, HealthSouth, Adelphia, Tyco, Parmalat, and WorldCom undertook risky, deceptive, and sometimes dishonest practices for the recording of earnings and/or obfuscation of liabilities, which ultimately led to their demise. Such practices also led to highly visible prosecutions of their CEOs, CFOs, accounting firms, legal advisors, and other related parties. This destructive short-term focus by both management and investors has been correctly labeled *impatient capitalism*. This point of debate is also sometimes referred to as the firm's *investment horizon*, in reference to how long it takes the firm's actions, its investments and operations, to result in earnings.

In contrast to impatient capitalism is *patient capitalism*, which focuses on long-term shareholder wealth maximization. Legendary investor Warren Buffett, through his investment vehicle Berkshire Hathaway, represents one of the best of the patient capitalists. Buffett has become a multibillionaire by focusing his portfolio on mainstream firms that grow slowly but steadily with the economy, such as Coca-Cola. He was not lured into investing in the high-growth but risky dot-coms of 2000 or the "high-tech" sector that eventually imploded in 2001.

Stakeholder Capitalism Model

In the non-Anglo-American markets, controlling shareholders also strive to maximize long-term returns to equity. However, they are more constrained by powerful other stakeholders. In particular, labor unions are more powerful than in the Anglo-American markets. Governments interfere more in the marketplace to protect important stakeholder groups, such as local communities, the environment, and employment. Banks and other financial institutions are more important creditors than securities markets. This model has been labeled the *stakeholder capitalism model* (SCM).

MARKET EFFICIENCY   The SCM model does not assume that equity markets are either efficient or inefficient. Their inefficiency does not really matter, because the firm's financial goals are not exclusively shareholder-oriented, because they are constrained by the other stakeholders. In any case, the SCM model assumes that long-term "loyal" shareholders—typically controlling shareholders—should influence corporate strategy, rather than the transient portfolio investor.

RISK   The SCM model assumes that *total risk*—that is, operating and financial risk—does count. It is a specific corporate objective to generate growing earnings and dividends over the long run with as much certainty as possible, given the firm's mission statement and goals. Risk is measured more by product market variability than by short-term variation in earnings and share price.

SINGLE VERSUS MULTIPLE GOALS   Although the SCM model typically avoids a flaw of the SWM model—namely, impatient capital that is short-run oriented—it has its own flaw. Trying to meet the desires of multiple stakeholders leaves management without a clear signal about the tradeoffs. Instead, management tries to influence the tradeoffs through written and oral disclosures and complex compensation systems.

THE SCORE CARD   In contrast to the SCM model, the SWM model requires a single goal of value maximization with a well-defined score card. In the words of Michael Jensen:

> *Maximizing the total market value of the firm – that is, the sum of the market values of the equity, debt, and any other contingent claims outstanding on the firm is the objective function that will guide managers in making the optimal tradeoffs among*

multiple constituencies (or stakeholders). It tells the firm to spend an additional dollar of resources to satisfy the desires of each constituency as long as that constituency values the result at more than a dollar. In this case, the payoff to the firm from the investment of resources is at least a dollar (in terms of market value).[2]

Although both models have their strengths and weaknesses, two trends in recent years have led to an increasing focus on the shareholder wealth form. First, as more of the non-Anglo-American markets have increasingly privatized their industries, the shareholder wealth focus is seemingly needed to attract international capital from outside investors, many of whom are from other countries. Second, and still quite controversial, many analysts believe that shareholder-based MNEs are increasingly dominating their global industry segments. Nothing attracts followers like success. *Global Finance in Practice 1.1* illustrates the movement toward shareholder wealth in Germany.

Global Finance in Practice 1.1

Changing Values: Satisfying Shareholders

Ulrich Hartmann, the chief executive of industrial giant Veba AG, is doing something unheard of in Germany: he's worrying about shareholder value. He has laid off thousands of workers, fired longtime managers, and closed divisions that date back to Veba's beginnings—all in the name of investors. "Our commitment," he said in last year's annual report, "is to create value for you, our shareholders."

The developments at Veba, Germany's fourth-largest company in revenue terms, underscore a trend catching hold in German boardrooms. Mr. Hartmann believes the trend will pick up in Germany if only, he says, because the pursuit of shareholder value is in everyone's interest. "Satisfying the shareholders is the best way to make sure that other stakeholders are served as well," he says. "It does no good when all the jobs are at sick companies."

But the German public—used to a fabled "German model" of management that advocates describe as "capitalism with a human face"—remains deeply suspicious of the alternative way of doing business. "A number of people are left behind," says Norbert Wieczorek, a member of Germany's lower house of parliament and an economic expert with the opposition Social Democratic Party. "That's not the German way."

Mr. Hartmann is one of a new breed of German managers who are enthusiastically embracing the shareholder-value concept. Others are Juergen Dormann at Hoescht AG and Juergen Schrempp at Daimler-Benz AG. During a recent interview, a secretary interupted the conversation to notify Mr. Schrempp of Daimler's opening stock price. "A year ago, no one in the company knew what the stock price was," he says. Now, he adds, the company keeps stockholders in mind with everything it does.

Driving companies to change are ever-growing capital requirements. Unable to raise enough money in Germany, companies are turning to foreigners. Nearly half the shares of drug companies Hoechst, Bayer AG, and Schering AG are owned by non-Germans, who want more than just a dividend check. "There is no German or French or American capital market anymore," says Veba's Mr. Hartmann. "It is a global capital market, and we all have to play by the same rules."

Source: Greg Steinmetz, "Changing Values: Satisfying Shareholders Is a Hot New Concept at Some German Firms," *The Wall Street Journal*, 3/6/96, pp. A1, A10.

---

[2]Michael C. Jensen, "Value Maximization, Stakeholder Theory, and the Corporate Objective Function," *Journal of Applied Corporate Finance*, Volume 14, No. 3, Fall 2001, p. 12.

Operational Goals for MNEs

The MNE must be guided by operational goals suitable for various levels of the firm. Even if the firm's goal is to maximize shareholder value, the manner in which investors value the firm is not always obvious to the firm's top management. Many top executives believe that the stock market moves in mysterious ways and is not always consistent in its conclusions. Therefore, most firms hope to receive a favorable investor response to the achievement of operational goals that can be controlled by the way in which the firm performs.

The MNE must determine for itself the proper balance between three common operational financial objectives:

1. Maximization of consolidated after-tax income.
2. Minimization of the firm's effective global tax burden.
3. Correct positioning of the firm's income, cash flows, and available funds as to country and currency.

These goals are frequently incompatible, in that the pursuit of one may result in a less-desirable outcome in regard to another. Management must make decisions about the proper tradeoffs between goals about the future (which is why people rather than computers are employed as managers). The operational goals should be guided by an understanding of what variables create or destroy value as detailed in *Global Finance in Practice 1.2.*

CONSOLIDATED PROFITS   The primary operational goal of the MNE is to maximize consolidated profits, aftertax. *Consolidated profits* are the profits of all the individual units of the firm originating in many different currencies expressed in the currency of the parent company. This is not to say that management is not striving to maximize the present value of all future cash flows. It is simply the case that most of the day-to-day decision making in global management is about current earnings. The leaders of the MNE, the senior management team who are developing and implementing the firm's strategy, must think far beyond current earnings.

For example, foreign subsidiaries have their own set of traditional financial statements: (1) a statement of income, summarizing the revenues and expenses experienced by the firm over the year; (2) a balance sheet, summarizing the assets employed in generating the unit's revenues, and the financing of those assets; and (3) a statement of cash flows, summarizing those activities of the firm that generate and then use cash flows over the year. These financial statements are expressed initially in the local currency of the unit for tax and reporting purposes to the local government, but must be consolidated with the parent company's financial statements for reporting to shareholders.

1.4   CORPORATE GOVERNANCE

Although the governance structure of any company—domestic, international, or multinational—is fundamental to its very existence, this subject has become a lightning rod for political and business debate in the past few years, as failures in governance in a variety of forms have led to corporate fraud and failure. Abuses and failures in corporate governance have dominated global business news in recent years. Beginning with the accounting fraud and questionable ethics of business conduct at Enron, culminating in its bankruptcy in the fall of 2001, failures in corporate governance have raised issues about the very ethics and culture of the conduct of business.

The Goal of Corporate Governance

The single overriding objective of corporate governance is the optimization over time of the returns to shareholders. In order to achieve this goal, good governance practices should focus the attention

Global Finance in Practice 1.2

What Drives Value?

The concept of *shareholder value* is often misunderstood by business executives and investors alike. Measurements of capital gains (share price movements) and dividends (current income distributions) do not tell the entire story of how shareholder value is created. Analysts and investors, however, look far beyond the basics of financial performance in their assessment of corporate value. They look to the knowledge assets of the firm.

Knowledge assets are the company's intangible assets, the sources and uses of its intellectual talent—its competitive advantage. Experts argue that there are at least 10 categories of knowledge assets:

1. Innovation
2. Quality
3. Customer care
4. Management skill
5. Alliances
6. Research and product/service development
7. Technology to streamline operations
8. Brand value
9. Employee relations
10. Environmental and community awareness

The investor is not looking at past performance as demonstrated by the numbers, but the prospects for the future, and their probable returns on investment. It is therefore critical for management to communicate their visions regarding the prospects for the future to investors and analysts. And what is it that the analyst and investor want? They want transparency, honesty, and openness. They want management to demonstrate their abilities to do what they say they will do. They want clearly defined strategies, measurable results, and a value proposition.

What Destroys Value?

Sometimes the most important thing to know is what *not* to do. Although there are countless books, periodicals, courses, and seminars to help key decision makers define and refine their strategies and implementation plans, there are still lessons to be learned from past mistakes. A recent Forrester survey of Fortune 1000 global companies separated the primary causes of stock value losses (25% or more) into four categories: strategic (58% of total causes), operational (31%), financial (6%), and hazard (5%).

Strategic

Customer demand shortfall	24%
Competitive pressure	12%
Mergers and acquisitions integration problems	7%
Misaligned products	6%
Customer pricing pressure	4%
Loss of key customer	2%
Regulatory problems	1%
Research and development delays	1%
Supplier problems	1%

Operational

Cost overruns	11%
Accounting irregularities	7%
Management ineffectiveness	7%
Supply chain issues	6%

Financial

Foreign macroeconomic issues	3%
High-input commodity prices	2%
Interest rate fluctuations	1%

Hazard

Lawsuits	1%
Natural disasters	1%

Source: www.forrester.com (undated).

of the board of directors of the corporation on this objective by developing and implementing a strategy for the corporation that ensures corporate growth and improvement in the value of the corporation's equity. At the same time, good governance practices should assure an effective relationship with stakeholders.[3]

---

[3]This definition of the corporate objective is based on that supported by the International Corporate Governance Network (ICGN), a nonprofit organization committed to improving corporate governance practices globally.

The most widely accepted statement of good corporate governance practices are those established by the Organisation for Economic Cooperation and Development (OECD):[4]

1. **The rights of shareholders.** The corporate governance framework should protect shareholders' rights.

2. **The equitable treatment of shareholders.** The corporate governance framework should ensure the equitable treatment of all shareholders, including minority and foreign shareholders. All shareholders should have the opportunity to obtain effective redress for violation of their rights.

3. **The role of stakeholders in corporate governance.** The corporate governance framework should recognize the rights of stakeholders as established by law and encourage active cooperation between corporations and stakeholders in creating wealth and jobs, and the sustainability of financially sound enterprises.

4. **Disclosure and transparency.** The corporate governance framework should ensure that timely and accurate disclosure is made on all material matters regarding the corporation, including the financial situation, performance, ownership, and governance of the company.

5. **The responsibilities of the board.** The corporate governance framework should ensure the strategic guidance of the company, the effective monitoring of management by the board, and the board's accountability to the company and the shareholders.

These principles obviously focus on several key areas—shareholder rights and roles, disclosure and transparency, and the responsibilities of boards—which we will discuss in more detail in the following sections.

The Structure of Corporate Governance

Our first challenge is to try and capture what people mean when they use the expression "corporate governance." Figure 1-1 provides an overview of the various parties and their responsibilities associated with the governance of the modern corporation. The modern corporation's actions and behaviors are directed and controlled by both internal forces and external forces.

The *internal forces*, the officers of the corporation (such as the chief executive officer, or CEO) and the board of directors of the corporation (including the chairman of the board), are those directly responsible for determining both the strategic direction and the execution of the company's future. But they are not acting within a vacuum; they are subject to the constant prying eyes of the *external forces* in the marketplace, who question the validity and soundness of their decisions and performance. These forces include the equity markets in which the shares are traded, the analysts who critique their investment prospects, the creditors and credit agencies who lend them money, the auditors and legal advisors who testify to the fairness and legality of their reporting, and the multitude of regulators who oversee their actions in order to protect the investing public.

THE BOARD OF DIRECTORS   The legal body that is accountable for the governance of the corporation is its board of directors. The board is composed of both employees of the organization (inside members) and senior and influential non-employees (outside members). Areas of debate surrounding boards include the following: (1) the proper balance between inside and outside members; (2) the means by which board members are compensated for their service; and (3) the actual ability of a board to adequately monitor and manage a corporation when board members are spending sometimes less than five days a year in board activities. Outside members, very often the current or retired chief executives of other major companies, might bring with them a healthy sense of distance and impartiality, which although refreshing can also result in limited understanding of the true issues and events within the company.

---

[4]"OECD Principles of Corporate Governance," The Organisation for Economic Cooperation and Development, 1999, revised 2004. http://www.oecd.org. Available free online.

FIGURE 1-1   The Structure of Corporate Governance.

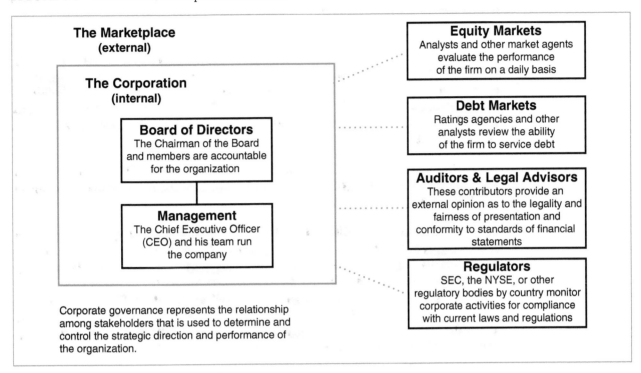

Corporate governance represents the relationship among stakeholders that is used to determine and control the strategic direction and performance of the organization.

OFFICERS AND MANAGEMENT   The senior officers of the corporation—the chief executive officer (CEO) the chief financial officer (CFO), and the chief operating officer (COO)—are not only the employees most knowledgeable of the business, but the creators and directors of its strategic and operational direction. The management of the firm is, according to theory, acting as a contractor—as an *agent*—of shareholders to pursue value creation. They are motivated by salary, bonuses, and stock options (positively) or the risk of losing their jobs (negatively). They might, however, have biases of self-enrichment or personal agendas that the board and other corporate stakeholders are responsible for overseeing and policing. Interestingly enough, in more than 80% of the companies in the Fortune 500, the CEO is also the chairman of the board. This is, in the opinion of many, a conflict of interest and not in the best interests of the company and its shareholders.

EQUITY MARKETS   A publicly traded company, regardless of country of residence, is highly susceptible to the changing opinion of the marketplace. The equity markets themselves, whether they be the New York Stock Exchange, London Stock Exchange, or Mexico City Bolsa, should reflect the market's constant evaluation of the promise and performance of the individual company. The analysts are those self-described experts employed by the many investment banking firms who also trade in the client company shares. They are expected (sometimes naively) to evaluate the strategies, plans for execution of the strategies, and financial performance of the firms on a real-time basis. Analysts depend on the financial statements and other public disclosures of the firm for their information.

DEBT MARKETS   Although the debt markets (banks and other financial institutions providing loans and various forms of securitized debt, like corporate bonds) are not specifically interested in building shareholder value, they are indeed interested in the financial health of the company. Their interest, specifically, is in the company's ability to repay its debt in a timely and efficient manner. These markets, like the equity markets, must rely on the financial statements and other disclosures (public and private, in this case) of the companies with which they work.

AUDITORS AND LEGAL ADVISORS   Auditors and legal advisors are responsible for providing an external professional opinion as to the fairness, legality, and accuracy of corporate financial statements. In this process, they attempt to determine whether the firm's financial records and practices follow what in the United States is termed *generally accepted accounting principles* (GAAP) in regard to accounting procedures. But auditors and legal advisors are hired by the firms they are auditing, leading to a rather unique practice of policing their employers. An additional difficulty that has arisen in recent years is that the major accounting firms pursued the development of large consulting practices, often leading to a conflict of interest. An auditor not giving a clean bill of health to a client could not expect to gain many lucrative consulting contracts from that same firm in the near future.

REGULATORS   Publicly traded firms in the United States and elsewhere are subject to the regulatory oversight of both governmental organizations and nongovernmental organizations. In the United States, the Securities and Exchange Commission (SEC) is a careful watchdog of the publicly traded equity markets, both of the behavior of the companies themselves in those markets and of the various investors participating in those markets. The SEC and other authorities like it outside of the United States require a regular and orderly disclosure process of corporate performance, so that all investors may evaluate the company's investment value with adequate, accurate, and fairly distributed information. This regulatory oversight is often focused on when and what information is released by the company, and to whom.

A publicly traded firm in the United States is also subject to the rules and regulations of the exchange upon which they are traded (New York Stock Exchange, American Stock Exchange, and NASDAQ being the largest). These organizations, typically categorized as "self-regulatory" in nature, construct and enforce standards of conduct for both their member companies and themselves in the conduct of share trading. Unfortunately, as the recent case of Richard Grasso (former New York Stock Exchange Chairman) and his retirement package of $148 million highlighted, it often appears that the "fox is in charge of the hen house."

Comparative Corporate Governance

The origins of the need for a corporate governance process arise from two sources: (1) the separation of ownership from management; and (2) the varying views by culture of who the stakeholders are and their relative significance. These two distinct features of global business assure that corporate governance practices will differ—sometimes dramatically—across countries, economies, and cultures. Table 1-2 provides one method of classifying corporate governance regimes. The four regimes described here are primarily based on the evolution of business ownership within the countries noted over time.[5]

Market-based regimes, like those of the United States, Canada, Australia, and the United Kingdom, are characterized by relatively efficient capital markets in which the ownership of publicly traded companies is widely dispersed. *Family-based systems*, like those characterized in many of the emerging markets, Asian markets, and Latin American markets, not only started with strong concentrations of family ownership (as opposed to partnerships or small investment groups that are not family-based), but have continued to be largely controlled by families even after going public. *Bank-based* and *government-affiliated* regimes reflect markets in which government ownership of

[5]For a summary of comparative corporate governance, see R. La Porta, F. Lopez-de-Silanes, and A. Schleifer, "Corporate Ownership Around the World," *Journal of Finance*, 54, 1999, pp. 471–517. See also A. Schleifer and R. Vishny, "A Survey of Corporate Governance," *Journal of Finance*, 52, 1997, pp. 737–783.

TABLE 1-2
Comparative
Corporate
Governance
Regimes.

REGIME BASIS	CHARACTERISTICS	EXAMPLES
Market-based	Efficient equity markets; dispersed ownership	United States, United Kingdom, Canada, Australia
Family-based	Management & ownership is combined; family/majority and minority shareholders	Hong Kong, Indonesia, Malaysia, Singapore, Taiwan, France
Bank-based	Government influence in bank lending; lack of transparency; family control	Korea, Germany
Government-affiliated	State ownership of enterprise; lack of transparency; no minority influence	China, Russia

Source: Based on "Corporate Governance in Emerging Markets: An Asian Perspective," by J. Tsui and T. Shieh, *International Finance and Accounting Handbook,* Third Edition, Frederick D.S. Choi, editor, Wiley, 2004, pp. 24.4–24.6.

property and industry has been the constant force over time, resulting in only marginal "public ownership" of enterprise that is even then subject to significant restrictions on business practices.

These regimes are therefore a function of at least four major factors in the evolution of corporate governance principles and practices globally: (1) financial market development; (2) the degree of separation between management and ownership; (3) the concept of disclosure and transparency; and (4) the historical development of the legal system.

FINANCIAL MARKET DEVELOPMENT   The depth and breadth of capital markets is critical to the evolution of corporate governance practices. National markets that have had relatively slow growth (such as in the emerging markets), or have industrialized rapidly utilizing neighboring capital markets (as is the case of Western Europe), might not form large public equity market systems. Without significant public trading of ownership shares, high concentrations of ownership are preserved and few disciplined processes of governance developed.

SEPARATION OF MANAGEMENT AND OWNERSHIP   In countries and cultures in which the ownership of the firm has continued to be an integral part of management, agency issues and failures have been less of a problem. In countries like the United States, in which ownership has become largely separated from management (and widely dispersed), aligning the goals of management and ownership is much more difficult.

DISCLOSURE AND TRANSPARENCY   The extent of disclosure regarding the operations and financial results of a company vary dramatically across countries. Disclosure practices reflect a wide range of cultural and social forces, including the degree of ownership that is public, the degree to which government feels the need to protect investors' rights versus ownership rights, and the extent to which family-based and government-affiliated business remains central to the culture. Transparency, a parallel concept to disclosure, reflects the visibility of decision-making processes within the business organization.

HISTORICAL DEVELOPMENT OF THE LEGAL SYSTEM   Investor protection is typically better in countries in which *English common law* is the basis of the legal system, compared to the *codified civil law* that is typical in France and Germany (the so-called *Code Napoleon*). English common law is typically the basis of the legal systems in the United Kingdom and its former colonies, including the United States and Canada. The Code Napoleon is typically the basis of the legal systems in former French colonies and the European countries that Napoleon once ruled, such as Belgium, Spain, and Italy. In countries with weak investor protection, controlling shareholder ownership is often a substitute for a lack of legal protection.

Note that the word "ethics" has not been used. All of the principles and practices described so far have assumed that the individuals in roles of responsibility and leadership pursue them truly and fairly. That, however, has not always been the case.

Family Ownership and Corporate Governance

Although much of the discussion about corporate governance concentrates on the market-based regimes (see Table 1-2), family-based regimes are arguably more common and more important worldwide, including in the United States and Western Europe. For example, in a study of 5,232 corporations in 13 Western European countries, family-controlled firms represented 44% of the sample, compared to 37% that were widely held.[6]

Recent research indicates that, as opposed to popular belief, family-owned firms in some highly developed economies typically outperform publicly owned firms. This higher performance is true not only in Western Europe but also in the United States. A recent study of firms included in the Standard and Poors 500 (S&P500) found that families are present in fully one-third of the S&P500 and account for 18% of their outstanding equity. And, as opposed to popular opinion, family firms outperform nonfamily firms. (An added insight is that firms possessing a CEO from the family also perform better than those with outside-CEOs.) Interestingly, it seems that minority shareholders are actually better off according to this study when part of a family-influenced firm.[7]

Another study based on 120 Norwegian, founding-family-controlled and non-founding-family-controlled firms concluded that founding family control was associated with higher firm value. Furthermore, the impact of founding family directors on firm value is not affected by corporate governance conditions such as firm age, board independence, and number of share classes. The authors also found that the positive relation between founding family ownership and firm value is greater among older firms and firms with larger boards, particularly when these firms have multiple classes of stock.[8] It is common for Norwegian firms and firms based in several other European countries to have dual classes of stock with differential voting rights.

Failures in Corporate Governance

Failures in corporate governance have become increasingly visible in recent years. The Enron scandal in the United States is described in the Mini-Case at the end of this chapter. In addition to Enron, other firms that have revealed major accounting and disclosure failures, as well as executives looting the firm, are WorldCom, Parmalat, Global Crossing, Tyco, Adelphia, and HealthSouth.

In each case, prestigious auditing firms, such as Arthur Andersen, missed the violations or minimized them, possibly because of lucrative consulting relationships or other conflicts of interest. Moreover, security analysts and banks urged investors to buy the shares and debt issues of these and other firms that they knew to be highly risky or even close to bankruptcy. Even more egregiously, most of the top executives that were responsible for the mismanagement that destroyed their firms walked away (initially) with huge gains on shares sold before the downfall, and with overly generous severance payments.

---

[6]Mara Faccio and Larry H. P. Lang, "The Ultimate Ownership of Western European Corporations," *Journal of Financial Economics*, 65, 2002, p. 365. See also Torben Pedersen and Steen Thomsen, "European Patterns of Corporate Ownership," *Journal of International Business Studies*, Vol. 28, No. 4, Fourth Quarter 1997, pp. 759–778.
[7]Ronald C. Anderson and David M. Reeb, "Founding Family Ownership and Firm Performance from the S&P500," *The Journal of Finance*, June 2003, p. 1,301.
[8]Chandra S. Mishra, Trond Randøy, and Jan Inge Jenssen, "The Effect of Founding Family Influence on Firm Value and Corporate Governance," *Journal of International Financial Management and Accounting*, Volume 12, Number 3, Autumn 2001, pp. 235–259.

It appears that the day of reckoning has come. The first to fall was Arthur Andersen, one of the former "Big Five" U.S. accounting firms, due to its involvement with Enron. However, many more legal actions against former executives are underway. Although the corruption scandals were first revealed in the United States, they have spread to Canada and the European Union countries. These scandals are described in *Global Finance in Practice 1.3*.

Good Corporate Governance and Reputation

Does good corporate governance matter? This is actually a difficult question, and the realistic answer has been largely dependent on outcomes historically. For example, as long as Enron's share price continued to rise dramatically throughout the 1990s, questions over transparency, accounting propriety, and even financial facts were largely overlooked by all of the stakeholders of the corporation. Yet eventually, the fraud, deceit, and failure of the multitude of corporate governance practices resulted in the bankruptcy of the firm. It not only destroyed the wealth of investors, but the careers, incomes, and savings of so many of its basic stakeholders—its own employees. Ultimately, *yes*, good governance does matter. A lot.

A second way of valuing good governance is by measuring the attitudes and tendencies of the large global institutional investors who make the largest decisions about where capital may go. A recent McKinsey study surveyed more than 200 institutional investors as to the value they placed on good governance. The survey results, presented in Figure 1-2, quantify good governance in the premium that institutional investors would be willing to pay for companies with good governance within specific national markets. Although this is not exactly equivalent to

Global Finance in Practice 1.3

When Scandals Go Global

The cockroach theory of financial scandals says that for every one you see, hundreds more are hiding in the woodwork. So it was in the United States, when the scandal at Enron was followed by blowups at WorldCom, HealthSouth, and elsewhere. And so it is now abroad; first Dutch grocer Ahold, then Italian dairy-products company Parmalat, and now Hollinger International Inc., the newspaper company controlled by Conrad M. Black, a Canadian-born British lord.

Scandals break out in bunches because they have common causes. They occur when insiders take advantage of weak corporate governance, feeble government oversight, and a financial system that too often looks the other way. Indeed, Parmalat's failure reflects badly on what were some of the biggest names in international finance in the 1990s. Bank of America, Barclays, and Merrill Lynch sold billions of dollars in Parmalat debt over the years. Although there's no evidence that the financial giants broke rules, a little skeptical probing would have revealed the rot at the heart of Parmalat years ago.

The slow-motion fall of Conrad Black appears to be a case of high-handedness and questionable governance. The press baron is denying allegations in a lawsuit that he arranged payments to himself and others that weren't properly authorized by the board of directors. If the board let Black run Hollinger for his own benefit, it reflects badly on luminary directors such as Henry A. Kissinger and Richard N. Perle.

There is obvious harm to these companies' shareholders and creditors, such as Parmalat bondholder AFLAC Inc. Less visible but more serious is the destruction of trust, which makes it harder for honest companies to raise the money they need to grow. Overseas, as in the United States, the solutions are clear: transparency, accountability, tough audits, and criminal penalties for those who cheat. Halfway measures are an invitation to more cheating.

Source: "When Scandals Go Global," *Business Week*, February 2, 2004, p. 96.

FIGURE 1-2   The Value of Good Governance.

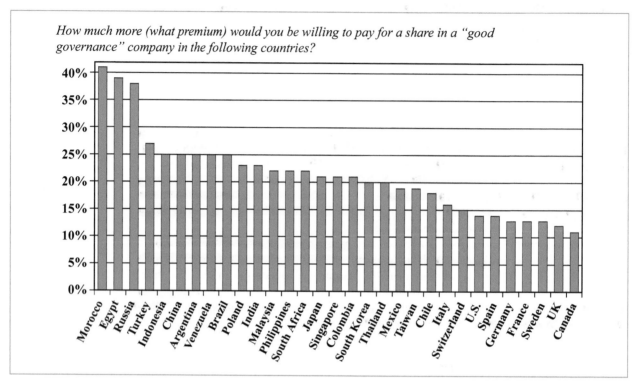

How much more (what premium) would you be willing to pay for a share in a "good governance" company in the following countries?

Source: "McKinsey Global Investor Opinion Survey on Corporate Goverance, 2002," McKinsey & Company, July 2002.

saying who has "good" or "bad" corporate governance globally, it does provide some insight as to which countries' institutional investors see good governance as scarce. It is again important to note that most of the emerging market nations have relatively few publicly traded companies, even today.

A third way to signal good corporate governance in non-Anglo-American firms is to elect one or more Anglo-American board members. This theory was shown to be true for a select group of Scandinavian firms. A study by Oxelheim and Randøy of a database of Norwegian and Swedish firms concluded the following:

> ***This study examines the influence of foreign (Anglo-American) board membership on corporate performance measured in terms of valuation (Tobin's Q). Based on firms headquartered in Norway and Sweden, this study indicates a significantly higher value for firms having outsider Anglo-American board member(s) after controlling for a variety of firm-specific and corporate governance—related factors. We argue that the superior performance reflects that these companies have successfully broken away from a partly segmented domestic capital market by "importing," through their outsider Anglo-American board member(s), an Anglo-American corporate governance system offering improved monitoring opportunities and enhanced investor recognition.[9]***

---

[9]Lars Oxelheim and Trond Randøy, "The Impact of Foreign Board Membership on Firm Value," *Journal of Banking and Finance*, Vol. 27, No. 12, 2003, pp. 2,369–2,392.

A follow-up study of the same firms found that CEO pay increased because of the perceived reduction in tolerance for bad performance and increased monitoring required.[10]

Corporate Governance Reform

Within the United States and United Kingdom, the main corporate governance problem is the one treated by agency theory: with widespread share ownership, how can a firm align management's interest with that of the shareholders? Because individual shareholders do not have the resources or the power to monitor management, the U.S. and U.K. markets rely on regulators to assist in the agency theory monitoring task. Outside the United States and United Kingdom, large controlling shareholders are in the majority (including Canada). They are able to monitor management in some ways better than regulators. However, controlling shareholders pose a different agency problem: how can minority shareholders be protected against the controlling shareholders?

In recent years, reform in the United States and Canada has been largely regulatory. Reform elsewhere has been largely adoption of principles rather than stricter legal regulations. The principles approach is softer, less costly, and less likely to conflict with other existing regulations.

SARBANES-OXLEY ACT   The U.S. Congress passed the Sarbanes-Oxley Act (SOX) in July 2002. Named after its two primary congressional sponsors, SOX had four major requirements: (1) CEOs and CFOs of publicly traded firms must vouch for the veracity of the firm's published financial statements; (2) corporate boards must have audit and compensation committees drawn from independent (outside) directors; (3) companies are prohibited from making loans to corporate officers and directors; and (4) companies must test their internal financial controls against fraud.

The first provision—the so-called *signature clause*—has already had significant impacts on the way in which companies prepare their financial statements. The provision was intended to instill a sense of responsibility and accountability in senior management (and therefore fewer explanations of "the auditors signed-off on it"). The companies themselves have pushed the same procedure downward in their organizations, often requiring business unit managers and directors at lower levels to sign their financial statements. Severe penalties are enacted in cases of noncompliance.

SOX has been much more expensive to implement than was originally expected during the debate in the U.S. Congress. Apart from the obvious costs of filling out more forms, many critics argue that too much time is consumed in meeting the new regulations, modifying internal controls to combat fraud, and restating past earnings, rather than running the operations of the firms. This cost may be disproportionately high for smaller firms that must meet the same regulatory requirements as large firms. In particular, auditing and legal fees have skyrocketed.

Everyone is afraid of following in the footsteps of Arthur Andersen, which collapsed as a result of the Enron scandal. The "Big Five" accounting firms became the "Big Four" overnight! The net result may lead to more small but growing firms choosing to sell out to larger firms instead of going the initial public offering (IPO) route. Other firms may simply choose to stay private, feeling that the costs of public offerings outweigh the benefits. Moreover, many firms may become more risk-averse. Lower-level employees might pass all risky decisions up the line to a more central risk assessment level. Such an action would slow decision making and also potentially slow growth.

---

[10]Lars Oxelheim and Trond Randøy, "The Anglo-American Financial Influence on CEO Compensation in Non-Anglo-American Firms," *Journal of International Business Studies*, Vol. 36, No. 4, July 2005, pp. 470–483.

SOX has been quite controversial internationally. Its "one size fits all" style conflicts with a number of the corporate governance practices already in place in markets that view themselves as having better governance records than the United States. A foreign firm wishing to list or continue listing their shares on a U.S. exchange must comply with the law. Some companies, such as Porsche, withdrew plans for a U.S. listing specifically in opposition to SOX. Other companies, however, including many of the largest foreign companies traded on U.S. exchanges such as Unilever, Siemens, and ST Microelectronics, have stated their willingness to comply—if they can find acceptable compromises between U.S. law and the governance requirements and principles in their own countries. One example is Germany, where supervisory board audit committees must include employee representatives. But according to U.S. law, employees are not independent. Many of these listed firms have concluded that they need access to the U.S. capital market and therefore must comply.

BOARD STRUCTURE AND COMPENSATION   Many critics have argued for the United States to move more towards structural reforms more consistent with European standards. For example, prohibiting CEOs from also being chairmen of the board directors. Although this is increasingly common, there is no regulatory or other legal requirement to force the issue. Secondly, and more radically, would be to move towards the two-tiered structure of countries like Germany, in which there is a supervisory board (mostly outsiders, and typically large—Siemens has 18 members) and a management board (predominantly insiders, and smaller—Siemens has 8 members). As illustrated by Table 1-3, it is not clear that the director composition of boards is truly the problem.

Although SOX addresses the agency theory problem of transparency, it does not address the agency theory problem of aligning the goals of boards and managers with the interests of shareholders. In the past, the U.S. firm was characterized by compensation schemes to reward directors and management with a combination of an annual stipend or salary with significant stock options. However, when stock options go *underwater* (become essentially valueless, because they are so far out of the money), it does not cause the recipient any direct cost—only the loss of a potential future benefit. Indeed, some firms simply rewrite the options so that they have higher values immediately. It now appears that many firms are changing their compensation schemes to replace options with restricted stock. *Restricted stock* cannot be sold publicly until after a specified period of time. If the price of the firm's shares falls, the recipient has actually lost money and is normally not recompensated by receiving more restricted shares.

TRANSPARENCY, ACCOUNTING, AND AUDITING   The concept of *transparency* is also one that has been raised in a variety of different markets and contexts. Transparency is a rather common term used to describe the degree to which an investor—either existing or potential—can

TABLE 1-3
Board Composition and Compensation, Fortune 100.

SIZE OF COMPANY (SALES)	TOTAL DIRECTORS	OUTSIDE DIRECTORS	AVG. ANNUAL RETAINER
Less than $3 billion	9	7	$33,792
$3 – $4.9 billion	10	8	$37,567
$5 – $9.9 billion	12	10	$42,264
$10 – 19.9 billion	12	10	$47,589
$20 billion and over	13	11	$6,587

Source: Korn/Ferry International, as quoted in "The Way We Govern Now," *The Economist*, January 9, 2003 (print edition).

discern the true activities and value drivers of a company from the disclosures and financial results reported. For example, Enron was often considered a "black box" when it came to what the actual operational and financial results and risks were for its multitude of business lines. The consensus of corporate governance experts is that all firms, globally, should work towards increasing the transparency of the firm's risk-return profile.

The accounting process itself has now come under debate. The U.S. system is characterized as strictly rule-based, rather than conceptually based, as is common in Western Europe. Many critics of U.S. corporate governance practices point to this as a fundamental flaw, in which constantly more clever accountants find ways to follow the rules, while not meeting the underlying purpose for which the rules were intended. An extension of the accounting process debate is that of the role and remuneration associated with auditing. This is the process of using third parties, paid by the firm, to vet their reporting practices as being consistent with generally accepted accounting principles. As the collapse of Arthur Andersen illustrated following the Enron debacle, serious questions remain as to the validity of this current practice.

MINORITY SHAREHOLDER RIGHTS Finally, the issue of minority shareholder rights continues to rage in many of the world's largest markets. Many of the emerging markets are still characterized by the family-based corporate governance regime, where the family remains in control even after the firm has gone public. But what of the interests and voices of the other shareholders? How are their interests preserved in organizations where families or controlling investors make all true decisions, including the boards? As *Global Finance in Practice 1.4* points out, minority shareholder rights are threatened in all markets, industrialized and emerging.

Poor performance of management usually requires changes in management, ownership, or both. Figure 1-3 illustrates some of the alternative paths available to shareholders dissatisfied with firm performance. Depending on the culture and accepted practices, it is not unusual for many investors to—at least for an extended time—remain quietly disgruntled regarding share price performance. If more active in response, they might sell their shares. It is the third and fourth responses, shareholder activist responses, in which management hears a much louder voice of the dissatisfied shareholder.

Global Finance in Practice 1.4

Conrad Black and Minority Shareholder Rights

Conrad Black was CEO of Hollinger International, a Canadian corporation listed on the New York Stock Exchange. Black controlled the company via a complex management agreement and through a holding company that he controlled that held a majority of Hollinger's voting shares. He was known to have little patience for shareholder questions, particularly when they were about how he was managing the firm. In a 2003 stockholder meeting he responded to continued questions with the following: "You have a right to say whatever it is that is on your mind, all of you," he informed his investors. "You don't know what you are talking about, but you are still welcome as shareholders." He resigned as chairman and CEO in November 2003, under pressure.

Source: Adapted from David Leonard, "Hollinger Black & Blue," Fortune, September 29, 2003.

FIGURE 1-3
Potential Responses to
Shareholder
Dissatisfaction.

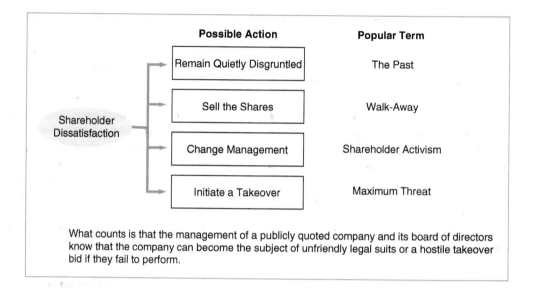

Possible Action	Popular Term
Remain Quietly Disgruntled	The Past
Sell the Shares	Walk-Away
Change Management	Shareholder Activism
Initiate a Takeover	Maximum Threat

What counts is that the management of a publicly quoted company and its board of directors know that the company can become the subject of unfriendly legal suits or a hostile takeover bid if they fail to perform.

1.5 NOTE ON CURRENCY TERMINOLOGY

Explanation of some basic terms will help prevent confusion in reading future chapters:

- A *foreign currency exchange rate*, or *simply exchange rate*, is the price of one country's currency in units of another currency or commodity (typically gold or silver). If the government of a country—for example, Argentina—regulates the rate at which the peso is exchanged for other currencies, the system or *regime* is classified as a *fixed* or *managed exchange rate regime*. The rate at which the currency is fixed, or pegged, is frequently referred to as its *par value*. If the government does not interfere in the valuation of its currency in any way, the currency is classified as *floating* or *flexible*.
- The *spot exchange rate* is the quoted price for foreign exchange to be delivered at once, or in two days for interbank transactions. For example, ¥114/$ is a quote for the exchange rate between the Japanese yen and the U.S. dollar. One needs 114 yen to buy one U.S. dollar for immediate delivery.
- *Devaluation* of a currency refers to a drop in foreign exchange value of a currency that is pegged to gold or to another currency. In other words, the par value is reduced. The opposite of devaluation is *revaluation.*
- *Weakening, deterioration*, or *depreciation* of a currency refers to a drop in the foreign exchange value of a floating currency. The opposite of weakening is *strengthening* or *appreciating*, which refers to a gain in the exchange value of a floating currency.
- *Soft* or *weak* describes a currency that is expected to devalue or depreciate relative to major currencies. It also refers to currencies whose values are being artificially sustained by their governments. A currency is considered *hard* if it is expected to revalue or appreciate relative to major trading currencies.
- *Eurocurrencies* are sometimes viewed as another kind of money, although in reality they are domestic currencies of one country on deposit in a bank in a second country. Their value is identical to that of the same currency "at home." For example, a *Eurodollar* is a U.S. dollar–denominated interest-bearing deposit in a bank outside the United States. A *Euroyen* is a yen-denominated deposit in a bank outside Japan. The bank may be a foreign bank or the overseas branch of a U.S. or Japanese bank.

- *Measuring a Change in Spot Exchange Rates* When working with exchange rates, the calculation of a percentage change can be a bit tricky. Assume that the Swiss franc, recently quoted at SF1.6351/$ (which is the same as $0.61158/SF), suddenly strengthens to SF1.5000/$ (which is the same as $0.66667/SF). What is the percent increase in the dollar value of the franc, and thus in the value of Swiss franc-denominated accounts receivable or payable held by Americans? The designation of the "home currency" is critical to the proper calculation.

QUOTATIONS EXPRESSED IN HOME CURRENCY TERMS (I.E., DIRECT QUOTATIONS): When the home currency price for a foreign currency is used, the formula for the percent change (Δ) in the foreign currency is:

$$\%\Delta = \frac{\text{Ending rate} - \text{Beginning rate}}{\text{Beginning rate}} \times 100$$

$$= \frac{\$0.66667/SF - \$0.61158/SF}{\$0.61158/SF} + 100 = +9.008\%$$

In this instance, the Swiss franc is 9.008% stronger at the ending rate. Holders of U.S. dollar receivables will receive 9.008% more dollars—but those who owe Swiss francs will have to pay 9.008% more to buy them.

QUOTATIONS EXPRESSED IN FOREIGN CURRENCY TERMS (I.E., INDIRECT QUOTATIONS): When the foreign currency price of the home currency is used, the formula for the percent change in the foreign currency becomes:

$$\%\Delta = \frac{\text{Beginning rate} - \text{Ending rate}}{\text{Ending rate}} \times 100$$

$$= \frac{SF1.6351/\$ - SF1.5000/\$}{SF1.5000/\$} \times 100 = +9.008\%$$

By both methods of calculation, the Swiss franc increased 9.008% in value relative to the dollar.

SUMMARY

- Financial management is an integral part of a firm's strategy. The main theme of this book is to analyze how a firm's financial management tasks evolve as it pursues global strategic opportunities and new constraints unfold.
- Some of the main differences between international and domestic financial management are institutions, foreign exchange and political risk, and the modifications required of finance theory and financial instruments.
- International financial management requires an understanding of cultural, historical, and institutional differences with a potential effect on corporate governance.

- The U.S. and U.K. stock markets are characterized by widespread ownership of shares. In the rest of the world, ownership is usually characterized by controlling shareholders. Typical controlling shareholders are government, institutions, family, and consortiums.
- The definitions of "return" and "risk" are not universally accepted. Indeed, they may be culturally determined norms that vary by country.
- In the Anglo-American markets, the shareholder wealth maximization model is the culturally determined norm. In many non-Anglo-American markets, the stakeholder capitalism model is the culturally determined norm. Distinct differences exist as to how these models treat return and risk. Additionally, these culturally determined norms are in process of evolution within many countries.
- As MNEs become more dependent on global capital markets for financing, they may need to modify their policies of corporate governance. A trend exists for firms resident in non-Anglo-American markets to become more "shareholder-friendly." Simultaneously, firms from the Anglo-American markets may becoming more "stakeholder-friendly."
- An MNE must be guided by operational goals suitable for various levels of the firm.
- An MNE must determine for itself the proper balance between three common operational objectives: maximization of consolidated after-tax income; minimization of the firm's effective global tax burden; and correct positioning of the firm's income, cash flows, and in each currency and country of activity.
- The relationship among stakeholders used to determine and control the strategic direction and performance of an organization is termed "corporate governance."
- Dimensions of corporate governance include agency theory; composition and control of boards of directors; and cultural, historical and institutional variables.
- Failures in corporate governance, especially in the United States, have recently been in the spotlight and have been given partial blame for the decline in value of the U.S. stock markets.
- Shareholders who are dissatisfied with their firm's performance have four typical choices: remain quietly disgruntled, sell their shares, change management, or initiate a takeover.
- The recent failures in corporate governance in the United States have spawned a flurry of government and private initiatives to prevent the same kind of future failures.
- The United States has already reacted to the recent failures in corporate governance by passing the Sarbanes-Oxley Act of 2002. The act specifically requires the CEOs of firms to vouch for their financial statements and to create audit committees from independent directors. The act, however, is inconsistent with the policies and practices employed in many other countries, and has been a point of contention for firms considering listing (or continued listings) in the United States.

QUESTIONS

1. **Corporate goals: shareholder wealth maximization.** Explain the assumptions and objectives of the shareholder wealth maximization model.
2. **Corporate goals: stakeholder capitalism.** Explain the assumptions and objectives of the stakeholder capitalism model.

3. **Corporate governance.** Define the following terms:
   a. Corporate governance
   b. The market for corporate control
   c. Agency theory
   d. Cronyism

4. **Operational goals.** What should be the primary operational goal of an MNE?

5. **Knowledge assets.** *Knowledge assets* are a firm's intangible assets, the sources and uses of its intellectual talent—its competitive advantage. What are some of the most important "knowledge assets" that create shareholder value?

6. **Labor unions.** In Germany and Scandinavia, and elsewhere, labor unions have representation on boards of directors or supervisory boards. How might such union representation be viewed under the shareholder wealth maximization model compared to the stakeholder capitalism model?

7. **Interlocking directorates.** In an interlocking directorate, members of the board of directors of one firm also sit on the boards of directors of other firms. How would interlocking directorates be viewed by the shareholder wealth maximization model compared to the stakeholder capitalism model?

8. **Leveraged buyouts.** A leveraged buyout is a financial strategy in which a group of investors gain voting control of a firm and then liquidate its assets in order to repay the loans used to purchase the firm's shares. How would leveraged buyouts be viewed by the shareholder wealth maximization model compared to the stakeholder capitalism model?

9. **High leverage.** How would a high degree of leverage (debt/assets) be viewed by the shareholder wealth maximization model compared to the stakeholder capitalism model?

10. **Conglomerates.** *Conglomerates* are firms that have diversified into unrelated fields. How would a policy of conglomeration be viewed by the shareholder wealth maximization model compared to the stakeholder capitalism model?

11. **Risk.** How is risk defined in the shareholder wealth maximization model compared to the stakeholder capitalism model?

12. **Stock options.** How would stock options granted to a firm's management and employees be viewed by the shareholder wealth maximization model compared to the stakeholder capitalism model?

13. **Shareholder dissatisfaction.** If shareholders are dissatisfied with their company, what alternative actions can they take?

14. **Dual classes of common stock.** In many countries, it is common for a firm to have two or more classes of common stock with differential voting rights. In the United States, the norm is for a firm to have one class of common stock with one-share-one-vote. What are the advantages and disadvantages of each system?

15. **Emerging markets corporate governance failures.** It has been claimed that failures in corporate governance have hampered the growth and profitability of some prominent firms located in emerging markets. What are some typical causes of these failures in corporate governance?

16. **Emerging markets corporate governance improvements.** In recent years, emerging-market MNEs have improved their corporate governance policies and become more shareholder-friendly. What do you think is driving this phenomenon?

17. **Developed markets corporate governance failures.** What have been the main causes of recent corporate governance failures in the United States and Europe?

PROBLEMS

Use the following formula for shareholder returns to answer questions 1 through 3, where P_t is the share price at time t, and D_t is the dividend paid at time t.

$$\text{Shareholder return} = \frac{P_2 - P_1 + D_2}{P_1}$$

1. **Shareholder returns.** If a share price rises from $16 to $18 over a one-year period, what was the rate of return to the shareholder if:

   a. The company paid no dividends?

   b. The company paid a dividend of $1 per share?

2. **Shareholder choices.** Wilford Fong, a prominent investor, is evaluating investment alternatives. If he believes an individual equity will rise in price from $62 to $74 in the coming one-year period, the share is expected to pay a dividend of $2.25 per share, and he expects at least a 12% rate of return on an investment of this type, should he invest in this particular equity?

3. **Microsoft's dividend.** In January 2003, Microsoft announced that it would begin paying a dividend of $0.16 per share. Given the following share prices for Microsoft stock in the recent past, how would a constant dividend of $0.16 per share per year have changed the company's return to its shareholders over this period?

FIRST TRADING DAY	CLOSING SHARE PRICE	FIRST TRADING DAY	CLOSING SHARE PRICE
1998 (Jan. 2)	$131.13	2001 (Jan. 2)	$43.38
1999 (Jan. 4)	$141.00	2002 (Jan. 2)	$67.04
2000 (Jan. 3)	$116.56	2003 (Jan. 2)	$53.72

4. **Dual classes of common stock (A).** Dual classes of common stock are common in a number of countries. Assume that Powlitz Manufacturing has the following capital structure at book value:

POWLITZ MANUFACTURING	LOCAL CURRENCY (MILLIONS)
Long-term debt	200
Retained earnings	300
Paid-in common stock: 1 million A-shares	100
Paid-in common stock: 4 million B-shares	400
Total long-term capital	1,000

The A-shares each have 10 votes per share, the B-shares each have 1 vote per share.

   a. What proportion of the total long-term capital has been raised by A-shares?

   b. What proportion of voting rights is represented by A-shares?

   c. What proportion of the dividends should the A-shares receive?

5. **Dual classes of common stock (B).** Assuming all of the same debt and equity values for Powlitz Manufacturing in problem 4, with the sole exception that both A-shares and B-shares have the same voting rights of 1 vote per share:

   a. What proportion of the total long-term capital has been raised by A-shares?

   b. What proportion of voting rights is represented by A-shares?

   c. What proportion of the dividends should the A-shares receive?

6. **Price/earnings ratios and acquisitions.** During the 1960s, many conglomerates were created by a firm enjoying a high price/earnings ratio (P/E). They then used their highly valued stock to acquire other firms that had lower P/E ratios, usually in unrelated domestic industries. These conglomerates went out of fashion during the 1980s when they lost their high P/E ratios, thus making it more difficult to find other firms with lower P/E ratios to acquire.

   During the 1990s, the same acquisition strategy was possible for firms located in countries where high P/E ratios were common compared to firms in other countries where low P/E ratios were common. Assume the following hypothetical firms in the pharmaceutical industry.

	P/E RATIO	NUMBER OF SHARES	MARKET VALUE PER SHARE	EARNINGS	EPS	TOTAL MARKET VALUE
Pharm-Italy	20	10,000,000	$20	$10,000,000	$1.00	$200,000,000
Pharm-USA	40	10,000,000	$40	$10,000,000	$1.00	$400,000,000

   Pharm-USA wants to acquire Pharm-Italy. It offers 5,500,000 shares of Pharm-USA, with a current market value of $220,000,000 and a 10% premium on Pharm-Italy's shares, for all of Pharm-Italy's shares.

   a. How many shares would Pharm-USA have outstanding after the acquisition of Pharm-Italy?

   b. What would be the consolidated earnings of the combined Pharm-USA and Pharm-Italy?

   c. Assuming that the market continues to capitalize Pharm-USA's earnings at a P/E ratio of 40, what would be the new market value for Pharm-USA?

   d. What is the new earnings per share of Pharm-USA?

   e. What is the new market value of a share of Pharm-USA?

   f. How much did Pharm-USA's stock price increase?

   g. Assume that the market takes a negative view of the merger and lowers Pharm-USA's P/E ratio to 30. What would be the new market price per share of stock? What would be its percentage loss?

7. **Corporate governance: overstating earnings.** A number of firms, especially in the United States, have had to lower their previously reported earnings due to accounting errors or fraud. Assume that Pharm-USA (from the previous problem) had to lower their reported earnings to $5,000,000 from the previously reported $10,000,000. What might be its new market value prior to the acquisition? Could it still do the acquisition?

8. **Pacific Precision (A): European sales.** Pacific Precision is a Hong Kong–based exporter of machine tools; it files all of its financial statements in Hong Kong dollars (HK$).

The company's European sales director, Jacque Mayal, has been criticized of late for his performance. He argues that sales in Europe have grown steadily in recent years. Who is correct?

	2002	2003	2004
Total net sales, HK$	171,275	187,500	244,900
Percent of total sales from Europe	48%	44%	39%
Total European sales, HK$			
Average exchange rate, HK$/€	7.4	8.5	9.4
Total European sales, €			
Growth rate of European sales			

9. **Pacific Precision (B): Japanese yen debt.** Pacific Precision of Hong Kong borrowed Japanese yen under a long-term loan agreement several years ago. The company's new CFO believes, however, that what was originally thought to have been relatively "cheap debt" is no longer true. What do you think?

	2002	2003	2004
Annual yen payments on debt agreement (¥)	12,000,000	12,000,000	12,000,000
Average exchange rate, ¥/HK$	15.9	14.7	13.7
Annual yen debt service, HK$			

10. **Chinese sourcing and the yuan.** Harrison Equipment of Denver, Colorado, purchases all of its hydraulic tubing from manufacturers in mainland China. The company has recently (June 2005) completed a corporate-wide initiative in six sigma/lean manufacturing. Completed oil field hydraulic system costs were reduced by 4% over a one-year period, from $880,000 to $844,800. The company is now worried that all of the hydraulic tubing that goes into these systems (making up 20% of their total costs) will be hit by the potential revaluation of the Chinese yuan, if some in Washington get their way. How would a 12% revaluation of the yuan against the dollar affect total system costs?

A 12% revaluation of the yuan would be calculated as follows:

$$\frac{Yuan8.28/\$}{1 + \% \, change} = \frac{Yuan8.28/\$}{1.012} = Yuan7.39/\$$$

11. **Mattel's global performance.** Mattel (a U.S. firm) achieved significant sales growth in its major international regions between 2001 and 2004. In its filings with the U.S. SEC, it reported both the amount of regional sales and the percentage change in regional sales that occurred as a result of exchange rate changes.

   a. What was the percentage change in sales, in U.S. dollars, by region?

   b. What was the percentage change in sales by region net of currency change impacts?

   c. What relative impact did currency changes have on the level and growth of Mattel's consolidated sales for the 2001–2004 period?

MATTEL'S GLOBAL SALES (THOUSANDS OF US$)	2001 SALES ($)	2002 SALES ($)	2003 SALES ($)	2004 SALES ($)
Europe	$ 933,450	$ 1,126,177	$ 1,356,131	$ 1,410,525
Latin America	471,301	466,349	462,167	524,481
Canada	155,791	161,469	185,831	197,655
Asia Pacific	119,749	136,944	171,580	203,575
Total international	$ 1,680,291	$ 1,890,939	$ 2,175,709	$ 2,336,236
United States	3,392,284	3,422,405	3,203,814	3,209,862
Sales adjustments	(384,651)	(428,004)	(419,423)	(443,312)
Total net sales	$ 4,687,924	$ 4,885,340	$ 4,960,100	$ 5,102,786

| | IMPACT OF CHANGE IN CURRENCY RATES | | |
REGION	2001–2002	2002–2003	2003–2004
Europe	7.0%	15.0%	8.0%
Latin America	−9.0%	−6.0%	−2.0%
Canada	0.0%	11.0%	5.0%
Asia Pacific	3.0%	13.0%	6.0%

Source: Mattel, Annual Report, 2002, 2003, 2004.

Garrison Industries

Problems 12 through 15 are based on Garrison Industries. Garrison is a U.S.-based multinational manufacturing firm, with wholly owned subsidiaries in Brazil, Germany, and China, in addition to domestic operations in the United States. Garrison is traded on the NADSAQ. Garrison currently has 650,000 shares outstanding. The basic operating characteristics of the various business units are as follows:

(000S, local currency)	US (dollers, $)	BRASIL (reais, R$)	GERMANY (euros, €)	CHINA (yuan, ¥)
Earnings before tax (EBT)	$4,500	R$6,250	€4,500	¥2,500
Corporate income tax rate	35%	25%	40%	30%
Average exchange rate for period	——	R$3.50/$	€0.9260/$	¥8.10/$

12. **Garrison Corporation's consolidated earnings.** Garrison must pay corporate income tax in each country in which it currently has operations.
    a. After deducting taxes in each country, what are Garrison's consolidated earnings and consolidated earnings per share in U.S. dollars?
    b. What proportion of Garrison's consolidated earnings arise from each individual country?
    c. What proportion of Garrison's consolidated earnings arise from outside the United States?

13. **Garrison's EPS sensitivity to exchange rates.** Assume that a major political crisis wracks Brazil, first affecting the value of the Brazilian reais and subsequently inducing an economic recession within the country.

    a. What would be the impact on Garrison's consolidated EPS if the Brazilian reais were to fall to R$4.50/$, with all other earnings and exchange rates remaining the same?

    b. What would be the impact on Garrison's consolidated EPS if, in addition to the fall in the value of the reais to R$4.50/$, earnings before taxes in Brazil fell as a result of the recession to R$5,800,000?

14. **Garrison's earnings and the fall of the dollar.** The U.S. dollar has experienced significant swings in value against most of the world's currencies in recent years.

    a. What would be the impact on Garrison's consolidated EPS if all foreign currencies were to appreciate 20% against the U.S. dollar?

    b. What would be the impact on Garrison's consolidated EPS if all foreign currencies were to depreciate 20% against the U.S. dollar?

    Note: Calculate the percentage changes similar to Problem 10, dividing the initial currency value by (1 + the percentage change) to calculate the new currency value.

15. **Garrison's earnings and global taxation.** All MNEs attempt to minimize their global tax liabilities. Return to the original set of baseline assumptions and answer the following questions regarding Garrison's global tax liabilities.

    a. What is the total amount—in U.S. dollars—that Garrison is paying across its global business in corporate income taxes?

    b. What is Garrison's effective tax rate on a global basis (total taxes paid as a percentage of pretax profits)?

    c. What would be the impact on Garrison's EPS and global effective tax rate if Germany instituted a corporate tax reduction to 28%, and Garrison's earnings before tax in Germany rose to €5,000,000?

INTERNET EXERCISES

1. **Multinational firms and global assets/income.** The differences across MNEs is striking. Using a sample of firms such as those listed here, pull from firms' individual web pages the proportions of their incomes that are earned outside their country of incorporation. (Note how Nestlé calls itself a "transnational company.")

   Walt Disney http://disney.go.com

   Nestlé S.A. http://www.nestle.com

   Intel http://www.intel.com

   Daimler-Benz http://www.daimlerchrysler.de

   Mitsubishi Motors http://www.mitsubishi.com

   Nokia http://www.nokia.com

   Royal Dutch/Shell http://www.shell.com

   Also note the way in which international business is now conducted via the Internet. Several of the listed home pages allow the user to choose the language of the presentation viewed.

2. **Corporate governance.** There is no hotter topic in business today than corporate governance. Use the following sites to view recent research, current events and news items, and other information related to the relationships between a business and its stakeholders.

   Corporate Governance Net http://www.corpgov.net

3. **Fortune Global 500.** *Fortune* magazine is relatively famous for its listing of the Fortune 500 firms in the global marketplace. Use *Fortune's* website to find the most recent listing of which firms from which countries are in this distinguished club.

   Fortune http://www.fortune.com/fortune

4. **Financial Times.** The website *Financial Times*, based in London—the global center of international finance, provides a wealth of information. After going to the home page, go to the Markets Data & Tools page, and examine the recent stock market activity around the globe. Note the similarity in movement on a daily basis among the world's major equity markets.

   Financial Times http://www.ft.com

SELECTED READINGS

Jensen, M., "Eclipse of the Public Corporation," *Harvard Business Review*, September 1989, pp. 61–74.

Jensen, M. and W. Meckling, "Theory of the Firm: Managerial Behavior, Agency Cost, and Ownership Structure," *Journal of Financial Economics*, 3, 1976, pp. 305–360.

La Porta, R., F. Lopez-de-Silanes, and A. Schleifer, "Legal Determinants of External Finance," *Journal of Finance*, 52, 1997, pp. 1131–1150.

La Porta, R., F. Lopez-de-Silanes, and A. Schleifer, "Corporate Ownership Around the Globe," *Journal of Finance*, 54, 1999, pp. 471–517.

La Porta, R., F. Lopez-de-Silanes, and A. Schleifer, "Investor Protection and Corporate Valuation," *Journal of Finance*, 57, 1997, pp. 1,147–1,169.

Oxelheim, Lars and Trond Randøy, "The Anglo-American Financial Influence on CEO Compensation in Non-Anglo-American Firms," *Journal of International Business Studies*, Vol. 36, No. 4, July 2005, pp. 470–483.

Schleifer, A. and R. Vishny, "A Survey of Corporate Governance," *Journal of Finance*, 52, 1997, pp. 737–783.

MINICASE   THE FAILURE OF CORPORATE GOVERNANCE AT ENRON

The tragic consequences of the related-party transactions and accounting errors were the result of failures at many levels and by many people: a flawed idea, self-enrichment by employees, inadequately designed controls, poor implementation, inattentive oversight, simple (and not so simple) accounting mistakes, and overreaching in a culture that appears to have encouraged pushing the limits. Our review indicates that many of these consequences could and should have been avoided.

"Report of Investigation: Special Investigative Committee of the
Board of Directors of Enron Corporation," Board of Directors, Enron, February 1, 2002, pp. 27–28.

On December 2, 2001, Enron Corporation filed for bankruptcy protection under Chapter 11. Enron failed as a result of a complex combination of business and governance failures. As noted in the previous quotation from the board report, the failures involved organizations and individuals both inside and outside of Enron. But outside of the courts and sensational press, the question remains as to how the system allowed it to happen. Why did the many structures and safeguards within the U.S. corporate governance system not catch, stop, or prevent the failure of Enron?

ENRON'S COLLAPSE

According to former Enron CEO Jeffrey Skilling, Enron failed because of a "run on the bank." This, in fact, is probably technically correct. When Enron's credit rating was downgraded to below investment grade in November 2001 by the credit rating agencies, its business was effectively stopped. This effect occurred because as a trading company, it needed to maintain an investment grade rating in order for other companies to trade with it. No grade, no trade.

But that answer largely begs the question of *why* the company was downgraded. Enron's total indebtedness was now determined to be $38 billion, not $13 billion. Why was the debt suddenly so high? Much of the debt that had been classified as *off-balance sheet* was now reclassified to *on-balance sheet*. Why the reclassification? Many of the *special purpose entities* (SPEs) and off-balance sheet partnerships carrying this debt either were found to have been misclassified to begin with or were reconsolidated with the company as a result of their equity falling in value (Enron shares). Which leads us back to the beginning—why did Enron's share price tumble in 2001? Was it simply a natural result of a failing business, or had Enron's reported and prospective earnings, in combination with its general financial health, not been honestly reported and evaluated?

FAILURE OF CORPORATE GOVERNANCE AT ENRON

Enron's senior management team, primarily CEO Kenneth Lay and COO Jeffrey Skilling (later CEO), were responsible for the formulation and implementation of the company's strategy, including its operating and financial results. Like most companies of its size, it had literally hundreds of accountants and lawyers on its permanent staff. The concerns of one accountant, Sherron Watkins, became public in August and September 2001 and contributed to the rapidly escalating examination of Enron and its operations in the fall of 2001.

In the case of Enron, the following external corporate governance bodies have been the focus of much criticism:

1. **Auditor.** Arthur Andersen (one of the so-called Big Five) was Enron's auditing firm. Andersen's job was to determine and annually testify as to whether Enron had followed generally accepted accounting practices in the statements of its financial results. Andersen, like all auditors, was hired and paid by Enron itself. Andersen also provided a large variety of consulting activities for Enron, the sum of which was a much larger line of business than the basic audit practice itself.

2. **Legal counsel.** Enron's legal counsel, primarily the Houston firm Vinson & Elkins, also hired by the firm, was responsible for providing legal opinions on the many strategies, structures, and general legality of much of what Enron did. As was also the case with Arthur Andersen, when questioned later as to why it did not oppose certain ideas or practices, the company explained that it had not been fully informed of all of the details and complexities of the management and ownership of the SPEs.

3. **Regulators.** Enron actually fell between the cracks of most U.S. regulatory bodies, specifically the trading of electrical power across states. As a trader in the energy markets, the Federal Energy Regulatory Commission (FERC) had some distant oversight responsibilities in regard to some of the markets and trading that the company participated in, but these were largely separate issues from Enron's overall activities.

4. **Equity markets.** As a publicly traded company, Enron was subject to the rules and regulations of the SEC. The SEC, however, does little firsthand investigation or confirmation of reporting diligence itself, relying instead on the testimonials of other bodies like the company's auditor.

   As a share traded on the New York Stock Exchange (NYSE), Enron was governed by the rules and regulations of that exchange. At this time, however, the reporting requirements of the NYSE differed little, if at all, from those of the SEC. The NYSE did no firsthand verification of compliance on its own.

   Because the Enron shares were followed by a multitude of investment banking firms, analysts for these firms were responsible for following, analyzing, and evaluating Enron's results on a constant basis. Enron's relationships with its investment bankers involved frequent "tit-for-tat" behavior, in which those firms that cooperated with Enron and supported its performance stories were rewarded with new business and new mandates for other investment banking activities that were profitable to the firms.

5. **Debt markets.** Enron, like all companies that desire and need a credit rating, paid companies like Standard & Poors and Moody's to provide it with a credit rating. These ratings are needed for the company's debt securities to be issued and traded in the marketplace. Again, one of the problems that the credit ratings agencies had with Enron was that they could provide analysis only on what was known to them of Enron's operational and financial activities and results. And, in the case of debt knowingly held by off-balance sheet in special purposes entities, there is considerable debate continuing as to whether the credit rating agencies had full detail and knowingly chose to overlook it in the company's total indebtedness or not.

And finally, let's not forget the banks and bankers themselves, who provided the access to the debt capital. Most of these banks made millions and millions of dollars on interest and fee income as a result of leading and managing debt issuances for Enron.

FEEDING THE BEAST

A particularly troublesome feature of Enron's emerging business model in the late 1990s was that revenues grew much faster than earnings. The cost of undertaking large international power projects (such as Enron did in India), electrical power trading, and even new trading ventures such as the trading in water rights and broadband, were, in the word of one former executive, *hideous*. The salaries, bonuses, startup costs, and general lack of control over all operating costs drowned whatever profits arose from the new ventures. Even the more successful trading lines, including electricity, did not generate the margins the marketplace had come to expect from Enron and its older portfolio of businesses (primarily, natural gas trading). As illustrated in the following Figure A, the actual operating income (IBIT, or income before interest and taxes) by business line was not growing in line with revenues.

The growing deficit in corporate cash flows also led to a more fundamental financial management problem for Enron: the growing need for external capital, or, as it was described in-house, "feeding the beast." Rapidly escalating investments in new businesses, whether they be the Portland General Electric (PGE) acquisition of 1997 or the power projects pursued by Rebecca Mark (the director of Enron's international development group) globally, were absorbing more capital than the current business could self-finance. Enron's cash flows fell increasingly behind its investments and sales.

Enron needed additional external capital—new debt and new equity. Ken Lay and Jeff Skilling, however, were both reluctant to issue large amounts of new equity, because that would dilute earnings and the holdings of existing shareholders. The debt option was also limited, given the already high debt levels Enron was carrying (and that it had carried since its inception), which left it in the continuously precarious position of being rated BBB, just barely *investment grade* by credit agency standards.

Although Jeff Skilling had first employed the concept of a fund of capital to be created to support business development within Enron with the creation of the *Cactus Fund* in 1991, Andrew Fastow took the concept to a whole new level. Fastow's experience in banking, specifically in the use of special purpose entities (SPEs), a common tool in financial

FIGURE A   Enron's Earning by Segment (IBIT*, millions).

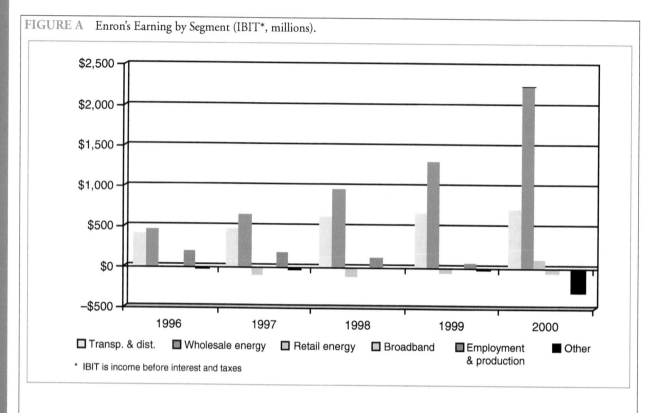

services, was his ticket up the corporate ladder at Enron. He eventually rose to the position of Chief Financial Officer.

Many of the transactions involve an accounting structure known as a "special purpose entity" or "special purpose vehicle" (referred to as an "SPE" in this Summary and in the Report). A company that does business with an SPE may treat that SPE as if it were an independent, outside entity for accounting purposes if two conditions are met: (1) an owner independent of the company must make a substantive equity investment of at least 3% of the SPE's assets, and that 3% must remain at risk throughout the transaction; and (2) the independent owner must exercise control of the SPE. In those circumstances, the company may record gains and losses on transactions with the SPE, and the assets and liabilities of the SPE are not included in the company's balance sheet, even though the company and the SPE are closely related. It was the technical failure of some of the structures with which Enron did business to satisfy these requirements that led to Enron's restatement.[11]

The SPEs created by Andy Fastow and his assistant Michael Kopper served two very important purposes. First, by selling troubled assets to the partnerships, Enron removed them from its balance sheet, taking pressure off the firm's total indebtedness and simultaneously hiding under-performing investments. This also freed additional room on the balance sheet to fund new investment opportunities. Secondly, the sale of the troubled investments to the partnerships generated income that Enron could then use to make its quarterly earnings commitments to Wall Street.

The problem with this solution was that it was only temporary. The SPEs were largely funded from three sources: (1) equity in the form of treasury shares; (2) equity in the form of a minimum 3% of assets by an unrelated third party (in principle, although this was later found to be untrue in a number of cases); and (3) large quantities of debt from major banks. This capital base made up the righthand side of the SPEs' balance sheet. On the lefthand side, the capital was used to purchase a variety of assets from Enron. Fastow sold these partnership deals to the banks on the premise that because he was uniquely positioned as both the CFO of Enron and the managing partner in the SPE, he could essentially cherry-pick the assets to

---

[11]Report of Investigation: Special Investigative Committee of the Board of Directors of Enron Corporation," Board of Directors, Enron, February 1, 2002 (often called The *Powers Report*), p. 5.

be purchased by the SPE. Fastow did indeed cherry-pick, but they were the rotten cherries. Most of the assets purchased by the SPEs were troubled or underperforming.

A final detail of the SPEs proved in the end devastating to the financial future of Enron. Because the primary equity in the SPEs was Enron stock, as the share price rose throughout 1999 and 2000, the SPEs could periodically be revalued using current market prices, resulting in an appreciation in the value of the SPE and contributing significant earnings to Enron. These same shares, once their price began sliding in 2001, resulted in partnerships that should have been marked-to-market for substantial losses, but were not. As Enron's share price plummeted in the early fall of 2001, the equity in the SPEs would no longer meet accounting guidelines for remaining off-balance sheet. The SPEs were becoming something of a synthetic business for Enron.

> *The trouble was, the Raptors, like the rest of LJM2, had become something of a dumping ground for bad properties. In an effort to make quarterly earnings (and, of course, annual bonuses), Enron originators were hooked on making deals with Fastow instead of outside third parties—who would have asked a lot of questions, slowed down the process, and, in many cases, killed deals. Again, none of this mattered to most people at Enron, as long as the stock kept rising.*[12]

THE FAILURE OF PEOPLE

As it turns out, much of what Enron reported as earnings were not. Much of the debt raised by the company via the partnerships that was not disclosed in corporate financial statements should have been. Simultaneous with the over-reporting of profits and the under-reporting of debt, was the massive compensation packages and bonuses earned by corporate officers. So how could this happen?

- It appears that the executive officers of the firm were successful in shepherding the Board of Directors toward management's own goals. Management had moved the company into a number of new markets in which the firm suffered substantial losses, resulting in redoubled attempts on their part to somehow generate the earnings needed to meet Wall Street's unquenchable thirst for profitable growth.

- The Board of Directors failed in its duties to protect shareholder interests, due to lack of due diligence and most likely also a faith in the competence and integrity of the company's senior officers. It is also notable that Enron's legal advisors, some of whom reported to the board directly, also failed to provide leadership in a number of instances of malfeasance.

- Enron's auditor, the firm Arthur Andersen, committed serious errors in its judgments regarding accounting treatment for many Enron activities, including the partnerships described previously. Andersen was reported to have had serious conflicts of interest, earning $5 million in auditing fees from Enron in 2001, but more than $50 million in consulting fees in the same year.

- Enron's analysts were, in a few cases, blinded by the sheer euphoria over Enron's successes in the mid to late 1990s, or working within investment banks that were earning substantial investment banking fees related to the complex partnerships. Although a few analysts continued to note that the company's earnings seemed strangely large relative to the falling cash flows reported, Enron's management was generally successful in arguing their point.

The rise and fall of Enron is a story that is far from complete. It may be in the end, however, that the true moral of the story is not in the failure of any specific process in place within the American system of corporate governance, nor in the mistaken focus on fair value accounting, nor in the lack of diligence of the board's own audit committee, but simply the failure of people in a wide variety of positions in a great many different organizations to act reputably and responsibly.

QUESTIONS

1. Which parts of the corporate governance system, both internal and external, do you believe failed Enron the most?

2. Describe how you think each of the individual stakeholders and components of the corporate governance system should have either prevented the problems at Enron or acted to resolve the problems before they reached crisis proportions.

3. If all publicly traded firms in the United States are operating within the same basic corporate governance system as Enron, why would some people believe this was an isolated incident, and not an example of many failures to come?

---

[12]Sherron Watkins, *Power Failure*, New York, N.Y.: Doubleday, p. 232. The *Raptors* and *LJM2* refer to special-purpose entities.

THE INTERNATIONAL MONETARY SYSTEM

2

This chapter begins with a brief history of the international monetary system from the days of the classical gold standard to the present time. The history includes the development of the Eurocurrency market and its reference rate of interest known as the London Interbank Offered Rate (LIBOR). The next section describes contemporary currency regimes, fixed versus flexible exchange rates, and the attributes of the ideal currency. The next section analyzes emerging markets and regime choices, including currency boards and dollarization. The following section describes the birth of the euro and the path toward monetary unification, including the expansion of the European Union on May 1, 2004. The final section analyzes the tradeoffs between exchange rate regimes based on rules, discretion, cooperation, and independence.

2.1 HISTORY OF THE INTERNATIONAL MONETARY SYSTEM

Over the ages, currencies have been defined in terms of gold and other items of value, and the international monetary system has been subject to a variety of international agreements. A review of these systems provides a useful perspective against which to understand today's system and to evaluate weaknesses and proposed changes in the present system.

The Gold Standard, 1876–1913

Since the days of the pharaohs (about 3000 B.C.), gold has served as a medium of exchange and a store of value. The Greeks and Romans used gold coins and passed on this tradition through the mercantile era to the nineteenth century. The great increase in trade during the free-trade period of the late nineteenth century led to a need for a more formalized system for settling international trade balances. One country after another set a par value for its currency in terms of gold and then tried to adhere to the so-called rules of the game. This later came to be known as the classical gold standard. The gold standard as an international monetary system gained acceptance in Western Europe in the 1870s. The United States was something of a latecomer to the system, not officially adopting the standard until 1879.

The "rules of the game" under the gold standard were clear and simple. Each country set the rate at which its currency unit (paper or coin) could be converted to a weight of gold. The United States, for example, declared the dollar to be convertible to gold at a rate of $20.67 per ounce of gold (a rate in effect until the beginning of World War I). The British pound was pegged at £4.2474 per ounce of gold. As long as both currencies were freely convertible into gold, the dollar/pound exchange rate was:

$$\frac{\$20.67 \text{ / ounce of gold}}{\pounds 4.2474 \text{ / ounce of gold}} = \$4.8665/\pounds$$

Because the government of each country on the gold standard agreed to buy or sell gold on demand with anyone at its own fixed parity rate, the value of each individual currency in terms of gold, and therefore exchange rates between currencies, was fixed. Maintaining adequate reserves of gold to back its currency's value was very important for a country under this system. The system also had the effect of implicitly limiting the rate at which any individual country could expand its money supply. Any growth in the amount of money was limited to the rate at which official authorities could acquire additional gold.

The gold standard worked adequately until the outbreak of World War I interrupted trade flows and the free movement of gold. This event caused the main trading nations to suspend operation of the gold standard.

The Interwar Years and World War II, 1914–1944

During World War I and the early 1920s, currencies were allowed to fluctuate over fairly wide ranges in terms of gold and each other. Theoretically, supply and demand for a country's exports and imports caused moderate changes in an exchange rate about a central equilibrium value. This was the same function that gold had performed under the previous gold standard. Unfortunately, such flexible exchange rates did not work in an equilibrating manner. On the contrary: international speculators sold the weak currencies short, causing them to fall further in value than warranted by real economic factors. *Selling short* is a speculation technique in which an individual speculator sells an asset such as a currency to another party for delivery at a future date. The speculator, however, does not yet own the asset, and expects the price of the asset to fall by the date when the asset must be purchased in the open market by the speculator for delivery.

The reverse happened with strong currencies. Fluctuations in currency values could not be offset by the relatively illiquid forward exchange market except at exorbitant cost. The net result was that the volume of world trade did not grow in the 1920s in proportion to world gross domestic product but instead declined to a very low level with the advent of the Great Depression in the 1930s.

The United States adopted a modified gold standard in 1934 when the U.S. dollar was devalued to $35 per ounce of gold from the $20.67 per ounce price in effect prior to World War I. Contrary to previous practice, the U.S. Treasury traded gold only with foreign central banks, not private citizens. From 1934 to the end of World War II, exchange rates were theoretically determined by each currency's value in terms of gold. During World War II and its chaotic aftermath, however, many of the main trading currencies lost their convertibility into other currencies. The dollar was the only major trading currency that continued to be convertible.

Bretton Woods and the International Monetary Fund, 1944

As World War II drew to a close in 1944, the Allied Powers met at Bretton Woods, New Hampshire, in order to create a new postwar international monetary system. The Bretton Woods Agreement established a U.S. dollar–based international monetary system and provided for two new institutions: the International Monetary Fund and the World Bank. The International Monetary Fund (IMF) aids countries with balance of payments and exchange rate problems. The International Bank for Reconstruction and Development (World Bank) helped fund postwar reconstruction and since then has supported general economic development.

The IMF was the key institution in the new international monetary system, and it has remained so to the present. The IMF was established to render temporary assistance to member countries trying to defend their currencies against cyclical, seasonal, or random occurrences. It also assists countries having structural trade problems if they promise to take adequate steps to correct their problems. If persistent deficits occur, however, the IMF cannot save a country from eventual devaluation. In recent years it has attempted to help countries facing financial crises. It has provided massive loans as well as advice to Russia and other former Russian republics, Brazil, Indonesia, and South Korea, to name but a few.

Under the original provisions of the Bretton Woods Agreement, all countries fixed the value of their currencies in terms of gold but were not required to exchange their currencies for gold. Only the dollar remained convertible into gold (at $35 per ounce). Therefore, each country established its exchange rate vis-à-vis the dollar, and then calculated the gold par value of its currency to create the desired dollar exchange rate. Participating countries agreed to try to maintain the value of their currencies within 1% (later expanded to $2\frac{1}{4}$%) of par by buying or selling foreign exchange or gold as needed. Devaluation was not to be used as a competitive trade policy, but if a currency became too weak to defend, a devaluation of up to 10% was allowed without formal approval by the IMF. Larger devaluations required IMF approval. This became known as the *gold-exchange standard*.

The *Special Drawing Right* (SDR) is an international reserve asset created by the IMF to supplement existing foreign exchange reserves. It serves as a unit of account for the IMF and other international and regional organizations, and is also the base against which some countries peg the exchange rate for their currencies.

Defined initially in terms of a fixed quantity of gold, the SDR has been redefined several times. It is currently the weighted average of four major currencies: namely, the U.S. dollar, the euro, the Japanese yen, and the British pound. The weights are updated every five years by the IMF. Individual countries hold SDRs in the form of deposits in the IMF. These holdings are part of each country's international monetary reserves, along with official holdings of gold, foreign exchange, and its reserve position at the IMF. Members may settle transactions among themselves by transferring SDRs.

Eurocurrencies

Eurocurrencies are domestic currencies of one country on deposit in a second country. Eurodollar time deposit maturities range from call money and overnight funds to longer periods. Certificates of deposit are usually for three months or more and in million-dollar increments. A Eurodollar deposit is not a demand deposit; it is not created on the bank's books by writing loans against required fractional reserves, and it cannot be transferred by a check drawn on the bank having the deposit. Eurodollar deposits are transferred by wire or cable transfer of an underlying balance held in a correspondent bank located within the United States. A domestic analogy in most countries would be the transfer of deposits held in nonbank savings associations. These are transferred by having the association write its own check on a commercial bank.

Any convertible currency can exist in "Euro-" form. (Note that this use of the expression "Euro-" should not be confused with the new common European currency called the *euro*.) The Eurocurrency market includes Eurosterling (British pounds deposited outside the United Kingdom), Euroeuros (euros on deposit outside the euro zone), and Euroyen (Japanese yen deposited outside Japan), as well as Eurodollars. The exact size of the Eurocurrency market is difficult to measure because it varies with daily decisions by depositors on where to hold readily transferable liquid funds, and particularly on whether to deposit dollars within or outside the United States.

Eurocurrency markets serve two valuable purposes: (1) Eurocurrency deposits are an efficient and convenient money market device for holding excess corporate liquidity; and (2) the Eurocurrency market is a major source of short-term bank loans to finance corporate working capital needs, including the financing of imports and exports.

Banks in which Eurocurrencies are deposited are called *Eurobanks*. A Eurobank is a financial intermediary that simultaneously bids for time deposits and makes loans in a currency other than that of the currency in which it is located. Eurobanks are major world banks that conduct a Eurocurrency business in addition to all other banking functions. Thus the Eurocurrency operation that qualifies a bank for the name "Eurobank" is in fact a department of a large commercial bank, and the name springs from the performance of this function.

The modern Eurocurrency market was born shortly after World War II. Eastern European holders of dollars, including the various state trading banks of the Soviet Union, were afraid to deposit their dollar holdings in the United States because these deposits might be attached by U.S. residents with claims against communist governments. Therefore, Eastern European holders deposited their dollars in Western Europe, particularly with two Soviet banks: the Moscow Narodny Bank in London, and the Banque Commerciale pour l'Europe du Nord in Paris. These banks redeposited the funds in other Western banks, especially in London. Additional dollar deposits were received from various central banks in Western Europe, which elected to hold part of their dollar reserves in this form to obtain a higher yield. Commercial banks also placed their dollar balances in the market for the same reason, as well as because specific maturities could be negotiated in the Eurodollar market. Additional dollars came to the market from European insurance companies with a large volume of U.S. business. Such companies found it financially advantageous to keep their dollar reserves in the higher-yielding Eurodollar market. Various holders of international refugee funds also supplied funds.

Although the basic causes of the growth of the Eurocurrency market are economic efficiencies, a number of unique institutional events during the 1950s and 1960s helped its growth.

- In 1957, British monetary authorities responded to a weakening of the pound by imposing tight controls on U.K. bank lending in sterling to nonresidents of the United Kingdom. Encouraged by the Bank of England, U.K. banks turned to dollar lending as the only alternative that would allow them to maintain their leading position in world finance. For this they needed dollar deposits.

- Although New York was home base for the dollar and had a large domestic money and capital market, London became the center for international trading in the dollar because of that city's expertise in international monetary matters and its proximity in time and distance to major customers.
- Additional support for a European-based dollar market came from the balance of payments difficulties that the United States experienced during the 1960s, which temporarily separated the U.S. domestic capital market from that of the rest of the world.

Ultimately, however, the Eurocurrency market continues to thrive because it is a large international money market relatively free from governmental regulation and interference.

Eurocurrency Interest Rates: LIBOR

In the Eurocurrency market, the reference rate of interest is the *London Interbank Offered Rate* (LIBOR). LIBOR is now the most widely accepted rate of interest used in standardized quotations, loan agreements, and financial derivatives valuations. LIBOR is officially defined by the *British Bankers Association* (BBA). For example, U.S. dollar LIBOR is the mean of 16 multinational banks' interbank offered rates as sampled by the BAA at 11 A.M. *London time in London.* Similarly, the BBA calculates the Japanese yen LIBOR, euro LIBOR, and other currency LIBOR rates at the same time in London from samples of banks.

The interbank interest rate is not, however, confined to London. Most major domestic financial centers construct their own interbank offered rates for local loan agreements. These rates include PIBOR (Paris Interbank Offered Rate), MIBOR (Madrid Interbank Offered Rate), SIBOR (Singapore Interbank Offered Rate), and FIBOR (Frankfurt Interbank Offered Rate), to name but a few.

The key factor attracting both depositors and borrowers to the Eurocurrency loan market is the narrow interest rate spread within that market. The difference between deposit and loan rates is often less than a 1%. Interest spreads in the Eurocurrency market are small for a number of reasons. Low lending rates exist because the Eurocurrency market is a *wholesale market*, where deposits and loans are made in amounts of $500,000 or more on an unsecured basis. Borrowers are usually large corporations or government entities that qualify for low rates because of their credit standing and because the transaction size is large. In addition, overhead assigned to the Eurocurrency operation by participating banks is small.

Deposit rates are higher in the Eurocurrency markets than in most domestic currency markets because the financial institutions offering Eurocurrency activities are not subject to many of the regulations and reserve requirements imposed on traditional domestic banks and banking activities. With these costs removed, rates are subject to more competitive pressures, deposit rates are higher, and loan rates are lower. A second major area of cost avoided in the Eurocurrency markets is the payment of deposit insurance fees (such as the Federal Deposit Insurance Corporation or FDIC assessments paid on deposits in the United States). Figure 2-1 provides an illustration of how Eurodollar deposit and loan rates, including dollar LIBOR and LIBID rates, compared with traditional domestic interest rates in June 2005.

Fixed Exchange Rates, 1945–1973

The currency arrangement negotiated at Bretton Woods and monitored by the IMF worked fairly well during the post–World War II period of reconstruction and rapid growth in world trade. However, widely diverging national monetary and fiscal policies, differential rates of inflation, and various unexpected external shocks eventually resulted in the system's demise. The U.S. dollar was the main reserve currency held by central banks and was the key to the web of exchange rate values. Unfortunately the United States ran persistent and growing deficits in its balance of payments. A heavy capital outflow of dollars was required to finance these deficits and

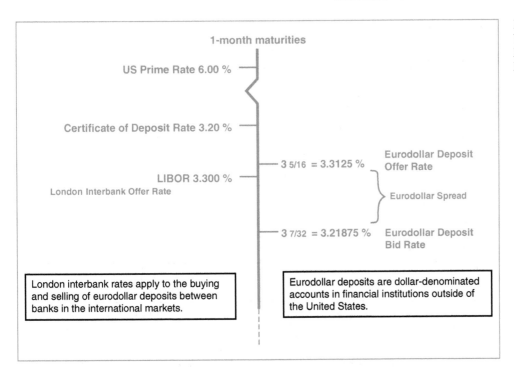

FIGURE 2-1
U.S. Dollar-
Denominated Interest
Rates, June 2005.

Source: *The Financial Times*, June 22, 2005, p. 23. Note: U.S. Federal Funds Rate 3.00%.

to meet the growing demand for dollars from investors and businesses. Eventually the heavy overhang of dollars held by foreigners resulted in a lack of confidence in the ability of the United States to meet its commitment to convert dollars to gold.

This lack of confidence forced President Richard Nixon to suspend official purchases or sales of gold by the U.S. Treasury on August 15, 1971, after the United States suffered outflows of roughly one third of its official gold reserves in the first seven months of the year. Exchange rates of most of the leading trading countries were allowed to float in relation to the dollar and thus indirectly in relation to gold. By the end of 1971, most of the major trading currencies had appreciated vis-à-vis the dollar. This change was—in effect—a devaluation of the dollar.

A year and a half later, the U.S. dollar once again came under attack, thereby forcing a second devaluation on February 12, 1973; this time by 10% to $42.22 per ounce of gold. By late February 1973, a fixed-rate system no longer appeared feasible given the speculative flows of currencies. The major foreign exchange markets were actually closed for several weeks in March 1973. When they reopened, most currencies were allowed to float to levels determined by market forces. Par values were left unchanged. The dollar floated downward an average of another 10% by June 1973.

An Eclectic Currency Arrangement, 1973–Present

Since March 1973, exchange rates have become much more volatile and less predictable than they were during the "fixed" exchange rate period, when changes occurred infrequently. Figure 2-2 illustrates the wide swings exhibited by the IMF's nominal exchange rate index of the U.S. dollar since 1957. Clearly, volatility has increased for this currency measure since 1973.

Table 2-1 summarizes the key events and external shocks that have affected currency values since March 1973. The most important shocks in recent years have been the European Monetary System (EMS) restructuring in 1992 and 1993; the emerging market currency crises, including that of Mexico in 1994, Thailand (and a number of other Asian currencies) in 1997, Russia in 1998, and Brazil in 1999; the introduction of the euro in 1999; Turkey in 2001; and Argentina and Venezuela in 2002.

FIGURE 2-2
The IMF's Nominal
Exchange Rate Index of
the U.S. Dollar and
Significant Events,
1957–2005.

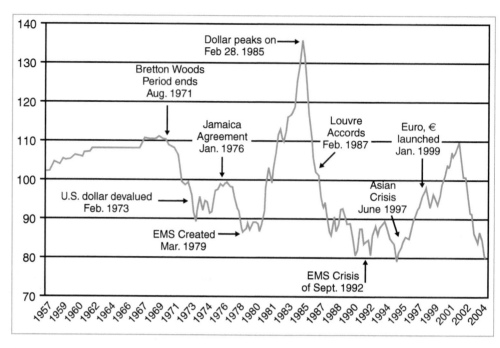

Source: International Monetary Fund, *International Financial Statistics*, http://www.imfstatistics.org.

TABLE 2-1   World Currency Events, 1971–2005.

DATE	EVENT	IMPACT
August 1971	Dollar Floated	Nixon closes the U.S. gold window, suspending purchases or sales of gold by U.S. Treasury; temporary imposition of 10% import surcharge.
December 1971	Smithsonian Agreement	Group of Ten reaches compromise whereby the US$ is devalued to $38/oz. of gold; most other major currencies are appreciated versus US$.
February 1973	U.S. dollar devalued	Devaluation pressure increases on US$, forcing further devaluation to $42.22/oz. of gold.
February–March 1973	Currency markets in crisis	Fixed exchange rates no longer considered defensible; speculative pressures force closure of international foreign exchange markets for nearly two weeks; markets reopen on floating rates for major industrial currencies.
June 1973	U.S. dollar depreciation	Floating rates continue to drive the now freely floating US$ down by about 10% by June.
Fall 1973–1974	OPEC oil embargo	Organization of Petroleum Exporting Countries (OPEC) impose oil embargo, eventually quadrupling the world price of oil; because world oil prices are stated in US$, value of US$ recovers some former strength.
January 1976	Jamaica Agreement	IMF meeting in Jamaica results in the "legalization" of the floating exchange rate system already in effect; gold is demonetized as a reserve asset.
1977–1978	U.S. inflation rate rises	Carter administration reduces unemployment at the expense of inflation increases; rising U.S. inflation causes continued depreciation of the US$.

TABLE 2-1 *Continued*

DATE	EVENT	IMPACT
March 1979	EMS created	The European Monetary System (EMS) is created, establishing a cooperative exchange rate system for participating members of the European Economic Community (EEC).
Summer 1979	OPEC raises prices	OPEC nations raise price of oil again.
Spring 1980	U.S. dollar begins rise	Worldwide inflation and early signs of recession coupled with real interest differential advantages for dollar-denominated assets contribute to increased demand for dollars.
August 1982	Latin American debt crisis	Mexico informs U.S. Treasury on Friday 13, 1982, that it will be unable to make debt service payments; Brazil and Argentina follow within months.
February 1985	U.S. dollar peaks	The U.S. dollar peaks against most major industrial currencies, hitting record highs against the deutsche mark and other European currencies.
September 1985	Plaza Agreement	Group of Ten members meet at the Plaza Hotel in New York City to sign an international cooperative agreement to control the volatility of world currency markets and to establish target zones.
February 1987	Louvre Accords	Group of Six members state they will "intensify" economic policy coordination to promote growth and reduce external imbalances.
December 1991	Maastricht Treaty	European Union concludes a treaty to replace all individual currencies with a single currency—the euro.
September 1992	EMS crisis	High German interest rates induce massive capital flows into deutsche mark–denominated assets, causing the withdrawal of the Italian lira and British pound from the EMS's common float.
July 31, 1993	EMS realignment	EMS adjusts allowable deviation band to ±15% for all member countries (except the Dutch guilder); U.S. dollar continues to weaken; Japanese yen reaches ¥100.25/$.
1994	EMI founded	European Monetary Institute (EMI), the predecessor to the European Central Bank, is founded in Frankfurt, Germany.
December 1994	Peso collapse	Mexican peso suffers major devaluation as a result of increasing pressure on the managed devaluation policy; peso falls from Ps3.46/$ to Ps5.50/$ within days. The peso's collapse results in a fall in most major Latin American exchanges in a contagion process—the "tequila effect."
August 1995	Yen peaks	Japanese yen reaches an all-time high versus the U.S. dollar of ¥79/$; yen slowly depreciates over the following two-year period, rising to over ¥130/$.
June 1997	Asian crisis	The Thai baht is devalued in July, followed soon after by the Indonesian rupiah, Korean won, Malaysian ringgit, and Philippine peso. Following the initial exchange rate devaluations, the Asian economy plummets into recession.
August 1998	Russian crisis	On Monday, August 17, the Russian Central Bank devalues the ruble by 34%. The ruble continues to deteriorate in the following days, sending the already weak Russian economy into recession.
January 1, 1999	Euro launched	Official launch date for the single European currency, the euro. Eleven European Union member states elect to participate in the system, which irrevocably locks their individual currencies rates between them.
January 1999	Brazilian reais crisis	The reais, initially devalued 8.3% by the Brazilian government on January 12, is allowed to float against the world's currencies.

TABLE 2-1   *Continued*

DATE	EVENT	IMPACT
January 1, 2002	Euro coinage	Euro coins and notes are introduced in parallel with home currencies. National currencies are phased out during the six-month period beginning January 1.
January 8, 2002	Argentine peso crisis	The Argentine peso, its value fixed to the U.S. dollar at 1:1 since 1991 through a currency board, is devalued to Ps1.4/$, then floated.
February 13, 2002	Venezuelan bolivar floated	The Venezuelan bolivar, fixed to the dollar since 1996, is floated as a result of increasing economic crisis.
February 14, 2004	Venezuelan bolivar devalued	Venezuela devalues the bolivar by 17% versus the U.S. dollar, in an attempt to deal with its growing fiscal deficit.
May 1, 2004	EU enlargement	Ten more countries join the European Union, thereby enlarging it to 25 members. In the future, when they qualify, most of these countries are expected to adopt the euro.
July 21, 2005	Yuan reform	The Chinese government and the People's Bank of China abandon the peg of the Chinese yuan (renminbi) to the U.S. dollar, announcing that it will be instantly revalued from Yuan8.28/$ to Yuan8.11/$, and reform the exchange rate regime to a managed float in the future. Malaysia announces a similar change to its exchange rate regime.

2.2   CONTEMPORARY CURRENCY REGIMES

The international monetary system today is composed of national currencies, artificial currencies (such as the SDR), and one entirely new currency (euro) that replaced the 11 national European Union currencies on January 1, 1999. All of these currencies are linked to one another via a "smorgasbord" of currency regimes.

IMF's Exchange Rate Regime Classifications

The IMF classifies all exchange rate regimes into eight specific categories. The eight categories span the spectrum of exchange rate regimes from rigidly fixed to independently floating.

1. **Exchange arrangements with no separate legal tender.** The currency of another country circulates as the sole legal tender or the member belongs to a monetary or currency union in which the same legal tender is shared by the members of the union.

2. **Currency board arrangements.** A monetary regime based on an implicit legislative commitment to exchange domestic currency for a specified foreign currency at a fixed exchange rate, combined with restrictions on the issuing authority to ensure the fulfillment of its legal obligation.

3. **Other conventional fixed peg arrangements.** The country pegs its currency (formally or *de facto*) at a fixed rate to a major currency or a basket of currencies (a *composite*), where the exchange rate fluctuates within a narrow margin or at most ±1% around a central rate.

4. **Pegged exchange rates within horizontal bands.** The value of the currency is maintained within margins of fluctuation around a formal or *de facto* fixed peg that are wider than ±1% around a central rate.

5. **Crawling pegs.** The currency is adjusted periodically in small amounts at a fixed, preannounced rate or in response to changes in selective quantitative indicators.

6. **Exchange rates within crawling pegs.** The currency is maintained within certain fluctuation margins around a central rate that is adjusted periodically at a fixed preannounced rate or in response to changes in selective quantitative indicators.

7. **Managed floating with no preannounced path for the exchange rate.** The monetary authority influences the movements of the exchange rate through active intervention in the foreign exchange market without specifying, or precommitting to, a preannounced path for the exchange rate.

8. **Independent floating.** The exchange rate is market-determined, with any foreign exchange intervention aimed at moderating the rate of change and preventing undue fluctuations in the exchange rate, rather than establishing a level for it.

The most prominent example of a rigidly fixed system is the euro area, in which the euro is the single currency for its member countries. However, the euro itself is an independently floating currency against all other currencies. Other examples of rigidly fixed exchange regimes include Ecuador and Panama, which use the U.S. dollar as their official currency; the Central African Franc (CFA) zone, in which countries such as Mali, Niger, Senegal, Cameroon, and Chad among others use a single common currency (the franc, tied to the euro) and the Eastern Caribbean Currency Union (ECCU), whose members use a single common currency (the Eastern Caribbean dollar).

At the other extreme are countries with independently floating currencies. These include many of the most-developed countries, such as Japan, the United States, the United Kingdom, Canada, Australia, New Zealand, Sweden, and Switzerland. However, this category also includes a number of unwilling participants—emerging market countries that tried to maintain fixed rates but were forced by the marketplace to let them float. Among these are Korea, the Philippines, Brazil, Indonesia, Mexico, and Thailand.

It is important to note that only the last two categories, including 80 of the 186 countries covered, are actually "floating" in any real degree. Although the contemporary international monetary system is typically referred to as a "floating regime," it is clearly not the case for the majority of the world's nations.

Fixed Versus Flexible Exchange Rates

A nation's choice as to which currency regime to follow reflects national priorities about all facets of the economy, including inflation, unemployment, interest rate levels, trade balances, and economic growth. The choice between fixed and flexible rates may change over time as priorities change.

At the risk of overgeneralizing, the following points partly explain why countries pursue certain exchange rate regimes. They are based on the premise that, other things being equal, countries would prefer fixed exchange rates.

- Fixed rates provide stability in international prices for the conduct of trade. Stable prices aid in the growth of international trade and lessen risks for all businesses.
- Fixed exchange rates are inherently anti-inflationary, requiring the country to follow restrictive monetary and fiscal policies. This restrictiveness, however, can often be a burden to a country wishing to pursue policies that alleviate continuing internal economic problems, such as high unemployment or slow economic growth.
- Fixed exchange rate regimes necessitate that central banks maintain large quantities of international reserves (hard currencies and gold) for use in the occasional defense of the fixed rate. As international currency markets have grown rapidly in size and volume, increasing reserve holdings has become a significant burden to many nations.
- Fixed rates, once in place, may be maintained at levels that are inconsistent with economic fundamentals. As the structure of a nation's economy changes, and as its trade relationships and balances evolve, the exchange rate itself should change. Flexible exchange rates allow this to happen gradually and efficiently, but fixed rates must be changed administratively—usually too late, too highly publicized, and at too large a one-time cost to the nation's economic health.

Attributes of the "Ideal" Currency

If the ideal currency existed in today's world, it would possess three attributes (illustrated in Figure 2-3), often referred to as *the impossible trinity*:

1. **Exchange rate stability.** The value of the currency would be fixed in relationship to other major currencies, so traders and investors could be relatively certain of the foreign exchange value of each currency in the present and into the near future.
2. **Full financial integration.** Complete freedom of monetary flows would be allowed, so traders and investors could willingly and easily move funds from one country and currency to another in response to perceived economic opportunities or risks.
3. **Monetary independence.** Domestic monetary and interest rate policies would be set by each individual country to pursue desired national economic policies, especially as they might relate to limiting inflation, combating recessions, and fostering prosperity and full employment.

The reason these qualities are termed "the impossible trinity": is that a country must give up one of the three goals described by the sides of the triangle: monetary independence, exchange rate stability, or full financial integration. The forces of economics do not allow the simultaneous achievement of all three. For example, a country with a pure float exchange rate regime can have monetary independence and a high degree of financial integration with the outside capital markets, but the result must be a loss of exchange rate stability (the case of the United States). Similarly, a country that maintains very tight controls over the inflow and outflow of capital will retain its monetary independence and a stable exchange rate, but at the loss of being integrated with global financial and capital markets (the case of Malaysia in the 1998–2002 period).

As illustrated in Figure 2-3, the consensus of many experts is that the force of increased capital mobility has been pushing more and more countries toward full financial integration in an attempt to stimulate their domestic economies and feed the capital appetites of their own MNEs. As a result, their currency regimes are being "cornered" into being either purely floating (like the United States) or integrated with other countries in monetary unions (like the European Union).

FIGURE 2-3
The Impossible Trinity.

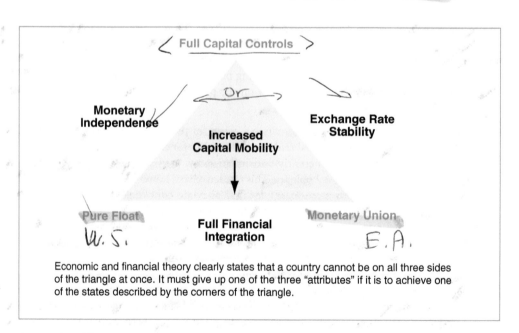

Source: Adapted from Lars Oxelheim, *International Financial Integration*, Springer-Verlag, 1990, p. 10.

2.3   EMERGING MARKETS AND REGIME CHOICES

The 1997–2005 period saw increasing pressures on emerging market countries to choose among more extreme types of exchange rate regimes. The increased capital mobility pressures noted in the previous section have driven a number of countries to choose between either a free-floating exchange rate (such as Turkey in February 2002) or the opposite extreme, a fixed-rate regime—such as a *currency board* (as in Argentina, which proved unsuccessful) or even *dollarization* (as in the case of Ecuador in 2000).

Currency Boards

A *currency board* exists when a country's central bank commits to back its monetary base—its money supply—entirely with foreign reserves at all times. This commitment means that a unit of domestic currency cannot be introduced into the economy without an additional unit of foreign exchange reserves being obtained first. Eight countries, including Hong Kong, utilize currency boards as a means of fixing their exchange rates.

ARGENTINA   In 1991, Argentina moved from its previous managed exchange rate of the Argentine peso to a currency board structure. The currency board structure fixed the Argentine peso's value to the U.S. dollar on a one-to-one basis. The Argentine government preserved the fixed rate of exchange by requiring that every peso issued through the Argentine banking system be backed by either gold or U.S. dollars held on account in banks in Argentina. This 100% reserve system made the monetary policy of Argentina dependent on the country's ability to obtain U.S. dollars through trade or investment. Only after Argentina had earned these dollars through trade could its money supply be expanded. This requirement eliminated the possibility of the nation's money supply growing too rapidly and causing inflation.

An additional feature of the Argentine currency board system was the ability of all Argentines or foreigners to hold dollar-denominated accounts in Argentine banks. These accounts were in actuality *Eurodollar accounts*—dollar-denominated deposits in non-U.S. banks. These accounts provided savers and investors with the ability to choose whether to hold pesos.

From the very beginning, however, there was substantial doubt in the market that the Argentine government could maintain the fixed exchange rate. Argentine banks regularly paid slightly higher interest rates on peso-denominated accounts than on dollar-denominated accounts. This interest differential represented a market-determined *risk premium* of the system itself. Depositors were rewarded for accepting risk—for keeping their money in peso-denominated accounts. This was an explicit signal by the marketplace that there was a perceived possibility that what was then "fixed" would not always be so.

The market proved to be correct. In January 2002, after months of economic and political turmoil and nearly three years of economic recession, the Argentine currency board was ended. The peso was first devalued from Peso1.00/$ to Peso1.40/$, then floated completely. It fell in value dramatically within days. The Argentine decade-long experiment with a rigidly fixed exchange rate was over. The devaluation followed months of turmoil, including continuing bank holidays and riots in the streets of Buenos Aires.

Dollarization

Several countries have suffered currency devaluation for many years, primarily as a result of infla-tion, and have taken steps toward dollarization. *Dollarization* is the use of the U.S. dollar as the official currency of the country. Panama has used the dollar as its official currency since 1907. Ecuador, after suffering a severe banking and inflationary crisis in 1998 and 1999, adopted the

U.S. dollar as its official currency in January 2000. One of the primary attributes of dollarization was summarized well by *Business Week* in a December 11, 2000, article entitled "The Dollar Club":

> *One attraction of dollarization is that sound monetary and exchange-rate policies no longer depend on the intelligence and discipline of domestic policymakers. Their monetary policy becomes essentially the one followed by the U.S., and the exchange rate is fixed forever.*

The arguments for dollarization follow logically from the previous discussion of the impossible trinity. A country that dollarizes removes any currency volatility (against the dollar) and would theoretically eliminate the possibility of future currency crises. Additional benefits are expectations of greater economic integration with the United States and other dollar-based markets, both product and financial. This last point has led many to argue in favor of regional dollarization, in which several countries that are highly economically integrated may benefit significantly from dollarizing together.

Three major arguments exist against dollarization. The first is the loss of sovereignty over monetary policy. This is, however, the point of dollarization. Secondly, the country loses the power of *seignorage*, the ability to profit from its ability to print its own money. Third, the central bank of the country, because it no longer has the ability to create money within its economic and financial system, can no longer serve the role of lender of last resort. This role carries with it the ability to provide liquidity to save financial institutions that may be on the brink of failure during times of financial crisis.

ECUADOR   Ecuador officially completed the replacement of the Ecuadorian sucre with the U.S. dollar as legal tender on September 9, 2000. This step made Ecuador the largest national adopter of the U.S. dollar, and in many ways set it up as a test case of dollarization for other emerging market countries to watch closely. As illustrated by Figure 2-4, this was the last stage of a massive depreciation of the sucre in a brief two-year period.

During 1999, Ecuador suffered a rising rate of inflation and a falling level of economic output. In March 1999, the Ecuadorian banking sector was hit with a series of devastating

FIGURE 2-4
The Ecuadorian Sucre Exchange Rate, November 1998–March 2000.

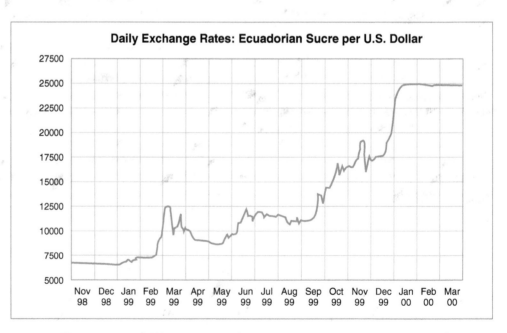

Source: Pacific Currency Exchange, http://pacific.commerce.ubc.ca/xr © 2001 by Prof. Werner Antweiler, University of British Columbia, Vancouver, BC, Canada.

"bank runs," financial panics in which all depositors attempted to withdraw all of their funds simultaneously. Although there were severe problems in the Ecuadorian banking system, the truth was that even the healthiest financial institution would fail under the strain of this financial drain. Ecuador's president at that time, Jamil Mahuad, immediately froze all deposits (what was termed a *bank holiday* in the United States in the 1930s, in which banks closed their doors). The Ecuadorian sucre, which in January 1999 was trading at roughly Sucre7,400/dollar, plummeted in early March to Sucre12,500/dollar. Ecuador defaulted on more than $13.6 billion in foreign debt in 1999 alone. President Mahuad moved quickly to propose dollarization to save the failing Ecuadorian economy.

By January 2000, when the next president took office (after a rather complicated military coup and subsequent withdrawal), the sucre had fallen in value to Sucre25,000/dollar. The new president, Gustavo Naboa, continued the dollarization initiative. Although unsupported by the U.S. government and the IMF, Ecuador completed its replacement of its own currency with the dollar over the next nine months.

The results of dollarization in Ecuador are still unknown. Ecuadorian residents did immediately return over $600 million into the banking system, money that they had withheld from the banks in fear of bank failure. This added capital infusion, along with new IMF loans and economic restructurings, allowed the country to actually close 2000 with a small economic gain of 1%. Inflation, however, remained high, closing the year at over 91% (up from 66% in 1999). Clearly, dollarization alone did not eliminate inflationary forces. Ecuador continues to struggle to find both economic and political balance with its new currency regime.

There is no doubt that for many emerging markets, a currency board, dollarization, and freely floating exchange rate regimes are all extremes. In fact, many experts feel that the global financial marketplace will drive more and more emerging market nations towards one of these extremes. As illustrated by Figure 2-5, there is a distinct lack of middle ground between rigidly fixed and freely floating extremes. In anecdotal support of this argument, a poll of the general population in Mexico in 1999 indicated that 9 out of 10 people would prefer dollarization over a floating-rate peso. Clearly, there are many in the emerging markets of the world who have little faith in their leadership and institutions to implement an effective exchange rate policy.

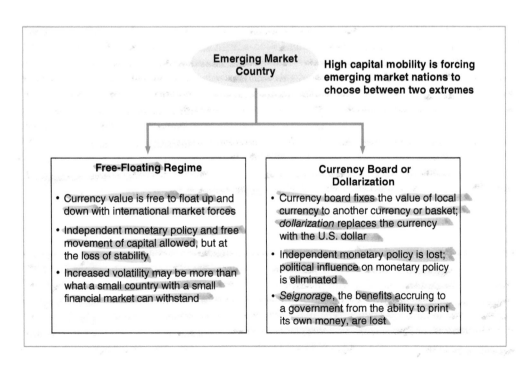

FIGURE 2-5
The Currency Regime Choices for Emerging Markets.

2.4 THE BIRTH OF A EUROPEAN CURRENCY: THE EURO

The original 15 members of the European Union (EU) are also members of the European Monetary System (EMS). This group has tried to form an island of fixed exchange rates among themselves in a sea of major floating currencies. Members of the EMS rely heavily on trade with each other, so they perceive that the day-to-day benefits of fixed exchange rates between them are great. Nevertheless the EMS has undergone a number of major changes since its inception in 1979, including major crises and reorganizations in 1992 and 1993, and conversion of 11 members to the euro on January 1, 1999 (Greece joined in 2001). In December 1991, the members of the EU met at Maastricht, the Netherlands, and concluded a treaty that changed Europe's currency future.

TIMETABLE The Maastricht Treaty specified a timetable and a plan to replace all individual ECU currencies with a single currency called the *euro*. Other steps were adopted that would lead to a full European Economic and Monetary Union (EMU).

CONVERGENCE CRITERIA To prepare for the EMU, the Maastricht Treaty called for the integration and coordination of the member countries' monetary and fiscal policies. The EMU would be implemented by a process called *convergence*. Before becoming a full member of the EMU, each member country was originally expected to meet the following convergence criteria:

1. Nominal inflation should be no more than 1.5% above the average for the three members of the EU with the lowest inflation rates during the previous year.
2. Long-term interest rates should be no more than 2% above the average for the three members with the lowest interest rates.
3. The fiscal deficit should be no more than 3% of gross domestic product.
4. Government debt should be no more than 60% of gross domestic product.

The convergence criteria were so tough that few, if any, of the members could satisfy them at that time, but 11 countries managed to do so just prior to 1999. Greece adopted the euro on January 1, 2001.

STRONG CENTRAL BANK A strong central bank, called the European Central Bank (ECB), has been established in Frankfurt, Germany, in accordance with the Treaty. The bank is modeled after the U.S. Federal Reserve System. This independent central bank dominates the countries' central banks, which continue to regulate banks resident within their borders; all financial market intervention and the issuance of euros remain the sole responsibility of the ECB. The single most important mandate of the ECB is to promote price stability within the European Union.

As part of its development of cross-border monetary policy, the ECB has formed the Transeuropean Automated Real-time Gross settlement Express Transfer system (TARGET). TARGET is the mechanism by which the ECB will settle all cross-border payments in the conduct of EU banking business and regulation. It will allow the ECB to conduct monetary policy and other intrabanking system capital movements quickly and without cost.

Why Monetary Unification?

According to the EU, EMU is a single-currency area within the EU single market, now known informally as the *euro zone*, in which people, goods, services, and capital are supposed to move without restrictions. Beginning with the Treaty of Rome in 1957 and continuing with the Single European Act of 1987, the Maastricht Treaty of 1991–1992, and the Treaty of Amsterdam of 1997, a core set of European countries worked steadily toward integrating their individual countries into one larger, more efficient, domestic market. Even after the launch of the 1992 Single Europe program, however, a number of barriers to true openness remained. The use of different currencies required both consumers and companies to treat the individual markets separately. Currency risk of cross-border commerce still persisted. The creation of a single currency is designed to move beyond these vestiges of separated markets.

The official abbreviation of the euro, EUR, has been registered with the International Standards Organization (letter abbreviations are needed for computer-based worldwide trading). This is similar to the three-letter computer symbols used for the U.S. dollar, USD, and the British pound sterling, GBP. The official symbol of the euro is €. According to the EU, the symbol was inspired by the Greek letter *epsilon* (ε), simultaneously referring to Greece's ancient role as the source of European civilization and recalling the first letter of the word *Europe*.

The Launch of the Euro

On January 4, 1999, 11 member states of the EU initiated the EMU. They established a single currency, the euro, which replaced the individual currencies of the participating member states. The 11 countries were Austria, Belgium, Finland, France, Germany, Ireland, Italy, Luxembourg, the Netherlands, Portugal, and Spain. The United Kingdom, Sweden, and Denmark chose to maintain their individual currencies. Greece did not qualify for EMU but joined the Euro group in 2001. On December 31, 1998, the final fixed rates between the 11 participating currencies and the euro were put into place. On January 4, 1999, the euro was officially launched. Although it was the result of a long-term and methodical program for the alignment of all political and economic forces in the EU, the launch of the euro was only the first of many steps to come. The impacts of the euro on the economic environment and on society in general within the participating countries have been and will continue to be dramatic. It is only now becoming apparent what some of the impacts might be.

The euro affects markets in three ways: (1) countries within the euro zone enjoy cheaper transaction costs; (2) currency risks and costs related to exchange rate uncertainty are reduced; and (3) all consumers and businesses both inside and outside the euro zone enjoy price transparency and increased price-based competition.

Achieving Monetary Unification

If the euro is to be a successful replacement for the currencies of the participating EU states, it must have a solid economic foundation. The primary driver of a currency's value is its ability to maintain its purchasing power (money is worth what money can buy). The single largest threat to maintaining purchasing power is inflation. So, job one for the EU since the beginning has been to construct an economic system that would work to prevent inflationary forces from undermining the euro.

FISCAL POLICY AND MONETARY POLICY   Monetary policy for the EMU is conducted by the ECB, which has one responsibility: to safeguard the stability of the euro. Following the basic structures that were used in the establishment of the Federal Reserve System in the United States and the Bundesbank in Germany, the ECB is free of political pressures that have historically caused monetary authorities to yield to employment pressures by inflating economies. The ECB's independence allows it to focus simply on the stability of the currency without falling victim to this historical trap.

FIXING THE VALUE OF THE EURO   The December 31, 1998, fixing of the rates of exchange between national currencies and the euro were permanent fixes for these currencies. The United Kingdom has been skeptical of increasing EU infringement on its sovereignty, and has opted to not participate. Sweden, which has failed to see significant benefits from EU membership (although it is one of the newest members), has also been skeptical of EMU participation. Denmark, like the United Kingdom and Sweden, has a strong political element that is highly nationalistic, and so far has opted to not participate. Norway has twice voted down membership in the EU and thus does not participate in the euro.

On January 4, 1999, the euro began trading on world currency markets. Its introduction was a smooth one. The euro's value slid steadily following its introduction, however, primarily as a result of the robustness of the U.S. economy and U.S. dollar, and continuing sluggish economic sectors in the EMU countries. Figure 2-6 illustrates the euro's value since its introduction in January 1999. After declining in value against the U.S. dollar over 1999 and 2000, the euro traded in a relatively narrow band throughout 2001. Beginning in early 2002, however, the euro started a strong and steady rise in value versus the dollar, peaking at $1.36/€ in late 2004.

CAUSES OF THE DOLLAR DECLINE   During the whole period since the introduction of the euro to the present time, the United States has experienced severe balance of payments deficits on current account. The biggest deficits were with China and Japan. However, in order to protect their export competitiveness, both China and Japan followed macroeconomic policies that would maintain fixed exchange rates between their currencies and the U.S. dollar. In order to accomplish this result, both China and Japan had to intervene in the foreign exchange market by buying up massive amounts of U.S. dollars while selling corresponding amounts of their own currencies, the Chinese yuan and the Japanese yen. These purchases showed up as capital inflows into the United States. However, as the United States continued to maintain historically low interest rates to stimulate its domestic economy, some critics wondered if China and Japan would continue to hold so many U.S. dollars.

EXPANSION OF THE EUROPEAN UNION AND THE EURO   On May 1, 2004 the European Union added 10 more countries to its ranks. Although none of the new countries is qualified at the moment to adopt the euro as its currency, expansion of the euro is expected over the next six years. *Global Finance in Practice 2.1* lists these 10 countries, their currency regimes, and their likely time frame for transition to the euro.

The transition to the euro may have been damaged a bit in 2005 when the effort to create a single constitution for all 25 member states of the EU foundered. The proposed constitution must be ratified by all 25 member states. As of June 2005, nine states had approved the proposal, but France and the Netherlands had voted "no."

FIGURE 2-6
The U.S. Dollar/Euro Spot Exchange Rate, 1999–2005 (Monthly Average).

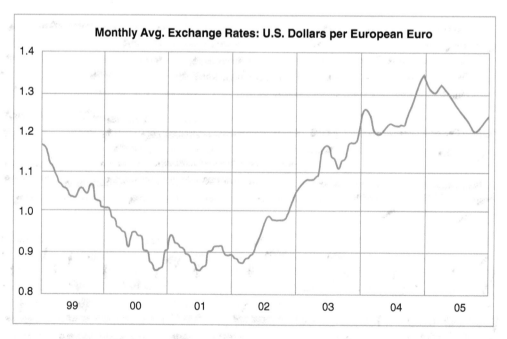

Source: © 2005 by Prof. Werner Antweiler, University of British Columbia, Vancouver, BC, Canada. The time period shown in diagram: 1/Jan/1999–31/Dec/2005.

Global Finance in Practice 2.1

Will the New Member States of the EU Automatically Adopt the Euro?

Country	Currency	EU Expected Entry Date	Current Exchange Rate Regime
Cyprus	pound	2007	Pegged to the euro
Czech Republic	koruna	2009/10	Free-floating, references the euro
Estonia	kroon	2007	Pegged to the euro in early 1999
Hungary	forint	2009/10	ERM-II type bank since May 2001
Latvia	lat	2008	Pegged to the IMF's SDR since 1994
Lithuania	litas	2007	Pegged to the euro since February 2002
Malta	lira	2007/08	Pegged to a basket (70% euro, 20% sterling, 10% dollar)
Poland	zloty	2008/09	Free-floating since April 2000
Slovakia	koruna	2009	Free-floating since October 1998
Slovenia	tolar	2008	Managed float, euro reference rate

The 10 new member states acceding to the EU on May 1, 2004 (Czech Republic, Estonia, Cyprus, Latvia, Lithuania, Hungary, Malta, Poland, Slovenia, and Slovakia) will not automatically adopt the euro by joining the EU. They will do so only once they have achieved the high degree of sustainable economic convergence with the euro area required for membership of the single currency.

They will thus need to fulfill the same Maastricht convergence criteria that were applied to the existing euro area members; namely, a high degree of price stability, sustainable government finances (in terms of both public deficit and public debt levels), a stable exchange rate, and convergence in long-term interest rates. There is no predefined timetable for adoption of the euro by the new member states, but the levels of convergence required for membership will be assessed by the Council of the EU on a proposal from the European Commission and on the basis of convergence reports by the Commission and the European Central Bank. These reports are produced at least every two years or at the request of a member state wishing to adopt the euro.

Sources: "EU Enlargement and the Adoption of the Euro," *AIG Global Treasury*, Economic Research Unit; and http://europa.eu.int/comm/economy_finance/euro/faqs/faqs_19_en.htm (accessed May 19, 2004).

The "no" votes were a big blow to those Europeans that saw the European Union as potentially more than just an economic, monetary, and currency union. The original founders of the EU were hoping eventually to create a political union, as a sort of "United States of Europe." In addition to establishing the euro, many non-trade barriers had been reduced in the runup to the 1992 Single European Market as part of the plan.

THE EURO AND GROWTH   Prior to the introduction of the euro, opponents thought political and economic conditions were unfavorable for a common currency. Most of the countries that eventually adopted the euro, such as Germany, France, and Italy, lacked the flexible labor markets they would need to compensate for losing individual (country-level) control over monetary policy as a tool to promote growth. Because the individual members of the EU cannot devalue their currencies, they need to rely mainly on coordinated fiscal policies to stimulate growth. It is probably

Global Finance in Practice 2.2

Calculating the Euro's Success

PROS	CONS
• Lower interest rates for countries such as Italy	• Strong euro deadly for exporters who face competition from China
• Europe is better able to absorb shocks such as the 9/11 attacks	• Average folks still don't like it; the euro feeds resentment toward EU
• Eliminates exchange rate risk within euro zone	• Encourages politicians to procrastinate on unpopular reforms
• Helps create deeper capital markets, making bigger deals possible	• Risk that a financial crisis in one nation will infect whole zone
• The euro is becoming a popular reserve currency, representing 19.7% of central bank holdings as of Feb. 2004	• The unified monetary policy is a straitjacket for slow-growth countries and spurs inflation in high-growth ones

Source: "Squeezed by the Euro," *Business Week*, June 6, 2006, p. 53.

impossible to conduct a centralized monetary policy that fits all member countries, as illustrated by the impossible trinity discussed earlier. Some member countries are growing and some are not. Unemployment has been fairly high in some member countries, but lower in others.

EVALUATING THE EURO   Apart from issues of growth and employment, the euro has had a mixed record of success and failure. *Global Finance in Practice 2.2* summarizes the pros and cons of the European Monetary Union and the euro to date.

2.5   EXCHANGE RATE REGIMES: WHAT LIES AHEAD?

All exchange rate regimes must deal with the tradeoff between *rules* and *discretion*, as well as between *cooperation* and *independence*. Figure 2-7 illustrates the tradeoffs between exchange rate regimes based on rules, discretion, cooperation, and independence.

- Vertically, different exchange rate arrangements may dictate whether the country's government has strict intervention requirements—*rules*—or whether it may choose whether, when, and to what degree to intervene in the foreign exchange markets—*discretion*.
- Horizontally, the tradeoff for countries participating in a specific system is between consulting and acting in unison with other countries—*cooperation*—or operating as a member of the system, but acting on their own—*independence*.

Regime structures like the gold standard required no cooperative policies among countries, only the assurance that all would abide by the "rules of the game." Under the gold standard in effect prior to World War II, this assurance translated into the willingness of governments to buy or sell gold at parity rates on demand. The Bretton Woods Agreement, the system in place between 1944 and 1973, required more in the way of cooperation, in that gold was no longer the "rule," and countries were required to cooperate to a higher degree to maintain the dollar-based system. Exchange rate systems, like the European Monetary System's fixed exchange rate band system used from 1979 to 1999, were hybrids of these cooperative and rule regimes.

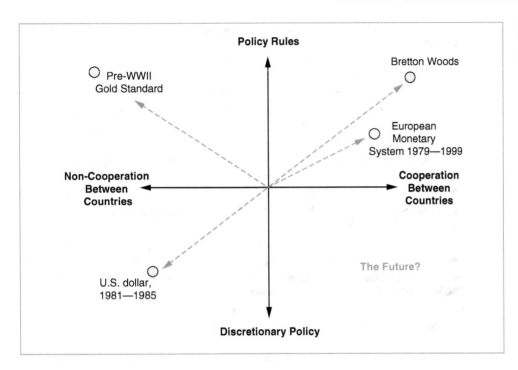

FIGURE 2-7
The Tradeoffs Between
Exchange Rate Regimes.

The present international monetary system is characterized by no rules, with varying degrees of cooperation. Although there is no present solution to the continuing debate over what form a new international monetary system should take, many believe that it could succeed only if it combined cooperation among nations with individual discretion to pursue domestic social, economic, and financial goals.

SUMMARY

- Under the gold standard (1896–1913), the rules of the game stated that each country set the rate at which its currency unit could be converted to a weight of gold.
- During the interwar years (1914–1944), currencies were allowed to fluctuate over fairly wide ranges in terms of gold and each other. Supply and demand forces determined exchange rate values.
- The Bretton Woods Agreement (1944) established a U.S. dollar–based international monetary system. Under the original provisions of the Bretton Woods Agreement, all countries fixed the values of their currencies in terms of gold but were not required to exchange their currencies for gold. Only the dollar remained convertible into gold (at $35 per ounce).
- A variety of economic forces led to the suspension of the convertibility of the dollar into gold in August 1971. Exchange rates of most of the leading trading countries were then allowed to float in relation to the dollar and thus indirectly in relation to gold. Since a series of continuing crises in 1972 and 1973, the U.S. dollar and the other leading currencies of the world have floated in value.
- Eurocurrencies are domestic currencies of one country on deposit in a second country.
- Although the basic causes of the growth of the Eurocurrency market are economic efficiencies, a number of unique institutional events during the 1950s and 1960s helped its

growth. In 1957, British monetary authorities responded to a weakening of the British pound sterling by imposing tight controls on U.K. bank lending in pounds sterling to non-residents of the United Kingdom. Encouraged by the Bank of England, U.K. banks turned to dollar lending as the only alternative that would allow them to maintain their leading position in world finance. For this they needed dollars. Although New York was home base for the dollar and had a large domestic money and capital market, London became the center for international trading in the dollar because of that city's expertise in international monetary matters and its proximity in time and distance to major multinational businesses.

- If the ideal currency regime existed in today's world, it would possess three attributes: a fixed value, convertibility, and independent monetary policy.

- Emerging market countries must often choose between two extreme exchange rate regimes—either a free-floating regime or an extremely fixed regime such as a currency board or dollarization.

- The 15 original members of the European Union (EU) are also members of the European Monetary System (EMS). This group has tried to form an island of fixed exchange rates among themselves in a sea of major floating currencies. Members of the EMS rely heavily on trade with each other, so the day-to-day benefits of fixed exchange rates between them are perceived to be great.

- The EU expanded to 25 members in May 2004. Eventually, all of these new members might adopt the euro.

- The euro affects markets in three ways: (1) countries within the euro zone enjoy cheaper transaction costs; (2) currency risks and costs related to exchange rate uncertainty are reduced; and (3) all consumers and businesses both inside and outside the euro zone enjoy price transparency and increased price-based competition.

- The euro has had mixed success. Because individual member countries cannot devalue their currencies, and cannot use independent monetary policy, they have experienced uneven growth and employment results.

QUESTIONS

1. **The gold standard and the money supply.** Under the gold standard, all national governments promised to follow the "rules of the game." This meant defending a fixed exchange rate. What did this promise imply about a country's money supply?

2. **Causes of devaluation.** If a country follows a fixed exchange rate regime, what macroeconomic variables could cause the fixed exchange rate to be devalued?

3. **Fixed versus flexible exchange rates.** What are the advantages and disadvantages of fixed exchange rates?

4. **The impossible trinity.** Explain what is meant by the concept of the "impossible trinity."

5. **Currency board or dollarization.** Fixed exchange rate regimes are sometimes implemented through a currency board (Hong Kong) or dollarization (Ecuador). What is the difference between the two approaches?

6. **Emerging market exchange rate regimes.** High capital mobility is forcing emerging market nations to choose between free-floating regimes and currency board or dollarization regimes. What are the main outcomes of each of these regimes from the perspective of emerging market nations?

7. **Argentine currency board.** How did the Argentine currency board function from 1991 to January 2002 and why did it collapse?

8. **The euro.** On January 4, 1999, 11 member states of the EU initiated the European Monetary Union (EMU) and established a single currency, the *euro*, which replaced the individual currencies of participating member states. Describe three of the main ways that the euro affects the members of the EMU.

9. **Mavericks.** The United Kingdom, Denmark, and Sweden have chosen not to adopt the *euro* but rather maintain their individual currencies. What are the motivations of each of these three countries that are also members of the EU?

10. **International Monetary Fund (IMF).** The IMF was established by the Bretton Woods Agreement (1944). What were its original objectives?

11. **Special Drawing Rights.** What are *special drawing rights*?

12. **Exchange rate regime classifications.** The IMF classifies all exchange rate regimes into eight specific categories that are summarized in this chapter. Under which exchange rate regime would you classify each of the following countries?
    a. France
    b. The United States
    c. Japan
    d. Thailand

13. **Bretton Woods failure.** Why did the fixed exchange rate regime of 1945–1973 eventually fail?

14. **EU and euro expansion.** With so many new countries joining the EU in 2004, when will they officially move to the euro—if ever?

PROBLEMS

1. **Amsterdam and New York.** In Amsterdam, one can buy a U.S. dollar for 0.8200. In New York, one can buy a euro for $1.22. What is the foreign exchange rate between the dollar and the euro?

2. **Peso exchange rate changes.** In December 1994, the government of Mexico officially changed the value of the Mexican peso from Peso3.2/$ to Peso5.5/$. Was this a devaluation, revaluation, depreciation, or appreciation? Explain.

3. **Good as gold.** Under the gold standard, the price of an ounce of gold in U.S. dollars was $20.67, while the price of that same ounce in British pounds was £4.2474. What would the exchange rate between the dollar and the pound be if the U.S. dollar price had been $38.00 per ounce?

4. **Gold standard.** Before World War I, U.S. $20.67 was needed to buy one ounce of gold. If at the same time one ounce of gold could be purchased in France for FF310.00, what was the exchange rate between French francs and U.S. dollars?

5. **Spot rate—customer.** The spot rate for Mexican pesos is Peso10.80/$. If your company buys Peso180,000 spot from your bank on Monday, how much must your company pay and on what date?

6. **Hong Kong dollar and the Chinese yuan.** The Hong Kong dollar has long been pegged to the U.S. dollar at HK$7.80/$. When the Chinese yuan was revalued in July 2005 against the U.S. dollar from Yuan8.28/$ to Yuan8.11/$, how did the value of the Hong Kong dollar change against the yuan?

7. **Toyota exports to the U.K.** Toyota manufactures most of the vehicles it sells in the United Kingdom in Japan. The base platform for the Toyota Tundra truck line is ¥1,650,000. The spot rate of the Japanese yen against the British pound has recently

moved from ¥197/£ to ¥190/£. How does this change the price of the Tundra to Toyota's British subsidiary in British pounds?

8. **Ranbaxy (India) in Brazil.** Ranbaxy, an India-based pharmaceutical firm, has continuing problems with its cholesterol reduction product's price in one of its rapidly growing markets, Brazil. All product is produced in India, with costs and pricing initially stated in Indian rupees (Rps), but converted to Brazilian reais (R$) for distribution and sale in Brazil. In 2004, the unit volume was priced at Rps12,500, with a Brazilian reais price set at R$825. But in 2005, the reais appreciated in value versus the rupee, averaging Rps17.5/R$. In order to preserve the reais price and product profit margin in rupees, what should the new rupee price be set at?

9. **Chunnel choices.** The Channel Tunnel, or *Chunnel*, passes underneath the English Channel between Great Britain and France, a land-link between the Continent and the British Isles. One side is therefore an economy of British pounds, the other euros. If you were to check the Chunnel's rail ticket price at Internet rates you would find that they would be denominated in U.S. dollars (US$). For example, a first-class round-trip fare for a single adult from London to Paris via the Chunnel through RailEurope may cost US$170.00. This currency neutrality, however, means that customers on both ends of the Chunnel pay differing rates in their home currencies from day to day. What are the British pound- and euro-denominated prices for the US$170 round-trip fare in local currency if purchased on the following dates at the accompanying spot rates drawn from the *Financial Times*:

DATE	POUND SPOT RATE	EURO SPOT RATE
July 17, 2005	£0.5702/$	€0.8304/$
July 18, 2005	£0.5712/$	€0.8293/$
July 19, 2005	£0.5756/$	€0.8340/$

10. **Saudi import.** A European-based manufacturer ships a machine tool to a buyer in Jordan. The purchase price is €375,000. Jordan imposes a 12% import duty on all products purchased from the European Union. The Jordanian importer then re-exports the product to a Saudi Arabian importer, but only after imposing their own resale fee of 22%. Given the following spot exchange rates, what is the total cost to the Saudi Arabian importer in Saudi Arabian riyal, and what is the U.S. dollar equivalent of that price?

Spot rate, Jordanian dinar (JD) per euro (€)	JD0.8700/€
Spot rate, Jordanian dinar (JD) per U.S. dollar ($)	JD0.7080/$
Spot rate, Saudi Arabian riyal (SRI) per U.S. dollar ($)	SRI3.750/$

11. **Chinese yuan revaluation.** Many experts believe that the Chinese currency should not only be revalued again against the U.S. dollar as it was in July 2005, but that it should be revalued by 20% or 30%. What would the new exchange rate value be if the yuan were revalued an additional 20% or 30% from its initial post-revaluation rate of Yuan8.11/$?

12. **Vietnamese coffee coyote.** Many people were surprised when Vietnam became the second largest coffee-producing country in the world in recent years, second only to Brazil. The Vietnamese dong, VND or d, is managed against the U.S. dollar but is not

widely traded. If you were a traveling coffee buyer for the wholesale market (a *coyote*, by industry terminology), which of the following currency rates and exchange commission fees would be in your best interest if traveling to Vietnam on a buying trip:

CURRENCY EXCHANGE	RATE	COMMISSION
Vietnamese bank rate	d14,000	1.50%
Saigon Airport exchange bureau rate	d13,800	2.00%
Hotel exchange bureau rates	d13,750	1.50%

INTERNET EXERCISES

1. The IMF's Special Drawing Rights. The Special Drawing Right (SDR) is a composite index. Use the IMF's website to find the current weights and valuation of the SDR.

   International Monetary Fund http://www.imf.org/external/np/fin/rates/rms_sdrv.com

2. Capital controls. One of the key "sides" of the impossible trinity is the degree of capital mobility into and out of a country. Use the International Finance subsection of Yahoo to determine the current state of capital movement freedom for the following countries: Chile, China, Malaysia, Taiwan, and Russia.

   Yahoo http://biz.yahoo.com/ifc/

3. Dollarization and currency boards. Use the following websites, and any others you may find, to track the ongoing debate of the relative success of dollarization and currency boards.

   International Monetary Fund http://www.imf.org/external/pubs/

   National Bureau of Economic Research http://papers.nber.org/papers/

4. Malaysian currency controls. The institution of currency controls by the Malaysian government in the aftermath of the Asian currency crisis is a classic response by government to unstable currency conditions. Use the following website to increase your knowledge of how currency controls work.

   EconEdLink http://www.econedlink.org/lessons/index.cfm?lesson=EM25

5. Personal transfers. As anyone who has traveled internationally learns, the exchange rates available to private retail customers are not always as attractive as those accessed by companies. The OzForex website includes a section on "customer rates," which illustrates the difference. Use the site to calculate the percentage difference between Australian dollar/U.S. dollar spot exchange rates for retail customers versus interbank rates.

   OzForex http://www.ozforex.com

SELECTED READINGS

Miller, Merton H., "Financial Markets and Economic Growth," *Journal of Applied Corporate Finance*, Fall 1998, Volume 11, No. 3, pp. 8–15.

Rajan, Raghuram G. and Luigi Zingales, "Which Capitalism? Lessons from the East Asia Crisis," *Journal of Applied Corporate Finance*, Fall 1998, Volume 11, No. 3, pp. 40–48.

Singal, Vijay, "Floating Currencies, Capital Controls, or Currency Boards: What's the Best Remedy for the Currency Crisis," *Journal of Applied Corporate Finance*, Winter 1999, Volume 11, No. 4, pp. 49–56.

MINICASE   THE CREATION OF EURODOLLARS

Eurodollar creation can be explained with a simple example. Assume that a French firm (FF) has $10 million in a soon-maturing certificate of deposit (CD) in a New York bank (NYB) on which it is earning 5% interest. The $10,000,000 shows on the books of the two entities as follows (000 omitted):

New York Bank (NYB)

	$CD_{FF @ 5.00\%}$	10,000

French Firm (FF)

$CD_{NYB @ 5.00\%}$	10,000	

FF wants to continue holding U.S. dollars but would like a higher rate of interest. A London bank (LB) offers to pay 5.25% on dollar-denominated deposits with a three-month maturity. When the New York bank CD matures, FF instructs its NYB to transfer funds to the London bank, where the sum is placed in a three-month Eurodollar deposit account paying 5.25%. Because the London bank maintains a correspondent account with the New York bank, the actual transfer is effected by the New York bank debiting the account of the French firm and crediting the demand deposit (DD) correspondent account of the London Bank. The books now look like this:

New York Bank (NYB)

	$\cancel{CD}_{FF @ 5.00\%}$	10,000
	DD_{LB}	10,000

London Bank (LB)

DD_{NYB}	10,000	$CD_{FF @ 5.25\%}$	10,000

French Firm (FF)

$CD_{LB @ 5.25\%}$	10,000	

Transfer of the dollar deposit from the New York bank to the London bank creates a Eurodollar deposit: a bank outside of the United States (the London bank) now has a deposit liability denominated in dollars rather than in British pounds. Behind this dollar liability lies a dollar asset in the form of a demand deposit held by the London bank with the New York bank. Hence total deposits in the United States have not diminished, but a NYB liability to a foreign firm has become a liability to a foreign bank. In three months the London bank must return $10,000,000 (plus interest) to FF, which it will do by giving FF a demand deposit on a New York bank or by transferring a New York deposit to any party specified by FF.

At this point, the London bank is temporarily holding a dollar demand deposit in New York, on which it is earning nothing, while simultaneously owing dollars to the FF on which it has promised to pay 5.25%. If the London bank is not to lose on the transaction, it must loan its dollar asset (the New York demand deposit) to an entity at a rate higher than the 5.25% it is paying. Suppose that the London bank loans $10,000,000 to an Italian bank (IB) at 5.50%. The books would then look like this:

New York Bank (NYB)

	$\cancel{CD}_{FF @ 5.00\%}$	10,000
	$\cancel{DD}_{LB}$	10,000
	$\cancel{DD}_{IB}$	10,000
	DD_{IM}	10,000

London Bank (LB)

$\cancel{DD}_{NYB}$	10,000	$CD_{FF @ 5.25\%}$	10,000
$Loan_{IB @ 5.50\%}$	10,000		

French Firm (FF)

$CD_{LB @ 5.25\%}$	10,000	

Italian Bank (IB)

$\cancel{DD}_{NYB}$	10,000	$Loan_{LB @ 5.50\%}$	10,000
$Loan_{IM @ 5.75\%}$	10,000		

Italian Manufacturer (IM)

DD_{NY}	10,000	$Loan_{IB @ 5.75\%}$	10,000

The New York bank's deposit liability has now shifted to the Italian bank, and the London bank owns a dollar asset in the form of a dollar loan to the Italian bank on which it is earning one quarter of a percent more than it is paying the FF for the funds. The Italian bank is paying 5.50% for the dollars and (for the moment) is earning nothing.

This chain of lending and relending at slightly higher interest rates can continue for some time. To end the sequence, assume that the Italian bank loans dollars to an Italian manufacturer (IM) at 5.75%. The dollars in New York are transferred to the account of the Italian manufacturer, and the books look like this:

New York Bank (NYB)

	~~CD~~ FF @ 5.00%	~~10,000~~
	~~DD~~ LB	~~10,000~~
	~~DD~~ IB	~~10,000~~
	DD IM	10,000

London Bank (LB)

~~DD~~ NYB	~~10,000~~	CD FF @ 5.25%	10,000
Loan IB @ 5.50%	10,000		

French Firm (FF)

CD LB @ 5.25%	10,000	

Italian Bank (IB)

~~DD~~ NYB	~~10,000~~	Loan LB @ 5.50%	10,000
Loan IM @ 5.75%	10,000		

Italian Manufacturer (IM)

DD NY	10,000	Loan IB @ 5.75%	10,000

The Italian manufacturer (IM) borrowed the funds for a business purpose—perhaps to pay for the purchase of new machine tools from the United States. If so, the Italian manufacturer transfers the money to the machine tool manufacturer and the deposit in New York becomes a bank liability to that domestic firm. The residual value of the Eurodollar deposit is that any U.S. person or firm will accept it as payment for goods or services.

Each bank in the chain between the New York bank and the Italian manufacturer has a dollar asset as well as a dollar liability and is earning a profit on the spread between the interest rates. The underlying dollar deposit remains in the New York bank (or in some other U.S. bank), but ownership of it shifts from one depositor to another and eventually back to an American entity.

To repay the loan in six months, the Italian manufacturer must either buy or accumulate (perhaps from exports to the United States) dollars and transfer them to the Italian bank, which will transfer the dollars to the London bank, which will transfer the dollars back to the French firm in the form of a deposit in New York.

The sequence of events just described could have evolved in other directions. Any holder of Eurodollar balances could have invested them in the New York money market, in shares of common stock traded in the United States, in the U.S. real estate market, or directly in a U.S. subsidiary. In all these cases, as in the original, a demand deposit in a U.S. bank is behind each Eurodollar transaction. Foreign banks accepting time deposits in Eurodollars do not "create" funds or expand the dollar money supply in the fashion described in textbooks on domestic money and banking. That is, they do not create new demand deposits in return for loans, as do domestic banks, but simply transfer deposits held in New York at a markup in interest rates.

One might ask why the French firm did not deposit its dollars directly in the Italian bank to earn a higher rate, or why the Italian manufacturer did not borrow directly from the London bank at the lower rate being charged there. Part of the answer lies in the imperfections of international capital markets and part in participants' different perceptions of risk. The French firm may not have known of the Italian bank or have had any easy way to find out that a bank in Italy was paying a higher rate for Eurodollar deposits. In addition, the French firm may simply have had more confidence in British banks—a confidence born of geographic proximity and a long history of association, or it may have wanted to be a good bank client so that the London bank would provide other services in the future.

The Italian bank may or may not have aggressively pursued the dollar deposit of the French firm. The Italian manufacturer might be unknown in London and thus unable to borrow there without first going through a long process of establishing a credit rating. If the Italian manufacturer were unknown in London, it might have to pay the London bank a rate higher than the rate paid to the Italian bank.

MINICASE   THE REVALUATION OF THE CHINESE YUAN

"They started talking about something that wasn't very useful, then started to collect mobile phones and BlackBerrys," said a banker who was briefed later. The Chinese then distributed a four-point statement: Beijing was unlinking the yuan from the U.S. dollar effective immediately.

"Behind Yuan Move,
Open Debate and Closed Doors,"
The Wall Street Journal, July 25, 2005, p. A1.

"This a cautious move," said Zhong Wei, a finance expert at Beijing Normal University. "This is more like a political stance than real currency reform."

"China Ends Fixed-Rate Currency,"
Peter S. Goodman, *The Washington Post*,
July 22, 2005, p. A01.

On July 21, 2005, the Chinese government and the People's Bank of China officially changed the value of the Chinese yuan (or renminbi, RMB). On the morning of July 21, a number of key foreign banks in Beijing were asked to send representatives to the People's Bank of China for a meeting with an unannounced agenda. The People's Bank announced to the assembled banking group that it would abandon the peg of the yuan to the dollar, allow the value of the yuan to rise to Yuan8.11/$ immediately, and allow the value of the yuan to fluctuate 0.3% per day over the previous day's closing price going forward (see appendix for complete text of announcement). The change in value and regime—a revaluation against the U.S. dollar and a movement to an unknown basket of currencies peg—was both expected and a surprise.

THE REVALUATION DEBATE

Throughout 2004 and 2005, the U.S. government had continued to urge China to revalue the yuan from its decade-long peg to the U.S. dollar of Yuan8.28/$. The U.S. argued that the growing Chinese trade surplus with the U.S. indicated that the yuan was significantly overvalued. The political sparring had reached levels of veiled threats, as members of the U.S. Treasury had warned Chinese officials that a revaluation of at least 10% would be needed to prevent protectionist legislation in Congress. Even many within China acknowledged that maintaining the pegged rate was costly, as China's central bank continued to buy up the U.S. dollars that continued to pour in from trade and investment. By early 2005, China's foreign exchange reserves had swelled to more than $700 billion, including $190 billion in U.S. government bonds.

The Chinese government and many international trade experts, however, did not agree that the yuan was overvalued, arguing that the bilateral trade surplus with the United States was a result of competitiveness, cost of production, and changing global industry structures. Regardless, the move to revalue the yuan was seen as a political move to reduce pressures growing between governments, while simultaneously starting the process of moving the Chinese economy into a prominent role in the global economy.

In May 2004, the Chinese government had convened a panel of academic experts in Dalian to debate the future of the Chinese yuan. The debate boiled down to a "stay the course" philosophy advocated by Ronald McKinnon of Stanford University and Robert Mundell of Columbia University, as opposed to the "pro-revaluation" position of Jeffrey Frankel of Harvard University and Morris Goldstein of the Institute for International Economics. Interestingly, the risk that both camps agreed upon was that if the revaluation was too small, the currency markets—specifically, speculators—would demand more, leading to additional instability. That risk was now a clear possibility.

Pressure had continued to mount and rumors circulated. As recently as July 15, the headlines of the *Financial Times* had proclaimed "U.S. Expects Chinese Currency Revaluation," speculating that it would occur sometime in August. China moved even faster. Late on Wednesday, July 20, 2005, the U.S. Treasury and Hong Kong banking authorities were both informed, just hours before the rest of the world, that China was on the brink of altering its exchange regime from a dollar-peg to a managed float.

Copyright © 2005 Thunderbird, The Garvin School of International Management. All rights reserved. This case was prepared by Professor Michael Moffett for the purpose of classroom discussion only, and not to indicate either effective or ineffective management.

FIGURE A   Monthly Avg. Exchange Rates: Chinese Renminbi per U. S. Doller.

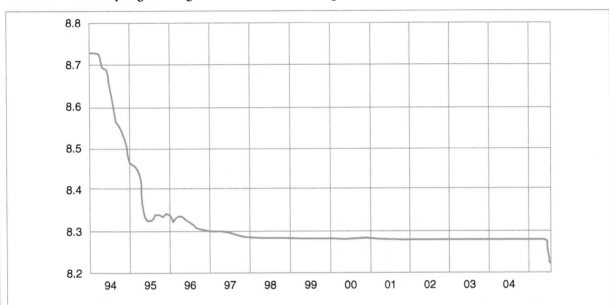

Source: © 2005 by Prof. Werner Antweiler, University of British Columbia, Vancouver, BC, Canada.

NEW CURRENCY REGIME

The Chinese yuan had been pegged to the U.S. dollar at Yuan8.28/$ since early 1997. This peg had been sustained through the Asian Financial Crisis of 1997/1998, and had provided a fixed and stable currency base for the rapid development and growth of the Chinese economy into the new millennium. The Chinese economy continued to grow extremely rapidly—more than 10% in real GDP terms—and the growth rate was expected to continue at this rate for at least a decade to come. Clearly, the economy was increasingly too large to remain a second-rate exchange rate country. More and more voices from outside China called for the Chinese yuan to be transitioned to a floating exchange rate and join the U.S. dollar, the euro, and the Japanese yen in the forefront of the global financial system.

The new currency regime announced by the People's Bank of China would change how the currency's value was managed. Although not saying exactly how the value would be determined, it was clear that the Chinese policymakers would consider the values of other major currencies such as the euro and the yen in addition to the dollar in moving to a *managed float*. Without knowing the contents of this *conceptual basket*, however, outsiders would be unable to predict specific policymaker movements on the currency's value.

The immediate change, however, was a revaluation of approximately 2.1%, a much smaller change than the 10% to 20% suggested by Chinese critics like the United States government:

$$\frac{\text{Yuan}8.28/\$ - \text{Yuan}8.11/\$}{\text{Yuan}8.11/\$} \times 100 = 2.096\% \approx 2.1\%$$

The implication of the 0.3% accepted deviation was potentially more significant. Although this deviation would limit the day-to-day movement of the yuan's value (in many ways protecting investors and companies alike against large sudden changes), it would permit the yuan to begin a minimal float. And it would not prevent the yuan from slowly and gradually *appreciating* against other currencies like the dollar over time. A number of currency experts were quick to point out that the previous yuan regime also officially allowed gradual rate adjustment, and that the yuan had actually been revalued from Yuan8.70/$ to Yuan8.28/$ between 1994 and 1997.

REGIONAL IMPACTS

The Chinese economy has become increasingly integral to the economies of Asia; specifically, to the economies of Thailand, Malaysia, Korea, and Taiwan. In recent years, a number of major industries have migrated from other Southeast Asian countries to China, so the revaluation of the yuan alters the competitive dynamics in the region. Several countries immediately reacted to the revaluation by announcing exchange rate changes of their own. Hong Kong, however, maintained its peg to the dollar.

The Malaysian government, within hours, announced the introduction of a similar managed-float exchange rate regime like that of China. Malaysia had maintained a fixed exchange rate since the onslaught of the Asian Financial Crisis in 1997. The new regimes in China and Malaysia were both remarkably similar to Singapore's regime, the so-called "basket, band, and crawl" or BBC, which that country had used successfully since the 1980s.

COMPETITIVE IMPLICATIONS

One well-known U.S. company with a big exposure to China is Mattel Inc., the world's largest toy manufacturer, which gets about 70% of its Barbie Dolls, Hot Wheels cars, and other toys from China, including from factories it owns there. A Mattel spokeswoman said the stronger yuan could mean higher materials costs next year when it renegotiates contracts with factories that it doesn't own. At its own plants, the impact "is mostly labor-related, rather than raw-material related, and is not sizeable," she added.

"Companies See Little Impact from
Costlier Yuan—For Now," *The Wall Street Journal,*
July 22, 2005, p. B1.

The revaluation of the Chinese yuan had not been something most multinational companies had sought. Most multinational companies operating in China had invested for the purpose of using China as a manufacturing base for global sourcing. As such, they wished the currency to remain both stable and relatively "cheap." A foreign multinational company like Mattel, one of the world's foremost toy manufacturers, sourced more than 70% of its toys from within China. Any revaluation of the yuan would mean that in dollar or euro terms, the cost of goods sold would rise and the resulting margins and profitability reduced when those same products were sold in euro or dollar markets.

For some companies, like Boeing, revaluation would have a marginally positive impact, if any. Boeing did little sourcing in China, but had been making larger and larger sales to China. The revaluation of the yuan would slightly increase the purchasing power of Boeing's Chinese customers, as it used U.S. dollar–based pricing for its export sales, including those to China. Other companies anticipated more complex competitive impacts. For example, General Motors actually welcomed the revaluation.

Although GM did increasingly source parts and subassemblies from China, the 2.1% revaluation was thought to be a small cost increase. Simultaneously, the revaluation of the yuan was expected to give the Japanese yen a substantial boost in the international financial markets, driving the value of the yen up against the dollar and the euro. From GM's perspective, any increase in the value of the yen would benefit it by hurting arch-competitor Toyota, with much of its global manufacturing still in Japan.

The competitive impacts on Chinese companies—specifically, Chinese multinationals like the Haier Group (manufacturer of small appliances like the mini-refrigerators in many college dorm rooms around the globe)—were potentially major over the long term. Although they would suffer only a 2% increase in cost versus foreign market pricing immediately, the yuan 's new freedom to float incrementally over time presented them with a new and growing operational risk from exchange rates over time.

Clearly, for all companies moving rapidly into China for either access to manufacturing or markets, only time would tell whether the yuan's newfound freedom would represent an opportunity or a threat.

QUESTIONS

1. Many Chinese critics had urged China to revalue the yuan by 20% or more. What would the Chinese yuan's value be in U.S. dollars if it had indeed been devalued by 20%?

2. Do you believe that the revaluation of the Chinese yuan was politically or economically motivated?

3. If the Chinese yuan were to change by the maximum allowed per day, 0.3% against the U.S. dollar, consistently over a 30- or 60-day period, what extreme values might it reach?

4. Chinese multinationals would now be facing the same exchange rate-related risks borne by U.S., Japanese, and European multinationals. What impact do you believe this rising risk will have on the strategy and operations of Chinese companies in the near-future?

MiniCase Appendix

Public Announcement of the People's Bank of China on Reforming the RMB Exchange Rate Regime
July 21, 2005

With a view to establish and improve the socialist market economic system in China, enable the market to fully play its role in resource allocation as well as to put in place and further strengthen the managed floating exchange rate regime based on market supply and demand, the People's Bank of China, with authorization of the State Council, is hereby making the following announcements regarding reforming the RMB exchange rate regime:

1. Starting from July 21, 2005, China will reform the exchange rate regime by moving into a managed floating exchange rate regime based on market supply and demand with reference to a basket of currencies. RMB will no longer be pegged to the U.S. dollar and the RMB exchange rate regime will be improved with greater flexibility.

2. The People's Bank of China will announce the closing price of a foreign currency such as the U.S. dollar traded against the RMB in the interbank foreign exchange market after the closing of the market on each working day, and will make it the central parity for the trading against the RMB on the following working day.

3. The exchange rate of the U.S. dollar against the RMB will be adjusted to 8.11 yuan per U.S. dollar at the time of 19:00 hours of July 21, 2005. The foreign exchange designated banks may since adjust quotations of foreign currencies to their customers.

4. The daily trading price of the U.S. dollar against the RMB in the interbank foreign exchange market will continue to be allowed to float within a band of ±0.3 percent around the central parity published by the People's Bank of China, while the trading prices of the non–U.S. dollar currencies against the RMB will be allowed to move within a certain band announced by the People's Bank of China.

The People's Bank of China will make adjustment of the RMB exchange rate band when necessary according to market development as well as the economic and financial situation. The RMB exchange rate will be more flexible based on market condition with reference to a basket of currencies. The People's Bank of China is responsible for maintaining the RMB exchange rate basically stable at an adaptive and equilibrium level, so as to promote the basic equilibrium of the balance of payments and safeguard macroeconomic and financial stability.

Source: http://www.pbc.gov.cn/english/xinwen/.

ACCOUNTING, CASH FLOWS, AND TAXES

3

No matter how large and complex it is, a firm's accounting system serves two basic purposes:

- reporting the firm's financial activities to its various stakeholders, and
- providing information to assist the firm's decision makers.

This chapter reviews material from basic accounting classes. We outline the basics of the accounting statements, without going into the details of how they are prepared. We describe important differences between accounting and economic information. Our focus in corporate financial management is on how to use and interpret this information, rather than on operating an accounting system and creating financial reports.

Accounting statements are important, as actions by firms such as WorldCom, Enron, and Arthur Andersen, among others, have all too often demonstrated. Accounting statements are used to communicate with stakeholders outside the firm, such as stockholders, bondholders, and other creditors. They are used within the firm to help plan and organize its activities. Accounting statements are used to monitor employees in connection with such things as performance or even theft. And they are used by the Internal Revenue Service to determine the firm's taxes.

Finally, we review the federal income tax system. Because taxes affect value, they affect many of a firm's decisions. At the most basic level, taxes are a significant cost of doing business. Throughout the book, we point out situations when taxes can affect decisions.

FOCUS ON PRINCIPLES

- *Two-Sided Transactions:* Recognize that the accounting system always records two sides to every transaction, a debit and a credit, and there are real people or real firms on each side of the transaction.
- *Incremental Benefits:* Use financial statements and the accounting system to help identify and estimate the incremental expected cash flows for making financial decisions.
- *Risk-Return Trade-Off:* Keep in mind that managerial decisions are based on future risks and returns. Accounting tends to measure historical or past returns. Consequently, many decisions require information and perspectives that are unavailable from the accounting system.
- *Behavioral Principle:* Use the wealth of financial information available from thousands of other firms to apply this principle.
- *Signaling:* Recognize that financial information provides many observable signals about customers, competitors, and suppliers.

3.1   THE LAYOUT OF ACCOUNTING STATEMENTS

Accounting statements in the United States are prepared according to **generally accepted accounting principles (GAAP)**. GAAP includes the conventions, rules, and procedures that define how firms should maintain records and prepare financial reports.[1] In the United States, these rules and procedures are based on guidelines issued by the *Financial Accounting Standards Board (FASB)*. FASB is the U.S. accounting profession's rule-making organization.

Internationally, the set of generally accepted accounting principles varies from one country to another. In some cases U.S. GAAP is quite different from international accounting standards (IAS) used in some other countries. As a result, you cannot compare the information contained in the financial statements of two firms when the statements were prepared under different systems of GAAP until you first adjust for the differences.

Even under U.S. GAAP, it is possible for accounting numbers to distort economic reality. One of the tasks facing a good manager is to use accounting information effectively. Managers must know how accounting information can—and cannot—be used. This is a balancing act. They have to combine their knowledge of accounting with other sources of information to make sound business decisions.

Financial Statements

A firm's published **annual report** includes, at a minimum, an income statement, a balance sheet, a statement of cash flows, and accompanying notes.[2] We review these statements, using a basic set of statements for OutBack SportWear, Inc., as an example.[3] They are the "raw material" for a variety

---

[1]According to the American Institute of Certified Public Accountants (AICPA), the "phrase 'generally accepted accounting principles' is a technical accounting term that encompasses the conventions, rules, and procedures necessary to define accepted accounting practice at a particular time. It includes not only broad guidelines of general application, but also detailed practices and procedures. . . . Those conventions, rules, and procedures provide a standard by which to measure financial presentations."

[2]A firm's annual report includes income statements and statements of cash flows for the latest three years and balance sheets for the latest two years. It also includes a separate statement of stockholders' equity. This shows how the firm's total stockholders' equity changed from one balance sheet to the next during the past three years.

[3]Publicly traded firms also publish quarterly reports and make public announcements of important information. And they file, with the Securities and Exchange Commission (SEC), disclosures that investors use. Such disclosures include 10-K annual reports (the information in the annual report plus more disclosures), 10-Q reports (the information in quarterly reports plus more), 8-K statements (describing significant events of interest to investors as the events occur), and registration statements (large documents containing financial and business information that must be filed before new securities can be publicly issued).

of techniques and procedures that managers and analysts use in financial statement analysis. But first, let us introduce some basic terms we will need.

The **maturity** of an asset is the end of its life. When a financial asset is issued (created), the length of its life is called its **original maturity**. The amount of time remaining until maturity is called the **remaining maturity**. Often, "maturity" is used to mean remaining maturity.

The **liquidity** of an asset expresses how quickly and easily it can be sold without loss of value. Cash is the most liquid asset.

Market value is the price for which something could be bought or sold in a "reasonable" length of time. A reasonable length of time is defined in terms of the asset's liquidity. It might be several months or even a year for buildings and land, but only a few days for publicly traded stocks and bonds. **Book value (net book value)** is a net amount shown in the accounting statements.

Balance Sheet

The **balance sheet** reports the financial position of a firm at a particular point in time. The balance sheet shows the firm's **assets**, which are the productive resources used in its operations. The balance sheet also shows the firm's **liabilities and stockholders' equity**, which are the total claims of creditors and owners against the assets.

A typical balance sheet, that of OutBack SportWear, is shown in Table 3-1. Note that the *balance sheet identity* is satisfied:

(3.1)   Assets = Liabilities + Stockholders' equity

Assets and liabilities are both broken down into short-term and long-term parts. In accounting statements, **current (short-term)** refers to a period of up to one year. **Long-term** refers to more than one year. Current assets are expected to become cash within one year. Current liabilities are expected to be paid off (mature) within one year. Assets and liabilities are usually arranged in approximate order of remaining maturity, from shortest to longest. This arrangement reflects the fact that, generally, the book values of the short-remaining-maturity assets and liabilities tend to be closer to their market values than those that have long maturities. For example, the book value of receivables may be fairly close to the market value. In contrast, the market value of net fixed assets can be very different from the book value.

TABLE 3-1   OutBack SportWear, Inc., annual balance sheet ($ millions) December 31.

	LATEST YEAR	PREVIOUS YEAR		LATEST YEAR	PREVIOUS YEAR
ASSETS			LIABILITIES & STOCKHOLDERS' EQUITY		
Cash and equivalents	$ 9.5	$ 12.0	Accounts payable	$ 18.8	$ 14.7
Accounts receivable	233.2	203.3	Notes payable	66.2	33.2
Inventories	133.9	118.8	Accrued expenses	77.7	62.0
Total current assets	$376.6	$334.1	Total current liabilities	$162.7	$109.9
Net plant and equipment	203.8	167.0	Long-term bonds	74.4	70.2
Total assets	$580.4	$501.1	Other long-term liabilities	19.6	17.7
			Total liabilities	$256.7	$197.8
			Preferred stock	10.0	10.0
			Common stock	45.4	45.4
			Retained earnings	268.3	247.9
			Total common equity	$323.7	$303.3
			Liabilities and stockholders' equity	$580.4	$501.1

The liabilities and stockholders' equity (right-hand) side of the balance sheet shows the firm's **capital structure**: the debt versus equity financing and the mixture of debt maturities, short-term versus long-term.

The difference between current assets and current liabilities is the firm's net working capital, often simply called **working capital**:

(3.2) Working capital = Current assets − Current liabilities

Working capital provides a measure of the firm's liquidity, or its ability to meet its short-term obligations as they come due.

Income Statement

The **income statement** reports the revenues, expenses, and profit (or loss) for a firm over a specific interval of time, typically a year or a quarter of a year. Net income, sometimes referred to as profit, is the difference between total revenue and total cost during the period. Table 3-2 shows the income statement for OutBack SportWear. In this income statement, the gross profit is the net sales minus the cost of goods sold. The cost of goods sold is the direct cost for the materials, labor, and other expenses directly associated with the production of the goods or services sold by the firm.

To compute the operating profit, subtract from gross profit (1) the indirect costs associated with selling, general, and administrative expenses and (2) depreciation and amortization (which are noncash items). **Earnings before interest and taxes (EBIT)** equals operating profit plus non-operating profit (such as investment income). Subtracting interest expense from EBIT gives pre-tax income of $44.0 million in the latest year. Finally, subtracting income taxes yields net income: $25.9 million, up from $18.0 million in the previous year.

If the firm has preferred stock outstanding, preferred dividends paid are subtracted from net income to get net income available for common stock. After subtracting whatever common stock dividends the firm paid, the remaining earnings are the current period's addition to retained earnings on the balance sheet.

	LATEST YEAR	PREVIOUS YEAR
Sales	$546.9	$485.8
Cost of goods sold	286.3	247.3
Gross profit	$260.6	$238.5
Selling, general & administrative exp.	186.2	180.5
Depreciation & amortization	22.7	20.1
Earnings before interest and taxes (EBIT)	$ 51.7	$ 37.9
Interest expense	7.7	8.0
Earnings before tax	$ 44.0	$ 29.9
Total income tax	18.1	11.9
Net income	$ 25.9	$ 18.0
Preferred dividends	1.0	1.0
Net income available for common	$ 24.9	$ 17.0
Dividends on common stock	4.5	3.6
Addition to retained earnings	$ 20.4	$ 13.4
Per-share data:		
Earnings per share	$ 2.77	$ 1.89
Dividends per share	$ 0.50	$ 0.40
Shares outstanding (millions)	9.000	9.000

TABLE 3-2
OutBack SportWear, Inc., annual income statement ($ millions, except per-share data) years ended December 31.

Dividends per share and earnings per share (EPS) are given in the bottom part of the income statement. The firm's common stockholders have a residual claim to the firm's assets after all debts and preferred stock dividends have been paid. The stockholders' welfare, then, depends on the current and future profitability and dividends of the firm. The per-share figures indicate how large the net income is relative to the number of common shares.[4] With nine million shares outstanding, OutBack shows $2.77 in EPS in the latest year.

Corporations occasionally declare an extraordinary gain or loss in addition to income or loss from their normal operations. OutBack SportWear did not report any extraordinary income. If a corporation had an extraordinary gain or loss, the income statement would show net income before and after (that is, without and with) the extraordinary gain or loss. In addition, EPS would be reported before and after the extraordinary income. For valuation purposes, EPS before extraordinary items (without taking them into account) is a more meaningful measure of the firm's sustainable profit.

Finally, dividends per share divided by EPS gives the firm's **payout ratio**. The payout ratio is the proportion of earnings that the firm paid out to common shareholders as cash dividends. OutBack's latest payout ratio is about 18% (= 0.50/2.77).

Statement of Cash Flows

The **statement of cash flows** indicates how the cash position of the firm has changed during the period covered by the income statement. Thus, it complements the income statement and the balance sheet. Changes in a firm's cash position can be the result of any of the firm's many transactions.

The statement of cash flows breaks down the sources and uses of cash into three components. These are cash flows from (1) operating, (2) investing, and (3) financing activities. The flows of funds between a firm and its investors, creditors, workers, customers, and other stakeholders serve as a fundamental starting point for the analysis of the firm, its capital investment projects, corporate acquisitions, and many other decisions.

Table 3-3 shows the statement of cash flows for OutBack SportWear. The sources and amounts of cash flows from operating activities, investing activities, and financing activities are itemized.[5]

Let us look more closely at the cash flow from operating activities. The net income is taken from OutBack's income statement (Table 3-2). To arrive at net income, various items are deducted from sales, including some that are noncash expenses. Depreciation is usually the largest of these items. Because these items are not cash flows, they must be added back to net income to determine cash flow. Dividends are *not* subtracted from operating activities. Instead, they are a discretionary part of financing activities. The other items represent changes in several working capital accounts, which are part of operating activities. Decreases (increases) in asset (liability) accounts are positive cash flows (*inflows*). The opposites are negative cash flows (*outflows*). One short-term liability, notes payable, is considered a financing activity and is not included in operating activities.

Investing activities cash flows include those connected with buying or selling long-term assets, acquiring other firms, and selling subsidiaries. OutBack used $59.5 million to purchase plant and equipment, which is an outflow (negative cash flow).

---

[4]The earnings-per-share calculation can be fairly complicated. Basic earnings per share is net income divided by the weighted average number of common shares outstanding during the period. Other definitions, such as diluted earnings per share, take into account what are called the *dilutive effects* of option-like instruments (warrants, convertibles, executive stock options). The rules for computing earnings per share are given in Accounting Principles Board, "Earnings per share," APB Opinion No. 15 (New York: AICPA, 1969). Most analysts regard diluted earnings per share as more informative than basic earnings per share.

[5]The format of the statement of cash flows shown in Table 3-3 is a presentation called the *indirect* method. Another method, called the *direct method*, sums the cash inflows and outflows associated with operating the firm. The first part of the statement of cash flows (cash flows from operating activities) looks different depending on whether the direct or the indirect method is used; the other two parts are the same. Although their formats differ, the methods give the same numerical result. We use the indirect method here because it is used most widely in published financial statements.

TABLE 3-3
OutBack SportWear,
Inc., statement of
cash flows
($ millions) year
ended December 31.

Cash Flows from Operating Activities	
Net income	$ 25.9
Depreciation and amortization	22.7
Accounts receivable decrease (increase)	(29.9)
Inventories decrease (increase)	(15.1)
Accounts payable increase (decrease)	4.1
Accrued expenses increase (decrease)	15.7
Net cash provided by (used in) operating activities	23.4
Cash Flows from Investing Activities	
Purchase of plant and equipment	(59.5)
Net cash provided by (used in) investing activities	(59.5)
Cash Flows from Financing Activities	
Notes payable increase (decrease)	33.0
Issuance of long-term debt, net	4.2
Increase in other long-term liabilities	1.9
Cash dividends (preferred and common)	(5.5)
Net cash provided by (used in) financing activities	33.6
Net increase (decrease) in cash and equivalents	(2.5)
Cash and equivalents, beginning of year	12.0
Cash and equivalents, end of year	$ 9.5

Financing activities cash flows include those connected with selling or repurchasing common and preferred stock, issuing or retiring long-term debt, issuing and repaying short-term notes, and paying dividends on common and preferred stock. For example, OutBack borrowed $33.0 million in notes payable, which was an inflow.

Net increase (decrease) in cash and equivalents is the sum of the cash flows from the three sections: 23.4 − 59.5 + 33.6 = $(2.5) million. This change is then added to the beginning cash balance of $12.0 million, leaving the ending cash balance of $9.5 million.

In many financial decisions, such as long-term investments, we separate the investing, financing, and operating cash flows. It is important to understand that such separations in the statement of cash flows are somewhat arbitrary, particularly in the case of the first part of the statement, which shows the cash flows from operating activities. For example, dividends are included with financing cash flows, whereas interest expense is treated as an operating cash flow.

Notes to the Financial Statements

The **notes to the financial statements** are an integral part of the statements. The notes disclose the significant accounting policies used to prepare the financial statements. They also provide additional detail concerning several of the items in the accounting statements. Table 3-4 lists subjects usually included in such notes.

Published annual reports also include **management's discussion** of recent operating results. Management's discussion is included along with the financial statements. Usually there is also a letter to the stockholders, which appears at the front of the annual report. This letter and the management's discussion can help you interpret the accounting statements. They can also provide insights into management's philosophy and strategy that simply do not appear in the numerical sections of the annual report.

The notes to the financial statements and management's discussion contain a wealth of useful information. You cannot fully appreciate the information contained in a firm's accounting statements unless you read the notes to the financial statements and the management's discussion.[6]

---

[6]This is why accounting and securities regulations require firms to furnish this information!

TABLE 3-4
Subjects typically covered as notes to financial statements in annual reports.

- Summary of significant accounting policies
- More-detailed breakdowns of other income, interest and other financial charges, and provision for income taxes
- A description of the earnings-per-share calculation
- Details concerning any extraordinary items, such as gain (or loss) on sales of assets or subsidiaries, and foreign exchange gains or losses
- Breakdown of inventories, investments (including nonconsolidated subsidiaries), property, plant, and equipment, and other assets
- Costs and amounts of short-term borrowings
- Schedules of long-term debt, preferred stock, and capitalized and operating lease obligations
- Schedule of capital stock issued or reserved for issuance and statement of changes in shareholders' equity (which is usually included as a separate financial statement)
- Details concerning significant acquisitions or disposals of assets
- Details concerning the use of derivatives
- Information concerning employee pension and stock option plans
- Commitments and contingent liabilities
- Events subsequent to the balance sheet date, but prior to the release of the financial statements to the public, that might significantly affect their interpretation
- Quarterly operating results
- Business segment information (by line of business and by geographical region)
- A five-year summary comparison of financial performance and financial position

3.2   MARKET VALUES VERSUS BOOK VALUES

Accounting statements are invaluable aids to analysts and managers. But the statements do not provide certain critical information, and as a result they have inherent limitations. Accounting statements are historical. They do not provide any information about cash flows that might be expected in the future. They also do not provide critically important information about the *current* market values of assets and liabilities. Thus, accounting statements not only fail to look ahead, they do not even report the current situation. Such missing information limits the usefulness of accounting information.

There are several reasons why accounting statements are historical, but we will not contribute here to the debate over how accounting statements might be better prepared. We will simply review the information accounting statements provide, based on today's practice, and note important implications of the procedures.

Market Versus Book Value of Assets

The current market value of an asset can be *very* different from its book value. Four factors affect the likelihood of a difference between market and book values: the time since the asset was acquired, inflation, the asset's liquidity, and whether the asset is tangible or intangible.

TIME SINCE ACQUISITION   As a rule, the more time that has passed since an asset was acquired, the greater the chance that the asset's current market value will be more or less than its book value. When an asset is acquired, it is recorded in the accounting statements at its cost. And that cost is a market value, at least in some sense. Therefore, the initial book value is quite likely to be similar to the market value of the asset *at the time it is acquired*. Over time, however, the market value can diverge significantly from the book value. This is because changes in the book value (depreciation each period) are specified by GAAP rather than by economic considerations.

EXAMPLE Differences in Car Usage

Two firms buy identical cars. In one case, a sales representative is going to drive the car about 10,000 miles per month. In the other, a manager is going to drive the car about 1,000 miles per month. GAAP specifies identical depreciation rules for these cars. The rule is based on the type of asset (an automobile), not on how it will be used. Thus, after any significant time, say a year, the book values of the cars will be identical, but the more heavily used car will have a much lower market value. The more time that passes, the larger the difference is likely to be.

EXAMPLE The Sampson Company Waterfront Warehouse

The Sampson Company purchased a warehouse 15 years ago. Since then, the area surrounding the building has changed dramatically from an industrial area of factories and shipping warehouses into an exclusive high-rise condominium area overlooking the waterfront. Sampson's building and land currently have a combined book value of $231,000 (after accounting for depreciation on the building; depreciation cannot be claimed on land). Today the building could be sold for $15 million. Such a difference fundamentally changes the value of the firm. It also has profound implications for the best use of the firm's assets at this point in time. Sampson should consider moving its operations elsewhere and selling the current location. Of course, in other cases the market value may be well *below* the book value, which could have very different policy implications!

INFLATION   Inflation during the time since the asset was acquired is a second important factor that can cause a significant difference between market value and book value. When prices change because of inflation, the market values of existing assets also change to reflect the difference in purchasing power. Such changes can be dramatic. For example, from 1964 until 2006, inflation caused the purchasing power of a dollar to change by about a factor of 8. This means that what could be purchased for $1.00 in 1964 cost about $8.00 in 2006.

EXAMPLE SunTrust's Shares of Coca-Cola Stock

Many years ago, when the Coca-Cola Company first issued shares of its common stock to the public, some of the shares went to a predecessor of SunTrust Banks in Atlanta. At the time, the value of the stock was recorded at its current market value of $100,000. Until relatively recently, the stock was shown on SunTrust's balance sheet as an asset with a book value of $100,000. However, the stock had since gone up in value. Seventy-five years later, those shares were worth about $1.5 billion, an increase of about 15,000 times over their original value. We know that the stock value increased well in excess of inflation over the intervening years. However, inflation during the same time period was substantial, perhaps changing purchasing power by a factor of 50 or more. Therefore, even if the value of the shares had increased only in step with inflation, the shares would be worth in excess of $5 million. In that case, then, only the remaining 300-times increase (= 15,000/50) is due to the success of the Coca-Cola Company!

LIQUIDITY   An asset's liquidity is a third factor that affects the likelihood that an asset's market value will differ from its book value. Less-liquid assets have higher transaction costs when they are sold, so there is greater uncertainty about the *net* proceeds from a sale. As a consequence, if all else is equal, the market values of less-liquid assets can differ more from their book values than those of more-liquid assets.

For example, compare a 2-year-old pickup truck to a unique patented process for producing plastic bags. The pickup truck is a more-liquid asset, because it could be easily sold in a used-truck market with low transaction costs. Contrast this with the plastic-bag production process. Such a production process may be worth much more than its book value if it is the leading production technology. Or it may be essentially worthless if another technology has made it obsolete. But in either case, it could be very costly and time consuming to find the buyer who will pay the most for the process because there is not an established market for used plastic-bag production processes.

TANGIBLE VERSUS INTANGIBLE ASSETS   Whether an asset is tangible or intangible affects the likelihood of there being a significant difference between market and book values. The market values of intangible assets are much more variable than those of tangible assets. As with our example of the plastic-bag production process, intangible assets can be extremely valuable or essentially worthless. Intangible assets also tend to be extremely illiquid. Even long-term assets such as plant and equipment are more likely to have established markets (real estate and used equipment) than are intangible assets such as patents or the design for a new product. Intangible assets tend to be unique. There are no active markets for selling them. Therefore, the current market value of an intangible asset is especially likely to differ from its book value.

EXAMPLE   **Developing a New Product at Murray Corporation**

Murray Corporation has spent $14 million developing a new product. Now, it can more accurately estimate that the product will provide only about $5 million in profit to offset the development cost. At this point, Murray would like to sell the rights to its product to another firm and let that firm manufacture and market the new product. Would you pay $14 million for something that is worth only $5 million? Despite the $14 million historical cost on Murray's balance sheet, a potential buyer will assess the value of the new product on the basis of its *future* potential.[7]

We noted earlier that placement on the balance sheet reflects the general remaining maturity of the assets. We should now point out that balance sheet placement also reflects the general likelihood that there will be a difference between the asset's book value and its market value. As you move down the list of assets, they are less liquid and generally have been held longer. Intangible assets are shown last.

Consider two types of assets that represent opposite extremes in liquidity: cash and a manufacturing plant. Cash is extremely liquid (actually, it is the very *definition* of liquidity), whereas it would probably require considerable effort to find a buyer for the plant.[8] However, despite the fact that the market values of other current assets are generally less likely to differ from their book values, care is always in order when valuing a firm. Accounts receivable can include bad debts. Inventory can be obsolete or can be shown at very low values because of a "last-in first-out" policy of accounting for inventory. Thus, even the book values of current assets other than cash and equivalents can be poor approximations of market value. Therefore, it is wise to look especially carefully at assets other than cash and equivalents when trying to value them.

---

[7]This problem is a major reason why GAAP calls for expensing (depreciating) research and development costs over a relatively short time period. Of course, the other side to this is that when a firm does make a great and valuable discovery, its book value grossly *under*states its market value.

[8]Of course, if the firm really wanted to sell the plant quickly, it could probably find a buyer almost instantly for a low enough price, say $1.00. (But even this price might be too high if the plant sat on top of a chemical waste dump that would cost the new owner $100 million to clean up.)

Market Versus Book Value of Liabilities

As with assets, the current market value of a liability can differ from its book value. Generally, however, the potential divergence is smaller, and the relationship between the market and book values is less complex.

REMAINING MATURITY   The time until a liability must be paid off—its remaining maturity—is the main factor that affects the difference between the market and book values of a healthy firm's liabilities. Liabilities have explicit contractual amounts that must be paid at specific points in time. Failure to meet these contractual obligations creates the possibility of bankruptcy. Therefore, when a liability becomes due, the market value of the liability is essentially equal to its book value. In contrast, the market value of liabilities that do not have to be repaid for a long time reflects current economic conditions, as well as expectations about the future.

Consider a loan for $10 million that is due to be paid off in four months. Because the remaining maturity is short, the cost of interest is relatively insignificant compared to the amount borrowed. Now consider a long-term loan for $10 million at 6% interest per year that does not have to be repaid for another 25 years, except for yearly interest. If the borrowing rate today is 10%, the market value of this liability is smaller than its book value because its remaining maturity of 25 years provides the firm with 25 more years over which to enjoy the low 6% interest cost on the existing loan.

FINANCIAL DISTRESS   In our discussion of the impact of remaining maturity, we referred to a *healthy* firm's liabilities. A second factor that affects the difference between the market and book values of liabilities is the firm's financial health. The market values of a financially distressed firm's liabilities are likely to be below their book values because of the uncertainty about the firm's long-term viability and the likelihood that liability holders will not be fully repaid. Thus financial distress can intensify the effect of remaining maturity on the market value of a firm's liabilities.

Total Value

The total value of a firm is simply the sum of the market values of all its assets. Because the market values of the individual assets can be very different from their book values, the balance sheet amount *Total Assets* should *never* be taken as a reliable estimate of the market value of the firm.

Equity Value

The current book value of the firm's equity is probably the least informative item on a balance sheet. Every factor that affects the difference between the market and book values of each individual item on the balance sheet affects the difference between the market and book values of the firm's equity. This is because the difference between the market and book values of equity is the sum of the differences between the market and book values of all the other items on the balance sheet.

Look back at Equation (3.1), the balance sheet identity. We can rewrite that equation as

$$\text{Stockholders' equity} = \text{Assets} - \text{Liabilities}$$

This form makes it easy to see the residual nature of the equity value. We have just said that the Assets amount is not the market value of the firm's assets and that the Liabilities amount is not the market value of the firm's liabilities. Therefore, it should be clear that the difference between the two is not miraculously going to become an accurate measure of market value, either!

If instead of being book (historical) values, the Assets and Liabilities amounts were current market values, this equation would provide the true residual value of the stockholders' equity. In a GAAP balance sheet, however, the value of Stockholders' equity is simply the result of applying the required rules to the historical cost of the assets and liabilities—in essence, an amount that forces the balance sheet identity to hold. In a sense, the book value of stockholders' equity is a "plug" figure that enforces the balance sheet identity.

As we will explain in detail later, stock prices observed in public market trading are a much more accurate basis for estimating the current market value of a firm.

REVIEW

1. Why might the market value of an asset differ from its book value?
2. Why might the market value of a liability differ from its book value?

3.3   ACCOUNTING NET INCOME VERSUS CASH FLOW

The income statement contains noncash expenses and accruals. Because of this, net income is not an accurate measure of cash inflow. In fact, this is part of the reason for requiring a Statement of Cash Flows.

Noncash Items

Certain items in the income statement are called noncash items, wherein the cash flow for the expense occurs outside of the reporting period. Depreciation is the most significant of these items. The use of certain assets, such as plant and equipment, spans multiple income statement periods. GAAP requires that the total expense be spread over multiple income periods, such as 5, 10, or even 30 years.

The only thing at issue here is *timing*. The claim of expense for accounting purposes is separated in time from when the cash flow actually occurs. The cash flow for the item occurs at the time of purchase. The expense charged against income occurs in stages over several income statement periods. Therefore, noncash items make the firm's net income figure very different from its cash inflow. Deferred and accrued taxes are two other examples of noncash items.

Accruals

The revenues and expenses on the income statement include items for which no cash has yet been received. For example, a sale of merchandise that has been agreed to and perhaps even delivered, but that has not yet been paid for, can be included. Also, a sale for which some cash has already been received may not be included, because it has not met certain GAAP requirements. Despite this, the revenues shown over a long time are a good estimate of the actual revenue that will *ultimately* be collected. However, within a limited time period of, say, one or two years, the revenue shown on the income statement can be significantly different from the cash revenue that actually came into the firm.

Estimating Cash Flow

Cash flow is often estimated by adding back noncash items to the net income, as in the first two lines of the operating activities part of the statement of cash flows (Table 3-3). This is because the distortion from accruals typically is relatively small.

Accounting Income Versus Economic Income

A firm's economic income is its total realized profit on an investment. It is made up of the cash inflow plus the change in the market value of the assets and liabilities. As we have just discussed, net income is not cash flow, and book changes in the firm's assets and liabilities do not reflect changes in market values. Thus Net Income is not economic income. As with the balance sheet, however, some items on the income statement are more or less likely than others to be good estimates of economic reality.

OPERATING INCOME Operating income can be a good estimate of economic operating income, provided that (1) the firm has made no changes in its accounting procedures, such as switching inventory accounting from a "last-in first-out" (LIFO) to a "first-in first-out" (FIFO) basis, and (2) the accounting period is sufficiently long. Changes in accounting procedures can increase or decrease the amounts reported in that period. With respect to the length of the accounting period, several years is preferable. Good or poor performance may not be revealed in income statements of one or two years. However, over time, significant changes in performance are likely to be revealed in any extended series of income statements—as many notorious fraud cases remind us.

EXTRAORDINARY INCOME Interpreting the economic meaning of extraordinary income requires an understanding of its nature and origin. For example, consider an extraordinary item that is the sale of some land that was worth much more than its current book value. This windfall could have come from good decision making—or dumb luck. If it was good decision making, it may mean a brighter future. Luck may not continue.

In general, extraordinary items occur only once. They do not reflect the firm's *sustainable net income*. We therefore recommend that you use *net income before extraordinary items* when making analytical calculations that involve net income.

REVIEW

1. What are the main differences between net income and cash flows?
2. Why might the economic income of the firm differ significantly from its net income?

SUMMARY

The purpose of Chapter 3 is to review the major financial statements, emphasize the difference between accounting and economic concepts of value and income, and detail the major corporate and personal tax features that affect a firm's financial policy.

- The primary financial statements are the balance sheet, income statement, and statement of cash flows. The footnotes and management's discussion are also important parts of the firm's annual report.
- The balance sheet shows the assets, liabilities, and stockholders' equity of the firm. The balance sheet shows the firm's financial position at a specific point in time.
- The income statement reports the firm's revenues, costs, and net income for a period of time, such as during one year or one quarter.
- The statement of cash flows shows the cash flows that result in a period's change in cash balances. The cash flows are broken into three parts, cash flows from operating activities, investing activities, and financing activities.
- Market values are based on expected future cash flows. Book values are based on historical costs. The market value and book value for an asset, liability, and stockholders' equity can be substantially different.
- Economic income (cash flow plus capital gain) differs from accounting income.

EQUATION SUMMARY

(3.1) $$Assets = Liabilities + Stockholders'\ equity$$

(3.2) $$Working\ capital = Current\ assets - Current\ liabilities$$

QUESTIONS

1. Explain the purpose of each of the following financial statements: income statement, balance sheet, and statement of cash flows.

2. What is the balance sheet identity?

3. Assume that interest rates have increased substantially. Would this tend to increase or decrease the market value of a firm's liabilities (relative to the book value of liabilities)?

4. Assume that inflation rates have been fairly high. Would this tend to increase or decrease the market value of a firm's assets (relative to their book values)?

5. Describe the difference between economic income and accounting net income.

6. Explain why the notes to a firm's financial statements are an integral part of the financial statements.

7. What primarily distinguishes:

   a. Current assets from the other classes of assets on the balance sheet?

   b. Current liabilities from the other classes of liabilities on the balance sheet?

8. Define the term *cash flow*. Explain the difference between cash flow and earnings.

9. Define the term *working capital*. How is working capital calculated? What does working capital measure?

CHALLENGING QUESTIONS

10. In a corporation's annual report, what do you think would be the order of presentation of the following items: balance sheet, income statement, statement of cash flows, management's discussion, notes to the financial statements?

11. Cite and briefly discuss four factors that affect the likelihood that the market and book values of an asset will differ.

12. Cite and briefly discuss two factors that affect the likelihood that the market and book values of a liability will differ.

PROBLEMS

■ **LEVEL A (BASIC)**

A1. (Balance sheet and income statement) Johnson's Scuba Co. has a weird accountant who reported the balance sheet and income statement items in alphabetical order. Please put these items in the correct format for a balance sheet and income statement for Johnson's Scuba Co. for the year ending January 31. All of the data are in thousands of dollars.

Accounts payable	500
Accounts receivable	700
Addition to retained earnings	400
Cash and equivalents	300
Common stock	500
Cost of goods sold	2,000
Depreciation	200
Dividends on common shares	100
Earnings before interest and taxes	800
Earnings before taxes	750
Gross profit	2,000
Interest expense	50

Inventories	500
Long-term debt	1,000
Net income	500
Net plant and equipment	3,000
Notes payable	250
Other current liabilities	400
Retained earnings	1,850
Sales	4,000
Selling, general, and administrative expenses	1,000
Taxes	250
Total assets	4,500
Total current assets	1,500
Total liabilities and equity	4,500
Total current liabilities	1,150
Total liabilities	2,150

A2. (Statement of cash flows) Johnson's accountant also presented all of the items in the statement of cash flows in alphabetical order. Please put these items in the correct format for a statement of cash flows for Johnson's Scuba Co. for the year ending January 31. All data are in thousands of dollars.

Accounts payable increase	100
Accounts receivable increase	(50)
Cash dividends (common stock)	(200)
Cash and equivalents at beginning of year	300
Cash and equivalents at end of year	150
Depreciation and amortization	200
Increase in other long-term liabilities	0
Inventories increase	(200)
Issuance of long-term debt, net	100
Net cash provided by (used in) financing activities	0
Net cash provided by (used in) investing activities	(700)
Net cash provided by (used in) operating activities	550
Net income	500
Net increase in cash and equivalents	(150)
Notes payable increase	100
Purchase of plant and equipment	(700)

A3. (Financial statements) For the year ended December 31, Dutch Retail, Inc., recorded the items listed here. Prepare an income statement for the year ended December 31 for Dutch Retail, Inc. Please use an appropriate format, such as the one in Table 3-2.

Cost of goods sold	$200
Interest expense	100
Preferred dividends paid	50
Common dividends paid	100
Selling expenses	65
Administrative expenses	100
Depreciation expense	150
Sales revenues	900
Taxes = 40% of taxable income	

A4. (Financial statements) Construct a balance sheet for Falken Computers, Inc., from the following data. Use a format similar to the balance sheet in Table 3-1. What is stockholders' equity?

Cash	$500
Inventory	100
Accounts receivable	300

Fixed assets	700
Accounts payable	300
Accrued expenses	100
Long-term debt	500

A5. (Financial statements) For the year, Pennsylvania Construction has a cash flow from operating activities of $1,000,000, a cash flow from investing activities of −$600,000, and a cash flow from financing activities of −$200,000. If Pennsylvania Construction has a beginning cash balance for the year of $500,000, what is the company's ending cash balance?

A6. (Financial statements) Ivan Brick Company earned net income after taxes of $850,000 during the latest year. Retained earnings on its balance sheet equaled $1,740,000 on December 31, last year and $2,040,000 on December 31, the latest year. What cash dividends did Ivan Brick Company pay during the latest year?

■ LEVEL B

B1. (Financial statements) Consider the following financial information for Sunny Fruit Co.

Balance Sheet, December 31
(Figures in millions of dollars)

ASSETS	LATEST YEAR	PREVIOUS YEAR	LIABILITIES AND STOCKHOLDERS' EQUITY	LATEST YEAR	PREVIOUS YEAR
Current assets	$400	$200	Current liabilities	$150	$195
Net fixed assets	600	400	Long-term debt	500	100

Partial Income Statement,
latest year ending December 31
(Figures in millions of dollars)

Sales	$900
Cost of goods sold	200
Selling and administrative expenses	200
Depreciation	100
Interest expense	50

a. What is stockholders' equity in the previous and latest years?

b. Assume a tax rate of 40%. What are income taxes paid and net income after taxes for the latest year?

c. The company did not issue or repurchase any stock during the latest year. What dividend was paid?

d. Given the change in net fixed assets and depreciation expense, what is the amount of fixed assets purchased during the latest year?

e. What is net working capital in the previous and latest years?

f. What is cash provided (used) by operations during the latest year (the increase in working capital is a use of cash)? What is cash provided (used) by investing activities? What is cash provided (used) by financing activities?

B2. (Book and market values) Bill's Lanes, a Louisiana corporation that owns several bowling alleys, has the following balance sheet:

Bill's Lanes Corporation
Balance Sheet, December 31
(Figures in thousands of dollars)

ASSETS		LIABILITIES AND STOCKHOLDERS' EQUITY	
Current assets	$1,200	Current liabilities	$ 800
Net fixed assets	3,000	Long-term debt	1,000
Total	$4,200	Stockholders' equity	2,400
		Total	$4,200

Assume that the market value of the current assets is equal to the book value and that the market value of the net fixed assets is three times the book value. The market value of current liabilities is equal to the book value and the market value of long-term debt is 90% of its book value.

   a. What is the market value of Bill's Lanes' assets?

   b. What is the market value of Bill's Lanes' liabilities?

   c. If the market value of equity is equal to the market value of assets minus the market value of liabilities, what is the market value of the equity in Bill's Lanes?

B3. (Book and market values) Consider the following information about the Dilbert Printing Company. All data are in millions of dollars.

	BOOK VALUE	MARKET VALUE
Assets, December 31, previous year	1,000	2,000
Assets, December 31, latest year	1,200	1,400
Liabilities, December 31, previous year	600	900
Liabilities, December 31, latest year	650	1,050

   a. What is the book value of stockholders' equity at the end of the previous and latest years?

   b. What is the market value of stockholders' equity at the end of the previous and latest years?

   c. For the latest year ending December 31, net income was $175 million. If Dilbert paid its stockholders cash dividends of $50 million, what is the total economic income of the stockholders during this year?

■ LEVEL C (ADVANCED)

C1. (Accounting versus economic income) During the latest year, McGowan Construction earned net income of $250,000. The firm neither bought nor sold any capital assets, and the book value of its assets declined by the year's depreciation charge, which was $200,000. The firm's operating cash flow for the year was $450,000, and the market value of its assets increased by $300,000. What was McGowan Construction's economic income for the year? Why is this figure different from its accounting net income?

APPENDIX
ANALYZING FINANCIAL STATEMENTS

Despite the built-in limitations of accounting information, published accounting statements can reveal a great deal about a firm. Financial analysts and managers find it helpful to calculate financial ratios when interpreting a firm's accounting statements. A **financial ratio** is simply one quantity divided by another. Financial statement analysis can be useful in at least two ways. First, it can help structure your thinking about business decisions. Second, it can provide some information that is helpful in making those decisions.

The number of financial ratios that could be created is virtually limitless, but certain basic ratios are used frequently. These ratios fall into six classes: *liquidity, asset activity, leverage, coverage, profitability, and market value.* The calculation and interpretation of these six classes of ratios are discussed here. Our sample calculations are made on an actual balance sheet and income statement of Anheuser-Busch, which are shown in Tables 3A-1 and 3A-2.

Liquidity Ratios

Liquidity ratios measure a firm's liquidity. The purpose is to assess the firm's ability to meet its financial obligations on time. Four widely used liquidity ratios are the current ratio, the quick ratio, the working capital ratio, and the cash ratio. The most commonly used measure of overall liquidity is the **current ratio**.

$$\text{Current ratio} = \frac{\text{Current assets}}{\text{Current liabilities}} = \frac{1,816}{1,460} = 1.24x$$

TABLE 3A-1
Anheuser-Busch Companies, Inc., annual balance sheet (millions of dollars, rounded), December 31.

	LATEST YEAR	PREVIOUS YEAR
ASSETS		
Cash and equivalents	$ 215.0	$ 97.3
Accounts receivable	649.8	654.8
Inventories	660.7	635.6
Other current assets	290.3	240.0
Total current assets	$ 1,815.8	$ 1,627.7
Gross fixed assets	11,385.1	10,589.6
Accumulated depreciation	(3,861.4)	(3,393.1)
Net fixed assets	7,523.7	7,196.5
Other assets	1,198.4	1,162.3
Total assets	$10,537.9	$ 9,986.5
LIABILITIES & STOCKHOLDERS' EQUITY		
Accounts payable	$ 737.4	$ 709.8
Taxes payable	38.8	45.2
Accrued expenses	426.7	392.7
Other current liabilities	256.9	255.1
Total current liabilities	$ 1,459.8	$ 1,402.8
Long-term debt	2,642.5	2,644.9
Deferred taxes	1,276.9	1,500.7
Other liabilities	538.3	0.0
Total liabilities	$ 5,917.5	$ 5,548.4
Preferred stock	$ 0.0	$ 0.0
Common stock	341.3	338.5
Capital surplus	328.5	193.3
Retained earnings	5,793.5	5,230.5
Less: Treasury stock	(1,842.9)	(1,324.2)
Total common equity	$ 4,620.4	$ 4,438.1
Total liabilities & stockholders' equity	$10,537.9	$ 9,986.5

	LATEST YEAR	PREVIOUS YEAR
Sales	$ 11,394	$ 10,996
Cost of goods sold	6,742	6,614
Gross profit	4,652	4,382
Selling, general, & administrative expenses	2,309	2,126
Depreciation, depletion, & amortization	567	534
Operating profit	1,776	1,722
Interest expense	(200)	(239)
Capitalized interest	48	47
Nonoperating profit (loss)	(9)	(9)
Earnings before tax	1,615	1,521
Total income tax	621	581
Net income	994	940
Preferred dividends	0	0
Available for common	$ 994	$ 940
Earnings per share	$3.48	$3.26
Dividends per share	$1.20	$1.06
Shares outstanding (000)	285,690	288,282

TABLE 3A-2
Anheuser-Busch Companies, Inc., annual income statement (millions of dollars, rounded, except per-share amounts), December 31.

The current ratio measures the number of times the firm's current assets "cover" its current liabilities. Presumably, the higher the current ratio, the greater the firm's ability to meet its short-term obligations as they come due. A widely held but rough rule of thumb is that a current ratio of 2.0 is an appropriate target for most firms.

Inventories are considered current assets, so they are included in the current ratio calculation. Inventories, however, are less liquid than marketable securities and accounts receivable. This is because it is normally more difficult to turn inventory into cash on short notice. Thus, analysts often exclude inventories from the numerator in the current ratio and calculate the **quick ratio** (also called the **acid test ratio**):

$$\text{Quick (acid test) ratio} = \frac{\text{Current assets} - \text{Inventories}}{\text{Current liabilities}} = \frac{1,816 - 661}{1,460} = 0.79x$$

Another widely held but rough rule of thumb says a quick ratio of 1.0 or more is healthy.

Equation (3.2) defines working capital as the difference between current assets and current liabilities. The **working capital ratio** is

$$\text{Working capital ratio} = \frac{\text{Current assets} - \text{Current liabilities}}{\text{Sales}} = \frac{1,816 - 1,460}{11,394} = 3.1\%$$

Working capital is often considered a measure of liquidity by itself. This ratio shows the amount of liquidity relative to sales.

The **cash ratio** is

$$\text{Cash ratio} = \frac{\text{Cash and equivalents}}{\text{Total assets}} = \frac{215}{10,538} = 2.0\%$$

Cash and equivalents (such as marketable securities) are the most liquid assets. The cash ratio shows the proportion of assets held in the most liquid possible form.

Ratios for other firms in the same industry and time period are often compared to judge a firm's relative strengths and weaknesses. For example, we can compare Anheuser-Busch's ratios to average ratios for the other large firms in the alcoholic beverages industry.[9]

	ANHEUSER-BUSCH	OTHER ALCOHOLIC BEVERAGE FIRMS
Current ratio	1.24x	2.12x
Quick ratio	0.79x	0.93x
Working capital ratio	3.1%	24.0%
Cash ratio	2.0%	3.0%

Anheuser-Busch has lower liquidity ratios than the other alcoholic beverage firms. Nevertheless, Anheuser-Busch is a healthy firm; nobody expects it to have trouble meeting its obligations as they come due. Its health allows it to carry much greater current liabilities, and it simply does not need as much liquidity as the rules of thumb prescribe, a current ratio of 2.0 and a quick ratio of 1.0. Note that the other alcoholic beverage firms have current and quick ratios that are very close to 2.0 and 1.0, respectively.

Asset Activity Ratios

Asset activity ratios are designed to measure how effectively a firm manages its assets. There are several ratios focusing on the management of specific assets as well as total assets.

The **receivables turnover ratio** is

$$\text{Receivables turnover} = \frac{\text{Annual credit sales}}{\text{Accounts receivable}} = \frac{11,394}{650} = 17.53x$$

It measures the number of times the accounts receivable balance "turns over" during the year. Note that annual credit sales, which give rise to receivables, are used in the numerator. If a figure for annual credit sales is not available, the firm's net sales figure is used instead. Making that substitution is like assuming that all sales were credit sales.

A closely related figure is the **days' sales outstanding** (DSO):[10]

$$\text{Days' sales outstanding} = \frac{365}{\text{Receivables turnover}} = \frac{\text{Accounts receivable}}{\text{Annual credit sales}/365} = \frac{365}{17.53} = 20.8 \text{ days}$$

The days' sales outstanding shows approximately how long it takes, on average, to collect a receivable. The days' sales outstanding is also called the **average collection period**.

A more detailed picture of the firm's accounts receivable can be obtained by preparing an **aging schedule**. An aging schedule shows the amounts of receivables that have been outstanding for

---

[9]Brown-Forman Corporation, Canandaigua Wine Co., Adolph Coors Company, The Molson Companies Ltd., and Seagram Co. are the other firms followed by *The Value Line Investment Survey*. The enormous difference between the working capital ratios for Anheuser-Busch and the other alcoholic beverage firms may look odd. You will find in a moment that Anheuser-Busch also has relatively high receivables and inventory turnover ratios.

[10]Before calculators and computers were widely used, analysts often used a 360-day year for simplicity. Although much of the financial press has continued this practice so far, it is becoming less popular. We always use a 365-day year.

AGE (DAYS)	ACCOUNTS RECEIVABLE	PERCENTAGE OF TOTAL
0–30	$1,500	50.0%
30–60	900	30.0
60–90	450	15.0
over 90	150	5.0
Total	$3,000	100.0%

different periods, such as 0 to 30 days, 30 to 60 days, 60 to 90 days, and more than 90 days. An example of an accounts receivable aging schedule is given in Table 3A-3. An external analyst typically lacks the detailed information in an aging schedule unless the firm has chosen to provide it. Of course, managers within the firm want this information to help monitor their accounts receivable.

A measure of the effectiveness of inventory management is the **inventory turnover ratio**:

$$\text{Inventory turnover} = \frac{\text{Cost of goods sold}}{\text{Inventory}} = \frac{6,742}{661} = 10.20x$$

Inventory turnover is a good estimate of how many times per year the inventory is physically turning over. In the past, some analysts calculated the inventory turnover by dividing net sales by inventory. However, this calculation overstates the turnover rate of physical inventory.[11]

Another way to measure inventory turnover is the **days' sales in inventory ratio**:

$$\text{Day's sales in inventory} = \frac{365}{\text{Inventory turnover}} = \frac{365}{10.20} = 35.8 \text{ days}$$

This ratio is the average time, in days, that inventory stays with the firm before it is sold.

Finally, the **fixed asset turnover ratio** and the **total asset turnover ratio** are

$$\text{Fixed asset turnover} = \frac{\text{Sales}}{\text{Net fixed assets}} = \frac{11,394}{7,524} = 1.51x$$

$$\text{Total asset turnover} = \frac{\text{Sales}}{\text{Total assets}} = \frac{11,394}{10,538} = 1.08x$$

These ratios show the sales generated per book-value dollar of fixed assets and total assets, respectively. We can again compare Anheuser-Busch's ratios to those of the other alcoholic beverage firms.

	ANHEUSER-BUSCH	OTHER ALCOHOLIC BEVERAGE FIRMS
Receivables turnover	17.53x	8.11x
Days' sales outstanding	20.8 days	50.9 days
Inventory turnover	10.20x	2.89x
Days' sales in inventory	35.8 days	189.2 days
Fixed asset turnover	1.51x	3.84x
Total asset turnover	1.08x	1.01x

[11]An example illustrates the problem: 60 units of the firm's product were sold last year; sales were $600; cost of goods sold on these units was $360; and inventory was $120 with 20 units in it. Dividing *sales* by inventory, 600/120 = 5.0x. Dividing *cost of goods sold* by inventory, 360/120 = 3.0x. From knowing the number of units, we can see that the physical turnover rate is in fact 60/20 = 3.0x. The turnover rate of 5.0x is larger than the physical turnover rate, because sales are on a different basis; sales include profit. Cost of goods sold does not include profit. Cost of goods sold is on the same cost basis as inventory.

Anheuser-Busch turns over its receivables and inventory more rapidly than the other firms.[12] Anheuser-Busch's fixed assets turn over more slowly. This implies that Anheuser-Busch has a larger investment in fixed assets (relative to sales) than these other firms.

Leverage Ratios

Financial leverage is the extent to which a firm is financed with debt. The amount of debt a firm uses has both positive and negative effects. The more debt, the more likely it is that the firm will have trouble meeting its obligations. Thus the more debt, the higher the probability of financial distress and even bankruptcy. Furthermore, the chance of financial distress, and even the existence of debt obligations, can create conflicts of interest among the stakeholders.

Despite this, debt is a major source of financing. It provides a significant tax advantage because interest is tax deductible. Debt also has lower transaction costs and is generally easier to arrange. Finally, debt affects how the firm's stakeholders bear the risk of the firm. One particular effect is that debt makes the stock riskier because of the increased chance of financial distress. These factors are discussed at length later in the book. At this point, suffice it to say that leverage is very important. **Leverage ratios** measure the amount of (financial) leverage.

Three common leverage ratios are the debt ratio, the debt/equity ratio, and the equity multiplier. The **debt ratio** is the proportion of debt financing.

$$\text{Debt ratio} = \frac{\text{Total debt}}{\text{Total assets}} = \frac{5,918}{10,538} = 0.56x$$

The **debt/equity ratio** is a simple rearrangement of the debt ratio and expresses the same information on a different scale. Whereas the debt ratio can be as small as zero but, assuming positive equity, is always less than 1.0, the debt/equity ratio ranges from zero to infinity. The debt/equity ratio is

$$\text{Debt/equity ratio} = \frac{\text{Total debt}}{\text{Stockholders'equity}} = \frac{5,918}{4,620} = 1.28x$$

The **equity multiplier** is yet another representation of the same information. It shows how much total assets the firm has for each dollar of equity.

$$\text{Equity multiplier} = \frac{\text{Total assets}}{\text{Stockholders'equity}} = \frac{10,538}{4,620} = 2.28x$$

All three of these leverage ratios are widely used. As we have said, they are simply different representations of the same information. If you know any one of them, you can derive the other two. For example, suppose a firm has a debt ratio of $0.40x$ and so is 40% debt financed. From this we know that the firm is 60% equity financed. Therefore, the firm's debt/equity ratio is 40/60 = $0.67x$. Because total assets equal 100% of the financing (the balance sheet equation, A = L + SE), the equity multiplier is 100/60 = 1.67. Generalizing, we have

$$\text{Debt/equity ratio} = \frac{\text{Debt ratio}}{1.0 - \text{Debt ratio}}$$

$$\text{Equity multiplier} = \text{Debt/equity ratio} + 1.0 = \frac{1}{1 - \text{Debt ratio}}$$

---

[12]We suggest you draw your own conclusions concerning the reasons for this rapid turnover in inventory.

Because it does not make any difference which of the three measures is used, we use the debt ratio throughout this book for simplicity and consistency.

Here again we compare Anheuser-Busch to the other alcoholic beverage firms.

	ANHEUSER-BUSCH	OTHER ALCOHOLIC BEVERAGE FIRMS
Debt ratio	0.56x	0.24x
Debt/equity ratio	1.28x	0.51x
Equity multiplier	2.28x	1.51x

The debt ratio shows that Anheuser-Busch is 56% debt financed. The debt/equity ratio shows that the firm has $1.28 in debt for each $1.00 of equity. The equity multiplier shows that the firm has about $2.28 in total assets for each $1.00 of equity. The comparison shows that Anheuser-Busch has more leverage than the other firms.

Coverage Ratios

Coverage ratios show the number of times a firm can "cover" or meet a particular financial obligation. The **interest coverage ratio**, which is also called the **times-interest-earned ratio**, measures the coverage of the firm's interest expense. It is earnings before interest and income taxes (EBIT) divided by the firm's interest expense. For Anheuser-Busch, EBIT equals operating profit (1,776) plus nonoperating profit (−9):

$$EBIT = 1,776 - 9 = 1,767$$

The interest coverage ratio is

$$\text{Times-interest-earned ratio} = \text{Interest coverage ratio} = \frac{\text{EBIT}}{\text{Interest expense}} = \frac{1,767}{200} = 8.84x$$

Many firms lease or rent assets that require contractual payments. Long-term leases are reported on the balance sheet, and the periodic lease payments are included in the firm's interest expense. Rental agreements are different. They are not on the balance sheet. Renting an asset is an alternative to owning it. (Rental payments are therefore an alternative to the interest payments the firm would make if it borrowed the money to buy the same assets.) Rental expense is reported in the notes to the financial statements. For these firms, the **fixed-charge coverage ratio** is useful, where fixed charges consist of interest expense plus rental payments:[13]

$$\text{Fixed-charge coverage ratio} = \frac{\text{EBIT} + \text{Rental payments}}{\text{Interest expense} + \text{Rental payments}} = \frac{1,767 + 5}{200 + 5} = 8.64x$$

---

[13]Rental expense in the previous year is $5 million.

The **cash flow coverage ratio** is the firm's operating cash flows divided by its payment obligations for interest, principal, preferred stock dividends, and rent.[14]

$$\text{Cash flow coverage ratio} = \frac{\text{EBIT} + \text{Rental payments} + \text{Depreciation}}{\text{Rental payments} + \text{Interest expense} + \dfrac{\text{Preferred stock dividends}}{1-T} + \dfrac{\text{Debt repayment}}{1-T}}$$

$$\text{Cash flow coverage ratio} = \frac{1{,}767 + 5 + 567}{5 + 200 + \dfrac{0}{1-0.4} + \dfrac{344}{1-0.4}} = 3.01x$$

Note that two of the financial obligations in the denominator of the cash flow coverage ratio are divided by $(1 - T)$, where T is the marginal income tax rate. Rental payments and interest charges are tax-deductible expenses. Only one dollar of before-tax cash flow is required to meet one dollar of these obligations. In contrast, preferred stock dividends and principal repayments must be made out of after-tax cash flows. They are divided by $(1 - T)$ to get the equivalent before-tax operating cash flow necessary to meet them. This is similar to the difference in tax treatment between interest expense and dividends that we noted in the chapter.

Comparing Anheuser-Busch with the other alcoholic beverage firms, we have:

	ANHEUSER-BUSCH	OTHER ALCOHOLIC BEVERAGE FIRMS
Interest coverage ratio	8.84x	6.28x
Fixed-charge coverage ratio	8.64x	6.17x
Cash flow coverage ratio	3.01x	8.26x

Anheuser-Busch has comparatively better coverage of its interest and fixed-charge obligations. Its cash flow coverage ratio is lower because it had greater long-term debt repayment obligations.

Profitability Ratios

Profitability ratios focus on the profit-generating performance of the firm. These ratios measure how effectively the firm is able to generate profits. They reflect the operating performance, its riskiness, and the effect of leverage. We will look at two kinds of profitability ratios. These are *profit margins*, which measure performance in relation to sales, and *rate-of-return ratios*, which measure performance relative to some measure of the size of the investment.

Gross profit is the difference between sales and the cost of goods sold. Gross profit is critical to the firm because it represents the amount of money remaining to pay operating costs, financing costs, and taxes and to provide for profit. The **gross profit margin** is

$$\text{Gross profit margin} = \frac{\text{Gross profit}}{\text{Sales}} = \frac{\text{Sales} - \text{Cost of goods sold}}{\text{Sales}} = \frac{4{,}652}{11{,}394} = 40.8\%$$

The **net profit margin** measures the profit that is available from each dollar of sales after *all* expenses have been paid.

$$\text{Net profit margin} = \frac{\text{Net income before extraordinary items}}{\text{Sales}} = \frac{994}{11{,}394} = 8.7\%$$

---

[14]Debt repayment in the previous year is $344 million.

Here is how Anheuser-Busch stacks up against the other alcoholic beverage firms:

	ANHEUSER-BUSCH	OTHER ALCOHOLIC BEVERAGE FIRMS
Gross profit margin	40.8%	40.5%
Net profit margin	8.7%	7.2%

Anheuser-Busch has done well. Its gross profit margin is about the same, but its net profit margin is higher.

Unlike profit margins, *rate-of-return ratios* express profitability in relation to various measures of investment in the firm. Their potential usefulness is inherently limited, however, because they are based on book values. Three ratios are commonly used: return on assets, earning power, and return on equity.

Return on assets (ROA)

$$ROA = \text{Return on assets} = \frac{\text{Net income}}{\text{Total assets}} = \frac{994}{10{,}538} = 9.4\%$$

Earning power is EBIT divided by total assets.

$$\text{Earning power} = \frac{\text{EBIT}}{\text{Total assets}} = \frac{1{,}767}{10{,}538} = 16.8\%$$

The difference between ROA and earning power is due to debt financing. Net income is EBIT minus interest and taxes, so ROA will always be less than earning power. Earning power represents the "raw" operating results, whereas ROA represents the combined results of operating and financing.

Return on equity (ROE) is

$$ROE = \frac{\text{Earnings available for common stock before extraordinary items}}{\text{Common stockholders' equity}} = \frac{994}{4{,}620} = 21.5\%$$

where common stockholders' equity includes common stock (at par value), capital surplus, and retained earnings. ROE shows the residual profits of the firm as a proportion of the book value of common stockholders' equity. The amount of leverage affects both the numerator and the denominator of ROE. Typically, ROE is greater than ROA for healthy firms. In bad years, however, ROE can fall below ROA. This is because financial leverage increases the risk of the stock, as we noted earlier.

Comparing Anheuser-Busch with the other alcoholic beverage firms, we have

	ANHEUSER-BUSCH	OTHER ALCOHOLIC BEVERAGE FIRMS
Return on assets (ROA)	9.4%	5.8%
Earning power	16.8%	10.6%
Return on equity (ROE)	21.5%	11.4%

Anheuser-Busch has higher profitability than the other firms. Note once again, however, that these ratios collectively reflect not only the operating performance and its riskiness but also the effect of the firm's financial leverage.

Market Value Ratios

Analysts use several **market value ratios** that relate the market value of the firm's common stock to earnings per share (EPS), dividends per share (DPS), and book value per share, which is total common equity divided by the number of common shares outstanding. Book value per share is $16.17 (= 4,620/285.69). At the time the statements were prepared, the market price of Anheuser-Busch common stock was $58.50 per share. With 285.69 million shares outstanding, Anheuser-Busch's **market capitalization** (market cap.), which is an estimate of the market value of equity, is $16,713 million [= (58.50)285.69].

The **market value leverage ratio** uses the firm's market value of equity (market cap.) in place of the book value of equity in the debt ratio:

$$\frac{\text{Market value}}{\text{leverage ratio}} = \frac{\text{Book value of debt}}{\text{Book value of debt} + \text{Market value of equity}} = \frac{5,918}{5,918 + 16,713} = 26.15\%$$

This ratio typically uses the book value of debt because the market value of debt can be difficult to determine and, in any case, does not often differ a great deal from the book value.

The **price/earnings ratio (P/E)** is

$$P/E = \text{Price/earnings ratio} = \frac{\text{Market price per share}}{\text{Earnings per share}} = \frac{58.50}{3.48} = 16.8x$$

When earnings are negative, earnings per share (EPS) is of course negative, which makes the P/E negative as well. Also, when EPS gets close to zero, the P/E becomes extremely large because of dividing by the EPS. The P/E is not generally reported when EPS is negative or very small, because it is not considered to be economically meaningful under those conditions.

Another form of the same information is **earnings yield**, which is the reciprocal of the P/E.

$$\text{Earnings yield} = \frac{\text{Earnings per share}}{\text{Market price per share}} = \frac{3.48}{58.50} = 5.95\%$$

Unlike the P/E, earnings yield does not "break down" when EPS is very small or negative. EPS is the numerator, avoiding the division-by-zero problem. A negative EPS is a loss per share, in which case earnings yield is a negative rate of return, a rate of losing value.

The **dividend yield** is

$$\text{Dividend yield} = \frac{\text{Dividend per share}}{\text{Market price per share}} = \frac{1.20}{58.50} = 2.05\%$$

Many firms do not pay a cash dividend. Such firms simply have a dividend yield of zero. The decision to pay cash dividends is essentially a choice between paying out earnings to the owners or reinvesting the money in the firm. We will have more to say about dividends later on.

Finally, the **market-to-book ratio** is

$$\text{Market-to-book ratio} = \frac{\text{Market price per share}}{\text{Book value per share}} = \frac{58.50}{16.17} = 3.62x$$

The market-to-book ratio is a very rough index of a firm's historical performance. A high ratio says the firm has created more in market value than the GAAP rules have recorded in book value. The implied message is that the firm has done well. Of course, as we noted earlier, there are many possible explanations for a difference between market and book values. Although the implied message of a high market-to-book ratio is likely to be correct in most cases, additional information is generally needed to reach a confident conclusion.

Comparing Anheuser-Busch with other alcoholic beverage firms, we have:

	ANHEUSER-BUSCH	OTHER ALCOHOLIC BEVERAGE FIRMS
Market value leverage ratio	26.15%	18.21%
Price/earnings ratio	16.8x	15.4x
Earnings yield	5.95%	6.40%
Dividend yield	2.05%	2.00%
Market-to-book ratio	3.62x	1.93x

Past increases in the market value of Anheuser-Busch's common stock have significantly exceeded increases in the book value per share. This makes Anheuser-Busch's market value leverage and market-to-book ratios higher than those of the other firms. Its P/E, earnings yield, and dividend yield are about the same.

Common-Statement Analysis

Another technique used in financial statement analysis is called common-statement analysis. Common-statement analysis makes some comparisons more meaningful because it puts the things being compared on a common basis. There are two widely used methods of common-statement analysis. **Common-size analysis** shows items as percentages rather than as amounts of money. Balance sheet items are expressed as percentages of total assets, and income statement items are expressed as percentages of sales. Common-size analysis makes possible a more meaningful comparison of firms that are of significantly different sizes and enables us to track a single firm through time.

    Common-base-year analysis shows each item as a percentage of its amount in an initial year, such as five years ago. Common-base-year analysis makes it easy to see which items are growing relatively faster or slower, because items that are more (less) than 100% have increased (declined).

SUMMARY

Despite the inherent limitations of accounting information, financial statement analysis can provide important insights into the firm. Numerous widely used financial ratios are given in Table 3A-4.

- Financial statement analysis can be useful in two fundamental ways. First, it can help structure your thinking about business decisions. Second, it can provide some information that is helpful in making those decisions.
- Financial ratio analysis focuses on specific relationships in the financial statements.
- Liquidity ratios show the firm's ability to meet its maturing short-term obligations. These ratios include the current ratio, the quick ratio, the working capital ratio, and the cash ratio.
- Asset turnover ratios show how effectively the firm is using its assets. These ratios include the receivables turnover, days' sales outstanding, inventory turnover, days' sales in inventory, fixed asset turnover, and total asset turnover ratios.
- Leverage ratios show the relative contribution of creditors and owners to the firm's financing. These include ratios such as the market value leverage ratio, the debt ratio, the debt-to-equity ratio, and the equity multiplier.
- Coverage ratios show the amount of funds available to "cover" a particular financial obligation compared to the size of that obligation. These include the interest coverage, fixed-charge coverage, and cash flow coverage ratios.

- Profitability ratios include profit margins and rate-of-return ratios. The profit margin ratios are the gross profit margin and the net profit margin. The rate-of-return ratios include return on assets, earning power, and return on equity.
- Market-value ratios are based on the market price of the company's common stock. These ratios include the market value leverage ratio, the price/earnings ratio, the earnings yield, the dividend yield, and the market-to-book ratio.
- Common-size financial statements show percentage breakdowns of the income statement and balance sheet that allow easier comparisons across companies.
- Common-base-year financial statements show each item as a percentage of its amount in an initial year, which permits easier comparisons across years.

TABLE 3A-4
Summary of
financial ratios.

LIQUIDITY RATIOS

$$\text{Current ratio} = \frac{\text{Current assets}}{\text{Current liabilities}}$$

$$\text{Quick ratio} = \frac{\text{Current assets} - \text{Inventories}}{\text{Current liabilities}}$$

$$\text{Working capital ratio} = \frac{\text{Current assets} - \text{Current liabilities}}{\text{Sales}}$$

$$\text{Cash ratio} = \frac{\text{Cash and equivalents}}{\text{Total assets}}$$

ASSET ACTIVITY RATIOS

$$\text{Receivables turnover} = \frac{\text{Annual credit sales}}{\text{Accounts receivable}}$$

$$\text{Days' sales outstanding} = \frac{365}{\text{Receivables turnover}}$$

$$\text{Inventory turnover} = \frac{\text{Cost of goods sold}}{\text{Inventory}}$$

$$\text{Days' sales in inventory} = \frac{365}{\text{Inventory turnover}}$$

$$\text{Fixed asset turnover} = \frac{\text{Sales}}{\text{Net fixed assets}}$$

$$\text{Total asset turnover} = \frac{\text{Sales}}{\text{Total assets}}$$

LEVERAGE RATIOS

$$\text{Debt ratio} = \frac{\text{Total debt}}{\text{Total assets}}$$

$$\text{Debt/equity ratio} = \frac{\text{Total debt}}{\text{Stockholders' equity}} = \frac{\text{Debt ratio}}{1.0 - \text{Debt ratio}}$$

$$\text{Equity multiplier} = \frac{\text{Total assets}}{\text{Stockholders' equity}} = \text{Debt/equity ratio} + 1.0$$

COVERAGE RATIOS

$$\text{Interest coverage ratio} = \frac{\text{EBIT}}{\text{Interest expense}}$$

$$\frac{\text{Fixed-charge}}{\text{coverage ratio}} = \frac{\text{EBIT} + \text{Rental payments}}{\text{Interest expense} + \text{Rental payments}}$$

$$\frac{\text{Cash flow}}{\text{coverage ratio}} = \frac{\text{EBIT} + \text{Rental payments} + \text{Depreciation}}{\text{Rental} + \text{Interest} + \dfrac{\text{Preferred stock dividends}}{1-T} + \dfrac{\text{Debt repayment}}{1-T}}$$

PROFITABILITY RATIOS

$$\text{Gross profit margin} = \frac{\text{Gross profit}}{\text{Sales}} = \frac{\text{Sales} - \text{Cost of goods sold}}{\text{Sales}}$$

$$\text{Net profit margin} = \frac{\text{Net income before extraordinary items}}{\text{Sales}}$$

$$\text{Return on assets} = \frac{\text{Net income}}{\text{Total assets}}$$

$$\text{Earning power} = \frac{\text{EBIT}}{\text{Total assets}}$$

$$\text{Return on equity} = \frac{\text{Earnings available for common stock before extraordinary items}}{\text{Common stockholders' equity}}$$

MARKET VALUE RATIOS

$$\frac{\text{Market value}}{\text{leverage ratio}} = \frac{\text{Book value of debt}}{\text{Book value of debt} + \text{Market value of equity}}$$

$$\text{P/E} = \text{Price/earnings ratio} = \frac{\text{Market price per share}}{\text{Earnings per share}}$$

$$\text{Earnings yield} = \frac{\text{Earnings per share}}{\text{Market price per share}}$$

$$\text{Dividend yield} = \frac{\text{Dividend per share}}{\text{Market price per share}}$$

$$\text{Market-to-book ratio} = \frac{\text{Market price per share}}{\text{Book value per share}}$$

APPENDIX REVIEW

Compute each of the ratios in Table 3A-4 for OutBack SportWear, using the information given in Tables 3-1, 3-2, and 3-3, and assuming the common stock has a current market value of $47.25. To calculate the book value per share, subtract the preferred stock from total stockholders' equity to get common stockholders' equity.

FOREIGN DIRECT INVESTMENT THEORY AND STRATEGY

4

This chapter analyzes the decisions whether, where, and how to undertake foreign direct investment (FDI).

The internationalization process begins with international trade. This chapter first reviews the theory of comparative advantage, the theoretical foundation of trade. Only after highlighting the limitations of international trade is it possible to understand why firms move beyond the geographic boundaries of their home country in order to license or manufacture abroad; that is, to engage in *foreign direct investment*.

The second section of the chapter analyzes how market imperfections create a rationale for the existence of multinational enterprises. Here we explain what motivates firms to become multinational. We then demonstrate how key competitive advantages support a firm's strategy to undertake foreign direct investment. We follow this by showing how the *OLI Paradigm* provides a theoretical foundation for foreign direct investment. Then we analyze how a firm decides where to invest abroad through various types of foreign involvement. At the end of the chapter is a mini-case on how one company pursued the global licensing of its product.

4.1   THE THEORY OF COMPARATIVE ADVANTAGE

The *theory of comparative advantage* provides a basis for explaining and justifying international trade in a model world assumed to enjoy free trade, perfect competition, no uncertainty, costless information, and no government interference. The theory contains the following features:

- Exporters in Country A sell goods or services to unrelated importers in Country B.
- Firms in Country A specialize in making products that can be produced relatively efficiently, given Country A's endowment of factors of production; that is, land, labor, capital, and technology. Firms in Country B do likewise, given the factors of production found in Country B. In this way, the total combined output of A and B is maximized.
- Because the factors of production cannot be moved freely from Country A to Country B, the benefits of specialization are realized through international trade.
- The way the benefits of the extra production are shared depends on the *terms of trade*, the ratio at which quantities of the physical goods are traded. Each country's share is determined by supply and demand in perfectly competitive markets in the two countries. Neither Country A nor Country B is worse off than before trade, and typically both are better off, albeit perhaps unequally.

An Example of Comparative Advantage

For an example of the benefits of free trade based on comparative advantage, assume that Thailand is more efficient than Brazil at producing sports shoes and stereo equipment. With one unit of production (a mix of land, labor, capital, and technology), efficient Thailand can produce either 12 shipping containers (ctrs) of shoes or 6 shipping containers of stereo equipment. Brazil, being less efficient in both, can produce only 10 containers of shoes or 2 containers of stereo equipment with one unit of input. These production capabilities are as follows:

	PRODUCTION CAPABILITY	
	CONTAINERS OF SPORTS SHOES	**CONTAINERS OF STEREO EQUIPMENT**
Thailand (1,000 production units)	12/unit	6/unit
Brazil (1,000 production units)	10/unit	2/unit

A production unit in Thailand has an *absolute advantage* over a production unit in Brazil in both shoes and stereo equipment. Thailand also has a larger *relative advantage* over Brazil in producing stereo equipment (6 to 2) than shoes (12 to 10). As long as these ratios are unequal, comparative advantage exists.

Assume that no trade takes place, and each country divides its own production units between shoes and stereo equipment. Each country elects to allocate 300 production units to shoes and 700 production units to stereo equipment, resulting in the production and consumption outcomes in the top of Table 4-1.

Now assume complete specialization. Thailand produces only stereo equipment and Brazil produces only shoes. World production would be higher for both shoes and stereo equipment, as illustrated by the bottom half of Table 4-1.

Clearly the world in total is better off because there are now 10,000 containers of shoes—instead of just 6,600. And there are 6,000 containers of stereo equipment—instead of just 5,600. But distribution is quite distorted. The Thais now tap only bare feet to their music, and the Brazilians dance through Carnival with good shoes but no recorded music!

TABLE 4-1
The Theory of
Comparative
Advantage:
A Numerical
Example of Brazil
and Thailand.

PRODUCTION IF NO TRADE

	Shoe Production	Stereo Production
Thailand produces and consumes	$300 \times 12 = 3,600$ ctrs	$700 \times 6 = 4,200$ ctrs
Brazil produces and consumes	$300 \times 10 = \underline{3,000}$	$700 \times 2 = \underline{1,400}$
Total world production and consumption	6,600 ctrs	5,600 ctrs

COMPLETE SPECIALIZATION

	Shoe Production	Stereo Production
Thailand produces only stereo equipment		$1,000 \times 6 = 6,000$ ctrs
Brazil produces only shoes	$1,000 \times 10 = \underline{10,000}$ ctrs	
Total world production and consumption	10,000 ctrs	6,000 ctrs

TABLE 4-2
Trade at Thailand's
Domestic Price.

FOR EACH CONTAINER OF STEREO EQUIPMENT EXPORTED, THAILAND IMPORTS TWO CONTAINERS OF SHOES FROM BRAZIL.

	Shoe Production Plus/Minus Trade	Stereo Production Plus/Minus Trade
Thailand produces 6,000 containers of stereo equipment and exports 1,800 containers	$0 + 3,600 = 3,600$ ctrs	$6,000 - 1,800 = 4,200$ ctrs
Brazil produces 10,000 containers of shoes and exports 3,600 containers	$10,000 - 3,600 = \underline{6,400}$	$0 + 1,800 = \underline{1,800}$
World production and consumption	10,000 ctrs	6,000 ctrs

Trade can resolve this distribution problem. Assume initially that trade between Thailand and Brazil takes place at the ratio of two containers of shoes for one container of stereo equipment. This exchange rate of two containers of shoes for one container of stereo equipment is Thailand's domestic price; that is, the ratio of trade within Thailand should it produce both items and not engage in international trade. Assume further that Thailand exports 1,800 containers of stereo equipment to Brazil and imports 3,600 containers of shoes from Brazil. The situation would be as depicted in Table 4-2.

At this price all gains go to Brazil, which consumes 6,400 containers of shoes (instead of 3,000 with no trade) and consumes 1,800 containers of stereo equipment (instead of 1,400 with no trade). Thailand's consumption, 3,600 containers of shoes and 4,200 containers of stereos, is just as it was with no trade. Thailand has gained nothing from trade at this price, although it has lost nothing, either!

Assume now that trade takes place at Brazil's domestic price of five containers of shoes for each container of stereo equipment. This is illustrated in Table 4-3. At Brazil's internal price, all gains go to Thailand, which now consumes 7,000 containers of shoes (instead of 3,600 with no trade) and 4,600 containers of stereo equipment (instead of 4,200 with no trade). Brazil's consumption, 3,000 containers of shoes and 1,400 containers of stereo equipment, is the same as with no trade. Brazil has gained nothing from trade at this price—although it has lost nothing, either.

TABLE 4-3
Trade at Brazil's
Domestic Price.

FOR EACH CONTAINER OF STEREO EQUIPMENT EXPORTED, THAILAND IMPORTS FIVE CONTAINERS OF SHOES FROM BRAZIL.

	Shoe Production Plus/Minus Trade	Stereo Production Plus/Minus Trade
Thailand produces 6,000 containers of stereo equipment and exports 1,400 containers	$0 + 7,000 = 7,000$ ctrs	$6,000 - 1,400 = 4,600$ ctrs
Brazil produces 10,000 containers of shoes and exports 7,000 containers	$10,000 - 7,000 = \underline{3,000}$	$0 + 1,400 = \underline{1,400}$
World production and consumption	10,000 ctrs	6,000 ctrs

TABLE 4-4
Trade at a Price
Reached by Free
Bargaining.

FOR EACH CONTAINER OF STEREO EQUIPMENT EXPORTED, THAILAND IMPORTS FOUR CONTAINERS OF SHOES FROM BRAZIL.

	Shoe Production Plus/Minus Trade	Stereo Production Plus/Minus Trade
Thailand produces 6,000 containers of stereo equipment and exports 1,600 containers	$0 + 6,400 = 6,400$ ctrs	$6,000 - 1,600 = 4,400$ ctrs
Brazil produces 10,000 containers of shoes and exports 6,400 containers	$10,000 - 6,400 = \underline{3,600}$	$0 + 1,600 = \underline{1,600}$
World production and consumption	10,000 ctrs	6,000 ctrs

Now let trade take place at a price in between Thailand's domestic price of 2-to-1 and Brazil's domestic price of 5-to-1. Assume that free bargaining leads to a price of 4-to-1, as seen in Table 4-4.

At any price between the boundaries of 2-to-1 and 5-to-1, both countries benefit from specializing and trading. At a 4-to-1 price, Thailand consumes 2,800 more containers of shoes as well as 200 more containers of stereo equipment than it has consumed with no trade. Brazil consumes 600 more containers of shoes as well as 200 more containers of stereo equipment than it has consumed with no trade. Total combined production of both shoes and stereo equipment has increased through the specialization process, and it only remains for the exchange ratio to determine how this larger output is distributed between the two countries.

Limitations of Comparative Advantage

Although international trade might have approached the comparative advantage model during the nineteenth century, it certainly does not today, for the following reasons:

- Countries do not appear to specialize only in those products that could be most efficiently produced by that country's particular factors of production. Instead, governments interfere with comparative advantage for a variety of economic and political reasons, such as to achieve full employment, economic development, national self-sufficiency in defense-related industries, and protection of an agricultural sector's way of life. Government interference takes the form of tariffs, quotas, and other nontariff restrictions.
- At least two of the factors of production—capital and technology—now flow directly and easily between countries, rather than only indirectly through traded goods and services. This direct flow occurs between related subsidiaries and affiliates of multinational firms,

as well as between unrelated firms via loans, and license and management contracts, as we will discuss later in this chapter.

- Modern factors of production are more numerous than in this simple model. Factors considered in the location of production facilities worldwide include local and managerial skills, a dependable legal structure for settling contract disputes, research and development competence, educational levels of available workers, energy resources, consumer demand for brand-name goods, mineral and raw material availability, access to capital, tax differentials, supporting infrastructure (roads, ports, communication facilities), and possibly others.
- Although the terms of trade are ultimately determined by supply and demand, the process by which the terms are set is different from that visualized in traditional trade theory. They are determined partly by administered pricing in oligopolistic markets.
- Comparative advantage shifts over time as less developed countries become more developed and realize their latent opportunities. For example, over the past 150 years, comparative advantage in producing cotton textiles has shifted from the United Kingdom to the United States, to Japan, to Hong Kong, to Taiwan, and to China.
- The classical model of comparative advantage did not really address certain other issues, such as the effect of uncertainty and information costs, the role of differentiated products in imperfectly competitive markets, and economies of scale.

Although the world is a long way from the classical trade model, the general principle of comparative advantage is still valid. The closer the world gets to true international specialization, the more world production and consumption can be increased, provided the problem of equitable distribution of the benefits can be solved to the satisfaction of consumers, producers, and political leaders. Complete specialization, however, remains an unrealistic limiting case, just as perfect competition is a limiting case in microeconomic theory.

Supply Chain Outsourcing: Comparative Advantage Today

Comparative advantage is still a relevant theory to explain why particular countries are most suitable for exports of goods and services that support the global supply chain of both MNEs and domestic firms. The comparative advantage of the twenty-first century, however, is based more on services and their cross- border facilitation by telecommunications and the Internet. The source of a nation's comparative advantage, however, still is created from the mixture of its own labor skills, access to capital, and technology.

Many locations for supply chain outsourcing exist today. Figure 4-1 presents a geographical overview of this modern reincarnation of trade-based comparative advantage. To prove that these countries should specialize in the activities shown, you would need to know how costly the same activities would be in the countries that are importing these services compared to their own other industries. Remember that it takes a relative advantage in costs, not just an absolute advantage, to create comparative advantage.

For example, India has developed a highly efficient and low-cost software industry. This industry supplies not only the creation of custom software, but also call centers for customer support and other information technology services. The Indian software industry is composed of subsidiaries of MNEs and of independent companies.

If you own a computer and call the customer support center number for help, you are highly likely to reach a call center in India. Answering your call will be a knowledgeable Indian software engineer or programmer who will walk you through your problem. India has a large number of well-educated, English- speaking technical experts who are paid only a fraction of the salary and overhead earned by their U.S. counterparts. The overcapacity and low cost of international telecommunication networks today further enhances the comparative advantage of an Indian location.

As illustrated by *Global Finance in Practice 4-1*, the extent of global outsourcing is already reaching out to every corner of the globe. From financial back offices in Manila to information technology engineers in Hungary, modern telecommunications now take business activities to labor, rather than labor migrating to the places of business.

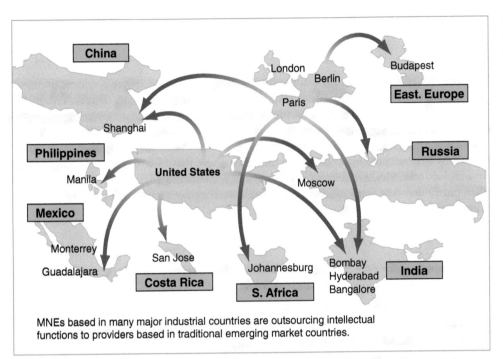

FIGURE 4-1
Global Outsourcing of
Comparative Advantage.

MNEs based in many major industrial countries are outsourcing intellectual functions to providers based in traditional emerging market countries.

Global Finance in Practice 4.1

Examples of Global Outsourcing of Comparative Advantage in Intellectual Skills

Country	Activity
China	Chemical, mechanical, and petroleum engineering services; business and product development centers for companies like GE.
Costa Rica	Call centers for Spanish-speaking consumers in many industrial markets; Accenture has IT support and back-office operations call centers.
Eastern Europe	American and IT service providers operate call centers for customer and business support in Hungary, Poland, and the Czech Republic, and Romanian and Bulgarian centers for German-speaking IT customers in Europe.
India	Software engineering and support; call centers for all types of computer and telecom services; medical analysis and consultative services; Indian companies such as Tata, Infosys, and Wipro are already global leaders in IT design, implementation, and support.
Mexico	Automotive engineering and electronic sector services.
Philippines	Financial and accounting services; architecture services; telemarketing and graphic arts.
Russia	Software and engineering services; R&D centers for Boeing, Intel, Motorola, and Nortel.
South Africa	Call and user support services for French, English, and German-speaking consumers throughout Europe.

Source: Abstracted from "Is Your Job Next?" *Business Week*, February 3, 2003.

4.2 MARKET IMPERFECTIONS: A RATIONALE FOR THE EXISTENCE OF THE MULTINATIONAL FIRM

MNEs strive to take advantage of imperfections in national markets for products, factors of production, and financial assets. Imperfections in the market for products translate into market opportunities for MNEs. Large international firms are better able to exploit such competitive factors as economies of scale, managerial and technological expertise, product differentiation, and financial strength than are their local competitors. In fact, MNEs thrive best in markets characterized by international oligopolistic competition, where these factors are particularly critical. In addition, once MNEs have established a physical presence abroad, they are in a better position than purely domestic firms to identify and implement market opportunities through their own internal information network.

Why Do Firms Become Multinational?

Strategic motives drive the decision to invest abroad and become an MNE. These motives can be summarized under the following five categories.

1. **Market seekers** produce in foreign markets either to satisfy local demand or to export to markets other than their home market. U.S. automobile firms manufacturing in Europe for local consumption are an example of market-seeking motivation.
2. **Raw material** seekers extract raw materials wherever they can be found, either for export or for further processing and sale in the country in which they are found—the host country. Firms in the oil, mining, plantation, and forest industries fall into this category.
3. **Production efficiency seekers** produce in countries where one or more of the factors of production are underpriced relative to their productivity. Labor-intensive production of electronic components in Taiwan, Malaysia, and Mexico is an example of this motivation.
4. **Knowledge seekers** operate in foreign countries to gain access to technology or managerial expertise. For example, German, Dutch, and Japanese firms have purchased U.S. located electronics firms for their technology.
5. **Political safety seekers** acquire or establish new operations in countries that are considered unlikely to expropriate or interfere with private enterprise. For example, Hong Kong firms invested heavily in the United States, United Kingdom, Canada, and Australia in anticipation of the consequences of China's 1997 takeover of the British colony.

These five types of strategic considerations are not mutually exclusive. Forest products firms seeking wood fiber in Brazil, for example, would also find a large Brazilian market for a portion of their output.

In industries characterized by worldwide oligopolistic competition, each of the previous strategic motives should be subclassified into proactive and defensive investments. *Proactive* investments are designed to enhance the growth and profitability of the firm itself. *Defensive* investments are designed to deny growth and profitability to the firm's competitors. Examples of the latter are investments that try to preempt a market before competitors can get established there, or attempt to capture raw material sources in order to deny them to competitors.

4.3 SUSTAINING AND TRANSFERRING COMPETITIVE ADVANTAGE

In deciding whether to invest abroad, management must first determine whether the firm has a sustainable competitive advantage that enables it to compete effectively in the home market. The competitive advantage must be firm-specific, transferable, and powerful enough to compensate the firm for the potential disadvantages of operating abroad (foreign exchange risks, political risks, and increased agency costs).

Based on observations of firms that have successfully invested abroad, we can conclude that some of the competitive advantages enjoyed by MNEs are: (1) economies of scale and scope arising from their large size; (2) managerial and marketing expertise; (3) superior technology, owing to their heavy emphasis on research; (4) financial strength; (5) differentiated products; and sometimes (6) competitiveness of their home markets.

Economies of Scale and Scope

Economies of scale and scope can be developed in production, marketing, finance, research and development, transportation, and purchasing. In each of these areas, there are significant competitive advantages to being large, whether size is due to international or domestic operations. Production economies can come from the use of large-scale automated plant and equipment or from an ability to rationalize production through worldwide specialization. For example, some automobile manufacturers, such as Ford, rationalize manufacturing by producing engines in one country, transmissions in another, bodies in another, and assembling still elsewhere, with the location often being dictated by comparative advantage.

Marketing economies occur when firms are large enough to use the most efficient advertising media to create worldwide brand identification, as well as to establish worldwide distribution, warehousing, and servicing systems. Financial economies derive from access to the full range of financial instruments and sources of funds, such as the Eurocurrency, Euroequity, and Eurobond markets. In-house research and development programs are typically restricted to large firms, because of the minimum-size threshold for establishing a laboratory and scientific staff. Transportation economies accrue to firms that can ship in carload or shipload lots. Purchasing economies come from quantity discounts and market power.

Managerial and Marketing Expertise

Managerial expertise includes skill in managing large industrial organizations from both a human and a technical viewpoint. It also encompasses knowledge of modern analytical techniques and their application in functional areas of business. Managerial expertise can be developed through prior experience in foreign markets. In most empirical studies, multinational firms have been observed to export to a market before establishing a production facility there. Likewise, they have prior experience sourcing raw materials and human capital in other foreign countries either through imports, licensing, or FDI. In this manner, the MNEs can partially overcome the supposed superior local knowledge of host country firms.

Advanced Technology

Advanced technology includes both scientific and engineering skills. It is not limited to MNEs, but firms in the most industrialized countries have had an advantage in terms of access to continuing new technology spin-offs from the military and space programs. Empirical studies have supported the importance of technology as a characteristic of MNEs.

Financial Strength

Companies demonstrate financial strength by achieving and maintaining a global cost and availability of capital. This is a critical competitive cost variable that enables them to fund FDI and other foreign activities. MNEs that are resident in liquid and unsegmented capital markets are normally blessed with this attribute. However, MNEs that are resident in small industrial or emerging market countries can still follow a proactive strategy of seeking foreign portfolio and corporate investors.

FIGURE 4-2
Determinants of
National Competitive
Advantage: Porter's
Diamond.

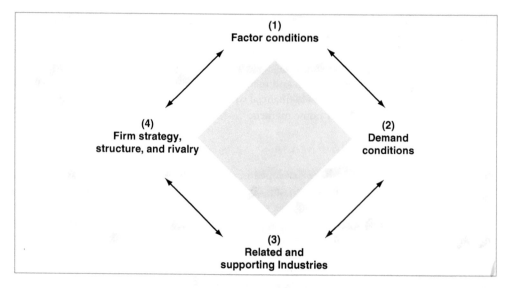

Source: Adapted and reprinted by permission of Harvard Business Review. From Michael Porter, *The Competitive Advantage of Nations* March–April 1990. Copyright © 1990 by the Harvard Business School Publishing Corporation. All Rights Reserved.

Small- and medium-size firms often lack the characteristics that attract foreign (and maybe domestic) investors. They are too small or unattractive to achieve a global cost of capital. This limits their ability to fund FDI, and their higher marginal cost of capital reduces the number of foreign projects that can generate the higher required rate of return.

Differentiated Products

Firms create their own firm-specific advantages by producing and marketing differentiated products. Such products originate from research-based innovations or heavy marketing expenditures to gain brand identification. Furthermore, the research and marketing process continues to produce a steady stream of new differentiated products. It is difficult and costly for competitors to copy such products, and they always face a time lag if they try. Having developed differentiated products for the domestic home market, the firm may decide to market them worldwide, a decision consistent with the desire to maximize return on heavy research and marketing expenditures.

Competitiveness of the Home Market

A strongly competitive home market can sharpen a firm's competitive advantage relative to firms located in less competitive home markets. This phenomenon is known as the "diamond of national advantage." The diamond has four components, as illustrated in Figure 4-2.[1]

A firm's success in competing in a particular industry depends partly on the availability of factors of production (land, labor, capital, and technology) appropriate for that industry. Countries that are either naturally endowed with the appropriate factors or able to create them will probably spawn firms that are both competitive at home and potentially so abroad. For example, a well-educated work force in the home market creates a competitive advantage for firms in certain high- tech industries.

Firms facing sophisticated and demanding customers in the home market are able to hone their marketing, production, and quality control skills. Japan is such a market.

---

[1]Michael Porter, *The Competitive Advantage of Nations*, London: Macmillan Press, 1990.

Firms in industries that are surrounded by a critical mass of related industries and suppliers will be more competitive because of this supporting cast. For example, electronic firms located in centers of excellence, such as in the San Francisco Bay area, are surrounded by efficient, creative suppliers and enjoy access to educational institutions at the forefront of knowledge.

A competitive home market forces firms to fine-tune their operational and control strategies for their specific industry and country environment. Japanese firms learned how to organize to implement their famous just-in-time inventory control system. One key was to use numerous subcontractors and suppliers that were encouraged to locate near the final assembly plants.

In some cases, home country markets have not been large or competitive, but MNEs located there have nevertheless developed global niche markets served by foreign subsidiaries. Global competition in oligopolistic industries substitutes for domestic competition. For example, a number of MNEs resident in Scandinavia, Switzerland, and the Netherlands fall in this category. Some of these are Novo Nordisk (Denmark), Norsk Hydro (Norway), Nokia (Finland), L.M. Ericsson (Sweden), Astra (Sweden), ABB (Sweden/Switzerland), Roche Holding (Switzerland), Royal Dutch Shell (the Netherlands), Unilever (the Netherlands), and Philips (the Netherlands).

Emerging market countries have also spawned aspiring global MNEs in niche markets even though they lack competitive home country markets. Some of these are traditional exporters in natural resource fields such as oil, agriculture, and minerals, but they are in transition to becoming MNEs. They typically start with foreign sales subsidiaries, joint ventures, and strategic alliances. Examples are Petrobrás (Brazil), YPF (Argentina), and Cemex (Mexico). Another category of firms is those that have been recently privatized in the telecommunications industry. Examples are Telefonos de Mexico and Telebras (Brazil). Still others started as electronic component manufacturers but are making the transition to manufacturing abroad. Examples are Samsung Electronics (Korea) and Acer Computer (Taiwan).

4.4   THE OLI PARADIGM AND INTERNALIZATION

The OLI Paradigm is an attempt to create an overall framework to explain why MNEs choose FDI rather than serving foreign markets through alternative modes such as licensing, joint ventures, strategic alliances, management contracts, and exporting.[2]

The *OLI Paradigm* states that a firm must first have some competitive advantage in its home market—"O" or *owner-specific*—that can be transferred abroad if the firm is to be successful in foreign direct investment. Second, the firm must be attracted by specific characteristics of the foreign market—"L" or *location-specific*—that will allow it to exploit its competitive advantages in that market. Third, the firm will maintain its competitive position by attempting to control the entire value chain in its industry—"I" or *internalization*. This attempt leads it to foreign direct investment rather than licensing or outsourcing.

Definitions

The "O" in OLI stands for owner-specific advantages. As described earlier, a firm must have competitive advantages in its home market. These must be firm-specific, not easily copied, and in a form that allows them to be transferred to foreign subsidiaries. For example, economies of scale and financial strength are not necessarily firm-specific, because they can be achieved by many other firms. Certain kinds of technology can be purchased, licensed, or copied. Even differentiated products can lose their advantage to slightly altered versions, given enough marketing effort and the right price.

---

[2]Peter J. Buckley and Mark Casson, *The Future of the Multinational Enterprise*, London: McMillan, 1976; and John H. Dunning, "Trade Location of Economic Activity and the MNE: A Search for an Eclectic Approach," in *The International Allocation of Economic Activity*, Bertil Ohlin, Per-Ove Hesselborn, and Per Magnus Wijkman, eds., New York: Holmes and Meier, 1977, pp. 395–418.

The "L" in OLI stands for location-specific advantages. These factors are typically market imperfections or genuine comparative advantages that attract FDI to particular locations. These factors might include a low-cost but productive labor force, unique sources of raw materials, a large domestic market, defensive investments to counter other competitors, or centers of technological excellence.

The "I" in OLI stands for internalization. According to the theory, the key ingredient for maintaining a firm-specific competitive advantage is possession of proprietary information and control of the human capital that can generate new information through expertise in research. Needless to say, once again large research-intensive firms are most likely to fit this description.

Minimizing transactions costs is the key factor in determining the success of an internalization strategy. Wholly owned FDI reduces the agency costs that arise from asymmetric information, lack of trust, and the need to monitor foreign partners, suppliers, and financial institutions. Self-financing eliminates the need to observe specific debt covenants on foreign subsidiaries that are financed locally or by joint venture partners. If a multinational firm has a low global cost and high availability of capital, why share it with joint venture partners, distributors, licensees, and local banks, all of which probably have a higher cost of capital?

The Financial Strategy

Financial strategies are directly related to the OLI Paradigm in explaining FDI, as shown in Table 4-5. Proactive financial strategies can be controlled in advance by the MNE's financial managers. These include strategies necessary to gain an advantage from lower global cost and

TABLE 4-5   Finance-Specific Factors and the OLI Paradigm: "X" indicates a connection between FDI and finance-specific strategies.

	OWNERSHIP ADVANTAGES	LOCATION ADVANTAGES	INTERNALIZATION ADVANTAGES
Proactive Financial Strategies			
1. Gaining and maintaining a global cost and availability of capital			
• Competitive sourcing of capital globally	X	X	
• Strategic preparatory cross-listing	X		
• Providing accounting and disclosure transparency	X		
• Maintaining competitive commercial and financial banking relationships	X		
• Maintaining a competitive credit rating	X	X	X
2. Negotiating financial subsidies and/or reduced taxation to increase free cash flow	X	X	
3. Reducing financial agency cost through FDI			X
4. Reducing operating and transaction exposure through FDI	X		
Reactive Financial Strategies			
1. Exploiting undervalued or overvalued exchange rates		X	
2. Exploiting undervalued or overvalued stock prices		X	
3. Reacting to capital control that prevents the free movement of funds		X	
4. Minimizing taxation		X	X

Source: Reprinted from Lars Oxelheim, Arthur Stonehill and Trond Randøy, "On the Treatment of Finance Specific Factors Within the OLI Paradigm," *International Business Review*, Vol. 10, pages 381–398, © 2001, with permission from Elsevier Science.

greater availability of capital. Other proactive financial strategies are negotiating financial subsidies and/or reduced taxation to increase free cash flows, reducing financial agency costs through FDI, and reducing operating and transaction exposure through FDI.

Reactive financial strategies, as illustrated in Table 4-5, depend on discovering market imperfections. For example, the MNE can exploit misaligned exchange rates and stock prices. It also needs to react to capital controls that prevent the free movement of funds and react to opportunities to minimize worldwide taxation.

4.5 DECIDING WHERE TO INVEST

The decision about where to invest abroad is influenced by behavioral factors. The decision about where to invest abroad for the first time is not the same as the decision about where to reinvest abroad. A firm learns from its first few investments abroad and what it learns influences subsequent investments.

In theory, a firm should identify its competitive advantages. Then it should search worldwide for market imperfections and comparative advantage until it finds a country where it expects to enjoy a competitive advantage large enough to generate a risk-adjusted return above the firm's hurdle rate.

In practice, firms have been observed to follow a sequential search pattern as described in the behavioral theory of the firm. Human rationality is bounded by one's ability to gather and process all the information that would be needed to make a perfectly rational decision based on all the facts. This observation lies behind two related behavioral theories of FDI: the behavioral approach and international network theory, described next.

Behavioral Approach to FDI

The *behavioral approach* to analyzing the FDI decision is typified by the so-called Swedish School of economists.[3] The Swedish School has rather successfully explained not just the initial decision to invest abroad but also later decisions to reinvest elsewhere and to change the structure of a firm's international involvement over time. Based on the internationalization process of a sample of Swedish MNEs, the economists observed that these firms tended to invest first in countries that were not too far distant in psychic terms. *Close psychic distance* defined countries with a cultural, legal, and institutional environment similar to Sweden's, such as Norway, Denmark, Finland, Germany, and the United Kingdom. The initial investments were modest in size to minimize the risk of an uncertain foreign environment. As the Swedish firms learned from their initial investments, they became willing to take greater risks with respect to both the psychic distance of the countries and the size of the investments.

International Network Theory

As the Swedish MNEs grew and matured, so did the nature of their international involvement. Today each MNE is perceived as being a member of an international network, with nodes based in each of the foreign subsidiaries, as well as the parent firm itself. Centralized (hierarchical) control has given way to decentralized (heterarchical) control. Foreign subsidiaries compete with each other and with the parent for expanded resource commitments, thus influencing the strategy and reinvestment decisions. Many of these MNEs have become political coalitions with competing internal and external networks. Each subsidiary (and the parent) is embedded in its host country's network

---

[3]John Johansen, and F. Wiedersheim-Paul, "The Internationalization of the Firm: Four Swedish Case Studies," *Journal of Management Studies*, Vol. 12, No. 3, 1975; and John Johansen and Jan Erik Vahlne, "The Internationalization of the Firm: A Model of Knowledge Development and Increasing Foreign Market Commitments," *Journal of International Business Studies*, Vol. 8, No. 1, 1977.

of suppliers and customers. It is also a member of a worldwide network based on its industry. Finally, it is a member of an organizational network under the nominal control of the parent firm. Complicating matters still further is the possibility that the parent itself may have evolved into a *transnational firm*, one that is owned by a coalition of investors located in different countries.[4]

Asea Brown Boveri (ABB) is an example of a Swedish-Swiss firm that has passed through the international evolutionary process all the way to being a transnational firm. ABB was formed through a merger of Sweden-based ASEA and Switzerland-based Brown Boveri in 1991. Both firms were already dominant players internationally in the electrotechnical and engineering industries. ABB has literally hundreds of foreign subsidiaries, which are managed on a very decentralized basis. ABB's "flat" organization structure and transnational ownership encourage local initiative, quick response, and decentralized FDI decisions. Although overall strategic direction is the legal responsibility of the parent firm, foreign subsidiaries play a major role in all decision making. Their input in turn is strongly influenced by their own membership in their local and worldwide industry networks.

4.6 HOW TO INVEST ABROAD: MODES OF FOREIGN INVOLVEMENT

The globalization process includes a sequence of decisions regarding where production is to occur, who is to own or control intellectual property, and who is to own the actual production facilities. Figure 4-3 provides a roadmap to explain this FDI sequence.

FIGURE 4-3
The FDI Sequence: Foreign Presence and Foreign Investment.

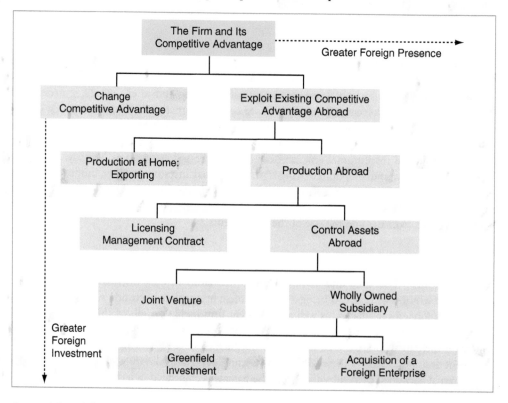

Source: Adapted from Gunter Dufey and R. Mirus, "Foreign Direct Investment: Theory and Strategic Considerations," unpublished, University of Michigan, 1985. Reprinted with permission from the authors. All Rights Reserved.

---

[4]Mats Forsgren, *Managing the Internationalization Process: The Swedish Case*, London: Routledge, 1989.

Exporting versus Production Abroad

There are several advantages to limiting a firm's activities to exports. *Exporting* has none of the unique risks facing FDI, joint ventures, strategic alliances, and licensing. Political risks are minimal. Agency costs, such as monitoring and evaluating foreign units, are avoided. The amount of front-end investment is typically lower than in other modes of foreign involvement. Foreign exchange risks remain, however.

The fact that a significant share of exports (and imports) are executed between MNEs and their foreign subsidiaries and affiliates further reduces the risk of exports compared to other modes of involvement. For example, *Global Finance in Practice 4-2* shows the extent of exports and imports from U.S.-based MNEs to their foreign subsidiaries and affiliates.

There are also disadvantages. A firm is not able to internalize and exploit the results of its research and development as effectively as if it invested directly. The firm also risks losing markets to imitators and global competitors that might be more cost-efficient in production abroad and distribution. As these firms capture foreign markets, they might become so strong that they can export back into the domestic exporter's own market. Remember that defensive FDI is often motivated by the need to prevent this kind of predatory behavior as well as to preempt foreign markets before competitors can get started.

Licensing and Management Contracts versus Control of Assets Abroad

Licensing is a popular method for domestic firms to profit from foreign markets without the need to commit sizable funds. Because the foreign producer is typically wholly owned locally,

Global Finance in Practice 4.2

Keeping It in the Family: American Exports to and Imports from American-Owned Affiliates Abroad (Billions of US$)

	Intracompany	Intercompany	Total
All countries			
Exports	145.5	24.5	170.0
Imports	123.9	19.4	143.3
Balance	21.6	5.1	26.7
High-income countries			
Exports	129.0	20.8	149.9
Imports	54.0	15.1	129.1
Balance	35.0	5.7	40.7
Middle-income countries			
Exports	28.9	5.4	34.3
Imports	31.5	1.9	33.4
Balance	−2.6	3.5	0.8
Low-income countries			
Exports	1.6	0.2	1.8
Imports	1.8	0.4	2.2
Balance	−0.2	−0.2	−0.4

Source: Edward M. Graham, Institute for International Economics, as cited in "Globalisation and Its Critics: A Survey of Globalisation," *The Economist*, September 29, 2001, p. 9. © 2001 The Economist Newspaper Ltd. All Rights Reserved. Reprinted with permission. Further reproduction prohibited. http://www.economist.com

political risk is minimized. In recent years, a number of host countries have demanded that MNEs sell their services in "unbundled form" rather than only through FDI. Such countries would like their local firms to purchase managerial expertise and knowledge of product and factor markets through management contracts, and purchase technology through licensing agreements.

The main disadvantage of licensing is that license fees are likely to be lower than FDI profits, although the return on the marginal investment might be higher. Other disadvantages include:

- Possible loss of quality control
- Establishment of a potential competitor in third-country markets
- Possible improvement of the technology by the local licensee, which then enters the original firm's home market
- Possible loss of opportunity to enter the licensee's market with FDI later
- Risk that technology will be stolen
- High agency costs

MNEs have not typically used licensing of independent firms. On the contrary, most licensing arrangements have been with their own foreign subsidiaries or joint ventures. License fees are a way to spread the corporate research and development cost among all operating units and a means of repatriating profits in a form more acceptable to some host countries than dividends.

Management contracts are similar to licensing, insofar as they provide for some cash flow from a foreign source without significant foreign investment or exposure. Management contracts probably lessen political risk, because repatriation of managers is easy. International consulting and engineering firms traditionally conduct their foreign business on the basis of a management contract.

Whether licensing and management contracts are cost-effective compared to FDI depends on the price host countries will pay for the unbundled services. If the price were high enough, many firms would prefer to take advantage of market imperfections in an unbundled way, particularly in view of the lower political, foreign exchange, and business risks. Because we observe MNEs continuing to prefer FDI, we must assume that the price for selling unbundled services is still too low.

Why is the price of unbundled services too low? The answer may lie in the synergy created when services are bundled as FDI in the first place. Managerial expertise is often dependent on a delicate mix of organizational support factors that cannot be transferred abroad efficiently. Technology is a continuous process, but licensing usually captures the technology only at a particular point in time. Most important of all, however, is that economies of scale cannot be sold or transferred in small bundles. By definition, they require large-scale operations. A relatively large operation in a small market can hardly achieve the same economies of scale as a large operation in a large market.

Despite the handicaps, some MNEs have successfully sold unbundled services. An example is sales of managerial expertise and technology to the OPEC countries. In this case, however, the OPEC countries are both willing and able to pay a price high enough to approach the returns on FDI (bundled services) while receiving only the lesser benefits of the unbundled services.

Joint Venture versus Wholly Owned Subsidiary

A *joint venture* is here defined as shared ownership in a foreign business. A foreign business unit that is partially owned by the parent company is typically termed a *foreign affiliate*. A foreign business unit that is 50% or more owned (and therefore controlled) by the parent company is typically designated a *foreign subsidiary.*

A joint venture between an MNE and a host country partner is a viable strategy if, and only if, the MNE finds the right local partner. Some of the obvious advantages of having a compatible local partner are as follows:

1. The local partner understands the customs, mores, and institutions of the local environment. An MNE might need years to acquire such knowledge on its own with a wholly owned greenfield subsidiary (see next section).

2. The local partner can provide competent management, not just at the top but also at the middle levels of management.

3. If the host country requires that foreign firms share ownership with local firms or investors, 100% foreign ownership is not a realistic alternative to a joint venture.

4. The local partner's contacts and reputation enhance access to the host country's capital markets.

5. The local partner may possess technology that is appropriate for the local environment or perhaps can be used worldwide.

6. The public image of a firm that is partially locally owned may improve its sales possibilities if the purpose of the investment is to serve the local market.

Despite this impressive list of advantages, joint ventures are not as common as wholly owned foreign subsidiaries, because MNEs fear interference by the local partner in certain critical decision areas. Indeed, what is optimal from the viewpoint of the local venture may be suboptimal for the multinational operation as a whole. The most important potential conflicts or difficulties are these:

1. Political risk is increased rather than reduced if the wrong partner is chosen. Imagine the standing of joint ventures undertaken with the family or associates of Suharto in Indonesia or Saddan Hussein in Iraq just before their overthrow. The local partner must be credible and ethical or the venture is worse off for being a joint venture.

2. Local and foreign partners may have divergent views about the need for cash dividends, or about the desirability of growth financed from retained earnings versus new financing.

3. Transfer pricing on products or components bought from or sold to related companies creates a potential for conflict of interest.

4. Control of financing is another problem area. An MNE cannot justify its use of cheap or available funds raised in one country to finance joint venture operations in another country.

5. Ability of a firm to rationalize production on a worldwide basis can be jeopardized if such rationalization would act to the disadvantage of local joint venture partners.

6. Financial disclosure of local results might be necessary with locally traded shares, whereas if the firm is wholly owned from abroad, such disclosure is not needed. Disclosure gives nondisclosing competitors an advantage in setting strategy.

Valuation of equity shares is difficult. How much should the local partner pay for its share? What is the value of contributed technology, or of contributed land in a country like China where all land is state-owned? It is highly unlikely that foreign and host country partners have similar opportunity costs of capital, expectations about the required rate of return, or similar perceptions of appropriate premiums for business, foreign exchange, and political risks. Insofar as the venture is a component of the portfolio of each investor, its contribution to portfolio return and variance may be quite different for each.

Greenfield Investment versus Acquisition

A *greenfield investment* is establishing a production or service facility starting from the ground up; that is, from a green field. A *cross-border acquisition*, in contrast, is defined as the purchase of an existing foreign-based firm or facility. The advantages and disadvantages of these modes of international involvement are contrasted in Chapter 7, on cross-border mergers and acquisitions.

Strategic Alliances

The term *strategic alliance* conveys different meanings to different observers. In one form of cross-border strategic alliance, two firms exchange a share of ownership with one another. A strategic alliance can be a takeover defense if the prime purpose is for a firm to place some of its stock in stable and friendly hands. If that is all that occurs, it is just another form of portfolio investment.

In a more comprehensive strategic alliance, in addition to exchanging stock, the partners establish a separate joint venture to develop and manufacture a product or service. Numerous examples of such strategic alliances can be found in the automotive, electronics, telecommunications, and aircraft industries. Such alliances are particularly suited to high-tech industries where the cost of research and development is high and timely introduction of improvements is important.

A third level of cooperation might include joint marketing and servicing agreements in which each partner represents the other in certain markets. Some observers believe such arrangements begin to resemble the cartels prevalent in the 1920s and 1930s. Because they reduce competition, cartels have been banned by international agreements and many national laws.

SUMMARY

- The theory of comparative advantage is based on one country possessing a relative (not absolute) advantage in the production of goods intensive in either land, labor, or capital, compared to another country.
- Imperfections in national markets for products, factors of production, and financial assets translate into market opportunities for MNEs.
- Strategic motives drive the decision to invest abroad and become an MNE. Firms could be seeking new markets, raw material sources, production efficiency locations, access to state-of-the-art knowledge, or political safety.
- In order to invest abroad, a firm must have a sustainable competitive advantage in the home market. This advantage must be strong enough and transferable enough to overcome the disadvantages of operating abroad.
- Competitive advantages stem from economies of scale and scope arising from large size, managerial and marketing expertise, superior technology, financial strength, differentiated products, and competitiveness of the home market.
- The OLI Paradigm is an attempt to create an overall framework to explain why MNEs choose FDI rather than serving foreign markets through alternative modes, such as licensing, joint ventures, strategic alliances, management contracts, and exporting.
- Finance-specific strategies are directly related to the OLI Paradigm, including both proactive and reactive financial strategies.

- The decision about where to invest is influenced by economic and behavioral factors, as well as the stage of a firm's historical development.
- Psychic distance plays a role in determining the sequence of FDI and later reinvestment. As firms learn from their early investments, they venture further afield and are willing to risk larger commitments.
- The most internationalized firms can be viewed from a network perspective. The parent firm and each of the foreign subsidiaries are members of networks. The networks are composed of relationships within a worldwide industry, within the host countries with suppliers and customers, and within the multinational firm itself.
- Exporting avoids political risk, but not foreign exchange risk. It requires the least up-front investment, but it might eventually lose markets to imitators and global competitors that might be more cost-efficient in production abroad and distribution.
- Alternative (to 100%-owned foreign subsidiaries) modes of foreign involvement exist. They include joint venture, strategic alliances, licensing, management contracts, and traditional exporting.
- Licensing enables a firm to profit from foreign markets without a major front-end investment. However, disadvantages include limited returns, possible loss of quality control, and the potential of establishing a future competitor.
- The success of a joint venture depends primarily on the right choice of a partner. For this reason and a number of issues related to possible conflicts in decision making between a joint venture and a multinational parent, the 100%-owned foreign subsidiary approach is more common.

QUESTIONS

1. **Evolving into multinationalism.** As a firm evolves from purely domestic into a true multinational enterprise, it must consider (a) its competitive advantages, (b) where it wants to locate production, (c) the type of control it wants to have over any foreign operations, and (d) how much monetary capital to invest abroad. Explain how each of these four considerations is important to the success of foreign operations.

2. **Theory of comparative advantage.** What is the essence of the theory of comparative advantage?

3. **Market imperfections.** MNEs strive to take advantage of market imperfections in national markets for products, factors of production, and financial assets. Large international firms are better able to exploit such imperfections. What are their main competitive advantages?

4. **Strategic motives for foreign direct investment (FDI).**
   a. Summarize the five main motives that drive the decision to initiate FDI.
   b. Match these motives with the following MNEs:
      General Motors (USA)
      Royal Dutch Shell (Netherlands/UK)
      Kentucky Fried Chicken (USA)
      Jardine Matheson (Hong Kong)
      Apple Computer (USA)
      NEC (Japan)

5. Competitive advantage. In deciding whether to invest abroad, management must first determine whether the firm has a sustainable competitive advantage that enables it to compete effectively in the home market. What are the necessary characteristics of this competitive advantage?

6. Economies of scale and scope. Explain briefly how economies of scale and scope can be developed in production, marketing, finance, research and development, transportation, and purchasing.

7. Competitiveness of the home market. A strongly competitive home market can sharpen a firm's competitive advantage relative to firms located in less competitive markets. This phenomenon is known as Porter's "diamond of national advantage." Explain what is meant by the "diamond of national advantage."

8. OLI Paradigm. The OLI Paradigm is an attempt to create an overall framework to explain why MNEs choose FDI rather than serving foreign markets through alternative modes.
   a. Explain what is meant by the "O" in the OLI Paradigm.
   b. Explain what is meant by the "L" in the OLI Paradigm.
   c. Explain what is meant by the "I" in the OLI Paradigm.

9. Financial links to OLI. Financial strategies are directly related to the OLI Paradigm.
   a. Explain how proactive financial strategies are related to OLI.
   b. Explain how reactive financial strategies are related to OLI.

10. Where to invest. The decision about where to invest abroad is influenced by behavioral factors
    a. Explain the behavioral approach to FDI.
    b. Explain the international network theory explanation of FDI.

11. Exporting versus producing abroad. What are the advantages and disadvantages of limiting a firm's activities to exporting, compared to producing abroad?

12. Licensing and management contracts versus producing abroad. What are the advantages and disadvantages of licensing and management contracts, compared to producing abroad?

13. Joint venture versus wholly owned production subsidiary. What are the advantages and disadvantages of forming a joint venture to serve a foreign market, compared to serving that market with a wholly owned production subsidiary?

14. Greenfield investment versus acquisition. What are the advantages and disadvantages of serving a foreign market through a greenfield foreign direct investment, compared to an acquisition of a local firm in the target market?

15. Cross-border strategic alliance. The term "cross-border strategic alliance" conveys different meanings to different observers. What are these meanings?

PROBLEMS

Comparative advantage. Problems 1–5 illustrate an example of trade induced by comparative advantage. They assume that China and France each have 1,000 production units. With one unit of production (a mix of land, labor, capital, and technology), China can produce either 10 containers of toys or 7 cases of wine. France can produce either 2 cases of toys or 7 cases of wine. Thus, a production unit in China is five times as efficient compared to France when producing toys, but equally efficient when producing wine. Assume at first that no trade takes place. China allocates 800 production units to building toys and 200 production units to producing wine. France allocates 200 production units to building toys and 800 production units to producing wine.

1. **Production and consumption.** What is the production and consumption of China and France without trade?

2. **Specialization.** Assume complete specialization, in which China produces only toys and France produces only wine. What would be the effect on total production?

3. **Trade at China's domestic price.** China's domestic price is 10 containers of toys per 7 cases of wine. Assume that China produces 10,000 containers of toys and exports 2,000 to France. Assume that France produces 7,000 cases of wine and exports 1,400 cases to China. What happens to total production and consumption?

4. **Trade at France's domestic price.** France's domestic price is 2 containers of toys per 7 cases of wine. Assume that China produces 10,000 containers of toys and exports 400 containers to France. Assume that France in turn produces 7,000 cases of wine and exports 1,400 cases to China. What happens to total production and consumption?

5. **Trade at negotiated mid-price.** The mid-price for exchange between France and China can be calculated as follows:

	TOYS		WINE
China's domestic price	10	to	7
France's domestic price	2	to	7
Negotiated mid-price	6	to	7

What happens to total production and consumption?

INTERNET EXERCISES

1. **International capital flows: public and private.** Major multinational organizations (some of which are listed) attempt to track the relative movements and magnitudes of global capital investment. Using these websites and others you may find, prepare a two-page executive briefing on the question of whether capital generated in the industrialized countries is finding its way to the less-developed and emerging markets. Is there some critical distinction between less-developed and emerging?

   The World Bank http://www.worldbank.org

   Organisation for Economic Co-operation and Development http://www.oecd.org

   European Bank for Reconstruction and Development http://www.ebrd.org

2. **International management and strategy consultancies.** The management consulting industry has been a primary resource for MNEs throughout the world in the 1990s to design and develop their corporate strategies. The following firm websites provide some insight into the industry, the job opportunities available for professionals in consulting, as well as some interesting features such as the Boston Consulting Group's online interactive case study.

   A.T. Kearney http://www.atkearney.com

   Bain & Company http://www.bain.com

   Booz Allen Hamilton http://www.bah.com

   The Boston Consulting Group http://www.bcg.com

   McKinsey & Company http://www.mckinsey.com

SELECTED READINGS

Brouthers, K. D. and L. E. Brouthers, "Explaining the Natural Culture Difference Paradox," *Journal of International Business Studies*, No. 32, 2001, pp. 177–190.

Buckley, Peter J., "The Limits of Explanation: Testing the Internalization Theory of the Multinational Enterprise," *Journal of International Business Studies*, Summer 1988, pp. 181–193.

Buckley, Peter J., and Mark Casson, "An Economic Model of International Joint Venture Strategy," *Journal of International Business Studies*, Vol. 27, No. 5, Special Issue 1996, pp. 849–876.

Dunning, John H., "Location and the Multinational Enterprise: A Neglected Factor?" *Journal of International Business Studies*, Vol. 29, No. 1, First Quarter 1998, pp. 45–66.

Dunning, John H., "The Eclectic Paradigm of International Production: A Restatement and Some Possible Extensions," *Journal of International Business Studies*, Spring 1988, pp. 1–32.

Hezai, W. and P. Pauly, "Motivations for FDI and Domestic Capital Formation," *Journal of International Business Studies*, Vol. 34, No. 3, 2003, pp. 282–289.

Sethi, D., S. E. Gunslinger, L. E. Whelan, and D. M. Berg, "Trends in Foreign Direct Investment Flows: A Theoretical and Empirical Analysis," *Journal of International Business Studies*, Vol. 34, No. 4, 2003, pp. 315–326.

Wells, Louis T., Jr., "Multinationals and the Developing Countries," *Journal of International Business Studies*, Vol. 29, No. 1, First Quarter 1998, pp. 101–114.

MINICASE   BENECOL'S GLOBAL LICENSING AGREEMENT

In November 1996, a Finnish company by the name of Raisio introduced a revolutionary new product into supermarkets across Finland—a cholesterol-reducing margarine called Benecol. Deriving its name from *bene* from the Latin for good, and *col* for cholesterol, the margarine could potentially reduce a regular consumer's blood cholesterol levels by 14%–15%. All that was needed was for the consumer to consume a few grams of the margarine roughly three times a day—essentially with meals.

Although priced at roughly three times the price of most other margarine products, Raisio could not keep store shelves stocked with the level of immediate demand. The global potential for the product was thought to be enormous. Raisio, traditionally a relatively quiet share on the Helsinki Stock Exchange, skyrocketed in the following months.

The problem, however, was that Raisio itself was primarily a regional producer of industrial chemicals and foodstuffs, with margarine being its only retail product. Simultaneously, there were a number of potential competitive products in various stages of pipeline development around the world by large and capable companies like Novartis and Unilever. Raisio quickly came to the conclusion that if it were to reap the benefits of Benecol quickly and effectively in the global marketplace, it would need a global partner.

After continued negotiations, in March 1997 Raisio signed a global licensing agreement with McNeil Consumer Products, a healthcare products subsidiary of Johnson & Johnson (USA). The global licensing agreement gave exclusive rights to McNeil for the global distribution and sale of all products containing Benecol. The licensing agreement had three key elements, as described in the following table.

The agreement made Raisio responsible for ensuring an adequate supply of stanol ester for all McNeil product needs. Raisio would have no other responsibilities under the agreement, other than the usual commitments associated with continued product development, testing, and certification. McNeil would be responsible for product development, manufacturing, regulatory approvals for national and international distribution, and marketing globally.

Global Licensing: Agreement Between Raisio (Finland) and McNeil Consumer Products (USA)

1. Raisio would provide at an agreed-upon price all stanol ester (the key chemical ingredient of Benecol), which McNeil would use in producing all Benecol-based products.
2. Raisio would receive a royalty calculated as a percentage of the retail sales price of all Benecol products sold in any marketplace outside of Finland (the exact royalty rate was not disclosed, but is thought to be about 5%).
3. Raisio would receive a series of milestone payments from McNeil totaling roughly $60 million from 1997 to 1999.

QUESTIONS

1. How does the global licensing agreement split risk and return, in a financial sense, between Raisio and McNeil?
2. How will the returns to Raisio accrue over the short, medium, and long terms under the agreement, assuming the product meets with relative success?
3. What are some of the possible motivations to Raisio and McNeil behind a milestone agreement? Assume the milestone payments are agreed-upon payments from McNeil to Raisio if:
   a. Raisio successfully completes the expansion of its manufacturing capabilities for stanol ester.
   b. McNeil successfully introduces Benecol products in major industrial markets, overcoming regulatory hurdles or reaching specific sales goals.

THE TIME VALUE OF MONEY

5

Have you ever paid for something with monthly payments? Suppose you wanted to buy a $30,000 car and were told the payments would be $656.10 per month for 48 months. How would you know whether you were being offered a great deal, a fair deal, or a bad deal?

Now suppose you have $30,000 to invest for a long time and someone tells you about an investment that will double your money without any risk: Invest your $30,000 now, and you will get back $60,000 in 15 years. How does this compare with other no-risk investments?

This chapter will teach you how to answer such questions; it is devoted entirely to the Time-Value-of-Money Principle. You will learn how to determine the present value of future cash flows and, more generally, how to value at one point in time cash flows that actually occur at other points in time. We develop the logic underlying these calculations and show you procedures for solving problems using a financial calculator or a spreadsheet. We urge you, however, not to use these procedures like cookbook recipes. Understanding the logic will prepare you to apply the Time-Value-of-Money Principle in the business world to new types of problems, ones that don't fit neatly into classroom examples.

Like you, firms also have to choose among investments and borrowing alternatives. In fact, their success *depends* on those choices. Financial decisions are measured by their net present value (NPV). NPV is the difference between what something is worth and what it costs. Most of us like to buy things that are worth more than they cost! The value of something is the present value of its expected future cash flows. NPV is the value created or lost by a decision. Therefore, to be successful, firms must find positive-NPV opportunities and avoid negative-NPV choices.

NPV = value − cost

FOCUS ON PRINCIPLES

- *Time Value of Money:* Note that the value of a cash flow depends on when it will occur.
- *Two-Sided Transactions:* Be specific about the timing of cash flows to be fair to both sides of a transaction.
- *Risk-Return Trade-Off:* Recognize that a higher-risk investment has a higher required return. The time value of money is especially important to the profitability of long-term investments.
- *Capital Market Efficiency:* Use efficient capital markets to estimate an investment's expected and required rates of return.

5.1 RATES OF RETURN AND NET PRESENT VALUE

Most investors want to know about an investment's rate of return. An investment's *return* for a period equals its income during the period (its cash flows plus its increase or decrease in value) divided by its starting value. Thus,

$$(5.1) \qquad \text{Return} = \text{Rate of return} = \frac{\text{Cash flow} + (\text{Ending value} - \text{Beginning value})}{\text{Beginning value}}$$

For example, suppose you bought a share of stock for $20, it paid you a $0.50 dividend during the next year, and was worth $24.50 at the end of one year. Your rate of return for the year would be

$$\text{Return} = \frac{0.50 + (24.50 - 20.00)}{20.00} = \frac{5.00}{20.00} = 25\%$$

$$\frac{4.5 + .5}{20} \times 100 = 25\%.$$

Your total income consists of $0.50 of dividend and $4.50 in increased value, for a total of $5.00. With $5.00 of income and an original investment of $20.00, your rate of return is 25%.

Realized, Expected, and Required Returns

The example we just gave is of a realized (or actual) return. There are, however, other concepts of returns. We describe and discuss here three different rates of returns. Distinguishing among these three concepts is critical.

REALIZED RETURN The **realized return** is the rate of return actually earned on an investment during a given time period. The realized return depends on what the future cash flows actually turn out to be. In the preceding return example, with the same $0.50 dividend but an unchanged stock price, the realized return would be 2.5% (= 0.50/20.00). Or, if the stock price had declined to $16.00, the realized return would be *minus* 17.5% (= [0.50 + (16.00 − 20.00)]/20.00).

rate = × 100%
for percentage

$\frac{.5}{20} = .025 \times 100 = 2.5\%$

It is critical to understand that a realized return is an outcome, the result of having made the decision to invest. You cannot go back and change the realized rate of return. You can only make new decisions in reaction to it.

EXPECTED RETURN The **expected return** is the rate of return you expect to earn if you make the investment. If you expected to make 15% in our example investment, including an expected $0.50 dividend, you would be expecting the value of the stock next year to be $22.50 (15% = [0.50 + (22.50 − 20.00)]/20.00).

REQUIRED RETURN   The **required return** is the rate of return that exactly reflects the riskiness of the expected future cash flows. This is the return the market would require of an investment of identical risk. The market evaluates all of the available information about an investment and prices it in comparison with all other investments. This pricing process establishes an investment's required return, the fair return for an investment.

EXAMPLE Stock Investment Rates of Return

An investment of $20 in K-Tron common stock is expected to pay no dividend and have a value of $24 in one year. An investment of $70 in ITT is expected to generate a $2.50 dividend next year, and the price of the stock is expected to be $78. What are the expected returns for these investments? If the required return is 10%, which stocks should be profitable investments? One year from now, K-Tron has paid no dividend and is selling for $19. ITT has paid a $3.00 dividend and is selling for $81. What are the realized returns for the two stocks?

Using Equation (5.1):

Expected return for K-Tron = [0 + (24 − 20)]/20 = 4/20 = 20%
Expected return for ITT = [2.50 + (78 − 70)]/70 = 10.5/70 = 15%

Both stocks are good investments because in each case the expected return exceeds the required return.

Finally, again using Equation (5.1):

Realized return for K-Tron = [0 + (19 − 20)]/20 = −1/20 = −5%
Realized return for ITT = [3.00 + (81 − 70)]/70 = 14.00/70 = 20%

Net Present Value

Using the required return to calculate the present value of an asset's expected future cash flows—Equation (2.3)—is one way to value the asset. Another way is to find out what it would cost to *buy* such an asset. The difference between an asset's value (the present value of its expected future cash flows) and its cost is the asset's **net present value (NPV)**.

(5.2)   NPV = Present value of expected future cash flows − Cost

A positive NPV increases wealth because the asset is worth more than it costs. A negative NPV decreases wealth because the asset costs more than it is worth.

The net-present-value concept is important because it provides a framework for decision making. NPV appears in connection with virtually every topic in this book, and most financial decisions can be viewed in terms of net present value. NPV measures the value created or lost by a financial decision. However, NPV is measured from the benchmark of a "normal" market return. Therefore, a zero-NPV decision earns the required return and is "fair." A decision that earns less than the required return is undesirable and has a negative NPV. Positive-NPV decisions earn more than the appropriate return. Firms that pursue the goal of maximizing shareholder wealth seek to make positive-NPV decisions.

Another way to state the Principle of Capital Market Efficiency is to say that financial securities are priced fairly. A **fair price** is a price that does not favor either the buyer's or seller's side of the transaction. A fair price makes the NPV from investing equal zero. Sometimes, people ask, "If the NPV is zero, why would anyone purchase a financial security?" The answer is to earn a profit. Remember, a zero NPV implies that the investor will earn the required return for the investment risk, *not* a zero return.

The Principle of Risk-Return Trade-Off implies that investors who take more risk can expect to earn a larger profit, on average. The decision to invest in (purchase) a financial security with NPV = 0 often involves risk. But in exchange for that risk, you get a higher expected return.

EXPECTED VERSUS REQUIRED RETURNS   Confusion between the expected and required returns arises because, if capital markets were *perfect*, an investment's expected return would *always* equal its required return and the investment's NPV would be zero. In fact, financial analysis often starts off assuming a perfect capital market environment, where everyone can expect to earn the required return for the risk they bear. Although this is a good starting place for analysis, and the capital markets are efficient, we must add that they are not, in fact, perfect.

EXPECTED VERSUS REALIZED RETURNS   Confusion between the expected and realized returns is created by risk. Because of risk, the outcome rarely equals the expected amount. In fact, one way to think about risk is to consider how different the outcome can be from the expected amount. The risk is high when the difference can be great. The risk is low when there cannot be much difference.

AN ILLUSTRATION   Let us review and summarize the relationships among these concepts by using an investment you might make. First, on the basis of alternative market investments of the same risk, you determine a minimum return you would have to earn to be willing to invest. (Otherwise, you would simply invest your money in one of these alternatives.) This is the *required* return. Next, you estimate the return if you were to make the investment. This is the *expected* return. Then you decide whether to make the investment. If the expected return is more than the required return, the investment is worth more than its cost, and the NPV is positive. A positive NPV creates value, whereas a negative NPV loses value. Let us say the NPV is positive, and you make the investment.

Later, the investment pays off. The payoff is the *realized* return. If the realized return is bad (low, negative, or perhaps even −100% when you get nothing back), you are not happy, but that is the fundamental nature of risk! After the return is realized, you cannot turn back the clock and decide not to make the investment after all. Of course, if the realized return is good (equal to or greater than the expected return), you are glad you made the investment. Therefore, the realized return is disconnected—by risk—from the required and expected returns, despite its vital importance and our desire for it to be large.

> **REVIEW**
>
> 1. Distinguish among the concepts of *realized*, *expected*, and *required returns*.
> 2. If the expected return is above the required return, does this mean that the realized return also will be above the required return?
> 3. Why would anyone ever make a *zero*-NPV investment?

5.2   VALUING SINGLE CASH FLOWS

In this section, we explain how time affects the value of a cash flow. That is, given a cash flow at one point in time, we show how to determine its value at some other point in time. For example, suppose you expect to receive $10,000 six years from today. We show how to calculate what that expected $10,000 is worth now.

Assumptions, Notation, and Some Advice

We need several additional definitions and underlying assumptions. Please read through the complete list of notation and assumptions now, even though we will not explain some of the terms until later.

Cash Flows Occur at the End of the Time Period   Unless otherwise stated, cash flows occur at the end of the time period.

Cash Outflows Are Negative Values   From the decision maker's viewpoint, positive cash flows are inflows and negative cash flows are outflows. The decision maker can be a firm or an individual. In other words, the algebraic sign indicates whether the amount is an inflow ($+$) or an outflow ($-$) to the decision maker.

The Decision Point Is $t = 0$ Unless otherwise stated, "now" is the instant before $t = 0$. That is, $t = 0$ cash flows (in or out) are just about to occur. In other words, you can still make a decision that affects them, such as choosing to make an investment.

Compounding Frequency Is the Same as Payment Frequency   Unless otherwise stated, financial transactions assume the compounding frequency is identical to the payment frequency. For example, if payments are monthly, compounding is also monthly.

Notation

APR	The annual percentage rate (nominal annual rate). The APR equals r times m.
APY	The annual percentage yield (effective annual rate). The APY is the amount you would actually earn if you invested for exactly one year and the investment earned interest at r per period for m periods.
CF_t	The net cash flow at time t. For example, CF_3 is the net cash flow at the end of time period 3.
FV	A future-value amount.
$FVAF_{r,n}$	The future-value-annuity factor for an n-period annuity at r per period.
FVA_n	The future value of an n-period annuity (at $t = n$).
$FVF_{r,n}$	The future-value factor for n periods at r per period.
FV_n	A future value at time n. For example, FV_5 is a future value at the end of time period 5.
I	The discount rate per period for a calculator. For example, $I = 2$ is 2% per time period.
m	The number of compounding periods per year.
n	A number of time periods. For example, n might be 36 months.
N	The number of periods for a calculator.
NPV	The net present value.
PMT	The net cash flow each period for an annuity in a calculator.
PV	A present-value amount.
$PVAF_{r,n}$	The present-value-annuity factor for an n-period annuity at r per period.
PVA_n	The present value of an n-period annuity.
$PVF_{r,n}$	The present-value factor for n periods at r per period.
r	The discount rate per period. For example, $r = 0.02$ is 2% per time period.
t	A time period. For example, $t = 3$ is time period 3.

Advice

1. Always use a time line. Valuation problems are easier to understand and the error rate is lower with the visual aid of a time line.
2. When making calculations, be careful to match the rate of return with the size of time periods. For example, use a monthly rate of return when periods are in months.
3. Make the calculations in the chapter yourself. It will help develop your abilities.
4. Follow the conceptual development carefully to build your understanding of finance.

Future Values

A future value (FV) is a value at the end of a given time period. If you invest $1,000 today, Table 5-1 shows the amount of money you will have at the end of each of the next six years if you earn 10% interest per year. After one year:

$$FV_1 = \$1,000 + \$100 = \$1,100$$

In the second year, you will earn $110 more—10% interest on your accumulated investment [$= (0.10)1,100$], for a total of

$$FV_2 = \$1,100 + \$110 = \$1,210$$

The extra $10 of interest earned in the second year is called compound interest. **Compound interest** is a method of interest computation wherein interest is earned on both the original investment *and* on the reinvested interest. As you can see in Table 5-1, the interest earned each year grows because of compound interest.

Table 5-1 also shows how fast your $1,000 investment grows if invested funds earn simple interest instead of compound interest. **Simple interest** is a method of interest computation wherein interest is earned on *only* the original investment. Note that in year 1 with simple interest, the interest earned is $100, the same as with compound interest. However, after that, the story changes. In year 2 with simple interest, the interest earned is again $100. No interest is earned on the first year's $100 interest. All other years also earn only $100, 10% of the original investment.

Would you rather earn compound interest or simple interest? Obviously, if the interest rates are the same, you will have more money with compound interest than with simple interest. Because of today's technology, the use of simple interest has largely disappeared.

TABLE 5-1 Future value of an investment of $1,000.

YEAR	COMPOUND INTEREST, $r = 10\%$			SIMPLE INTEREST, $r = 10\%$		
	BEGINNING BALANCE	INTEREST EARNED	ENDING BALANCE	BEGINNING BALANCE	INTEREST EARNED	ENDING BALANCE
1	$1,000	$100	$1,100	$1,000	$100	$1,100
2	1,100	110	1,210	1,100	100	1,200
3	1,210	121	1,331	1,200	100	1,300
4	1,331	133.10	1,464.10	1,300	100	1,400
5	1,464.10	146.41	1,610.51	1,400	100	1,500
6	1,610.51	161.05	1,771.56	1,500	100	1,600

FIGURE 5-1
The future-value factor,
$FVF_{r,n}$, as a function of
time and various dis-
count rates.

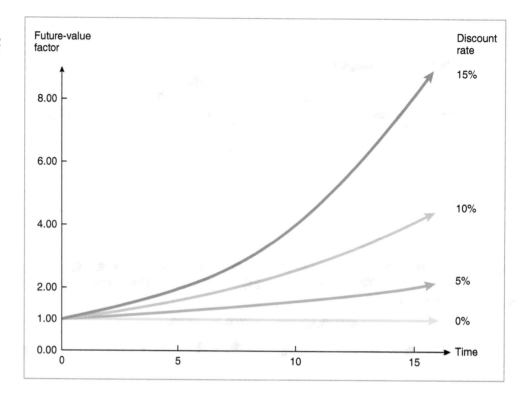

One way to find a future value is to calculate interest each year, adding it to the previous year's balance, and accumulating the result for the desired number of years. In Table 5-1, we stopped at six years. Suppose you were investing for 20 years. Calculating the value would be tedious and error prone. Consequently, we use shortcut methods whenever we can. One shortcut method of finding future values is to use the **future-value formula**:

The Future-Value Formula

(5.3) $$FV_n = PV(1 + r)^n = PV(FVF_{r,n})$$

The amount $(1 + r)^n$ is called the future-value factor. The **future-value factor**, $FVF_{r,n}$, is the value $1.00 will grow to if it is invested at r per period for n periods. Figure 5-1 is a graph of $FVF_{r,n}$ as a function of n and r. As you can see, future value is directly related to both time and the discount rate. The larger the discount rate, the larger the future value. For positive discount rates, the more time, the larger the future value.

EXAMPLE Calculating a Future Value

What is the future value of $1,000 invested at 10% per year for six years?
  Use the future-value formula with these values:

$$FV_n = PV(FVF_{r,n}) = PV(1 + r)^n = 1,000(1.10)^6 = 1,000(1.771561) = \$1,771.56$$

To do this on a calculator, you can first raise 1.10 (= 1 + the discount rate) to the power six, using the y^x key where y = 1.10 and x = 6. Then multiply the answer by 1,000 to get 1771.56.

CALCULATOR SOLUTION	
Data Input	**Function Key**
6	N
10	I
1,000	PV
0	PMT
−1,771.56	FV

An easier way to make our future-value calculation is to use a financial calculator: Put in PV = 1,000, N = 6, I = 10%, and PMT = 0, then compute FV = −1,771.56. Note the negative

Financial Calculators

There are five basic input variables to a financial (sometimes called business) calculator:

N	The number of time periods
I	The discount rate per period. This corresponds to the *r* in the text's equations. (Note that the calculator key will show I/YR.)
PV	Present value
PMT	The cash flow (payment) for an annuity
FV	Future value

The basic calculator formula encompasses each of the four basic time-value-of-money formulas we explain in this chapter. For this reason, in many cases, you need to put in a zero for some variables—especially if we have not explained the variable yet! Even though you may not fully appreciate the basic calculator formula right away, we state it now so you can refer back to it. Then, you can see how each of the basic time-value-of-money formulas is part of it, as we explain that formula.

The Basic Calculator Formula

$$PV + PMT\left[\frac{(1+I)^N - 1}{I(1+I)^N}\right] + FV\left[\frac{1}{(1+I)^N}\right] = 0$$

The calculator solves this equation for each time-value-of-money calculation. It computes the variable you want on the basis of the values you put in for all the other variables. Amounts can be positive or negative. However, to use your calculator, you must understand how it handles positive and negative amounts.

Confusion about positives and negatives can occur because the basic calculator formula sums to zero. As a result, the three terms cannot all be positive. You can think of this in terms of the decision maker's cash flows we described earlier: You are paying out (−) one amount to get in (+) another. For example, if you borrow $10,000 (PV), the money is an inflow, which is a positive. But when you pay back $248.85 per month for 48 months, the payments are outflows, which are negatives. If you enter PV as a positive value, the calculator calculates FV (or PMT) as a negative value. Appendix A at the end of the book shows the key strokes for standard calculations on a calculator of this type, the BAII PLUS.

Another common problem that can arise is when a calculator retains one or more values from previous calculations. If you do not put in a value for a variable, your calculator may use a value from a previous calculation and give you an incorrect answer. You can avoid this problem in two ways. One way is to use the "CLR TVM" function to zero all the variables. (Be sure to use "clear-time-value-of-money" rather than "clear-the-latest-entry." The calculator's "how-to" book will describe both.) Another way to avoid the problem is to enter a zero for any variables not otherwise used. We will use this approach for our calculator computations.

sign on the FV amount. This is because the formula sums to zero. You can think of this as getting PV and paying back FV. Also, note again that the discount rate is entered as a percentage, 10, *not* as a decimal number, 0.10. Throughout the rest of the book, we will show such calculations in a standardized format. The amount the calculator solves for is given in the bottom line in bold type. The other amounts are inputs.

CALCULATOR SOLUTION

Data Input	Function Key
15	N
6	I
1,000	PV
0	PMT
−2,396.56	FV

CALCULATOR SOLUTION

Data Input	Function Key
15	N
10	I
1,000	PV
0	PMT
−4,177.25	FV

CALCULATOR SOLUTION

Data Input	Function Key
2	N
8	I
0	PMT
2,000	FV
−1,714.68	PV

EXAMPLE Grandma's Savings Bond

Suppose your grandma just gave you a $1,000 savings bond. If the bond earns 6% interest, what will the bond be worth in 15 years?

Using the future-value formula, the bond will be worth:

$$FV_n = PV(FVF_{r,n}) = PV(1+r)^n$$
$$FV_{15} = 1,000(1.06)^{15} = 1,000(2.39656) = \$2,396.56$$

What would your bond be worth if it earned 10% instead of 6%? Do this one on your calculator. The answer is $4,177.25.

Present Values

Now, let's find the *present* value of an expected *future* cash flow. A present value (PV) is an amount invested today at r per period that would provide a given future value at time n. We can compute a PV using the **present-value formula**:

The Present-Value Formula

(5.4)
$$PV = FV_n \left[\frac{1}{(1+r)^n} \right] = FV_n (PVF_{r,n})$$

The present-value formula is simply a rearrangement of the future-value formula where we solve for PV instead of FV. In the present-value formula, the amount $[1/(1+r)^n]$ is called the present-value factor. The **present-value factor**, $PVF_{r,n}$, is the amount that, if invested today at r per period, will grow to exactly $1.00 n years from today.

Figure 5-2 is a graph of $PVF_{r,n}$ as a function of time and various discount rates. It shows that present value is inversely related to both time and the discount rate. That is, the larger the discount rate, the smaller the present value. For positive discount rates, the more time until the cash flow, the smaller is the present value. Like two kids on a seesaw, when one goes up the other goes down.

EXAMPLE Present Value of a Future Cash Flow

What is the present value of $2,000 to be received two years from today if the required return is 8% per year?

Using the present-value formula,

$$PV = FV_n(PVF_{r,n}) = FV_n \left[\frac{1}{(1+r)^n} \right] = 2,000 \left[\frac{1}{(1.08)^2} \right] = 2,000(0.857339) = \$1,714.68$$

$PVF_{8\%,2}$ is 0.857339, and the present value of the future $2,000 is $1,714.68.

Solving for a Return

If you look back at the basic calculator formula, you can see how the present-value formula is part of it. You can also see that if you know any four of the five input variables, the formula can be solved for the fifth.

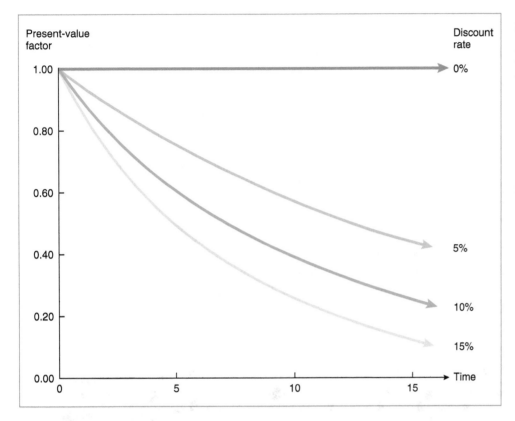

FIGURE 5-2
The present-value factor, $PVF_{r,n}$, as a function of time and various discount rates.

For example, to find a PV, we put in FV (the expected future cash flow), N (the time the cash flow will occur), I (the required return), and PMT = 0. However, suppose you already know PV, but you do not know the discount rate. You can rearrange the present value formula (5.4) and solve for the expected return. Solving for r, with PMT = 0, we get

$$r = \left[\frac{FV}{PV}\right]^{1/n} - 1$$

EXAMPLE **The Expected Return for a Bank One Certificate of Deposit**

Suppose Bank One offers a certificate of deposit that pays $10,000 in three years in exchange for $7,938.32 today. What interest rate is Bank One offering? In other words, what is the expected return from investing in this certificate of deposit?

Using our rearranged formula, with $n = 3$, FV = 10,000, and PV = 7,938.32, we find that the expected return is

$$r = \left[\frac{10,000}{7,938.32}\right]^{0.3333} - 1 = 1.08 - 1 = 8.00\%$$

CALCULATOR SOLUTION	
Data Input	Function Key
3	N
7,938.32	PV
0	PMT
–10,000	FV
8.00	I

Note again the negative FV and positive PV. This calculation is from the bank's viewpoint: getting the PV and paying back the FV. The 8.00% answer is the same if we use the consumer viewpoint with a negative PV and positive FV: paying the PV and getting back the FV.

Solving for the Number of Time Periods

We could also rearrange the basic calculator formula to solve for n using natural logarithms. However, it is much easier to let the calculator do the work.

CALCULATOR SOLUTION

Data Input	Function Key
6	I
1	PV
0	PMT
−2	FV
11.9	N

EXAMPLE **How Long to Double Your Salary?**

Are you earning a salary currently? If you are, and your salary grows at 6% per year, how many years will it take to double?

Even though we do not know how much you make, so long as it is more than zero, we can tell you it will take 11.9 years to double if it is growing at 6% per year. Try it.

REVIEW

1. What is the future-value formula? What is the present-value formula?
2. Is the present-value factor the reciprocal of the future-value factor?
3. Explain why present value and the discount rate are inversely related.

5.3   VALUING ANNUITIES

Annuity payments are a very common financial arrangement. An **annuity** is a series of equal, periodic cash flows. The cash flows occur regularly, such as every month or every year.

Annuities occur in many different financial transactions. Monthly payments on a car loan, a student loan, or a mortgage are annuities. Monthly rent is an annuity. A paycheck, with a fixed salary, is an annuity. Lease, interest, and dividend payments are annuities. Any series of equal, periodic cash flows is an annuity.

The majority of annuities have end-of-period payments. For example, car loans usually require end-of-month payments. For a 48-month loan, the first payment is made at the end of the first month and the 48th (and last) is made at the end of month 48. This kind of annuity, whose payments occur at the end of each period, is called an **ordinary annuity**. An annuity whose first payment is different than one period in the future is called a **deferred annuity**.

Other annuities, such as a rental, require beginning-of-period payments. For a 12-month apartment lease, the first rent payment is due at the beginning of the first month, and the 12th (and last) is due at the beginning of the 12th month. This kind of annuity, whose payments occur at the beginning of each period, is called an **annuity due**.

We know the timing of payments affects value. Therefore, it is critical to know whether you are dealing with an ordinary annuity or an annuity due. We will start by analyzing the future and present values of an ordinary annuity. Later, we will show you how to handle an annuity due.

The Future Value of an Annuity

We started our discussion of the time value of money with an example of depositing money in a savings account. Now consider a savings plan for depositing the same amount every period for n periods. How much will you have at the end of the n periods?

Let the periodic cash flow, PMT, be the amount deposited at the end of each time period (that is, $CF_1 = CF_2 = \ldots = CF_n = PMT$). Figure 5-3 illustrates the future value of an n-period annuity.

The future value of an annuity is the total value that will have accumulated at the end of the annuity if the annuity payments are all invested at r per period. The future value of an annuity can be computed using the future-value formula to value each payment and then adding up

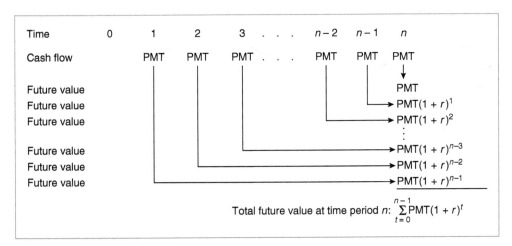

FIGURE 5-3
The future value of an
n-period annuity.

the individual values to get the total. If we start with the last payment at time $t = n$ and proceed backward to the first payment at time $t = 1$, the future value of the annuity at time n, FVA_n, is

$$FVA_n = PMT(1 + r)^0 + PMT(1 + r)^1 + \ldots + PMT(1 + r)^{n-1}$$

Figure 5-3 illustrates this calculation. Note that the first payment (at $t = 1$) earns interest for $(n - 1)$ periods, *not n* periods. Each subsequent payment earns interest for one less period than the previous one. Note that the last payment occurs exactly at the end of the annuity, so it does not earn any interest—$(1 + r)^0 = 1$.

The equation for FVA_n has a PMT in every term on the right-hand side. If the PMT is factored out, the equation can be rewritten as

$$FVA_n = PMT[(1+r)^0 + (1+r)^1 + \quad + (1+r)^{n-1}] = PMT\sum_{t=0}^{n-1}(1+r)^t$$

where Σ is a summation. This equation can be simplified to

(5.5) $$FVA_n = PMT\sum_{t=0}^{n-1}(1+r)^t = PMT\left[\frac{(1+r)^n - 1}{r}\right] = PMT(FVAF_{r,n})$$

The quantity in large brackets in Equation (5.5) is called the future-value-annuity factor. The **future-value-annuity factor**, $FVAF_{r,n}$, is the total future value of $1.00 per period for n periods invested at r per period. The particular values for PMT, n, and r along with Equation (5.5) are all that are needed to determine the future value of the annuity.

EXAMPLE Saving for Retirement at Citibank

Suppose you save $2,000 per year at the end of each year for 30 years at Citibank, and the money earns 5% interest per year. How much will you have at the end of the 30 years?

The cash flows are like those in Figure 5-3 with $n = 30$. Therefore, using Equation (5.5)

$$FVA_{30} = PMT(FVAF_{5\%,30}) = 2,000\left[\frac{(1.05)^{30} - 1}{0.05}\right] = 2,000(66.43885) = \$132,877.70$$

$FVAF_{5\%,30}$ is 66.43885, and the future value of the annuity is $132,877.70.

What would be the future value if the interest rate were 6% instead of 5%? Compute the answer of $158,116.37 on your calculator.

CALCULATOR SOLUTION	
Data Input	Function Key
30	N
5	I
0	PV
2,000	PMT
−132,877.70	FV

CALCULATOR SOLUTION	
Data Input	Function Key
30	N
6	I
0	PV
2,000	PMT
−158,116.37	FV

The Present Value of an Annuity

The present value of an annuity is the amount that, if invested today at r per period, could exactly provide equal payments every period for n periods. The present value of an annuity, PVA_n, is simply the sum of the present values of the n individual payments:

$$PVA_n = PMT\frac{1}{(1+r)^1} + PMT\frac{1}{(1+r)^2} + \quad + PMT\frac{1}{(1+r)^n}$$

The present value of an n-period annuity is illustrated in Figure 5-4. Because the cash flows or payments are all identical, we can rewrite this as

$$PVA_n = PMT\left[\frac{1}{(1+r)^1} + \frac{1}{(1+r)^2} + \quad + \frac{1}{(1+r)^n}\right] = PMT\sum_{t=1}^{n}\frac{1}{(1+r)^t}$$

This equation for PVA_n can be simplified to

(5.6) $$PVA_n = PMT\sum_{t=1}^{n}\frac{1}{(1+r)^t} = PMT\left[\frac{(1+r)^n - 1}{r(1+r)^n}\right] = PMT(PVAF_{r,n})$$

The quantity in large brackets in Equation (5.6) is called the present-value-annuity factor.[1] The **present-value-annuity factor**, $PVAF_{r,n}$, is the total present value of an annuity of $1.00 per period for n periods discounted at r per period. The particular values for PMT, n, and r are all that are needed to determine the present value of the annuity.

> **EXAMPLE Computing the Present Value of a Car Loan from GMAC**
>
> Suppose General Motors Acceptance Corporation (GMAC) expects to receive future car-loan payments of $200 per month for the next 36 months from one of its customers. The first payment is due one month from today. The interest rate on the loan is 1% per month. How much money is being borrowed? In other words, what is the present value of the loan?

FIGURE 5-4
The present value of an n-period annuity.

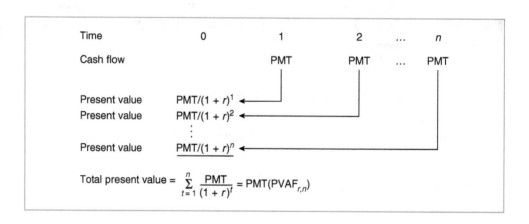

---

[1]The present value of an annuity can also be expressed as the PV of FVA_n. To see this, show that $PVAF_{r,n} = FVAF_{r,n}$ times $PVF_{r,n}$.

(handwritten margin note) to calculate PVA = need r = % n = time pmt value

Using Equation (5.6) with PMT = $200, $n = 36$, and $r = 1\%$:

$$PVA_{36} = PMT(PVAF_{1\%,36}) = 200\left[\frac{(1.01)^{36}-1}{0.01(1.01)^{36}}\right] = 200(30.1075) = \$6,021.50$$

$PVAF_{1\%,36}$ is 30.1075, and the present value is $6,021.50.

CALCULATOR SOLUTION

Data Input	Function Key
36	N
1	I
200	PMT
0	FV
-6,021.50	PV

Calculating Annuity Payments

We have shown how to compute the present and future values of an annuity, given a set of payments and a discount rate. When you borrow money, the amount is the present value, and the annuity is the loan payments. We can solve for the payments by rearranging Equation (5.6):

.014

(5.7)
$$PMT = PVA_n\left[\frac{r(1+r)^n}{(1+r)^n - 1}\right] = \frac{PVA_n}{PVAF_{r,n}}$$

EXAMPLE Computing Loan Payments

Consider a $260,000 mortgage requiring equal payments at the end of each month for 15 years—180 months [= 15(12)]. If the interest rate is 0.5% per month, what are the payments?

Using Equation (5.7), we get:

$$PMT = PVA_{180}\left[\frac{(0.005)(1.005)^{180}}{(1.005)^{180} - 1}\right] = \$2,194.03$$

$PVAF_{0.5\%,180}$ is 118.50351, and the payments are $2,194.03.

CALCULATOR SOLUTION

Data Input	Function Key
180	N
0.5	I
260,000	PV
0	FV
-2,194.03	PMT

Now suppose you are getting ahead of the game and saving money regularly rather than paying off a loan. The accumulated amount is a future value. We can solve for the amount that must be saved regularly to accumulate a given future value, this time by rearranging Equation (5.5):

1.454

(5.8)
$$PMT = FVA_n\left[\frac{r}{(1+r)^n - 1}\right] = \frac{FVA_n}{FVAF_{r,n}}$$

EXAMPLE Saving at the IBM Credit Union for a Down Payment on a House

Dina Naples is saving money at the IBM Credit Union for a down payment on a house. How much does she have to save at the end of every month to accumulate a total of $12,000 at the end of five years if the money is invested at 0.5% per month?

Using Equation (5.8), we get:

$(.014) \times 12000 =$

$$PMT = FVA_{60}\left[\frac{(0.005)}{(1.005)^{60} - 1}\right] = \$171.99 \leftarrow$$

CALCULATOR SOLUTION

Data Input	Function Key
60	N
0.5	I
0	PV
12,000	FV
-171.99	PMT

$FVAF_{0.5\%,60}$ is 69.77, and the payments are $171.99.

REVIEW

1. What is an annuity?
2. Explain why the future value of an annuity, FVA_n, discounted back over n periods at r per period must equal the present value of the annuity, PVA_n.

Amortizing a Loan

A **loan amortization schedule** shows how a loan is paid off over time. That is, it shows the relationships among a loan's payments, principal, and interest rate.

To create an amortization schedule, start with the amount borrowed. Add the first period's interest, and then subtract the first period's payment. The result is the remaining balance, which is the starting amount for the second period. Repeat this procedure each period until the remainder becomes zero at the end of the last period.

CALCULATOR SOLUTION	
Data Input	**Function Key**
3	N
8.5	I
1,000	PV
0	FV
−391.54	PMT

EXAMPLE Amortizing a Loan

Suppose a $1,000 loan with an interest rate of 8.5% requires equal payments at the end of each of the next three years. The annual loan payments will be $391.54.

This loan's amortization schedule is given in Table 5-2. Each period's interest increases the remaining balance by the interest rate times the previous period's remaining balance. The loan payment then reduces the remaining balance. Because the loan payment exceeds the first year's interest charge, the remaining balance is sequentially reduced to zero after n periods. Note how the interest amount declines and the principal reduction increases over the loan's life.

Calculating the Discount Rate and Number of Annuity Payments

In addition to solving for the payments, future value, or present value of an annuity, we can solve for the discount rate or the number of annuity payments. However, unlike the payments, we cannot always rearrange our equation to solve for these variables. Instead, the equation must be solved using trial and error. A financial calculator is especially convenient for calculating these variables because it performs the tedious trial-and-error calculations automatically.

TABLE 5-2
A loan amortization schedule.

YEAR	1	2	3
a. Principal at start of period	$1,000.00	$693.46	360.86
b. Interest for the period (8.5% of starting principal)	85.00	58.94	30.68
c. Balance (a + b)	1,085.00	752.40	391.54
d. Payment	−391.54	−391.54	−391.54
e. Principal at end of this period and start of next period (c − d)	693.46	360.86	0.00
f. Principal reduction (d − b)	306.54.	332.60	360.86

note = payment is (−).

EXAMPLE **Computing the Interest Rate on a Mortgage from Chase Home Mortgage**

Chase Home Mortgage offers a $100,000 home mortgage loan. Payments will be $678.79 per month for 30 years (360 payments). What interest rate is Chase charging?

Using Equation (5.6):

$$100,000 = 678.79(\text{PVAF}_{r,360}) = 678.98 \left[\frac{(1+r)^{360} - 1}{r(1+r)^{360}} \right]$$

An r of 0.6% solves this equation, so Chase is charging 0.6% per month.

CALCULATOR SOLUTION	
Data Input	Function Key
360	N
100,000	PV
−678.79	PMT
0	FV
0.6	I

EXAMPLE **Computing the Remaining Life of a Car Loan**

Suppose you borrowed $15,000 to buy a car. The loan was originally a 48-month loan charging 0.75% per month on the unpaid balance. Your monthly payment is $373.28.

Now you do not remember how many payments are remaining, but your statement says that your remaining balance is now $9,092.81. How many more monthly payments are left?

Again, using Equation (5.6):

$$9,092.81 = 373.28(\text{PVAF}_{0.75\%,n}) = 373.28 \left[\frac{(1+0.0075)^{n} - 1}{0.0075(1+0.0075)^{n}} \right]$$

An n of 27 solves this equation, so you have to make 27 more monthly payments.

CALCULATOR SOLUTION	
Data Input	Function Key
48	N
0.75	I
15,000	PV
0	FV
−373.28	PMT

CALCULATOR SOLUTION	
Data Input	Function Key
0.75	I
9,092.81	PV
−373.28	PMT
0	FV
27	N

Valuing Deferred Annuities

Deferred annuities start at a time other than right away (where the first payment is at $t = 1$). The present value of such an annuity can be computed by first calculating the annuity's future value and then calculating the present value of that lump-sum future value.

EXAMPLE **Computing the Present Value of an Annuity Starting in the Future**

What is the present value of $5,000 per year to be received at the end of each of the years 4 through 7 if the required return is 12% per year?

This deferred annuity is equivalent to its future value at the end of its life, year 7, which is $23,896.64.

The present value of the annuity is then the present value of this lump sum, $10,809.63.

Figure 5-5 shows the equivalence of the three amounts: annuity cash flows, lump-sum value at year 7, and present value.

CALCULATOR SOLUTION	
Data Input	Function Key
4	N
12	I
0	PV
5,000	PMT
−23,896.64	FV

CALCULATOR SOLUTION	
Data Input	Function Key
7	N
12	I
0	PMT
−23,896.64	FV
10,809.63	PV

Perpetuities

An annuity that goes on forever is called a **perpetuity**. Although perpetuities actually exist in some situations, the most important reason for studying them is that they can be used as a simple and fairly accurate approximation of a long-term annuity.

FIGURE 5-5
Valuing a deferred
annuity.

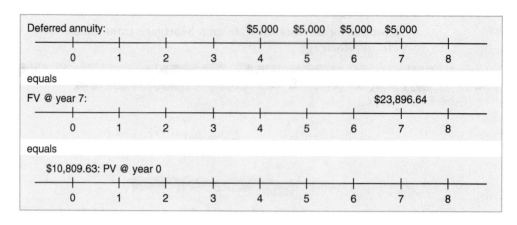

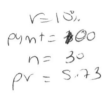

$r = 10\%$.
$pymt = \$100$
$n = 30$
$pv = 5.73$

Figure 5-2 showed that the present-value factor becomes smaller as n becomes larger. Therefore, later payments in a long annuity add little to the present value of the annuity. For example, at a required return of 10% per year, the present value of getting $100 in 30 years is $5.73. It is only 85 cents if payment is in 50 years, and less than a penny for 100 years.

To examine the present value of a perpetuity, we can start with the present value of an annuity and see what happens when the life of the annuity, n, becomes very large. Start by rewriting Equation (5.6), the present value of an annuity formula:

$$PVA_n = PMT\left[\frac{(1+r)^n - 1}{r(1+r)^n}\right] = PMT\left[\frac{(1+r)^n}{r(1+r)^n}\right] - PMT\left[\frac{1}{r(1+r)^n}\right]$$

$$PVA_n = \left[\frac{PMT}{r}\right] - \left[\frac{PMT}{r(1+r)^n}\right]$$

Written this way, you can see what happens when n becomes large. The first term on the right-hand side of the last line is not affected by n. But the second term gets smaller because $(1 + r)^n$ gets larger when n increases. As n gets really big, the second term goes to zero. Therefore, the present value of a perpetuity is

(5.9)
$$PVA_{perpetuity} = \frac{PMT}{r}$$

EXAMPLE Present Value of a Perpetuity

What is the present value of $1,000 per year, forever, if the required return is 8% per year?
   Using Equation (5.9):

$$PVA_{perpetuity} = \frac{PMT}{r} = \frac{1,000}{0.08} = \$12,500.00$$

Now suppose the $1,000 per year only lasted for 50 years. What would be the present value, and how well would the present value of the perpetuity approximate this present value?
   The actual present value for the 50-year annuity is

$$PVA_{50} = PMT(PVAF_{8\%,50}) = 1,000\left[\frac{(1.08)^{50} - 1}{(0.08)(1.08)^{50}}\right] = 1,000(12.23348) = \$12,233.48$$

CALCULATOR SOLUTION	
Data Input	Function Key
50	N
8	I
1,000	PMT
0	FV
−12,233.48	PV

In this case, the perpetuity is worth only about 2% more than a 50-year annuity. This is because the present value of the very distant (the fifty-first and subsequent) payments is very small.

Valuing an Annuity Due

The payments for an annuity due occur at the beginning of each period instead of at the end. Because each payment occurs one period earlier, an annuity due has a higher present value than a comparable ordinary annuity. Likewise, an annuity due has a higher future value than a comparable ordinary annuity because each payment has an additional period to compound. In fact, a simple way to value an annuity due is to multiply the value of a comparable ordinary annuity by $(1 + r)$.

EXAMPLE **Computing the Future Value and Present Value of an Annuity Due**

What are the future and present values of an annuity due of $100 per year for seven years, if the required return is 10% per year?

If this were an ordinary annuity, the future and present values would be:

$$FVA_n = PMT(FVAF_{10\%,7}) = 100\left[\frac{(1.10)^7 - 1}{0.10}\right] = \$948.72$$

$$PVA_n = PMT(PVAF_{10\%,7}) = 100\left[\frac{(1.10)^7 - 1}{0.10(1.10)^7}\right] = \$486.84$$

CALCULATOR SOLUTION	
Data Input	Function Key
7	N
10	I
0	PV
100	PMT
−948.72	FV

Then, for the annuity due:

Future value of annuity due = $FVA_n(1 + r) = 948.72(1.10) = \$1,043.59$
Present value of annuity due = $PVA_n(1 + r) = 486.84(1.10) = \$535.53$

You can also use a financial calculator to compute the FV and PV of an annuity due directly. To do so, put your calculator into the BEGIN mode, and make the FV and PV calculations in the usual way.

CALCULATOR SOLUTION	
Data Input	Function Key
7	N
10	I
100	PMT
0	FV
−486.84	PV

REVIEW

1. Describe the layout of a loan amortization schedule.
2. Why is the value of a perpetuity a good estimate of the value of an otherwise comparable long-term annuity?

5.4 MULTIPLE EXPECTED FUTURE CASH FLOWS

Unlike an annuity, in some cases, future cash flows vary in size. In this section, we demonstrate a few common-sense methods for computing the value of a set of unequal future cash flows using the following example.

FIGURE 5-6
Computing the present
value of a set of unequal
future cash flows.

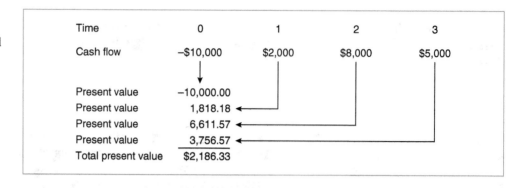

EXAMPLE Computing the Present Value of a Set of Unequal Future
Cash Flows

You have an opportunity to invest $10,000. If you make the investment, you expect to get
$2,000 next year, $8,000 the year after, and $5,000 in the third year. If the required return is
10%, what is the net present value (NPV) of your investment?

The NPV is the sum of the present values of all the cash flows:

$$NPV = \frac{-10,000}{(1.1)^0} + \frac{2,000}{(1.1)^1} + \frac{8,000}{(1.1)^2} + \frac{5,000}{(1.1)^3}$$

$$NPV = -10,000 + 1,818.182 + 6,611.570 + 3,756.574 = \$2,186.326$$

This calculation is illustrated in Figure 5-6.

A second method for calculating the total present value of our set of unequal future cash flows
is called the "rollback" method: Start with the most distant cash flow ($5,000 at time 3) and dis-
count it back one period (at 10%). Its value at $t=2$ is $4,545.45 (= 5,000/1.10). Add this amount
to the time 2 cash flow of $8,000 to get $12,545.45. Discount this amount back one period. Its
value at $t=1$ is $11,404.96 (= 12,545.45/1.10). Add the time 1 cash flow to this amount to get
$13,404.96. Discount this amount back one period. Its value is $12,186.33 (= 13,404.96/1.10).
Finally, this amount minus the $10,000 time 0 cash flow equals the total present value of
$2,186.33. Figure 5-7 illustrates the rollback method of calculating a present value.

Finally, many financial calculators provide a third method for valuing this unequal set of
future cash flows. Because calculators are not identical, you will have to use your own calculator's manual to learn how to use this method. There is an important advantage to using this
calculator feature: If you already know the present value but do not know the discount rate,
the calculator can automatically compute the expected return for the set of unequal cash
flows. This can eliminate the hassle of very tedious trial-and-error calculations.

FIGURE 5-7
The rollback method for
calculating a present
value.

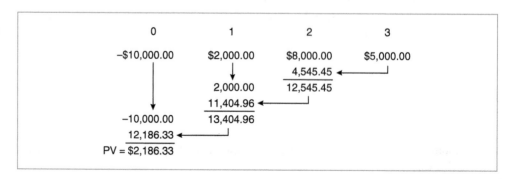

Valuing Cash Flows at Other Points Along the Time Line

Thus far, we have calculated a present value ($t = 0$) or a future value at $t = n$. But suppose we want to know the total value of a set of cash flows at some other point in time. Calculating such a value directly may require extra care, but it uses the same formulas. And if you already know the present or future value, calculating such values is quite straightforward. Our next example illustrates this process, by building on our last example.

EXAMPLE Computing Total Value at Other Points in Time

Let us reconsider the value of our set of unequal cash flows. What is their total value at $t = 2$? Cash flows before $t = 2$ must be compounded forward. Cash flows on or after $t = 2$ must be discounted back. The sum of these compounded and discounted cash flows plus the $t = 2$ cash flow equals FV_2, the total value at $t = 2$:

$$FV_2 = -10,000(1.10)^2 + 2,000(1.10)^1 + 8,000(1.10)^0 + 5,000\frac{1}{(1.10)^1}$$

$$= -12,100 + 2,200 + 8,000 + 4,545.45 = \$2,645.45$$

CALCULATOR SOLUTION	
Data Input	Function Key
2	N
10	I
2,186.326	PV
0	PMT
−2,645.45	FV

This calculation is illustrated in Figure 5-8.

In this case, there is a shortcut for computing FV_2. In our previous example, we computed the present value of this set of cash flows. The PV can be used directly to find FV_2. Simply compound the total present value forward two periods, just as though it is a single cash flow at $t = 0$:

$$FV_n = PV(FVF_{r,n}) = PV(1 + r)^n$$
$$FV_2 = 2,186.326(1.10)^2 = \$2,645.45$$

CALCULATOR SOLUTION	
Data Input	Function Key
1	N
10	I
2,645.45	PV
0	PMT
−2,910.00	FV

In a parallel way, FV_2 can also be used to find FV_3. Simply compound 2,645.45 forward one period, just as though it is a single cash flow at $t = 2$:

$$FV_3 = FV_2(FVF_{10\%,1}) = 2,645.45(1.10)^1 = \$2,910.00$$

Finally, note that FV_3 can also be calculated from the PV.

CALCULATOR SOLUTION	
Data Input	Function Key
3	N
10	I
2,186.326	PV
0	PMT
−2,910.00	FV

This example illustrates a very important point we want to emphasize. Once you have the total value of a set of cash flows at *any* point in time, you can easily compute the total value at any *other* point in time. Simply *treat the value you know as though it is a single cash flow* and compound or discount it for the difference in time to compute the value you are looking for.

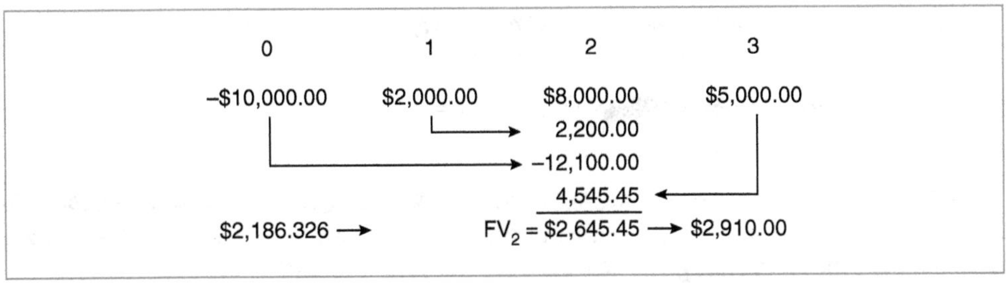

FIGURE 5-8
Computing the future value at time period 2 of an unequal set of future cash flows.

0	1	2	3
−$10,000.00	$2,000.00	$8,000.00	$5,000.00
		2,200.00	
		−12,100.00	
		4,545.45	
$2,186.326 →		$FV_2 = \$2,645.45$ → $2,910.00	

5.5   COMPOUNDING FREQUENCY

Thus far, we have been careful to use a discount rate that is consistent with the frequency of the cash flows—for example, 1% per *month* with *monthly* payments or 10% per *year* with *annual* payments. In practice, interest rates are typically stated in one of two ways, as an annual percentage rate (APR) or as an annual percentage yield (APY), even though interest may be calculated and paid more often than annually.

Annual Percentage Rate (APR)

The **annual percentage rate (APR)** is the periodic rate times the number of periods in a year. The APR is a nominal rate, a rate "in name only." The true (effective) annual rate may be different from the APR because of the compounding frequency.

The **compounding frequency** is how often interest is compounded. For example, the compounding frequency might be monthly (12 times per year), quarterly (4 times), or annually (once). The periodic rate is an effective rate, but recall that two periods of interest is more than double one. The second period's interest includes interest on the first period's interest.

With *m* compounding periods per year and a periodic rate of *r*, the APR is:

(5.10)
$$APR = (m)(r)$$

> **EXAMPLE Computing an APR at Bank of America**
>
> Bank of America offers a loan, charging 1% per month. What is the APR?
> Using Equation (5.10), the APR is 12%:
>
> $$APR = 12(0.01) = 0.12 = 12.00\%$$
>
> *Note: The compounding frequency is the same as the payment frequency, unless it is otherwise specified.*

Annual Percentage Yield (APY)

The **annual percentage yield (APY)** is the effective (true) annual rate of return. It is the rate you *actually* earn or pay in one year, taking into account the effect of compounding. The APY is computed by compounding the periodic rate for the compounding frequency:

(5.11)
$$APY = \left[1 + \frac{APR}{m}\right]^{m} - 1$$

If interest is compounded once per year, $m = 1$, and the APY equals the APR. When compounding is more often, the APY, the true rate, exceeds the APR.

> **EXAMPLE Computing the APY from Bank of America's APR**
>
> What is the APY on Bank of America's 12% APR loan, with monthly compounding?
> Using Equation (5.11), the APY is 12.6825%:
>
> $$APY = (1 + r)^{m} - 1 = (1.01)^{12} - 1 = 0.126825 = 12.6825\%$$

CALCULATOR SOLUTION

Data Input	Function Key
12	N
1	I
100	PV
0	PMT
−112.6825	FV

CALCULATING THE APY USING A CALCULATOR   We can also compute the APY using the calculator's future value function. If you start with 100% of your money and compound it at *r* per period for *m* periods (one year), the increase is the true rate of return.

After one year, you would have 112.6825% of the 100% you started with, so you would earn an APY of 12.6825%.

EXAMPLE Computing the APY for a Credit Card

A credit card charges 1.50% per month on unpaid balances. The periodic rate $r = 1.5\%$ and $m = 12$. The APR $= 0.015(12) = 0.18 = 18.00\%$. What is the APY? That is, what is the true, or effective, annual return?

The credit card is charging 19.562% per year, as shown in the Calculator Solution.

CALCULATOR SOLUTION	
Data Input	**Function Key**
12	N
1.5	I
100	PV
0	PMT
−119.562	FV

The Effect of Compounding Frequency on Future Value

How does compounding frequency affect future value? To answer this question, we will compare yearly, semiannually, quarterly, monthly, weekly, daily, and continuous compounding for saving $10,000 for a year at a 12% APR.

The future value of $10,000 in one year is shown in Table 5-3 for all of these compounding frequencies. The APY equals the 12% APR for yearly compounding. But the table shows how the future value and APY increase as the compounding frequency increases.

Another way to understand an APY is to say that it is the total interest earned in a year (annual interest) divided by the principal. That is

$$APY = \frac{\text{Annual interest}}{\text{Principal}}$$

For example, the annual interest for monthly compounding is $1,268.25, which, divided by $10,000, gives the same 12.68% we got using Equation (5.11), and the calculator.

Continuous Compounding

If more frequent compounding increases the future value, what if we compound daily, hourly, or even every minute? These are all examples of *discrete compounding*, where interest is compounded a finite number of times per year. If we use *continuous compounding*, interest is compounded an infinite number of times per year. How can we do that?

COMPOUNDING FREQUENCY	m	PV	FV$_{\text{YEAR}}$	ANNUAL INTEREST	APY
Yearly	1	$10,000	$11,200.00	$1,200.00	12.0000%
Semiannually	2	10,000	11,236.00	1,236.00	12.3600
Quarterly	4	10,000	11,255.09	1,255.09	12.5509
Monthly	12	10,000	11,268.25	1,268.25	12.6825
Weekly	52	10,000	11,273.41	1,273.41	12.7341
Daily	365	10,000	11,274.75	1,274.75	12.7475
Continuous	∞	10,000	11,274.97	1,274.97	12.7497

TABLE 5-3
Future values and APYs for various compounding frequencies.

The APR is 12%.
m = number of times interest is compounded per year
FV$_{\text{year}}$ = PV$(1 + \text{APR}/m)^m = 10,000(1 + 0.12/m)^m$
Annual Interest = FV − PV
APY $= (1 + \text{APR}/m)^m - 1 = $ Annual interest/PV
For continuous compounding, FV = PV $e^{\text{APR}} = 10,000e^{0.12}$
For continuous compounding, APY $= e^{\text{APR}} - 1 = e^{0.12} - 1$

THE APR AND APY WITH CONTINUOUS COMPOUNDING   Without giving the proof, it turns out that with continuous compounding:

(5.12)
$$APY = e^{APR} - 1$$

where e is approximately 2.718.[2] The function e^x is called an exponential function. It is usually found on a calculator with either an "e^x" or "exp" on the key. When m, the compounding frequency, becomes large enough, compounding becomes essentially continuous. So a way to approximate continuous compounding is to use a very large value for m, such as 100,000.

CALCULATOR SOLUTION	
Data Input	**Function Key**
100,000	N
12/100,000	I
100	PV
0	PMT
−112.74968	FV

EXAMPLE Computing an APY with Continuous Compounding

What is the APY for a 12% APR continuously compounded?
   Using Equation (5.12), we have

$$APY = e^{APR} - 1 = e^{0.12} - 1 = 0.1274969 = 12.74969\%$$

An alternative to the above calculation is to approximate APY using a very large value for m. For example, $m = 100,000$ (compounding about 274 times per day) yields APY = 12.74968%.

Figure 5-9 shows how compounding frequency affects future value by graphing future value as a function of annual, semiannual, and continuous compounding for 20% APR.

FIGURE 5-9
Future value as a function of annual, semiannual, and continuous compounding for 20% APR.

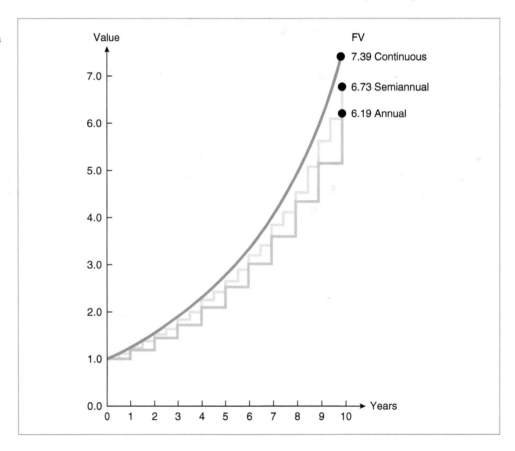

---

[2]This number occurs frequently in the mathematical and natural sciences. It is the base for what are called *natural logarithms*, usually denoted *ln*; *ln* is the inverse function of *e*. That is, $ln(e^x) = x$.

Note how the "stair steps" are smaller and more frequent for semiannual compounding and how they become a smooth curve with continuous compounding. Note also that the amount increases with more frequent compounding.

REVIEW

1. What is the APR (annual percentage rate)? Does it reflect the frequency of compounding?
2. What is the APY (annual percentage yield)? How does it take into account the effect of compounding?
3. Suppose a bank offers you a 10% APR certificate of deposit. You can specify annual, semiannual, quarterly, monthly, or daily compounding. Which would you choose?
4. Suppose you are going to borrow from a bank at 10% APR. You can specify annual, semiannual, quarterly, monthly, or daily compounding. Which would you choose?

5.6   PARTIAL TIME PERIODS

Using the time-value-of-money formulas with partial time periods requires care and an understanding of the assumptions underlying the formulas. A time line can be essential to solving problems involving partial time periods.

Single Cash Flows

Computing present and/or future values of single cash flows between partial time periods is straightforward because a fractional exponent can be used directly in modern calculators.

EXAMPLE **Computing the Present Value of a Single Future Cash Flow**

What is the present value of $1,000 to be received 46 months from today if the required return is 12% APY?

Using the present-value formula with $n = 3.8333 \ (= 46/12)$:

$$PV = 1,000 \left[\frac{1}{(1.12)^{3.8333}} \right] = \$647.64$$

$PV = pmt \left(\frac{1}{(r)n} \right)$

CALCULATOR SOLUTION	
Data Input	Function Key
3.8333	N
12	I
0	PMT
1,000	FV
−647.64	PV

EXAMPLE **Using a Partial Period to Compute an APY**

We showed one way to calculate an APY based on how much money will grow in one year. An alternative way to compute an APY is to calculate the yearly rate for money that grows at the periodic rate for one period. Let's illustrate using the same 1% per month example.

A PV of 100 grows to 101 in 1/12 of a year (one month). Therefore, as shown in the Calculator Solution, the true yearly rate, the APY, is 12.6825%.

CALCULATOR SOLUTION	
Data Input	Function Key
1/12	N
100	PV
0	PMT
−101	FV
12.6825	I

Annuities with Partial Time Periods

Unfortunately, calculator treatment of annuities with partial time periods is not consistent. Some "round down" and treat the partial time period and payment as though they are not there. Others "round up" and treat the partial time period and payment as though they are a full

FIGURE 5-10
Solution using a time
line.

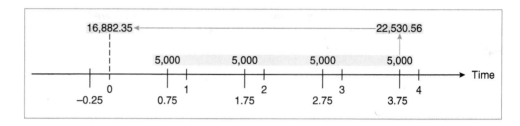

CALCULATOR SOLUTION	
Data Input	Function Key
4	N
8	I
0	PV
5,000	PMT
−22,530.56	FV

period and payment. Still others account for the partial time period but assume no payment. Our advice is to either (1) carefully study how your calculator works and use it successfully, or (2) "take matters into your own hands" and account for annuities with partial time periods in other ways. Here are two examples of how to compute a future value using a two-step process, without relying on whatever assumptions are programmed into your calculator.

EXAMPLE Computing the Present Value of an Annuity with Early Cash Flows

CALCULATOR SOLUTION	
Data Input	Function Key
3.75	N
8	I
−22,530.56	PV
0	PMT
16,882.35	FV

What is the present value of a four-year annuity, with the first $5,000 payment being made nine months from today, if the required return is 8% APY?
 The future value of this four-year annuity at the end of its life is $22, 530.56.
 The present value can then be computed by simply treating $22,530.56 as a single cash flow 3.75 years from now to get $16,882.35.
 Figure 5-10 illustrates the solution using a time line.

CALCULATOR SOLUTION	
Data Input	Function Key
3	N
10	I
1,000	PMT
0	FV
−2,486.85	PV

EXAMPLE Computing the Future Value of an Annuity After It Has Ended

What is the value 3.75 years from now of a three-year annuity, with the first $1,000 payment being made one year from today, if the expected return is 10% APY?
 The present value is $2,486.85.
 The future value in 3.75 years can then be computed by simply treating the $2,486.85 as though it is a single cash flow at $t = 0$ and compounding that amount for 3.75 time periods to get: $3,555.27.
 Figure 5-11 illustrates the solution to this example using a time line.

CALCULATOR SOLUTION	
Data Input	Function Key
3.75	N
10	I
−2,486.85	PV
0	PMT
3,555.27	FV

REVIEW

1. How can you compute the present or future value of a single cash flow when there is a partial time period involved?
2. Why must you be especially careful when using a calculator to compute the present or future value of an annuity when there is a partial time period involved?

FIGURE 5-11
Solution using a time
line.

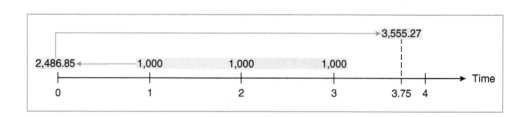

5.7 EVALUATING "SPECIAL-FINANCING" OFFERS

"Special-financing" offers are often used as part of a sales promotion for consumer goods, such as cars, furniture, and even condominiums. In short, special financing has become part of the package in many types of consumer purchases. But how can you tell whether the financing is really special in anything but name only? In this section, we provide an example and some guidelines for dealing with special financing.

Often the interest rate creates the most confusion with special financing. This is because the special rate offered, such as 0.9% APR, is not the opportunity cost for borrowing money. You cannot really borrow money at that rate. The special financing is simply a promotional gimmick. In essence, the firm is lowering the effective price to encourage sales. It is just that the lower price is expressed in the form of special financing. The key question, then, is how much does the interest savings lower the price?

To evaluate a special-financing deal, you need the interest rate at which you can borrow money for *any* comparable use. That is, you need the market interest rate for such loans. The market interest rate provides a way to measure the opportunity cost of the special financing. You use the market rate to compute the "real" price for the product. The real price is the present value of the payments you would have to make using the special-financing offer. If the present value is smaller than the cash price, the special financing is a better deal; the real price with special financing is lower than the cash price.

CALCULATOR SOLUTION	
Data Input	Function Key
36	N
0.075	I
20,000	PV
0	FV
−563.30	PMT

EXAMPLE **Cash Back or 0.9% APR from Chevy**

Chevy is offering a choice of either "special financing" or "cash back" to buy a car you have already decided to buy. The stated price is $20,000. Either you can have $2,000 cash back, for a cash price of $18,000, or you can borrow the "$20,000" at 0.9% APR, 0.075% per month (= 0.9/12). Monthly payments would be $563.30 for the next 36 months.

Or, you could borrow $18,000 from Citibank (or any of several other banks) at 7.2% APR and pay cash for the car. Should you take the special-financing offer or take the cash-back offer and borrow from a bank?

The best choice has the lowest present-value cost. The difference between the two costs is the NPV of the choice. On the basis of 7.2% APR (0.60% per month), the present value of the special-financing loan payments is $18,189.38.

This is more than the $18,000 cash-back-offer price, so taking the cash-back offer and borrowing from the bank is the better deal. The NPV is $189.38.

There is another way to see the difference between the two alternatives: Compute what the payments would be on the Citibank loan if Citibank required the same 36 monthly payments.[3] The payments for such a Citibank loan would be $557.44.

So the bank loan would be $5.865 per month cheaper (= 563.30 − 557.435). Note that the monthly savings have a present value of $189.38, which is the NPV for the bank loan.

CALCULATOR SOLUTION	
Data Input	Function Key
36	N
0.60	I
−563.30	PMT
0	FV
18,189.38	PV

CALCULATOR SOLUTION	
Data Input	Function Key
36	N
0.60	I
18,000	PV
0	FV
−557.435	PMT

$$\frac{7.2}{12} = .6$$

CALCULATOR SOLUTION	
Data Input	Function Key
36	N
0.60	I
5.865	PMT
0	FV
−189.38	PV

In the preceding example, you had already decided to purchase that particular car. But what if you are still shopping? In the next example, we will show how to evaluate competing product offers.

---

[3]To make a "fair" comparison possible, the repayment process for the bank loan *must* be identical to that for the special-financing offer: 36 equal monthly payments. If the length of the period is different (say weekly), if the maturity of the loan is different (say 48 months), or if the payments are not identical each period, a comparison of payments can lead to the wrong choice.

CALCULATOR SOLUTION	
Data Input	Function Key
48	N
0.0	I
22,000	PV
0	FV
–458.33	PMT

EXAMPLE **Computing the Value of a Special-Financing Offer from Chrysler**

Suppose that just before you "sign on the dotted line" for the Chevy, you hear about another offer from Chrysler. It is a nicer model that you actually like better—except for its higher price of $22,000. Now Chrysler is offering 0% APR for 48 months on this "$22,000" model. Therefore, you could buy the nicer model for $458.33 per month for the next 48 months.

However, because the loan on the more expensive model is over a different period, the lower monthly payment is not necessarily the best deal.[4]

Is Chrysler's price on the better model less than the $18,000 cash price on Chevy's more basic model? It is a lower monthly payment at a "lower" interest rate, but it is for 12 more months. What is the real price for the Chrysler? There is no cash-back offer on this nicer model to give a guideline for the price discount.

Again, the real price with the special financing is the present value of the loan payments at the opportunity cost (market) interest rate. On the basis of the bank's 7.2% APR interest rate, the real price is $19,065.99.

Therefore, Chrysler's 0% APR special-financing offer on the nicer model costs $1,065.99 more (= 19,065.99 – 18,000) than the best deal (cash back) on Chevy's model.

CALCULATOR SOLUTION	
Data Input	Function Key
48	N
0.60	I
–458.33	PMT
0	FV
19,065.99	PV

SUMMARY

This chapter explored the Time-Value-of-Money Principle and established the following concepts:

- The expected rate of return is what you expect to earn, the required rate of return is the return the marketplace demands for securities with similar characteristics, and the realized rate of return is what you actually get.
- NPV (net present value) is the present value minus the cost. NPV measures the value created by a financial decision. A positive (negative) NPV creates (destroys) value.
- An annuity is a set of equal periodic payments for a given number of periods. Annuities are common in financial contracts. Annuity formulas allow complex problems to be solved in a routine manner.
- The present-value and future-value formulas can be used to compute the value of cash flows at times other than when they will be paid or received. These formulas can be used to find PV (present value), FV (future value), PMT (annuity cash flow), n (number of periods), or r (the periodic rate of return).
- Time-value-of-money formulas can also be used to find a loan's payments or true interest cost—its APY.
- A loan's APY—its true annual cost—can differ from its APR, which is a nominal rate.
- Present value and the discount rate are inversely related: Present value goes down when r goes up, and vice versa—like two kids on a seesaw.

---

[4]We also want to caution that you must *never* multiply the payment amount times the number of payments. Remember, even identical cash flows, if they occur at different times, do not have the same value—because of the time value of money.

EQUATION SUMMARY

The Basic Calculator Formula

$$PV + PMT\left[\frac{(1+I)^N - 1}{I(1+I)^N}\right] + FV\left[\frac{1}{(1+I)^N}\right] = 0$$

(5.1) $\quad$ Return = Rate of return = $\dfrac{\text{Cash flow} + (\text{Ending value} - \text{Beginning value})}{\text{Beginning value}}$

(5.2) $\quad$ NPV = Net present value = Present value of expected future cash flows − Cost

The Future-Value Formula

(5.3) $\qquad\qquad FV_n = PV(1 + r)^n = PV(FVF_{r,n})$

The Present-Value Formula

(5.4) $\qquad\qquad PV = FV_n\left[\dfrac{1}{(1+r)^n}\right] = FV_n(PVF_{r,n})$

(5.5) $\qquad FVA_n = PMT\left[\dfrac{(1+r)^n - 1}{r}\right] = PMT(FVAF_{r,n})$

(5.6) $\qquad PVA_n = PMT\left[\dfrac{(1+r)^n - 1}{r(1+r)^n}\right] = PMT(PVAF_{r,n})$

(5.7) $\qquad PMT = PVA_n\left[\dfrac{r(1+r)^n}{(1+r)^n - 1}\right] = \dfrac{PVA_n}{PVAF_{r,n}}$

(5.8) $\qquad PMT = FVA_n\left[\dfrac{r}{(1+r)^n - 1}\right] = \dfrac{FVA_n}{FVAF_{r,n}}$

(5.9) $\qquad\qquad PVA_{\text{perpetuity}} = \dfrac{PMT}{r}$

(5.10) $\qquad\qquad APR = (m)(r)$

(5.11) $\qquad\qquad APY = \left[1 + \dfrac{APR}{m}\right]^m - 1$

(5.12) $\qquad\qquad APY = e^{APR} - 1$

QUESTIONS

1. Why is the present value of a future cash flow inversely related to the discount rate?
2. What is an ordinary annuity? What is an annuity due? Why is the present value of an annuity due greater than the present value of an ordinary annuity?

3. Dewey Noe computed the value of a 10-year annuity of $100 per year. The value was $700. Now he cannot remember whether it was a *present* value or a *future* value. Which is it? Why?

4. Why should a business undertake an investment that has a positive net present value?

5. Explain the format or layout of a loan amortization table.

PROBLEMS

■ **LEVEL A (BASIC)**

A1. (PV and FV of single payments) Fill in the missing information:

	PV	FV	*r*	*n*
a.	—	20	10%	10
b.	10	—	10%	10
c.	10	20	—	10
d.	10	20	10%	—

A2. (PV and FV of single payments) Fill in the missing information:

	PV	FV	*r*	*n*
a.	—	20	10%	15
b.	10	—	10%	15
c.	10	20	—	15
d.	15	20	10%	—

A3. (PV and FV of single payments) Fill in the missing information:

	PV	FV	*r*	*n*
a.	—	22,000	5.6%	3.0
b.	1,000	—	12.1%	5.5
c.	400	400	—	4.0
d.	25,000	50,000	7.75%	—

A4. (PV and FV of single payments) Fill in the missing information:

	PV	FV	*r*	*n*
a.	—	45,000	5.6%	3.0
b.	250	—	12.1%	5.5
c.	500	500	—	4.0
d.	25,000	78,000	7.75%	—

A5. (Calculating FVs) If you invest $1,000 in a savings account paying 12% APY, what will be your account balance at the end of the following periods?

a. 1 year

b. 5 years

c. 1.75 years

A6. (Calculating PVs) What is the present value of $20,000 discounted back at 6% if the money is received at the end of the following periods?

a. 1 year

b. 5 years

c. 1.75 years

A7. (Expected, required, and realized returns) If you buy shares of Rivas Resorts, it will cost you $45 per share and you can expect to receive $1.00 in dividends and sell the stock for $56 in one year. If you invest in Carreras Holdings, the investment will be $125 per share with an expected dividend of $5.00 and stock price of $132 in one year.

    a. What are the expected returns for Rivas and Carreras?

    b. If the required rate of return is 15%, which stocks should be profitable investments?

    c. One year from now, Rivas has paid a $1.00 dividend and is selling for $52. Carreras has paid a $5.00 dividend and is selling for $155. What were the realized returns for the two stocks?

A8. (Rate of return) Adrian Trennepohl bought shares of a small firm's stock three years ago for $12.00 per share. What will be Adrian's annual rate of return if she sells the stock today for each of the following prices?

    a. $72.00

    b. $13.50

    c. $15.00

    d. $6.00

A9. (Rate of return) After graduation, Adrian moved across the country to Brownville and bought a small house for $208,000. Bill moved to Columbus and bought a house for $195,000. Four years later, they both sold their houses. Adrian netted $256,000 when she sold her house and Bill netted $168,000 on his.

    a. What annual rate of return did Adrian realize on her house?

    b. What annual rate of return did Bill realize on his house?

A10. (PV of lump sum) George Jetson invests $100 for one year at 10%. He expects to have $110 in one year.

    a. What is the present value of this future amount discounted at 10%?

    b. What is the present value discounted at 8%?

    c. What is the present value discounted at 12%?

A11. (Calculating the PV and FV of an annuity) Assume an ordinary annuity of $500 at the end of each of the next three years.

    a. What is the present value discounted at 10%?

    b. What is the future value at the end of year 3 if cash flows can be invested at 10%?

A12. (PV of an annuity) What is the present value of $500 per year for eight years if the required return is 8.5% per year?

A13. (PV of an annuity) What is the present value of $100 per year for 10 years if the required return is 6.5% per year?

A14. (FV of an annuity) What is the future value at the end of year 6 of a six-year annuity of $1,000 per year if the expected return is 10%?

A15. (FV of an annuity) What is the future value, at the end of year 7, of $1,500 per year for each of the next seven years if the expected return is 9% per year?

A16. (FV of an annuity) What is the future value 25 years from now of an annuity of $600 per year for each of the next 25 years if the expected return is 10% per year?

A17. (PV of an annuity) What is the present value of a six-year annuity of $1,000 per year, if the required return is 10% per year?

A18. (Remaining life of an annuity) You borrowed $225,000 to buy a house. The loan was originally a 30-year loan charging 0.60% per month on the unpaid balance. Your monthly payment is $1,527.27. Now you do not remember how many payments are remaining, but your statement says that your remaining balance is $215,407.67. How many more monthly payments are left?

A19. (Finding loan payments) What are the monthly payments on a 15-year $35,000 loan if the interest rate is 1% per month?

A20. (Loan payments and amortization schedule) What are the annual payments for a four-year $4,000 loan if the interest rate is 9% per year? Make up a loan amortization schedule for this loan.

A21. (Loan payments and amortization schedule) Create a loan amortization schedule for borrowing $9,500 at an interest rate of 15% per year, to be paid off in four equal annual payments.

A22. (Ordinary annuity and annuity due) Assume an annuity payment of $300, an annuity life of 10 years, and a required return of 8%.

   a. If the annuity is an ordinary annuity, what is the future value of the annuity?

   b. If the annuity is an ordinary annuity, what is its present value?

   c. If the annuity is an annuity due, what is its future value?

   d. If the annuity is an annuity due, what is its present value?

A23. (PV of a perpetuity) What is the present value of a perpetuity of $800 per year if the required return is 11% per year?

A24. (PV of a perpetuity) What is the present value of a perpetuity of $2,500 per year if the required return is 15% per year?

A25. (Loan payment) What are the monthly payments on a $15,000 four-year loan if the required return is 9% APR?

A26. (PV of loan) What is the present value of $100 per week for five years if the required return is 10% APR?

A27. (FV of an annuity) What is the future value after 10 years of $200 per month if the expected return is 6% APR?

A28. (Finding mortgage payment) What are the monthly payments on a $150,000 25-year mortgage if the required return is 7.5% APR?

A29. (PV of single payment) What is the present value of $10,000 to be received 7.8 years from today, if the required return is 8.2% APY?

A30. (PV of single payment) What is the present value of $10,000 to be received 9.2 years from today, if the required return is 6.8% APY?

A31. (PV of a perpetuity) What is the present value of $10,000 per year received at the end of each year in perpetuity with a required return of 7.4% APY?

A32. (PV of a perpetuity) What is the present value of $200,000 per year received at the end of each year in perpetuity with a required return of 4% APY?

■ LEVEL B

B1. (Finding the APY) You expect to receive $16,000 three years from today. If the present value of this amount is $12,701.13, what is the APY? What is the monthly return?

B2. (PV of a deferred annuity) What is the present value of a stream of $1,500 payments received at the end of each of years 3 through 9 if the required return is 10% per year?

B3. (PV of an annuity) If the required return is 8% per year, what is the present value of $1,000 per year for:

   a. 10 years?

   b. 20 years?

   c. 50 years?

   d. 100 years?

   e. forever?

B4. (PV of an annuity due) Congratulations! You have just won a $10 million lottery prize. The prize is paid out to you in 20 equal installments at the beginning of each of the next 20 years.

   a. What is the present value of your lottery winnings if the discount rate is 7%?

b. The lottery commission claims that lottery prizes are 50% of lottery tickets sold. If this claim is based on all prizes having a 20-year payout schedule like yours without regard to the time value of money, the present value of lottery prizes is less than 50% of tickets sold. The PV of lottery prizes is what percentage of lottery revenue?

B5. (Finding a monthly return) A bank offers to pay you $1,000.00 per month for 10 years if you will give them $69,700.52 today. What return would you earn per month if you accept the bank's offer? What is the APR?

B6. (Finding loan interest rates) Suppose you are paying $31.73 per week for 10 years to repay a $10,000 loan.

   a. What is the weekly interest rate on this loan?

   b. What is the APR?

   c. What is the APY?

B7. (Annuity due)

   a. What is the present value of a six-year *annuity due* of $650 per year if the required return is 9% APY?

   b. What is the future value at the end of five years of a five-year *annuity due* of $900 per year if the expected return is 9.8% APY?

B8. (FV of a PV with a partial time period) What is the future value, 1.75 years from now, if the present value is $900 and the expected return is 12% APR, compounded semiannually?

B9. (Value of cash flows at various points in time) You expect to receive the following future cash flows at the end of the years indicated: −$1,500 in year 0, $1,300 in year 2, $600 in year 3, and $1,700 in year 4. If the discount rate is 9% per year,

   a. What is the present value of all four expected future cash flows?

   b. What is the value of the four flows at year 4?

   c. What is the value of the four flows at year 1?

B10. (Value of cash flows at various points in time) You expect to receive the following future cash flows at the end of the years indicated: $500 in year 2, $1,200 in year 4, $800 in year 5, and $1,500 in year 6. If the discount rate is 7% per year,

   a. What is the present value of all four expected future cash flows?

   b. What is the value of the four flows at year 5?

   c. What is the value of the four flows at year 10?

B11. (Value of cash flows at various points in time) The following future cash flows will be received at the end of the years indicated: $1,000 in year 0, $1,400 in year 1, $900 in year 2, and $600 in year 3. If the discount rate is 8% per year,

   a. What is the present value of all four expected future cash flows?

   b. What is the value of the four flows at year 3?

   c. What is the value of the four flows at year 2?

B12. (Calculating the PV) A scam artist collected $20 million from gullible investors for an oil-well-drilling scheme. The scam artist promised that he would pay off the investors in full within eight years if the oil wells, for some reason, were not drilled. He purchased zero-coupon bonds that paid off the $20 million in a single payment at the end of eight years. He then mailed the bonds to his investors, pocketing the difference between the price of the bonds and the $20 million, and skipped the country. The rate of return on the bonds was 9%.

   a. What is the present value of $20 million in 8 years discounted at 9%?

   b. How much did the scam artist pocket?

B13. (APR and APY) Corey Christian has a $4,000 balance on a credit card. The APR on the card is 18%, compounded monthly.

   a. What is the APY?

   b. If he makes no payments and no further charges, what will be the credit card balance in one year?

   c. What will be the balance in four years?

B14. (Finding APR and APY of a loan) Suppose a bank offers to loan you $18,000 if you will pay back $439.43 per month for 48 months.

   a. What monthly interest rate is the bank charging?

   b. What APR interest rate is the bank charging on this loan?

   c. What APY interest rate is the bank charging on this loan?

B15. (PV of a deferred annuity) What is the present value of $1,000 to be received at the end of each of years 6 through 15 with 10% APY.

B16. (Finding interest rates) Find the APY for the following:

   a. The APR is 8% compounded semiannually.

   b. The APR is 21.6% compounded monthly.

   c. The APR is 6% compounded continuously.

B17. (Finding the APY) Find the APY for:

   a. 15% APR with monthly compounding.

   b. 9% APR with monthly compounding.

B18. (Finding the APY) Find the APY for:

   a. 15% APR with continuous compounding.

   b. 9% APR with continuous compounding.

B19. (Finding the APR and APY for a mortgage) Suppose a bank offers a $130,000 20-year mortgage if you will pay back $1,007.89 per month.

   a. What monthly interest rate is the bank charging?

   b. What APR interest rate is the bank charging on this mortgage?

   c. What APY interest rate is the bank charging on this loan?

B20. (PV of single payment with continuous compounding) What is the present value of $3,400 to be received three years from today if the required return is 11% APR compounded continuously?

B21. (PV of a single payment) What is the present value of $4,500 to be received 31 months from today if the required return is 10% APY?

B22. (FV of discrete payments with continuous compounding) What is the future value of $20,000 received as a lump sum at the end of each year for five years if the expected return is 10% per year compounded continuously?

B23. (PV of a deferred annuity) What is the present value of a five-year annuity, with the first $3,000 payment being made three months from today, if the required return is 7% APY?

B24. (FV of an annuity) What is the value 4.35 years from now of a four-year annuity, with the first $1,200 payment being made one year from today, if the expected return is APY = 10%?

B25. (FV of an annuity) What is the value seven years from now of a four-year annuity, with the first $1,600 payment being made one year from today, if the expected return is APY = 10%?

B26. (PV of a deferred annuity) What is the present value of a six-year annuity, with the first $2,500 payment being made seven months from today, if the required return is APY = 12%?

B27. (PV of a deferred annuity) What is the present value of a six-year annuity, with the first $3,000 payment being made four months from today, if the required return is APY = 12%?

B28. (PV of a deferred annuity) What is the present value of a stream of $1,900 payments received at the end of each of years 4 through 9 if the required return is 10% per year?

B29. (Finding the APY) You expect to receive $2,000 three years from today. If the present value of this amount is $1,423.56, what is the APY?

B30. (Finding the time period) You expect to receive $1,000 sometime in the future. If the present value of this amount is $592.03 and the discount rate is 10% APY, when is the cash flow expected to occur?

B31. (Time to double your money) How long does it take a present-value amount to double if the expected return is 4%, 9%, and 15%?

B32. (Finding the APY) If an annuity of $5,000 per year for eight years has a present value of $27,469.57, what is the expected APY?

B33. (PV of a deferred annuity) What is the present value of a 15-year annuity with payments of $1,800 per year, where the first payment is expected to occur four years from today and the required return is 7.3% APY?

B34. (Finding the PV of an annuity with missing payments) Suppose you expect to receive $1,000 per year for each of the next 15 years, except that you will not receive any payments in years 3 and 5. What is the present value of this stream if the required return is 12% APR?

B35. (Finding the PV of an annuity with missing payments) Suppose you expect to receive $1,000 per year for each of the next 13 years, except that you will not receive any payments in years 3 and 5. What is the present value of this stream if the required return is 11% APR?

B36. (Mortgage loan interest rates) Peter's Bank has offered you a $200,000 mortgage on a house. Payments are to be $2,057.23 per month for 30 years.

   a. What monthly interest rate is Peter charging?

   b. What is the APR on this loan?

   c. What is the APY on this loan?

B37. (Special-financing offer) Chrysler is offering "42-month 2.2% APR" financing or "$2,000 cash back" on a car you have decided to buy. The stated price for the car is $23,000.

   a. What are the monthly payments required for Chrysler's special-financing deal?

   b. If you can borrow the cash to buy the car from several different banks at 8.3% APR, would you be better off taking the cash-back offer?

B38. (Special-financing offer) Honda is offering "42-month 2.5% APR" financing or "$2,000 cash back" on a car you have decided to buy. The stated price for the car is $23,000.

   a. What are the monthly payments required for Honda's special-financing deal?

   b. If you can borrow the cash to buy the car from several different banks at 8.3% APR, would you be better off taking the cash-back offer?

B39. (Special-financing offer) You have negotiated a price of $20,000 to buy a car. Ford will either give you $1,500 cash back, or a 48-month loan of the "$20,000" at 3.9% APR. Alternatively, you can borrow $18,500 from Citibank (or any of several other banks) at 8% APR and pay cash for the car.

   a. What are the monthly payments required for Ford's special-financing deal?

   b. If you can borrow the cash to buy the car from several different banks at 8% APR, would you be better off taking the cash-back offer?

B40. (Special-financing offer) Performance Auto is offering you a choice of either special financing or a price discount on their new sports car, the QT-123. The stated price for the car is $31,000, but you can pay $25,500 cash and "drive it home today." Alternatively, you can borrow the $31,000 from Performance Auto and make monthly payments for three years with a 1% APR. Suppose the best financing currently available is to borrow money from Bob's Bank for three years at 12% APR with monthly installment payments, and you have decided to buy a QT-123 from Performance Auto. Should you take the special financing or borrow the money from Bob's Bank and pay the cash price?

B41. (Special-financing offer) Performance Auto is offering you a choice of either special financing or a price discount on their new "artistic" van, the Van-Go. The stated price for the van is $23,000, but you can pay $19,500 cash and "drive it home today." Alternatively, you can borrow the $23,000 from Performance Auto and make monthly payments for four years with a 0.9% APR. Suppose the best financing currently available is to borrow money from Barb's Bank for four years at 7.2% APR with monthly installment payments, and you have decided to buy a Van-Go from Performance Auto. Should you take the special financing or borrow the money from Barb's Bank and pay the cash price?

B42. (Monthly loan installment) What are the monthly payments on a three-year $10,000 loan (36 equal payments) if the interest rate is a 10% APY?

B43. (Monthly loan installment) What are the monthly payments on a three-year $20,000 loan (36 equal payments) if the interest rate is an 8% APY?

B44. (FV and PV of an annuity) Suppose you would like to be paid $40,000 per year during your retirement, which starts in 20 years. Assume the $40,000 is an annual perpetuity and that the expected return is 5% APY. How much should you save per year for the next 20 years so that you can achieve your retirement goal?

B45. (Special-financing offer) Toyota is offering "36-month 1.9% APR" financing or "$1,400 cash back" on a car you have decided to buy. The stated price for the car is $18,000. You can borrow the cash to buy the car from several different banks at 8.1% APR. Which alternative has the lower "real" price, the special-financing deal or the cash-back offer?

B46. (Excel: amortization table) You borrow $20,000 for a 36-month car loan.

    a. If the APR is 9%, what is your monthly loan payment?

    b. Prepare a loan amortization schedule that shows, for each month, your loan payment, interest expense, loan amortization, and remaining loan balance.

    c. What is the APY on your loan?

B47. (Excel: amortization table) Bill Welch is buying out his partner in an avocado orchard. Bill is borrowing $200,000 and will pay 10% interest on the outstanding balance. Bill has agreed to pay $25,000 per year for the first five years, $30,000 for the next four, and then will pay off the remaining balance at the end of the 10th year.

    a. Prepare a loan amortization schedule that shows, for the next 10 years, Bill's loan payment, interest expense, loan amortization, and remaining loan balance.

    b. What is the final (10th) loan payment?

■ LEVEL C (ADVANCED)

C1. (Loan payments) Harry's Home Finance is offering to loan you $10,000 for a home improvement. The loan is to be repaid in monthly installments over nine years. If the interest rate on this loan is 15% APR, compounded continuously, what would your monthly payments be if you accepted Harry's offer?

C2. (PV of an annuity) Jason won a lottery that will pay him $100,000 per year for 10 years. He got the first payment nine months ago, so the second payment will occur three months from today. Jason has decided to sell the rest of the payments. He is offering them to you for $602,000. If the appropriate required return on this stream of expected future cash flows is 10.8% APY,

    a. What is the present value of this set of cash flows?

    b. What is the net present value of buying this set of expected future cash flows from Jason for $602,000?

C3. (PV of an annuity) What is the present value of $5,000 per year received at the end of each year for 20 years if the required return is 8% APR, compounded continuously?

C4. (FV and PV of an annuity) Suppose your parents have decided that after you graduate at the end of this year, they will start saving money to help pay for your younger sister to attend college. They plan to save money for five years before she starts college. The instant after they make the last payment, they will withdraw the first payment for her. The payments to her will be $20,000 per year at the start of each of her four college years. They will save an equal amount at the end of every month for five years. The monthly interest rate they will earn on their savings is 0.45%. How much must they save each month in order to be able to make the four payments with no money left over?

C5. (Annuity payments) Suppose your parents have decided that after you graduate at the end of this year, they will start saving money to help pay for your younger brother to attend college. They plan to save money for five years before he starts college and to continue to save during his college years. They plan to give your brother $20,000 per year at the start of each of his four college years. Your parents will thus make monthly savings payments for eight years, five prior to and three during your brother's college education. (The sixtieth monthly savings payment happens simultaneously with the first $8,000 college payment.) The monthly interest rate earned on their savings is 0.45%. How much must the monthly savings be under these conditions?

C6. (PV of a perpetuity) What is the present value of $5,500 every two years forever, with the first payment two years from today, if the required return is 8% APY?

C7. (PV of a deferred perpetuity) What is the present value of $500 every four years forever, with the first payment two years from today, if the required return is 12% APY?

C8. (PV of a deferred perpetuity) What is the present value of $6,500 every four years forever, with the first payment six years from today, if the required return is 11% APY?

C9. (Finding an APY) A firm advertising early-retirement programs promises to repay you forever, whatever amount you pay them per year for 12 years. What interest rate are they promising?

C10. (Finding an annuity payment) Suppose you would like to be paid $30,000 per year during your retirement, which starts in 25 years. Assume the $30,000 is an annual perpetuity and that the expected return is 6% APY. What should you save *per month* for the next 25 years so that you can achieve your retirement goal?

C11. (Excel: PV of income stream) Cynthia Fisher is purchasing an asset that will pay her $1,000 in one year, $1,500 in two years, $2,000 in three years, and $2,500 in four years.

   a. If the required rate of return is 10%, what is the present value of this income stream?

   b. If Cynthia purchases this asset for $3,500, what rate of return will she earn on her investment?

C12. (Excel: PV of income stream) Eduardo Garcia has a starting salary of $45,000. He expects the salary to grow at 10% annually for the next nine years. Then for years 11 through 30, the salary will grow at 8% annually. Finally, for years 31 through 35, the salary will decline by 5% annually. Assume that the payments are received at the end of the year and that the required rate of return is 6%. What is the PV of Eduardo's projected income stream?

C13. (Excel: FV of variable cash flows) Gary French wants to have $1.0 million in 10 years. Currently, he has an investment portfolio of $200,000. He will also invest an additional $25,000 at the end of each of the next 10 years. If he has the following annual returns, how much will his investment portfolio be worth at the end of 10 years?

Year 1	12%	Year 6	8%
Year 2	−6%	Year 7	4%
Year 3	3%	Year 8	1%

MINICASE   THE $125 BILLION SWISS SURPRISE

Imagine getting a bill for $125 billion you did not know you owed. That actually happened to the residents, called "burghers," of the town of Ticino, Switzerland. The New York Supreme Court in Brooklyn ordered Ticino to pay a group of American investors. The investors had sued in the Brooklyn court over a loss they claimed in connection with the failure 27 years earlier of Inter Change Bank, a tiny bank in Ticino. The burghers had known about the suit, but thought the matter was trivial, and were naturally stunned by the bill. Their lead lawyer quipped that "if the judgment was upheld by the higher courts, all of Ticino's citizens would have to spend the rest of their lives flipping real burgers (the kind you eat) at McDonald's and Burger King to pay off the debt."

The root of Ticino's problem was a deposit made 28 years earlier, one year before the bank failed. The estate of one Sterling Granville Higgins deposited $600 million of options on Venezuelan oil and mineral deposits. The bank agreed to pay an interest rate of 1% per week. (No wonder the bank failed the next year!) The Brooklyn court ruled that Ticino had to pay 1% interest per week compounded weekly for the seven years between the date of deposit and the date Ticino had the bank liquidated and interest at the rate of 8.54% APY for the subsequent 21 years.

QUESTIONS

1. The $125 billion reported in the press was rounded, but the original amount was precisely $600 million. Assuming the time periods are exactly seven years at 1% per week and exactly 21 years at 8.54% APY, how much was the bill to the nearest dollar?

2. What was the APY over the entire 28 years as the $600 million grew to the exact amount you calculated in question 1?

3. Suppose Ticino could pay $5 billion per year. How long would it take to pay off the debt, assuming interest continued to be charged at 8.54% APY? How long would it take at $12 billion per year?

Postscript: To the burghers' relief, the judgment was thrown out on appeal. This no doubt restored the confidence of the good burghers of Ticino in the American system of justice!

MULTINATIONAL CAPITAL BUDGETING

6

T his chapter describes in detail the issues and principles related to the investment in real productive assets in foreign countries, generally referred to as *multinational capital budgeting*.

Although the original decision to undertake an investment in a particular foreign country may be determined by a mix of strategic, behavioral, and economic decisions, the specific project, as well as all reinvestment decisions, should be justified by traditional financial analysis. For example, a production efficiency opportunity may exist for a U.S. firm to invest abroad, but the type of plant, mix of labor and capital, kinds of equipment, method of financing, and other project variables must be analyzed within the traditional financial framework of discounted cash flows. The firm must also consider the impact of the proposed foreign project on consolidated net earnings, on cash flows from subsidiaries in other countries, and on the market value of the parent firm.

Multinational capital budgeting, like traditional domestic capital budgeting, focuses on the cash inflows and outflows associated with prospective long-term investment projects. Multinational capital budgeting techniques are used in traditional FDI analysis, such as the construction of a manufacturing plant in another country, as well as in the growing field of international mergers and acquisitions.

Capital budgeting for a foreign project uses the same theoretical framework as domestic capital budgeting—with a few very important differences. The basic steps are:

1. Identify the initial capital invested or put at risk.
2. Estimate cash flows to be derived from the project over time, including an estimate of the terminal or salvage value of the investment.
3. Identify the appropriate discount rate for determining the present value of the expected cash flows.
4. Apply traditional capital budgeting decision criteria such as net present value (NPV) and internal rate of return (IRR) to determine the acceptability of or priority ranking of potential projects.

This chapter first describes the complexities of budgeting for a foreign project. Second, we describe the insights gained by valuing a project from both the project's viewpoint and the parent's viewpoint. We then use a hypothetical investment by Cemex of Mexico in Indonesia to detail the process of multinational capital budgeting in practice. We conclude the chapter with an introduction to the concept of real options analysis, an alternative method for evaluating the potential returns to a project or investment.

6.1 COMPLEXITIES OF BUDGETING FOR A FOREIGN PROJECT

Capital budgeting for a foreign project is considerably more complex than the domestic case. Several factors contribute to this greater complexity:

- Parent cash flows must be distinguished from project cash flows. Each of these two types of flows contributes to a different view of value.
- Parent cash flows often depend on the form of financing. Thus we cannot clearly separate cash flows from financing decisions, as we can in domestic capital budgeting.
- Additional cash flows generated by a new investment in one foreign subsidiary may be in part or in whole taken away from another subsidiary, with the net result that the project is favorable from a single subsidiary's point of view but contributes nothing to worldwide cash flows.
- The parent must explicitly recognize remittance of funds because of differing tax systems, legal and political constraints on the movement of funds, local business norms, and differences in the way financial markets and institutions function.
- An array of nonfinancial payments can generate cash flows from subsidiaries to the parent, including payment of license fees and payments for imports from the parent.
- Managers must anticipate differing rates of national inflation because of their potential to cause changes in competitive position, and thus changes in cash flows over a period of time.
- Managers must keep the possibility of unanticipated foreign exchange rate changes in mind because of possible direct effects on the value of local cash flows, as well as indirect effects on the competitive position of the foreign subsidiary.
- Use of segmented national capital markets may create an opportunity for financial gains or may lead to additional financial costs.
- Use of host-government-subsidized loans complicates both capital structure and the parent's ability to determine an appropriate weighted average cost of capital for discounting purposes.
- Managers must evaluate political risk, because political events can drastically reduce the value or availability of expected cash flows.
- Terminal value is more difficult to estimate, because potential purchasers from the host, parent, or third countries, or from the private or public sector, may have widely divergent perspectives on the value to them of acquiring the project.

Because the same theoretical capital budgeting framework is used to choose among competing foreign and domestic projects, it is critical that we have a common standard. Thus all foreign complexities must be quantified as modifications to either expected cash flow or the rate of discount. Although in practice many firms make such modifications arbitrarily, readily available information, theoretical deduction, or just plain common sense can be used to make less arbitrary and more reasonable choices.

6.2 PROJECT VERSUS PARENT VALUATION

A strong theoretical argument exists in favor of analyzing any foreign project from the viewpoint of the parent. Cash flows to the parent are ultimately the basis for dividends to stockholders, reinvestment elsewhere in the world, repayment of corporate-wide debt, and other purposes that affect the firm's many interest groups. However, because most of a project's cash flows to its parent, or to sister subsidiaries, are financial cash flows rather than operating cash flows, the parent viewpoint usually violates a cardinal concept of capital budgeting; namely, that financial cash flows should not be mixed with operating cash flows. Often the difference is not important, because the two are almost identical, but in some instances a sharp divergence in these cash flows will exist. For example, funds that are permanently blocked from repatriation, or "forcibly reinvested," are not available for dividends to the stockholders or for repayment of parent corporate debt. Therefore shareholders will not perceive the blocked earnings as contributing to the value of the firm, and creditors will not count on them in calculating interest coverage ratios and other evidence of ability to service debt.

Evaluation of a project from the local viewpoint serves some useful purposes, but it should be subordinated to evaluation from the parent's viewpoint. In evaluating a foreign project's performance relative to the potential of a competing project in the same host country, we must pay attention to the project's local return. Almost any project should at least be able to earn a cash return equal to the yield available on host government bonds with a maturity the same as the project's economic life, if a free market exists for such bonds. Host government bonds ordinarily reflect the local risk-free rate of return, including a premium equal to the expected rate of inflation. If a project cannot earn more than such a bond yield, the parent firm should buy host government bonds rather than invest in a riskier project—or, better yet, invest somewhere else!

Multinational firms should invest only if they can earn a risk-adjusted return greater than locally based competitors can earn on the same project. If they are unable to earn superior returns on foreign projects, their stockholders would be better off buying shares in local firms, where possible, and letting those companies carry out the local projects. Apart from these theoretical arguments, surveys over the past 35 years show that in practice multinational firms continue to evaluate foreign investments from both the parent and project viewpoint.

The attention paid to project returns in various surveys probably reflects emphasis on maximizing reported consolidated net earnings per share as a corporate financial goal. As long as foreign earnings are not blocked, they can be consolidated with the earnings of both the remaining subsidiaries and the parent. As mentioned previously, U.S. firms must consolidate foreign *subsidiaries* that are 50% or more owned. If a firm is owned between 20% and 49% by a parent, it is called an *affiliate*. Affiliates are consolidated with the parent owner on a pro rata basis. Subsidiaries less than 20% owned are normally carried as unconsolidated investments. Even in the case of temporarily blocked funds, some of the most mature MNEs do not necessarily eliminate a project from financial consideration. They take a very long-run view of world business opportunities.

If reinvestment opportunities in the country where funds are blocked are at least equal to the parent firm's required rate of return (after adjusting for anticipated exchange rate changes), temporary blockage of transfer may have little practical effect on the capital budgeting outcome, because future project cash flows will be increased by the returns on forced reinvestment. Because large multinationals hold a portfolio of domestic and foreign projects, corporate liquidity is not impaired if a few projects have blocked funds; alternate sources of funds are available to meet all planned uses of funds. Furthermore, a long-run historical perspective on blocked funds does indeed lend support to the belief that funds are almost never permanently blocked. However, waiting for the release of such funds can be frustrating, and sometimes the blocked funds lose value while blocked because of inflation or unexpected exchange rate deterioration, even though they have been reinvested in the host country to protect at least part of their value in real terms.

In conclusion, most firms appear to evaluate foreign projects from both parent and project viewpoints. The parent's viewpoint gives results closer to the traditional meaning of net present value in capital budgeting. Project valuation provides a closer approximation of the effect on consolidated earnings per share, which all surveys indicate is of major concern to practicing managers. To illustrate the foreign complexities of multinational capital budgeting, we analyze a hypothetical market-seeking foreign direct investment by Cemex in Indonesia.

6.3   ILLUSTRATIVE CASE: CEMEX ENTERS INDONESIA[1]

It is early in 1998. Cementos Mexicanos, or Cemex, is considering the construction of a cement manufacturing facility on the Indonesian island of Sumatra. The project, Semen Indonesia (the Indonesian word for "cement" is *semen*), would be a wholly owned greenfield investment with a total installed capacity of 20 million metric tons per year (mmt/y). Although that is large by Asian production standards, Cemex believes that its latest cement manufacturing technology would be most efficiently utilized with a production facility of this scale.

Cemex has three driving reasons for the project: (1) the firm wishes to initiate a productive presence of its own in Southeast Asia, a relatively new market for Cemex; (2) the long-term prospects for Asian infrastructure development and growth appear very good over the longer term; and (3) there are positive prospects for Indonesia to act as a produce-for-export site as a result of the depreciation of the Indonesian rupiah (Rp) in 1997.

Cemex, the world's third-largest cement manufacturer, is an MNE headquartered in an emerging market but competing in a global arena. The firm competes in the global marketplace for both market share and capital. The international cement market, like markets in other commodities such as oil, is a dollar-based market. For this reason, and for comparisons against its major competitors in both Germany and Switzerland, Cemex considers the U.S. dollar to be its functional currency.

Cemex's shares are listed in both Mexico City and New York (OTC: CMXSY). The firm has successfully raised capital—both debt and equity—outside Mexico in U.S. dollars. Its investor base is increasingly global, with the U.S. share turnover rising rapidly as a percentage of total trading. As a result, its cost and availability of capital are internationalized and dominated by U.S. dollar investors. Ultimately, the Semen Indonesia project will be evaluated—in both cash flows and capital cost—in U.S. dollars.

Overview

A roadmap of the complete multinational capital budgeting analysis for Cemex in Indonesia is illustrated in Figure 6-1. The basic principle is that, starting at the top left, the parent company invests U.S. dollar—denominated capital, which flows clockwise through the creation and operation of an Indonesian subsidiary, which then generates cash flows that are eventually returned in a variety of forms to the parent company—in U.S. dollars. The first step is to construct a set of

FIGURE 6-1
A Roadmap to the Construction of Semen Indonesia's Capital Budget.

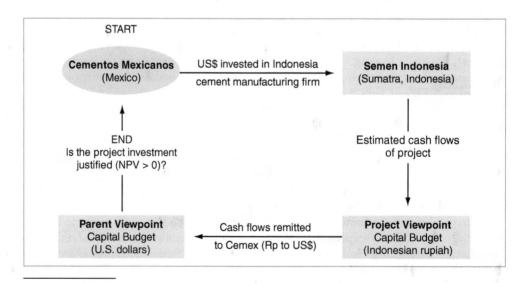

[1]Cemex is a real company; the greenfield investment described here is hypothetical.

pro forma financial statements for Semen Indonesia, all in Indonesian rupiah (Rp). The next step is to create two capital budgets: the project viewpoint and the parent viewpoint.

Semen Indonesia will take only one year to build the plant, with actual operations commencing in year 1. The Indonesian government has only recently deregulated the heavier industries to allow foreign ownership. The following analysis is conducted assuming that purchasing power parity (PPP) holds for the Rp/US$ exchange rate for the life of the Indonesian project. This is a standard financial assumption made by Cemex for its foreign investments. The projected inflation rates for Indonesia and the United States are 30% per annum and 3% per annum, respectively.

If we assume an initial spot rate of Rp10,000/US$, and Indonesian and U.S. inflation rates of 30% and 3% per annum, respectively, for the life of the project, forecasted spot exchange rates follow the usual PPP calculation. For example, the forecasted exchange rate for year 1 of the project would be:

$$\text{Spot rate (year 1)} = \text{Rp10,000/US\$} \times \frac{1 + 0.30}{1 + 0.03} = \text{Rp12,621/US\$}$$

Financial Assumptions

The series of financial statements in this section is based on these assumptions.

CAPITAL INVESTMENT Although the cost of building new cement manufacturing capacity anywhere in the industrial countries was estimated at roughly $150/ton of installed capacity, Cemex believed that it could build a state-of-the-art production and shipment facility in Sumatra at roughly $110/ton (see Table 6-1). Assuming a 20 million metric tons per year capacity and a year 0 average exchange rate of Rp10,000/$, this cost will constitute an investment of

TABLE 6-1

Investment and Financing of the Semen Indonesia Project (all values in 000s unless otherwise noted).

Investment		Financing		
Average exchange rate, Rp/$	10,000	Equity	Rp 11,000,000,000	
Cost of installed capacity, $/ton	$110	Debt		
Installed capacity	20,000	Rupiah debt	2,750,000,000	
Investment in US$	$2,200,000	US$ debt, Rp	8,250,000,000	
Investment in rupiah	22,000,000,000	Total	Rp 22,000,000,000	
Plant and equipment, Rp	17,600,000,000			
Annual depreciation, Rp	1,760,000,000			
Costs Of Capital: Cemex				
Risk-free rate	6.000%	Cemex beta	1.500	
Credit premium	2.000%	Equity risk premium	7.000%	
Cost of debt	8.000%	Cost of equity	16.500%	
Cost of debt, after tax	5.200%	Percent equity	60%	
Percent debt	40%	WACC	11.980%	
Costs Of Capital: Semen Indonesia				
Risk-free rate	33.000%	Semen Indonesia beta	1.000	
Credit premium	2.000%	Equity risk premium	6.000%	
Cost of rupiah debt	35.000%	Cost of equity	40.000%	
Cost of US$ debt, after tax	5.200%	Percent equity	50%	
Cost of US$ debt (rupiah equivalent)	38.835%			
Cost of US$ debt, after tax (rup. equiv.)	27.184%			
Percent debt	50%	WACC	33.257%	

Note: Assumes corporate income tax rates of 35% and 30% in Mexico and Indonesia, respectively. The cost of the US$ loan is stated in rupiah terms assuming purchasing power parity and U.S. dollar and Indonesian rupiah inflation rates of 3% and 30%, respectively, throughout the subject period.

Rp22 trillion ($2.2 billion). This figure includes an investment of Rp17.6 trillion in plant and equipment, giving rise to an annual depreciation charge of Rp1.76 trillion if we assume a 10-year straight-line depreciation schedule. The relatively short depreciation schedule is one of the policies of the Indonesian tax authorities meant to attract foreign investment.

FINANCING This massive investment would be financed with 50% equity, all from Cemex, and 50% debt, 75% from Cemex and 25% from a bank consortium arranged by the Indonesian government. Cemex's own U.S. dollar–based weighted average cost of capital (WACC) was estimated at 11.98%. The WACC on a local Indonesian level in rupiah terms, for the project itself, was estimated at 33.257%. The details of this calculation are discussed later in this chapter.

The explicit debt structures, including repayment schedules, are presented in Table 6-2. The loan arranged by the Indonesian government, part of the government's economic development incentive program, is an eight-year loan, in rupiah, at 35% annual interest, fully amortizing. The interest payments are fully deductible against corporate tax liabilities.

The majority of the debt, however, is being provided by the parent company, Cemex. After raising the capital from its financing subsidiary, Cemex will relend the capital to Semen

TABLE 6-2 Semen Indonesia's Debt Service Schedules and Foreign Exchange Gains/Losses.

Spot rate (Rp/$)	10,000	12,621	15,930	20,106	25,376	32,028
Project year	*0*	*1*	*2*	*3*	*4*	*5*
Indonesian loan @ 35% for 8 years (millions of Rp)						
Loan principal	2,750,000					
Interest payment		(962,500)	(928,921)	(883,590)	(822,393)	(739,777)
Principal payment		(95,939)	(129,518)	(174,849)	(236,046)	(318,662)
Total payment		(1,058,439)	(1,058,439)	(1,058,439)	(1,058,439)	(1,058,439)
Cemex loan @ 10% for 5 years (millions of US$)						
Principal	825					
Interest payment		(82.5)	(69.0)	(54.1)	(37.8)	(19.8)
Principal payment		(135.1)	(148.6)	(163.5)	(179.9)	(197.8)
Total payment		(217.6)	(217.6)	(217.6)	(217.6)	(217.6)
Cemex loan converted to Rp at scheduled and current spot rates (millions of Rp):						
Scheduled at Rp10,000/$:						
Interest payment		(825,000)	(689,867)	(541,221)	(377,710)	(197,848)
Principal payment		(1,351,329)	(1,486,462)	(1,635,108)	(1,798,619)	(1,978,481)
Total payment		(2,176,329)	(2,176,329)	(2,176,329)	(2,176,329)	(2,176,329)
Actual (at current spot rate):						
Interest payment		(1,041,262)	(1,098,949)	(1,088,160)	(958,480)	(633,669)
Principal payment		(1,705,561)	(2,367,915)	(3,287,494)	(4,564,190)	(6,336,691)
Total payment		(2,746,823)	(3,466,864)	(4,375,654)	(5,522,670)	(6,970,360)
Cash flows in Rp on Cemex loan (millions of Rp):						
Total actual cash flows	8,250,000	(2,746,823)	(3,466,864)	(4,375,654)	(5,522,670)	(6,970,360)
IRR of cash flows	38.835%					
Foreign exchange losses on Cemex loan (millions of Rp):						
Foreign exchange losses on interest		(216,262)	(409,082)	(546,940)	(580,770)	(435,821)
Foreign exchange losses on principal		(354,232)	(881,453)	(1,652,385)	(2,765,571)	(4,358,210)
Total foreign exchange losses on debt		(570,494)	(1,290,535)	(2,199,325)	(3,346,341)	(4,794,031)

Note: The loan by Cemex to the Indonesian subsidiary is denominated in U.S. dollars. The loan will therefore have to be repaid in U.S. dollars, not rupiah. At the time of the loan agreement, the spot exchange rate is Rp10,000/$. This is the assumption used in calculating the "scheduled" repaying of principal and interest in rupiah. The rupiah, however, is expected to depreciate in line with purchasing power parity. As it is repaid, the "actual" exchange rate will therefore give rise to a foreign exchange loss as it takes more and more rupiah to acquire U.S. dollars for debt service, both principal and interest. The foreign exchange losses on this debt service will be recognized on the Indonesian income statement.

Indonesia. The loan is denominated in U.S. dollars, at five years maturity, with an annual interest rate of 10%. Because the debt will have to be repaid from the rupiah earnings of the Indonesian enterprise, the pro forma financial statements are constructed so that the expected costs of servicing the dollar debt are included in the firm's pro forma income statement. The dollar loan, if the rupiah follows the purchasing power parity forecast, will have an effective interest expense in rupiah terms of 38.835%. We find this rate by determining the internal rate of return of repaying the dollar loan in full in rupiah (see Table 6-2).

REVENUES   Given that the existing cement manufacturing in Indonesia is depressed, all sales are based on export. The 20 mmt/y facility is expected to operate at only 40% capacity (producing 8 million metric tons). Cement produced will be sold in the export market at $58/ton (delivered). Note also that, at least for the conservative baseline analysis, we assume no increase in the price received over time.

COSTS   The cash costs of cement manufacturing (labor, materials, power, etc.) are estimated at Rp115,000 per ton for 1999, rising at about the rate of inflation, 30% per year. Additional production costs of Rp20,000 per ton for year 1 are also assumed to rise at the rate of inflation. As a result of all production being exported, loading costs of $2.00/ton and shipping of $10.00/ton must also be included. Note that these costs are originally stated in U.S. dollars, and for the purposes of Semen Indonesia's income statement, they must be converted to rupiah terms. This is the case because both ship-loading and shipping costs are international services governed by contracts denominated in dollars. As a result, they are expected to rise over time only at the U.S. dollar rate of inflation (3%).

Semen Indonesia's pro forma income statement is illustrated in Table 6-3. This is the typical financial statement measurement of the profitability of any business, whether domestic or international. The baseline analysis assumes a capacity utilization rate of only 40% (year 1), 50% (year 2), and 60% in the following years. Management believes this is necessary, because existing in-country cement manufacturers are averaging only 40% of capacity at this time.

Additional expenses in the pro forma financial analysis include license fees paid by the subsidiary to the parent company of 2.0% of sales, and general and administrative expenses for Indonesian operations of 8.0% per year (and growing an additional 1% per year). Foreign exchange gains and losses are those related to the servicing of the U.S. dollar—denominated debt provided by the parent and are drawn from the bottom of Table 6-2. In summary, the subsidiary operation is expected to begin turning an accounting profit in its third year of operations.

Project Viewpoint Capital Budget

The capital budget for the Semen Indonesia manufacturing project from a project viewpoint is shown in Table 6-4. We find the net cash flow, or *free cash flow* (FCF) as it is often called, by summing EBITDA (earnings before interest, taxes, depreciation, and amortization), recalculated taxes, and changes in net working capital (the sum of the net additions to receivables, inventories, and payables necessary to support sales growth).

Note that EBITDA, not EBT, is used in the capital budget, which contains both depreciation and interest expense. Depreciation and amortization are noncash expenses of the firm and therefore contribute positive cash flow. Because the capital budget creates cash flows that will be discounted to present value with a discount rate, and the discount rate includes the cost of debt—interest—we do not wish to subtract interest twice. Therefore, taxes are recalculated on the basis of EBITDA. (This issue highlights the distinction between an income statement and a capital budget. The project's income statement shows losses the first two years of operations as a result of interest expenses and forecast foreign exchange losses, so it is not expected to pay taxes. But the capital budget, constructed on the basis of EBITDA, before these financing and foreign exchange expenses, calculates a positive tax payment.) The firm's cost of capital used in discounting also includes the deductibility of debt interest in its calculation.

TABLE 6-3   Semen Indonesia's Pro Forma Income Statement (millions of rupiah).

Exchange Rate (Rp/$)	10,000	12,621	15,930	20,106	25,376	32,038
Project year	*0*	*1*	*2*	*3*	*4*	*5*
Sales volume		8,000	10,000	12,000	12,000	12,000
Sales price (US$)		58.00	58.00	58.00	58.00	58.00
Sales price (Rp)		732,039	923,933	1,166,128	1,471,808	1,857,627
Total revenue		5,856,311	9,239,325	13,993,541	17,661,751	22,291,530
Less cash costs		(920,000)	(1,495,000)	(2,332,200)	(3,031,860)	(3,941,418)
Less other production costs		(160,000)	(260,000)	(405,600)	(527,280)	(685,464)
Less loading costs		(201,942)	(328,155)	(511,922)	(665,499)	(865,149)
Less shipping costs		(1,009,709)	(1,640,777)	(2,559,612)	(3,327,495)	(4,325,744)
Total production costs		(2,291,650)	(3,723,932)	(5,809,334)	(7,552,134)	(9,817,774)
Gross profit		3,564,660	5,515,393	8,184,207	10,109,617	12,473,756
Gross margin		61%	60%	58%	57%	56%
Less license fees		(117,126)	(184,787)	(279,871)	(353,235)	(445,831)
Less general and administrative		(468,505)	(831,539)	(1,399,354)	(1,942,792)	(2,674,984)
EBITDA		2,979,029	4,499,067	6,504,982	7,813,589	9,352,941
Less depreciation and amortization		(1,760,000)	(1,760,000)	(1,760,000)	(1,760,000)	(1,760,000)
EBIT		1,219,029	2,739,067	4,744,982	6,053,589	7,592,941
Less interest on Cemex debt		(825,000)	(689,867)	(541,221)	(377,710)	(197,848)
Foreign exchange losses on debt		(570,494)	(1,290,535)	(2,199,325)	(3,346,341)	(4,794,031)
Less interest on local debt		(962,500)	(928,921)	(883,590)	(822,393)	(739,777)
EBT		(1,138,965)	(170,256)	1,120,846	1,507,145	1,861,285
Less income taxes (30%)		—	—	—	(395,631)	(558,386)
Net income		(1,138,965)	(170,256)	1,120,846	1,111,514	1,302,900
Net income (millions of US$)		(90)	(11)	56	44	41
Return on sales		−19%	−2%	8%	6%	6%

Note: EBITDA = earnings before interest, taxes, depreciation, and amortization; EBIT = earnings before interest and taxes; EBT = earnings before taxes. Tax credits resulting from current period losses are carried forward toward next year's tax liabilities. Dividends are not distributed in the first year of operations as a result of losses, and are distributed at a 50% rate in years 2000–2003. All calculations are exact, but may appear not to add due to reported decimal places and rounding. The tax payment for year 3 is zero, and year 4 is less than 30%, as a result of tax loss carry-forwards from previous years.

TABLE 6-4   Semen Indonesia's Capital Budget: Project Viewpoint (millions of rupiah).

Exchange Rate (Rp/$)	10,000	12,621	15,930	20,106	25,376	32,038
Project year	*0*	*1*	*2*	*3*	*4*	*5*
EBITDA		2,979,029	4,499,067	6,504,982	7,813,589	9,352,941
Less recalculated taxes		(893,709)	(1,349,720)	(1,951,495)	(2,344,077)	(2,805,882)
Net operating cash flow		2,085,320	3,149,347	4,553,487	5,469,512	6,547,059
Less additions to NWC		(240,670)	(139,028)	(436,049)	(289,776)	(626,314)
Initial investment	(22,000,000)					
Terminal value						19,686,451
Free cash flow (FCF)	(22,000,000)	1,844,650	3,010,319	4,117,438	5,179,736	25,607,196
NPV @ 33.257%	(9,443,538)					
IRR	15.4 %					

Note: NWC = net working capital. NPV = net present value. Discount rate is Semen Indonesia's WACC of 33.257%. IRR = internal rate of return, the rate of discount yielding an NPV of exactly zero. Values in exhibit are exact and are rounded to the nearest million.

The initial investment of Rp22 trillion is the total capital invested to support these earnings. Although receivables average 50 to 55 days sales outstanding (DSO) and inventories 65 to 70 DSO, payables and trade credit are also relatively long at 114 DSO in the Indonesian cement industry. Semen Indonesia expects to add approximately 15 net DSO to its investment with sales growth. The remaining elements to complete the project viewpoint's capital budget are the terminal value (discussed next) and the discount rate of 33.257% (the firm's WACC).

TERMINAL VALUE   The terminal value (TV) of the project represents the continuing value of the cement manufacturing facility in the years after year 5, the last year of the detailed pro forma financial analysis shown here. This value, like all asset values according to financial theory, is the present value of all future free cash flows that the asset is expected to yield. We calculate the TV as the present value of a perpetual net operating cash flow (NOCF) generated in the fifth year by Semen Indonesia, the growth rate assumed for that net operating cash flow (g), and the firm's weighted average cost of capital (k_{WACC}):

$$\text{Terminal value} = \frac{\text{NOCF}_5(1+g)}{k_{WACC} - g} = \frac{6{,}547{,}059(1+0)}{0.33257 - 0} = \text{Rp}19{,}686{,}451$$

or Rp19.686 trillion (Rp19,686,450,933,000). The assumption that g = 0—that is, that NOCFs will not grow past year 5—is probably not true, but it is a prudent assumption for Cemex to use when estimating future cash flows so far into the future.

The results of the capital budget from the project viewpoint indicate a negative net present value (NPV) of Rp9,443,538 million (or about Rp9.4 trillion) and an internal rate of return (IRR) of only 15.4% compared to the 33.257% cost of capital. These are the returns the project would yield to a local or Indonesian investor in Indonesian rupiah. The project, from this viewpoint, is not acceptable.

Repatriating Cash Flows to Cemex

Table 6-5 now collects all incremental earnings to Cemex from the prospective investment project in Indonesia. As described in the section preceding the case, a foreign investor's assessment of a project's returns depends on the actual cash flows that are returned to it, in its own currency. For Cemex, this means that the investment must be analyzed in terms of U.S. dollar cash inflows and outflows associated with the investment over the life of the project, after tax, discounted at its appropriate cost of capital.

We build this *parent viewpoint capital budget* in two steps. First, we isolate the individual cash flows, adjusted for any withholding taxes imposed by the Indonesian government and converted to U.S. dollars. (Statutory withholding taxes on international transfers are set by bilateral tax treaties, but individual firms may negotiate lower rates with governmental tax authorities. In the case of Semen Indonesia, dividends will be charged a 15% withholding tax, 10% interest payments, and 5% license fees.) Mexico does not tax repatriated earnings, as they have already been taxed in Indonesia. (The United States does levy a contingent tax on repatriated earnings of foreign source income. This is a complex calculation and is covered in Chapter 8.)

The second step, the actual parent viewpoint capital budget, combines these U.S. dollar after-tax cash flows with the initial investment to determine the net present value of the proposed Semen Indonesia subsidiary in the eyes (and pocketbook) of Cemex. This is illustrated in Table 6-5, which shows all incremental earnings to Cemex from the prospective investment project. A specific peculiarity of this parent viewpoint capital budget is that only the capital invested into the project by Cemex itself, $1,925 million, is included in the initial investment (the $1,100 million in equity and the $825 million loan). The Indonesian debt of Rp2.75 billion ($275 million) is not included in the Cemex parent viewpoint capital budget.

TABLE 6-5   Semen Indonesia's Remittance and Capital Budget: Parent Viewpoint (millions of rupiah and US$).

Exchange Rate (Rp/$)	10,000	12,621	15,930	20,106	25,376	32,038
Project year	*0*	*1*	*2*	*3*	*4*	*5*
Dividend Remittance						
Dividends paid (Rp)	—	—		560,423	555,757	651,450
Less withholding tax				(84,063)	(83,364)	(97,717)
Net dividend remitted (Rp)	—	—		476,360	472,393	553,732
Net dividend remitted (US$)	—	—		23.7	18.6	17.3
License Fees Remittance						
License fees remitted (Rp)		117,126	184,787	279,871	353,235	445,831
Less withholding tax		(5,856)	(9,239)	(13,994)	(17,662)	(22,292)
Net dividend remitted (Rp)		111,270	175,547	265,877	335,573	423,539
Net license fees remitted (US$)		8.8	11.0	13.2	13.2	13.2
Debt Service Remittance						
Promised interest paid (US$)		82.5	69.0	54.1	37.8	19.8
Less withholding tax @ 10%		(8.25)	(6.90)	(5.41)	(3.78)	(1.98)
Net interest remitted (US$)		74.25	62.09	48.71	33.99	17.81
Principal payments remitted (US$)		135.1	148.6	163.5	179.9	197.8
Capital Budget: Parent Viewpoint (Millions of US$)						
Dividends		—	—	23.7	18.6	17.3
License fees		8.8	11.0	13.2	13.2	13.2
Debt service		209.4	210.7	212.2	213.9	215.7
Total earnings		218.2	221.8	249.1	245.7	246.2
Initial investment	(1,925.0)					
Terminal value						614.7
Free cash flow (FCF)	(1,925.0)	218.2	221.8	249.1	245.7	860.8
NPV @ 17.98%	(925.6)					
IRR	−1.84 %					

Note: NPV calculated using a company-determined discount rate of WACC + foreign investment premium, or 11.98% + 6.00% = 17.98%.

Parent Viewpoint Capital Budget

Finally, all cash flow estimates are now constructed to form the parent viewpoint's capital budget, detailed in Table 6-5. The cash flows generated by Semen Indonesia from its Indonesian operations, dividends, license fees, debt service payments, and terminal value are now valued in U.S. dollar terms after tax.

In order to evaluate the project's cash flows that are returned to the parent company, Cemex must discount these at the corporate cost of capital. Remembering that Cemex considers its functional currency to be the U.S. dollar, it calculates its cost of capital in U.S. dollars. The customary weighted average cost of capital formula is as follows:

$$k_{WACC} = k_e \frac{E}{V} + k_d(1-t)\frac{D}{V}$$

where

k_e = risk-adjusted cost of equity
k_d = before-tax cost of debt

t = marginal tax rate
E = market value of the firm's equity
D = market value of the firm's debt
V = total market value of the firm's securities (E + D)

Cemex's cost of equity is calculated using the capital asset pricing model (CAPM):

$$k_e = k_{rf} + (k_m - k_{rf})\beta_{Cemex} = 6.00\% + (13.00\% - 6.00\%)1.5 = 16.50\%$$

where

k_e = risk-adjusted cost of equity
k_{rf} = risk-free rate of interest (U.S. Treasury intermediate bond yield)
k_m = expected rate of return in U.S. equity markets (large stock)
β_{Cemex} = measure of Cemex's individual risk relative to the market

The calculation assumes the current risk-free rate to be 6.00%, the expected return on U.S. equities to be 13.00%, and Cemex's beta to be 1.5. The result is a cost of equity—required rate of return on equity investment in Cemex—of 16.50%.

The investment will be funded internally by the parent company, roughly in the same debt/equity proportions as the consolidated firm: 40% debt (D/V) and 60% equity (E/V). The current cost of debt for Cemex is 8.00%, and the effective tax rate is 35%. The cost of equity, when combined with the other components, results in a weighted average cost of capital for Cemex of:

$$k_{WACC} = k_e\frac{E}{V} + k_d(1-t)\frac{D}{V} = (16.50\%)(0.60) + (8.00\%)(1 - 0.35)(0.40) = 11.98\%$$

Cemex customarily uses this weighted average cost of capital of 11.98% to discount prospective investment cash flows for project ranking purposes. The Indonesian investment poses a variety of risks, however, which the typical domestic investment does not.

If Cemex were undertaking an investment of the same relative degree of risk as the firm itself, a simple discount rate of 11.98% might be adequate. Cemex, however, generally requires new investments to yield an additional 3% over the cost of capital for domestic investments, and 6% more for international projects. The discount rate for Semen Indonesia's cash flows repatriated to Cemex will therefore be discounted at 11.98% + 6.00%, or 17.98%. The project's baseline analysis indicates a negative NPV of US$925.6 million (IRR of –1.84%), which means that it is an unacceptable investment from the parent's viewpoint.

Most corporations require that new investments cover more than the cost of the capital employed in their undertaking. It is therefore not unusual for the firm to require a hurdle rate of 3% to 6% above its cost of capital in order to identify potential investments that will literally add value to stockholder wealth. A NPV of zero means the investment is "acceptable," but NPV values that exceed zero are literally the present value of wealth that is expected to be added to that of the firm and its shareholders. For foreign projects, as discussed previously, we must adjust for agency costs and foreign exchange risks and costs.

Sensitivity Analysis: Project Viewpoint Measurement

So far the project investigation team has used a set of "most likely" assumptions to forecast rates of return. It is now time to subject the most likely outcome to sensitivity analyses. The same probabilistic techniques are available to test the sensitivity of results to political and foreign exchange risks as are used to test sensitivity to business and financial risks. Many decision makers feel more uncomfortable about the necessity to guess probabilities for unfamiliar political and foreign exchange events than they do about guessing their own more familiar business or financial risks. Therefore it is more common to test sensitivity to political and foreign exchange risk by simulating what would happen to net present value and earnings under a variety of "what if" scenarios.

POLITICAL RISK   What if Indonesia should impose controls on the payment of dividends or license fees to Cemex? The impact of blocked funds on the rate of return from Cemex's perspective would depend on when the blockage occurs, what reinvestment opportunities exist for the blocked funds in Indonesia, and when the blocked funds would eventually be released to Cemex. We could simulate various scenarios for blocked funds and rerun the cash flow analysis in Table 6-5 to estimate the effect on Cemex's rate of return.

What if Indonesia should expropriate Semen Indonesia? The effect of expropriation would depend on the following five factors:

1. When the expropriation occurs, in terms of number of years after the business began operation.
2. How much compensation the Indonesian government will pay, and how long after expropriation the payment will be made.
3. How much debt is still outstanding to Indonesian lenders, and whether the parent, Cemex, will have to pay this debt because of its parental guarantee.
4. The tax consequences of the expropriation.
5. Whether the future cash flows are forgone.

Many expropriations eventually result in some form of compensation to the former owners. This compensation can come from a negotiated settlement with the host government or from payment of political risk insurance by the parent government. Negotiating a settlement takes time, and the eventual compensation is sometimes paid in installments over a further period of time. Thus the present value of the compensation is often much lower than its nominal value. Furthermore, most settlements are based on book value of the firm at the time of expropriation rather than the firm's market value.

Repayment of parent guaranteed local debt would usually receive first claim on any compensation funds paid. If Cemex had guaranteed Semen Indonesia's debt to Indonesian lenders, they would be paid before Cemex could receive any settlement funds. In fact, the settlement agreement would probably provide for this. Alternatively, Cemex might have refused to guarantee Semen Indonesia's debt, protecting itself in the case of an expropriation but probably causing Semen Indonesia to pay a higher rate of interest and making the subsidiary less profitable to its parent.

If no compensation agreement is negotiated, Semen Indonesia, as an independently incorporated subsidiary of Cemex, might default on its debt. Cemex would not be obligated for Semen Indonesia's own debt, lacking a parent guarantee. As a practical matter, this is likely to occur only when the subsidiary's debt is borrowed locally, as in the case of Semen Indonesia. If Semen Indonesia had borrowed from banks in Singapore, for instance, parent Cemex would feel an obligation to repay the debt even if it were not technically obligated.

The tax consequences of expropriation would depend on the timing and amount of capital loss recognized by Mexico. This loss would usually be based on the uncompensated book value of the Indonesian investment. The problem is that there is often some doubt as to when a write-off is appropriate for tax purposes, particularly if negotiations for a settlement drag on. In some ways a nice clear expropriation without hope of compensation, such as occurred in Cuba in the early 1960s, is preferred to a slow "bleeding death" in protracted negotiations. The former leads to an earlier use of the tax shield and a one-shot write-off against earnings, whereas the latter tends to depress earnings for years, as legal and other costs continue and no tax shelter is achieved.

FOREIGN EXCHANGE RISK   The project team assumed that the Indonesian rupiah would depreciate versus the U.S. dollar at the purchasing power parity "rate" (approximately 20.767% per year in the baseline analysis). What if the rate of rupiah depreciation were greater? Although this event would make the assumed cash flows to Cemex worth less in dollars, operating exposure analysis would be necessary to determine whether the cheaper rupiah made Semen Indonesia more competitive. For example, because Semen Indonesia's exports to Taiwan are denominated in U.S. dollars, a weakening of the rupiah versus the dollar could result in greater rupiah earnings from those export sales. This process serves to somewhat offset the imported components that Semen Indonesia purchases from the parent company that are also denominated in U.S. dollars. Semen Indonesia is representative of firms today that have both cash inflows and outflows denominated in foreign currencies, providing a partial natural hedge against currency movements.

What if the rupiah should appreciate against the dollar? The same kind of economic exposure analysis is needed. In this particular case, we might guess that the effect would be positive on both local sales in Indonesia and the value in dollars of dividends and license fees paid to Cemex by Semen Indonesia. Note, however, that an appreciation of the rupiah might lead to more competition within Indonesia from firms in other countries with now-lower cost structures, lessening Semen Indonesia's sales.

OTHER PROJECT SENSITIVITY VARIABLES The project rate of return to Cemex would also be sensitive to a change in the assumed terminal value, the capacity utilization rate, the size of the license fee paid by Semen Indonesia, the size of the initial project cost, the amount of working capital financed locally, and the tax rates in Indonesia and Mexico. Because some of these variables are within control of Cemex, it is still possible that the Semen Indonesia project could be improved in its value to the firm and become acceptable.

Sensitivity Analysis: Parent Viewpoint Measurement

When a foreign project is analyzed from the parent's point of view, the additional risk that stems from its "foreign" location can be measured in at least two ways: *adjusting the discount rates or adjusting the cash flows.*

ADJUSTING DISCOUNT RATES The first method is to treat all foreign risk as a single problem by adjusting the discount rate applicable to foreign projects relative to the rate used for domestic projects to reflect the greater foreign exchange risk, political risk, agency costs, asymmetric information, and other uncertainties perceived in foreign operations. However, adjusting the discount rate applied to a foreign project's cash flow to reflect these uncertainties does not penalize net present value in proportion either to the actual amount at risk or to possible variations in the nature of that risk over time. Combining all risks into a single discount rate may thus cause us to discard much information about the uncertainties of the future.

In the case of foreign exchange risk, changes in exchange rates have a potential effect on future cash flows because of operating exposure. The direction of the effect, however, can either decrease or increase net cash inflows, depending on where the products are sold and where inputs are sourced. To increase the discount rate applicable to a foreign project, on the assumption that the foreign currency might depreciate more than expected, ignores the possible favorable effect of a foreign currency depreciation on the project's competitive position. Increased sales volume might more than offset a lower value of the local currency. Such an increase in the discount rate also ignores the possibility that the foreign currency may appreciate (two-sided risk).

ADJUSTING CASH FLOWS In the second method, we incorporate foreign risks in adjustments to forecasted cash flows of the project. The discount rate for the foreign project is risk-adjusted only for overall business and financial risk, in the same manner as for domestic projects. Simulation-based assessment utilizes scenario development to estimate cash flows to the parent arising from the project over time under different alternative economic futures.

Certainty regarding the quantity and timing of cash flows in a prospective foreign investment is, to quote from *The Maltese Falcon*, the stuff that dreams are made of. Due to the complexity of economic forces at work in major investment projects, it is paramount that the analyst realize the subjectivity of the forecast cash flows. Humility in analysis is a valuable trait.

SHORTCOMINGS OF EACH   In many cases, however, neither adjusting the discount rate nor adjusting cash flows is optimal. For example, political uncertainties are a threat to the entire investment, not just the annual cash flows. Potential loss depends partly on the terminal value of the unrecovered parent investment, which will vary depending on how the project was financed, whether political risk insurance was obtained, and what investment horizon is contemplated. Furthermore, if the political climate were expected to be unfavorable in the near future, any investment would probably be unacceptable. Political uncertainty usually relates to possible adverse events that might occur in the more distant future, but that cannot be foreseen at the present. Adjusting the discount rate for political risk thus penalizes early cash flows too heavily while not penalizing distant cash flows enough.

REPERCUSSIONS TO THE INVESTOR   Apart from anticipated political and foreign exchange risks, MNEs sometimes worry that taking on foreign projects may increase the firm's overall cost of capital because of investors' perceptions of foreign risk. This worry seemed reasonable if a firm had significant investments in Iraq, Iran, Russia, Serbia, or Afghanistan in the 1990s. However, the argument loses persuasiveness when applied to diversified foreign investments with a heavy balance in the industrial countries of Canada, Western Europe, Australia, Latin America, and Asia where, in fact, the bulk of FDI is located. These countries have a reputation for treating foreign investments by consistent standards, and empirical evidence confirms that a foreign presence in these countries may not increase the cost of capital. In fact, some studies indicate that required returns on foreign projects may even be lower than those for domestic projects.

MNE PRACTICES   Surveys of MNEs over the past 35 years have shown that about half of them adjust the discount rate and half adjust the cash flows. One recent survey indicated a rising use of adjusting discount rates over adjusting cash flows. However, the survey also indicated an increasing use of multifactor methods—discount rate adjustment, cash flow adjustment, real options analysis, and qualitative criteria—in evaluating foreign investments.[2]

Portfolio Risk Measurement

The field of finance has distinguished two definitions of risk: (1) the risk of the individual security (standard deviation of expected return) and (2) the risk of the individual security as a component of a portfolio (*beta*). A foreign investment undertaken in order to enter a local or regional market—*market-seeking*—will have returns that are more or less correlated with those of the local market. A portfolio-based assessment of the investment's prospects would then seem appropriate. A foreign investment undertaken for *resource-seeking* or *production-seeking* purposes may have returns related to those of the parent company or units located somewhere else in the world and have little to do with local markets. Cemex's proposed investment in Semen Indonesia is both *market-seeking* and *production-seeking* (for export). The decision about which approach is to be used by the MNE in evaluating prospective foreign investments may be the single most important analytical decision it makes. An investment's acceptability may change dramatically from one criteria to the other.

For comparisons within the local host country, we should overlook a project's actual financing or parent-influenced debt capacity, because these would probably be different for local investors than they are for a multinational owner. In addition, the risks of the project to local investors might differ from those perceived by a foreign multinational owner because of the opportunities an MNE has to take advantage of market imperfections. Moreover, the local project

---

[2]Tom Keck, Eric Levengood, and Al Longfield, "Using Discounted Cash Flow Analysis in an International Setting: A Survey of Issues in Modeling the Cost of Capital," *Journal of Applied Corporate Finance*, Vol. 11, No. 3, Fall 1998, pp. 82–99.

may be only one out of an internationally diversified portfolio of projects for the multinational owner; if undertaken by local investors, it might have to stand alone without international diversification. Because diversification reduces risk, the MNE can require a lower rate of return than is required by local investors.

Thus the discount rate used locally must be a hypothetical rate based on a judgment as to what independent local investors would probably demand, were they to own the business. Consequently, application of the local discount rate to local cash flows provides only a rough measure of the value of the project as a standalone local venture, rather than an absolute valuation.

6.4   REAL OPTION ANALYSIS

The discounted cash flow (DCF) approach used in the valuation of Semen Indonesia—and capital budgeting and valuation in general—has long had its critics. Investments that have long lives, cash flow returns in later years, or higher levels of risk than those typical of the firm's current business activities are often rejected by traditional DCF financial analysis. More importantly, when MNEs evaluate competitive projects, traditional discounted cash flow analysis is typically unable to capture the *strategic options* that an individual investment option may offer. This lack has led to the development of real option analysis. *Real option analysis* is the application of option theory to capital budgeting decisions.

Real options is a different way of thinking about investment values. At its core, it is a cross between decision-tree analysis and pure option-based valuation. It is particularly useful for analyzing investment projects that will follow very different value paths at decision points in time where management decisions are made regarding project pursuit. This wide range of potential outcomes is at the heart of real option theory. These wide ranges of value are *volatilities*, the basic element of option pricing theory.

Real option valuation also allows us to analyze a number of managerial decisions that in practice characterize many major capital investment projects:

1. The option to defer
2. The option to abandon
3. The option to alter capacity
4. The option to start up or shut down (switching)

Real option analysis treats cash flows in terms of future value in a positive sense, whereas DCF treats future cash flows negatively (on a discounted basis). Real option analysis is a particularly powerful device when addressing potential investment projects with extremely long life spans, or investments that do not commence until future dates. Real option analysis acknowledges the way information is gathered over time to support decision making. Management learns from both active (searching it out) and passive (observing market conditions) knowledge gathering and then uses this knowledge to make better decisions. The mini-case that follows illustrates an application of real option analysis.

SUMMARY

- The proposed greenfield investment in Indonesia by Cemex was analyzed within the traditional capital budgeting framework (base case).
- Foreign complications, including foreign exchange and political risks, were introduced to the analysis.

- Parent cash flows must be distinguished from project cash flows. Each of these two types of flows contributes to a different view of value.
- Parent cash flows often depend on the form of financing. Thus cash flows cannot be clearly separated from financing decisions, as is done in domestic capital budgeting.
- Additional cash flows generated by a new investment in one foreign subsidiary may be in part or wholly taken away from another subsidiary, with the net result that the project is favorable from a single subsidiary point of view but contributes nothing to worldwide cash flows.
- Remittance of funds to the parent must be explicitly recognized because of differing tax systems, legal and political constraints on the movement of funds, local business norms, and differences in how financial markets and institutions function.
- Cash flows from subsidiaries to parent can be generated by an array of nonfinancial payments, including payment of license fees and payments for imports from the parent.
- Differing rates of national inflation must be anticipated because of their importance in causing changes in competitive position and thus cash flows over a period of time.
- A foreign project's capital budgeting analysis should be adjusted for potential foreign exchange and/or political risks associated with the investment.
- A number of alternative methods are used for adjusting for risk, including adding an additional risk premium to the discount factor used, decreasing expected cash flows, and conducting detailed sensitivity and scenario analysis on expected project outcomes.
- Real option is a different way of thinking about investment values. At its core, it is a cross between decision-tree analysis and pure option-based valuation.
- Real option valuation also allows us to evaluate the option to defer, the option to abandon, the option to alter capacity, and the option to start up or shut down a project.

QUESTIONS

1. **Capital budgeting theoretical framework.** Capital budgeting for a foreign project uses the same theoretical framework as domestic capital budgeting. What are the basic steps in domestic capital budgeting?

2. **Foreign complexities.** Capital budgeting for a foreign project is considerably more complex than for a domestic project. What are the factors that add complexity?

3. **Project versus parent valuation.**

   a. Why should a foreign project be evaluated from both a project and a parent viewpoint?

   b. Which viewpoint, project or parent, gives results closer to the traditional meaning of net present value in capital budgeting?

   c. Which viewpoint gives results closer to the effect on consolidated earnings per share?

4. **Cash flow.** Capital projects provide both operating cash flows and financial cash flows. Why are operating cash flows preferred for domestic capital budgeting but financial cash flows given major consideration in international projects?

5. **Risk-adjusted return.** Should the anticipated internal rate of return (IRR) for a proposed foreign project be compared to (a) alternative home country proposals, (b) returns earned by local companies in the same industry and/or risk class, or (c) both of the above? Justify your answer.

6. **Blocked cash flows.** In the context of evaluating foreign investment proposals, how should a multinational firm evaluate cash flows in the host foreign country that are blocked from being repatriated to the firm's home country?

7. **Host country inflation.** How should an MNE factor host country inflation into its evaluation of an investment proposal?

8. **Cost of equity.** A foreign subsidiary does not have an independent cost of capital. However, in order to estimate the discount rate for a comparable host country firm, the analyst should try to calculate a hypothetical cost of capital. As part of this process, the analyst can estimate the subsidiary's proxy cost of equity by using the traditional equation: $k_e = k_{rf} + \beta(k_m - k_{rf})$. Define each variable in this equation and explain how the variable might be different for a proxy host country firm compared to the parent MNE.

9. **Viewpoints.** What are the differences in the cash flows used in a project point of view analysis and a parent point of view analysis?

10. **Foreign exchange risk.** How is foreign exchange risk sensitivity factored into the capital budgeting analysis of a foreign project?

11. **Expropriation risk.** How is expropriation risk factored into the capital budgeting analysis of a foreign project?

12. **Real option analysis.** What is real option analysis? How is it a better method of making investment decisions than traditional capital budgeting analysis?

PROBLEMS

1. **Sarasota Corporation.** Sarasota Corporation (U.S.) expects to receive cash dividends from a French joint venture over the coming three years. The first dividend, to be paid December 31, 2004, is expected to be €720,000. The dividend is then expected to grow 10.0% per year over the following two years. The current exchange rate (December 30, 2003) is $1.25/€. Sarasota's weighted average cost of capital is 12%.

   a. What is the present value of the expected euro dividend stream if the euro is expected to appreciate 4.00% per annum against the dollar?

   b. What is the present value of the expected dividend stream if the euro were to depreciate 3.00% per annum against the dollar?

2. **Trefica de Honduras.** Texas Pacific, a U.S.-based private equity firm, is trying to determine what it should pay for a tool manufacturing firm in Honduras named Trefica. Texas Pacific estimates that Trefica will generate a free cash flow of 13 million Honduran lempiras (Lp) next year, and that this free cash flow will continue to grow at a constant rate of 8.0% per annum indefinitely.

   A private equity firm like Texas Pacific, however, is not interested in owning a company for long, and plans to sell Trefica at the end of three years for approximately 10 times Trefica's free cash flow in that year. The current spot exchange rate is Lp14.80/$, but the Honduran inflation rate is expected to remain at a relatively high rate of 16.0% per annum compared to the U.S. dollar inflation rate of only 2.0% per annum. Texas Pacific expects to earn at least a 20% annual rate of return on international investments like Trefica.

   a. What would Trefica be worth if the Honduran lempira were to remain fixed over the three-year investment period?

   b. What would Trefica be worth if the Honduran lempira were to change in value over time according to purchasing power parity?

3. **Baltimore Tile Company.** Baltimore Tile Company (U.S.) is considering investing Rs 50,000,000 in India to create a wholly owned tile manufacturing plant to export to the European market. After five years the subsidiary would be sold to Indian investors for

Rs 100,000,000. A pro forma income statement for the Indian operation predicts the generation of Rs 7,000,000 of annual cash flow, as follows:

Annual sales revenue	Rs 30,000,000
Less cash operating expenses	– 17,000,000
Less depreciation	– 1,000,000
Income before interest and taxes	Rs 12,000,000
Less Indian taxes at 50%	– 6,000,000
Net income	Rs 6,000,000
Add back depreciation	+ 1,000,000
Annual cash flow	Rs 7,000,000

The initial investment will be made on December 31, 2002, and cash flows will occur on December 31 of each succeeding year. Annual cash dividends to Baltimore Tile from India will equal 75% of accounting income.

The U.S. corporate tax rate is 40% and the Indian corporate tax rate is 50%. Because the Indian tax rate is greater than the U.S. tax rate, annual dividends paid to Baltimore Tile will not be subject to additional taxes in the United States. There are no capital gains taxes on the final sale. Baltimore Tile uses a weighted average cost of capital of 14% on domestic investments, but will add six percentage points for the Indian investment because of perceived greater risk. Baltimore Tile forecasts the rupee/dollar exchange rate for December 31 on the next six years to be

YEAR	EXCHANGE RATE	YEAR	EXCHANGE RATE
2002	Rs50.00/$	2005	Rs62.00/$
2003	Rs54.00/$	2006	Rs66.00/$
2004	Rs58.00/$	2007	Rs70.00/$

What is the net present value and internal rate of return on this investment?

4. Berkeley Devices. Berkeley Devices, Inc., manufactures design components for personal computers. Until now, manufacturing has been subcontracted to other companies, but for reasons of quality control, Berkeley Devices has decided to manufacture the components itself in Asia. Analysis has narrowed the choice to two possibilities; Penang in Malaysia and Manila in the Philippines. At the moment, only the following summary of expected, after-tax, cash flows is available. Although most operating outflows would be in Malaysian ringgit or Philippine pesos, some additional U.S. dollar cash outflows would be necessary, as shown.

BERKELEY IN PENANG	2002	2003	2004	2005	2006	2007
Net ringgit cash flows	(26,000)	8,000	6,800	7,400	9,200	10,000
Net dollar cash flows	—	(100)	(120)	(150)	(150)	—

BERKELEY IN MANILA	2002	2003	2004	2005	2006	2007
Net peso cash flows	(560,000)	190,000	180,000	200,000	210,000	200,000
Dollar cash outflows	—	(100)	(200)	(300)	(400)	—

The Malaysia ringgit currently trades at RM3.80/$ and the Philippine peso trades at Rs 50.00/$. Berkeley expects the Malaysian ringgit to appreciate 2.0% per year against the dollar and the Philippine peso to depreciate 5.0% per year against the dollar. If the weighted average cost of capital for Berkeley Devices is 14.0%, which project looks most promising?

5. **Superior Machine Oil Company.** Privately owned Superior Machine Oil Company is considering investing in the Czech Republic so as to have a refinery source closer to its European customers. The original investment in Czech korunas would amount to K250 million, or $7,692,308 at the current spot rate of K32.50/$, all in fixed assets, which will be depreciated over 10 years by the straight-line method. An additional K100,000,000 will be needed for working capital.

For capital budgeting purposes, Superior assumes sale as a going concern at the end of the third year, at a price (after all taxes) equal to the net book value of fixed assets alone (not including working capital). All free cash flow will be repatriated to the United States as soon as possible. In evaluating the venture, Superior uses the following U.S. dollar forecasts:

END OF YEAR	UNIT DEMAND	UNIT SALES PRICE	EXCHANGE RATE (KORUNAS/$)	FIXED CASH OPERATING EXPENSES	DEPRECIATION
0			32.5		
1	700,000	$10.00	30.0	$1,000,000	$500,000
2	900,000	10.30	27.5	1,030,000	500,000
3	1,000,000	10.60	25.0	1,060,000	500,000

Variable manufacturing costs are expected to be 50% of sales. No additional funds need be invested in the U.S. subsidiary during the period under consideration. The Czech Republic imposes no restrictions on repatriation of any funds of any sort. The Czech corporate tax rate is 25% and the U.S. rate is 40%. Both countries allow a tax credit for taxes paid in other countries. Superior uses 18% as its weighted average cost of capital, and its objective is to maximize present value. Is the investment attractive to Superior?

6. **Tostadas de Baja, S.A.** Tostadas de Baja, S.A., located in the state of Baja California, Mexico, manufactures frozen Mexican food, which enjoys a large following in the U.S. states of California and Arizona to the north. In order to be closer to its U.S. market, Tostadas de Baja is considering moving some of its manufacturing operations to southern California. Operations in California would begin in 2003 and have the following attributes:

a. The 2003 sales price in the United States would average $5.00 per package, and prices would increase 3.0% per annum.

b. 2003 production and sales would be 1 million packets. Unit sales would grow at 10.0% per annum through 2004 and then stabilize forever.

c. Production costs are estimated at $4.00 per packet in 2003, and would increase by 4.0% per year.

d. General and administration expenses would be $100,000 per year, and depreciation expenses were estimated at a constant $80,000 per year.

e. Tostadas de Baja has assigned a weighted average cost of capital of 16.0% to the project.

f. Tostadas de Baja will assign an after-tax value to its California plant at the end of 2005 equal to an infinite stream of 2005 dividends, discounted at 20% per annum. The higher discount rate is because the company is concerned about the political risk of a Mexican firm manufacturing in California.

g. All production is for sale (production volume equals sales volume), and all sales are for cash.

h. Combined federal and state tax rate in the United States is 30%; Mexico's is 25%.

i. Actual and expected exchange rates, by year, are:

2002: Ps8.00/$ 2004: Ps10.00/$

2003: Ps9.00/$ 2005: Ps11.00/$

j. Tostadas de Baja will remit 80.0% of its reported profits each period back to the parent company as an annual cash dividend.

What is the maximum U.S. dollar cost that Tostadas de Baja can afford in 2002 for the investment?

Santa Clara Electronics. Use the following problem and assumptions to answer questions 7 through 10.

Santa Clara Electronics, Inc., of California exports 24,000 sets of low-density lightbulbs per year to Argentina under an import license that expires in five years. In Argentina, the lightbulbs are sold for the Argentine peso equivalent of $60 per set. Direct manufacturing costs in the United States and shipping together amount to $40 per set. The market for this type of bulb in Argentina is stable, neither growing nor shrinking, and Santa Clara holds the major portion of the market.

The Argentine government has invited Santa Clara to open a manufacturing plant so that imported bulbs can be replaced by locally produced bulbs. If Santa Clara makes the investment, it will operate the plant for five years and then sell the building and equipment to Argentine investors at net book value at the time of sale plus the value of any net working capital. (Net working capital is the amount of current assets less any portion financed by local debt.) Santa Clara will be allowed to repatriate all net income and depreciation funds to the United States each year. Santa Clara traditionally evaluates all foreign investments in U.S. dollar terms.

- *Investment.* Santa Clara's anticipated cash outlay in U.S. dollars in 2003 would be:

Building and equipment	*$1,000,000*
Net working capital	*1,000,000*
Total investment	*$2,000,000*

All investment outlays will be made in 2003, and all operating cash flows will occur at the end of years 2004 through 2008.

- *Depreciation and investment recovery.* *Building and equipment will be depreciated over five years on a straight-line basis. At the end of the fifth year, the $1,000,000 of net working capital may also be repatriated to the United States, as may the remaining net book value of the plant.*

- *Sale price of bulbs.* *Locally manufactured bulbs will be sold for the Argentine peso equivalent of $60 per set.*

- *Operating expenses per set of bulbs.* *Material purchases are as follows:*

Materials purchased in Argentina	
(U.S. dollar equivalent)	*$20 per set*
Materials imported from	
Santa Clara	*+$10 per set*
Total variable costs	*$30 per set*

- *Transfer prices.* *The $10 transfer price per set for raw material sold by the parent consists of $5 of direct and indirect costs incurred in the United States on their manufacture, creating $5 of pretax profit to Santa Clara.*

- *Taxes.* *The corporate income tax rate is 40% in Argentina and in the United States (combined federal and state/province). There are no capital gains taxes on the future sale of the Argentine subsidiary, either in Argentina or in the United States.*

- *Discount rate.* *Santa Clara Electronics uses a 15% discount rate to evaluate all domestic and foreign projects.*

7. **Santa Clara Electronics: Baseline analysis.** Evaluate the proposed investment in Argentina by Santa Clara Electronics (U.S.). Santa Clara's management wishes the baseline analysis to be performed in U.S. dollars (and implicitly also assumes that the exchange rate remains fixed throughout the life of the project). Create a project viewpoint capital budget and a parent viewpoint capital budget. What do you conclude from your analysis?

8. **Santa Clara Electronics: Revenue growth scenario.** As a result of their analysis in the previous question, Santa Clara wishes to explore the implications of being able to grow sales volume by 4% per year. Argentine inflation is expected to average 5% per year, so sales price and material cost increases of 7% and 6% per year, respectively, are thought reasonable. Although material costs in Argentina are expected to rise, U.S.-based costs are not expected to change over the five-year period. Evaluate this scenario for both the project and parent viewpoints. Under this revenue growth scenario, is the project acceptable?

9. **Santa Clara Electronics: Revenue growth and sales price scenario.** In addition to the assumptions employed in Problem 8, Santa Clara now wishes to evaluate the prospect of being able to sell the Argentine subsidiary at the end of year 5 at a multiple of the business's earnings in that year. Santa Clara believes that a multiple of 6 is a conservative estimate of the market value of the firm at that time. Evaluate the project and parent viewpoint capital budgets.

10. **Santa Clara Electronics: Revenue growth, sales price, and currency risk scenario.** One of the new analysts at Santa Clara, a recent business school graduate, believes that it is a fundamental error to evaluate the Argentine project's prospective earnings and cash flows in dollars, rather than first estimating their Argentine peso (Ps) value and then converting cash flow returns to the U.S. in dollars. She believes the correct method is to use the end-of-year spot rate in 2003 of Ps3.50/$ and assume that it will change in relation to purchasing power. (She is assuming U.S. inflation to be 1% per annum and Argentine inflation to be 5% per annum). She also believes that Santa Clara should use a risk-adjusted discount rate in Argentina that reflects Argentine capital costs (20% is her estimate) and a risk-adjusted discount rate for the parent viewpoint capital budget (18%), on the assumption that international projects in a risky currency environment should require a higher expected return than other, lower-risk projects. How do these assumptions and changes alter Santa Clara's perspective on the proposed investment?

INTERNET EXERCISES

1. **Capital projects and the EBRD.** The European Bank for Reconstruction and Development (EBRD) was established to "foster the transition towards open market-oriented economies and to promote private and entrepreneurial initiative in the countries of central and eastern Europe and the Commonwealth of Independent States (CIS) committed to and applying the principles of multiparty democracy, pluralism and market economics." Use the EBRD website to determine which projects and companies EBRD is currently undertaking.

   European Bank for Reconstruction and Development http://www.ebrd.org

2. **Emerging markets: China.** Long-term investment projects abroad such as electrical power generation require a thorough understanding of all attributes of doing business in that country. These include import/export restrictions, labor relations, supplier financing, tax rules, depreciation schedules, currency properties and restrictions, and sources of short-term and long-term debt, to name a few. China is currently the focus of investment and market penetration strategies of multinational firms worldwide. Using the Web (start with the sites listed), build a database on doing business in China, and prepare an update of many of the factors, such as average receivables outstanding and currency convertibility, discussed in this chapter.

Ministry of Foreign Trade and Economic Cooperation, PRC
http://www.chinamarket.com.cn/E

China Investment Trust & Investment Corporation
http://www.citic.com/english/index.asp

China Net Investment Pages
http://www.business-china.com/invest

SELECTED READINGS

Amram, Martha and Nalin Kulatilaka, "Strategy and Shareholder Value Creation: The Real Options Frontier,"*Journal of Applied Corporate Finance*, Vol. 13, No. 2, Summer 2000, pp. 15–28.

Brealey, Richard A., Ian A. Cooper, and Michael A. Habib, "Using Project Finance to Fund Infrastructure Investments," *Journal of Applied Corporate Finance*, Vol. 9, No. 5, Fall 1996, pp. 25–38.

Brounen, Dirk, Abe de Jong, and Kees Koedjik, "Corporate Finance in Europe: Confronting Theory with Practice," *Financial Management*, Vol. 33, No. 4, Winter 2004, pp. 71–101.

Damodaran, Aswath, "The Promise of Real Options," *Journal of Applied Corporate Finance*, Vol. 13, No. 2, Summer 2000, pp. 29–43.

Dixit, Avinash K., and Robert S. Pindyck, "The Options Approach to Capital Investment," *Harvard Business Review*, May/June 1995, pp. 105–115.

Godfrey, Stephen, and Ramon Espinosa, "A Practical Approach to Calculating the Cost of Equity for Investments in Emerging Markets," *Journal of Applied Corporate Finance*, Vol. 9, No. 3, Fall 1996, pp. 80–89.

Hodder, James E., Antonio S. Mello, and Gordon Sick, "Valuing Real Options: Can Risk-Adjusted Discounting Be Made to Work?" *Journal of Applied Corporate Finance*, Vol. 14, No. 2, Summer 2001, pp. 90–101.

Keck, Tom, Eric Levengood, and Al Longfield, "Using Discounted Cash Flow Analysis in an International Setting: A Survey of Issues in Modeling the Cost of Capital," *Journal of Applied Corporate Finance*, Vol. 11, No. 3, Fall 1998, pp. 82–99.

Luehrman, Timothy A., "What's It's Worth?: A General Manager's Guide to Valuation," *Harvard Business Review*, May 1997.

Luehrman, Timothy A., "Strategy as a Portfolio of Real Options," *Harvard Business Review*, September–October 1998, pp. 89–99.

MINICASE   CARLTON'S CHINESE MARKET ENTRY—AN APPLICATION OF REAL OPTION ANALYSIS

Carlton is evaluating the possibility of entering the Chinese market. The senior management team, headed by CEO Charles Darwin, has concluded from a number of preliminary studies (code named *Beagle*) performed by a consultant that within three to five years this market could well determine who the major players are to be in Carlton's telecommunications industry. The corporate finance team, headed by CFO Caitlin Kelly, has concluded a preliminary financial analysis of its own on the basis of the numbers presented by the consultants.

The results of the corporate finance team's expected value analysis were not, however, encouraging. As illustrated in Table A, the expected gross profits of the venture were estimated to be only $10 million.

- Revenues were expected to follow one of two paths— either high (approximately $130 million at a 50% probability) or low ($50 million at a 50% probability). Therefore, using expected value analysis, revenues were estimated to be $90 million.

- Costs were expected to be either high ($120 million), medium ($80 million), or low ($40 million), all with an equal 33.3% expected probability of occurrence. The expected value of costs were $80 million.

What made this $10 million gross profit all the more unattractive was that the market development group was requesting an additional $15 million for up-front research and development (R&D). This capital expense could not be justified. The expected total return on the project would then be a negative $5 million: ($15) + $ 10 = ($5). The

corporate finance team concluded that the project was not an acceptable investment in its present form.

Charles was clearly frustrated with the corporate finance team during the presentation of their results. After some heated debate over individual values, Charles asked what specifically would be learned if the added $15 million in market research and development were actually spent. Would it improve the expected profitability of the project?

After some additional analysis, the corporate finance team concluded that nothing significant would be learned about the market which would change either the probabilities or expected values of revenues. However, after the additional R&D expenditure, the team felt certain that the cost of operations would be better known.

Charles then asked the corporate finance team about an alternative approach to viewing the project.

What if the expenditure of $15 million were looked upon as the purchase of a call option on the project? What I mean is, if we spend the $15 million, we would then have the ability to identify the actual cost associated with undertaking the project? Even though we still would not really know the revenues—we still have business risk—we would be able to decide more intelligently whether to stop or proceed with the project at that point in time.

As illustrated in Figure A, after the investment (or expenditure) of the $15 million in market research and development, the firm would know which of the three cost paths it would be on—high, medium, or low. Regardless of

TABLE A   Carlton's Analysis of Chinese Market Entry.

REVENUES	VALUE (IN MILLIONS)	PROBABILITY	EXPECTED VALUE (IN MILLIONS)
High	$130	0.50	$65.00
Low	50	0.50	25.00
Expected value			$90.00
Costs			
High	$120	0.33	$40.00
Medium	80	0.33	26.67
Low	40	0.33	13.33
Expected value			$80.00

Expected project gross profit = revenues − costs = $90 − $80 = $10.

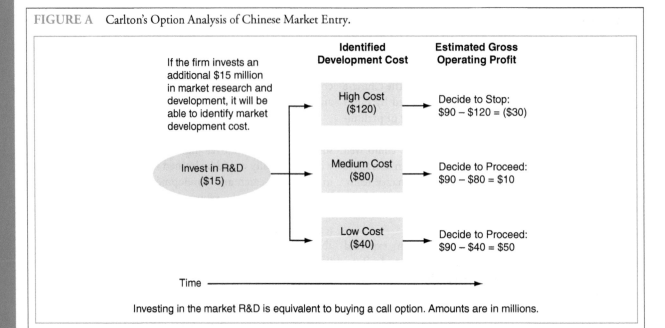

FIGURE A   Carlton's Option Analysis of Chinese Market Entry.

Investing in the market R&D is equivalent to buying a call option. Amounts are in millions.

the expected revenue, still assumed to be $90 million, the firm could make an intelligent choice to either stop or proceed at that point. This was, in Charles's opinion, a much more logical way to pursue the analysis.

Caitlin Kelly and her finance team, however, were still not convinced. Caitlin said, "But we would still be spending the $15 million up front and still be looking at the same expected outcomes. I don't see how your approach changes anything."

Charles continued, "It changes a lot. After spending the $15 million we would know—with added certainty— what the likely outcome would be. If it is either the medium- or low-cost path, we would proceed and end up with a gross operating profit of either $10 or $50 million, depending on revenues. If it is the high-cost path, we would stop all work immediately, before incurring additional operating costs. The expected value, at least according to my calculations, is a positive $20 million."

Expected value = ($15) + [(0.333 × $0)
+ (0.333 × $10) + (0.333 × $50)] = $20

It then dawned upon Caitlin what Charles was saying. The purchase of the call option, the expenditure of the $15 million, would allow Carlton to avoid the loss-making option (the high-cost path with an expected outcome of negative $30 million), so the high-cost path would enter the calculation of expected value as zero. The purchase of the call option would indeed allow Carlton to undertake the investment, if it wished, only after gaining additional time and knowledge.

Charles and the senior management team then concluded that they had won the argument (as senior management always does) and approved the project.

THE POTENTIAL OF REAL OPTION ANALYSIS
Real options analysis, like DCF and other investment analysis techniques, is nothing other than a tool. The two techniques are complementary. Management should employ both methods in the analysis of potential investments and gather information from both.

Unlike our example, real option analysis is not ordinarily a simple technique. There is an enormous amount of technical "comfort" required on the part of the analyst in order to implement the technique correctly. Like most techniques derived from financial theory, it is easily abused. Those who will utilize the information provided by real option analysis must be trained in the proper interpretation of its results.

But real option analysis is gaining in use and popularity. Consistent with the example of Carlton, it is often favored first by senior management, because it has two characteristics they like. Its structure acknowledges the time sequence of a project, describing cash inflows and outflows at different points in time. This structure is more consistent with the way management frequently sees a project unfold. Real option analysis also seems to value "management" by its very nature; it credits the ability of management to gain new information and make good business decisions at the points in time when those decisions must be made.

QUESTIONS

1. How does real option analysis differ from traditional expected value analysis?

2. How does real option analysis use information gathering differently from discounted cash flow analysis?

3. Recalculate both the expected return analysis and the real option analysis for the Chinese market entry assuming that the revenue probabilities were 25% high and 75% low. Is the project acceptable under either of the decision-making methodologies?

APPENDIX
ADJUSTING FOR RISK IN FOREIGN INVESTMENTS

In this chapter, Cemex added a 6% risk premium to its 11.98% domestic cost of capital when evaluating foreign investments. This addition resulted in an arbitrary 17.98% risk-adjusted cost of capital that was then used to calculate the expected rate of return on its proposed Semen Indonesia project from the parent firm's perspective. However, it is possible to design a more sophisticated calculation of the cost of capital that could be selectively risk-adjusted in order to evaluate investments in a variety of international markets, particularly emerging markets like Indonesia.

The risks associated with the prospective Indonesian investment can be subdivided into two-sided risks (symmetric risks) and one-sided risks.[1] *Symmetric risks* include operating risk, demand markets and pricing risk, and macroeconomic and macro political risks, risk components that can cause the cash flow returns of the investment to be higher or lower than generally expected (most likely). *One-sided risks* (those variables that are likely to result in decreased cash flows only from those expected) include expropriation, cross-border payment restrictions or prohibitions, political chaos, or upheaval. If the prospective Indonesian investment is to be evaluated on a risk-adjusted cost of capital basis, both symmetric and one-sided risks must be incorporated into Cemex's weighted-average cost of capital.

Risk-Adjusting Cemex's Cost of Capital

Cemex needs to adjust both its cost of debt and its cost of equity to reflect the additional risks posed by the Indonesian investment.[2]

Adjusting Debt Costs (Required Returns)

The simplest and most straightforward estimate of the risk premium on risks associated with debt in Indonesia is based on the Indonesian government's cost of borrowing U.S. dollars. The Indonesian government's risk premium would be that additional interest it pays to borrow U.S. dollars in the Eurobond market above that paid by the U.S. Treasury. Because both parties are committing to repayment in the same currency, U.S. dollars, the differential in their debt costs reflects the higher perceived risk associated with repayment of U.S. dollar-denominated debt by the government of Indonesia. These interest rate spreads are termed *sovereign spreads*.[3] Table 6A-1

---

[1] This approach follows that of the following sources: Stephen Godfrey and Ramon Espinosa, "A Practical Approach to Calculating Costs of Equity for Investments in Emerging Markets," *Journal of Applied Corporate Finance,* Vol. 9, No. 3 Fall 1996, pp. 80–89; and Donald R. Lessard, "Incorporating Country Risk in the Valuation of Offshore Projects," *Journal of Applied Corporate Finance,* Vol. 9, No. 3, Fall 1996, pp. 52–63.

[2] There are a number of alternative approaches to cost of capital calculations for international projects and investments. See, for example, ibbotson (http://www.ibbotson.com) or Harvey (http://www.duke.edu/_charvey/Country_risk).

[3] The sovereign spread used here is from J.P. Morgan for issues outstanding on August 30, 1996. Strangely, sovereign spreads are readily available for emerging market countries, but not for the majority of industrialized nations.

TABLE 6A-1   The Cost Borrowing U.S. Dollars by selected Emerging Market Countries (1996).

Country	(1) U.S. Treasury Cost of Funds (basis points)	(2) Country's Sovereign Spread (basis points)	(3) Country's U.S. Dollar Total Cost of Funds (basis points)	(3) Country's U.S. Dollar Total Cost of Funds (percent)
Argentina	600	718	1318	13.18
Brazil	600	610	1210	12.10
Indonesia	600	400	1000	10.00
Mexico	600	597	1197	11.97
Philippines	600	226	826	8.26
Venezuela	600	811	1411	14.11
United States	600	—	600	6.00

Source: Abstracted by authors from Lessard (1996), op. cit. Original data from J.P. Morgan and the International Finance Corporation's *Emerging Stock Markets Factbook*, 1996. Column (3) = column (1) + column (2).

illustrates sovereign spreads and U.S. dollar borrowing costs by a selected group of emerging market countries, including Indonesia.

The sovereign spread for Indonesia, according to Table 6A-1, is 400 basis points or 4.00%. The risk-free rate of interest applicable to Cemex's prospective Indonesian investment is then:

$$k_{rf}^{Indo} = k_{rf}^{US} + \text{(Indonesian sovereign spread)} = 6.00\% + 4.00\% = 10.00\%$$

If we assume that the project risk of Cemex's prospective Indonesian investment is the same as that of other investments by Cemex, we would add the same credit spread Cemex pays above the risk-free Treasury rate in the United States (200 basis points or 2.00%) to the risk-free rate in Indonesia. This yields a risk-adjusted cost of debt for Cemex's Indonesian investment of:[4]

$$k_d^{Indo} = k_{rf}^{Indo} + \text{(credit spread)} = 10.00\% + 2.00\% = 12.00\%$$

Although this cost appears at first glance to be prohibitively high, it does reflect current costs for high-grade Indonesian corporate borrowers in the Eurobond market. And again, this includes the risks associated with borrowing U.S. dollars (the sovereign risk premium) and the risks associated with the project (the credit risk premium).

Adjusting Equity Costs (Required Returns)

Adjusting the required return on equity is not quite as simple as adding a sovereign spread to an existing corporate cost of debt. Again using the capital asset pricing model as the theoretical foundation, we need to find what Lessard calls an offshore project beta. In our numerical example here, the *offshore project beta* attempts to measure the risk associated with a U.S.–dollar based company investing in a cement manufacturing facility (the *project* component) in Indonesia (the *offshore* component).

THE OFFSHORE PROJECT BETA   In order to create this new beta (it is too specific to have been previously measured), we utilize one of the basic mathematical characteristics of betas, that betas are multiplicative (one beta may be multiplied by a second beta). Assuming that the risk of the project relative to the Indonesian market (a cement plant in Indonesia) is the same *relative risk* as that project would represent in the United States market (a cement plant in the U.S.), we calculate the offshore project beta as the product of Cemex's own beta and the *Indonesia-to-U.S. country beta*.

Emerging market spreads are found most easily by published spreads on Brady bond issuances (see for example the daily *Financial Times*). Industrialized country governments, however, rarely issue dollar-denominated Eurobonds (and definitely not Brady bonds), making their sovereign spreads much harder to capture empirically.
[4]This assumption may be a bit heroic. The credit spread of Cemex in the U.S. over U.S. treasuries may not be a good proxy for the credit spread that Cemex Indonesia would pay over the dollar risk-free rate in Indonesia.

The *Indonesia-to-U.S. country beta*, β^{Indo}, is rather difficult to empirically estimate, because of the limited data on the covariance between U.S. equity markets and Indonesian equity markets. Luckily, an equivalent method of calculating beta is to find the ratio of the standard deviations of each of the individual markets—the United States and Indonesia, in this case—and to then multiply this ratio by the correlation coefficient between the two markets. The correlation of the Indonesian equity markets to the U.S. equity markets is here assumed to be 0.26 ($\rho_{\text{Indo, USA}} = 0.26$). This number is then multiplied by the ratio of market standard deviations ($\sigma_{\text{Indo}} = 30.55$, $\sigma_{\text{USA}} = 10.08$):[5]

$$\beta^{\text{Indo}} = \frac{\text{Cov}(k_{\text{Indo}}, k_{\text{USA}})}{\text{Var}(k_{\text{USA}})} = \rho_{\text{Indo, USA}} \frac{\sigma_{\text{Indo}}}{\sigma_{\text{USA}}} = [0.26]\frac{30.55}{10.08} = 0.7880$$

The country beta for Indonesia is found to be 0.7880. We now multiply this country beta with the beta value for Cemex itself, β_{Cemex}, the same 1.5 value used in the parent company's cost of equity calculation. Cemex's offshore project beta for Indonesia is now calculated as 1.182:

$$\beta_{\text{Cemex}}^{\text{Offshore}} = \beta_{\text{Cemex}} \times \beta^{\text{Indo}} = 1.5(0.7880) = 1.182$$

THE EQUITY RISK PREMIUM   The final input to the CAPM approach is the equity risk premium demanded by a U.S. investor on an Indonesian equity investment, $\text{RPM}_{\text{US}}^{\text{Indo}}$. The offshore project beta calculated in the previous section will now be multiplied by the following risk premium:

$$\text{RPM}_{\text{US}}^{\text{Indo}} = k_m - K_{\text{rf}}^{\text{Indo}}$$

Empirically, we are confronted with making a choice between two approaches. We could infer that the applicable RPM is that found by subtracting the Indonesian risk-free rate of 10.0% (calculated earlier) from the U.S. equity return of 13.0%, a premium of 3.0%. Such a small risk premium for the Indonesian market is, however, troubling. Alternatively, we could use the U.S. market's equity risk premium of 13.0% − 6.0% = 7.0%, and assume that this RPM is what would be demanded by a U.S.-based investor when establishing the required return on equity investments in the Indonesian marketplace.[6] We choose the latter.

THE ADJUSTED COST OF CAPITAL   We now have all of the components for estimating the risk-adjusted cost of equity for Cemex's prospective investment in Indonesia:

$$K_e^{\text{Indo}} = k_{\text{rf}}^{\text{Indo}} + \text{RMP}_{\text{US}}^{\text{Indo}} \beta_{\text{Cemex}}^{\text{Offshore}} = 10.0\% + (7.0\%)1.182 = 18.274\%$$

With all components in place, the weighted-average cost of capital, adjusted for offshore application to Indonesia, assuming the same 35% effective tax rate as the parent company, is calculated as:

$$K_{\text{WACC}}^{\text{Indo}} = (18.274\%)(0.60) + (12.000\%)(1 - 0.35)(0.40) = 14.084\%$$

The relatively surprising result is that the Indonesian risk-adjusted weighted-average cost of capital is only 2.104% higher than the parent company's own cost of capital (14.084% − 11.980%). This amount is substantially less than if the simple sovereign spread of 4.00% were added to the parent's own cost of capital. This is not to say that this will always be the case. This is not a simple cost of capital plus 3% or 6% premium process. Because the costs of equity are adjusted on the basis of

---

[5]Godfrey and Espinosa (1996) argue that MNEs are often not interested in their investors' ability to diversity internationally, and therefore the correlation coefficient between country markets should be assumed to be equal to one in this type of analysis. In our opinion, this would tend to rob the approach to international risk measurement of its theoretical foundations, as it would ignore the fact that equity markets in different countries are not perfectly correlated (for example, in this case, the correlation between the United States and Indonesia is 0.26, not 1.00).
[6]It should also be noted that the first approach could actually result in a negative premium (for example, Brazil/U.S.), which would be even more troubling.

relative volatilities and correlations with the home country capital market, the relative direction and magnitude of the risk-adjusted WACC to that of the parent's is purely an empirical issue on a case-by-case basis.

Adjusting Costs of Capital for Cemex's Portfolio of Potential Projects

But what if Cemex wanted to evaluate projects across a number of emerging markets, and not just Indonesia? It would then need to repeat the capital cost adjustment process just demonstrated for Indonesia across the subject country-set. This calculation, although somewhat cumbersome initially, is quite tractable for Cemex or any other MNE attempting to evaluate a wide spectrum of potential investments globally.

Table 6A-2 presents the needed data for a small set of emerging market countries, including Indonesia, used in the Cemex-Indonesia numerical illustration. The data presented in Table 6A-2 is generally applicable to any U.S.-based or U.S. dollar-based MNE. The MNE need only contribute its own cost of capital components, plus the appropriate beta value comparable to the industry-specific beta of the prospective investment. (Under most applications, the MNE parent company will simply use its own beta from its home market as a proxy for this relative measure of risk.)

Table 6A-3 summarizes the next step, the calculation of the adjusted cost of equity for Cemex in evaluating prospective investments across the countries listed. As in the previous numerical example, the CAPM approach uses the same basic U.S. Treasury risk-free rate and adds to it the individual country's sovereign risk premium. This country-specific risk-free cost of U.S. dollar debt is then added to the product of the equity market risk premium for the United States (7.000%) and the offshore beta to the U.S. market (Table 6A-2). As Table 6A-3 illustrates, this calculation results in a wide range of adjusted cost of equity estimates across these countries, with the highest in Brazil (37.458%) and the lowest in Venezuela (12.206%). Note that the reason the Venezuelan adjusted cost of equity is so low is a direct result of the negative correlation the Venezuelan equity markets have with U.S. equity markets.

Finally, with the risk-adjusted costs of debt and equity calculated for each country, it is now possible to calculate the weighted-average cost of capital to be applied to each of the individual emerging market countries. Table 6A-4 reports the results of this last step. Clearly this methodology, internally consistent with domestic capital cost estimation, results in substantially different (generally lower) discount rates on foreign projects than the traditional WACC + 3% (or even 6%) rule of thumb utilized by many MNEs in the past.

The adjusted costs of Table 6A-4 do indeed present some surprises. All but one country's cost ends up higher than that of the parent company's 11.98%. The adjusted cost of equity in one country,

TABLE 6A-2 Risk-Adjustment Component Inputs for Selected Emerging Countries.

Country	(1) Sovereign Spread (basis points)	(2) Market Volatility (%)	(3) Relative to U.S.	(4) Correlation with U.S.	(5) Country Beta to U.S.	(6) Offshore Beta to U.S. Market
Argentina	718	61.63	6.11	0.32	1.9565	2.935
Brazil	610	60.86	6.04	0.40	2.4151	3.623
Indonesia	400	30.55	3.03	0.26	0.7880	1.182
Mexico	597	37.90	3.76	0.22	0.8272	1.241
Philippines	226	34.16	3.39	0.22	0.7456	1.118
Venezuela	811	60.93	6.04	−0.03	−0.1813	−0.272
United States	—	10.08	1.00	1.00	1.0000	1.500

Source: Columns (1), (2), and (4) are from Lessard (1996). Original data from J.P. Morgan and the International Finance Corporation's Emerging Stock Markets Factbook, 1996. Correlations are based on 50 months ending December 1995. Column (3) is the ratio of the individual country's volatility shown in Column (2) divided by U.S. volatility (10.08) shown in column (2). For example, Argentina's relative volatility of 6.11 = 61.63 ÷ 10.08.
Column (5) = Column (3) × Column (4).
Column (6) = Column (5) × U.S. beta of 1.500.

TABLE 6A-3 Cemex's Calculated Risk-Adjusted Cost of Equity for Selected Emerging Market Countries.

Country	(1) Risk-free U.S. Treasury rate (%)	(2) Sovereign Spread (%)	(3) Adjusted Risk-Free Rate (%)	(4) Equity Risk Premium (%)	(5) Offshore Beta (%)	(6) Adjusted Cost of Equity (%)
Argentina	6.00	7.18	13.18	7.00	2.935	33.723
Brazil	6.00	6.10	12.10	7.00	3.623	37.458
Indonesia	6.00	4.00	10.00	7.00	1.182	18.274
Mexico	6.00	5.97	11.97	7.00	1.241	20.655
Philippines	6.00	2.26	8.26	7.00	1.118	16.088
Venezuela	6.00	8.11	14.11	7.00	−0.272	12.206
United States	6.00	—	6.00	7.00	1.500	16.500

Source: Columns (1) and (2) are drawn from Table 6A-1.
Column (3) = Column (1) + Column (2)
Column (4) is the same U.S. equity market risk premium used in Table 6A-2.
Column (5) is taken from Table 6A-2.
Column (6) = Column 3 + [Column (4) × Column (5)].

TABLE 6A-4 Cemex's Calculated Risk-Adjusted Cost of Capital for Selected Emerging Market Countries.

Country	(1) Adjusted Cost of Debt (%)	(2) Adjusted Cost of Equity (%)	(3) Adjusted Cost of Capital (%)	(4) Spread Over U.S. WACC (%)
Argentina	15.180	33.723	24.181	12.201
Brazil	14.100	37.458	26.141	14.161
Indonesia	12.000	18.274	14.084	2.104
Mexico	13.970	20.655	16.025	4.045
Philippines	10.260	16.088	12.321	0.341
Venezuela	16.110	12.206	11.512	−0.468
United States	8.000	16.500	11.980	—

Source: Column (1) and Column (2) from Table 6A-3.
Column (3) = [0.40 × (1 − 0.35) × Column (1)] + [0.60 × Column (2)], where 0.40 and 0.60 are the proportions of debt and equity, respectively, in the weighted-average cost of capital, and the tax rate is assumed to be 35%.
Column (4) = the adjusted cost of capital—United States cost of capital. For example, Argentina's spread over U.S. WACC is 24.181 − 11.980 = 12.201.

Venezuela, is actually lower than that in the United States. This is a result of Venezuela's country beta and a negative correlation with U.S. equity market returns. It is critical to remember, however, that the adjusted cost of capital in Venezuela is lower *only* when evaluated in the context of Cemex's portfolio of foreign investments and the commensurate correlations with the U.S. dollar markets.

Reservations on the Country-Beta Approach

The *country-beta approach* has a number of implicit assumptions that need to be appreciated by any MNE considering its application. First, as we mentioned previously, if the purpose of the foreign investment is either to source raw material or natural resources, or to produce a product for further processing and sale in some other country market, the returns on the specific investment under consideration may have little association with the host-country market and its observable equity returns and correlations. Secondly, beta values are highly sensitive to leverage. If leverage levels and value differ dramatically in the host market from that of the parent company, resulting equity adjustments will be biased. Finally, MNEs operate in specific industry segments, segments that may or may not be typical of the returns and correlations represented by country-level summary statistics.

CROSS-BORDER MERGERS, ACQUISITIONS, AND VALUATION

7

Although there are many pieces to the puzzle of building shareholder value, ultimately it comes down to growth. Chapter 7 described the process of how an MNE will "go global" in search of new markets, resources, productive advantages, and other elements of competition and profit. A more and more popular route to this global growth and expansion is through *cross-border mergers and acquisitions*. The process of identifying, valuing, and acquiring a foreign firm is the subject of this chapter.

This chapter focuses on identifying and completing a cross-border acquisition transaction. In addition, it details both the valuation techniques employed and the management of the acquisition process, we describe both the theory and the management of the acquisition process.

Cross-border mergers, acquisitions, and strategic alliances all face similar challenges: they must value the target enterprise on the basis of its projected performance in its market. This process of enterprise valuation combines elements of strategy, management, and finance. Strategically, the potential core competencies and competitive advantages of the target firm attract the acquisition. An enterprise's potential value is a combination of the intended strategic plan and the expected operational effectiveness to be implemented after acquisition.

The first section of this chapter details the arguments and identify the trends in cross-border acquisitions. This discussion focuses on the particularly unique factors in the cross-border acquisition environment. Second, we review the acquisition process. The third section explains the corporate governance and shareholder rights issues raised in cross-border acquisitions. In the fourth section, we perform a valuation using an illustrative case, Tsingtao Brewery Company Ltd. of China. We cover the many different valuation methods employed in industry—and their limitations.

7.1 CROSS-BORDER MERGERS AND ACQUISITIONS

The 1980s and 1990s were characterized by a spate of mergers and acquisitions (M&A) with both domestic and foreign partners. Cross-border mergers have played an important role in this activity. The 1992 completion of the European Union's Internal Market stimulated many of these investments, as European, Japanese, and U.S. firms jockeyed for stronger market positions within the EU. However, the long-run U.S. growth prospects and political safety in the United States motivated more takeovers of U.S. firms by foreign firms, particularly from the United Kingdom and Japan, than vice versa. This trend showed a reversal of historical trends when U.S. firms were net buyers of foreign firms rather than net sellers to foreign firms.

The latter half of the 1990s saw a number of mega-mergers between multinationals—for example, DaimlerChrysler and Exxon-Mobil—which virtually changed the entire competitive landscapes of their respective global markets. The 1990s also saw the rise of privatization of enterprise in many emerging markets, creating growth opportunities for MNEs to gain access to previously closed markets of enormous potential.

The Driving Force: Shareholder Value Creation

What is the true motivation for cross-border mergers and acquisitions? The answer is the traditional one: to build shareholder value.

Figure 7-1 tries, in a simplistic way, to model this global expansion. Publicly traded MNEs live and die, in the eyes of their shareholders, by their share price. If the MNE's share price is a combination of the earnings of the firm and the market's opinion of those earnings, the price-to-earnings multiple, then management must strive to grow both.

Management's problem is that it does not directly influence the market's opinion of its earnings. Although management's responsibility is to increase its P/E ratio, this is a difficult, indirect, and long-term process of communication and promise fulfillment. Over the long term, the market—analysts, investors, and institutional stakeholders—will look to the ability of the management to deliver on the promises made in meetings, advertisements, annual reports, and at the stockholders' meetings. But the opinion of markets as reflected in P/E ratios is infamously fickle. (The astronomic share prices garnered by many dot-com firms in recent years before the bubble burst is the most obvious example.)

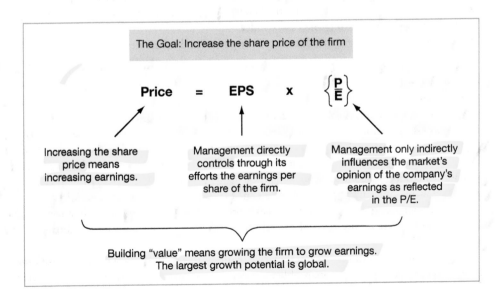

FIGURE 7-1
Building Shareholder Value Means Building Earnings.

But management does directly affect earnings. Increasing the earnings per share (EPS) is within the direct control of the firm. In many of the developed country markets today, the growth potential for earnings in the traditional business lines of the firm is limited. Competition is fierce; margins are under continual pressure. Senior management of the firm cannot ignore these pressures. Indeed, they must continually undertake activities to promote brand, decrease inventory investments, increase customer focus and satisfaction, streamline supply chains, and manage all the other drivers of value in global business. Nevertheless, they must also look outward to build value.

In contrast to the fighting and scraping for market shares and profits in traditional domestic markets, the global marketplace offers greater growth potential—greater "bang for the buck." As Chapter 4 described, there are a variety of paths by which the MNE can enter foreign markets, including greenfield investment and acquisition.

7.2   CROSS-BORDER MERGERS AND ACQUISITIONS DRIVERS

In addition to the desire to grow, MNEs are motivated to undertake cross-border mergers and acquisitions by a number of other factors. The United Nations Conference on Trade and Development (UNCTAD, formerly the U.N. Centre for Transnational Corporations) has summarized the mergers and acquisitions drivers and forces relatively well, as shown in Figure 7-2.

The drivers of M&A activity are both *macro* in scope—the global competitive environment—and *micro* in scope—the variety of industry and firm-level forces and actions driving individual firm value. The primary forces of change in the global competitive environment—technological change, regulatory change, and capital market change—create new business opportunities for MNEs, which they pursue aggressively.

But the global competitive environment is really just the playing field, the ground upon which the individual players compete. MNEs undertake cross-border mergers and acquisitions for a variety of reasons. As shown in Figure 7-2, the drivers are strategic responses by MNEs to defend and enhance their global competitiveness by:

- Gaining access to strategic proprietary assets
- Gaining market power and dominance
- Achieving synergies in local/global operations and across different industries
- Becoming larger, and then reaping the benefits of size in competition and negotiation
- Diversifying and spreading their risks wider
- Exploiting financial opportunities they may possess and others desire

As opposed to greenfield investment, a cross-border acquisition has a number of significant advantages. First and foremost, it is quicker. Greenfield investment frequently requires extended periods of physical construction and organizational development. By acquiring an existing firm, the MNE shortens the time required to gain a presence and facilitate competitive entry into the market. Second, acquisition may be a cost-effective way of gaining competitive advantages such as technology, brand names valued in the target market, and logistical and distribution advantages, while simultaneously eliminating a local competitor. Third, specific to cross-border acquisitions, international economic, political, and foreign exchange conditions may result in market imperfections, allowing target firms to be undervalued. Many enterprises throughout Asia have been the target of acquisition, as a result of the Asian economic crisis's impact on their financial health. Many enterprises were in dire need of capital injections from so-called White Knights for competitive survival.

Cross-border acquisitions are not, however, without their pitfalls. As with all acquisitions—domestic or cross-border—there are problems of paying too much or suffering excessive financing

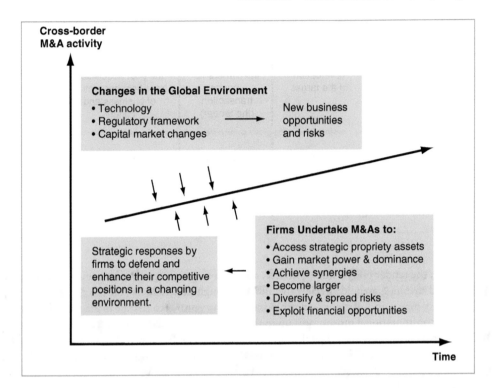

FIGURE 7-2

Driving Forces
Behind Cross-
Border M&A.

Source: UNCTAD, World Development Report 2000: Cross-border Mergers and Acquisitions and Development, figure V. 1., p. 154.

costs. Melding corporate cultures can be traumatic. Managing the postacquisition process is frequently characterized by downsizing to gain economies of scale and scope in overhead functions. This approach results in nonproductive impacts on the firm as individuals attempt to save their own jobs. Internationally, additional difficulties arise from host governments intervening in pricing, financing, employment guarantees, market segmentation, and general nationalism and favoritism. In fact, the ability to successfully complete cross-border acquisitions may itself be a test of competency of the MNE in the twenty-first century.

7.3   THE CROSS-BORDER ACQUISITION PROCESS

Although the field of finance has sometimes viewed acquisition as mainly an issue of valuation, it is a much more complex and rich process than simply determining what price to pay. As depicted in Figure 7-3, the process begins with the strategic drivers discussed in the previous section. The process of acquiring an enterprise anywhere in the world has three common elements: (1) identification and valuation of the target, (2) completion of the ownership change transaction—the *tender*, and (3) management of the postacquisition transition.

Stage 1: Identification and Valuation

Identification of potential acquisition targets requires a well-defined corporate strategy and focus.

IDENTIFICATION   The identification of the target market typically precedes the identification of the target firm. Entering a highly developed market offers the widest choice of publicly traded firms with relatively well-defined markets and publicly disclosed financial and operational data.

FIGURE 7-3

The Cross-Border
Acquisition Process.

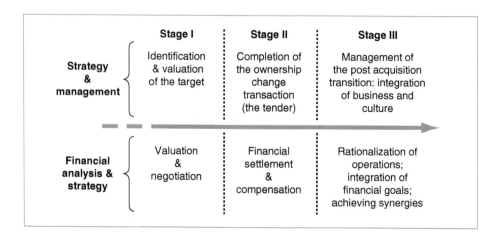

In this case, the tender offer is made publicly, although target company management may openly recommend that its shareholders reject the offer. If enough shareholders take the offer, the acquiring company may gain sufficient ownership influence or control to change management. During this rather confrontational process, it is up to the board of the target company to continue to take actions consistent with protecting the rights of shareholders. The board may need to provide rather strong oversight of management during this process to ensure that management does not take actions consistent with its own perspective but inconsistent with protecting and building shareholder value.

VALUATION   Once identification has been completed, the process of valuing the target begins. A variety of valuation techniques are widely used in global business today, each with its relative merits. In addition to the fundamental methodologies of discounted cash flow (DCF) and multiples (earnings and cash flows), there are also a variety of industry-specific measures that focus on the most significant elements of value in business lines.

For example, the case of Tsingtao Brewery in China, analyzed later in this chapter, focuses on the valuation of a brewery business. In this industry, the cost per ton of brewing capacity of the business is a frequently employed industry-specific valuation method. In the field of valuation, more is better when using valuation methods. The completion of a variety of alternative valuations for the target firm aids not only in gaining a more complete picture of what price must be paid to complete the transaction, but also in determining whether the price is attractive.

Stage 2: Settlement of the Transaction

The term "settlement" is actually misleading. Once an acquisition target has been identified and valued, the process of gaining approval from management and ownership of the target, getting approvals from government regulatory bodies, and finally determining method of compensation can be time-consuming and complex.

TENDER PROCESS   Gaining the approval of the target company has itself been the subject of some of the most storied acquisitions in history. The critical distinction here is whether the acquisition is supported or not by the target company's management.

Although there is probably no "typical transaction," many acquisitions flow relatively smoothly through a friendly process. The acquiring firm will approach the management of the target company and attempt to convince them of the business logic of the acquisition. (Gaining their support is sometimes difficult, but assuring target company management that it will not be replaced is often quite convincing!) If the target's management is supportive, they may then recommend to stockholders that they accept the offer of the acquiring company. One problem that does occasionally surface at this stage is that influential shareholders may object to the offer, either in principle or based on price, and therefore feel that management is not taking appropriate steps to protect and build their shareholder value.

The process takes on a very different dynamic when the acquisition is not supported by target company management—the so-called *hostile takeover*. The acquiring company may choose to pursue the acquisition without the target's support and go directly to the target shareholders. In this case the tender offer is made publicly, although target company management may openly recommend that its shareholders reject the offer. If enough shareholders take the offer, the acquiring company may gain sufficient ownership influence or control to change management. During this rather confrontational process it is up to the board of the target company to continue to take actions consistent with protecting the rights of shareholders. The board may need to provide rather strong oversight of management during this process, to ensure that management does not take actions consistent with its own perspective but not with protecting and building shareholder value.

REGULATORY APPROVAL   The proposed acquisition of Honeywell International (a recent merger of Honeywell U.S. and Allied-Signal U.S.) by General Electric (U.S.) in 2001 was something of a watershed event in the field of regulatory approval. General Electric's acquisition of Honeywell had been approved by management, ownership, and U.S. regulatory bodies.

The final stage was the approval of European Union antitrust regulators. Jack Welch, the charismatic chief executive officer and president of General Electric, did not anticipate the degree of opposition that the merger would face from EU authorities. After a continuing series of demands by the EU that specific businesses within the combined companies be sold off to reduce anticompetitive effects, Welch withdrew the request for acquisition approval, arguing that the liquidations would destroy most of the value-enhancing benefits of the acquisition. The acquisition was canceled. This case may have far-reaching affects on cross-border M&A for years to come, as the power of regulatory authorities within strong economic zones like the EU to block the combination of two MNEs may foretell a change in regulatory strength and breadth.

COMPENSATION SETTLEMENT   The last act within this second stage of cross-border acquisition is the payment to shareholders of the target company. Shareholders of the target company are typically paid either in shares of the acquiring company or in cash. If a share exchange occurs, which exchange may be defined by some ratio of acquiring company shares to target company shares (say, two shares of acquirer in exchange for three shares of target), the stockholder is typically not taxed. The shareholder's shares of ownership have simply been replaced by other shares in a nontaxable transaction.

If cash is paid to the target company shareholder, it is the same as if the shareholder had sold the shares on the open market, resulting in a capital gain or loss (a gain, it is hoped, in the case of an acquisition) with tax liabilities. Because of the tax ramifications, shareholders are typically more receptive to share exchanges so that they may choose whether and when tax liabilities will arise.

A variety of factors go into the determination of type of settlement. The availability of cash, the size of the acquisition, the friendliness of the takeover, and the relative valuations of both acquiring firm and target firm affect the decision. One of the most destructive forces that sometimes arise at this stage is regulatory delay and its impact on the share prices of the two firms. If regulatory body approval drags out over time, the possibility of a drop in share price increases and can change the attractiveness of the share swap. *Global Finance in Practice 7.1* illustrates the problems firms confronted recently in settling cross-border acquisition with shares.

Global Finance in Practice 7.1

Cash or Shares in Payment

One factor influencing not only the number but the method of payment used in cross-border mergers and acquisitions is the equity "altitudes" of many MNEs. One of the major drivers of cross-border M&A growth in 1999 and 2000 was the lofty levels of equity values. Many MNEs found the higher equity prices allowed what the financial press termed "shopping sprees," in which the acquiring firms could afford more M&As as a result of inflated equity prices. This ability allowed them to bid higher for potential targets and then pay with their own shares.

But 2001 was different. Falling equity prices in most of the major equity markets of the world made acquisitions much more costly prospects than in the previous years.

Shareholders of target firms were no longer interested in being paid in shares, demanding cash payments at significant premiums. (Premiums over the latter half of the 1990s and into 2000 and 2001 averaged between 48% and 55% over existing share values prior to the acquisition offers.)

With slower economies and lower growth prospects, even the banking sectors were increasingly critical of grandiose promises of M&A synergies and benefits in general. As banks and other potential cash providers looked upon potential M&A deals with increasing scrutiny, sources of debt for cash payments also became more scarce. The financing for settlement made cross-border M&A activity much tougher to complete.

Stage 3: Postacquisition Management

Although the headlines and flash of investment banking activities are typically focused on the valuation and bidding process in an acquisition transaction, posttransaction management is probably the most critical of the three stages in determining an acquisition's success or failure. An acquiring firm can pay too little or too much, but if the posttransaction is not managed effectively, the entire return on the investment is squandered. Postacquisition management is the stage in which the motivations for the transaction must be realized. Those reasons, such as more effective management, synergies arising from the new combination, or the injection of capital at a cost and availability previously out of the reach of the acquisition target, must be effectively implemented after the transaction. The biggest problem, however, is nearly always melding corporate cultures.

As painfully depicted in the case of British Petroleum (United Kingdom) and Amoco (United States) in *Global Finance in Practice 7.2*, the clash of corporate cultures and personalities pose both the biggest risk and the biggest potential gain from cross-border mergers and acquisitions. Although not readily measurable like price/earnings ratios or share price premiums, in the end the value is either gained or lost in the hearts and minds of the stakeholders.

7.4 CORPORATE GOVERNANCE AND SHAREHOLDER RIGHTS

> By takeover bid (tender offer) we mean an unsolicited offer by an unaffiliated third party and/or his group ('Bidder') to acquire enough voting shares of a target company ('Target') in another jurisdiction so that the shares acquired, plus the shares held before the offer was made, give Bidder control in fact or in law of the Target.
>
> "Constraints on Cross Border Takeovers and Mergers," International Bar Association for International Capital Markets Group, *International Business Lawyer*, 1991

Global Finance in Practice 7.2

Clashing Corporate Cultures at British Petroleum and Amoco

A popular joke in Amoco hallways goes: What's the British pronunciation of BP Amoco? BP—the Amoco is silent.

LONDON—BP and Amoco called it a merger of equals. But over coffee and sandwiches one day in the BP cafeteria here, Amoco Corp. executives discovered that British Petroleum PLC had other plans.

During a conference of 20 top executives from both companies last fall, Rodney Chase, then BP's deputy chief executive, unveiled the blueprint for the merged company. It would be led by BP management, run with BP's structure, and infused with BP's do-or-die culture. Anyone who didn't agree was welcome to join the 10,000 other workers who were being fired.

In Chicago during negotiations, Mr. Browne, BP's chief executive, and Amoco Chief Executive Lawrence Fuller wrestled with the question of management control. It was clear that BP would be the acquirer, since it was larger, but Mr. Fuller wondered whether the two companies could combine the "best of both" management worlds. Mr. Browne was unequivocal. "It was not negotiable for us," he said in a recent interview. "We had developed a structure and systems that had worked for us, and we were anxious to apply it to a larger company."

Indeed, at the heart of BP is an unusual management structure and culture that it aims to stamp on other companies. The system grew from the company's near-fatal crisis in 1992, when then-CEO Robert Horton was ousted in a boardroom coup, the company's dividend was cut in half and a single quarter's loss topped $1 billion. The subsequent restructuring essentially turned the company into a giant family of entrepreneurial small businesses.

The system clashed badly with Amoco. More like a classic pyramid, Amoco had strict reporting lines and heavy internal bureaucracy. Managers often spent months negotiating contracts with internal businesses. Amoco's executive suite on the 30th floor in Chicago was a formal corridor of closed doors and strict schedules. BP's fourth-floor suite in London is an open-plan space with glass walls, where top executives breeze in and out of each other's offices.

Company memos began showing up with British spellings, prompting complaints in the BP-Amoco newsletter about use of the words "organisation" and "labour." BP jargon was lost on some Amoco executives. In meetings, BP's managers lived on "hard targets" that had to be met, while Amoco talked about "aspirations" that were only occasionally reached. BP raved about "peer groups," while Amoco talked about "strategic-planning councils."

The culture clash came to a head in the cafeteria meeting last fall at BP headquarters. Although most managers expected BP would dominate the merged company, few anticipated that its grip would be so strong. During the all-day conference, Amoco managers argued the case for a centralized structure, while their BP counterparts said it wouldn't work. "You're not interested at all in our ideas," said one Amoco executive. Another said: "We weren't prepared for this." Sensing a crisis, Mr. Fuller stood up, a BP executive says, and gave his troops a final order: "We're going to use the BP systems, and that's that."

The Tender and Shareholder Rights

One of the most controversial issues in shareholder rights is at what point in the accumulation of shares is the bidder required to make all shareholders a tender offer. For example, a bidder may slowly accumulate shares of a target company by gradually buying shares on the open market over time. Theoretically, this share accumulation could continue until the bidder had (1) the single largest block of shares among all individual shareholders, (2) majority control, or (3) all the shares outright. Every country possesses a different set of rules and regulations for the transfer of control of publicly traded corporations. This market, the *market for corporate control*, has been the subject of enormous debate in recent years.

The regulatory approach taken towards the market for corporate control varies widely across countries. The elements of the regulation of cross-border takeovers typically includes the following ten elements.

1. Creeping tenders. Many countries prohibit *creeping tenders*, the secret accumulation of relatively small blocks of stock, privately or in the open market, in a preliminary move towards a public bid. This element is intended to promote public disclosure of bids for takeovers.

2. Mandatory offers. Many countries require that the bidder make a full public tender offer to all shareholders when a certain threshold of ownership is reached. This practice is intended to extend the opportunity to all shareholders to sell their shares at a tender price to a bidder gaining control, rather than have the bidder pay the tender price only to those shareholders it needs to garner control.

3. Timing of takeovers. A wide spectrum of different time frames apply to takeover bids. This is typically the time period over which the bid must be left open for each individual tender, withdrawal of tender, or revision of tender. This time is in place to allow bidders and targets alike to consider all potential offers and for information regarding the tender to reach all potential shareholders.

4. Withdrawal rights. Most countries allow any security to be withdrawn as long as the bid is open. In some countries, a competing bid automatically revokes all acceptances as long as the bid remains open. This practice is intended to protect shareholders against tendering their shares early at lower prices than may be garnered by waiting to a later offer by any competing bidder.

5. Market purchases during bid. Some countries allow the bidder to purchase shares in the open market during the public tender with public disclosure. Many countries, however, prohibit purchases absolutely during this period. This rule is enacted to protect against any potential market manipulation by either bidder or target during the tender period.

6. Market sales during bid. Some countries prohibit the sale of the target company's shares by the bidder during the tender offer period. This prohibition is intended to protect against any potential market manipulation by either bidder or target during the tender period.

7. Limitation of defenses. Some jurisdictions limit the defensive tactics that a target may take during a public tender offer. In many countries, this limit has not been stated in law, but has been refined through shareholder law suits and other court rulings subsequent to measures taken by target company management to frustrate bidders. This restriction is intended to protect shareholders against management taking defensive measures that are not in the best interests of shareholders.

8. Price integration. Most countries require that the highest price paid to any shareholder for their shares be paid to all shareholders tendering their shares during the public tender. Some countries require that this price be provided also to those selling shares to the bidder in the prebid purchases as well. Although intended in principle to guarantee equity in price offerings, this is a highly complex provision in many countries that allow two-tier bids and so-called front-end back-end bids.

9. Proration of acceptances. Most countries that regulate takeovers require *proration* when a bid is made for less than all the shares and more than that maximum is tendered. Some countries do not allow a bid to be made for less than all the shares once the mandatory offer percentage is reached.

10. Target responses. Many countries require that the board of directors of the target company make a public statement regarding their position on a public tender offer within a time frame following the tender. This requirement is intended to disclose the target's opinions and attitudes towards the tender to the existing shareholders. As illustrated in *Global Finance in Practice 7.3*, the complexity of issues over minority shareholder rights and the constant changes in regulatory policy continue globally.

Global Finance in Practice 7.3

Vodafone's Hostile Acquisition of Mannesmann

Once a firm has gained majority control of a target, many countries require that the remaining minority shareholders tender their shares. This requirement is undertaken to prevent minority shareholders from hindering the decision-making process of the owners, or requiring the owners to continue to take actions or incur expenses to serve a few remaining minority shareholders.

One example of this abuse was the case of Vodafone's acquisition of Mannesmann of Germany in 2000. By August 2001, Vodafone had gained ownership of 99.4% of Mannesmann's outstanding shares. Because minority shareholders holding a total of 7,000 shares refused to sell, and were not required to sell under German law even though the majority of shareholders had decided to sell the firm, Vodafone was required to continue to hold stockholders' meetings in Germany for their benefit. Under German corporate governance laws, because this was a cross-border acquisition, minority shareholders could not be forced to tender their shares. If, however, the acquisition had been domestic, these same minority shareholders would have been required to sell their shares at the publicly tendered price.

The Vodafone acquisition of Mannesmann is considered by many as a watershed event in Continental European mergers and acquisitions history. The acquisition marked the first large-scale cross-border hostile takeover in recent times. After Vodafone's takeover, the German federal government initiated legislation for the governance of acquisitions and a procedure for the future "squeeze-out" of minority shareholders.

7.5 ILLUSTRATIVE CASE: THE POTENTIAL PARTIAL ACQUISITION OF TSINGTAO BREWERY COMPANY LTD., CHINA

In January 2001, Anheuser Busch (AB) was considering acquiring a larger minority interest in Tsingtao Brewery Company Ltd., China, the largest brewer in China. AB had originally acquired a 5% equity interest (US$16.4 million) in 1993 when Tsingtao had first been partly privatized. AB now considered Tsingtao an even more attractive investment. The key questions to be answered were:

- The valuation of Tsingtao's share price in an illiquid Chinese equity market
- The percentage of Tsingtao's total equity that could be purchased
- The terms of settling the transaction
- The prospects for AB to contribute its management skills to Tsingtao after the acquisition of a larger equity stake
- The degree of future compatibility between the two corporate cultures
- The potential for future rationalization of operations

The Challenge and the Opportunity

Tsingtao Brewery Company Ltd. is the largest brewer in China. The first beer manufacturer in modern times, Tsingtao traces its roots to the Tsingtao Brewery Factory established in 1903 in Qinqdao, China, by German immigrants. But much had changed in a century of Chinese history and development. Tsingtao in January 2001 was a publicly traded company in an increasingly open marketplace. It operated 43 breweries, 2 malt plants, and 49 distribution companies covering 15 provinces in China. It was considered to be the number-one branded consumer product exported from China, selling a variety of brews including Dragon, Phoenix, and Premium.

Tsingtao was also China's largest single consumer-product exporter and was continuing to expand, with exports to more than 30 countries. With its two largest rivals, Beijing Yanjing and Guangzhou Zhujiang, Tsingtao was now in a highly competitive market. There were an estimated 800 different breweries in China. Consolidation was the only method of survival.

The company was gaining the attention of investors inside and outside China. The value proposition for Tsingtao was increasingly clear: it had gained the upper hand in its market through recent acquisitions, acquisitions that would now begin to add earnings with rationalization and modernization through Tsingtao's operational excellence. Tsingtao seemed positioned for strong earnings growth and was increasingly viewed as a potential acquisition target.

Chinese Brewery Consolidation

Chinese per capita consumption of beer was only 9 liters per person per year, compared to 90 liters in the United States and 154 liters in Germany. But the sheer magnitude of the Chinese market represented an enormous profit potential (or to quote one analyst, "there were simply so many capitas"). China in 2001 was the second-largest beer market in the world after the United States. Tsingtao believed that if it did not move quickly and aggressively, it could lose its opportunity to expand its share of a market poised for growth.

By early 2001, Tsingtao was struggling with the postmerger digestion of this acquisition binge, in addition to finding itself under heavy debt-service pressures from the rising debt used to finance the acquisitions. Two other current trends were adding pressure to this debt burden: (1) consolidation had resulted in a series of price wars, putting pressure on operating margins; and (2) the majority of acquired brewers were on the bottom end of the market with high growth potential but low or negative margins when acquired. Management concluded that the company's debt burden—and bright prospects for future earnings and cash flows—made raising additional equity both necessary and feasible.

- Tsingtao was known for its operational excellence—it knew brewing and distribution. It had worked constantly throughout the 1990s to increase the efficiency of its operations, specifically in its use of net working capital. But the task was compounded by the multitudes of acquisitions of small regional operators that were small in scale and low in technology. Although sales per day had more than doubled from Rmb4.4 million (1998) to Rmb9.4 million (2000), total net working capital had actually fallen by two-thirds, from Rmb 676.7 million to Rmb 201.5 million. The net working capital to sales ratio had fallen from 0.42 to only 0.06 in 2000.
- Tsingtao had enjoyed rapid sales growth, both from existing business units and through acquisition. The company's gross margin and operating margin had remained stable over recent years. This was a significant accomplishment, given the many acquisitions made in recent years.

In general, it appeared that Tsingtao had: (1) been growing rapidly; (2) maintaining a gross margin that was healthy for its industry—despite taking on 34 acquisitions in the past four years; (3) suffered from higher depreciation and amortization expenses related to modernization and acquisition efforts, respectively; and (4) demonstrated a declining overall profitability as a result.

Measures of Cash Flow

Financial theory has traditionally defined value as the present value of expected future cash flows. We then need to isolate the gross and free cash flows of Tsingtao for valuation purposes, and Tsingtao's statement of cash flows is a good place to start.

The *statement of cash flows* is constructed in three segments: operating activities, investing activities, and financing activities. Tsingtao's *operating activities* are illustrated in the top portion of Table 7-1. They begin with earnings before tax, then reduce cash flows by taxes paid (cash taxes), add back depreciation and amortization expenses, and finally add changes in net working capital.

TABLE 7-1   Tsingtao Brewing Company Ltd., Measures of Cash Flow (millions of Rmb).

FROM THE STATEMENT OF CASH FLOWS

Operating Cash Flow Calculation	Acronym	1998	1999	2000
Earnings before taxes	EBT	63.2	72.9	113.3
Less corporate income tax		(21.4)	(29.0)	(34.0)
Add back depreciation and amortization		132.1	180.4	257.6
Less additions to net working capital	Chg. NWC	(148.3)	475.7	134.8
Operating cash flow		25.6	700.0	471.7

CASH FLOWS FOR VALUATION

Calculation of NOPAT	Acronym	1998	1999	2000
Earnings before interest and taxes	EBIT	111.3	127.9	207.3
Less taxes (recalculated)	30%	(33.4)	(38.4)	(62.2)
Net operating profit after tax	NOPAT	77.9	89.5	145.1
Calculation of Operating Cash Flow				
Net operating profit after-tax	NOPAT	77.9	89.5	145.1
Add back depreciation and amortization		132.1	180.4	257.6
Operating cash flow	OCF	210.0	269.9	402.7
Calculation of Free Cash Flow				
Net operating profit after tax	NOPAT	77.9	89.5	145.1
Add back depreciation and amortization	D&A	132.1	180.4	257.6
Less additions to net working capital	Chg. NWC	(148.3)	475.7	134.8
Less capital expenditures	Capex	(286.1)	(1,530.0)	(1,330.0)
Free cash flow	FCF	(224.4)	(784.4)	(792.5)

Depreciation and amortization are defined as *noncash expenses.* Cash expenses are for labor or materials purchased by the firm, where cash payments must be paid to the providers of these inputs. Depreciation and amortization are accounting-based expenses (noncash). *Depreciation* is a charge for investments made in capital equipment. *Amortization* is a charge for investments made in other companies (acquisitions) over and above the value of the assets purchased. Although they are deductible expenses for tax purposes, cash is never paid out by the firm. The depreciation and amortization expenses must therefore be added back in for calculation of actual cash flows.

Net working capital (NWC) is the net amount of capital that the firm invests in the actual production and sales of its product. It is calculated as follows:

$$NWC = (\text{Accounts receivable} + \text{Inventories}) - (\text{Accounts payable})$$

Intuitively, these are the line items of the company's balance sheet that change spontaneously with sales. For example, for Tsingtao to make a sale, it must purchase hops and barley (accounts payable), brew its various beers (inventory), and make sales to distributors (accounts receivable). Net working capital is typically a positive number, because receivables and inventories exceed accounts payable for most firms in most industries (about 99% of the time).

VALUATION CASH FLOWS   *Operating cash flow* as calculated and recorded on the statement of cash flows is not the measure of cash flow we need for valuation purposes. The lower half of Table 7-1 illustrates the calculation of *net operating profit after tax (NOPAT)* and *free cash flow (FCF)* for valuation purposes. NOPAT is calculated as follows:

$$NOPAT = EBIT - Taxes$$

For Tsingtao in 2000, NOPAT was 207.3 − 62.2 = 145.1, or a positive Rmb145.1 million. This calculation is shown in the lower half of Table 7-1. NOPAT is a cash flow measure of basic business profitability. What it does not contain, however, are the two areas of investment made by Tsingtao as the company continues to sustain and grow the business. Sustaining a business requires investment in NWC and capital expenditures (capex). *Capex* is any new investment to replace old equipment, to acquire new equipment and technology, or to acquire other businesses; it reduces available free cash flow. The addition of these new investment drains on cash flow to NOPAT create the desired measure of cash flow for valuation purposes, or *free cash flow (FCF)*:

FCF = NOPAT + Depreciation & amortization + Changes in NWC − Capex

Tsingtao's free cash flow in 2000 was a negative Rmb792.5 million. Although Tsingtao's operations are generating a substantial positive cash flow, the firm's modernization and acquisition strategies have required substantial capital expenditures. The net result is a negative free cash flow for the year 2000.

Tsingtao's Discounted Cash Flow Valuation

Now that Tsingtao's current financial results have been analyzed and decomposed, we turn our attention to what Tsingtao's discounted future will look like. There are three critical components to constructing a discounted cash flow valuation of Tsingtao: (1) expected future free cash flows; (2) terminal value; and (3) the risk-adjusted discount rate.

FREE CASH FLOW FORECAST   Forecasting Tsingtao's future free cash flows requires forecasting NOPAT, net working capital, and capital expenditures individually. The source of value of Tsingtao was its operating profits, and given the recent acquisitions which were expected to only grow and improve in both sales and profitability with continued technology and management injections, NOPAT was expected to grow 25% in 2001, 20% in 2002, 15% in 2003, and 10% in 2004 and 2005. The NOPAT forecast and discounted cash flow valuation is shown in Table 7-2. With rapid growth forecast, NWC was now expected to be maintained at roughly 5.8% of sales throughout the analysis period.

Most firms have relatively poor capabilities to plan for needed replacement investment or technological upgrades with innovations. Capital expenditures had been enormous in 1999 and 2000 as a result of the 29 acquisitions made in those two years alone. Although few additional acquisitions were planned by Tsingtao beginning in 2001, the capital investment needed to modernize many of the acquired properties would require substantial outlays for years to come. Capital expenditures were estimated to be 2.5% of total sales through 2005.

DISCOUNT RATE   The discount rate to be used for Tsingtao's valuation would be the company's weighted average cost of capital. Assuming a 34% corporate tax rate and a pretax cost of debt of 7.00% per annum (the cost of Tsingtao's most recent debt), the after-tax cost of debt was estimated at 4.62% per annum.

The cost of equity was calculated using the capital asset pricing model. Using the Hong Kong market as the best indicator of equity valuation, the risk-free rate is 7.800% per annum, the equity risk premium is 6.100% per annum, and the beta of Tsingtao's H-shares on the Hong Kong stock exchange is 0.80:

$$\text{Cost of equity} = k_e^{\text{Tsingtao}} = k_{rf} + \beta \, (k_m - k_{rf}) = 7.800 + 0.80 \, (13.900 - 7.800) = 12.68\%$$

The final component needed for the calculation of Tsingtao's weighted average cost of capital is the weights of debt and equity in its target capital structure. The firm had increased its degree of leverage in recent years, but management and analysts considered a $\frac{1}{3}$ debt and $\frac{2}{3}$

equity capital structure appropriate over the long term. Using these weights, Tsingtao's weighted average cost of capital (WACC) was calculated as:

$$WACC = \left(\frac{Equity}{Capital} \times k_e\right) + \left(\frac{Debt}{Capital} \times k_d \times (1-tax)\right)$$

Plugging in the 12.68% cost of equity and the 4.62% cost of debt, after tax:

$$WACC = (0.667 \times 12.68\%) + (.333 \times 4.62\%) = 10.00\%.$$

This WACC is used to discount the future cash flows of Tsingtao for valuation purposes.

TERMINAL VALUE   The terminal value is critical in discounted cash flow valuation because it must capture all free cash flow value flowing indefinitely into the future (past the 2001–2005 period shown). Assuming a discount rate of 10.00%, a free cash flow growth rate into the future of 1.00% per annum (conservative), the terminal value as captured in year 5 of the analysis, using a constant dividend growth model formulation is:

$$\text{Terminal value} = \frac{FCF_{2005}(1+g)}{k_{wacc}-g} = \frac{420.2(1+0.0100)}{0.1000-0.0100} = \text{Rmb } 4,715.6$$

This terminal value enters the discounted cash flow in 2005 in Table 7-2 and represents all expected free cash flows arising in all years after that.

TABLE 7-2   Discounted Cash Flow Valuation of Tsingtao Brewing Company Ltd. (millions of Rmb).

SALES FORECAST	ASSUMPTION	ACTUAL 2000	1 2001	2 2002	3 2003	4 2004	5 2005
Sales growth rate assumption			25%	20%	15%	10%	10%
Sales		3,448.3	4,310.4	5,172.5	5,948.3	6,543.1	7,197.5
Discounted Cash Flow Valuation							
NOPAT	4.2%	145.1	181.0	217.2	249.8	274.8	302.3
Depreciation and amortization	7.5%	257.6	276.9	297.7	320.0	344.0	369.8
Operating cash flow		402.7	458.0	514.9	569.8	618.8	672.1
Less additions to net working capital	1.0%	134.8	(43.1)	(51.7)	(59.5)	(65.4)	(72.0)
Less capital expenditures	2.5%	(1,330.0)	(107.8)	(129.3)	(148.7)	(163.6)	(179.9)
Free cash flow (FCF)		(792.5)	307.1	333.9	361.7	389.8	420.2
Terminal value (and assumed growth rate)	1.0%						4,715.6
Expected FCF for discounting			307.1	333.9	361.7	389.8	5,135.8
Present value factor (and discount rate)	10.0%		0.9091	0.8264	0.7513	0.6830	0.6209
Discounted FCF			279.2	275.9	271.7	266.3	3,188.9
Cumulative discounted FCF		4,282.0					
Less present value of debt capital		(2,093.0)					
Residual equity value		2,189.0					
Shares outstanding (millions)		900.0					
Equity value (Rmb/share)		2.43					
Spot exchange rate (Rmb/HK$)		1.0648					
Equity value (HK$/share)		2.28					

Note: The discounted cash flow analysis is based primarily on sales expectations. Sales growth rate assumptions are used to generate sales expectations, which are in turn used for estimates of NOPAT (assumed as 4.2% of sales), depreciation and amortization (assumed as 7.5% of sales), additions to net working capital (assumed 1.0% of sales), and capital expenditures (assumed 2.5% of sales). Free cash flow is discounted at the 10% weighted average cost of capital. The terminal value for this baseline analysis assumes a 1% perpetual growth rate in free cash flow.

DCF VALUATION   The present value of all future expected cash flows is the total enterprise value. Enterprise value is the sum of the present values of both debt and equity in the enterprise. Tsingtao's equity value is then found by deducting the net debt due creditors and any minority interests. Total equity value divided by total shares outstanding is the fair value of equity per share. The baseline discounted cash flow valuation of Tsingtao is Rmb2.43/share (HK$2.28).

Valuation by Multiples of Earnings and Cash Flows

The valuation of businesses of all kinds, small or large, domestic or multinational, goods or services, has long been as much art as science. The use of multiples, in which a ratio for the subject firm is compared to comparable ratios for competitors or recent acquisitions, is one of the more artistic processes. Similar in logic to ratio analysis used in traditional financial analysis, multiples simply present the way the firm stacks up against industry comparables. Some of the most widely used measures include the PE (price/earnings-per-share) ratio, PS (price/sales) ratio, market-to-book (M/B) ratio, and a variety of ratios that compare enterprise value (EV) to either earnings or cash flows. Each of these ratios includes a market-determined value—price—either explicitly in the numerator or in calculating market capitalization. The price is then combined with values taken from the firm's own financials, in the form of either earnings (such as EPS), cash flow (such as FCF), or market capitalization.

PE RATIO   The PE ratio is by far the most widely used of the valuation ratios. Simply stated, the PE ratio is an indication of what the market is willing to pay for a currency unit of earnings. But more importantly, it is an indication of how secure the market's perception is about the future earnings of the firm. Coca-Cola has long been a prime example of an MNE whose PE ratio, typically ranging between 35 and 42, is an indicator of how sustainable global earnings and earnings growth are in the eyes of shareholders. Markets do not pay for past or present earnings. An investor purchasing a share today is taking a long position on the basis of what earnings are expected to do in the future—from that moment on.

Because Tsingtao is traded most heavily on the Hong Kong stock exchange, and that exchange is relatively more liquid and open to global investors than the Shanghai stock exchange, we shall focus on the PE ratio calculations and comparisons of the Hong Kong listing for Tsingtao. Tsingtao's earnings per share for 2000 were Rmb61.3 million on 900 million outstanding shares (EPS of Rmb0.068 or HK$0.0640 assuming an exchange rate of Rmb1.0648/HK$). The closing share price for 2000 in Hong Kong was HK$2.20/share. The closing PE ratio for Tsingtao in Hong Kong for 2000 was then:

$$\text{PE ratio}_{\substack{\text{Hong Kong}}}^{\text{Tsingtao}} = \frac{\text{Current share price in HK\$}}{\left[\dfrac{\text{Earnings for 2000 in HK\$}}{\text{Outstanding shares}}\right]} = \frac{\text{HK\$2.20}}{\left[\dfrac{\text{HK\$57,569,497}}{900,000,000 \text{ shares}}\right]} = 34$$

Tsingtao's PE ratio of 34 was quite high compared to the Hong Kong stock exchange's H-share PE average of 12 (a ratio of 2.83:1).

Recalling our earlier statement that markets do not pay for past or present earnings, we should also probably calculate Tsingtao's PE ratio not on current earnings but on future earnings. This ratio would then be compared to the Hong Kong stock exchange's share prices recalculated on expected earnings. Deutsche Bank Securities estimated the 2001 forecast PE ratio for Tsingtao as 28.8, compared to its forecast of the Hong Kong H-share market's average of 8.2. This ratio is 3.5:1, an even higher relative measure than before. Clearly, regardless of the precise calculation of Tsingtao's PE ratio, the market believes that Tsingtao's earnings would be either relatively riskless compared to the market or significantly higher in the near future.

M/B RATIO   The market-to-book (M/B) ratio is nearly as widely used in valuation as the PE ratio. It provides some measure of the market's assessment of the employed capital per share versus what the capital cost. The book value of a firm is the value of common stock as recorded on the firm's balance sheet plus the retained earnings (cumulative capital reinvested from earnings). If the M/B ratio exceeds 1, it implies that the firm's equity is currently valued in excess of what stockholders invested in the firm. Like the PE ratio, the magnitude of the M/B ratio, as compared to its major competitors, reflects the market's perception of the quality of the firm's earnings, management, and general strategic opportunities.

The M/B ratio focuses on equity in both the numerator, and denominator, and is a mix of market value (numerator) and historical accounting value (denominator). It is calculated as the ratio of share price to book value per share. The M/B ratio for Tsingtao in 2000 is:

$$\text{M/B ratio}^{\text{Tsingtao}} = \frac{\text{Current share price}}{\text{Book value per share}} = \frac{\text{HK\$2.34/share}}{\text{HK\$2.35/share}} = 0.9957 \approx 1$$

According to this equation, Tsingtao is selling for the historical cost of the capital invested in the business. Under most typical business conditions, a M/B ratio is interpreted as a signal that the company may be "undervalued" and therefore a true investment opportunity.

OTHER MULTIPLES   Two other comparison ratios or multiples may provide additional insights into Tsingtao's value. The 2001 forecast price-to-sales ratio (price per share versus forecast sales per share) for Tsingtao by Deutschebank Securities was 0.56. The Hong Kong H-share forecast was 0.85. This ratio would imply an undervaluation of Tsingtao if the other firms in the comparison are truly compatible.

A similar type of ratio, the ratio of 2001 forecast enterprise value (market value of debt and equity, EV) to basic business earnings (EBITDA) for Tsingtao was 7.5 compared to the Hong Kong H-share forecast of 3.7. The higher ratio for Tsingtao implied that its shares were overvalued. Again, the difficulty in interpreting these relative measures of value is in knowing how well Tsingtao compares to the other firms traded as H-shares on the Hong Kong stock exchange.

Summary of Valuation Measures

Table 7-3 summarizes the various measures of Tsingtao's valuation we have discussed. As is often the case in corporate valuations—domestic or cross-border—much of the information is conflicting. What is Tsingtao worth? Value, like beauty, is in the eyes of the beholder.

TABLE 7-3   Summary of Valuation Measures for Tsingtao Brewing Company Ltd. (Rmb/share and HK\$/share).

VALUATION METHOD	SHARE PRICE	OBSERVATIONS
Current market price	Rmb 2.34	Baseline
Discounted cash flow	Mean = Rmb 2.43 (wide range)	Implies Tsingtao is undervalued
Price-to-earnings ratio	34 to market's 12	Tsingtao's potential may already be included in the price
Market-to-book ratio	0.9957 or 1	Tsingtao is undervalued
Price-to-sales ratio	0.56 to market's .85	Tsingtao is undervalued
Enterprise value-to-EBITDA ratio	07.5 to market's 3.7	Tsingtao is overvalued

SUMMARY

- The number and dollar value of cross-border mergers and acquisitions has grown rapidly in recent years, but the growth and magnitude of activity is taking place in the developed countries, not the developing countries.

- As opposed to the fighting and scraping for market share and profits in traditional domestic markets, an MNE can expect greater growth potential in the global marketplace. There are a variety of paths by which the MNE can enter foreign markets, including greenfield investment and acquisition.

- The drivers of M&A activity are both macro in scope—the global competitive environment—and micro in scope—the variety of industry and firm-level forces and actions driving individual firm value.

- The primary forces of change in the global competitive environment—technological change, regulatory change, and capital market change—create new business opportunities for MNEs, which they pursue aggressively.

- The process of acquiring an enterprise anywhere in the world has three common elements: (1) identification and valuation of the target; (2) completion of the ownership change transaction (the tender); and (3) the management of the postacquisition transition.

- The settlement stage of a cross-border merger or acquisition requires gaining the approval and cooperation of management, shareholders, and eventually regulatory authorities.

- Cross-border mergers, acquisitions, and strategic alliances all face a similar challenge: they must value the target enterprise on the basis of its projected performance in its market. This process of enterprise valuation combines elements of strategy, management, and finance.

- One of the most controversial issues in shareholder rights is at what point in the accumulation of shares is the bidder required to make all shareholders a tender offer. For example, a bidder may slowly accumulate shares of a target company by gradually buying shares on the open market over time. Theoretically, this share accumulation could continue until the bidder has: (1) the single largest block of shares among all individual shareholders, (2) majority control, or (3) all the shares outright.

- Every country possesses a different set of rules and regulations for the transfer of control of publicly traded corporations. This market, the market for corporate control, has been the subject of enormous debate in recent years.

- There are a variety of valuation techniques widely used in global business today, each with its relative merits. In addition to the fundamental methodologies of discounted cash flow (DCF) and multiples (earnings and cash flows), there are also a variety of industry-specific measures that focus on the most significant elements of value in business lines.

- The DCF approach to valuation calculates the value of the enterprise as the present value of all future free cash flows less the cash flows due creditors and minority interest holders.

- The PE ratio is an indication of what the market is willing to pay for a currency unit of earnings. It is also an indication of how secure the market's perception is about the future earnings of the firm and its riskiness.

- The market-to-book ratio (M/B) is a method of valuing a firm on the basis of what the market believes the firm is worth over and above its capital its original capital investment and subsequent retained earnings.

QUESTIONS

1. **Cross-border trends.** According to recent trends in cross-border mergers and acquisitions, would you say that MNEs are moving into emerging markets in a big way?

2. **Shareholder value.** If most bidders pay the owners of the target firm the "true value" of the firm, how does a bidder create value for its own shareholders through the acquisition?

3. **Management and shareholder value.** Why is it that acquisitions provide management with a greater potential for shareholder value creation than internal growth?

4. **Cross-border drivers.** List and explain at least six drivers for cross-border mergers and acquisitions.

5. **Stages of acquisition.** The three stages of a cross-border acquisition combine all elements of business (finance, strategy, accounting, marketing, management, organizational behavior, etc.), but many people believe that finance is relevant only in the first stage. List specific arguments why finance is just as important as any other business field in stages two and three of a cross-border acquisition.

6. **Shareholder rights.** Why do many national governments create specific laws and processes for one company to acquire the control and ownership of another company? Why not just let the market operate on its own?

7. **Settlement.** What factors are considered when deciding how to settle an acquisition in cash or shares?

8. **Corporate cascades.** Why do some countries object to multiple levels of ownership control? Do minority shareholders get treated any differently in these cascades than without them?

9. **Free cash flow versus profit.** Consider the following statement: Academia always focuses on the present value of free cash flow as the definition of value, yet companies seem to focus on "earnings" or "profits."

    a. Do you think this statement is true?

    b. What is the basic distinction between cash flow and profit?

    c. How do we convert a measure of profit (say, net income on a profit and loss statement) into a measure of cash flow?

10. **Discounted cash flow valuation.** Discounted cash flow (DCF) valuation requires the analyst to estimate and isolate the expected free cash flows a specific asset or investment will produce in the future. The analyst then must discount these back to the present.

    a. Are the cash flows and discount rate before or after tax? Do both need to be the same or should one be before tax and the other after tax?

    b. Where does the discount rate for the investment come from? What assumptions should it make about the way the investment will actually be financed?

    c. A very common criticism of DCF is that it "punishes future value and therefore is biased against long-term investments." Construct an argument refuting this statement.

11. **Comparables and market multiples.** What valuation insight or information is gained by looking at market multiples like PE ratios that is not captured in the information gained through discounted cash flow analysis?

12. **Market-to-book.** What is the market-to-book ratio, and why is it considered so useful in the valuation of companies?

13. **Tsingtao (A).** Recommend the valuation measure, or combination of valuation methods, that Anheuser-Busch (AB) should use.

14. **Tsingtao (B).** What share price should AB offer? Is this an opening offer or best offer in negotiations?

15. **Tsingtao (C).** Identify the postacquisition (Phase III) problems that AB is likely to face if it acquires a larger minority ownership position in Tsingtao.

PROBLEMS

1. **PE valuation of Global.com.** A new worldwide cellular phone company, Global.com (U.S.), is one of the new high-flying telecommunication stocks that are valued largely on the basis of price/earnings multiples. Other firms trading on U.S. exchanges in its similar industry segment are currently valued at PE ratios of 35 to 40. Given the following earnings estimates, what would you estimate the value of Global.com to be?

LAST YEAR'S	THIS YEAR'S	NEXT YEAR'S
EPS	EPS	EPS
$(1.20)	$0.75	$1.85

2. **Bidding on Sao Paulo cellular rights.** A consortium of global telecommunication firms is about to submit a bid to purchase the rights to provide cellular telephone services to central Sao Paulo. The bid must be submitted, and payment made if awarded the bid, in U.S. dollars, not in Brazilian reais (R$). The consortium has finalized the following forecasts of cash flows, exchange rates, and potential discount rates.

	YEAR 0	YEAR 1	YEAR 2	YEAR 3
Estimated CF				
(millions of R$):				
Best case	(1,350)	550	2,000	3,800
Moderate case	(1,350)	550	1,600	3,200
Worst case	(1,350)	550	1,000	1,500
Expected Exchange				
Rate (R$/US$):				
Best case	1.70	1.70	1.70	1.70
Moderate case	1.70	1.80	1.90	2.00
Worst case	1.70	2.00	2.20	2.50
Discount rate				
(R$ terms)	32.0%			
Discount rate				
(US$ terms)	18.0%			

Perform a DCF analysis on the potential investment and propose a final bid for submission.

Private equity in Latin America—The Soto Group. *(Use the following private equity problem to answer Questions 3 through 5.) Private equity focuses on purchasing small privately held firms, restructuring them with infusions of capital and professional management, and reselling them several years later (either to another private buyer or through a public offering). Thus their value to the private equity investors is in their terminal value—their value when taken public several years from now.*

The Soto Group is a Mexico City–based private equity fund. The group is evaluating the prospects for purchasing Guga Avionics (Buenos Aires), an aviation operating and management firm with current business operations throughout Argentina and southern Brazil. The Soto Group has, through their due diligence process, acquired the needed financial statements, inventory of assets, and assessment of operations. Soto's valuation staff typically values the potential target on both an a priori basis (current structure and management strategy) and an ex post basis (expected values after capital and management expertise injections).

The second major set of "ifs" associated with acquiring Guga is what it could sell for in three years. The Soto Group has an unbending internal discipline that every firm acquired must be restructured, revitalized, and ready for public sale in three years from deal consummation or less. Given market multiples on the Buenos Aires Bolsa at this time, a value of 18 to 20 times current free cash flow (year 3) would be considered aggressive. The a priori analysis, acquired from Guga Avionics and adjusted by Soto's own valuation and market experts, appears in the following table.

A priori financial forecast: Guga Avionics, Buenos Aires, Argentina (millions of Argentine pesos)

	YEAR 0	YEAR 1	YEAR 2	YEAR 3
Gross revenues	210	235	270	325
Less direct costs	(132)	(144)	(162)	(190)
Gross profit	78	91	108	135
Gross margin	37%	39%	40%	41%
Less G&A	(16)	(17)	(18)	(19)
Less depreciation	(24)	(24)	(24)	(24)
EBIT	38	50	66	92
Less interest	(28)	(30)	(30)	(28)
EBT	10	20	36	64
Less taxes @ 30%	(3)	(6)	(11)	(19)
Net profit	7	14	26	45
Return on sales	3%	6%	9%	14%

The Soto Group believes that it can reduce financing expenses by 25% in years 1 and 2, and 25% in year 3. It also believes that by using its own operational experience, it can reduce direct costs by 15%, 20%, and 25%, in years 1, 2, and 3, respectively. The big question is revenue enhancement. Guga has done a solid job of promoting and expanding service revenues in the past several years. At most, the Soto Group believes it may be able to expand gross revenues by 5% per annum over current forecasts.

3. **Guga Avionics valuation (A).** Using this data, as the lead member of the Soto Group's valuation staff, what is the difference between a priori and ex post earnings and cash flows?

4. **Guga Avionics valuation (B).** What is the difference between a priori and ex post sale value at the end of year 3?

5. **Soto Group and Guga Avionics.** What would you recommend—in addition to the current Soto plan—to enhance the profit and cash flow outlook for Guga if acquired?

Tsingtao Brewery Company. *Use the spreadsheet analysis of Tsingtao Brewery Company used throughout the chapter to answer questions 6 through 10.*

6. **Tsingtao Brewery Company (A).** As described in the chapter, Anheuser-Busch (AB) is interested in further analysis of the potential value represented by the newfound strategic and operational direction of Tsingtao. The baseline analysis assumed some rather aggressive growth rates in sales. AB wishes to find out what are the implications of slower sales growth, such as 15% per annum throughout the 2001–2005 period, on the discounted cash flow equity value of the company. And, assuming that sales growth is indeed slower, AB wishes to determine the compounded impact of a declining NOPAT margin, such as

3.6% of sales, rather than the baseline assumption of 4.2% of sales, on equity value. Perform the analysis.

7. **Tsingtao Brewery Company (B).** Returning to the original set of assumptions, AB is now focusing on the capital expenditure and depreciation components of the valuation. Tsingtao has invested heavily in brewery upgrades and distribution equipment in recent years, and hopes that its capital expenditures are largely done. However, if a number of the recent acquisitions require higher capex levels, AB wants to run a scenario to focus on that possibility. What is the impact on Tsingtao's discounted cash flow value if capex expenditures are assumed to be 3.5% of sales rather than the baseline assumption of 2.5%? What is the result of combining that with an assumed depreciation level of 8.5%, as opposed to 7.5% (baseline), for the time period of the analysis?

8. **Tsingtao Brewery Company (C).** Returning to the original set of assumptions: one of the truly controversial components of all discounted cash flow analysis is the impact that terminal value calculations have on equity value. AB wishes to explore the following sensitivities to the DCF valuation:

   a. Assuming no terminal value, what is the DCF equity value per share?

   b. Assuming a terminal value growth rate of 0%, what is the DCF equity value per share? What percentage of the total DCF value is the terminal value?

9. **Tsingtao Brewery Company (D).** One of AB's analysts is quite pessimistic on the outlook for Tsingtao. Although the company did indeed make major strides in reducing net working capital needs in recent years, much of that was accomplished before really tackling the complexity of absorbing many of these new acquisitions. The analyst argues that, at best, sales growth will average 12% for the coming five-year period and that net working capital will most likely rise to 3% of sales (baseline assumption was 1%). What does this do to the equity valuation of Tsingtao?

10. **Tsingtao Brewery Company (E).** Finally, the valuation staff wants to address a full scenario of what they consider best-case and worst-case analysis, assuming that the baseline analysis is somewhere in between (moderate).

	BEST CASE	BASELINE	WORST CASE
Sales growth	20%	Variable	10%
NOPAT of sales	4.4%	4.2%	3.6%
Depreciation	8.5%	7.5%	6.5%
NWC of sales	0.8%	1.0%	3.0%
Capex of sales	1.5%	2.5%	3.5%
Terminal value growth	2.0%	1.0%	0.0%

Evaluate the best-case and worst-case scenarios for Tsingtao.

INTERNET EXERCISES

1. **Intellectual property & valuation.** The late 1990s saw the rise of corporate valuations arising from ownership of various forms of intellectual property, rather than the traditional value arising from goods or services production and sale. Use the following website as a start to prepare a management brief on the current state of valuing intellectual property.

   Intellectual Property Valuation http://valuationcorp.com

2. **Market capitalization of Brahma of Brazil.** Brahma is one of the largest publicly traded firms in Brazil. It is listed on both the Bovespa and the New York Stock Exchange (ADRs). Using historical data that can be found on one of the following sources, answer the following questions.

   Hoovers http://www.hoovers.com

   Yahoo http://www.yahoo.com

   a. How did Brahma's share price—in both real and U.S. dollar terms—react to the January 1999 Brazilian reais devaluation?

   b. Would a firm like Brahma be a more or less attractive target of foreign investors after the reais's devaluation?

SELECTED READINGS

Bank of America Roundtable on Evaluating and Financing Foreign Direct Investment," *Journal of Applied Corporate Finance*, Volume 9, No. 3, Fall 1996, pp. 64–79.

Brouthers, K.D. and L.E. Brouthers, "Acquisition or Greenfield Startup? Institutional, Cultural, and Transaction Cost Influences," *Strategic Management Journal*, No. 21, 2000, pp. 89–98.

Bruner, Robert, "Where M&A Pays and Where It Strays: A Survey of the Research," *Journal of Applied Corporate Finance*, Vol. 16, No. 4, Fall 2004, pp. 63–76.

Doukas, J. and N.G. Travlos, "The Effect of Corporate Nationalism on Shareholders' Wealth: Evidence From International Acquisitions," *Journal of Finance*, No. 43, 1988, pp. 1161–1175.

Lee, Tung-Jean and Richard E. Caves, "Uncertain Outcomes of Foreign Investment: Determinants of Profits After Large Acquisitions," *Journal of International Business Studies*, Volume 29, No. 3, Third Quarter 1998, pp. 563–582.

Luehrman, Timothy A., "What's It Worth?: A General Manager's Guide to Valuation," *Harvard Business Review*, May–June 1997, pp. 132–142.

Luehrman, Timothy A., "Strategy as a Portfolio of Real Options," *Harvard Business Review*, September–October 1998, pp. 89–99.

Reuer, Jeffrey J., Oded Shenkar and Robert Ragozzino, "Mitigating Risk in International Mergers and Acquisitions: The Role of Contingent Payouts," *Journal of International Business Studies*, Vol. 35, no. 1, January 2004, pp. 19–32.

Seth, A, K. P. Song, and R. Pettit, "Value Creation and Destruction in Cross-Border Acquisitions: An Empirical Analysis of Foreign Acquisitions of U.S. Firms," *Strategic Management Journal*, No. 23, 2002, pp. 921–940.

Tolmunen, Pasi and Sami Torstila, "Cross-Listings and M&A Activity: Transatlantic Evidence," *Financial Management*, Vol 34, No. 1, Spring 2005, pp. 123–142.

MINICASE   THE BIDDING WAR FOR HARBIN BREWERY GROUP (CHINA)

There is great disorder under heaven. The situation is excellent.

Mao Tse-tung

The Harbin Brewery Group was a dominant player in the Northeastern part of China, and the fourth largest brewer in China in 2004 with a 4% market share for the country. Harbin held a 76% market share in its home city of Harbin City and a 43% share in the Heilongjiang region. Harbin was publicly traded on the Hong Kong Stock Exchange. But no one expected the bidding war to come in the early summer of 2004.

Hapi, as it was commonly known, was Harbin's number-one selling beer in Northeastern China (see Figure A). This region, Heilongjiang, had the highest per capita consumption of beer within the country at 36 liters, double the national average of 18 liters. The market, however, was now mature and saturated. The high per capita consumption rate allowed little room for organic growth. This situation had forced Harbin to either live with its regional label or launch aggressive expansion elsewhere to claim national status.

Harbin Brewery Group had always been controlled by the Harbin City government, but the remaining shares had seen many different hands. Harbin Brewery Group Ltd. first went public in June 2002, eventually having a full 41% of its ownership publicly floated. Harbin came into play in June 2003 when SABMiller, the South African—based beer conglomerate, acquired 29% of Harbin's shares in a highly controversial investment. SABMiller's purchase was considered to be hostile by brewery management. SABMiller's actual purchase was made by Gardwell, a financial investment company that was 95% owned by SABMiller and 5% Harbin Brewery management. Accusations of conflict of interest and self-dealing followed. SABMiller unhappily agreed to a five-year standstill agreement preventing it from acquiring additional shares.

On March 23, 2004, Harbin's management announced that it had reached agreement to sell itself in a friendly sale to Global Conduit Holdings—but would not divulge who Global Conduit represented. Five weeks later, on May 2, Anheuser-Busch mysteriously and surprisingly announced that it would purchase the 29% interest held by Global Conduit for $139 million (an effective price of HK$3.70/share, which was above the current market price). SABMiller responded quickly with an offer of HK$4.30/share on May 5 (see Figure B). In the following weeks, Anheuser-Busch acquired additional shares, raising its total interest to

37.4% (including the share options held by the Harbin management team). The Mayor of Harbin City announced that "Anheuser-Busch was the right strategic partner" for Harbin.[1]

On June 1, Anheuser-Busch announced a mandatory general tender offer for all outstanding shares at HK$5.58/share. A *mandatory general tender offer* is when the buyer is offering a stated price to all current public share owners. The offer was contingent on the buyer gaining control; in this case, more than 50% of issued voting share capital. Under Chinese law, once Anheuser-Busch took control of more than 90% of Harbin's voting shares, the remaining shares would be required to be sold to Anheuser-Busch. The Hong Kong Stock Exchange required the company be delisted once voting share free float fell below 25%. This tender offer price (HK$5.58/share) was an additional 30% premium over and above the SABMiller offer price (HK$4.30/share). Harbin had been trading at roughly HK$3.30 per share over the recent quarter.

On June 2, SABMiller announced it was withdrawing from the bidding for Harbin. The CEO of SABMiller, Graham Mackay, stated, "We remain fully committed to the Chinese beer market and we must evaluate every potential acquisition on its merits. We believe that the AB offer price for Harbin more than fully values the business, even after taking into account the significant synergies uniquely available to us." Meanwhile Harbin Brewery's CEO, Peter Lo, summarized management's position very clearly: "The SABMiller offer was wholly unsolicited and not welcomed by the management or employees of Harbin. I am therefore delighted that Anheuser-Busch has stepped in as a white knight with a counterbid." But the question remained: what had Anheuser-Busch bought?

. . . We believe Harbin will be privatized at the takeover offer price. More importantly, instead of the strong synergies anticipated under SABMiller, we see AB's victory creating uncertainty over Harbin's operations. The reason: we expect competition between Harbin (under AB) and China Resources Brewery (under SABMiller)—together dominating the northeast China market—to intensify.

"AB takes over, the end of the story," Nomura International, June 4, 2004

---

[1]"Anheuser wins stake and PR battle in China," Media, June 18, 2004, p. 8.

FIGURE A   Major Chinese Beer Markets.

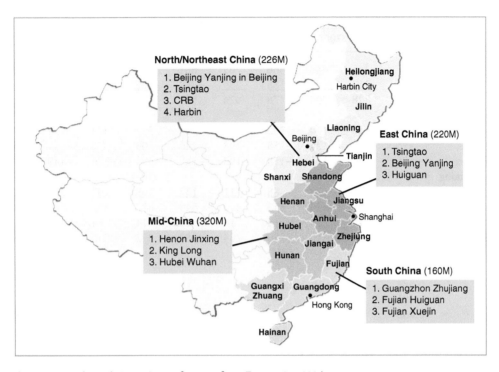

Source: Regional population estimates for 2002 from *Euromonitor*, 2004.

FIGURE B   Bidding for Harbin Brewery Group, 2004.

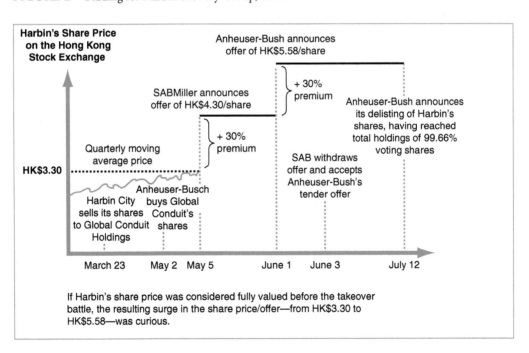

TABLE C   Citigroup's Valuation of Harbin, March 2004 (millions of HK$).

	2004E	2005E	2006E	2007E	2008E	2009E	2010E	2011E	2012E	2013E	2014E
					HARBIN BREWERY—DCF VALUATION						
EBIT	237	345	448	566	709	881	1,086	1,328	1,610	1,986	2,308
Cash taxes	−86	−117	−149	−188	−235	−292	−360	−441	−534	−642	−766
NOPAT	150	228	300	378	474	589	726	887	1,076	1,293	1,542
Depreciation and amortization	139	150	160	202	253	314	387	473	574	690	823
Maintenance capex	−75	−100	−125	−158	−198	−246	−303	−370	−449	−540	−643
Expansionary capex	−175	−150	−125	−158	−198	−246	−303	−370	−449	−540	−643
Change in net working capital	43	57	70	88	111	137	169	207	251	302	360
Free cash flow (FCF)	83	185	279	353	442	549	677	827	1,003	1,206	1,438
WACC	14	14	14	14	14	14	14	14	14	14	14
Present value	83	163	216	240	264	288	312	336	358	378	396
Constant growth	3										
Terminal value	3,687										
DCF firm value	6,324										
Less net debt	291										
Equity value	6,032										
EV per share	6.02										

Source: Citigroup Smith Barney, "Harbin Brewery," March 19, 2004, p. 8.

QUESTIONS

1. Did AB pay too much for a mature business?

2. Because Harbin's major competitor is controlled by SABMiller, will a price war likely result from the new competitive structure in the region? What will this do to Harbin's value?

3. Table C is Citigroup's valuation of Harbin at the start of the bidding war. Analyze their valuation of HK$6.02/share compared to the HK$5.58/share Anheuser-Busch finally paid.

MULTINATIONAL TAX MANAGEMENT

8

T ax planning for multinational operations is an extremely complex but vitally important aspect of international business. To plan effectively, MNEs must understand not only the intricacies of their own operations worldwide, but also the different structures and interpretations of tax liabilities across countries. *The primary objective of multinational tax planning is the minimization of the firm's worldwide tax burden.* This objective, however, must not be pursued without full recognition that decision making within the firm must always be based on the economic fundamentals of the firm's line of business, and not on convoluted policies undertaken purely for the reduction of tax liability. As evident from previous chapters, taxes have a major impact on corporate net income and cash flow through their influence on foreign investment decisions, financial structure, determination of the cost of capital, foreign exchange management, working capital management, and financial control.

The purpose of this chapter is to provide an overview of the way taxes are applied to MNEs globally, how the United States taxes the global earnings of U.S.-based MNEs, and how U.S.-based multinationals manage their global tax liabilities. We do this in four parts. The first section acquaints you with the overall international tax environment. This includes a brief overview of the tax environments that an MNE is likely to encounter globally and the basics of most intercountry tax treaties. The second part examines transfer pricing. The third part of the chapter describes how the United States government taxes income generated abroad by U.S.-based multinationals, highlighting the tax management dilemma faced by Carlton. Although we use U.S. taxes as illustrations, our intention is not to make this chapter or this book U.S.-centric. Most of the U.S. practices that we describe have close parallels in other countries, albeit modified to fit their specific national overall tax system. The fourth and final part of the chapter examines the use of tax-haven subsidiaries and international offshore financial centers.

8.1   TAX PRINCIPLES

The following sections explain the most important aspects of the international tax environments and specific features that affect MNEs. Before we explain the specifics of multinational taxation in practice, however, it is necessary to introduce two areas of fundamental importance: *tax morality and tax neutrality.*

Tax Morality

The MNE faces not only a morass of foreign taxes but also an ethical question. In many countries, taxpayers—whether corporate or individual—do not voluntarily comply with the tax laws. Smaller domestic firms and individuals are the chief violators. The MNE must decide whether to follow a practice of full disclosure to tax authorities or adopt the philosophy of "when in Rome, do as the Romans do." Given the local prominence of most foreign subsidiaries and the political sensitivity of their position, most MNEs follow the full disclosure practice. Some firms, however, believe that their competitive position would be eroded if they did not avoid taxes to the same extent as their domestic competitors. There is obviously no prescriptive answer to the problem, as business ethics are partly a function of cultural heritage and historical development.

Some countries have imposed what seem to be arbitrary punitive tax penalties on MNEs for presumed violations of local tax laws. Property or wealth tax assessments are sometimes perceived by the foreign firm to be excessively large when compared with those levied on locally owned firms. The problem is then how to respond to tax penalties that are punitive or discriminatory.

Tax Neutrality

When a government decides to levy a tax, it must consider not only the potential revenue from the tax, or how efficiently it can be collected, but also the effect that the proposed tax can have on private economic behavior. For example, the U.S. government's policy on taxation of foreign source income does not have as its sole objective the raising of revenue but instead has multiple objectives. These include the following:

- Neutralizing tax incentives that might favor (or disfavor) U.S. private investment in developed countries
- Providing an incentive for U.S. private investment in developing countries
- Improving the U.S. balance of payments by removing the advantages of artificial tax havens and encouraging repatriation of funds
- Raising revenue

The ideal tax should not only raise revenue efficiently but also have as few negative effects on economic behavior as possible. Some theorists argue that the ideal tax should be completely neutral in its effect on private decisions and completely equitable among taxpayers. However, other theorists claim that national policy objectives such as balance of payments or investment in developing countries should be encouraged through an active tax incentive policy. Most tax systems compromise between these two viewpoints.

One way to view neutrality is to require that the burden of taxation on each dollar, euro, pound, or yen of profit earned in home country operations by an MNE be equal to the burden of taxation on each currency-equivalent of profit earned by the same firm in its foreign operations. This policy is called *domestic neutrality*. A second way to view neutrality is to require that the tax burden on each foreign subsidiary of the firm be equal to the tax burden on its competitors in the same country. This policy is called *foreign neutrality*. The latter interpretation is often supported by MNEs, because it focuses more on the competitiveness of the individual firm in individual country markets.

The issue of *tax equity* is also difficult to define and measure. In theory, an equitable tax is one that imposes the same total tax burden on all taxpayers who are similarly situated and located in the same tax jurisdiction. In the case of foreign investment income, the U.S. Treasury argues that because the United States uses the nationality principle to claim tax jurisdiction, U.S.-owned foreign subsidiaries are in the same tax jurisdiction as U.S. domestic subsidiaries. Therefore a dollar earned in foreign operations should be taxed at the same rate and paid at the same time as a dollar earned in domestic operations.

National Tax Environments

Despite the fundamental objectives of national tax authorities, it is widely agreed that taxes do affect economic decisions made by MNEs. Tax treaties between nations, and differential tax structures, rates, and practices all result in a less than level playing field for the MNEs competing on world markets.

Table 8-1 provides an overview of corporate tax rates as applicable to Japan, Germany, and the United States. The categorizations of income (e.g., distributed versus undistributed profits), the differences in tax rates, and the discrimination in tax rates applicable to income earned in specific countries serve to introduce the critical dimensions of tax planning for the MNE.

Nations typically structure their tax systems along one of two basic approaches: the worldwide approach or the territorial approach. Both approaches are attempts to determine which firms, foreign or domestic by incorporation, or which incomes, foreign or domestic in origin, are subject to the taxation of host country tax authorities.

TABLE 8-1 Comparison of Corporate Tax Rates for Japan, Germany, and the United States.

TAXABLE INCOME CATEGORY	JAPAN	GERMANY	UNITED STATES
Corporate income tax rates:			
Profits distributed to stockholders	30.0%	30.5%	35.0%
Undistributed profits	30.0%	30.5%	35.0%
Branches of foreign corporations	30.0%	30.5%	35.0%
Withholding taxes on dividends (portfolio):			
with Japan	—	20.0%	10.0%
with Germany	10.0%	—	5.0%
with United States	10.0%	15.0%	—
Withholding taxes on dividends (substantial holdings):			
with Japan	—	15.0%	15.0%
with Germany	15.0%	—	15.0%
with United States*	15.0%	5.0%	—
Withholding taxes on interest:			
with Japan	—	10.0%	10.0%
with Germany	10.0%	—	0.0%
with United States	10.0%	0% to 25%	—
Withholding taxes on royalties:			
with Japan	—	10.0%	10.0%
with Germany	10.0%	—	0.0%
with United States	10.0%	0.0%	—

Source: PricewaterhouseCoopers, Corporate Taxes 2003–2004, Worldwide Summaries, 2004.

* "Substantial holdings" for the United States applies only to intercorporate dividend payments. In Germany and Japan, "substantial holdings" applies to corporate shareholders of greater than 25% interest in the enterprise. The German corporate tax rate of 30.5% is the sum of a 25.0% basic income tax rate plus a 5.5% solidarity levy.

WORLDWIDE APPROACH   The *worldwide approach*, also referred to as the *residential* or *national approach*, levies taxes on the income earned by firms that are incorporated in the host country, regardless of where the income was earned (domestically or abroad). An MNE earning income both at home and abroad would therefore find its worldwide income taxed by its home country tax authorities. For example, a country like the United States taxes the income earned by firms based in the United States regardless of whether the income earned by the firm is domestically sourced or foreign-sourced. In the case of the United States, ordinary foreign-sourced income is taxed only as remitted to the parent firm. As with all questions of tax, however, numerous conditions and exceptions exist. The primary problem is that this approach does not address the income earned by foreign firms operating within the United States. Countries like the United States then apply the principle of territorial taxation to foreign firms within their legal jurisdiction, taxing all income earned by foreign firms within their borders as well.

TERRITORIAL APPROACH   The *territorial approach*, also termed the *source approach*, focuses on the income earned by firms within the legal jurisdiction of the host country, not on the country of firm incorporation. Countries like Germany that follow the territorial approach apply taxes equally to foreign and domestic firms on income earned within the country but in principle not on income earned outside the country. The territorial approach, like the worldwide approach, results in a major gap in coverage if resident firms earn income outside the country but are not taxed by the country in which the profits are earned. In this case, tax authorities extend tax coverage to income earned abroad if it is not covered by foreign tax jurisdictions. Once again, a mix of the two tax approaches is necessary for full coverage of income.

TAX DEFERRAL   If the worldwide approach to international taxation is followed to the letter, it would end the *tax-deferral* privilege for many MNEs. Foreign subsidiaries of MNEs pay host country corporate income taxes, but many parent countries defer claiming additional income taxes on that foreign source income *until it is remitted to the parent firm*. For example, U.S. corporate income taxes on some types of foreign source income of U.S.-owned subsidiaries incorporated abroad are deferred until the earnings are remitted to the U.S. parent. However, in October 2004 the U.S. tax laws were modified to encourage foreign source tax-deferred income earned before 2003 to be repatriated to the United States at a low 5.25% tax rate. This money has to be repatriated before the end of 2005 and be used to stimulate job creation in the United States to qualify for the low rate. It has been estimated that as much as $520 billion will be returned, depending on the final U.S. Treasury tax guidelines that will determine exactly how the repatriated funds can be used.[1] *Global Finance in Practice 8.1* describes what has transpired recently with this repatriation act.

Tax Treaties

A network of bilateral tax treaties, many of which are modeled after one proposed by the Organisation for Economic Cooperation and Development (OECD), provides a means of reducing double taxation. Tax treaties normally define whether taxes are to be imposed on income earned in one country by the nationals of another, and if so, how. Tax treaties are bilateral, with the two signatories specifying what rates are applicable to which types of income between themselves alone. Table 8-1's specification of withholding taxes on dividends, interest, and royalty payments between resident corporations of Japan, Germany, and the United States, is a classic example of the structure of tax treaties. Note that Germany, for example, imposes a 10% withholding tax on royalty payments to Japanese investors, and royalty payments to U.S. investors are withheld at a 0% rate.

The individual bilateral tax jurisdictions as specified through tax treaties are particularly important for firms that are primarily exporting to another country rather than doing business there through a "permanent establishment." The latter would be the case for manufacturing operations.

---

[1] *Business Week*, August 1, 2005, p 34.

Global Finance in Practice 8.1

Profits Head Homeward, But Where Are the Jobs?

When it comes to corporate income taxes, it sure pays to be a multinational these days. U.S. companies fork over up to 35% of their domestic income in federal taxes. But for earnings from abroad, the tax rate is just 5.25% this year, thanks to the American Jobs Creation Act of 2004. The election-year bill was aimed at spurring the U.S. economy by encouraging U.S. companies with international operations to bring home profits they had parked in lower tax countries.

The one-year tax break has clearly opened the floodgates: U.S. based companies are on track to repatriate upwards of $520 billion by the end of December, estimates Henry "Chip" Dickson, chief U.S. equity strategist at Lehman Brothers Inc. The drug industry is far and away ahead of the pack. Led by Pfizer Inc., which is returning $36.9 billion in foreign earnings alone, pharmaceutical and biotech companies could bring $120.5 billion into their U.S. coffers at the lower tax rate. High-tech equipment makers such as IBM and Hewlett-Packard Co. come next, with an estimated $62.9 billion in repatriated earnings.

But if there's little doubt the money is pouring in, figuring out exactly where it's going is another matter. Though the bill was promoted as a job-creation measure, regulations set by the U.S. Treasury leave companies wide leeway in how they use their repatriated profits, Hiring, capital investment, research and development, marketing, acquisitions, pension funding, and debt repayment all qualify—and companies do not have to disclose specifics of their spending plans. They also have three years to allocate the cash. Moreover, if a company plows its foreign profits into research and development, for instance, it could take money previously earmarked for research and use it elsewhere. "You can't trace the money," points out Mickey D. Levy, chief economist at Bank of America Corp.

Still, some companies are starting to show how they're putting their newfound treasure to use. In June, Pfizer paid $1.9 billion for Vicuron Pharmaceuticals Inc., a King of Prussia (Pa.) biotech firm. Pfizer also has initiated a $5 billion stock buyback—though the company says that isn't a direct result of the profits it's shipping home, since share repurchases aren't allowed under the Treasury regs. But a spokesman for the New York-based drugmaker acknowledges: "It's hard to say where money is going to and coming from."

One thing is clear, however: The money piling in from abroad as the result of the Jobs Creation Act has done little to actually spur hiring. In fact, six of the 10 companies repatriating the biggest totals are axing workers in the U.S. They include HP, which announced July 19 that it would cut its head count by 14,500 in the U.S. and abroad, and Pfizer, which has said it will shutter 20 factories with undisclosed U.S. job losses to lower costs by $4 billion by 2008.

Oddly, the repatriation is also cutting into profits. The reason: Even that measly 5.25% rate means companies must pay higher taxes than they had budgeted when the earnings were tucked away outside the U.S. Pfizer has taken a $1.7 billion charge to cover taxes on its foreign profits in the first half, while Merck & Co. has said it would have to take a one-time charge of $1 billion if it goes ahead with plans to bring home $15 billion.

Back to the U.S.

Estimated amount of repatriated profits in 2005, in billions

Pfizer	$36.9
Merck	15.0
Hewlett-Packard	14.5
Johnson & Johnson	10.8
DuPont	10.0
Schering-Plough	9.4
Bristol-Myers Squibb	9.0
IBM	8.0
Eli Lilly	8.0
PepsiCo	7.5

Data: Company reports

Altogether, if Corporate America returns the $520 billion that Dickson says it could, the government could collect an extra $27.3 billion in income taxes this year. But next year, the tax rate on overseas earnings snaps back to 35%. Every holiday, after all, must come to an end.

Source: Michael Arndt, "Profits Head Homeward, But Where Are the Jobs?" *Business Week*, Aug. 1, 2005, p. 34.

A firm that only exports would not want any of its other worldwide income taxed by the importing country. Tax treaties define what is a "permanent establishment" and what constitutes a limited presence for tax purposes.

Tax treaties also typically result in reduced withholding tax rates between the two signatory countries, the negotiation of the treaty itself serving as a forum for opening and expanding business relationships between the two countries. This practice is important to both MNEs operating through foreign subsidiaries, earning *active income*, and individual portfolio investors simply receiving *passive income* in the form of dividends, interest, or royalties.

Tax Types

Taxes are classified on the basis of whether they are applied directly to income, called *direct taxes*, or on the basis of some other measurable performance characteristic of the firm, called *indirect taxes*. Table 8-2 illustrates the wide range of corporate income taxes in the world today.

INCOME TAX   Many governments rely on personal and corporate income taxes for their primary revenue source. Corporate income taxes are widely used today. Some countries impose different corporate tax rates on distributed income versus undistributed income. Corporate income tax rates vary over a relatively wide range, rising as high as 45% in Guyana and falling as low as 16% in Hong Kong, 15% in the British Virgin Islands, 10% in Cyprus, and effectively 0% in a number of offshore tax havens (discussed later in this chapter).

WITHHOLDING TAX   Passive income (dividends, interest, royalties) earned by a resident of one country within the tax jurisdiction of a second country are normally subject to a withholding tax in the second country. The reason for the institution of withholding taxes is actually quite simple: governments recognize that most international investors will not file a tax return in each country in which they invest, and the government therefore wishes to assure that a minimum tax payment is received. As the term *withholding* implies, the taxes are withheld by the corporation from the payment made to the investor, and the withheld taxes are then turned over to government authorities. Withholding taxes are a major subject of bilateral tax treaties, and generally range between 0% and 25%.

VALUE-ADDED TAX   One type of tax that has achieved great prominence is the *value-added tax (VAT)*. The value-added tax is a type of national sales tax collected at each stage of production or sale of consumption goods in proportion to the value added during that stage. In general, production goods such as plant and equipment have not been subject to the value-added tax. Certain basic necessities such as medicines and other health-related expenses, education and religious activities, and the postal service are usually exempt or taxed at lower rates. The value-added tax has been adopted as the main source of revenue from indirect taxation by all members of the European Union, most other countries in Western Europe, a number of Latin American countries, Canada, and scattered other countries. A numerical example of a value-added tax computation is shown in Table 8-3.

OTHER NATIONAL TAXES   There are a variety of other national taxes, which vary in importance from country to country. The *turnover tax* (tax on the purchase or sale of securities in some country stock markets) and the *tax on undistributed profits* were mentioned before. *Property* and *inheritance taxes*, also termed *transfer taxes*, are imposed in a variety of ways to achieve intended social redistribution of income and wealth as much as to raise revenue. There are a number of red-tape charges for public services that are in reality user taxes. Sometimes foreign exchange purchases or sales are in effect hidden taxes, inasmuch as the government earns revenue rather than just regulates imports and exports for balance of payments reasons.

TABLE 8-2 Corporate Tax Rates for Selected Countries (percentage of taxable income).

COUNTRY	TAX RATE	COUNTRY	TAX RATE	COUNTRY	TAX RATE
Antigua & Barbuda	40	Ghana	32.5	Panama	30
Argentina	25	Greece	35	Papua New Guinea	25
Australia	30	Guatemala	31	Paraguay	30
Austria	34	Guyana	45	Peru	27
Azerbaijan	25	Hong Kong	16	Philippines	32
Bahamas	0	Hungary	18	Poland	27
Bahrain	0	India	36.75	Portugal	33
Barbados	36	Indonesia	30	Puerto Rico	20
Belgium	34	Iran	25	Qatar	35
Bermuda	0	Ireland	12.5/25	Romania	25
Bolivia	25	Isle of Man	18	Russian Federation	24
Botswana	5/15	Israel	36	St. Lucia	33.33
Brazil	15	Italy	34	Saudi Arabia	30
British Virgin Islands	15/1	Ivory Coast (Côte d'Ivore)	35	Singapore	22
Brunei Darussalam	30	Jamaica	33.3	Slovak Republic	25
Bulgaria	23.5	Japan	30	Slovenia	25
Cambodia	20	Kazakhstan	30	Solomon Islands	30
Canada	33/38	Kenya	30	South Africa	30
Cayman Islands	0	Korea	27	Spain	35
Channel Islands, Guernsey	20	Latvia	15	Sri Lanka	30
Channel Islands, Jersey	20	Liechtenstein	15	Swaziland	30
Chile	17	Lithuania	15	Sweden	28
China	30	Luxembourg	22	Switzerland	17–30
Colombia	36.7	Macau	15	Tahiti	35
Congo	40	Malaysia	28	Taiwan	25
Costa Rica	30	Malta	35	Tanzania	30
Croatia	20	Mauritius	25	Thailand	30
Cyprus	10	Mexico	35	Trinidad & Tobago	30
Czech Republic	31	Morocco	35	Turkey	30
Denmark	30	Mozambique	32	Ukraine	30
Dominican Republic	25	Namibia	35	United Kingdom	33
Ecuador	25	Netherlands	34.5	United States	35
Egypt	40	Netherlands Antilles	34.5	Uruguay	35
Estonia	35	New Caledonia	30	Uzbekistan	20
Faroe Islands	20	New Zealand	33	Venezuela	34
Fiji	32	Norway	28	Vietnam	25
Finland	29	Oman	30	Zambia	35
France	33.33	Pakistan	35p/45np	Zimbabwe	30.9
Germany	26.5				

Notes: Botswana rates differ between manufacturing (5%) and nonmanufacturing (15%); the British Virgin Islands impose a 1% tax on foreign-source income; Canada imposes a 33% rate on manufacturing and processing industries, 38% on all others; Chile imposes a 35% withholding tax on income remitted to foreign residents from domestic operations; Ireland imposes a 12.5% rate on trading companies, 25% on nontrading companies; Pakistan rates differ between publicly owned (p, 35%) and nonpublic ownership (np, 45%); Switzerland's effective rate depends greatly on the canton of residence. These rates are representative rates, and often vary by industry and activities within each country. For actual tax liability calculations, see original source.

Source: PricewaterhouseCoopers, *Corporate Taxes 2003–2004, Worldwide Summaries,* 2004.

TABLE 8-3
Value-Added Tax Applied to the Sale of a Wooden Fence Post.

This is an example of how a wooden fence post would be assessed for value-added taxes in the course of its production and subsequent sale. A value-added tax rate of 10% is assumed.

Step 1. The original tree owner sells to the lumber mill, for $0.20, that part of a tree that ultimately becomes the fence post. The grower has added $0.20 in value up to this point by planting and raising the tree. After collecting $0.20 from the lumber mill, the grower must set aside $0.02 to pay the value-added tax to the government.

Step 2. The lumber mill processes the tree into fence posts and sells each post for $0.40 to the lumber wholesaler. The lumber mill has added $0.20 in value ($0.40 less $0.20) through its processing activities. Therefore the lumber mill owner must set aside $0.02 to pay the mill's value-added tax to the government. In practice, the owner would probably calculate the mill's tax liability as 10% of $0.40, or $0.04, with a tax credit of $0.02 for the value-added tax already paid by the tree owner.

Steps 3 and 4. The lumber wholesaler and retailer also add value to the fence post through their selling and distribution activities. They are assessed $0.01 and $0.03, respectively, making the cumulative value-added tax collected by the government $0.08, or 10% of the final sales price.

STAGE OF PRODUCTION	SALES PRICE	VALUE ADDED	VALUE-ADDED TAX AT 10%	CUMULATIVE VALUE-ADDED TAX
Tree owner	$0.20	$0.20	$0.02	$0.02
Lumber mill	$0.40	$0.20	$0.02	$0.04
Lumber wholesaler	$0.50	$0.10	$0.01	$0.05
Lumber retailer	$0.80	$0.30	$0.03	$0.08

Foreign Tax Credits

To prevent double taxation of the same income, most countries grant a *foreign tax credit* for income taxes paid to the host country. Countries differ on how they calculate the foreign tax credit and what kinds of limitations they place on the total amount claimed. Normally foreign tax credits are also available for withholding taxes paid to other countries on dividends, royalties, interest, and other income remitted to the parent. The value-added tax and other sales taxes are not eligible for a foreign tax credit but are typically deductible from pretax income as an expense.

A *tax credit* is a direct reduction of taxes that would otherwise be due and payable. It differs from a *deductible expense,* which is an expense used to reduce taxable income before the tax rate is applied. A $100 tax credit reduces taxes payable by the full $100, whereas a $100 deductible expense reduces taxable income by $100 and taxes payable by $100 $\times$ t, where t is the tax rate. Tax credits are more valuable on a dollar-for-dollar basis than are deductible expenses.

If there were no credits for foreign taxes paid, sequential taxation by the host government and then by the home government would result in a very high cumulative tax rate. To illustrate, assume that the wholly owned foreign subsidiary of an MNE earns $10,000 before local income taxes and pays a dividend equal to all of its after-tax income. The host country income tax rate is 30%, and the home country of the parent tax rate is 35%. For simplicity, we will assume no withholding taxes. Total taxation with and without allowances for tax credits is shown in Table 8-4.

If tax credits are not allowed, sequential levying of a 30% host country tax and then a 35% home country tax on the income that remains results in an effective 54.5% tax, a cumulative rate that would render many MNEs uncompetitive with single-country local firms. The effect of allowing tax credits is to limit total taxation on the *original* before-tax income to no more than the highest single rate among jurisdictions. In the case depicted in Table 8-4, the effective overall tax rate of 35% with foreign tax credits is equivalent to the higher tax rate of the home country (and is the tax rate payable if the income had been earned at home).

The $500 of additional home country tax under the tax credit system in Table 8-4 is the amount needed to bring total taxation ($3,000 already paid plus the additional $500) up to but not beyond 35% of the original $10,000 of before-tax foreign income.

TABLE 8-4   Foreign Tax Credits.

	WITHOUT FOREIGN TAX CREDITS	WITH FOREIGN TAX CREDITS
Before-tax foreign income	$10,000	$10,000
Less foreign tax at 30%	−3,000	−3,000
Available to parent and paid as dividend	$ 7,000	$ 7,000
Less additional parent-country tax at 35%	−2,450	
Less incremental tax (after credits)	—	−500
Profit after all taxes	$ 4,550	$ 6,500
Total taxes, both jurisdictions	$ 5,450	$ 3,500
Effective overall tax rate (total taxes paid ÷ foreign income)	54.5%	35.0%

8.2   TRANSFER PRICING

The pricing of goods, services, and technology transferred to a foreign subsidiary from an affiliated company, called *transfer pricing,* is the first and foremost method of transferring funds out of a foreign subsidiary. These costs enter directly into the cost-of-goods-sold component of the subsidiary's income statement. This problem is particularly sensitive for MNEs. Even purely domestic firms find it difficult to reach agreement on the best method for setting prices on transactions between related units. In the case of MNEs, managers must balance conflicting considerations such as fund positioning and income taxes.

Fund Positioning Effect

A parent company wishing to transfer funds out of a particular country can charge higher prices on goods sold to its subsidiary in that country, to the degree that government regulations allow. A foreign subsidiary can be financed by the reverse technique, a lowering of transfer prices. Payment by the subsidiary for imports from its parent or sister subsidiary transfers funds out of the subsidiary. A higher transfer price permits funds to be accumulated in the selling country. Transfer pricing may also be used to transfer funds between sister subsidiaries. Multiple sourcing of component parts on a worldwide basis allows switching between suppliers from within the corporate family to function as a device to transfer funds.

Income Tax Effect

A major consideration in setting a transfer price is the *income tax effect.* Worldwide corporate profits may be influenced by setting transfer prices to minimize taxable income in a country with a high income tax rate and maximize income in a country with a low income tax rate. A parent company wishing to reduce the taxable profits of a subsidiary in a high-tax environment may set transfer prices at a higher rate to increase the costs of the subsidiary thereby reducing taxable income. *Global Finance in Practice 8.2* illustrates some apparent distortions to transfer prices by U.S. MNEs.

The income tax effect is illustrated in Table 8-5. Carlton Germany is operating in a relatively high-tax environment (German corporate income taxes are 45%). Carlton USA is in a significantly lower tax environment (U.S. corporate income tax rates are 35%), motivating Carlton to charge Carlton Germany a higher transfer price on goods produced in the United States and sold to Carlton Germany.

If Carlton adopts a high-markup policy by "selling" its merchandise at an intracompany sales price of $1,700,000, the same $800,000 of pretax consolidated income is allocated more heavily to low-tax Carlton USA and less heavily to high-tax Carlton Germany. As a consequence, total taxes drop by $30,000 and consolidated net income increases by $30,000 to $500,000—all while total sales remain constant.

Global Finance in Practice 8.2

Over- and Under-Invoicing

A recent study raises questions over the legitimacy of the invoicing practices of many importers and exporters operating in the United States. Import transactions were examined for *over-invoicing*, the use of a transfer price to pay more than is typical for that product or service. Over-invoicing is one method of moving funds out of the United States. Export transactions were examined for *under-invoicing*, the use of a lower-than-normal export price to reposition profits outside the United States.

The study examined approximately 15,000 import commodity code categories and 8,000 export commodity codes to determine the average selling prices—import and export—to determine implied prices. The study first calculated the medium price, lower export quartile price, and upper import quartile price by bilateral transfers (between the United States and nearly 230 individual countries). The following is a sample of some of the more suspicious results.

Over-Priced Imports			*Under-Priced Exports*		
Item	**From**	**Unit price**	**Item**	**To**	**Unit price**
Sunflower seeds	France	$5,519/kg	Truck caps	Mexico	$4.09/unit
Toothbrushes	U.K.	$5,655/unit	Turbojet engines	Romania	$10,000/unit
Hacksaw blades	Germany	$5,485/unit	Cameras (SLRs)	Mexico	$3.30/unit
Razor blades	India	$461/unit	Soybeans	Netherlands	$1.58/ton
Vinegar	Canada	$5,430/ltr	ATM machines	Salvador	$35.93/unit
Flashlights	Japan	$5,000/unit	Bulldozers	Mexico	$527.94/unit
Sawdust	U.K.	$642/kg	Rocket launchers	Bolivia	$40.00/unit
Iron/steel ladders	Slovenia	$15,852/unit	Toilets, porcelain	Hong Kong	$1.08/unit
Inkjet printers	Colombia	$179,000/unit	Prefabricated bldgs	St. Lucia	$0.82/unit
Lard	Canada	$484/kg	Video projectors	Malta	$28.71/unit
Hypodermic syringes	Switzerland	$2,306/unit	Radial bus tires	U.K.	$8.46/unit

Source: Simon Pak and John Zdanowicz, "U.S. Trade with the World: An Estimate of 2000 Lost U.S. Federal Income Tax Revenues Due to Over-Invoiced Imports and Under-Invoiced Exports," Florida International University, November 1, 2001, unpublished.

TABLE 8-5   Effect of Low versus High Transfer Price on Carlton Europe's Net Income (thousands of U.S. dollars).

LOW-MARKUP POLICY	CARLTON USA	CARLTON GERMANY	CARLTON
Sales	$1,400	$2,000	$2,000
Less cost of goods sold*	(1,000)	(1,400)	(1,000)
Gross profit	$ 400	$ 600	$ 1,000
Less operating expenses	(100)	(100)	(200)
Taxable income	$ 300	$ 500	$ 800
Less income taxes	35% (105)	45% (225)	(330)
Net income	$ 195	$ 275	$ 470
HIGH-MARKUP POLICY			
Sales	$1,700	$2,000	$2,000
Less cost of goods sold*	(1,000)	(1,700)	(1,000)
Gross profit	$ 700	$ 300	$ 1,000
Less operating expenses	(100)	(100)	(200)
Taxable income	$ 600	$ 200	$ 800
Less income taxes	35% (210)	45% (90)	(300)
Net income	$ 390	$ 110	$ 500

* Carlton USA's sales price becomes cost of goods sold for Carlton Germany.

Carlton would naturally prefer the high-markup policy for sales from the United States to Germany. Needless to say, government tax authorities are aware of the potential income distortion from transfer price manipulation. There are a variety of regulations and court cases on the reasonableness of transfer prices, including fees and royalties as well as prices set for merchandise. If a government taxing authority does not accept a transfer price, taxable income will be deemed larger than was calculated by the firm and taxes will be increased.

Section 482 of the U.S. Internal Revenue Code is typical of laws circumscribing freedom to set transfer prices. Under this authority, the Internal Revenue Service (IRS) can reallocate gross income, deductions, credits, or allowances between related corporations in order to prevent tax evasion or to reflect more clearly a proper allocation of income. Under the IRS guidelines and subsequent judicial interpretation, the burden of proof is on the taxpaying firm to show that the IRS has been arbitrary or unreasonable in reallocating income. This "guilty until proven innocent" approach means that MNEs must keep good documentation of the logic and costs behind their transfer prices. The "correct price" according to the guidelines is the one that reflects an *arm's length price*; that is, a sale of the same goods or service to a comparable unrelated customer.

Methods of Determining Transfer Prices

IRS regulations provide three methods to establish arm's length prices: comparable uncontrolled prices, resale prices, and cost-plus calculations. All three of these methods are recommended for use in member countries by the OECD Committee on Fiscal Affairs. In some cases, combinations of these three methods are used.

COMPARABLE UNCONTROLLED PRICE METHOD   A comparable, uncontrolled price is regarded as the best evidence of arm's length pricing. The transfer price is the same as prices of bona fide sales of the same items between the MNE and unrelated customers, or between two unrelated firms. Although such a market-determined price is ideal, in practice it is difficult to apply because of variations in quality, quantity, timing of sale, and proprietary trademarks. Perhaps even more important is the fact that sales between subsidiaries are often of custom-designed items—a generator sold by Ford USA for a European model is unlikely to be sold to, or even usable by, say, General Motors in Europe.

RESALE PRICE METHOD   The resale price method, a second-best approach to arm's length pricing, starts with the final selling price to an independent purchaser and subtracts an appropriate markup for the distribution subsidiary. The allowed markup is to cover the distribution subsidiary's costs and profits. This price is then used as the intracompany transfer price for similar, but not necessarily identical, items. Nevertheless, determination of an appropriate markup is difficult, especially if the distribution subsidiary adds value to the item through subsequent processing or packaging.

COST-PLUS METHOD   The cost-plus method sets the allowable transfer price by adding an appropriate profit markup to the seller's full cost, where *full cost* is the accounting definition of direct costs plus overhead allocation. This method is often used where semifinished products are sold between subsidiaries. Allocation of overhead in determining full cost is always a very subjective matter, especially when joint products are involved, so the method allows room for negotiation.

Other Transfer Pricing Considerations

Many tax authorities allow lower transfer prices when a new market is being established. For example, a manufacturing subsidiary may cut its price to the distribution subsidiary so that the latter can get market penetration. However, the price cut must be passed on to the final customer—it cannot be used to accumulate more profits in the distribution subsidiary. Another approach is to negotiate an advance pricing agreement (APA) with both home country and host country tax authorities. APAs involve time and expense to negotiate, but they do provide the firm with advanced assurance that its transfer pricing policies are acceptable. Without them, a firm may try to follow tax guidelines on transfer prices and still find itself in expensive tax appeals after the fact, defending a decision process it thought conformed to the letter of the tax rule.

Managerial Incentives and Evaluation

When a firm is organized with decentralized profit centers, transfer pricing between centers can disrupt evaluation of managerial performance. This problem is not unique to MNEs but is also a controversial issue in the "centralization versus decentralization" debate in domestic circles. In the domestic case, however, a modicum of coordination at the corporate level can alleviate some of the distortion that occurs when any profit center suboptimizes its profit for the corporate good. Also, in most domestic cases, the company can file a single (for that country) consolidated tax return, so the issue of cost allocation between related companies is not critical from a tax-payment point of view.

In the multinational case, coordination is often hindered by longer and less-efficient channels of communication, the need to consider the unique variables that influence international pricing, and separate taxation. Even with the best intentions, a manager in one country may find it difficult to know what is best for the firm as a whole when buying at a negotiated price from related companies in another country. Yet, if corporate headquarters establishes transfer prices and sourcing alternatives, one of the main advantages of a decentralized profit center system disappears: local management loses the incentive to act for its own benefit.

To illustrate, refer to Table 8-5, where an increase in the transfer price led to a worldwide income gain: Carlton's income rose by $195,000 (from $195,000 to $390,000) while Carlton Germany's income fell by only $165,000 (from $275,000 to $110,000), for a net gain of $30,000. Should the managers of the German subsidiary lose their bonuses (or even their jobs) because of their "sub-par" performance? Bonuses are usually determined by a companywide formula based in part on the profitability of individual subsidiaries, but in this case Carlton Germany "sacrificed" for the greater good of the whole. Arbitrarily changing transfer prices can create measurement problems.

Specifically, transferring profit from high-tax Carlton Germany to low-tax Carlton USA changes the following for one or both companies:

- Import tariffs paid (importer only) and hence profit levels
- Measurements of foreign exchange exposure, such as the amount of net exposed assets, because of changes in amounts of cash and receivables
- Liquidity tests, such as the current ratio, receivables turnover, and inventory turnover
- Operating efficiency, as measured by the ratio of gross profit to either sales or to total assets
- Income tax payments
- Profitability, as measured by the ratio of net income to either sales or capital invested
- Dividend payout ratio, in that a constant dividend will show a varied payout ratio as net income changes. Alternatively, if the payout ratio is kept constant, the amount of dividend is changed by a change in transfer price
- Internal growth rate, as meas.ured by the ratio of retained earnings to existing ownership equity

Effect on Joint-Venture Partners

Joint ventures pose a special problem in transfer pricing, because serving the interest of local stockholders by maximizing local profit may be suboptimal from the overall viewpoint of the MNE. Often, the conflicting interests are irreconcilable. Indeed, the local joint venture partner could be viewed as a potential Trojan horse if its management complains to local authorities about the MNE's transfer pricing policy.

Flexibility in Transfer Pricing

Although all governments have an interest in monitoring transfer pricing by MNEs, not all governments use these powers to the detriment of MNEs. In particular, transfer pricing has some political advantages over other techniques of transferring funds. Although the recorded transfer price is known to the governments of both the exporting and importing countries, the underlying cost data are not available to the importing country. Thus the importing country finds it difficult to judge the reasonableness of the transfer price, especially for nonstandard items such as specialized components.

Additionally, even if cost data could be obtained, some of the more sophisticated governments might continue to ignore the transfer pricing leak. They recognize that foreign investors must be able to repatriate a reasonable profit by their own standards, even if this profit seems unreasonable locally. An unknown or unproved transfer price leak makes it more difficult for local critics to blame their government for allowing the country to be "exploited" by foreign investors. Thus within the potential and actual constraints established by governments, opportunities may exist for MNEs to alter transfer prices away from an arm's length market price. On the other hand, if a host government sours on foreign investment, past transfer price leaks may be exploited to penalize the foreigners.

8.3   U.S. TAXATION OF FOREIGN SOURCE INCOME

As we noted previously, the United States employs the *worldwide approach* to international taxation of U.S. multinationals operating globally, but the *territorial approach* to foreign firms operating within its borders. This part of the chapter focuses on how U.S. tax authorities tax the foreign sourced income of U.S.-based multinationals.

U.S. Calculation of Foreign Tax Credits

Dividends received from U.S. corporate subsidiaries are fully taxable in the United States at U.S. tax rates but with credit allowed for direct taxes paid on income in a foreign country. The amount of foreign tax allowed as a credit depends on five tax parameters:

1. Foreign corporate income tax rate
2. U.S. corporate income tax rate
3. Foreign corporate dividend withholding tax rate for nonresidents (per the applicable bilateral tax treaty between the specific country and the United States)
4. Proportion of ownership held by the U.S. corporation in the foreign firm
5. Proportion of net income distributed, the dividend payout rate

The five cases depicted in Figure 8-1 are based on a foreign subsidiary of a U.S. corporation that earns $10,000 before local taxes. The U.S. corporate income tax rate is 35%. The foreign tax rate is 30% in Cases 1 through 4 and 40% in Case 5.

CASE 1: FOREIGN SUBSIDIARY WITH 100% PAYOUT (NO WITHHOLDING TAX)
Assuming the foreign subsidiary earns $10,000 before local taxes in its overall tax basket, it pays $3,000 in foreign taxes (30% foreign tax rate) and distributes all $7,000 in net income to its U.S. parent (100% payout rate). Because there are no withholding taxes, the U.S. parent receives a net remittance of the full $7,000.

The U.S. parent corporation takes the *full* before-tax foreign income of the foreign corporation—apportioned by its proportional ownership in the foreign corporation (in this case 100%)—into its taxable income. This is called *grossing-up*.

FIGURE 8-1 U.S. Taxation of Foreign Source Income.

	A	B	C	D	E	F
1	Figure 8.1 U.S. Taxation of Foreign Source Income					
2	**Baseline Values**	Case 1	Case 2	Case 3	Case 4	Case 5
3	Foreign corporate income tax rate	30%	30%	30%	30%	40%
4	U.S. corporate income tax rate	35%	35%	35%	35%	35%
5	Foreign dividend witholding tax rate	0%	10%	10%	10%	10%
6	U.S. ownership in foreign firm	100%	100%	100%	40%	40%
7	Dividend payout rate of foreign firm	100%	100%	50%	50%	50%
8	**Foreign Subsidiary Tax Computation**					
9	Taxable income of foreign subsidiary	$ 10,000	$ 10,000	$ 10,000	$ 10,000	$ 10,000
10	Less foreign corporate income tax	3,000	3,000	3,000	3,000	4,000
11	Net income available for distribution	$ 7,000	$ 7,000	$ 7,000	$ 7,000	$ 6,000
12	Retained earnings	-	-	3,500	3,500	3,000
13	Distributed earnings	7,000	7,000	3,500	3,500	3,000
14	Distribution to U.S. parent company	$ 7,000	$ 7,000	$ 3,500	$ 1,400	$ 1,200
15	Withholding taxes on dividends	-	700	350	140	120
16	Net remittance to U.S. parent	$ 7,000	$ 6,300	$ 3,150	$ 1,260	$ 1,080
17	**U.S. Corporate Tax Computation on Foreign Source Income**					
18	Dividend received (before withholding)	$ 7,000	$ 7,000	$ 3,500	$ 1,400	$ 1,200
19	Add-back foreign deemed-paid tax	3,000	3,000	1,500	600	800
20	Grossed-up foreign dividend	$ 10,000	$ 10,000	$ 5,000	$ 2,000	$ 2,000
21	Tentative U.S. tax liability	3,500	3,500	1,750	700	700
22	Less credit for foreign taxes					
23	Foreign income taxes paid	$ 3,000	$ 3,000	$ 1,500	$ 600	$ 800
24	Foreign withholding taxes paid	-	700	350	140	120
25	Total	$ 3,000	$ 3,700	$ 1,850	$ 740	$ 920
26	Additional U.S. taxes due	500	-	-	-	-
27	Excess foreign tax credits	-	200	100	40	220
28	After-tax income from foreign subsidiary	$ 6,500	$ 6,300	$ 3,150	$ 1,260	$ 1,080
29	**Tax Burden Measurement**					
30	Total taxes paid on remitted income	$ 3,500	$ 3,700	$ 1,850	$ 740	$ 920
31	Effective tax rate on foreign income	35%	37%	37%	37%	46%
32	**Key Cell Entries**					
33	Entries in Column B are to be copied across to Columns C, D, E, and F.					
34	B10: =B9*B3		B21: =B20*B4			
35	B11: =B9 – B10		B23: =B19			
36	B12: =B11*(1 – B7)		B24: =B15			
37	B13: =B11*B7		B25: =SUM(B23:B24)			
38	B14: =B13*B6		B26: =IF(B21>B25,B21 – B25,0)			
39	B15: =B14*B5		B27: =IF(B21<B25,B25 – B21,0)			
40	B16: =B14 – B15		B28: =B20 – B25 – B26			
41	B18: =B14		B30: =B21+B27			
42	B19: =(B14/B11)*B10		B31: =B30/B20			
43	B20: =SUM(B18:B19)					
44						

The U.S. parent then calculates a tentative U.S. tax against the grossed-up foreign income. Assuming a 35% U.S. tax rate, the tentative U.S. tax on a grossed-up income of $10,000 is $3,500. The U.S. parent is then entitled under U.S. tax law to reduce this U.S. tax liability by a *deemed-paid foreign tax credit* for taxes already paid on the same income in the foreign country. The deemed-paid tax credit is calculated as follows:

$$\text{Deemed-paid credit} = \frac{\text{Dividends received (including withholding tax)} \times \text{Creditable foreign taxes}}{\text{After-tax net profits of the foreign corporation}}$$

Creditable taxes are foreign income taxes paid on earnings by a foreign corporation that has paid a dividend to a qualifying U.S. corporation. In order to qualify, a U.S. corporation must own at least 10% of the voting power of the distributing foreign corporation.

The deemed-paid credit in Case 1 is calculated as follows:

$$\text{Deemed-paid credit} = \frac{\$7,000 \times \$3,000}{\$7,000} = \$3,000$$

The U.S. parent owes an additional $500 in U.S. taxes ($3,500 tentative U.S. tax less the deemed-paid credit of $3,000). The after-tax income earned by the U.S. parent corporation is $6,500, and the overall tax rate on the foreign income is 35% (total taxes of $3,500 on total income of $10,000). Note that although the foreign corporate tax rate was lower (30% to the U.S. 35% rate), the U.S. corporation ends up paying the higher effective rate.

CASE 2: FOREIGN SUBSIDIARY WITH 100% PAYOUT (10% WITHHOLDING TAX)   Assume that the same foreign corporation earns the same income, but now all dividends paid to the U.S. parent corporation are subject to a 10% withholding tax. All other values remain the same as in Case 1. Although the actual net remittance to the U.S. parent is now lower, $6,300 instead of $7,000, the U.S. parent calculates the tentative U.S. tax on a grossed-up dividend of $7,000.

The tentative U.S. tax liability is again $3,500. The U.S. corporation can then deduct the amount of the deemed-paid credit ($3,000) and the full amount of withholding tax ($700) from its U.S. tax liability. Because the total foreign tax credits of $3,700 are greater than the tentative U.S. tax of $3,500, the U.S. parent owes no additional U.S. taxes. The U.S. parent has, in fact, an *excess foreign tax credit* of $200 ($3,700 − $3,500) which it can carry back two years or carry forward five years. The effective foreign tax rate is now 37% as a result of paying higher taxes abroad than it would have theoretically paid at home, including the withholding tax.

CASE 3: FOREIGN SUBSIDIARY WITH 50% PAYOUT (10% WITHHOLDING TAX)   In this case it is assumed that all tax rates remain the same, but the foreign subsidiary chooses to pay out only 50% of net income rather than 100%. As a result, all dividends, withholding taxes, deemed-paid credits, tentative U.S. tax liabilities, foreign tax credits, after-tax income from the foreign subsidiary, and, finally, total taxes paid, are cut in half. The overall effective tax rate is again 37%, higher than what would have theoretically been paid if the income had been earned inside rather than outside the United States.

CASE 4: FOREIGN SUBSIDIARY WITH 50% PAYOUT (10% WITHHOLDING TAX)   Case 4 illustrates to what degree these cash flows change when the U.S. parent corporation owns only 40% of the foreign corporation. As illustrated in Table 8-5, the 40% ownership acts only as a "scale factor" in apportioning dividends paid, withholding tax withheld, and tax liabilities and credits resulting. Once again, the U.S. parent corporation has excess foreign tax credits as a result of paying more taxes abroad than it is liable for at home. The overall effective tax rate on the reduced after-tax net income for the foreign subsidiary of $1,400 is 37%.

CASE 5: FOREIGN SUBSIDIARY WITH 50% PAYOUT (40% FOREIGN CORPORATE TAX, 10% WITHHOLDING TAX)   This fifth and final case illustrates the increasing tax burden on the U.S. parent corporation when the corporate income tax in the foreign country is higher than that in the United States. The combined impact of a 40% foreign income tax and a 10% withholding tax, even after calculation of deemed-paid foreign tax credits, results in a rising excess foreign tax credit and a substantially higher effective tax rate of 46%. Clearly, when the implications of Case 5 are combined with the number of countries with corporate tax rates higher than that of the United States (see Table 8-2), the tax burden borne by U.S.-based MNEs is a significant competitive concern.

Excess Foreign Tax Credits

If a U.S.-based MNE receives income from a foreign country that imposes higher corporate income taxes than the United States (or combined income and withholding tax), total creditable taxes will exceed U.S. taxes on that foreign income. The result is *excess foreign tax credits*. All firms wish to manage their tax liabilities globally, however, so that they do not end up paying more on foreign-sourced income than they do on domestically sourced income. The proper management of global taxes is not simple, however, and combines three different components: (1) foreign tax credit limitations; (2) tax credit carry-forward/carry-back; and (3) foreign tax averaging.

FOREIGN TAX CREDIT LIMITATION   The amount of credit a taxpayer can use in any year is limited to the U.S. tax on that foreign income. Foreign tax credits *cannot* be used to reduce taxes levied on domestic income. The total foreign tax creditable in any one year is limited according to the following formula:

$$\text{Creditable tax limit} = \frac{\text{Total foreign taxable income}}{\text{Total taxable income}} \times \text{U.S tax on total income}$$

This formula requires the consideration of not only foreign source income, but the U.S. tax liabilities associated with the firm's domestic income.

TAX CREDIT CARRY-FORWARD/CARRY-BACK   Excess foreign tax credits, like domestic tax credits, may be carried forward five years and carried back two years against similar tax liabilities. Unfortunately, because excess foreign tax credits arise from tax differentials and tax rates typically change slowly, a firm experiencing an excess foreign tax credit one year may experience it year after year.

TAX AVERAGING   The good news is that under U.S. tax law, it is possible to offset foreign tax credits derived from one source against foreign tax liabilities from another source, assuming that they are derived from the same type of income. This practice is termed *tax averaging*. In principle, it means that if income is derived from a high-tax country, creating excess foreign tax credits, these credits can in turn be used against a deficit foreign tax credit position formed from repatriating income from a low-tax country.

The primary obstacle to tax averaging is the inability to average across different categories or "baskets" of income. The U.S. tax code specifies a *general limitation income basket*, which includes the majority of income derived by U.S. corporations abroad, such as manufacturing, services, and sales income. The U.S. tax code specifies eight other baskets of income into which foreign-sourced income may fall. For example, a U.S.-based firm cannot average deficit foreign tax credits on active income from a low-tax country against excess foreign tax credits on passive income from a high-tax country. This basket limitation provides fewer incentives for MNEs to position certain types of profits in low-tax countries. Many countries, however, do not restrict the use of foreign tax credits by income category, or ignore foreign-sourced income altogether.

Controlled Foreign Corporations and Subpart F Income

The rule that U.S. shareholders do not pay U.S. taxes on foreign-sourced income until that income is remitted to the United States was amended in 1962 by the creation of special *Subpart F income*. The revision was designed to prevent the use of arrangements between operating companies and base companies located in tax havens as a means of deferring U.S. taxes and to encourage greater repatriation of foreign incomes. A *controlled foreign corporation* (CFC) is any foreign corporation in which U.S. shareholders, including corporate parents, own more than 50% of the combined voting power or total value.

Subpart F income is subject to immediate U.S. taxation *even when not remitted.* It is income of a type otherwise easily shifted offshore to avoid current taxation. It includes (1) passive income received by the foreign corporation such as dividends, interest, rents, royalties, net foreign currency gains, net commodities gains, and income from the sale of non-income-producing property; (2) income from the insurance of U.S. risks; (3) financial service income; (4) shipping income; (5) oil-related income; and (6) certain related-party sales and service income.

Branch Versus Locally Incorporated Subsidiary

An MNE normally has a choice between organizing a foreign subsidiary as a branch of the parent or as a local corporation. Both tax and nontax consequences must be considered. Nontax factors include the locus of legal liability, public image in the host country, managerial incentive considerations, and local legal and political requirements.

One major tax consideration is whether the foreign subsidiary is expected to run at a loss for several years after startup. If so, it might be preferable to organize originally as a branch operation to permit these anticipated losses to be consolidated in the parent's income statement for tax purposes. For example, tax laws in the United States and many other countries do not permit a foreign corporation to be consolidated for tax purposes, even though it is consolidated for reporting purposes; yet do permit consolidation of foreign branches for tax purposes.

A second tax consideration is the net tax burden after paying withholding taxes on dividends. An MNE must weigh the benefit of potential tax deferral of home country taxes on foreign-source income from a fully incorporated foreign subsidiary versus the total tax burden of paying foreign corporate income taxes and withholding taxes once the income is distributed to the parent corporation. A foreign branch's income would typically bear only the burden of home-country taxation, because its income is concurrently consolidated with that of the parent, with no foreign corporate income taxes or withholding taxes applied.

Foreign Sales Corporations

Over the years, the United States has introduced into U.S. tax laws special incentives dealing with international operations. To benefit from these incentives, a firm may have to form separate corporations for qualifying and nonqualifying activities. The most important U.S. special corporation is a foreign sales corporation (FSC). FSCs were introduced in the Tax Reform Act of 1984 as a device to provide tax-exempt income for U.S. persons or corporations having export-oriented activities.

"Exempt foreign trade income" of an FSC is not subject to U.S. income taxes. Exempt foreign trade income is income from foreign sources that is not effectively connected with the conduct of a trade or business within the United States. Exempt income is limited to 34% of the FSC's total trade income.

An FSC's total foreign trade income is derived from gross receipts from the sale of export property, lease or rental of export property, incidental services provided with the sale or lease of export property, and fees for engineering, architectural, or managerial services. The exempt portion of the FSC's total foreign trade income depends on the pricing rules used. "Export property" is manufactured, produced, grown, or extracted from the United States by an entity other than the FSC and is sold, leased, or rented outside the United States.

In 1999, however, the World Trade Organization (WTO) ruled that FSCs were an illegal subsidy worth billions of dollars to thousands of U.S. exporters. Although it is unlikely that FSCs will be discontinued, their role in aiding U.S.-based exporters is increasingly controversial. The EU threatened to impose penalty tariffs in 2004 or later.

Possessions Corporation

A business carried on to a substantial extent in a U.S. possession can be carried on by a separate U.S. corporation, which, if it meets the requirements for a *possessions corporation,* is not subject to U.S. tax on income earned outside the United States unless the income is *received* in the United States. Although technically a U.S. corporation, a possessions corporation is treated like a foreign corporation in nearly every respect. The U.S. pharmaceutical industry, specifically, has made heavy use of Puerto Rican possessions corporations.

REQUIREMENTS   To qualify as a possessions corporation, a corporation must satisfy the following requirements:

1. It is a domestic U.S. corporation.
2. At least 80% of its gross income is derived from within a U.S. possession.
3. At least 75% of its gross income is derived from the active conduct of a trade or business in a U.S. possession.

EXCLUSION FROM GROSS INCOME   A corporation meeting these requirements excludes from U.S. gross income amounts earned outside the United States unless the income is received in the United States. Thus, a possessions corporation should arrange to receive income initially outside the United States, although it may subsequently transfer it from a foreign bank account to a bank account in the United States.

The possessions corporation's income is subject to U.S. tax, but a tax-sparing credit is allowed for U.S. taxes on foreign-source income attributable to the conduct of a trade or business in a U.S. possession and qualified possessions-source investment income. The net result is that nonqualified income is subject to U.S. tax but possessions income is exempt from tax. The income qualifying for this credit is as follows:

- Income from foreign sources that is attributable to the conduct of a trade or business in a possession.
- Qualified possessions-source investment income that is defined as investment income (a) from sources within the possession in which the business is carried on, and (b) which the taxpayer establishes is attributable to the funds derived from the business or investment in such possession.

Other investment is taxable in the United States on a current basis. No foreign tax credit is available to possessions corporations except to the extent that a foreign tax is imposed on income subject to U.S. tax but not eligible for the tax-sparing credit. For the U.S. parent company of a possessions corporation, foreign taxes paid with respect to distributions from the possessions subsidiary are neither creditable nor deductible.

Dividends from possessions corporations are eligible for the 100% or 85% dividends-received deduction, regardless of when the income was earned. Thus accumulated earnings from prior years can be repatriated by the possessions corporation to the U.S. parent with little or no U.S. tax.

U.S. Taxation: Summary Points

Figure 8-2 provides an overview of the primary tax issues facing a U.S.-based MNE.

- Domestic-source income and foreign-source income are separated. Tax credits or deficits in one category cannot be applied to net positions in the other category.
- Foreign source income is separated into active and passive categories. *Active* income is taxed by U.S. tax authorities only as it is remitted to the U.S. parent. *Passive* income is taxed as it is earned, regardless of whether it is remitted to the U.S. parent.

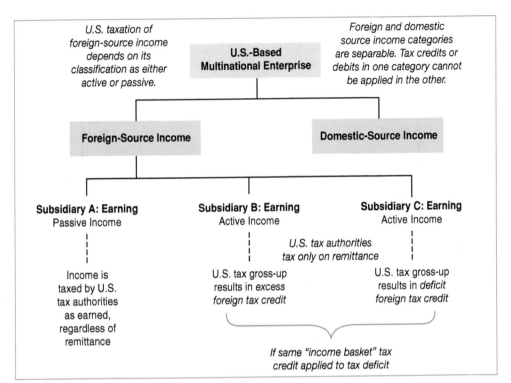

FIGURE 8-2
U.S. Taxation of a U.S.
-based Multinational
Enterprise.

- If the remittance of active income from one subsidiary results in an excess foreign tax credit, and the remittance from a second subsidiary results in a foreign tax deficit, the credit may be applied to the deficit if the incomes are of the same "basket" under U.S. tax law.

Although multinational taxation is complex, the global management of tax liabilities is one of the most important financial management tasks facing any MNE. A multinational enterprise that effectively manages its global tax liabilities by reducing its global tax payments creates share-holder value.

Tax Management at Carlton

Figure 8-3 summarizes the key tax management issue for Carlton when remitting dividend income back to the United States from Carlton Germany and Carlton Brazil.

- Because corporate income tax rates in Germany (40%) are higher than those in the United States (35%), dividends remitted to the U.S. parent result in *excess* foreign tax credits. Any applicable withholding taxes on dividends between Germany and the United States only increase the amount of the excess foreign tax credit.
- Because corporate income tax rates in Brazil (25%) are lower than those in the United States (35%), dividends remitted to the U.S. parent result in *deficit* foreign tax credits. If there are withholding taxes applied to the dividends by Brazil on remittances to the United States, this will reduce the size of the deficit, but not eliminate it.

Carlton's management would like to manage the two dividend remittances in order to match the deficits with the credits. The most straightforward method of doing this is to adjust the amount of dividend distributed from each foreign subsidiary so that, after all applicable income and withholding taxes have been applied, Carlton' excess foreign tax credits from Carlton Germany exactly match the excess foreign tax deficits from Carlton Brazil. There are a number of

FIGURE 8-3
Carlton's Tax
Management of Foreign-
Source Income.

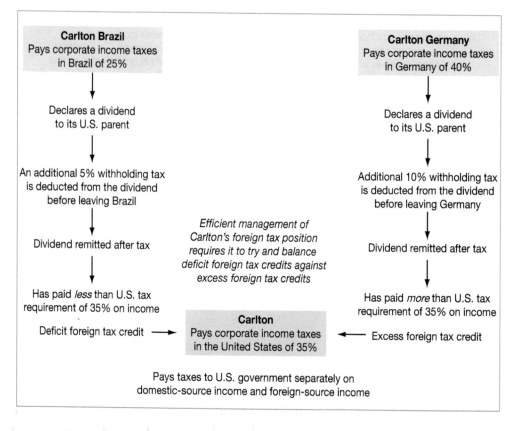

other methods of managing the global tax liabilities of Carlton, so-called *repositioning of funds,* which are examined in detail in the following chapter.

8.4   TAX-HAVEN SUBSIDIARIES AND INTERNATIONAL OFFSHORE FINANCIAL CENTERS

Many MNEs have foreign subsidiaries that act as tax havens for corporate funds awaiting reinvestment or repatriation. Tax-haven subsidiaries, categorically referred to as *international offshore financial centers,* are partially a result of tax-deferral features on earned foreign income allowed by some of the parent countries. Tax-haven subsidiaries are typically established in a country that can meet the following requirements:

- A low tax on foreign investment or sales income earned by resident corporations and a low dividend withholding tax on dividends paid to the parent firm.
- A stable currency to permit easy conversion of funds into and out of the local currency. This requirement can be met by permitting and facilitating the use of Eurocurrencies.
- The facilities to support financial services such as good communications, professional qualified office workers, and reputable banking services.
- A stable government that encourages the establishment of foreign-owned financial and service facilities within its borders.

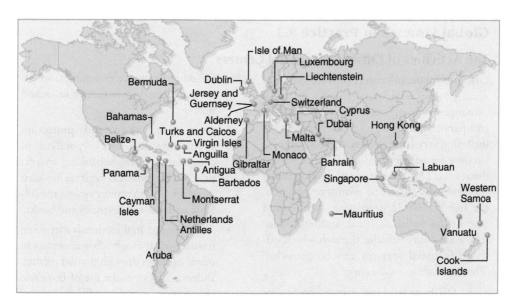

FIGURE 8-4
International Offshore
Financial Centers.

Figure 8-4 provides a map of most of the world's major offshore financial centers. The typical tax-haven subsidiary owns the common stock of its related operating foreign subsidiaries. There might be several tax-haven subsidiaries scattered around the world. The tax-haven subsidiary's equity is typically 100% owned by the parent firm. All transfers of funds might go through the tax-haven subsidiaries, including dividends and equity financing. Thus the parent country's tax on foreign source income, which might normally be paid when a dividend is declared by a foreign subsidiary, could continue to be deferred until the tax-haven subsidiary itself pays a dividend to the parent firm. This event can be postponed indefinitely if foreign operations continue to grow and require new internal financing from the tax-haven subsidiary. Thus MNEs are able to operate a corporate pool of funds for foreign operations without having to repatriate foreign earnings through the parent country's tax machine.

For U.S. MNEs, the tax deferral privilege operating through a foreign subsidiary was not originally a tax loophole. On the contrary, it was granted by the U.S. government to allow U.S. firms to expand overseas and place them on a par with foreign competitors, which also enjoy similar types of tax deferral and export subsidies of one type or another.

Unfortunately, some U.S. firms distorted the original intent of tax deferral into tax avoidance. Transfer prices on goods and services bought from or sold to related subsidiaries were artificially rigged to leave all the income from the transaction in the tax-haven subsidiary. This manipulation could be done by routing the legal title to the goods or services through the tax-haven subsidiary, even though physically the goods or services never entered the tax-haven country. This maneuver left no residual tax base for either exporting or importing subsidiaries located outside the tax-haven country. Needless to say, tax authorities of both exporting and importing countries were dismayed by the lack of taxable income in such transactions.

One purpose of the U.S. Internal Revenue Act of 1962 was to eliminate the tax advantages of these "paper" foreign corporations without destroying the tax-deferral privilege for those foreign manufacturing and sales subsidiaries that were established for business and economic motives rather than tax motives. Although the tax motive has been removed, some firms have found these subsidiaries useful as finance control centers for foreign operations. *Global Finance in Practice* 8.3 provides a categorization of the primary activities of offshore financial centers.

Global Finance in Practice 8.3

The Activities of Offshore Financial Centers

Offshore financial centers provide financial management services to foreign users in exchange for foreign exchange earnings. The comparative advantage for clients? Several, including very low tax rates, minimal administrative formalities, and confidentiality and discretion. This environment allows wealthy international clients to minimize potential tax liability while protecting income and assets from political, fiscal, and legal risks. There are many vehicles through which offshore financial services can be provided. These include the following:

- Offshore banking, which can handle foreign exchange operations for corporations or banks. These operations are not subject to either capital, corporate, capital gains, dividend, or interest taxes or to exchange controls.
- International business corporations, which are often tax-exempt, limited-liability companies used to operate businesses or raise capital through issuing shares, bonds, or other instruments.

- Offshore insurance companies, which are established to minimize taxes and manage risk.
- Asset management and protection allows individuals and corporations in countries with fragile banking systems or unstable political regimes to keep assets offshore to protect against the collapse of domestic currencies and banks.
- Tax planning: multinationals may route transactions through offshore centers to minimize taxes through transfer pricing. Individuals can make use of favorable tax regimes offered by offshore centers through trust and foundations.

The tax concessions and secrecy offered by offshore financial centers can be used for many legitimate purposes, but they have also been used for illegitimate ends, including money laundering and tax evasion.

Source: IMF, "Caribbean Centers: Stricter Rules Change Climate for Offshore Financial Centers," IMF Survey, August 5, 2002, p. 252.

SUMMARY

- MNEs face an ethical problem of tax morality.
- Governments attempt to attain tax neutrality.
- Nations typically structure their tax systems along one of two basic approaches: the worldwide approach or the territorial approach.
- Both approaches are attempts to determine which firms, foreign or domestic by incorporation, or which incomes, foreign or domestic in origin, are subject to the taxation of host country tax authorities.
- The worldwide approach, also referred to as the residential or national approach, levies taxes on the income earned by firms that are incorporated in the host country, regardless of where the income was earned (domestically or abroad).
- The territorial approach, also termed the source approach, focuses on the income earned by firms within the legal jurisdiction of the host country, not on the country of firm incorporation.
- Many countries defer taxes on foreign-sourced income until that income is remitted to the parent.
- A network of bilateral tax treaties, many of which are modeled after one proposed by the Organization for Economic Cooperation and Development (OECD), provides a means of reducing double taxation.

- Tax treaties normally define whether taxes are to be imposed on income earned in one country by the nationals of another, and if so, how. Tax treaties are bilateral, with the two signatories specifying what rates are applicable to which types of income between themselves alone.

- The value-added tax (VAT) is a type of national sales tax collected at each stage of production or sale of consumption goods in proportion to the value added during that stage.

- The United States differentiates between foreign-source income and domestic-source income. Each is taxed separately, and tax deficits or credits in one category may not be used against deficits or credits in the other category.

- If a U.S.-based MNE receives income from a foreign country that imposes higher corporate income taxes than does the United States (or combined income and withholding tax), total creditable taxes will exceed U.S. taxes on that foreign income. The result is an excess foreign tax credit.

- All firms wish to manage their tax liabilities globally so that they do not pay more on foreign-source income than they do on domestic-source income.

- Transfer pricing should be calculated on an arm's-length basis, if possible.

- Transfer pricing affects income taxes, funds positioning, managerial evaluation, and joint venture partners.

- Many MNEs have foreign subsidiaries that act as tax havens for corporate funds awaiting reinvestment or repatriation. Because tax havens have the potential to be misused by MNEs and by money launderers, they are carefully watched by all countries' tax authorities.

- U.S.-based MNEs can utilize possession corporations and foreign sales corporations to reduce their worldwide taxes.

- Tax considerations sometimes determine whether a foreign subsidiary is organized as a branch or a locally incorporated subsidiary.

QUESTIONS

1. **Tax morality.**
   a. What is meant by the term "tax morality"?
   b. Your company has a subsidiary in Russia, where tax evasion is a fine art. Discuss whether you should comply fully with Russian tax laws or should violate the laws, as do your local competitors.

2. **Tax neutrality.**
   a. Define the term "tax neutrality."
   b. What is the difference between domestic neutrality and foreign neutrality?
   c. What are a country's objectives when determining tax policy on foreign-sourced income?

3. **Worldwide versus territorial approach.** Nations typically structure their tax systems along one of two basic approaches: the worldwide approach or the territorial approach. Explain these two approaches and how they differ from each other.

4. **Tax deferral.**
   a. What is meant by the term "tax deferral"?
   b. Why do countries allow tax deferral on foreign-sourced income?

5. Tax treaties.

    a. What is a bilateral tax treaty?

    b. What is the purpose of a bilateral tax treaty?

    c. What policies do most tax treaties cover?

6. Tax types. Taxes are classified on the basis of whether they are applied directly to income, called direct taxes, or to some other measurable performance characteristic of the firm, called indirect taxes. Classify each of the following types of taxes as direct, indirect, or something else.

    a. Corporate income tax paid by a Japanese subsidiary on its operating income

    b. Royalties paid to Saudi Arabia for oil extracted and shipped to world markets

    c. Interest received by a U.S. parent on bank deposits held in London

    d. Interest received by a U.S. parent on a loan to a subsidiary in Mexico

    e. Principal repayment received by a U.S. parent from Belgium on a loan to a wholly owned subsidiary in Belgium

    f. Excise tax paid on cigarettes manufactured and sold within the United States

    g. Property taxes paid on the corporate headquarters building in Seattle

    h. A direct contribution to the International Committee of the Red Cross for refugee relief

    i. Deferred income tax, shown as a deduction on the U.S. parent's consolidated income tax

    j. Withholding taxes withheld by Germany on dividends paid to a U.K. parent corporation

7. Foreign tax credit. What is a foreign tax credit? Why do countries give credit for taxes paid on foreign-source income?

8. Tax averaging. How does tax averaging help or hinder a U.S.-based MNE in managing its global tax liabilities?

9. Passive versus active income. What is the difference between passive and active income?

10. Value-added tax.

    a. What is a value-added tax?

    b. What are the advantages and disadvantages of a value-added tax?

    c. Although the value-added tax has been proposed numerous times, the United States has never adopted one. Why do you think the attitude toward value-added tax is so negative in the United States when the value-added tax is widely used in the rest of the world?

11. Subpart F income. The rule that U.S. shareholders do not pay taxes on foreign-sourced income until that income is remitted to the United States (tax deferral) was amended in 1962 by the creation of special Subpart F income.

    a. Why was this revision adopted?

    b. What is included in Subpart F income?

    c. When is Subpart F income taxed?

12. Transfer pricing motivation. What is a transfer price? Can a government regulate it? What difficulties and motives does a parent multinational firm face in setting transfer prices?

13. Sister subsidiaries. Subsidiary Alpha in Country Able faces a 40% income tax rate. Subsidiary Beta in Country Baker faces only a 20% income tax rate. At present, each subsidiary imports from the other an amount of goods and services exactly equal in monetary value to what each exports to the other. This method of balancing intracompany trade was imposed by a management keen to reduce all costs, including the costs (spread between bid and ask) of foreign exchange transactions. Both subsidiaries are profitable, and both could purchase all components domestically at approximately the same prices as they are paying to their foreign sister subsidiary. Does this seem like an optimal situation to you?

14. **Correct pricing.** Section 482 of the U.S. Internal Revenue Code specifies use of a "correct" transfer price, and the burden of proof that the transfer price is "correct" lies with the company. What guidelines exist for determining the proper transfer price?

15. **Branch income.** Branches are often used as the organizational structure for foreign operations that are expected to lose substantial amounts of money in their first years of operation. Why would branches be preferable to wholly owned subsidiaries?

16. **Foreign sales corporation (FSC).** What is a foreign sales corporation? Why do many other countries argue that the U.S. FSCs are illegal under the World Trade Organization's current rules for the conduct of international trade?

17. **Tax haven subsidiary.**
    a. What is meant by the term "tax haven"?
    b. What are the desired characteristics for a country if it expects to be used as a tax haven?
    c. Identify five tax havens.
    d. What are the advantages leading an MNE to use a tax haven subsidiary?
    e. What are the potential distortions of an MNE's taxable income that are opposed by tax authorities in nontax haven countries?

18. **Tax treaties.** What do most bilateral tax treaties cover? How do they affect the operations and structure of MNEs?

19. **Passive.** Why do the U.S. authorities tax passive income generated offshore differently from active income?

PROBLEMS

1. **U.S. taxation of foreign-source income.** Using the structure for calculating U.S. taxes for foreign-source income from Exhibit 8.6, assume that a foreign subsidiary has $3,400,000 in gross earnings, U.S. and foreign corporate income taxes are 35% and 28%, respectively, and foreign withholding taxes are 15%.
    a. What is the total tax payment, foreign and domestic combined, for this income?
    b. What is the effective tax rate paid on this income by the U.S.-based parent company?
    c. What would be the total tax payment and effective tax rate if the foreign corporate tax rate were 45% and there were no withholding taxes on dividends?
    d. What would be the total tax payment and effective tax rate if the income were earned by a branch of the U.S. corporation?

2. **Discovery Bay Airlines (Hong Kong).** Discovery Bay Airlines is a U.S.-based air freight firm with a wholly owned subsidiary in Hong Kong. The subsidiary, DBay-Hong Kong, has just completed a long-term planning report for the parent company in San Francisco, in which it has estimated the following expected earnings and payout rates for the years 2004 to 2007.

   The current Hong Kong corporate tax rate on this category of income is 16.5%. Hong Kong imposes no withholding taxes on dividends remitted to U.S. investors (per the Hong Kong–United States bilateral tax treaty). The U.S. corporate income tax rate is 35%. The parent company wants to repatriate 75% of net income as dividends annually.
    a. Calculate the net income available for distribution by the Hong Kong subsidiary for the years 2004 to 2007.
    b. What is the amount of the dividend expected to be remitted to the U.S. parent each year?
    c. After gross-up for U.S. tax liability purposes, what is the total dividend after tax (all Hong Kong and U.S. taxes) expected each year?
    d. What is the effective tax rate on this foreign-source income per year?

DISCOVERY BAY–HONG KONG (MILLIONS OF U.S. DOLLARS)	2004	2005	2006	2007
Earnings before interest and taxes (EBIT)	8,000	10,000	12,000	14,000
Less interest expenses	(800)	(1,000)	(1,200)	(1,400)
Earnings before taxes (EBT)	7,200	9,000	10,800	12,600

3. **Jurgen-Strut of Germany.** Jurgen-Strut (JS) is a German-based company that manufactures electronic fuel-injection carburetor assemblies for several large automobile companies in Germany, including Mercedes, BMW, and Opel. The firm, like many firms in Germany today, is revising its financial policies in line with the increasing degree of disclosure required by firms if they wish to list their shares publicly in or out of Germany.

JS's primary problem is that the German corporate income tax code applies a different rate to income depending on whether it is retained (45%) or distributed to stockholders (30%).

Earnings before interest and taxes (EBIT)	€580,000,000
Less interest expenses	(96,500,000)
Earnings before taxes (EBT)	€483,500,000
Less corporate income taxes	_____
Net income	€_____
Retained earnings	_____
Distributed earnings	_____

a. If Jurgen-Strut planned to distribute 50% of its net income, what would be its total net income and total corporate tax bills?

b. If Jurgen-Strut were attempting to choose between a 40% and 60% payout rate to stockholders, what arguments and values would management use to convince stockholders which of the two payouts is in everyone's best interest?

Kowloon Blade Company. *Use the following company case to answer Questions 4 through 6. Kowloon Blade Company (Hong Kong) exports razor blades to its wholly owned parent company, Cranfield Eversharp (Great Britain). Hong Kong tax rates are 16% and British tax rates are 30%. Kowloon calculates its profit per container as follows (all values in British pounds):*

CONSTRUCTING PRICE	KOWLOON BLADE	CRANFIELD EVERSHARP
Direct costs	£10,000	£16,100
Overhead	4,000	1,000
Total costs	£14,000	£17,100
Desired markup (15%)	2,100	2,565
Transfer price (sales price)	£16,100	£19,665
Income statements (assumes a volume of 1,000 units)		
Sales revenue	£16,100,000	£19,665,000
Less total costs	(14,000,000)	(17,100,000)
Taxable income	£2,100,000	£2,565,000
Less taxes (16%)	(336,000)	(30%) (769,500)
Post-tax profit	£1,764,000	£1,795,500
Consolidated profit	£3,559,50	

4. **Kowloon Blade (A).** Corporate management of Cranfield Eversharp is considering repositioning profits within the multinational company. What happens to the profits of Kowloon Blade and Cranfield Eversharp, and the consolidated results of both if the markup at Kowloon were increased to 20% and the markup at Cranfield were reduced to 10%? What is the impact of this repositioning on consolidated tax payments?

5. **Kowloon Blade (B).** Encouraged by the results from the previous problem's analysis, corporate management of Cranfield Eversharp wishes to continue to reposition profit in Hong Kong. It is, however, facing two constraints. First, the final sales price in Great Britain must be £20,000 or less to remain competitive. Secondly, the British tax authorities—in working with Cranfield Eversharp's cost accounting staff—has established a maximum transfer price allowed (from Hong Kong) of £17,800. What combination of markups do you recommend for Cranfield Eversharp to institute? What is the impact of this repositioning on consolidated profits after tax and total tax payments?

6. **Kowloon Blade (C).** Not wanting to leave any potential tax repositioning opportunities unexplored, Cranfield Eversharp wants to combine the components of Question 4 with a redistribution of overhead costs. If overhead costs could be reallocated between the two units, but still total £5,000 per unit, and maintain a minimum of £1,750 per unit in Hong Kong, what is the impact of this repositioning on consolidated profits after tax and total tax payments?

7. **Gamboa's tax averaging.** Gamboa Incorporated is a relatively new U.S.-based retailer of specialty fruits and vegetables. The firm is vertically integrated with fruit- and vegetable-sourcing subsidiaries in Central America and distribution outlets throughout the southeastern and northeastern regions of the United States. Gamboa's two Central American subsidiaries are in Belize and Costa Rica.

   Emilia Gamboa, the daughter of the firm's founder, is being groomed to take over the firm's financial management in the near future. Like many firms of similar size, Gamboa has not possessed a very high degree of sophistication in financial management because of time and cost considerations. Emilia, however, has recently finished her MBA and is now attempting to put some specialized knowledge of U.S. taxation practices to work to save Gamboa money. Her first concern is tax averaging for foreign tax liabilities arising from the two Central American subsidiaries.

   Costa Rican operations are slightly more profitable than Belize operations, because Costa Rica is a relatively low-tax country. Costa Rican corporate taxes are a flat 30%, and no withholding taxes are imposed on dividends paid by foreign firms with operations there. Belize has a higher corporate income tax rate, 40%, and imposes a 10% withholding tax on all dividends distributed to foreign investors. The current U.S. corporate income tax rate is 35%.

	BELIZE	COSTA RICA
Earnings before taxes	$1,000,000	$1,500,000
Corporate income tax rate	40%	30%
Dividend withholding tax rate	10%	0%

   a. If Emilia Gamboa assumes a 50% payout rate from each subsidiary, what are the additional taxes due on foreign-sourced income from Belize and Costa Rica individually? How much in additional U.S. taxes would be due if Emilia averaged the tax credits/liabilities of the two units?

   b. Keeping the payout rate from the Belize subsidiary at 50%, how should Emilia change the payout rate of the Costa Rican subsidiary in order to most efficiently manage her total foreign tax bill?

   c. What is the minimum effective tax rate Emilia can achieve on her foreign-sourced income?

8. **Hazelnut, Incorporated.** Jerry Filbert is the Vice President of Tax Planning for the U.S.-based firm, Hazelnut, Inc. Mr. Filbert is attempting to determine what the actual tax liabilities of Hazelnut will be for 2005, given solid forecasts of all expected values (it is now December 15, 2004). Hazelnut (USA) has a wholly owned manufacturing subsidiary in Cádiz, Spain.

   The Spanish subsidiary, Hazelnut Cádiz, had earnings before tax (EBT) in 2004 of €40 million. The earnings were of two types: manufacturing and sales of chocolate-covered hazelnut candy bars (80% of the total) and dividend income from a wholly owned subsidiary in Switzerland (20% of the total). The average exchange rate for the year was $1.20/€. Corporate tax rates in Spain and the United States are both 35%. Dividends distributed from Spain to the United States are subject to a 15% withholding tax. Mr. Filbert was recently told that the Spanish subsidiary will declare an end-of-year dividend of 50% of net income available for distribution.

   a. What will be the amount in U.S. dollars of the net dividend remitted?

   b. What will be the U.S. tax liability associated with the Hazelnut Cádiz 2005 operations?

9. **Ballantyne Brand Services (A).** Ballantyne Brand Services is a U.S.-based brand development and management services consultancy. It is privately held and, although now incorporated was originally a small consulting firm started, by Sara Ballantyne. The company signs contracts for services well into the future and has estimated its income before tax for the 2005–2007 period as follows (note that it has a very large contract already committed for the 2004 year in Australia). All values have been converted to U.S. dollars for tax planning purposes.

ASSUMPTIONS	2005	2006	2007
U.S. domestic income for tax purposes	$2,500,000	$3,500,000	$2,500,000
Australian earnings before tax	$200,000	$2,000,000	$250,000

   The U.S. and Australian corporate income tax rates are 35% and 36%, respectively, in 2005. But the corporate income tax in Australia is scheduled to be reduced to 32% in 2006 and years after that. The reduction in tax rates will also apply to dividend withholding taxes on income remitted outside of Australia, currently 10%, to be reduced to 0% beginning in 2006. Ballantyne intends to remit 75% of all Australian earnings to its parent company each year.

   a. What is the net dividend Ballantyne expects to remit to the U.S. parent from its Australian subsidiary in each of the three years?

   b. What are the additional U.S. taxes due, or foreign tax credits arising from, the expected dividend remittance to the U.S. parent from Australia?

   c. Assuming excess foreign tax credits can be carried forward five years, what is the actual additional tax payment due on the Australian foreign-sourced income in each year?

   d. Assuming carry-forward, what is the cumulative excess foreign tax credits balance at the end of 2007?

   e. What is the creditable tax limit on Ballantyne's foreign-sourced income in each year?

10. **Ballantyne Brand Services (B).** Ballantyne Brand Services, the same firm and situation described in the previous problem, has just been informed by its Australian law firm that the Australian tax revision will not take place as previously expected. The Australian corporate

tax rate will stay at 36% for the foreseeable future, and there will be no reduction in the 10% withholding tax on dividend distributions.

   a. What net dividend can Ballantyne now expect to remit to the U.S. parent from its Australian subsidiary in each of the three years?

   b. What are the additional U.S. taxes due, or foreign tax credits arising from, the expected dividend remittance to the U.S. parent from Australia?

   c. Assuming that excess foreign tax credits can be carried forward five years, what is the actual additional tax payment due on the Australian foreign-sourced income in each year?

   d. Assuming carry-forward, what is the cumulative excess foreign tax credits balance at the end of 2007?

INTERNET EXERCISES

1. Official government tax authorities. Tax laws are constantly changing, and an MNE's tax-planning and management processes must therefore include a continual updating of tax practices by country. Use the following government tax sites to address specific issues related to those countries.

   Hong Kong's ownership change to China: http://www.info.gov.hk/eindex.htm

   Ireland's international financial services centre: http://www.revenue.ie

   Czech Republic's tax incentives for investment: http://www.czech.cz/index.php?section-2&menu-22

2. Tax practices for international business. Many of the major accounting firms provide online information and advisory services for international business activities as related to tax and accounting practices. Use the following websites to gain up-to-date information on tax law changes or practices.

   Ernst & Young http://www.ey.com/tax/

   Deloitte & Touche http://www.dttus.com

   KPMG http://www.kpmg.com

   PricewaterhouseCoopers http://www.pwcglobal.com

SELECTED READINGS

Devereux, P., C. Spengel, and L. Lammerson, "Corporate Taxes and Inefficiency in Europe," *National Tax Journal*, Proceedings of the 95th Annual Conference, 2003, pp. 226–235.

Isenbergh, Joseph, *International Taxation*, Foundation Press, New York, NY, 2000.

Lymer, Andrew, and John Hasseldine (editors), *The International Taxation System*, Kluwer Academic Publishers, 2002.

PricewaterhouseCoopers, *Corporate Taxes: A Worldwide Summary*, New York: PricewaterhouseCoopers, 2005.

Scholes, Myron S., Mark A. Wolfson, Merle M. Erickson, Edward L. Maydew, and Terrence J. Shevlin, *Taxes and Business Strategy: A Planning Approach*, third edition, Prentice Hall, 2004.

MINICASE   STANLEY WORKS AND CORPORATE INVERSION[1]

This strategic initiative will strengthen our company over the long term. An important portion of our revenues and earnings are derived from outside the United States, where nearly 50% of our people reside. Moreover, an increasing proportion of our materials are being purchased from global sources. This change will create greater operational flexibility, better position us to manage international cash flows and help us to deal with our complex international tax structure. As a result, our competitiveness, one of the three legs of our vision to become a Great Brand, will be enhanced. The business, regulatory, and tax environments in Bermuda are expected to create considerable value for share owners. In addition to operational flexibility, improved worldwide cash management and competitive advantages, the new corporate structure will enhance our ability to access international capital markets, which is favorable for organic growth, future strategic alliances and acquisitions, Finally, enhanced flexibility to manage worldwide tax liabilities should reduce our global effective tax rate from its current 32% to within the range of 23%–25%.

Stanley Works, Form 14A, Securities and Exchange Commission, 8 February 2002

Over and over again courts have said that there is nothing sinister in so arranging one's affairs as to keep taxes as low as possible. Everybody does so, rich and poor, and all do right, for nobody owes any public duty to pay more than the law demands: taxes are enforced extractions, not voluntary contributions. To demand more in the name of morals is mere cant.

Judge Learned Hand, Commissioner v. Newman, 159 F.2d 848 (CA-2, 1947)

On February 8, 2002, Stanley Works (USA) announced that it would enter into a *corporate inversion,* whereby the company would reincorporate itself as a Bermuda-based corporation. This was termed an *outbound inversion,* as the reincorporation was to move the company's incorporation out of the United States to a foreign country. Currently a U.S.-based corporation with head offices in New Britain, Connecticut, Stanley would make all U.S. operations a wholly owned subsidiary of a new parent company based in Bermuda—Stanley Tools, Ltd. Corporate headquarters, in fact all company offices and operational centers, would remain in Connecticut. The reasoning was simple: Stanley expected to save close to $30 million annually in corporate income taxes by changing its citizenship. On the date of the announcement, the market value of Stanley increased by $199 million.

But the announcement was met with heated opposition from employees, stockholders, and local, state, and federal authorities. The change required a two-thirds approval by its stockholders. Stanley suffered through a controversial vote on the move in May 2002. Due to confusing corporate communiques to shareholders, a second vote had to be scheduled. In August 2002, Stanley found itself a lightning rod for public debate on the responsibilities of a corporate citizen and the ethics of tax reduction and patriotism. Many regulators were now accusing the company of treaty shopping. The senior management team now wished to reevaluate their inversion decision.

CORPORATE INVERSION

The purpose of a *corporate inversion* was—for all intents and purposes—to reduce tax liability. The United States taxed U.S. based multinational companies on their worldwide income. As a U.S.-based company, Stanley paid corporate income taxes on all income generated in the United States (*domestic-source income*) and income earned abroad and repatriated or deemed repatriated to the parent company in the United States (*foreign-source income*). It was this latter tax on foreign source income which was at the heart of the dilemma for companies like Stanley.

Other countries, for example Germany, taxed only income deemed earned *within* the country, termed *territorial taxation.* Multinational companies with their parent company located in countries like Germany had lower effective tax burdens imposed by their home country tax structures. Offshore tax havens—countries such as Bermuda, the Cayman Islands, and British Virgin Islands—imposed no taxes on foreign-source income and few or negligible taxes on domestic income of multinational companies incorporated there. This provided a

---

[1]This mini-case was derived from *Stanley Works and Corporate Inversion,* Thunderbird Case Series. Copyright ©2003 Thunderbird, The American Graduate School of International Management, prepared by Professors Dale Davison and Michael H. Moffett. Reprinted with permission.

literal tax haven for a multinational company incorporated in that country although it had little or no operational or structural presence there.

HISTORY OF INVERSIONS

Corporate inversions were not a new tax strategy. The first outbound inversion of note was that undertaken by the McDermott Company in 1983. McDermott exchanged the shares held by its U.S. stockholders for shares in McDermott International, a Panamanian subsidiary of the company prior to the restructuring. The IRS had ruled the exchange of shares a taxable event, taxing all of the U.S. shareholders on the sale of their shares as capital gains. This unexpected consequence was thought to be a significant deterrent to future inversions, and the U.S. Congress soon followed with new tax legislation, Section 1248(i) of the IRS Code, which made it easier for the IRS to construe some inversions as taxable events for U.S. shareholders.

The next major corporate inversion of note was that undertaken by Helen of Troy, a beauty supply company located in Texas, in 1993. This was the first so-called *pure inversion,* in that the company set up a completely new company offshore as its corporate headquarters (instead of selling the company's shares to an existing company or subsidiary). Management hoped that this strategy would be ruled a *reorganization,* rather than a taxable sale. The IRS once again, however, ruled the transaction a taxable event: "if US transferors owned, in the aggregate, 50% or more in the vote of value of the transferee foreign corporation immediately after the exchange." Although the McDermott and Helen of Troy

tax rulings were thought to constitute significant deterrents to outbound corporate inversions, more and more companies have considered and, in some cases, completed the reorganization to offshore incorporation. The pace quickened in the late 1990s, with companies like Tyco and Ingersoll-Rand moving offshore to reduce tax liabilities.

An additional consideration was the equity market's response to inversions. On average the market rewarded the announcement of an outbound inversion with a 1.7% appreciation in the company's share price.[2] This share price reaction was thought to represent the present value of cash flow savings resulting from both reduction in taxes due on foreign source income and the reduction of domestic (U.S.) tax savings on domestic income as a result of the restructuring of operations postinversion.

TAX STRATEGY

Stanley, like many other U.S.-based multinational companies, felt increasingly burdened by the U.S. corporate income tax structure. Stanley's U.S. earnings were taxed at the U.S. corporate income tax rate of 35%. This U.S. corporate rate, which had only varied up or down by about 1% over 15 years, had become increasingly high relative to corporate tax rates globally, as many countries reduced corporate tax rates consistently and significantly throughout the 1990s.

The problem faced by Stanley and other multinationals was that more and more of their earnings were being generated outside of the United States, and U.S. tax authorities taxed those profits when remitted back to the parent company in the United States. As illustrated in Figure A, if

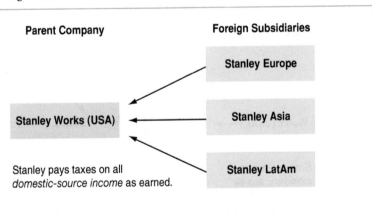

FIGURE A
Stanley Works U.S. Tax Liabilities Before the Outbound Corporate Inversion.

[2]Mihir A. Desai and James R. Hines, Jr., "Expectations and Expatriations: Tracing the Causes and Consequence of Corporate Inversions," *NBER Working Paper 9057,* July 2002, http://www.nber.org/papers/w9057.

Stanley's European operations generated a profit, they would first pay local taxes to the host government in, say, France or Germany, and then additional taxes on those profits when the earnings were remitted back to the U.S. parent company. However, under Subpart F of the U.S. Internal Revenue Service Tax Code, Sections 951–964, a U.S. parent company is subject to current U.S. tax on certain income earned by a foreign subsidiary, without regard to whether the income is remitted to the U.S. corporation or not.[3] This income, typically referred to as Subpart F income, was income generated by a controlled foreign corporation and earned primarily through ownership of assets, not through the active production of goods or services. The U.S. tax authorities taxed this income as earned, rather than waiting to tax it when (or if) it was remitted to the U.S. parent company. This Subpart F provision had been specifically constructed to prevent foreign source income from being permanently parked in offshore tax havens, such as Bermuda, which assesses no corporate income taxes.

The U.S. tax code did have a number of features to eliminate the potential for double taxation (taxes paid in both Europe and the U.S., for example) or at least to lessen the burden. Many of the corporate taxes paid to host governments were credited against potential U.S. tax liabilities. This had proven quite effective when corporate tax rates abroad were higher than in the United States, but as many countries lowered their rates below those in the U.S., profits returned to the United States now resulted in additional taxes due.

The specific tax goals of the outbound corporate inversion were (see Figure B):[4]

- First, Bermuda, as is typical of most offshore financial centers, does not tax foreign source income. (In fact, Bermuda does not have a corporate income tax.) Stanley's profits generated throughout the world could be freely redistributed throughout the global business, including the parent, without creating additional tax liabilities in the country of the parent company (now Bermuda instead of the United States).
- Second, the U.S. operations of Stanley would now be conducted as the U.S. subsidiary of a foreign corporation. This arrangement would most likely pose restructuring possibilities whereby the U.S. subsidiary would have increasing obligations to the Bermuda parent such as royalties, debt service, and licensing fees, which were legitimate deductible expenses in the U.S. but income to the parent company in Bermuda. The result would be a net reduction in U.S. tax liabilities from Stanley's business conducted in the United States.

This second dimension of the tax benefits of corporate inversion is often termed *earnings stripping*. The term refers to the practice of structuring operations within the United States to position as many corporate costs as legally possible to reduce taxable profits within the higher tax environment of the United States.

FIGURE B
Stanley Works U.S. Tax Liabilities After the Outbound Corporate Inversion.

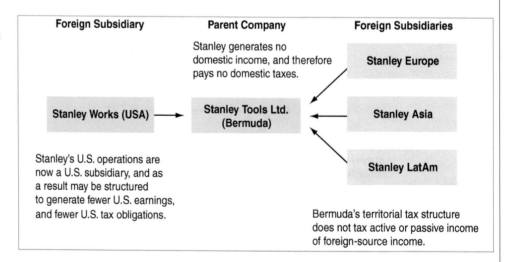

<hr />

[3]This code specifically applied to *controlled foreign corporations or CFCs.* A *CFC* was defined as any foreign corporation with more than 50% of its voting stock owned directly or indirectly by U.S. shareholders. Thus, most foreign subsidiaries of U.S.-based multinationals were classified as CFCs.
[4]"Special Report: Outbound Inversion Transactions." *Tax Notes*, New York State Bar Association Tax Section, July 1, 2002, pp. 127–149.

TABLE A   Prospective Changes in Stanley Works' Earnings After Inversion.

	PRO FORMA 2003 EARNINGS		
	BEFORE	AFTER	SAVINGS
Earnings before tax	$420	$420	
Tax liability (32%/24%)	(134)	(101)	
Earnings after tax	$286	$319	+ $33
Shares outstanding (millions)	88.0	88.0	
Earnings per share (EPS)	$3.250	$3.625	+ $0.375 or 11.5%

There was, however, considerable debate as to the actual tax benefits to be gained versus the growing public relations costs of inversion. The earnings per share (EPS) benefits had been touted by Stanley as a simple reduction in the effective tax rate for the overall organization. For example, using the pro forma earnings estimates for 2003, Stanley was expected to pay $134 million in taxes in 2003 on $420 million in earnings before tax, as shown in Table A. This assumed an effective tax rate of 32%. If Stanley were to reincorporate in Bermuda, Stanley estimated the effective tax rate would fall to 24%, yielding a $33 million savings for Stanley and its stockholders.[5]

PATRIOTISM AND INVERSION

How would you like to keep living in your current home, but tell the Internal Revenue Service to go pound sand in Bermuda, because you're a legal resident of that lovely island? You can't, but toolmaker Stanley Works plans to save $30 million a year by moving. So what if our country is at war against terrorism and is spending billions extra for defense and homeland security? That's our problem, not the tax dodgers'. Their problem is raising profits to get their stock price higher. What could possibly be more important, since a good stock market is good for America, right?

Allan Sloan, "The Tax-Free Bermuda Getaway,"
Newsweek, April 15, 2002

John Trani's other worries surrounded the image of Stanley. The move to reincorporate offshore was portrayed by many as unpatriotic—unsupportive of the United States during a time of recession and continuing terrorist threats in the post–September 11 world. In addition to the growing debate in Congress over the increasing use of corporate inversions, there was strong opposition to the move by Stanley workers and their unions. Although Stanley was not doing anything illegal, and was paying its taxes in accordance with current law, the company was portrayed as "working too hard" to avoid future income tax obligations.

John Trani and his senior management team returned to the conference room. Time was running out. Stanley needed to reschedule the stockholder vote now if it was to continue to pursue corporate inversion. The question remained as to whether the benefits exceeded the costs of moving offshore.

QUESTIONS

1. If Stanley did indeed reincorporate offshore, how do you think the company would restructure its operations, both inside and outside the United States?

2. Do you believe that the U.S. government should allow a company like Stanley to reincorporate outside the country in order to pay lower taxes?

3. If you were John Trani, would you continue to pursue the outbound inversion or choose to stay put?

---

[5]Stanley had consistently followed a conservative estimate in its public discussions of a $30 million tax savings, as opposed to the $33 million calculation here.

Working Capital Management

9

Working capital management in an MNE requires repositioning cash flows, as well as managing current assets and liabilities, when faced with political, foreign exchange, tax, and liquidity constraints. The overall goal is to reduce funds tied up in working capital while simultaneously providing sufficient funding and liquidity for the conduct of global business. This combination should enhance return on assets and return on equity. It also should improve efficiency ratios and other evaluation of performance parameters.

The first section of this chapter describes Carlton's operating cycle. The second section analyzes Carlton's fund repositioning decisions. The third section examines the constraints that affect the repositioning of Carlton's funds. The fourth section identifies alternative conduits for moving funds. The fifth section introduces the management of net working capital, including accounts receivable, inventory, and cash. The sixth and final section examines how working capital is financed, including the various types of banking services available.

9.1   CARLTON BRAZIL'S OPERATING CYCLE

The *operating* and *cash conversion cycles* for Carlton Brazil are illustrated in Figure 9-1. The operating cycle can be decomposed into five periods, each with business, accounting, and potential cash flow implications. The operating cycle periods are described in the following sections.

Quotation Period

The quotation period extends from the time of price quotation, t_0, to the point when the customer places an order, t_1. If the customer is requesting a price quote in foreign currency terms, such as Chilean pesos, Carlton Brazil would have a potential but uncertain foreign exchange transaction exposure. The quotation itself is not listed on any of the traditional financial statements of the firm, although a firm like Carlton Brazil would keep a worksheet of quotations extended and their time periods.

Input Sourcing Period

Once a customer has accepted a quotation, the order is placed at time t_1. The buyer and seller sign a contract describing the product to be delivered, likely timing of delivery, conditions of delivery, and price and financing terms. At this time, Carlton Brazil would order the material inputs that it requires to manufacture the product that it does not currently hold in inventory. Depending on the individual sale, the buyer may make a cash deposit or down payment. This would constitute the first actual cash flow associated with the order, a cash inflow to Carlton Brazil, which would initiate the cash conversion cycle for this transaction.

Inventory Period

As it receives inputs, Carlton Brazil assembles and manufactures the goods. The length of this inventory-manufacturing period, from t_1 to t_2, depends on the type of product (off-the-shelf versus custom built-to-specification), the supply-chain integration of Carlton Brazil with its various internal and external suppliers, and the technology employed by Carlton Brazil.

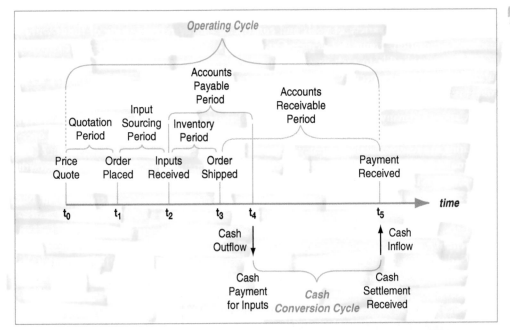

FIGURE 9-1
Operating and Cash Cycles for Carlton Brazil.

Accounts Payable Period

As inputs arrive, Carlton lists them as material and component inventories on the left-hand side of Carlton Brazil's balance sheet, with corresponding accounts payable entries on the right-hand side of the balance sheet. If the inputs are invoiced in foreign currencies, whether from Carlton USA, a sister subsidiary, or external suppliers, they constitute foreign currency transaction exposures to Carlton Brazil.

Note that the accounts payable period shown in Figure 9-1 begins at the same time as the inventory period, t_2, but may extend in time to t_4, after the inventory period ends. If Carlton Brazil's suppliers extend trade credit, Carlton Brazil would be able to postpone paying for the inventory for an extended period. Of course, if Carlton Brazil chooses not to accept trade credit, it may pay for the inputs as delivered. In this case, the accounts payable period would end before the inventory period—the manufacturing period—ends at time t_3. At whatever point in time Carlton Brazil chooses to settle its outstanding accounts payable, it incurs a cash outflow.

Accounts Receivable Period

When the goods are finished and shipped, Carlton Brazil records the transaction as a sale on its income statement and as an account receivable on its balance sheet. If it is a foreign currency–denominated invoice, the spot exchange rate on that date, t_4, is used to record the sale value in local currency. The exchange rate in effect on the date of cash settlement, t_5, would then be used in the calculation of any foreign exchange gains and losses associated with the transaction—the *transaction exposure*.

The length of the accounts receivable period depends on the credit terms offered by Carlton Brazil, the choice made by the buyer to either accept trade credit or pay in cash, and country-specific and industry-specific payment practices. At cash settlement, Carlton Brazil receives a cash inflow (finally) in payment for goods delivered. At time t_5 the transaction is concluded and all accounting entries—inventory items, accounts payable, accounts receivable—are eliminated.

9.2   CARLTON'S REPOSITIONING DECISIONS

Next we describe the variety of goals and constraints on the repositioning of funds within Carlton Corporation. Figure 9-2 depicts Carlton, its wholly owned subsidiaries, the currency and tax rates applicable to each unit, and management's present conclusions regarding each subsidiary's growth prospects. Carlton's three foreign subsidiaries each present a unique set of concerns:

- Carlton Germany, the oldest of the three, is operating in a relatively high-tax environment (compared in principle to the tax rate in the parent country, the United States). It is operating in a relatively stable currency—the euro—and is free to move capital in and out of the country with few restrictions. The business itself is mature, with few significant growth prospects in the near future.
- Carlton Brazil, the result of a recent acquisition, is operating in a low-tax environment, but historically a volatile currency environment. It is subject to only a few current capital restrictions. Carlton believes the business has very good growth prospects in the short to medium term if it is able to inject additional capital and managerial expertise into the business.
- Carlton China, a new joint venture with an in-country partner that is a former unit of the Chinese government, is operating in a relatively low-tax environment, with a fixed exchange rate (the renminbi is managed within a very narrow band relative to the U.S. dollar). It is subject to a number of restrictions on capital. The business is believed to have the greatest potential—in the long run.

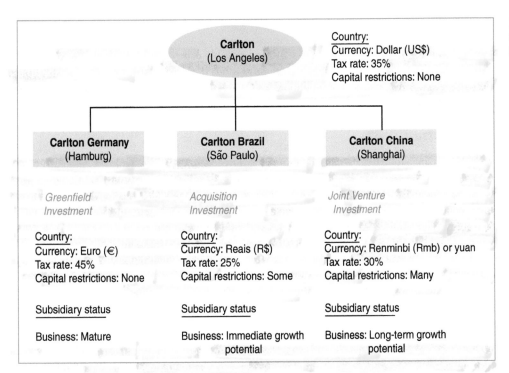

FIGURE 9-2
Carlton's Foreign
Subsidiaries.

In practice, Carlton's senior management in the parent company (*corporate*) will first determine its strategic objectives regarding the business developments in each subsidiary, and then design a financial management plan for the repositioning of profits, cash flows, and capital for each subsidiary. As a result of this process, Carlton will now attempt to pursue the following repositioning objectives by subsidiary:

- Carlton Germany: Reposition profits from Germany to the United States, while maintaining the value of the European market's maturity to Carlton Corporation.
- Carlton Brazil: Reposition or in some way manage the capital at risk in Brazil subject to foreign exchange rate risk, while providing adequate capital for immediate growth prospects.
- Carlton China: Reposition the quantity of funds in and out of China to protect against blocked funds (transfer risk), while balancing the needs of the joint venture partner.

9.3 CONSTRAINTS ON REPOSITIONING FUNDS

Fund flows between units of a domestic business are generally unimpeded, but that is not the case in a multinational business. A firm operating globally faces a variety of political, tax, foreign exchange, and liquidity considerations that limit its ability to move funds easily and without cost from one country or currency to another. These constraints are the reason that multinational financial managers must plan ahead for repositioning funds within an MNE. Advance planning is essential even when constraints do not exist, for at some future date political events may lead to unexpected restrictions.

Political Constraints

Political constraints can block the transfer of funds either overtly or covertly. Overt blockage occurs when a currency becomes inconvertible or is subject to government exchange controls that prevent its transfer at reasonable exchange rates. Covert blockage occurs when dividends or other forms of fund remittances are severely limited, heavily taxed, or excessively delayed by a bureaucratic approval process.

Tax Constraints

Tax constraints arise because of the complex and possibly contradictory tax structures of various national governments through whose jurisdictions funds might pass. A firm does not want funds in transit eroded by a sequence of nibbling tax collectors in every jurisdiction through which such funds might flow.

Transaction Costs

Foreign exchange transaction costs are incurred when one currency is exchanged for another. These costs, in the form of fees and/or the difference between bid and offer quotations, are revenue for the commercial banks and dealers that operate the foreign exchange market. Although usually a small percentage of the amount of money exchanged, such costs become significant for large or frequent transfers. Transaction costs are sufficiently large enough to warrant planning to avoid unnecessary back-and-forth transfers such as would occur if a subsidiary remitted a cash dividend to its parent at approximately the same time as the parent paid the subsidiary for goods purchased. Sending foreign exchange simultaneously in two directions is obviously a sheer waste of corporate resources, but it sometimes occurs when one part of a firm is not coordinated with another.

Liquidity Needs

Despite the overall advantage of worldwide cash handling, liquidity needs in each individual location must be satisfied and good local banking relationships maintained. The size of appropriate balances is in part a judgmental decision not easily measurable. Nevertheless, such needs constrain a pure optimization approach to worldwide cash positioning.

9.4 CONDUITS FOR MOVING FUNDS BY UNBUNDLING THEM

Multinational firms often *unbundle* their transfer of funds into separate flows for specific purposes. Host countries are then more likely to perceive that a portion of what might otherwise be called *remittance of profits* constitutes an essential purchase of specific benefits that command worldwide values and benefit the host country. Unbundling allows a multinational firm to recover funds from subsidiaries without piquing host country sensitivities over large dividend drains. For example, Carlton might transfer funds from its foreign subsidiaries to the parent, Carlton, by any of the conduits shown in Figure 9-3.

The conduits are separable into those that are before-tax and after-tax in the host country. Although not always the focus of intra-unit fund movement, tax goals frequently make this a critical distinction for foreign subsidiary financial structures. An increase in the funds flow (charges) in any of the before-tax categories reduces the taxable profits of the foreign subsidiary *if* the host country tax authorities acknowledge the charge as a legitimate expense. The before-tax/after-tax distinction is also quite significant to a parent company attempting to repatriate funds in the most tax-efficient method if it is attempting to manage its own foreign tax credit/deficits between foreign units.

An item-by-item matching of remittance to input, such as royalties for intellectual property with fees for patents and advice, is equitable to host country and foreign investor alike. It allows each party to see the reason for each remittance and to judge its acceptance independently. If all investment inputs are unbundled, part of what might have been classified as residual profits may turn out to be tax-deductible expenses related to a specific purchased benefit. Unbundling also facilitates allocation of overhead from a parent's international division, so-called *shared services*, to each operating subsidiary in accordance with a predetermined formula. Predetermination of the allocation method means a host country is less likely to view a given remittance as capricious and thus inappropriate. Finally, unbundling facilitates the entry of local capital into joint-venture projects, because total

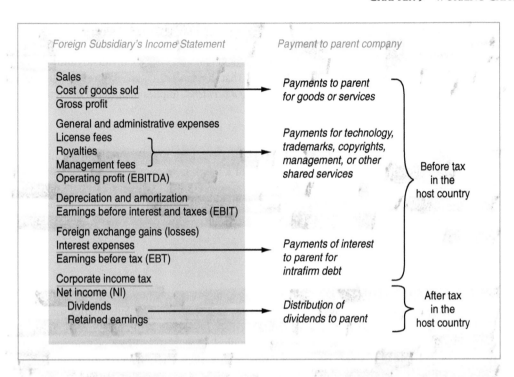

remuneration to different owners can be in proportion to the value of the varied contributions of each, rather than only in proportion to the amount of monetary capital they have invested.

9.5 INTERNATIONAL DIVIDEND REMITTANCES

Payment of dividends is the classic method by which firms transfer profit back to owners, be those owners individual shareholders or parent corporations. International dividend policy now incorporates tax considerations, political risk, and foreign exchange risk, as well as a return for business guidance and technology.

Tax Implications

Host country tax laws influence the dividend decision. Countries such as Germany tax retained earnings at one rate and distributed earnings at a lower rate. Most countries levy withholding taxes on dividends paid to foreign parent firms and investors. Again, most (but not all) parent countries levy a tax on foreign dividends received, but allow a tax credit for foreign taxes already paid on that income stream. That said, dividends remain the most tax inefficient method for repatriating funds, because they are distributed on an after-tax basis. This means that the parent company will frequently be faced with the generation of excess foreign tax credits on a dividend. Remittance of license or royalty fees is on a pretax basis in the foreign subsidiary; the only tax typically applied is that of withholding, a rate considerably below that of corporate income taxes.

Political Risk

Political risk may motivate parent firms to require foreign subsidiaries to remit all locally generated funds "beyond" or "in excess of" that required to finance growth internally in sales (working capital requirements) and planned capital expansions (capex, or capital expenditures). Such policies, however, are not universal.

One strategy employed by MNEs in response to potential government restrictions is to maintain a constant dividend payout ratio, so as to demonstrate that an established policy is being consistently carried out. This step establishes a precedent for remittance of dividends and removes the perception of some host country governments that dividend distributions are by managerial election. (Note that even the terminology, *declaring a dividend*, implies managerial discretion.)

Foreign Exchange Risk

If it anticipates a foreign exchange loss, an MNE may speed up the transfer of funds out of the country via dividends. This "lead" is usually part of a larger strategy of moving from weak currencies to strong currencies, and can include speeding up intrafirm payments on accounts receivable and payable. However, decisions to accelerate dividend payments ahead of what might be normal must take into account interest rate differences and the negative impact on host country relations.

Distributions and Cash Flows

Dividends are a cash payment to owners equal to all or a portion of earnings of a prior period. To pay dividends, a subsidiary needs both past earnings and available cash. Subsidiaries sometimes have earnings without cash, because earnings are measured at the time of a sale but cash is received later, when the receivable is collected (a typical distinction between accounting profits and cash flow). Profits of rapidly growing subsidiaries are often tied up in ever-increasing receivables and inventory (working capital). Hence rapidly growing foreign subsidiaries may lack the cash to remit a dividend equal to even a portion of earnings.

The reverse may also be true; firms may be receiving cash from the collection of old receivables even when profits are down, because current sales have fallen off or current expenses have risen relative to current sales prices. Such firms might want to declare a dividend in order to remove a bountiful supply of cash from a country, but lack the earnings against which to charge such payments. For either of these reasons, a firm must look at both measured earnings and available cash before settling on a cash dividend policy.

Joint Venture Factors

Existence of joint-venture partners or local stockholders also influences dividend policy. Optimal positioning of funds internationally cannot dominate the valid claims of independent partners or local stockholders for dividends. The latter do not benefit from the worldwide success of the MNE parent, but only from the success of the particular joint venture in which they own a share. Firms might hesitate to reduce dividends when earnings falter. They also might hesitate to increase dividends following a spurt in earnings because of possible adverse reaction to reducing dividends later should earnings decline. Many MNEs insist on 100% ownership of subsidiaries in order to avoid possible conflicts of interest with outside shareholders.

9.6 NET WORKING CAPITAL

If Carlton Brazil's business continues to expand, it will continually add to inventories and accounts payable (A/P) in order to fill increased sales in the form of accounts receivable (A/R). These three components make up *net working capital* (NWC). The combination is "net" as a result of the spontaneous funding capability of accounts payable; accounts payable provide part of the funding for increased levels of inventory and accounts receivable.

$$\text{Net working capital (NWC)} = (\text{A/R} + \text{Inventory}) - (\text{A/P})$$

Because both A/R and inventory are components of current assets on the left-hand side of the balance sheet, as they grow they must be financed by additional liabilities of some form on the right-hand side of the balance sheet. A/P may provide a part of the funding. Figure 9-4 illustrates Carlton Brazil's net working capital. Note that we do not include cash or short-term debt as part of net working capital. Although they are part of current assets and current liabilities, respectively, they are the result of management discretion, and do not spontaneously change with operations. Their determinates are discussed later in this chapter.

In principle, Carlton attempts to minimize its net working capital balance. It reduces A/R if collections are accelerated. It reduces inventories by carrying lower levels of unfinished and finished goods, and by speeding the rate at which goods are manufactured—reducing so-called *cycle time*. All of these measures must be balanced with their customer needs. Sales could be reduced if inventories are not on hand, or if credit sales are reduced. On the other side of the balance sheet, NWC can be reduced by stretching A/P out. Again, if not done carefully, this could potentially damage the company's relationship with its key suppliers, thereby reducing reliability and supply-chain partnerships.

A/P versus Short-Term Debt

Figure 9-4 also illustrates one of the key managerial decisions for any subsidiary: Should A/P be paid off early, taking discounts if offered by suppliers? The alternative financing for NWC balances is short-term debt.

For example, payment terms in Brazil are quite long by global standards, often extending 60 to 90 days. Paraña Electronics is one of Carlton Brazil's key suppliers. It delivers a shipment of electronic components and invoices Carlton Brazil R$180,000. Paraña Electronics offers credit terms of 5/10 net 60. This means that the entire amount of the A/P, R$180,000, is due in 60 days. Alternatively, if Carlton Brazil wishes to pay within the first 10 days, a 5% discount is given:

$$R\$180,000 \times (1 - 0.05) = R\$171,000$$

Carlton Brazil's financial manager, Caitlin Kelly, must decide which is the lower-cost method of financing the NWC. Short-term debt in Brazilian reais, because of the relatively higher inflationary conditions common in Brazil, costs 24% per year.

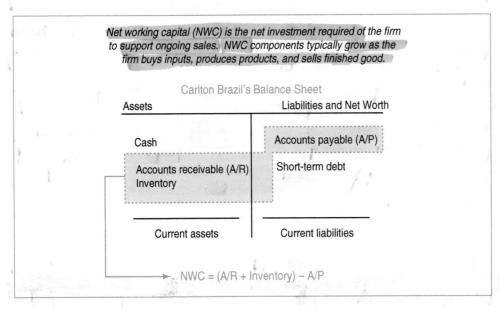

FIGURE 9-4
Carlton Brazil's Net
Working Capital
Requirements.

Net working capital (NWC) is the net investment required of the firm to support ongoing sales. NWC components typically grow as the firm buys inputs, produces products, and sells finished good.

Carlton Brazil's Balance Sheet

Assets — Liabilities and Net Worth

Cash

Accounts payable (A/P)

Accounts receivable (A/R)
Inventory

Short-term debt

Current assets — Current liabilities

NWC = (A/R + Inventory) – A/P

What is the annual cost of the discount offered by Paraña Electronics? Carlton Brazil is effectively paid 5% for giving up 50 days of financing (60 days less the 10-day period for discounts). Assuming a 365-day count for interest calculation,

$$\frac{365 \text{ days}}{50 \text{ days}} = 7.30$$

To calculate the effective annual interest cost of supplier financing, we must compound the 5% discount for 50 days 7.30 times, yielding a *cost of carry* provided by Paraña Electronics of

$$(1 + 0.05)^{7.3} = 1.428, \text{ or } 42.8\% \text{ per year}$$

Paraña Electronics is therefore charging Carlton Brazil 42.8% per year for financing. Alternatively, Carlton Brazil could borrow reais from local banks in São Paulo for 24% per year, use the funds to pay Paraña Electronics early, and take the discounts offered. The latter is the obvious choice in this case.

The choice between taking supplier-provided financing and short-term debt is not always purely a matter of comparing interest costs. In many countries, the foreign subsidiaries of foreign MNEs have limited access to local currency debt. In other cases, the subsidiary may be offered funds from the parent company at competitive rates. We will return to this topic of internal banking in the last section of this chapter.

Days Working Capital

A common method of benchmarking working capital management practice is to calculate the NWC of the firm on a "days sales" basis. If the value of A/R, inventories, and A/P on the balance sheet are divided by the annual daily sales (annual sales/365 days), we can summarize the firm's NWC in the number of days of sales NWC constitutes. Table 9-1 provides the results of a survey by *CFO Magazine* in both the United States and Europe in 2001 for the technology hardware and equipment industry segment.

We must use care in viewing the survey results. First, the days sales values are for the consolidated companies, not specific country-level subsidiaries. Therefore the averages could reflect very different working capital structures for individual subsidiaries of the firms listed. Secondly, without knowing the specific business and country areas included, we have difficulty evaluating the short-term financing decisions discussed in the previous section as made by management of the listed firms.

Despite these reservations, there are some clear differences between the U.S. and European averages, as well as between individual firms. The days working capital average for the selected U.S. firms of 29 days is less than half the 75 days for the European sample. A closer look at the subcategories indicates a radically sparse attitude toward inventory among the U.S. firms, averaging 19 days sales. Days sales held in accounts receivable at 53 days on average is nearly 20 days less than the European average of 70. Payables are essentially identical between the two groups. Clearly, European-based technology hardware firms are carrying a significantly higher level of net working capital in their financial structures than comparable U.S.-based firms to support the same level of sales.

Among individual firms, Dell lives up to its billing as one of the most aggressive working capital managers across all industries. Dell's net working capital level of negative two days indicates exactly what it says—a level of A/P that surpasses the sum of receivables and inventory. Even with that accomplishment, its inventory days of six is still three times that of Apple Computer's two days in inventory.

Intrafirm Working Capital

The MNE itself poses some unique challenges in the management of working capital. Many multinationals manufacture goods in a few specific countries and then ship the intermediate products to other facilities globally for completion and distribution. The payables, receivables,

TABLE 9-1 Days Working Capital for Selected U.S. and European Technology Hardware and Equipment Firms, 2001.

COMPANY	COUNTRY	DAYS WORKING CAPITAL	DAYS RECEIVABLES	DAYS INVENTORY	DAYS PAYABLES
Intel Corporation	U.S.	48	47	21	20
Cisco Systems	U.S.	54	46	20	12
Dell Computer	U.S.	(2)	41	6	49
Texas Instruments	U.S.	34	65	32	63
Applied Materials	U.S.	41	82	52	93
Apple Computer	U.S.	2	48	2	48
Sun Microsystems	U.S.	58	67	12	21
Gateway Inc.	U.S.	0	25	8	33
Average	U.S.	29	53	19	42
ST Microelectronics	France-Italy	58	65	52	59
Nokia	Finland	66	72	31	37
Philips Electronics	Netherlands	71	59	51	39
GN Store Nord	Denmark	100	92	40	32
Spirent	United Kingdom	107	66	63	22
Getronics	Netherlands	51	80	20	49
Infinecon Tech	Germany	75	57	69	51
Average	Europe	75	70	47	41

Source: *CFO Magazine*, "2001 Working Capital Survey," July 2, 2001, and *CFO Europe Magazine*, "2001 Working Capital Survey," July/August 2001. Days working capital = days receivables + days inventory – days payables.

and inventory levels of the various units are a combination of intrafirm and interfirm. The varying business practices observed globally regarding payment terms—both days and discounts—create severe mismatches in some cases.

For example, Figure 9-5 illustrates the challenges in working capital management faced by Carlton Brazil. Because Carlton Brazil purchases inputs from Carlton USA and then uses additional local material input to finish the products for local distribution, it must manage two different sets of payables. Carlton USA sells intrafirm on common U.S. payment terms, net 30 days. Local suppliers in Brazil, however, use payment terms closer to Brazilian norms of 60 days net (although this is in many cases still quite short for Brazilian practices, which have been known to extend to as long as 180 days). Similarly, as the customers of Carlton Brazil are Brazilian, they expect the same common payment terms of 60 days. Carlton Brazil is then "squeezed," having to pay Carlton USA much faster than it pays other local suppliers and long before it receives cash settlement from its customers.

In addition to Carlton's need to determine intrafirm payment practices that do not put undue burdens on their foreign subsidiaries, the question of currency of invoice will also be extremely important. If Carlton Brazil sells only domestically, it does not have natural inflows of U.S. dollars or other hard currencies—it earns only Brazilian reais. If Carlton USA then invoices it for inputs in U.S. dollars, Carlton Brazil will be constantly short dollars and will incur continuing currency management costs. Carlton USA should invoice in Brazilian reais and manage the currency exposure centrally (possibly through a reinvoicing center).

Managing Receivables

A firm's operating cash inflow is derived primarily from collecting its accounts receivable. Multinational accounts receivable are created by two separate types of transactions: sales to related subsidiaries and sales to independent or unrelated buyers.

FIGURE 9-5
Carlton's Multinational
Working Capital
Sequence.

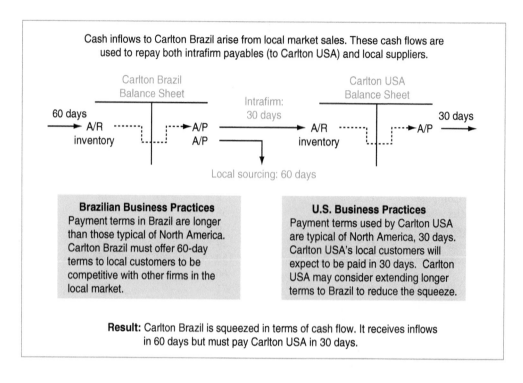

Cash inflows to Carlton Brazil arise from local market sales. These cash flows are used to repay both intrafirm payables (to Carlton USA) and local suppliers.

Brazilian Business Practices
Payment terms in Brazil are longer than those typical of North America. Carlton Brazil must offer 60-day terms to local customers to be competitive with other firms in the local market.

U.S. Business Practices
Payment terms used by Carlton USA are typical of North America, 30 days. Carlton USA's local customers will expect to be paid in 30 days. Carlton USA may consider extending longer terms to Brazil to reduce the squeeze.

Result: Carlton Brazil is squeezed in terms of cash flow. It receives inflows in 60 days but must pay Carlton USA in 30 days.

INDEPENDENT CUSTOMERS   Management of accounts receivable from independent customers involves two types of decisions: in what currency should the transaction be denominated, and what should be the terms of payment? Domestic sales are almost always denominated in the local currency. At issue is whether export sales should be denominated in the currency of the exporter, the currency of the buyer, or a third-country currency. Competition or custom will often dictate the answer, but if negotiating room exists, the seller prefers to price and to invoice in the strongest currency, while an informed buyer prefers to pay in the weakest currency.

PAYMENT TERMS   Terms of payment are another bargaining factor. Considered by themselves, receivables from sales in weak currencies should be collected as soon as possible to minimize loss of exchange value between sales date and collection date. Accounts receivable resulting from sales in hard currencies may be allowed to remain outstanding longer. In fact, if the seller is expecting an imminent devaluation of its home currency, it might want to encourage slow payment of its hard currency receivables, especially if the home government requires immediate exchange of foreign currency receipts into the home currency. An alternative, if legal, would be for the seller to accept the proceeds abroad and keep them on deposit abroad rather than return them to the home country.

In inflationary economies, the demand for credit usually exceeds the supply. Often, however, a large business (be it multinational or a large local concern) has better access to the limited, cheaper credit that is available locally than do smaller domestic businesses, such as local distributors, retail merchants, or smaller manufacturers.

SELF-LIQUIDATING BILLS   Some banking systems, often for reasons of tradition, have a predilection toward self-liquidating, discountable bills. In many European countries, it is easier to borrow from a bank on the security of bills (receivables in negotiable form) generated from sales than on the security of physical inventory. Napoleon is alleged to have had a philosophy that no good French merchant should be required to wait for funds if good merchandise has been sold to good people, provided a document exists showing sales of the items. The document must have the signature of the buyer and the endorsement of the seller and the rediscounting bank. Thus in France it is often possible to reduce net investment in receivables to zero by selling entirely on trade acceptances that can be discounted at the bank.

The European use of discountable bills has a very real rationale behind it. According to European commercial law, based on the Code Napoleon, the claim certified by the signature of the buyer on the bill is separated from the claim based on the underlying transaction. For example, a bill is easily negotiable, because objections about the quality of the merchandise by the buyer do not affect the claim of the bill holder. In addition, defaulted bills can be collected through a particularly speedy judicial process that is much faster than the collection of normal receivables.

OTHER TERMS   In many countries, government bodies facilitate inventory financing in the guise of receivable financing by extending export credit or by guaranteeing export credit from banks at advantageous interest rates. When the term of the special export financing can be extended to match the payment of the foreign purchaser, the foreign purchaser is in effect able to finance its inventory through the courtesy of the exporter's government.

In some environments, credit terms extended by manufacturers to retailers are of such long maturities as to constitute "purchase" of the retailer, such "purchase" being necessary to build an operational distribution system between manufacturer and ultimate customer. In Japan, for example, customer payment terms of 120 days are fairly common, and a manufacturer's sales effort is not competitive unless sufficient financial aid is provided to retailers to make it possible or beneficial for them to buy the manufacturer's product. Financial aid is reported to take the form of outright purchase of the retailer's capital stock, working capital loans, equipment purchase, subsidy or loan, and consideration of payment terms. Such manufacturer-supplied financing is a normal way of doing business in Japan—and contributes to the lack of domestic competition prevalent in that country.

Inventory Management

Operations in inflationary, devaluation-prone economies sometimes force management to modify its normal approach to inventory management. In some cases, management may choose to maintain inventory and reorder levels far in excess of what would be called for in an economic order-quantity model.

Under conditions where local currency devaluation is likely, management must decide whether to build up inventory of imported items in anticipation of the expected devaluation. After the devaluation, imported inventory will cost more in local currency terms. One tradeoff is a higher holding cost because of the bloated level of inventory and high local interest rates that normally reflect the expected devaluation. A less obvious tradeoff is the possibility that local government will enforce a price freeze following devaluation. This freeze would prevent the imported inventory from being sold for an appropriate markup above its now-higher replacement value. Still worse, the devaluation may not occur as anticipated, leaving management holding an excessive level of inventory until it can be worked down. Disposing of excessive inventory will be particularly painful if competitors have followed the same strategy of speculating on imported inventory.

Free-Trade Zones and Free Industrial Zones

A *free-trade zone* combines the old idea of duty-free ports with legislation that reduces or eliminates customs duties to retailers or manufacturers who structure their operations to benefit from the technique. Income taxes may also be reduced for operations in a free-trade zone. The old duty-free ports, typically located in the dock area of major seaports, were where goods were held, duty-free, until the owner was ready to deliver them within the country. Modern free-trade zones, by comparison, are often located away from a port area. For example, the Italian firm of Olivetti has such a zone in Harrisburg, Pennsylvania.

Free-trade zones function in several ways. As mentioned, they may be a place to offload merchandise for subsequent sale within the country where the zone is located. An example of such a zone would be a storage area for imported Toyota automobiles in the port of Los Angeles. A large quantity of differentiated models can be held until sold by a dealer, at which time the cars are "imported" into the United States from the free-trade zone. The advantage of such an arrangement is that a variety of models can be kept near the point of sale for quick delivery, but import duties need be paid only when the merchandise passes from the zone into California.

A second type of zone involves the assembly of components for subsequent sale within the country where the zone is located. An example would be the Mercedes assembly line in Alabama. Components are imported into the free-trade zone where assembly work is finished. The import duty is paid only when the finished car is removed from the zone. Furthermore, the duty is lower than it would be for a finished car, because the charges on components are less than the charge on a finished vehicle.

A third type of zone is a full-fledged manufacturing center with a major portion of its output reexported out of the country. Two examples are Penang, Malaysia, and Madagascar, where such zones are officially designated "free industrial zones." In Penang, companies as diverse as Dell, National Semiconductor, Sony, Bosch, and Trane Air Conditioning manufacture final products. A major portion of production is reexported, avoiding Malaysian customs altogether but providing jobs for Malaysian workers and engineers. The portion of production sold in Malaysia is assessed duties only on the components originally imported. However, the variety of firms permits one to buy from another; Dell buys Pentium chips from Intel and disk drives from Seagate, both of which are located less than a mile from the Dell plant.

9.7   INTERNATIONAL CASH MANAGEMENT

International cash management is the set of activities determining the levels of cash balances held throughout the MNE, and the facilitation of its movement cross-border. These activities are typically handled by the international treasury of the MNE.

Motives for Holding Cash

The level of cash maintained by an individual subsidiary is determined independently of the working capital management decisions discussed previously. Cash balances, including marketable securities, are held partly to enable normal day-to-day cash disbursements and partly to protect against unanticipated variations from budgeted cash flows. These two motives are called the *transaction motive* and the *precautionary motive*.

Cash disbursed for operations is replenished from two sources: (1) internal working capital turnover, and (2) external sourcing—traditionally, short-term borrowing. Short-term borrowing can also be "negative," as when excess cash is used to repay outstanding short-term loans. In general, individual subsidiaries of MNEs typically maintain only minimal cash balances necessary to meet the transaction purposes. Efficient cash management aims to reduce cash tied up unnecessarily in the system, without diminishing profit or increasing risk, so as to increase the rate of return on invested assets.

International Cash Settlements and Processing

Multinational business increases the complexity of making payments and settling cash flows between related and unrelated firms. Over time, a number of techniques and services have evolved that simplify and reduce the costs of making these cross-border payments. We focus here on four such techniques: wire transfers, cash pooling, payment netting, and electronic fund transfers.

Wire Transfers

Although there are a variety of computer-based networks used for effecting international transactions and settlements, two have come to dominate the international financial sector: CHIPS and SWIFT. The primary distinction among systems is whether they are for secure communications alone, or for actual transfer and settlement.

CHIPS CHIPS, the Clearing House Interbank Payment System, is a computerized network that connects major banks globally. CHIPS is owned and operated by its member banks, making it the single largest privately operated and final-payments system in the world. Developed in 1970 when international currency transactions were dominated by the U.S. dollar, CHIPS has continued to dominate the transfer and settlement of U.S. dollar transactions for more than 34 years.

CHIPS is actually a subsidiary of the New York Clearing House, the oldest and largest payments processor of bank transactions. The New York Clearing House was first established in 1853 to provide a central place—a clearinghouse—where all banks in New York City could daily settle transactions, such as the many personal checks written by private individuals and corporations, among themselves. CHIPS itself is simply a computer-based evolutionary result of this need. Because banks are still the primary financial service provider for MNEs, businesses transferring payments both interfirm and intrafirm globally use banks for effecting the payments and the banks in turn utilize CHIPS.

SWIFT The Society for Worldwide Interbank Financial Telecommunications, SWIFT, also facilitates the wire transfer settlement process globally. Whereas CHIPS actually clears financial transactions, SWIFT is purely a communications system. By providing a secure and standardized transfer process, SWIFT has greatly reduced the errors and associated costs of effecting international cash transfers.

In recent years, SWIFT has expanded its messaging services beyond banks to broker-dealers and investment managers. In the mid-1990s, its services gained wider breadth as SWIFT expanded market infrastructure to payments in treasury, derivatives, and securities and trade services. It is now in the forefront of the evolution of Internet-based products and services for e-payments, expanding beyond banks to nonfinancial sector customers conducting business-to-business electronic commerce.

Cash Pooling and Centralized Depositories

Any business with widely dispersed operating subsidiaries can gain operational benefits by centralizing cash management. Internationally, the procedure calls for each subsidiary to hold minimum cash for its own transactions and no cash for precautionary purposes. However, the central pool has authority to override this general rule. All excess funds are remitted to a central cash depository, where a single authority invests the funds in such currencies and money market instruments as best serve the worldwide firm.

A central depository provides an MNE with at least four advantages:

1. Obtaining information
2. Holding precautionary cash balances
3. Reducing interest rate costs
4. Locating cost in desirable financial centers

INFORMATION ADVANTAGE A central depository's size gives it an advantage in obtaining information. It should be located in one of the world's major financial centers so information needed for opinions about the relative strengths and weaknesses of various currencies can easily be obtained. Rate of return and risk information on alternative investments in each currency and facilities for executing orders must also be available. The information logic of centralization is that an office that specializes and operates with larger sums of money can get better information from banks, brokers, and other financial institutions, as well as better service in executing orders.

PRECAUTIONARY BALANCE ADVANTAGE A second reason for holding all precautionary balances in a central pool is that the total pool, if centralized, can be reduced in size without any loss in the level of protection. Carlton USA, for example, has subsidiaries in Germany, Brazil, and China. Assume each of these subsidiaries maintains its own precautionary cash balance equal to its expected cash needs plus a safety margin of three standard deviations of historical variability of actual cash demands. Cash needs are assumed to be normally distributed in each country, and the needs are independent from one country to another. Three standard deviations means there exists a 99.87% chance that actual cash needs will be met; that is, only a 0.13% chance that any subsidiary will run out of cash.

Cash needs of the individual subsidiaries, and the total precautionary cash balances held, are shown in Table 9-2. Total precautionary cash balances held by Carlton Germany, Brazil, and China, add up to $46,000,000, consisting of $28,000,000 in expected cash needs, and $18,000,000 in idle cash balances (the sum of three standard deviations of individual expected cash balances) held as a safety margin.

What would happen if the three Carlton subsidiaries maintained all precautionary balances in a single account with Carlton USA? Because variances are additive when probability distributions are independent (see footnote b to Table 9-2), cash needed would drop from $46,000,000 to $39,224,972, calculated as follows:

Centralized cash balance = *Sum of expected cash needs* + *Three standard deviations of expected sum*

$$= \$28,000,000 \qquad + (3 \times \$3,741,657)$$
$$= \$28,000,000 \qquad + \$11,224,972$$
$$= \$39,224,972$$

A budgeted cash balance three standard deviations above the aggregate expected cash need requires only $11,224,972 in potentially idle cash, as opposed to the previous cash balance of $18,000,000. Carlton saves $6,755,028 in cash balances without reducing its safety.

INTEREST RATE ADVANTAGE A third advantage of centralized cash management is that one subsidiary will not borrow at high rates at the same time that another holds surplus funds idle or

TABLE 9-2 Decentralized versus Centralized Cash Depositories.

DECENTRALIZED CASH DEPOSITORIES

Subsidiary	Expected cash need (A)	One standard deviation (B)	Cash balance budgeted for adequate protection[a] (A + 3B)
Carlton Germany	$10,000,000	$1,000,000	$13,000,000
Carlton Brazil	6,000,000	2,000,000	12,000,000
Carlton China	12,000,000	3,000,000	21,000,000
Total	$28,000,000	$ 6,000,000	$46,000,000

CENTRALIZED CASH DEPOSITORIES

Subsidiary	Expected cash need (A)	One standard deviation (B)	Cash balance budgeted for adequate protection[a] (A + 3B)
Carlton Germany	$10,000,000		
Carlton Brazil	6,000,000		
Carlton China	12,000,000		
Total	$28,000,000	$ 3,741,657[b]	$39,224,972

[a] Adequate protection is defined as the expected cash balance plus three standard deviations, assuming that the cash flows of all three individual units are normally distributed.
[b] The standard deviation of the expected cash balance of the centralized depository is calculated as follows:

$$\text{Standard deviation} = \sqrt{(1,000,000)^2 + (2,000,000)^2 + (3,000,000)^2} = \$3,741,657$$

invests them at low rates. Managers of the central pool can locate the least expensive locations to borrow and the most advantageous returns to be earned on excess funds. When additional cash is needed, the central pool manager determines the location of such borrowing. A local subsidiary manager can avoid borrowing at a rate above the minimum available to the pool manager. If the firm has a worldwide cash surplus, the central pool manager can evaluate comparative rates of return in various markets, transaction costs, exchange risks, and tax effects.

LOCATION   Central money pools are usually maintained in major money centers such as London, New York, Zurich, Singapore, and Tokyo. Additional popular locations for money pools include Liechtenstein, Luxembourg, the Bahamas, and Bermuda. Although these countries do not have strong diversified economies, they offer most of the other prerequisites for a corporate financial center: freely convertible currency, political and economic stability, access to international communications, and clearly defined legal procedures. Their additional advantage as a so-called tax haven is desirable.

The need for a centralized depository system means that multinational banks have an advantage over single-country banks in designing and offering competitive services. However single-country banks can be incorporated into the system if the desired results can still be achieved, for the essence of the operation is centralized information and decisions. MNEs can place actual funds in as many banks as they desire.

Multilateral Netting

Multilateral netting is defined as the process that cancels, via offset, all or part of the debt owed by one entity to another related entity. Multilateral netting of payments is useful primarily when a large number of separate foreign exchange transactions occur between subsidiaries in the normal course of business. Netting reduces the settlement cost of what would otherwise be a large number of crossing spot transactions.

Multilateral netting is an extension of bilateral netting. Assume that Carlton Brazil owes Carlton China $5,000,000, and Carlton China simultaneously owes Carlton Brazil $3,000,000. A bilateral settlement calls for a single payment of $2,000,000 from Brazil to China and the cancellation, via offset, of the remainder of the debt.

A multilateral system is an expanded version of this simple bilateral concept. Assume that payments are due between Carlton's operations at the end of each month. Each obligation reflects the accumulated transactions of the prior month. These obligations for a particular month might be as shown in Figure 9-6.

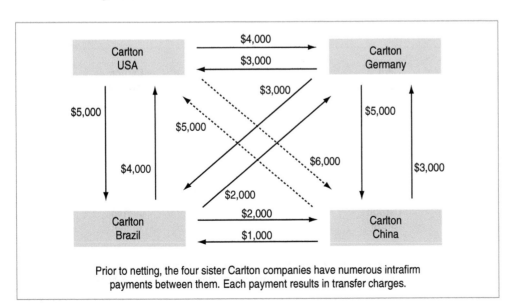

FIGURE 9-6
Multilateral Matrix Before Netting (thousands of U.S. dollars).

Prior to netting, the four sister Carlton companies have numerous intrafirm payments between them. Each payment results in transfer charges.

Without netting, Carlton Brazil makes three separate payments and receives three separate receipts at the end of the month. If Carlton Brazil paid its intracompany obligations daily, or even weekly, rather than accumulating a balance to settle at the end of the month, it would generate a multitude of costly small bank transactions. The daily totals would add up to the monthly accumulated balances shown in the diagram.

In order to reduce bank transaction costs, such as the spread between foreign exchange bid and ask quotations and transfer fees, MNEs like Carlton establish in-house multilateral netting centers. Other firms contract with banks to manage their netting system. Assume that Carlton's net intracompany obligations for a given month can be summarized as in Table 9-3.

Note that payment obligations and expected receipts add up to $43,000,000 because one subsidiary's debts are another's receivables. If the cost of foreign exchange transactions and transfer fees were 0.5%, the total cost of settlement would be $205,000. Using information from the netting matrix in Table 9-3, the netting center at Carlton USA can order three payments to settle the entire set of obligations. Carlton USA will itself remit $3,000,000 to China, and Germany will be instructed to send $1,000,000 each to Brazil and China. Total foreign exchange transfers are reduced to $5,000,000, and transaction costs at 0.5% are reduced to $25,000. This is shown in Figure 9-7.

Some countries limit or prohibit netting, while others permit netting on a "gross payment" basis only. For a single settlement period, all payments may be combined into a single payment, and all receipts will be received as a single transfer. However, these two may not be netted and thus must pass through the local banking system.

TABLE 9-3   Calculation of Carlton Intrasubsidiary Net Obligation (thousands of U.S. dollars).

	PAYING SUBSIDIARY					
Receiving Subsidiary	USA	Brazil	Germany	China	Total receipts	Net receipts (payments)
USA	—	$4,000	$3,000	$5,000	$12,000	($3,000)
Brazil	$5,000	—	3,000	1,000	9,000	$1,000
Germany	4,000	2,000	—	3,000	9,000	($2,000)
China	6,000	2,000	5,000	—	13,000	$4,000
Total payments	$15,000	$8,000	$11,000	$9,000	$43,000	—

FIGURE 9-7
Multilateral Matrix
After Netting (thousands
of U.S. dollars).

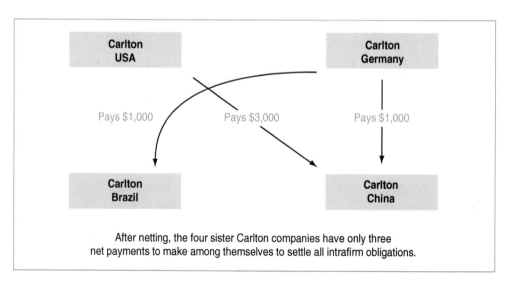

After netting, the four sister Carlton companies have only three
net payments to make among themselves to settle all intrafirm obligations.

9.8   FINANCING WORKING CAPITAL

The MNE enjoys a much greater choice of banking sources to fund its working capital needs than do domestic firms. Banking sources available to MNEs include in-house banks funded by unrepatriated capital, international banks, and local banks where subsidiaries are located. In-house banks and the various types of external commercial banking offices are described in the remainder of this chapter.

In-House Banks

Some MNEs have found that their financial resources and needs are either too large or too sophisticated for the financial services available in many locations where they operate. One solution to this has been the establishment of an *in-house* or *internal bank* within the firm. An in-house bank is not a separate corporation; rather, it is a set of functions performed by the existing treasury department. Acting as an independent entity, the central treasury of the firm transacts with the various business units of the firm on an arm's length basis. The purpose of the in-house bank is to provide bank-like services to the various units of the firm. The in-house bank may be able to provide services not available in many countries, and do so at lower cost when they are available. In addition to traditional banking activities, the in-house bank may be able to offer services to units of the firm which aid in the management of ongoing transaction exposures. Lastly, because it is in-house, credit analysis is not a part of the bank's decision making.

For example, the in-house bank of Carlton Corporation could work with Carlton Germany and Carlton Brazil. Carlton Brazil sells all its receivables to the in-house bank as they arise, reducing some of its domestic working capital needs. Additional working capital needs are supplied by the in-house bank directly to Carlton Brazil. Because the in-house bank is part of the same company, interest rates it charges may be significantly lower than what Carlton Brazil could obtain on its own. The source of funds for the in-house bank may arise from the deposits of excess cash balances from Carlton Germany. If the in-house bank can pay Carlton Europe a higher deposit rate than it could obtain on its own, and if the in-house bank can lend these funds to Carlton Brazil at an interest rate lower than it could obtain on its own in Brazil, then both operating units benefit. Assuming that the loan rate is greater than the deposit rate, the in-house bank profits by the margin between the two, but this margin or spread must be smaller than would be available from a commercial bank.

How can the in-house bank operate with a smaller spread than a regular commercial bank? First, its costs are lower, because it does not have to conform to the stringent capital requirements imposed on commercial banks worldwide. Second, in-house banks do not have the overhead costs of supporting large dealing rooms, branch networks, retail "store fronts," and other services required for commercial bank competitiveness. Third, they need not assess the creditworthiness of the corporate units with which they deal, since the units are all in the same family. Furthermore, they need not provide for credit losses.

In addition to providing financing benefits, in-house banks allow for more effective currency risk management. In the case of Carlton Brazil, the sale of foreign currency receivables to the in-house bank shifts transaction exposure to the bank. The in-house bank is better equipped to deal with currency exposures and has a greater volume of international cash flows allowing Carlton USA overall to gain from more effective use of netting and matching. This frees the units of the firm from struggling to manage transaction exposures and allows them to focus on their primary business activities.

Commercial Banking Offices

MNEs depend on their commercial banks to handle most of their trade financing needs, such as letters of credit, but also to provide advice on government support, country risk assessment, introductions to foreign firms and banks, and general financing availability. MNEs interface with their banks through a variety of types of banking offices, many of which perform specialized functions. Therefore it is important for financial managers to understand which bank offices provide which kinds of activities. The main points of bank contact are with correspondent banks, representative offices, branch banks, and subsidiaries. In the United States, a more specialized banking facility is available: the Edge Act Corporation.

CORRESPONDENT BANKS   Most major banks of the world maintain correspondent banking relationships with local banks in each of the major foreign cities of the world. The two-way link between banks is essentially one of correspondence via fax, cable, and mail, and a mutual deposit relationship. For example, a U.S. bank may have a correspondent bank in Kuala Lumpur, Malaysia, and the U.S. bank will in turn be the correspondent bank for the Malaysian bank. Each will maintain a deposit in the other in local currency.

Correspondent services include accepting drafts, honoring letters of credit, and furnishing credit information. Services are centered around collecting or paying foreign funds, often because of import or export transactions. However, a visiting business person can use the home bank's introduction to meet local bankers. Under a correspondent banking relationship, neither of the correspondent banks maintains its own personnel in the other country. Direct contact between the banks is usually limited to periodic visits between members of the banks' management.

For the businessperson, the main advantage of banking at home with a bank having a large number of foreign correspondent relationships is having the ability to handle financial matters in a large number of foreign countries through local bankers whose knowledge of local customs should be extensive. The disadvantages are the lack of ability to deposit in, borrow from, or disburse from a branch of one's own home bank. There is a possibility that correspondents will put a lower priority on serving the foreign banks' customer than on serving their own permanent customers.

REPRESENTATIVE OFFICES   A bank establishes a representative office in a foreign country primarily to help parent bank clients when they are doing business in that country or in neighboring countries. It also functions as a geographically convenient location from which to visit correspondent banks in its region rather than sending bankers from the parent bank at greater financial and physical cost. A representative office is not a bank office. It cannot accept deposits, make loans, commit the parent bank to a loan, or deal in drafts, letters of credit, or the Eurocurrency market. Indeed, a tourist cannot even cash a traveler's check from the parent bank in the representative office.

If the parent bank eventually decides to open a local general banking office, the existence of a representative office for some prior period usually provides a valuable base of contacts and expertise to facilitate the change. However, representative offices are not necessarily a prelude to a general banking office, and an eventual general banking office need not be the major reason for opening a representative office.

BRANCH BANKS   A foreign branch bank is a legal and operational part of the parent bank, with the full resources of that parent behind the local office. A branch bank does not have its own corporate charter, its own board of directors, or any shares of stock outstanding. Although for managerial and regulatory purposes it will maintain its own set of books, its assets and liabilities are in fact those of the parent bank. However, branch deposits are not subject to reserve requirements or FDIC insurance, in the case of U.S. banks, unless the deposits are reloaned to the U.S. parent bank.

Branch banks are subject to two sets of banking regulations. As part of the parent, they are subject to home-country regulations. However, they are also subject to regulations of the host country, which may provide any of a variety of restrictions on their operations.

The major advantage to a business of using a branch bank is that the branch will conduct a full range of banking services under the name and legal obligation of the parent. A deposit in a branch is a legal obligation of the parent. Services to customers are based on the worldwide value of the client relationship rather than just on the relationship to the local office. Legal loan limits are a function of the size of the parent, not of the branch.

From the point of view of a banker, the profits of a foreign branch are subject to immediate taxation at home, and losses of a foreign branch are deductible against taxable income at home. A new office expected to have losses in its early years creates a tax advantage if it is initially organized as a branch, even if eventually the intent is to change it to a separately incorporated subsidiary. From an organizational point of view, a foreign branch is usually simpler to create and staff than is a separately incorporated subsidiary.

The major disadvantage of a branch bank is one that accrues to the bank rather than to its customers. The parent bank (not just the branch) may be sued at the local level for debts or other activities of the branch.

BANKING SUBSIDIARIES A subsidiary bank is a separately incorporated bank, owned entirely or in major part by a foreign parent, that conducts a general banking business. As a separate corporation, the banking subsidiary must comply with all the laws of the host country. Its lending limit is based on its own equity capital rather than that of the parent bank. This limits its ability to service large borrowers, but local incorporation also limits the liability of the parent bank to its equity investment in the subsidiary.

A foreign banking subsidiary often appears as a local bank in the eyes of potential customers in host countries and is thus often able to attract additional local deposits. This likelihoood will especially be true if the bank was independent prior to being purchased by the foreign parent. Management may well be local, giving the bank greater access to the local business community. A foreign-owned bank subsidiary is more likely to be involved in both domestic and international business than is a foreign branch, which is more likely to appeal to the foreign business community but may well encounter difficulty in attracting banking business from local firms.

EDGE ACT CORPORATIONS Edge Act corporations are subsidiaries of U.S. banks, incorporated in the United States under Section 25 of the Federal Reserve Act as amended, to engage in international banking and financing operations. Not only may such subsidiaries engage in general international banking, they may also finance commercial, industrial, or financial projects in foreign countries through long-term loans or equity participation. Such participation, however, is subject to the day-to-day practices and policies of the Federal Reserve System.

Edge Act corporations generally engage in two types of activities: direct international banking, including acting as a holding company for the stock of one or more foreign banking subsidiaries, and financing development activities not closely related to traditional banking operations.

SUMMARY

- Working capital management in an MNE requires repositioning cash flows, as well as managing the many components of current assets and current liabilities, when faced with political, foreign exchange, tax, and liquidity constraints.
- The operating and cash conversion cycles can be decomposed into five periods: quotation, input sourcing, inventory, accounts payable, and accounts receivable.
- MNE's unbundle their transfer of funds into separate flows for specific purposes, rather than making all remittances to the parent only in the form of dividends.
- Net working capital (NWC) is defined as accounts receivable (A/R) plus inventories minus accounts payable (A/P).
- Most firms, including MNEs, try to minimize their net working capital balances by reducing cycle time.
- A common method of benchmarking working capital is to calculate and minimize the net working capital of a firm on a "days sales" basis.
- A firm's operating cash inflow is derived primarily from collecting its accounts receivable from independent customers and related subsidiaries.

- A free trade zone combines the old idea of duty-free ports with legislation that reduces or eliminates customs duties to retailers or manufacturers who structure their operations to benefit from the technique.
- MNEs focus on four techniques to reduce the costs of making cross-border payments: wire transfers, cash pooling, payment netting, and electronic fund transfers.
- A centralized cash depository provides an MNE with at least four advantages: obtaining information, holding precautionary cash balances, reducing interest costs, and locating cost in desirable financial centers.
- Multilateral netting is defined as the process that cancels, via offsets, all or part of the debt owed by one entity to another related entity.
- MNEs enjoy a much greater choice of banking sources to fund their working capital needs than do domestic firms.
- Banking sources available to MNEs include in-house banks funded by unrepatriated capital, international banks, and local banks where subsidiaries are located.
- Commercial banking offices available to MNEs include correspondent banks, representative offices, branch banks, subsidiary banks, and—in the United States only—Edge Act banks.

QUESTIONS

1. **Constraints on positioning funds.** Each of the following factors is sometimes a constraint on the free movement of funds internationally. Why would a government impose such a constraint? How might the management of a multinational argue that such a constraint is not in the best interests of the government that has imposed it?
   a. Government-mandated restrictions on moving funds out of the country
   b. Withholding taxes on dividend distributions to foreign owners
   c. Dual-currency regimes, with one rate for imports and another rate for exports
   d. Refusal to allow foreign firms in the country to net cash inflows and outflows into a single payment

2. **Unbundling.** What does this term mean? Why would unbundling be needed for international cash flows from foreign subsidiaries, but not for domestic cash flows between related domestic subsidiaries and their parent?

3. **Conduits.** In the context of unbundling cash flows from subsidiary to parent, explain how each of the following creates a conduit. What are the tax consequences of each?
   a. Imports of components from the parent
   b. Payment to cover overhead expenses of parent managers temporarily assigned to the subsidiary
   c. Payment of royalties for the use of proprietary technology
   d. Subsidiary borrowing of funds on an intermediate or long-term maturity from the parent
   e. Payment of dividends to the parent

4. **Sister subsidiaries.** Subsidiary Alpha in Country Able faces a 40% income tax rate. Subsidiary Beta in Country Baker faces only a 20% income tax rate. At present, each subsidiary imports from the other an amount of goods and services exactly equal in monetary value to what each exports to the other. This method of balancing intracompany trade was imposed by a management keen to reduce all costs, including the costs (spread between bid and ask) of foreign exchange transactions. Both subsidiaries are profitable, and both could purchase all components domestically at approximately the same prices as they are paying to their foreign sister subsidiary. Does this seem like an optimal situation to you?

5. Allocated fees (A). What is the difference between a license fee and a royalty fee? Do you think license and royalty fees should be covered by the tax rules that regulate transfer pricing? Why?

6. Allocated fees (B). What are the differences between a management fee, a technical assistance fee, and a license fee for patent usage? Should they be treated differently for income tax purposes?

7. Distributed overhead. What methods might the U.S. Internal Revenue Service use to determine whether allocations of distributed overhead are being fairly allocated to foreign subsidiaries?

8. Fee treatment. In the context of unbundling cash flows from subsidiary to parent, why might a host government be more lenient in its treatment of fees than in its treatment of dividends? What difference does it make to the subsidiary and to the parent?

9. The cycle. The operating cycle of a firm, domestic or multinational, consists of the following four time periods:

   a. Quotation period

   b. Input sourcing period

   c. Inventory period

   d. Accounts receivable period

   For each of these periods, explain whether a cash outflow or a cash inflow is associated with the beginning and the end of the period.

10. Accounts payable period. Figure 9-1 shows the accounts payable period to be longer than the inventory period. Could this be otherwise, and what would be the cash implications?

11. Payables and receivables. As a financial manager, would you prefer that the accounts payable period end before, at the same time, or after the beginning of the accounts receivable period? Explain.

12. Transaction exposure. Assuming the flow illustrated in Figure 9-1, where does transaction exposure begin and end if inputs are purchased with one currency at t_1 and proceeds from the sale are received at t_5? Is there more than one interval of transaction exposure?

13. Operating exposure. Is any operating exposure created during the course of a firm's operating cycle?

14. Accounting exposure. Is any translation exposure created during the course of a firm's operating cycle?

15. Reducing NWC. Assume that a firm purchases inventory with one foreign currency and sells it for another foreign currency, neither currency being the home currency of the parent or subsidiary where the manufacturing process takes place. What can the firm do to reduce the amount of net working capital?

16. Trade terms. Roberts and Sons, Inc., of Great Britain has just purchased inventory items costing Kronor 1,000,000 from a Swedish supplier. The supplier has quoted terms 3/15, net 45. Under what conditions might Roberts and Sons reasonably take the discount, and when might it be a reasonable idea to wait the full 45 days to pay?

17. Inventory turnover. Japanese industry is often praised for its just-in-time inventory practice between industrial buyers and industrial sellers. In the context of the "Days Receivables" turnover in Table 9-5, what is the comparative impact of the just-in-time system in Japan? Are there any risks associated with this system? Do you think this applies equally to Japanese manufacturing firms sourcing raw material and components in Japan and those sourcing similar items from Thailand and Malaysia?

18. Receivables turnover. Why might the time lag for multinational intrafirm accounts receivable and payable (i.e., all received or paid to a parent or sister subsidiary) differ substantially from the time lags reported for transactions with nonaffiliated companies?

19. Devaluation risk. Merlin Corporation of the United States imports raw material from Indonesia on terms of 2/10, net 30. Merlin expects a 36% devaluation of the Indonesian rupiah at any moment. Should Merlin take the discount? Discuss aspects of the problem.

20. Free-trade zones. What are the advantages of a free-trade zone? Are there any disadvantages?

21. Motives. Explain the difference between the transaction motive and the precautionary motive for holding cash.

22. Cash cycle. The operating cash cycle of a multinational firm goes from cash collection from customers, cash holding for anticipated transaction needs (the transaction motive for holding cash), possible cash repositioning into another currency, and eventual cash disbursements to pay operating expenses. Assuming that the initial cash collection is in one currency and the eventual cash disbursement is in another currency, what can a multinational firm do to shorten its cash cycle and what risks are involved?

23. Electro-Beam Company. Electro-Beam Company generates and disburses cash in the currencies of four countries: Singapore, Malaysia, Thailand, and Vietnam. What would be the characteristics you might consider if charged with designing a centralized cash depository system for Electro-Beam Company's Southeast Asian subsidiaries?

24. France. During the era of the French franc, France imposed a rule on its banks and subsidiaries of international companies operating in France that precluded those subsidiaries from netting cash flow obligations between France and non-French entities. Why do you suppose the French government imposed such a rule, and what, if anything, could subsidiaries in France have done about it?

25. Foreign bank office. What is the difference between a foreign branch and a foreign subsidiary of a home-country bank?

PROBLEMS

1. Quinlan Company. The following events take place:

March 1: Quinlan Company seeks a sale at a price of €10,000,000 for items to be sold to a long-standing client in Poland. To achieve the order, Quinlan offered to denominate the order in zlotys (Z), Poland's currency, for Z20,000,000. This price was arrived at by multiplying the euro price by Z2.00/€, the exchange rate on the day of the quote. The zloty is expected to fall in value by 0.5% per month versus the euro.

`April 1: Quinlan receives an order worth Z20,000,000 from that customer. On the same day, Quinlan places orders with its vendors for €4,000,000 of components needed to complete the sale.

May 1: Quinlan receives the components and is billed €4,000,000 by the vendor on terms of 2/20, net 60. During the next two months Quinlan assigns direct labor to work on the project. The expense of direct labor was €5,000,000.

July 1: Quinlan ships the order to the customer and bills the customer Z20,000,000. On its corporate books, Quinlan debits accounts receivable and credits sales.

Sept. 1: Quinlan's customer pays Z20,000,000 to Quinlan.

a. Draw a cash flow diagram for this transaction in the style of Figure 9-1 and explain the steps involved.

b. What working capital management techniques might Quinlan use to better its position vis-à-vis this particular customer?

2. Super-Do, K.K. Super-Do, K.K., the Japanese subsidiary of a U.S. company, has ¥100,000,000 in accounts receivable for sales billed to customers on terms of 2/30 net 60. Customers usually pay in 30 days. Super-Do also has ¥60,000,000 of accounts payable billed to it on terms of 3/10 net 60. Super-Do delays payment until the last minute because

it is normally short of cash. Super-Do, K.K. normally carries an average cash balance for transactions of ¥30,000,000. How much cash could Super-Do, K.K. save by taking the discount?

3. Alpine Ski Company. Alpine Ski Company of Grenoble, France, manufactures and sells in France, Switzerland, and Italy, and also maintains a corporate account in Frankfurt, Germany. Alpine has been setting a separate operating cash balance in each country at a level equal to expected cash needs plus two standard deviations above those needs, based on a statistical analysis of cash flow volatility. Expected operating cash needs and one standard deviation of those needs are

	EXPECTED CASH NEED	ONE STANDARD DEVIATION
Switzerland	€5,000,000	€1,000,000
Italy	3,000,000	400,000
France	2,000,000	300,000
Germany	800,000	40,000
	€10,800,000	€1,740,000

Alpine's Frankfurt bank suggests that the same level of safety could be maintained if all precautionary balances were combined in a central account at the Frankfurt headquarters.

a. How much lower would Alpine Ski Company's total cash balances be if all precautionary balances were combined? Assume that cash needs in each country are normally distributed and are independent of each other.

b. What other advantages might accrue to Alpine Ski Company from centralizing its cash holdings? Are these advantages realistic?

4. Futebal do Brasil, S.A., Futebal do Brazil, S.A., purchases newly sewn soccer balls from Pakistani manufacturers and distributes them in Argentina, Brazil, and Chile. All operations are through wholly owned subsidiaries. The three subsidiaries have submitted the following daily cash reports (all amounts in thousands of U.S. dollars), which the Brazilian company uses for cash management purposes. Each of the two foreign subsidiaries is allowed to carry a $1,000,000 cash balance overnight, with the remainder remitted to a U.S. dollar account maintained in São Paulo, unless instructed otherwise by the Brazilian financial staff. As a general matter, the cost of moving funds is such that funds should not be moved for one day and then returned the next, but a movement for two days which is then reversed is financially advantageous. The Brazilian headquarters invests surplus cash balance over US$5,000,000 in U.S. money market instruments purchased through the Miami correspondent bank of the firm's Brazilian bank. Anticipated cash flows, in thousands of U.S. dollars, are:

	COMPANHIA FUTEBAL DO BRASIL	COMPAÑÍA FÚTBAL DE AGRENTINA	COMPAÑÍA FÚTBAL DE CHILE
Day-end cash balance	$6,000	$5,000	$5,000
Minimum operating balance required:	$5,000	$1,000	$1,000
Expected receipts (+) or disbursements (−):			
+1 day	+3,000	−2,000	+5,000
+2 days	-0-	+1,000	−3,000
+3 days	−5,000	−3,000	+2,000

Design an advantageous cash movement plan that complies with Futebal do Brasil general policies.

5. **Earth Technology, Inc.** Earth Technology, Inc., manufactures basic farm equipment in China, Spain, and Iowa. Each subsidiary has monthly unsettled balances due to or from other subsidiaries. At the end of December, unsettled intracompany debts in U.S. dollars were as follows:

Earth Technology China:

　Owes $8 million to Spanish subsidiary

　Owes $9 million to Iowa parent

Earth Technology Spain:

　Owes $5 million to Chinese subsidiary

　Owes $6 million to Iowa parent

Earth Technology Iowa:

　Owes $4 million to Chinese subsidiary

　Owes $10 million to Spanish subsidiary

Foreign exchange transaction spreads average 0.4% of funds transferred.

　　a. How could Earth Technology net these intracompany debts? How much would be saved in transaction expenses over the no-netting alternative?

　　b. Before settling these accounts, Earth Technology decides to invest $6,000,000 of parent funds in a new farm equipment manufacturing plant in the new free industrial zone at Subic Bay, Philippines. How can this decision be incorporated into the settlement process? What would the total bank charges be? Explain.

6. **Crystal Publishing Company.** Crystal Publishing Company publishes books in Europe through separate subsidiaries in several countries. On a Europe-wide basis, Crystal Publishing experiences uneven cash flows. Any given book creates a cash outflow during the period of writing and publishing, followed by a cash inflow in subsequent months and years as the book is sold. To handle these imbalances, Crystal decided to create an in-house bank.

At the beginning of April Crystal's in-house bank held deposits, on which it paid 4.8% interest, as follows:

From Crystal Germany　　　€20,000,000

From Crystal Spain　　　　€5,000,000

From Crystal Britain　　　£12,000,000

At the beginning of April, Crystal's in-house bank advanced funds at an annual rate of 5.4%, as follows:

To Crystal France　　　　€12,000,000

To Crystal Italy　　　　　€8,000,000

To Crystal Greece　　　　€6,000,000

The exchange rate between pounds sterling and the euro is €1.6000/£.

　　a. What would be the net interest earnings (i.e., interest earned less interest paid, before administrative expenses), of Crystal's in-house bank for the month of April?

　　b. If parent Crystal Publishing subsidized the in-house bank for all of its operating expenses, how much more could the in-house bank loan at the beginning of April?

7. **Balanced Tire Company (A).** Balanced Tire Company manufactures automobile tires for sale to retail outlets in the United States and, through a wholly owned distribution subsidiary, in neighboring Canada. Annual capacity of the U.S. factory is 700,000 tires per year, but present production is only 450,000, of which 300,000 are sold in the United States and 150,000 are exported to Canada. Federal and state income tax rates in both countries add up to 40%.

Within the United States, Balanced Tire sells to retail outlets for the U.S. dollar equivalent of C$80 per tire. After-tax profit is equivalent to C$10.80 per tire calculated as follows, with all prices expressed in the Canadian dollar equivalent of U.S. dollars.

BALANCED TIRE'S U.S. PROFIT CALCULATION, EXPRESSED IN CANADIAN DOLLARS

Balanced Tire's U.S. sales price per tire	C$80.00
Less direct labor in U.S.	–20.00
Less direct material in U.S.	–20.00
Less U.S. manufacturing overhead	–12.00
Total manufacturing costs	52.00
U.S. factory margin	28.00
Less selling and administrative costs	–10.00
Pretax profit per set	18.00
Less 40% U.S. income taxes	–7.20
After-tax profit per tire in the United States	C$10.80

Direct labor consists of hourly payroll costs for factory workers, and direct material is for raw material purchased in the United States. Manufacturing overhead is a fixed cost that includes supervision and depreciation. Selling and administrative costs are fixed expenses for management salaries, office expenses, and rent.

For its exports to Canada, Balanced Tire sells sets to its Canadian subsidiary at a U.S. dollar transfer price equal to C$56 per tire, this being U.S. manufacturing cost of C$52 plus a C$4.00 profit. Transportation and distribution costs add an additional C$2.00 per tire, and the tires are resold to Canadian retail outlets for C$80, the equivalent of the U.S. price. This price was arrived at independently, based on the following analysis of elasticity of demand in Canada.

BALANCED TIRE (CANADIAN DOLLARS)

Unit sales price in Canada	$85.00	$80.00	$75.00	$70.00	$65.00
Less import	–56.00	–56.00	–56.00	–56.00	–56.00
Less shipping	–2.00	–2.00	–2.00	–2.00	–2.00
Unit profit before tax	27.00	22.00	17.00	12.00	7.00
Less 40% Canadian tax	–10.80	–8.80	–6.80	–4.80	–5.40
Unit profit after tax	16.20	13.20	10.20	7.20	4.20
Expected unit volume	×110,000	×150,000	×180,000	×250,000	×400,000
Total profit (000)	1,782	1,980	1,836	1,800	1,680

Maximum profit is at a sales price of C$80.00.

In making this calculation, Balanced Tire determined that unit demand in Canada was a function only of the sales price. Hence it seemed self-evident to Balanced Tire's management that a transfer price to Canada of C$80.00 per tire maximized Canada's contribution to profits at a total figure of C$1,980,000. Is Balanced Tire's present pricing strategy for Canada correct?

8. Balanced Tire Company (B). Assume that Balanced Tire (of the previous problem) wants to divide profits on export sales evenly between Canada and the United States so as to avoid difficulties with either tax authority.

   a. What final transfer price and unit price in Canada should the firm adopt?

   b. If Canada's income tax rate remains 40%, but the United States lowers its tax rate to 25%, should a new transfer price be adopted? What policy issues are involved?

9. **Surgical Tools, Inc.** Surgical Tools, Inc., of Illinois wants to set up a regular procedure for transferring funds from its newly opened manufacturing subsidiary in Korea to the United States. The precedent set by the transfer method or methods is likely to prevail over any government objections that might otherwise arise in future years. The Korean subsidiary manufactures surgical tools for export to all Asian countries. The following pro forma financial information portrays the results expected in the first full year of operations:

Sales	Won 2,684,000,000
Cash manufacturing expenses	1,342,000,000
Depreciation	335,500,000
Pretax profit	1,006,500,000
Korean taxes at 28%	281,820,000
Profit after taxes	Won 724,680,000
Exchange rate	Won 1342/$
Korean income tax rate	28%
U.S. income tax rate	34%

Compare the tax and income impacts of the following two alternatives:

a. Declare a dividend of Won 362,340,000, equal to 50% of profit after taxes. The dividend would be taxable in the United States after a gross up for Korean taxes already paid.

b. Add a license fee of Won 362,340,000 to the listed expenses, and remit that amount annually. The license fee would be fully taxable in the United States.

10. **Adams Corporation (A).** Adams Corporation (U.S.), a recently divested unit of Pfizer and the owner of a series of valuable consumer brands such as Listerine and Halls, owns 100% of Adams Brazil, S.A. This year Adams Brazil, S.A., earned R$52,000,000, equal to $20,000,000 at the current exchange rate of R$2.60/$. The exchange rate is not expected to change.

Adams Corporation wants to transfer half of its Brazilian earnings to the United States and wonders whether this sum should be remitted (1) by a cash dividend of $10,000,000 or (2) by a cash dividend of $5,000,000 and a royalty of $5,000,000. Brazilian income taxes are 15% and U.S. income taxes are 30%. Which do you recommend and why?

11. **Adams Corporation (B).** The Brazilian government under President Lula has instituted a new tax policy aimed at encouraging foreign MNEs to come to Brazil and reinvest their profits in the country, rather than pulling them out. Assume that all of the same conditions exist as in the previous problem, but now assume that Brazil has instituted the following withholding taxes on dividends, royalties, and licensing fee remittances.

TYPE OF REMITTANCE	WITHHOLDING TAX RATE
Dividends	30%
Royalty payments	5%
License fees	5%

Which of the alternatives do you recommend Adams use in remitting the $10 million to Adams (U.S.)?

INTERNET EXERCISES

1. **Working capital management.** Many major multinational banks provide a variety of working capital and multinational cash management services described in this chapter. Using the websites of a variety of these cross-border banks, research which banks offer multinational cash management services that would combine banking with foreign

exchange management. Which banks provide specific services through regional or geographic service centers?

Bank of America http://www.bankamerica.com/corporate/

Bank of Montreal http://www.bmo.com/cebssite/

2. Clearinghouse associations. Associations like the New York Clearinghouse Association have played major roles in the international financial system for centuries. Use the following websites to prepare a two-page executive briefing on the role of clearinghouses in history and in contemporary finance. Use the website for the Clearing House Interbank Payments System (CHIPS) to estimate the volume of international financial transactions.

New York Clearinghouse Association http://www.theclearinghouse.org

Clearing House Interbank Payments System http://www.chips.org

SELECTED READINGS

Gentry, James A., Dileep R. Mehta, S. K. Bhattacharya, Robert Cobbaut, and Jean-Louis Scaringella, "An International Study of Management Perceptions of the Working Capital Process," *Journal of International Business Studies,* Spring-Summer 1979, pp. 28–38.

Houpt, James V., "International Trends for U.S. Banks and Banking Markets," Staff Study of the Board of Governors of the Federal Reserve System, No. 156, May 1988.

"International Working Capital Practices of the Fortune 200," *Financial Practice & Education,* Vol. 6, Issue 2 Fall/Winter 1996.

Laporta, R., F. Lopez-de-Silanes, A. Schleifer, and R. Vishny, "Agency Problems and Dividend Policies Around the World," *Journal of Finance,* No. 55, 2000, pp. 1–33.

Srinivasan, VenKat, Susan E. Moeller, and Young H. Kim, "International Cash Management: State-of-the-Art and Research Directions," *Advances in Financial Planning and Forecasting.* Vol. 4, Part B, 1990, pp. 161–194.

MINICASE   HONEYWELL AND PAKISTAN INTERNATIONAL AIRWAYS

The Space and Avionics Control Group (SAC) of Honeywell, Incorporated (USA) was quite frustrated in June 1997. The cockpit retrofit proposal with Pakistan International Airlines had been under negotiation for seven months, and over the past weekend a new request had been thrown in—to accept payment in Pakistan rupee. This was against corporate policy at Honeywell, but if an exception was not made, the deal—worth $23.7 million—was most likely dead.

PAKISTAN INTERNATIONAL AIRLINES (PIA)

Pakistan International Airlines Corporation (PIA) was the national carrier of the Islamic Republic of Pakistan. Founded in 1954, PIA operated scheduled passenger and cargo services. The firm was 57% state-owned, with the remaining 43% held by private investors internal to Pakistan.

PIA's fleet was aging. Although the airline had planned a significant modernization program, recent restrictions placed on government spending by the International Monetary Fund (IMF) had killed the program. With the cancellation of the fleet modernization program, PIA now had to move fast to ensure compliance with U.S. Federal Aviation Administration (FAA) safety mandates. If it did not comply with the FAA mandates for quieter engines and upgraded avionics by June 30, 1998, PIA would be locked out of its very profitable U.S. gates. PIA would first retrofit the aircraft utilized on the long-haul flights to the United States, primarily the Boeing 747 classics. Due to SAC's extensive experience with a variety of control systems for Boeing and its recent work on cockpit retrofit for McDonnell Douglas aircraft, SAC felt it was the preferred supplier for PIA. However, SAC had not undertaken Boeing cockpit retrofits to date (no one had), and looked to the PIA deal as an opportunity to build a new competitive base. PIA's insistence on payment in local currency terms was now thought to be a tactic to extract better concessions from SAC and their agent, Makran.

IBRAHIM MAKRAN PVT. LTD

In countries like Pakistan, the use of an agent is often considered a necessary evil. The agent can often help to bridge two business cultures and provide invaluable information, but at some cost. Honeywell's agent, Ibrahim Makran Pvt. Ltd., based in Hyderabad, was considered one of the most reliable and well connected in Pakistan. Makran traced its roots back to a long association with the Sperry Aerospace and Marine Group, the precursor to Honeywell's SAC unit (Sperry was acquired in 1986). Makran was also one of the largest import/export trading houses in Pakistan. It was 100% family-owned and-managed.

Standard practice in the avionics business was to provide the agent with a 10% commission, although this was negotiable. The 10% was based on the final sales and was paid after all payments were received. Typically it was the agent who spotted the business opportunity and submitted a proposal to SAC Marketing.

When PIA contacted Makran regarding their latest demand, Makran knew that SAC would want to maintain the deal in U.S. dollars. Makran had therefore inquired as to the availability of dollar funds for a deal of this size from its own finance department. The finance department confirmed that they had the necessary U.S. dollar funds to pay SAC, but warned that policy was to charge 5% for services rendered and currency risks.

Makran advised SAC that it would be willing to purchase the receivable for an additional 5% (in addition to the 10% commission). Makran's U.S. subsidiary in Los Angeles would credit SAC within 30 days of SAC invoicing Makran. PIA advised Makran that if SAC accepted payment in Pakistan rupees, then local (Pakistan) payment terms would apply. This meant 180 days in principle, but often was much longer in practice. The agent also advised SAC that the Pakistan rupee was due for another devaluation. When pressed for more information, Makran simply replied that the company president, the elder Ibrahim Makran, had "good connections."

PAKISTAN RUPEE

A central part of the IMF's austerity program was a devaluation of the Pakistan rupee by 7.86% against the U.S. dollar on October 22, 1996. Now, roughly six months later, there was renewed speculation that another devaluation was imminent in order to limit imports and help the export sector earn badly needed hard currency. Another recent economic setback had been the ruling by the European Union that Pakistan was guilty of dumping cotton, and had imposed anti-dumping fines on Pakistani cotton. This was a painful blow to the export sector. The current exchange rate of 40.4795 Pakistan rupee (Rp) per dollar was maintained by the Pakistani Central Bank. The parallel market rate—*the black market rate*—was approaching Rp50/US$. At present, there was no forward market for the Pakistan rupee.

HONEYWELL'S WORKING CAPITAL

Honeywell's finance department was attempting to reduce net working capital and had just concluded a thorough review of existing payment terms and worldwide days sales receivable (DSR) rates. The department's goal was to reduce worldwide DSR rates from 55 to 45 days in the current fiscal year. The *pay for performance* target for the current year (the annual performance bonus system at Honeywell) included net working capital goals. There was concern in the organization that the net working capital goal could prove the obstacle to achieving a bonus despite excellent sales growth. The latest DSR report follows.

SAC CONTROL SYSTEMS' AVERAGE DAYS SALES RECEIVABLES BY REGION

Region	Actual	Target	Amount
North America	44	40	$31.0 million
South America	129	70	$2.1 million
Europe	55	45	$5.7 million
Middle East	93	60	$3.2 million
Asia	75	55	$11.0 million
PIA	264	180	$0.7 million
Boeing	39	30	$41.0 million
McDonnell Douglas	35	30	$18.0 million
Airbus Industries	70	45	$13.0 million

Notes
1. U.S.-based airline trading companies distort the actual local payment terms.
2. The spread between individual customers within regions can be extremely large.
3. Some collection activity is assumed. Specific customers are periodically targeted.
4. Disputed invoices are included. Amount is for all products, services, and exchanges.
5. One of the criteria for granting "preferred" pricing is a 30-day DSR. The 10% reduction can be substantial but typically only motivates the larger customers.

Honeywell payment terms were net 30 from date of invoice. However, payment terms and practices varied dramatically across country and region. Payment terms were generally not published, with the exception of some private reports by credit rating agencies. Honeywell had not in the past enforced stringent credit terms on many customers. For example, neither contracts nor invoices stated any penalties for late payment. Many airlines did pay on time, but others availed themselves of Honeywell's cheap financing.

A review of PIA's account receivable history indicated that they consistently paid their invoices late. The current average DSR was 264 days. PIA had been repeatedly put on hold by the collections department, forcing marketing staff representatives to press the agent who in turn pressed PIA for payment. Honeywell was very concerned about this deal. It had in fact asked for guarantees that PIA would pay promptly. Honeywell's concern was also reflected in the 20% advance

payment clause in the contract. Although marketing took the high DSR rate up with PIA and the agent, the current proposed deal was expected to be the same if not worse.

One positive attribute of the proposed contract was that delivery would not occur until one year after the contract was signed. The invoice for the full amount outstanding would be issued at that time. If the expected improvements to the DSR were made in the meantime, maybe the high DSR rate on the PIA deal could be averaged with the rest of Asia. The 20% advance payment would be used to fund the front-end engineering work.

Global treasury at Honeywell was headquartered along with corporate in Minneapolis, Minnesota. Corporate treasury was a profit center and charged 1% commission on all sales. Treasury, however, passed on the currency risk to the business unit. If a local subsidiary required local currency, treasury would try to match those requirements by accepting the A/R in the local currency. They had advised SAC that for many developing countries where Honeywell had little or no activities, such as Pakistan, this was done only on an exception basis. Global treasury also evaluated all deals in present value terms given the extended payment periods, and the corporate cost of capital was set at 12%.

NEGOTIATIONS

Honeywell now speculated that the local currency request was a result of the 20% advance payment clause. The project was considered one of the riskiest SAC had undertaken, and the 20% advance payment would help reach the group's DSR goals. The DSR was being watched on a daily basis by division management. This project had already been forced to secure group-level approval because it fell below the minimum return-on-sales target. SAC's management had counted on the deal to make its annual sales targets, and that now seemed in jeopardy. It would need to act soon if it was to reach its targets.

QUESTIONS

1. Estimate what cash flows in which currencies the proposal would probably yield. What is the expected U.S. dollar value that would, in the end, be received?

2. Do you think the services that Makran is offering are worth the costs?

3. What would you do if you were heading the Honeywell SAC group negotiating the deal?

BUSINESS INVESTMENT RULES

10

W hen making capital budgeting decisions, a firm evaluates the expected future cash flows in relation to the required initial investment. The objective is to find investment projects that will add value to the firm. These are projects that are worth more to the firm than they cost—projects that have a positive NPV.

The pivotal role of capital budgeting and the risks associated with capital investments are dramatically demonstrated by comparing the initial cash outflow, which can be huge, to that of the relatively much smaller expected periodic future cash inflows. The risk is especially obvious if you consider the tremendous uncertainty associated with the timing and size of the future cash flows. A firm might invest $200 million now, *hoping* to net $30 million per year *after* several years of development!

A firm's evaluation of a long-term investment project is like an individual's investment decision. The steps are the same:

1. Estimate the expected future cash flows from the project, like estimating the coupon payments for a bond or the dividend stream for a stock, and a maturity value or terminal sale price.

2. Assess the risk and determine a required return for discounting the expected future cash flows.

3. Compute the present value of the expected future cash flows.

4. Determine the cost of the project and compare it to what the project is worth. If the project is worth more than it costs—if it has a positive NPV—it will create value.

FOCUS ON PRINCIPLES

- *Valuable Ideas:* Look for new ideas to use as a basis for capital budgeting projects that will create value.
- *Comparative Advantage:* Look for capital budgeting projects that will use the firm's comparative advantage to create value.
- *Incremental Benefits:* Identify and estimate the expected future cash flows for a capital budgeting project on an incremental basis.
- *Risk-Return Trade-Off:* Incorporate the risk of a capital budgeting project into its *cost of capital* —the project's required return.
- *Time Value of Money:* Measure the current value a capital budgeting project will create, its NPV.
- *Options:* Recognize the value of options, such as the options to expand, postpone, or abandon a capital budgeting project.
- *Two-Sided Transactions:* Consider why the other party to a transaction is willing to participate.
- *Signaling:* Consider the products and actions of competitors.

In this chapter we present the process of capital budgeting as it is practiced in most corporations. We show you ways to measure the attractiveness of projects. As you will see, some badly flawed methods remain in practice and can lead to bad decisions. We also show how sound methods of evaluating business investments can be applied to both proposed projects and to current operations. When combined with reasonable estimates of future outcomes, these methods support good decisions.

Throughout this chapter on investment rules, we ignore taxes and certain other complications to focus on basic investment criteria and the process of capital budgeting.

10.1   THE CAPITAL BUDGETING PROCESS

We start by looking at how **capital budgeting** works in practice. The overall process can be broken down into five steps as a project moves from idea to reality:

1. Generating ideas for capital budgeting projects
2. Reviewing existing projects and facilities
3. Preparing proposals
4. Evaluating proposed projects and creating the **capital budget**, the firm's set of planned capital expenditures
5. Preparing appropriation requests

Idea Generation

The first—and most important—part of the capital budgeting process is generating new ideas. Its critical importance is obvious from the Principle of Valuable Ideas. Unfortunately, we cannot teach people how to come up with valuable new ideas. If we could, we would already be wealthy from having followed the procedure ourselves! However, although we don't have a process that ensures the creation of new ideas, it is important to stress their value. Such an emphasis makes it more likely that those ideas that do occur to us and to others will be given serious consideration.

Where do new ideas come from? Ideas for capital budgeting projects come from all levels within an organization. Figure 10-1 shows the desirable flow of capital investment ideas within

FIGURE 10-1
The desirable flow of
capital budgeting ideas
within a firm.

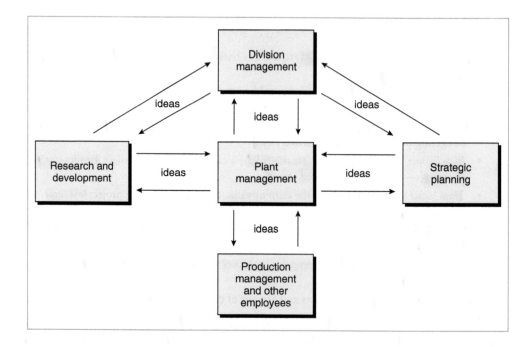

a firm. Often plant managers are responsible for identifying potential projects that will enable their plants to operate on a different scale or on a more efficient basis. For instance, a plant manager might suggest adding 10,000 square feet of production space to a plant or replacing a piece of equipment with a newer, more efficient machine. After screening out the less advantageous or less attractive ideas, the manager would send the ones that appear to be attractive to the divisional level, along with supporting documentation.

Division management not only reviews such proposals, but also adds ideas of its own. For example, division management may propose the introduction of a new product line or combining two plants and eliminating the less efficient one. Such ideas are less likely to come from the plant managers!

This bottom-up process results in ideas percolating upward through the organization. At each level, ideas submitted by lower-level managers are screened; some are forwarded to the next level. In addition, the managers at successively higher levels, who are in a position to take a broader view of the firm's business, add ideas that may not be visible to lower-level managers.

At the same time, there is also a top-down process at work in most firms. Strategic planners will generate ideas regarding new businesses the firm should enter, other firms it might acquire, and ways to modify its existing businesses to achieve greater profitability. Strategic planning is a critical element in the capital budgeting process. The processes complement one another; the top-down process generates ideas of a broader, more strategic nature, whereas the bottom-up process generates ideas of a more project-specific nature.

In addition, some firms have a research-and-development group, either within a production division or as a separate department. A research-and-development group often provides new ideas for products that can be sent on to a marketing research department. Table 10-1 lists the typical stages for the development and approval of a capital investment proposal.

TABLE 10-1
Development and
approval stages for a
proposed capital
budgeting project.

1. Approve funds for research that may result in a product *idea.*
2. Approve funds for market research that may result in a product *proposal.*
3. Approve funds for product development that may result in a usable *product.*
4. Approve funds for plant and/or equipment for the *production* and sale of the new product.

Each stage in Table 10-1 involves a capital budgeting decision at one or more levels of the firm. Therefore, at each stage, the firm reestimates the NPV of going ahead. With this kind of sequential appropriation of funds, an automatic progress review is enforced, which enables early cancellation of unsuccessful projects. So each stage includes options, for example, to abandon, postpone, change, or continue.

EXAMPLE Strategic Decisions at Boeing: Will It Fly?

Boeing Corporation is a world leader in commercial aircraft. In the heat of competition, Boeing often faces a critical capital budgeting decision: whether to develop a new generation of passenger aircraft. Developing new aircraft is very expensive.

For example, at one time, Boeing was considering the development of a new generation of its highly successful 747 jumbo jet. The estimated development cost was $7 billion. Its major competitor, Airbus Industrie, was developing larger, longer-range aircraft.

Boeing announced that it would undertake the project only if it would benefit shareholders. After sizing up the potential market, Boeing stopped its plans for a new 747 because of rising development costs and weak demand for the plane. Boeing had exercised its option to postpone because, several years later, it reanalyzed market conditions and then proceeded with the project.

Classifying Capital Budgeting Projects

Analysis costs money. Therefore, certain types of projects receive only cursory checks before approval, whereas others are subjected to extensive analysis. Generally, less costly and more routine projects are subjected to less extensive evaluation. As a result, firms typically categorize projects and analyze them at the level judged appropriate to their category. Investments in each category may have a lot in common and can be analyzed similarly. A useful set of investment classifications is

Maintenance projects
Cost-saving/revenue-enhancing projects
Capacity expansions in current businesses
New products and new businesses
Projects required by government regulation or firm policy

MAINTENANCE EXPENDITURES At a most basic level, a firm must make certain investments to continue to be a healthy, profitable business. Replacing worn-out or damaged equipment is necessary to continue in business. Therefore, the major questions concerning such investments are: "Should we continue in this business?" and if so, "Should we continue to use the same production process?" Because the answers to these questions are so frequently "yes," an elaborate decision-making process is not a good use of resources. Typically, such decisions are approved with only routine review.

COST SAVINGS/REVENUE ENHANCEMENT These projects include improvements in production technology to realize cost savings and marketing campaigns to achieve revenue enhancement. The central issue is increasing the difference between revenue and cost; the result must be sufficient to justify the investment. Cost-reducing investments involve not only the requirement that the purchase and installation of the equipment must be profitable, but also that current action is better than waiting until a later time—there may be a valuable option to postpone.

CAPACITY EXPANSION IN CURRENT BUSINESSES Deciding to expand the current business is inherently more difficult than approving maintenance or cost-savings proposals. Firms have to consider the economics of expanding or adding new facilities and must also prepare demand forecasts. The Principle of Two-Sided Transactions reminds us to consider competitors' likely strategies. Marketing consultants may help, but the cash flow projections for this type of project have naturally greater uncertainty than those for maintenance or replacement projects.

NEW PRODUCTS AND NEW BUSINESSES   These projects, which include research-and-development activities, are among the most difficult to evaluate. Their newness and long lead times make it very difficult to forecast product demand accurately. In many cases, the project may be of special interest because it would give the firm an option to break into a new market. For example, a firm that possesses a proprietary technology might spend additional research-and-development funds trying to develop new products based on this technology. If successful, these new products could pave the way for future profitable investment opportunities. Access to such follow-up opportunities creates options for the firm, which are valuable.

MEETING REGULATORY AND POLICY REQUIREMENTS   Government regulations and/or firm policies concerning such things as pollution control and health or safety factors are viewed as costs. Often, the critical issue in such projects is meeting the standards in the most efficient manner—at the minimum present-value cost—rather than realizing the value added by the project. Engineering analyses of alternative technologies often provide critical information in such cases. Of course, the firm must also consider the possibility that the option to abandon the business is worth more than making the required investments and continuing.

Capital Budgeting Proposals

Small expenditures may be handled informally but, in general, the originator presents a proposal in writing. Sometimes proposals are not formally written in smaller, privately owned firms, which tend to have relatively informal organizational structures. Most firms use standard forms, and these are typically supplemented by written memoranda for larger, more complex projects. Also, there may be consulting or other studies prepared by outside experts; for example, economic forecasts from economic consultants.

For a healthy firm, a maintenance project might require only limited supporting information. In contrast, a new product would require extensive information gathering and analysis. At the same time, within a category, managers at each level typically have upper limits on their authority regarding both expenditures on individual assets and the total expenditure for a budgeting period. In this way, larger projects require the approval of higher authority.

For example, at the lowest level, a department head may have the authority to approve $25,000 in total equipment purchases for the year but must obtain specific approval from higher authority for any single piece of equipment costing more than $5,000. A plant manager might have authorization limits of $250,000 per year and $50,000 per piece of equipment, and so forth.

A system of authorization such as this requires more extensive review and a greater number of inputs to improve important ideas. Multiple reviews make sense because a firm wishes to avoid making a negative-NPV investment. The hierarchical review structure reflects the obvious fact that misjudging a larger project is potentially more costly than misjudging a smaller one, hence, the need for a greater number of reviews before deciding to proceed.

Capital Budgeting and the Required Return

Recall that the required return is the minimum rate of return that you need to earn to be willing to make an investment. It is the rate of return that exactly reflects the riskiness of the expected future cash flows. In capital budgeting, the required return has several different names. The most widely used term is the **cost of capital**. Other names are the *hurdle rate* and the *appropriate discount rate*, or simply the *discount rate*. Although these terms may be used interchangeably, it is important to remember that the cost of capital reflects the riskiness of the capital budgeting project's cash flows, not the interest rate on its bonds or the riskiness of the firm's *existing* assets.

REVIEW

1. What are the five steps in the capital budgeting process? Which is most important?
2. Why are capital budgeting projects frequently classified into groups such as maintenance projects, cost savings/revenue-enhancement projects, capacity-expansion projects, new product/new business projects, and projects mandated by regulation or firm policy?
3. What other names are used to refer to the cost of capital, a capital budgeting project's required return?

10.2 NET PRESENT VALUE (NPV)

Recall that a net present value (NPV) is the difference between what something is worth (the present value of its expected future cash flows—its market value) and what it costs. Can something really be worth more than it costs? Yes, it happens. But being the skeptical and insightful person you are, you know that we are not going to give you a list of such opportunities; we would rather keep it for ourselves. In fact, the major difficulty of finding a project's NPV rests on the need to see situations differently from other people. That means taking some risk based on special knowledge or valuable ideas. At best, we can estimate a project's NPV in advance. We will not know its true market value, or what it is *really* worth, until the project is completed and the returns are collected.

EXAMPLE   **Discovering a Positive-NPV Opportunity**

Suppose you have noticed a run-down office building in downtown Asbury Park that you think has possibilities. You decide to buy it for $420,000 and invest $300,000 more in renovations over the next six months. After this, you offer the building for sale and sell it to the highest bidder for $910,000. Because the building turned out to be worth more than you paid for it, that is, its market value of $910,000 exceeded its cost of $720,000 (= $420,000 + 300,000), your management will have created about $190,000 (= $910,000 − 720,000) in value.

Although it is delightful to contemplate the money you made in our example, think about how you could have known enough to undertake this capital budgeting project in the first place. You could find the building's market value by offering it for sale—the highest offer you get is its market value. However, that is possible only after doing the renovations. Although you might be able to offer the building for sale before doing the renovations by describing your plans, at best this would be awkward, time-consuming, and expensive. Furthermore, keep in mind the Principle of Two-Sided Transactions: Once you pointed out the potential value of renovating the building to other people, some of them might decide to bid on the building now for more than the $420,000 you hoped to pay for it.

To estimate the market value after renovation, you might have looked at other buildings in good repair to see what they were worth and then adjusted for differences between them and the one you were considering. You would also estimate the cost of the needed renovations and add that to the cost of buying the building, to determine the total cost. Finally, you would compare your market value estimate to your total cost estimate.

If the estimates told you the project created value, and your estimates were correct, then you would get the value that was created. You can see right away how important accurate estimates are!

Another way to determine value is to use **discounted-cash-flow (DCF) analysis** and compute the present value of all the cash flows connected with ownership. This is like discounting the interest payments on a bond or dividends on a stock.

The NPV of a capital budgeting project is the present value of *all* of the cash flows connected with the project, all its costs and revenues, now and in the future:

$$\text{NPV} = \text{CF}_0 + \frac{\text{CF}_1}{(1+r)} + \frac{\text{CF}_2}{(1+r)^2} + \cdots + \frac{\text{CF}_n}{(1+r)^n}$$

(10.1)

$$= \sum_{t=0}^{n} \frac{\text{CF}_t}{(1+r)^t}$$

DECISION RULE   for net present value: Undertake a capital budgeting project if the NPV is positive.

EXAMPLE Computing an NPV

Suppose that instead of expecting to sell the building after you renovate it, you expect to lease it out for 20 years and then sell the building for $250,000. You expect the lease to pay you $110,000 per year. Finally, the cost of capital in this case is 12%. What is the NPV of this renovation project?

Using Equation (10.1), the NPV is $127,555.49:

$$\text{NPV} = -(420,000 + 300,000) + 110,000 \sum_{t=1}^{20} \frac{1}{(1.12)^t} + 250,000 \frac{1}{(1.12)^{20}}$$

$$= -720,000 + 821,639.80 + 25,916.69 = \$127,555.49$$

The NPV is the present value of the future cash flows, which is $847,555.49 minus the initial cost of $720,000.

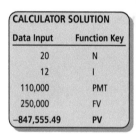

CALCULATOR SOLUTION	
Data Input	Function Key
20	N
12	I
110,000	PMT
250,000	FV
−847,555.49	PV

It is important to note that the risk connected with the estimates of revenues, costs, and selling price are included in the cost of capital (required return). That is to say, computing the NPV does *not* reduce the risk. If the estimates are realized, however, you will be richer for undertaking the project.

Adding Value per Share

If the firm undertakes the building renovation project, how much value does it add to a share of its stock? Typically, each share has a $1/n$ claim on the firm's value, where n is the number of outstanding shares. This claim extends to the project's NPV. In concept then, if the firm has 100,000 shares of common stock outstanding and our estimates are correct, the project would add $1.28 per share (= 127,555.49/100,000). If the project were completely unanticipated by the market and the market agreed with the NPV estimate, the price of the stock would jump by $1.28 per share. In practice, a share of stock does not typically change precisely by its fractional claim on the NPV of a new project. This is because prices are made on expectations, and rarely is it the case when a project is a complete surprise and the market makes the identical estimate of NPV.

REVIEW

1. What is the NPV of a capital budgeting project?
2. State the decision rule for net present value.
3. What is discounted-cash-flow analysis?

10.3 INTERNAL RATE OF RETURN (IRR)

Another method of evaluating a capital budgeting project is called the internal-rate-of-return method. The **internal rate of return (IRR)** is the project's expected return. If the cost of capital (required return) equals the IRR (expected return), the NPV equals zero. So, one way of viewing the IRR is to say that it is the discount rate that makes the total present value of all of a project's cash flows sum to zero. Of course, because of risk, the project's realized return will almost surely be different from its IRR. Recall how to compute a bond's yield to maturity (YTM). We use the same sort of procedure to compute an IRR:

(10.2)
$$CF_0 + \frac{CF_1}{(1+IRR)} + \frac{CF_2}{(1+IRR)^2} + \cdots + \frac{CF_n}{(1+IRR)^n} = 0$$

$$\sum_{t=0}^{n} \frac{CF_t}{(1+IRR)^t} = 0$$

DECISION RULE for internal rate of return: Undertake the capital budgeting project if the IRR exceeds r, the project's cost of capital.

In its simplest form, the IRR rule is intuitively appealing. In essence, it asks whether the capital budgeting project's expected return exceeds its required return. In other words, will it create value?

At first glance, this seems to be saying the same thing as the NPV rule. As we will see, this is generally true—but not always. The intuitive appeal of the IRR rule, however, probably accounts for its widespread use (in fact, many practitioners prefer it).

Like other expected returns, the IRR must be calculated by trial and error. Although many calculators and spreadsheets can solve for the IRR, they also are using trial and error.

EXAMPLE Computing an IRR for Reebok

Suppose Reebok can invest in a capital budgeting project that has a 12% cost of capital. The project's expected future net cash flows are shown in Figure 10-2. What is the project's IRR?

When in doubt, start by trying 10%. At a discount rate of 10%, the NPV of this project would be

$$NPV_{10\%} = -800 + \frac{300}{(1.10)^1} + \frac{300}{(1.10)^2} + \frac{300}{(1.10)^3} + \frac{150}{(1.10)^4} = +48.51$$

Year	0	1	2	3	4
Cash flows	−800	300	300	300	150

FIGURE 10-2
Expected future net cash flows for Reebok's capital budgeting project.

Because $NPV_{10\%}$ is positive, we need a larger rate. At 14%:

$$NPV_{14\%} = -800 + \frac{300}{(1.14)^1} + \frac{300}{(1.14)^2} + \frac{300}{(1.14)^3} + \frac{150}{(1.14)^4} = -14.70$$

Because 14% would make the NPV negative, it is too high. At 13%:

$$NPV_{13\%} = -800 + \frac{300}{(1.13)^1} + \frac{300}{(1.13)^2} + \frac{300}{(1.13)^3} + \frac{150}{(1.13)^4} = +0.34$$

CALCULATOR SOLUTION	
Data Input	Function Key
4	N
−800	PV
300	PMT
−150	FV
13.0225	I

This is pretty close, but you could keep going with this process and be more accurate. In this particular case, you could notice that the cash flows are very even and can be represented as an annuity of +300 per year for four years plus a terminal cash flow of −150. Then, using a calculator, calculate IRR = 13.0225%. With a cost of capital of 12%, then, the IRR decision rule would tell us to undertake this project, which is the same advice the NPV decision rule offers.

If you consider a project in which the cash flows are more complex and uneven, you can see the value of a spreadsheet. In practice, spreadsheets are used for all but the simplest projects.

REVIEW

1. What is a capital budgeting project's IRR?
2. State the decision rule for internal rate of return. What does it mean in practical terms?
3. Does the IRR rule usually lead to the same investment decisions as the NPV rule?

10.4 USING NPV AND IRR

In many applications, the NPV and IRR are both valuable guides to making capital budgeting decisions. Frequently, they agree and can be trusted to provide a valid assessment. There are some instances, however, when the NPV and IRR disagree on the relative merits of projects, and there are other instances when the IRR is very difficult to interpret. In this section, we discuss when both methods can be trusted. We also show cases where they disagree. When in doubt, as we show, use the NPV rule.

When IRR and NPV Agree: Independent, Conventional Projects

In the example just given, the IRR and NPV methods agree. This will happen whenever the projects are both independent and conventional. An **independent project** is one that can be chosen independently of other projects. That is, undertaking it neither requires nor precludes any other investment. A project that requires other investments is simply part of a larger capital budgeting project, which must be evaluated together with all of its parts. When undertaking one project prevents investing in another project, and vice versa, the projects are said to be **mutually exclusive projects**.

A **conventional project** has an initial cash outflow that is followed by one or more expected future cash inflows. That is, after making the investment, the total cash flow in each future year is expected to be positive. Purchasing a stock or bond is a simple example of a conventional capital budgeting project: You buy the security (a negative cash flow), and the terminal sale price and any dividends or interest payments while you own it will not be negative (you have limited liability).

NPV Profile

Another way to look at this problem is to graph NPV as a function of the discount rate. This graph is called an **NPV profile**, which is a very useful tool.

The NPV profile includes both NPV and IRR, as well as the project's value at various costs of capital. Therefore, if you are unsure about the project's cost of capital, you can use the NPV profile to identify costs of capital at which the project would not create value.

An NPV profile for our IRR computation example is presented in Figure 10-3. To construct this NPV profile, we use the calculations in the example and a couple more. One of the additional calculations assumes a cost of capital of 0%, in which case the NPV would be +250. This calculation is straightforward because it is simply the undiscounted sum of all the cash flows. We also calculated what the NPV would be at discount rates of 5% and 20%, to fill in the graph.

The NPV profile in Figure 10-3 shows the general relationship between IRR and NPV for independent, conventional projects. If the IRR exceeds the cost of capital, the NPV is positive. If the IRR is less than the cost of capital, the NPV is negative.

When IRR and NPV Can Differ: Mutually Exclusive Capital Budgeting Projects

Thus far, we have looked only at the question of whether or not to undertake an independent project. But often we must choose from a set of mutually exclusive projects. If we undertake one, we cannot undertake any of the others.

For example, a firm that plans to build a new assembly plant might have three possible locations and four possible plant configurations. But the firm needs only *one* plant. Therefore, it must choose one configuration in one location, and the alternatives are mutually exclusive. In such cases, we can get conflicting recommendations from the IRR and NPV methods.

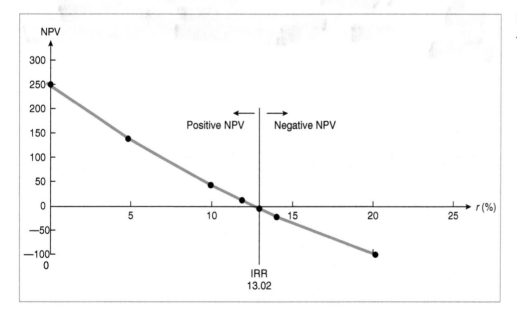

FIGURE 10-3
An NPV profile.

Conflicting recommendations can occur because there is a difference in (1) the *size* of the projects, or (2) the *cash flow timing*. An example of the latter occurs when cash flows from one project come in mostly early and cash flows from the other project come in later. We will look at each of these types of differences in turn.

SIZE DIFFERENCES   When one project is larger than another, the smaller project can have a larger IRR but a smaller NPV. For example, suppose project A has an IRR of 30% and an NPV of $100, and project B has an IRR of 20% and an NPV of $200. The choice between these two projects—and therefore the resolution of such conflicts—is fairly straightforward: You need only decide whether you would rather have more wealth or a larger IRR. Like you, we will take the wealth, thank you. Therefore, the NPV decision rule is the better rule to follow when mutually exclusive projects differ in size.

CASH FLOW TIMING DIFFERENCES   The problem of cash flow timing can arise because of the **reinvestment rate assumption**. The question is: "What will the cash inflows from the investment earn when they are subsequently reinvested in other projects?" The IRR method assumes the future cash inflows will earn the project's IRR. The NPV method assumes they will earn the cost of capital.

The following example illustrates the conflict in the reinvestment rate assumption that results from a difference in cash flow timing. As you will see, the NPV profiles diverge at a **crossover point**, a cost of capital at which the two projects have equal NPV.

EXAMPLE **Comparing IRR with NPV at Guess, Inc**

Suppose Guess, Inc., can invest in only one of two projects, S (for short term) and L (for long term). The cost of capital is 10%, and the projects have the expected future cash flows shown in Figure 10-4. Which is the better project?

Project S has an IRR of 22.08%, and project L has an IRR of 20.01%. But project S has an NPV of $76.29, and project L has an NPV of $94.08. Thus, the IRR method tells us to choose S, but the NPV method says choose L.

Take a look at Figure 10-5. It compares NPV and IRR. You can see there that project S will have a higher NPV than project L whenever the cost of capital is higher than 15.40%, the crossover point.[1] Both projects would have an NPV of $37.86 if the cost of capital were 15.40%. You can also see that project L has a steeper NPV profile than project S. This is because the present values of cash flows further in the future are more sensitive to the discount rate. We saw this in the case of bonds, where the market value of a long-term bond changes more than that of a short-term bond in response to a given interest rate change.

FIGURE 10-4
Alternative short- and long-term capital budgeting projects for Guess.

Year	0	1	2	3	4	5	6	IRR	NPV
Project S	−250	100	100	75	75	50	25	22.08%	76.29
Project L	−250	50	50	75	100	100	125	20.01%	94.08

---

[1]You can compute the crossover point by finding the rate that makes the present value of the cash flow differences equal zero. Thus, for this example, the yearly differences are

Year	0	1	2	3	4	5	6
Cash flow difference	0	50	50	0	−25	−50	−100

You can verify that 15.3985% will make the present value of this cash flow stream equal zero.

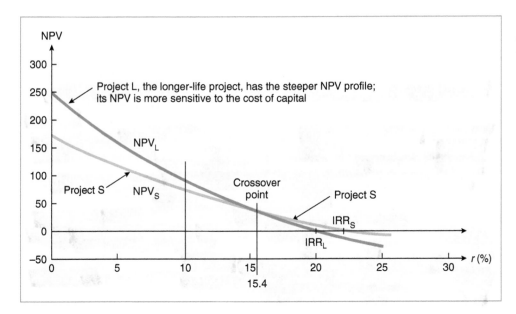

FIGURE 10-5
A comparison of NPV and IRR.

Which method makes the better assumption about what the reinvested cash flows will earn? If the cost of capital is computed correctly, it is the project's required return. In equilibrium, the required return equals the expected return and, over time, competitive forces drive investment returns to equilibrium.

Although new ideas can be very valuable, after a while most people will be using them, and they will no longer command a positive NPV. So the NPV from future projects based on the same sort of idea will tend toward zero. In the long run, then, reinvested cash flows can earn the cost of capital, but not the extra, positive, NPV. So the NPV method's assumption that the reinvestment rate will equal the cost of capital is the better assumption. And, again, the NPV decision rule is superior to the IRR decision rule.

Another Case When IRR and NPV Can Differ: Nonconventional Projects

We defined a conventional capital budgeting project earlier in the chapter. A **nonconventional project** has a cash flow pattern that is different in some way from conventional projects. Nonconventional projects can create a conflict between the NPV and IRR decision rules.

In some cases, a nonconventional project is simply the reverse conventional project, one in which the initial cash flow is positive and the subsequent flows are all negative. A lifetime annuity, which insurance firms sell to retired persons, is an example. From the insurance firm's viewpoint, it receives a lump-sum amount at the start of the investment. It then makes monthly payments to the annuity's owner for the rest of that person's life.

Analyzing such cases using IRR is straightforward: Simply reverse the IRR decision rule. That is, for a reverse conventional project, undertake the project if the IRR is *less than* the cost of capital. Of course, if you forget to reverse the IRR rule in such cases, you will make exactly the wrong decision.

Unfortunately, complications can arise. When some future cash flows are expected to be positive and others negative, there can be multiple IRRs. Such cases can occur, for example, when an environmental cleanup is necessary at the end of the project. The firm makes an initial investment, receives positive cash flows while the project is operating, and then must make a cash outlay to clean up when the project is terminated. Another example is a project that requires one or more major renovations during its life. Let's take a look at the kinds of conflicts that can arise in these more complex situations.

EXAMPLE Multiple IRRs for Triborg, Inc.

Triborg, Inc., can invest in a project that has an initial cash flow of –$24,000, with expected future cash flows of $58,000 after three years and –$51,000 after 10 years. So the net expected cash flows are negative, positive, and negative. Is this a problem? It can be.

The best way to see the problem we are illustrating here is to look at the NPV profile for this project, which is shown in Figure 10-6. You can see the problem right away. With possible discount rates from 0 to 30%, the NPV goes from negative to positive, and back to negative again. The project has two IRRs, 10.8% and 25.4%. That is, there are two points where the NPV would be zero if those points were the cost of capital.[2]

In this case, the IRR decision rule breaks down completely. If we applied the IRR decision rule blindly to this choice, we could make a serious mistake.

For example, if the cost of capital were 10% and both IRRs exceed this, we would undertake the project because both IRRs exceed this. However, at a 10% cost of capital, the project has a negative NPV. Reversing the rule as we did with reverse conventional projects does not help either. If the cost of capital exceeded 25.4%, the rule would again lead to an incorrect decision. Finally, even in the range where the NPV is positive, it is not very large, and the project would not create much wealth, anyway.

Unfortunately, calculators and currently available PC software generally are not fully equipped to handle the problem of multiple IRRs. They often report only the IRR their trial-and-error process happens to find first. However, they can be used to create an NPV profile. And, in any case, that provides a much more complete view of the project's potential value.

IRR, on Balance

At this point, you may ask, "Why use the IRR rule, when you may have to make several NPV calculations in the course of computing the IRR?" Our answer is that you should not use the IRR rule. Use NPV, instead.

In practice, however, the IRR rule is more widely used than the NPV rule. Many people prefer the intuitive feel of the IRR rule: After all, if the expected return is big enough, it will surely exceed the required return, and the project is a good investment. Such straightforward simplicity is appealing. For example, in cases when the cost of capital is especially uncertain, as in the case of

FIGURE 10-6
A capital budgeting project with multiple IRRs.

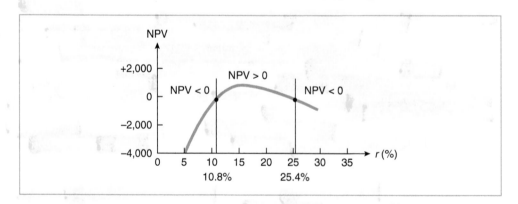

---

[2]The number of IRRs is never more than the number of sign reversals in the stream of cash flows. So conventional projects and reverse conventional projects have only one IRR because they have only one sign reversal—a negative followed by all positives, or a positive followed by all negatives. In this example, there can be at most two IRRs because there are two reversals, the flows go from negative to positive, and back to negative.

an entirely new product, using the IRR rule gets around having to compute the cost of capital carefully.

Also, if the IRR for a conventional project is large enough, say 88%, it is probably not worth the trouble to estimate the cost of capital accurately. Because the cost of capital would virtually never be that high, we can simply undertake the project without wasting additional resources on analysis. Those resources can be spent instead on making the project successful!

REVIEW

1. What is the difference between mutually exclusive projects and independent projects?
2. Distinguish between a conventional project and a nonconventional project.
3. When do the NPV and IRR methods agree? Under what circumstances can they differ?
4. When the NPV and IRR methods disagree, which is usually more reliable?
5. Describe an NPV profile in your own words. Why is it so useful?

10.5 OTHER CAPITAL BUDGETING CRITERIA

Several capital budgeting criteria besides the NPV and IRR are widely used. These include *modified internal rate of return, profitability index, payback, discounted payback,* and *urgency.* We will describe them here as background in case you encounter them. Because some of these are not economically sound, it is critical to know their strengths and weaknesses.

Profitability Index

Another time-value-of-money-adjusted method that can be used to evaluate capital budgeting projects is the **profitability index (PI)**, or **benefit-cost ratio** as it is sometimes called. The PI for a project equals the present value of the future cash flows divided by the initial investment. One way to view the PI is that it is 1 plus the NPV divided by the initial investment:

$$(10.3) \quad \text{Profitability Index} = PI = \frac{PV(\text{future cash flows})}{\text{Initial investment}} = 1 + \frac{NPV}{\text{Initial investment}}$$

If a project had an NPV of $240 and required an initial cash flow of −$1,000, the project's PI would be 1.24 (= 1 + 240/1,000).

DECISION RULE   for the profitability index: Undertake the capital budgeting project if the PI is greater than 1.0.

You probably wonder why we bother introducing this method, because it is obvious the NPV decision rule will give you the identical recommendation.[3] The idea underlying the PI is to measure the capital budgeting project's "bang for the buck." By scaling (dividing) the present value of the future cash flows by the initial outlay, you can see how much return is obtained *per dollar* invested. For example, with a PI of 1.24, you get $1.24 of present value back for each $1 invested, or an NPV of $0.24 for each $1 invested.

Although the PI works fine for independent projects, the scale problem of mutually exclusive projects we saw with IRR also occurs with PI. For example, suppose project A has a PI of 1.6 and an NPV of $100. Project B has a PI of 1.3 and an NPV of $200. The choice between these

---

[3]In fact, some people define the PI as simply the NPV divided by the initial investment. Such a definition changes the scale to center on zero, rather than 1.0. There is no substantive difference because such a definition simply changes the cutoff for the PI rule to zero from 1.0.

two projects is again straightforward: Would you rather have more wealth or a larger PI? (Again, like you, we will take the wealth.) Therefore, the NPV decision rule is the better rule to follow when mutually exclusive projects differ in size.

PROFITABILITY INDEX, ON BALANCE   Although PI offers a perspective on "bang for the buck," it is best used in conjunction with NPV, rather than in place of NPV. PI gets some use in practice, but less than IRR. Its most beneficial use is in situations when the firm is restricting the amount of investment it makes, rather than investing in all worthwhile projects. Such a situation is called *capital rationing*.

Modified Internal Rate of Return (MIRR)

We noted earlier that many practitioners prefer IRR because of its intuitive appeal. Modified internal rate of return (MIRR) was developed to have the same intuitive feel, but to provide a better measure of relative profitability than IRR. This method calculates the present value of all the cash outflows and the future value of all the cash inflows using the cost of capital. The MIRR is the rate of return that equates the two over the project life of N, so that

$$(10.4) \qquad \text{PV(cash outflows)} = \frac{\text{FV(cash inflows)}}{(1 + \text{MIRR})^N}$$

MIRR is used by some firms, such as FedEx, because it is a better measure than IRR but has the same intuitive appeal. The decision rule for MIRR is the same as for IRR.

DECISION RULE   for modified internal rate of return: Undertake the capital budgeting project if the MIRR exceeds the project's cost of capital.

CALCULATOR SOLUTION	
Data Input	Function Key
4	N
12	I
0	PV
300	PMT
−1,433.80	FV

CALCULATOR SOLUTION	
Data Input	Function Key
4	N
−800	PV
0	PMT
1,283.80	FV
12.5516	I

EXAMPLE **Computing the MIRR for Reebok's Project**

The cash flows for this project (Figure 10-2) for times 0 through 4 are, respectively, −800, 300, 300, 300, 150, and the cost of capital is 12%. The present value of the cash outflows is simply the 800 at time 0. The future value of 300 per year for four years at 12% is 1,433.80. So the future value of all the cash flows is 1,283.80 (= 1,433.80 − 150). The MIRR, which equates the present and future values, is 12.5516%.

MIRR, ON BALANCE   MIRR is a better measure than IRR, but it offers the same intuitive appeal. Still, like IRR and PI, although MIRR offers a good measure of "bang for the buck," it is best used in conjunction with NPV.

Payback

An appealing investment concept is that of "getting your money back." Of course, risk may intervene, but investors often want an estimate of the time it will take to recover the initial cash outflow. When this amount of time is calculated without regard to the time value of money, it is called a project's payback. **Payback** is computed by simply summing all the expected cash flows (without discounting them) in sequential order until the sum equals the initial outflow.

DECISION RULE   for payback: Undertake the capital budgeting project if the payback is less than a preset amount of time.

Year	0	1	2	3	4	5	6	7	8
Cash flows	−720	110	110	110	110	110	110	110	110
Cumulative	−720	−610	−500	−390	−280	−170	−60	+50	
Payback:								↑6.55 years	

FIGURE 10-7
Payback for the building renovation project.

EXAMPLE Computing a Payback

Let's return to the building-renovation example we used earlier in the chapter to illustrate the NPV method. We expected to purchase the building for $420,000 and spend $300,000 on renovations. After renovation, we expected to be able to lease the building out for $110,000 per year. Ignoring taxes, this would give the cash flows in Figure 10-7. What is this project's payback?

The payback is 6.55 years (= 720,000/110,000), because $110,000 per year for 6.55 years equals $720,000, the initial investment.

The idea underlying the payback method is simple: The shorter the payback the better. But, there are serious deficiencies in the payback method. You are probably already saying, "But, but, but—it ignores the time value of money!" This is true. And it also ignores risk differences. In fact, the cutoff is entirely arbitrary, and all cash flows beyond the cutoff are ignored.

PRACTICAL VALUE OF PAYBACK   Despite the drawbacks of the payback method, the gut reaction of wanting to "at least get your money back" is a powerful feeling to overcome. Moreover, payback provides a control on liquidity, offers a different type of risk control, is easy to compute, and is simple to understand.

Payback controls liquidity because it rejects excessively long-term projects. This may be important for a smaller, less liquid firm because it favors investments that will return cash sooner. That cash can be reinvested in other profitable projects.

Cash flows further in the future are arguably more risky. As a risk-control device, payback addresses this harshly by simply ignoring those beyond the payback period.

Finally, we would add two other practical considerations: First, most investments with a short payback, and additional benefits beyond that, will also have a positive NPV. Second, for relatively small investments, the cost of extensive analysis can exceed the potential loss from a mistake. This can make the simplicity of payback attractive.

PAYBACK, ON BALANCE   Probably because of the practical considerations just noted, the payback rule is still widely used in practice despite its serious deficiencies. However, very few firms use payback by itself. Most firms also require investments to be acceptable on the basis of other rules, such as NPV. Because of its weaknesses, payback should be viewed, at best, as a supplement to the discounted-cash-flow techniques.

Discounted Payback

If a firm wants to use the payback method, a better measure is a variation of payback called **discounted payback**. The discounted payback is the amount of time it takes for the project's *discounted* cash flows to equal the project's initial cost. The idea underlying the discounted payback period is to incorporate the time value of money into the basic notion of getting your money back.

DECISION RULE   for discounted payback: Undertake the capital budgeting project if the discounted payback is less than a preset amount of time.

CALCULATOR SOLUTION	
Data Input	Function Key
12	I
−720,000	PV
110,000	PMT
0	FV
13.58	N

EXAMPLE **Computing a Discounted Payback**

Consider once again our building renovation example. The initial outlay is $720,000, and we expect to lease the building out for $110,000 per year. Using a 12% cost of capital and ignoring taxes, what is the project's discounted payback?

As shown in the calculator solution, the discounted payback is 13.58 years because that is the estimate of how long it takes for the project's discounted cash flows to equal the initial outlay.

You can probably see that for conventional projects, which are the most common type, a project that meets a discounted payback cutoff will always have a positive NPV. This is because the present value of the future cash flows during the discounted payback period alone cover the initial cost. The project's NPV, then, is the present value of the remaining cash flows—those ignored by the discounted-payback-period computation.

Discounted payback is superior to the payback method because it includes the effects of the time value of money. However, it too is arbitrary and suffers from the weakness of ignoring all cash flows beyond the cutoff. This can be a significant problem when there are negative expected future cash flows. The rule can break down in such cases.

DISCOUNTED PAYBACK, ON BALANCE   Although it is better than payback, the discounted payback method is still not an adequate indicator by itself. It too should be viewed as, at best, a supplement to the NPV method. Discounted payback is neither as conceptually correct as NPV nor as simple as payback. If you can understand the notion of discounted payback, you can understand and use net present value. So why bother with discounted payback? This is probably why discounted payback is not very widely used in practice.

Urgency

The final method we look at can be described by inverting Ben Franklin's advice and asking, "Why do today what you can put off until tomorrow?" The corollary to this perverse statement as applied to capital budgeting is "Do not replace it until we *absolutely* have to." No need for replacement studies. Wait until the machine breaks down, then air-freight in a new one. At that point, the specter of costly downtime will be sufficient to convince management to skip the analysis and simply order the replacement equipment.

Such a policy has obvious disadvantages, yet stories of plants that have critical equipment held together by "chewing gum and baling wire" loom large in industrial folklore. Capital budgeting projects and key pieces of equipment should be reviewed at regular intervals. A firm should develop a program of preventive maintenance and should estimate a probable replacement date each time it acquires a significant piece of equipment. This will help to ensure that the assets are used with maximum efficiency and that equipment is replaced when it is most advantageous to do so—rather than when the baling wire finally snaps and the equipment stops working!

URGENCY, ON BALANCE   Urgency is a frequently used but extremely poor basis for making important decisions. Firms should instead plan ahead. Drawing on Ben Franklin again, with accuracy this time, "An ounce of prevention is worth a pound of cure."

REVIEW

1. What is the profitability index? How is it calculated? What is its decision rule?
2. What is the payback rule? Why is it inferior to NPV? Does it have any practical value? Does the discounted payback method avoid the shortcomings of the simple payback method?

10.6 BUSINESS INVESTMENT IN PRACTICE

In this section, we look at some other practical aspects of capital budgeting and provide some perspective on how it is actually done.

Methods of Evaluation

Just about all firms use the evaluation methods we have discussed, in one form or another. *The single most useful tool is the NPV profile.* This is because it provides the most complete view of the project. It incorporates both NPV and IRR, and it also sheds light on the problem of an uncertain required return.

Understandably, however, most firms use more than one evaluation technique. Over the last 30 years, the use of techniques based on the time value of money, especially the NPV method, has increased substantially. We hope that means that when you finish school and apply the things you have learned here, you will be able to convince your employer to use the better discounted-cash-flow techniques that are available for capital budgeting if they are not already being used.

Appropriations

A decision to include an investment in the capital budget seldom means automatic approval of the required expenditures. Most firms require that plant managers or division heads submit detailed appropriation requests before funds can be released for a project.

Firms often create manuals that specify how appropriation requests must be prepared. This helps maintain managerial control over investments and their associated costs.

Conducting a review of a budgeted capital expenditure just prior to releasing funds provides one last check before making the expenditure. This can be valuable in cases in which new information has come to light that might make one or more changes advantageous.

Review and Performance Measurement

As we have said, capital budgeting has a critical role in the firm's strategic plan. Therefore, firms must systematically review the status of all projects. Such a process is sometimes called a **postaudit**. Managers should examine projects not yet completely underway to determine whether or not development should continue.

They also must assess the performance of the firm's existing assets. Consideration should be given to whether projects should, for example, be expanded, contracted, liquidated, sold off, reconfigured, or simply continued. The basic capital budgeting techniques discussed in this chapter can be applied to the review and performance-measurement process.

The major goal of the postaudit is improvement. Improvements can come primarily in two areas: (1) forecasting and (2) operations. When people know that records of estimates, either forecasts or operational goals, will be maintained and later compared to the actual outcomes, they tend to be more careful making their estimates. The fact that they are being monitored and will be evaluated and held accountable for their work tends to motivate people to seek better methods and work to eliminate both conscious and unconscious biases. This kind of process is sometimes referred to as *continuous improvement*, and it is part of the concept of *total quality management (TQM)*.

Although very difficult in some situations, postaudits are extremely important because of their potential impact on value.

REVIEW

1. What is the single most useful capital budgeting evaluation tool?
2. Why are appropriation requests useful in the capital budgeting process?
3. What is a postaudit? Why are postaudits useful in the capital budgeting process?

SUMMARY

The capital budgeting process and the investment criteria used to make capital budgeting decisions are critical because firms are effectively defined by the products and services they provide using their capital assets.

- **Idea generation** is the first and most important part of the capital budgeting process. Sources of potential valuable ideas include production employees, managers at all levels, sales and marketing staff, research and development groups, and the strategic planning process.

- The **net present value** (NPV) method discounts all cash flows at the project's required return—its *cost of capital*. The NPV measures the value the project will create, which is the difference between what the project is worth and what it will cost to undertake. The NPV method recommends that all independent projects with a positive NPV be undertaken. The NPV method is widely used in practice.

- The **internal rate of return** (IRR) is the project's expected return. It is the return that would make the NPV zero if it were the project's cost of capital. The IRR method recommends that every conventional capital budgeting project with an IRR greater than its cost of capital be undertaken. Caution is needed because the IRR decision rule can break down when projects are mutually exclusive or nonconventional. IRR is widely used in practice, probably because of its "intuitive feel."

- The **profitability index** (PI) method calculates one plus the project's NPV divided by its initial cost. The idea is to measure the project's "bang for the buck." The PI rule can break down when projects are mutually exclusive.

- The **payback** method finds the length of time it takes to recover the initial investment, without regard to the time value of money. It recommends acceptance of projects that "return the investment" quickly. The payback method has several serious deficiencies that can cause bad recommendations, but it may have some practical value. In particular, it can provide a liquidity screen, which might be desirable in some situations. Although widely used in conjunction with other methods, payback is rarely used alone.

- The **discounted payback** method is like payback but it incorporates the effect of the time value of money. The discounted payback is the time it takes the project to earn a present value equal to its initial cost. Although this method is superior to the payback method, it is still inferior to NPV because it ignores the value of cash flows after the payback point. Discounted payback is not widely used in practice, probably because it is neither as conceptually correct as NPV nor as simple as payback.

- **Urgency** is a dangerous but widely used method of allocating resources. Its use is shortsighted. Many potential crises can be avoided through good planning.

- In practice, most firms use multiple evaluation methods for investments of any significance. However, the **NPV profile** is the single most useful tool. It provides the project's
  NPV, IRR, and sensitivity to the discount rate at a glance.
- The **postaudit** is a critical and ongoing part of capital budgeting. It provides a significant opportunity to create value through *continuous improvement* in forecasting outcomes and in choosing and operating projects.

EQUATION SUMMARY

(10.1)
$$NPV = CF_0 + \frac{CF_1}{(1+r)} + \frac{CF_2}{(1+r)^2} + \cdots + \frac{CF_n}{(1+r)^n}$$

$$= \sum_{t=0}^{n} \frac{CF_t}{(1+r)^t}$$

(10.2)
$$CF_0 + \frac{CF_1}{(1+IRR)} + \frac{CF_2}{(1+IRR)^2} + \cdots + \frac{CF_n}{(1+IRR)^n} = 0$$

$$\sum_{t=0}^{n} \frac{CF_t}{(1+IRR)^t} = 0$$

(10.3) $\text{Profitability Index} = PI = \dfrac{PV(\text{future cash flows})}{\text{Initial investment}} = 1 + \dfrac{NPV}{\text{Initial investment}}$

(10.4) $PV(\text{cash outflows}) = \dfrac{FV(\text{cash inflows})}{(1+MIRR)^N}$

QUESTIONS

1. Briefly describe the five steps in the capital budgeting process.
2. Why is the Principle of Valuable Ideas of critical importance to the capital budgeting process?
3. Define the term *independent project*.
4. Define the terms *conventional project* and *nonconventional project*.
5. Define the term *mutually exclusive projects*.
6. Define the term *profitability index* and describe the concept.
7. Define the term *payback* and describe the concept.
8. What is an internal rate of return (IRR)?
9. Briefly explain why capital budgeting projects are frequently classified into groups such as maintenance projects, cost savings/revenue-enhancement projects, capacity-expansion projects, new product/new business projects, and projects mandated by regulation or firm policy.
10. Why can the NPV and IRR methods disagree on the rankings for mutually exclusive projects?
11. What are the strengths and weaknesses of the payback and the discounted payback?
12. Which of the capital budgeting criteria are the most sound? Which are the least sound?

13. Suppose you were restricted to using only one method of analysis to evaluate a capital budgeting project. Briefly explain why the NPV profile is the best method to use.

14. Why do firms perform postaudits, reviewing and measuring the performance of their previous capital investments?

CHALLENGING QUESTION

15. A staff analyst has just brought you an incomplete capital budgeting analysis that shows you only that the discounted payback of this conventional project is 5.24 years. A moment later, before you can fully collect your thoughts and ask the analyst any questions, the marketing vice president calls you and asks if the project analysis shows a positive NPV. You answer yes. Explain how you know this.

PROBLEMS

■ LEVEL A (BASIC)

A1. (NPV and IRR) An investment of $100 at time 0 generates a cash flow of $150 at time 1. If the cost of capital is 10%, what is the NPV? What is the IRR?

A2. (Mutually exclusive projects) Consider the cash flows given below for the mutually exclusive projects, S and L.

a. If the cost of capital is 10%, what is the NPV of each investment?

b. What is the IRR of each investment?

c. Which investment should you accept?

YEAR	0	1	2
Project S	−100	160	0
Project L	−100	0	200

A3. (NPV and PI) Vu Trading Company is evaluating a project that has the estimated cash flows given here. The cost of capital is 14%.

a. What is the project's NPV?

b. What is the profitability index?

YEAR	0	1	2	3	4
Cash flow	−100,000	30,000	30,000	60,000	60,000

A4. (Investment criteria) An investment of $100 returns exactly $100 in one year. The cost of capital is 10%.

a. What are the payback, NPV, and IRR for this investment?

b. Is this a profitable investment?

A5. (Investment criteria) Compute the NPV, IRR, and payback period for the following investment. The cost of capital is 10%.

YEAR	0	1	2	3
Cash flow	−200,000	100,000	100,000	150,000

A6. (Payback and discounted payback) Find the payback and the discounted payback for a project with the cash flows given here. The cost of capital is 12%.

YEAR	0	1	2	3	4
Cash flow	−10	3	3	4	6

A7. (NPV and IRR) A project is expected to generate cash flows of $14,000 annually for five years plus an additional $27,000 in year 6. The cost of capital is 10%.

a. What is the most that you can invest in this project at time 0 and still have a positive NPV?

b. What is the most that you can invest in this project at time 0 if you want to have a 15% IRR?

A8. (Investment criteria) An investment of $100,000 generates cash flows of $30,000 annually for the next four years. Find the NPV using a 10% cost of capital, the IRR, and the payback.

A9. (NPV) An investment of $10 will generate an annual cash flow of $1 forever. If the cost of capital is 8%, what is the NPV of this investment?

A10. (NPV) An investment of $25 will generate an annual cash flow of $2 forever. If the cost of capital is 7%, what is the NPV of this investment?

A11. (Payback and NPV) Three projects have the cash flows given here. The cost of capital is 10%.

a. Calculate the paybacks for all three projects. Rank the projects from best to worst based on their paybacks.

b. Calculate the NPVs for all three projects. Rank the projects from best to worst based on their NPVs.

c. Why are these two sets of rankings different?

YEAR	0	1	2	3	4	5
Project 1	−10	4	3	2	1	5
Project 2	−10	1	2	3	4	5
Project 3	−10	4	3	2	1	10

▪ LEVEL B

B1. (Reverse conventional project) You have an opportunity to undertake a project that has a positive cash flow of $100 at time 0 and a negative cash flow of $100 at time 1. The cost of capital is 10%.

a. What is the IRR?

b. What is the NPV?

c. Should you accept this project?

B2. (Reverse conventional project) You can undertake a project with the following cash flows:

CF_0	CF_1	CF_2
+5,000	+5,000	−12,500

The cost of capital is 10%. The internal rate of return is 15.8%. Should you accept this project? Why or why not?

B3. (NPV) Truman State University is evaluating an investment in new air handling systems for some of its major buildings. The expected outlays and the expected savings, in millions of dollars, are given here:

TIME	0	1	2	3	4 THROUGH 10
Outlays	2.0	3.0	4.0	0	0
Savings	0	0.5	1.0	1.5	2.0

What is the net present value of this investment if the required return is 8%?

B4. (NPV and shareholder wealth) Stockholders are surprised to learn that the firm has invested $43 million in a project that has an expected payoff of $8 million per year for six years. The project's cost of capital is 12%.

a. What is the project's NPV?

b. There are 3 million outstanding shares. What should be the direct impact of this invest-ment on the per-share value of the common stock?

B5. (Investment criteria) Pierre Bouvier is evaluating four projects. The cash flows for the four projects are given here.

a. Pierre thinks you can rank these projects from best to worst by simply inspecting the cash flows (and not calculating anything). Try to do so.

b. Pierre next found the NPV of each project, discounting future cash flows at 10%. What is the NPV for each project?

c. Do your rankings in parts a and b agree?

TIME	0	1	2	3	4
Project K	−100	40	40	40	40
Project L	−100	40	80	0	40
Project M	−90	40	80	0	30
Project N	−90	40	80	0	40

B6. (Investment criteria) Consider the cash flows for the two capital budgeting projects given here. The cost of capital is 10%.

a. Calculate the NPV for both projects.

b. Calculate the IRR for both.

c. Calculate the PI for both.

d. Calculate the MIRR for both.

e. Calculate the payback for both.

f. Which is the better project? Why?

YEAR	0	1	2	3	4
Project A	−25,000	10,000	10,000	10,000	10,000
Project B	−12,500	5,000	5,000	5,000	5,000

B7. (NPV profile) Consider the projects shown here.

a. Based on a 10% cost of capital, which is the better project?

b. Is this an example of size differences or cash flow timing differences?

c. What is the crossover point, the discount rate that would have the same NPV for both projects? (Hint: Find the differential cash flows between the two projects. Then find the IRR for the differential cash flows.)

	CASH FLOWS ($)				
PROJECT	CF_0	CF_1	CF_2	NPV @ 10%	IRR
R1	−100	70	70	$21.49	25.7%
R2	−150	100	100	$23.55	21.5%

B8. (Investment criteria) Consider a project that has these cash flows. The required return on the investment is 10%. Compute the:

a. Payback

b. Discounted payback

c. NPV

d. Profitability index

e. IRR

f. MIRR

YEAR	0	1	2	3	4
Cash flow	−70,000	30,000	30,000	30,000	20,000

B9. (NPV) Bill Scott estimates that a project will involve an outlay of $125,000 and will return $40,000 per year for six years. The required return is 12%.

a. What is the NPV using Bill's estimates?

b. David Scott is less optimistic about the project. David thinks the outlay will be 10% higher, the annual cash flows will be 5% lower, and the project will have a five-year life. David does agree with Bill's required return. What is the NPV using David's estimates?

B10. (Investment criteria) Suppose Reebok has a possible capital budgeting project with a cost of capital of 10%, and the expected cash flows shown here.

a. Calculate the project's NPV. Should Reebok accept the project?

b. Calculate the project's IRR. Should Reebok accept the project according to the IRR rule?

c. Calculate the project's payback. What does payback tell you about the project's acceptability?

YEAR	0	1	2	3	4	5
Cash flow	−100	25	50	50	25	10

B11. (Investment criteria) Texaco has a capital budgeting project with a cost of capital of 12% and the following expected cash flow pattern:

a. Calculate NPV. Should the firm accept the project?

b. Calculate IRR. Should the firm accept the project?

c. Calculate payback period.

d. How would your answers to parts a or b change if you were told that the project is one of two mutually exclusive projects the firm has under consideration?

YEAR	0	1	2	3
Cash flow	50	100	−20	−50

B12. (Mutually exclusive projects) Sperry is considering two mutually exclusive capital budgeting projects with a cost of capital of 14% and the expected cash flows shown here. Which, if either, project should Sperry undertake? Justify your answer.

YEAR	0	1	2	3	4	5
Project A	−100	30	40	50	40	30
Project B	−150	45	60	75	60	60

B13. (Excel: NPV profile) Helix, Inc., is considering two mutually exclusive one-time projects. Both require an initial investment of $80,000. Project A will last for six years and has expected net future cash flows of $40,222 per year. Project B will last for five years and has expected net future cash flows of $44,967 per year. The cost of capital for this project is 12%.

a. Calculate the NPV for each project.

b. Calculate the IRR for each project.

c. Graph the NPV of the projects as a function of the discount rate, including solving for the crossover point by trial and error.

d. Which project should Helix take?

B14. (Excel: NPV profile) Watson, Inc., is considering two mutually exclusive one-time projects. Both require an initial investment of $50,000. Project A will last for six years and has expected net future cash flows of $25,000 per year. Project B will last for five years and has expected net future cash flows of $20,000 per year. The cost of capital for this project is 10%.

a. Calculate the NPV for each project.

b. Calculate the IRR for each project.

c. Which project should Watson, Inc., take?

B15. (Excel: Choosing among mutually exclusive projects) Suppose Kodak is considering two mutually exclusive capital budgeting projects with the following expected cash flow patterns:

TIME	0	1	2	3	4	5	6
Project A	−350	140	140	100	100	65	30
Project B	−350	65	65	100	140	140	175

a. Compute the IRR for each project.

b. Compute the NPV for each project, assuming the cost of capital is 10%.

c. Compute the NPV for each project, assuming costs of capital of 14%, 18%, and 22%. Create NPV profiles comparing the projects.

d. If the cost of capital is precisely 12%, which project should Kodak undertake?

B16. (Excel: Finding NPV and IRR) Use the worksheet functions in your spreadsheet to find the NPV, IRR, and PI of the following project. The cost of capital is 10%. Are you getting the correct values in your spreadsheet?

Time	0	1
Cash flow	−100	+120

B17. (Excel: Finding NPV and IRR) Kennesaw Instrument Company is looking at six projects with the following cash flows (investment outlays are negative cash flows):

TIME	0	1	2	3	4	5	6	7	8
Project A	−10	2	3	4	5	4	3	2	1
Project B	−8	−3	5	5	5	2	0	0	0
Project C	−45	25	20	15	5	0	0	0	0
Project D	−1	2	2	2	0	0	0	0	0
Project E	−30	6	6	6	6	6	0	0	0
Project F	−10	−20	5	5	8	8	8	8	8

The cost of capital for all of the projects is 10%.

a. Calculate the NPV for the six projects.

b. Calculate the IRR for the six projects.

c. Calculate the MIRR for the six projects.

B18. (Excel: Mutually exclusive projects) Gloria Brick is preparing an economic analysis of the two mutually exclusive projects shown here:

PROJECT	CF_0	CF_1	CF_2	CF_3
1	−200	300	0	0
2	−200	0	0	400

The cost of capital is 10%.

a. What is the NPV and IRR for each project?

b. Calculate the NPV for each project assuming required rates of return of 0%, 5%, 10%, etc., up to 50%.

c. Graph the NPV profile for each project.

■ **LEVEL C (ADVANCED)**

C1. (Investment criteria) Nassau Manufacturing Company is considering two capital budgeting projects with a cost of capital of 15% and the expected cash flows shown here.

a. Calculate the NPV and IRR for each project.

Which project(s) should Nassau accept, assuming they are:

b. Independent?

c. Dependent (both or neither are required)?

d. Mutually exclusive?

YEAR	0	1	2	3	4	5
Project A	−100	25	30	40	30	25
Project B	−50	10	15	25	15	15

C2. (Excel: Multiple rates of return) Consider the oil pump cash flows given here:

TIME	0	1	2
Cash flow	−1,600	10,000	−10,000

a. Calculate the NPV for the oil pump using discount rates between 0% and 500%, in 25% increments.
b. What are the two internal rates of return?
c. Where is the highest NPV?
d. Graph the NPV profile.

MINICASE GETTING OFF THE GROUND AT BOEING

When the Boeing Corporation announced its intention to build a new plane, the project was an enormous undertaking. Research and development had already begun two and a half years earlier, and Boeing had already spent $873 million. Aggregate development cost, disregarding the time value of money, was expected to be between $4 billion and $5 billion. Production facilities and personnel training would require an additional investment of $2.0 billion, and they would need $1.7 billion in working capital when deliveries began in six years. The following table shows projected future cash flows for the project at the time of Boeing's announcement. Boeing's cost of capital was 18%.

CASH FLOW PROJECTIONS FOR THE BOEING PROJECT
(DOLLAR AMOUNTS IN MILLIONS)

Year	After-Tax Profit[a]	Depreciation	Capital Expenditures[b]	Year	After-Tax Profit[a]	Depreciation	Capital Expenditures[b]
1	(597.30)	40.00	400.00	18	1,691.19	129.20	178.41
2	(947.76)	96.00	600.00	19	1,208.64	96.99	627.70
3	(895.22)	116.40	300.00	20	1,954.39	76.84	144.27
4	(636.74)	124.76	200.00	21	2,366.03	65.81	100.51
5	(159.34)	112.28	182.91	22	2,051.46	61.68	(463.32)
6	958.62	101.06	1,741.42	23	1,920.65	57.96	(234.57)
7	1,718.14	90.95	2.12	24	2,244.05	54.61	193.92
8	1,503.46	82.72	(327.88)	25	2,313.63	52.83	80.68
9	1,665.46	77.75	67.16	26	2,384.08	52.83	83.10
10	1,670.49	75.63	(75.21)	27	2,456.65	52.83	85.59
11	1,553.76	75.00	(88.04)	28	2,531.39	52.83	88.16
12	1,698.99	75.00	56.73	29	2,611.89	47.52	90.80
13	1,981.75	99.46	491.21	30	2,699.26	35.28	93.53
14	1,709.71	121.48	32.22	31	2,785.50	28.36	96.33
15	950.83	116.83	450.88	32	2,869.63	28.36	99.22
16	1,771.61	112.65	399.53	33	2,956.28	28.36	102.20
17	1,958.48	100.20	(114.91)	34	3,053.65	16.05	105.26

[a]Includes expenditure for research and development.
[b]Includes changes in working capital. Negative values are caused by reductions in working capital.

QUESTIONS

1. Calculate the NPV, IRR, and payback for the project.

2. On the basis of your analysis, do you think Boeing should have continued with this project? Explain your reasoning.

WHY CAPITAL STRUCTURE MATTERS

11

A firm's mix of financing methods is called its **capital structure**. In simple terms, capital structure is the proportion of firm value financed with debt, the leverage ratio. That capital structure does not affect firm value—*in a perfect capital market environment*. Capital structure choice is a pure risk-return trade-off. We then showed that this is equivalent to saying that leverage does not affect the cost of capital—in a perfect capital market environment.

The question of whether capital structure affects firm value in real capital markets has been called the *capital structure puzzle*. Puzzle is a particularly appropriate term because our understanding has evolved in much the same way that a puzzle is pieced together. Currently, pieces are still being added, and we still do not have the complete picture.

Capital structure matters in practice if for no other reason than that firms actually behave as though it does. The empirical evidence shows consistent patterns of leverage ratios, as though there are definite reasons for following certain policies. Some argue that firms are simply following the Behavioral Principle of Finance—just copying each other—and that these patterns continue from habit and imitation even though they do not affect firm value. We believe this is too simplistic.

We have found that firms manage their capital structures carefully. The factors involved with choosing a capital structure are complex, and the impact of each factor on the value of the firm is not clear-cut. However, we can describe such factors using the three persistent capital market imperfections: asymmetric taxes, asymmetric information, and transaction costs.

In principle, a firm should balance the incremental advantage of more financial leverage against the incremental costs. Unfortunately, we cannot precisely measure all the factors.

A number of methods exist for analyzing the impact of alternative capital structures, but in the end, the choice of capital structure requires expert judgment. The analytical models give us a range of reasonable capital structures, rather than pinpointing the absolute best. In this chapter, we show you how a firm can take into account the various relevant factors to select an appropriate capital structure. The next chapter describes a practical method for managing capital structure.

FOCUS ON PRINCIPLES

- *Incremental Benefits:* Consider the possible ways to minimize the value lost to capital market imperfections, such as asymmetric taxes, asymmetric information, and transaction costs. At the same time, be sure to include all of the transaction costs of making potentially beneficial financing transactions, because they reduce the *net* benefit from such transactions.

- *Capital Market Efficiency:* Recognize that the potential to increase firm value through capital structure is smaller than the potential to increase firm value through the introduction of *valuable new ideas* and wise use of the firm's *comparative advantages.*

- *Signaling:* Consider any possible change in capital structure carefully, because financing transactions and capital structure changes convey information to outsiders and can be misunderstood.

- *Time Value of Money:* Include any time-value-of-money tax benefits from capital structure choices.

- *Valuable Ideas:* Look for opportunities to create value by issuing securities that are in short supply, perhaps resulting from changes in tax laws.

- *Behavioral:* Look to the information contained in the capital structure decisions and financing transactions of other firms for guidance in choosing a capital structure.

- *Risk-Return Trade-Off:* Recognize that capital structure changes made at fair-market security prices also change equity–debt risk bearing, and they are simply a risk-return trade-off. Such transactions do not affect firm value (except for possible signaling effects).

11.1 DOES CAPITAL STRUCTURE MATTER?

Capital structure does not affect a firm's value in a perfect capital market environment. Our Per-Pet example demonstrates that leverage is a pure risk-return trade-off in such an environment. This result is called the **perfect market view of capital structure**. Firm value depends only on its expected future operating cash flows and the cost of capital, not on how those cash flows are divided between the debtholders and the shareholders. The fundamental concept underlying the perfect market view is value conservation.

Let us review our Per-Pet example. With or without leverage, the total value of the firm is $1,000. With leverage, the shareholders get $500 in exchange for half their claim on the firm. Figure 11-1 illustrates these cases in terms of "pies." The total size of the pie is the same whether the firm is leveraged or all-equity financed. The only difference is in the claims on that pie. Figure 11-1 expresses the perfect market view in terms of total firm value, the present value of the expected future cash flows.

Figure 11-2 illustrates the perfect market view, but it does so in terms of the cost of capital, WACC, and the required returns on the expected future cash flows.

Recall that present value depends on both the cost of capital and the expected cash flows. If the cash flows do not change and the cost of capital does not change, then the present value must also remain constant. However, also recall that even though the leverage ratio L [the market-value proportion of debt financing—$D/(D+E)$] does not affect WACC, it does affect how the risk of the firm is borne by the shareholders and debtholders. Therefore, the required returns on equity and debt (r_e and r_d, respectively) depend on L.

FIGURE 11-1
A "pie" representation of the perfect market view of capital structure.

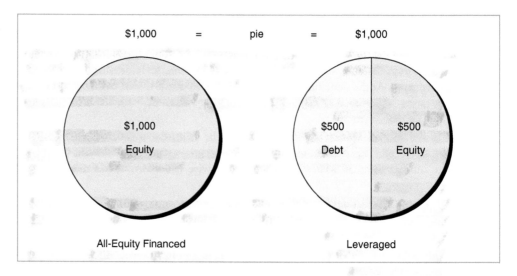

Finally, recall that the WACC can always be expressed as the weighted average cost of any financing package. With only equity and debt, the WACC is the weighted average of r_e and r_d adjusted for taxes,[1] or

(11.1)
$$WACC = (1 - L)r_e + L(1 - T)r_d$$

Note how the weight shifts from the higher return r_e to the lower return r_d as L increases and $(1 - L)$ decreases, leaving WACC unchanged.

Another way of illustrating capital structure irrelevance is with an arbitrage argument. We show below that if two firms have identical operating profitability but different capital structures, arbitrage among investors will ensure that the two firms have equal market values.

FIGURE 11-2
WACC (weighted average cost of capital), r_e (required return for equity), and r_d (required return for debt) as hypothetical functions of L (the leverage ratio) under the perfect market view of capital structure.

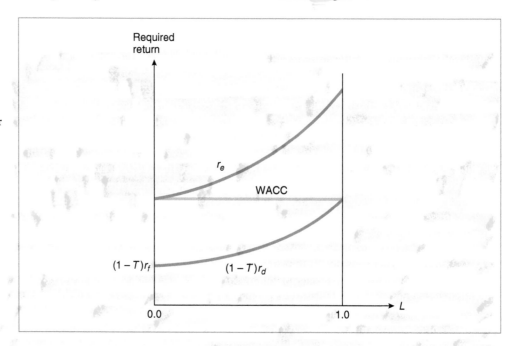

---

[1]The tax adjustment is necessary because interest payments are paid out *before* corporate taxes are levied on the firm's income, but dividends are not paid out until after taxes. See Figure 11-6 for a visual representation of this process that includes personal taxes.

	FIRM L	FIRM U
Leverage ratio [= debt/(debt + equity)]	50%	0
Operating income	$10,000,000	$10,000,000
− Interest expense[a]	3,600,000	0
Net income	$ 6,400,000	$10,000,000
Market value of equity	$30,000,000	$50,000,000
Market value of debt	30,000,000	0
Total market value	$60,000,000	$50,000,000

TABLE 11-1
An illustration of capital structure arbitrage.

[a]At a 12% interest rate.

An Arbitrage Argument

Consider two firms operating in a perfect capital market environment. Each will generate $10,000,000 of operating income. They are identical in every other respect except for their capital structures. Firm L is leveraged and has debt in its capital structure. Firm U is unleveraged; it has an all-equity capital structure. The two firms have the market values shown in Table 11-1. Firm L has a higher market value, supposedly because of its leverage.

According to the perfect market view, the situation shown in Table 11-1 cannot persist because of a profitable arbitrage opportunity. Shareholders of firm L can realize a greater return on their investment, with no increase in either their investment risk or the amount of funds they have invested, by making the following transactions. First, sell their shares of firm L. Second, borrow and create their own personal 50% leverage to duplicate firm L's capital structure. Third, use all the resulting cash to purchase shares of firm U. To illustrate this opportunity, consider the following example.

EXAMPLE Arbitraging Leverage-Valuation Differences

An investor owns 1% of the shares of firm L. The first step in the arbitrage process is to sell these shares at their market value of $300,000 (1% of $30,000,000). The second step is to borrow an identical amount, $300,000, at an interest rate of 12% per year. This creates a personal capital structure that is 50% debt and 50% equity, exactly firm L's capital structure. The final step is to use the total funds to purchase $600,000 (= 300,000 + 300,000) of firm U shares, which happens to be 1.20% (= 600,000/50,000,000) of firm U.

Now let us compare the return before and after. Before the three-step transaction, the investor's return per year is 1% of firm L's expected net income, $64,000. After, the return per year is $120,000 (1.20% of firm U's expected net income) minus an interest charge of $36,000 (12% of $300,000), or $84,000. Thus, without adding any funds, our investor has an investment with an identical amount of leverage (and therefore identical risk) that earns $20,000 (84,000 − 64,000) per year more after completing the arbitrage transaction.

With self-interested arbitrage activity, investors continue to sell firm L and buy firm U until their total market values (debt plus equity) are equal. Only when the total firm values are equal will there be no further profitable arbitrage opportunity.

Capital Market Imperfections

In our chapter introduction, we mentioned three persistent capital market imperfections: tax asymmetries, information asymmetries, and transaction costs. So an important place to look for value-changing market imperfections is in the tax code. Whenever tax rates differ for the two sides of a transaction, there is a tax asymmetry that might be used to enhance firm value. We will do this in the next section.

REVIEW

1. What is the perfect market view of capital structure?
2. What is the shape of the WACC curve according to the perfect market view?

11.2 THE ROLE OF INCOME TAXES

We have pointed out numerous times that interest payments are tax deductible to the firm, whereas dividend payments are not. This tax asymmetry gives rise to the **corporate tax view of capital structure**. In this view, corporate taxes cause debt to be cheaper than equity. The corporate tax view concludes that the maximum firm value results from being essentially all-*debt* financed.

Corporate Income Taxes

We will illustrate the corporate tax view by extending our Per-Pet example.

EXAMPLE **Corporate Taxes at Per-Pet, Inc.**

As in our Chapter 8 example, we will start with an all-equity firm and examine the effect of leverage on firm value. We assume that Per-Pet must pay corporate taxes on its net income at the rate of 37.5%, but it operates in an otherwise-perfect capital market environment. What is Per-Pet worth if it is all-equity financed, and what is it worth with leverage?

Per-Pet has a perpetual expected cash inflow each year of $150, which can be larger or smaller, but is never less than $50 per year. Therefore, its expected after-tax net income is $93.75 per year [= $(1 - 0.375)150$]. Per-Pet's cost of capital is 15%, so Per-Pet is worth $625 [= $93.75/0.15$], compared to a $1,000 value without corporate taxes.

Now suppose the firm borrows $500 at 10% per year and gives the $500 to the shareholders. This debt will require $50 per year in interest payments. Because the interest payments are made *before* corporate taxes are assessed, they cost only $31.25 [= $(1 - 0.375)50$] in after-tax cash flow. After the capital structure change, then, the residual expected future cash flow to be paid out to shareholders each year is $62.50 [= $93.75 - 31.25$].[2] Once again, the leverage would increase the shareholders' required return to 20%. Therefore, under the proposed leveraging, shareholders would get $500 from the debtholders in cash to invest as they wish and have a remaining invest-ment worth $312.50 [= $62.50/0.20$], for a total value of $812.50. Thus, in this environment, the proposed leveraging increases shareholder value by $187.50 [= $812.50 - 625.00$].

Simultaneously, the total value of Per-Pet would also increase by the same $187.50 amount. With no leverage, the firm is worth $625.00 [= $93.75/0.15$]. Under the proposed leveraging, total firm value is the value of the debt ($500) plus the value of the equity ($312.50), for a total value of $812.50.

The extra value for the Per-Pet shareholders can be traced directly to the tax asymmetry. The expected after-tax cash flows to investors increase because the government collects fewer tax dollars from the leveraged firm. Specifically, with the all-equity capital structure, the firm pays an

---

[2]This amount can also be computed starting with the firm's expected income of $150 per year: Subtract the $50 interest payment and apply the corporate tax rate so that $(1 - 0.375)(150 - 50) = 62.50.

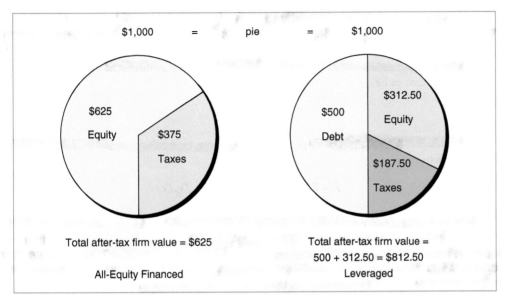

average tax of $56.25 [= (0.375)150] per year. It pays an average tax of only $37.50 [=(0.375)(150 − 50)] per year with the leveraged capital structure.

Figure 11-3 illustrates the corporate tax view of capital structure, showing the Per-Pet alternatives in terms of "pies." Once again, the total size of the pie is the same whether the firm is leveraged or all-equity financed, $1,000. The only difference is in the claims on the pie. However, this time, under the corporate tax view, there are three claimants: shareholders, debtholders, and the government. By selling part of the cash flow to the debtholders, the government collects less in taxes. This shrinks the government claim and leaves more for investors. Leverage increases the total after-tax firm value from $625 to $812.50.

The Cost of Capital with Corporate Income Taxes

Although leverage actually changes the after-tax cash flows, the effect can be equivalently accounted for by adjusting the cost of capital. Let $\bar{I}$ represent the expected perpetual cash inflow per year. Then the unleveraged firm pays taxes of $T\bar{I}$ each year, and the shareholders get the rest, an expected yearly after-tax cash flow $\bar{I}(1-T)$. The value of the unleveraged firm, V_U, is then

$$(11.2) \qquad V_U = \frac{\bar{I}(1-T)}{r}$$

where r is the unleveraged cost of capital (15% in the Per-Pet example).

In the Per-Pet example, we adjusted the after-tax cash flows and the required returns for equity (20%) and debt (10%) to find the value of the leveraged firm. Alternatively, we can represent the value of the leveraged firm, V_L, in terms of the "basic" after-tax cash flow to the firm and an appropriately adjusted cost of capital. The "basic" cash flow is the cash flow to the shareholders if the firm were unleveraged, $\bar{I}(1-T)$. This cash flow is what we called CFAT in capital budgeting. Then

$$(11.3) \qquad V_L = \frac{\bar{I}(1-T)}{\text{WACC}}$$

where WACC is the weighted average cost of capital, which has been adjusted for the effect of corporate taxes. Now we need to determine just what that adjustment is.

The firm uses an amount of debt, $D = LV_L$. Interest payments are $r_d D$, the interest rate times the amount of debt. The debtholders earn a *risky* (rather than riskless) amount each period, which has an expected payment of $r_d D$.

The firm pays taxes on all its income that is not paid out as interest. So the firm's annual taxes are expected to be

$$T(\bar{I} - r_d D)$$

The combined after-tax cash flow expected to be paid out to debtholders and shareholders is a yearly perpetuity of

$$\bar{I} - T(\bar{I} - r_d D) = \bar{I}(1 - T) + Tr_d D$$

The cash flows in this equation do not all have the same risk. The tax savings due to interest ($Tr_d D$) have exactly the same riskiness as the debt (because they are strictly proportional to the debt), so the tax savings are discounted at r_d. The "basic" after-tax cash flow to equity is discounted at r, because the equity cash flow is riskier than the debt payments. The value of the leveraged firm is then the present value of these two cash flow streams:

(11.4)
$$V_L = \frac{\bar{I}(1 - T)}{r} + \frac{Tr_d D}{r_d} = \frac{\bar{I}(1 - T)}{r} + TD$$

Because $\bar{I}(1 - T)/r$ is equal to the value of the unleveraged firm, from Equation (11.2):

(11.5)
$$V_L = V_U + TD$$

This is the most common way of mathematically expressing the corporate tax view. The value of the leveraged firm is equal to the value of the unleveraged firm plus the tax rate times the amount of debt.

We can build on this result. A value for WACC can be derived by setting Equations (11.3) and (11.4) equal to each other and solving for WACC. We will spare you the details, and just give you the result:

(11.6)
$$\text{WACC} = r(1 - TL)$$

Figure 11-4 illustrates the corporate tax view of capital structure in terms of the WACC and hypothetical functions for the required returns on equity and debt. Note that the function for WACC is a straight line. WACC decreases as leverage increases. The lowest value for WACC, $r(1 - TL)$ occurs when the firm is financed entirely with debt, that is, when $L = D/(D + E) = 1.0$. Under the corporate tax view, the optimal capital structure—the one that creates the most valuable firm—is the one that contains as much debt as possible.

EXAMPLE The Cost of Capital at Per-Pet, Inc.

Now we can check our work by applying the adjusted cost of capital given in Equation (11.6) to our Per-Pet example with corporate taxes. Under the proposed leveraging, the firm borrows $500, and leveraged firm value is $812.50. This means that Per-Pet's leveraged capital structure would be $L = D/(D + E) = 0.61538$ (= 500/812.50). (Remember, the leverage ratio is based on market values.) What is Per-Pet's cost of capital under the proposed leveraging?

From Equation (11.6), we have

$$\text{WACC} = r(1 - TL) = (0.15)[1 - (0.375)(0.61538)] = 0.115385 = 11.5385\%$$

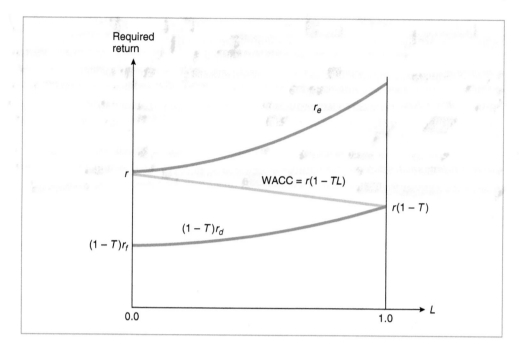

FIGURE 11-4
WACC (weighted average cost of capital), r_e (required return for equity), and r_d (required return for debt), as hypothetical functions of L (the leverage ratio) under the corporate tax view of capital structure.

Alternatively, we can also find the WACC using Equation (11.1):

$$\text{WACC} = (1 - L)r_e + L(1 - T)r_d$$
$$= (0.38462)(0.20) + (0.61538)(1 - 0.375)(0.10) = 0.115385 = 11.5385\%$$

We can also verify that our adjustment produces the correct value for V_L using this WACC and Per-Pet's CFAT of $93.75 in Equation (11.3):

$$V_L = \frac{\overline{I}(1 - T)}{\text{WACC}} = \frac{93.75}{0.115385} = \$812.50$$

Before moving on, we want to emphasize the equivalence between (1) adjusting the WACC and (2) adjusting the after-tax cash flows and required returns on equity and debt. The first method, adjusting the WACC, is more commonly used, probably because of convenience. It involves only a single adjustment.

Also, it is important to reemphasize that *the leverage ratio is based on market values.*

REVIEW

1. What is the corporate tax view of capital structure?
2. Why does the U.S. corporate tax system seem to favor debt financing over equity financing?
3. What is the shape of the WACC curve according to the corporate tax view?

Personal Income Taxes

From an income tax perspective, our Per-Pet corporate tax example is incomplete. There are other significant taxes besides corporate income taxes. The firm pays taxes on its income, but investors then pay personal income taxes on their income from the firm. And the rates investors pay are not all the same. The rates depend on the form of the investment, in particular whether it is equity or debt.

Interest and dividends are taxed when they are received, but capital gains are not taxed until the asset is sold. Therefore, a shareholder can postpone the tax on a gain by not selling the shares. At the same time, there is a mirror-image treatment of losses. The shareholder can claim the tax shield resulting from a loss right away by selling the asset. This creates a valuable tax-timing option. The capital gain tax-timing option lowers the effective tax rate on shareholder income. In turn, this lower effective rate leads to the **personal tax view of capital structure**. According to this view, the firm is still operating in a perfect capital market environment, except for corporate *and* personal income taxes.

The personal tax view concludes that the differential between tax rates on personal income from equity and from debt cancels out the corporate tax asymmetry. The outcome is that leverage has no effect on firm value in this environment and, once again, capital structure is irrelevant.

To illustrate the personal tax view of capital structure, let us extend our Per-Pet example one more time.

EXAMPLE **Personal Taxes at Per-Pet, Inc.**

Once again, we will start with an all-equity firm and examine the effect of leverage on firm value. Suppose Per-Pet's debtholders' tax rate is 50%, whereas the shareholders' rate is 20%. Per-Pet's corporate tax rate is the same 37.5%, and it operates in an otherwise-perfect capital market environment. What is Per-Pet worth if it is all-equity financed, and what is it worth with leverage?

After paying 20% in personal taxes, the shareholders get to keep 80% [= 1.0 − 0.20] of their cash flow from the firm, which after corporate taxes is expected to be $93.75 [= (1 − 0.375)150]. With an all-equity capital structure, then, the shareholders' expected cash flow after corporate *and* personal taxes is $75.00 [= (0.8)93.75]. On the basis of Per-Pet's 15% unleveraged cost of capital, Per-Pet is worth $500 [= 75.00/0.15].

Now suppose the firm borrows $250 at an after-personal-taxes required return of 10%. So the debtholders must receive 10% of $250, or $25 after taxes. Therefore, the interest payment from the firm must be $50 [= 25/(1 − 0.5)] per year. After the interest payment and corporate taxes, the shareholders have an expected income of $62.50 [= (1 − 0.375)(150 − 50)], on which they must pay personal taxes. Therefore, under the proposed leveraging, the shareholders have an expected annual cash flow after corporate and personal taxes of $50 [= (1 − 0.2)62.50]. Again, the leverage would increase the shareholders' required return to 20%. Under the proposed leveraging, then, shareholders would get $250 from the debtholders in cash to invest as they wish and have a remaining investment in Per-Pet worth $250 [= 50/0.20]. Thus, shareholders will have the same total value of $500 whether or not the firm is leveraged.

The total value of Per-Pet is not changed, and capital structure is irrelevant in this environment. In both cases, the firm is worth $500—either $500 worth of equity, or $250 worth of equity plus $250 worth of debt.

Figure 11-5 illustrates the personal tax view of capital structure, showing the alternatives in our Per-Pet example with personal taxes in terms of "pies." In this case, the total size of the pie is the same and the total taxes paid are the same. The only difference is the amounts paid of each type of tax. With all-equity financing, more corporate taxes and less personal taxes are paid than under the proposed leveraging. So in this case the total after-tax value is $500 either way.

If it occurs to you that the results illustrated in Figure 11-5 depend on the personal tax rates we use, you are right. The critical issue is the amount that reaches the investor after corporate and

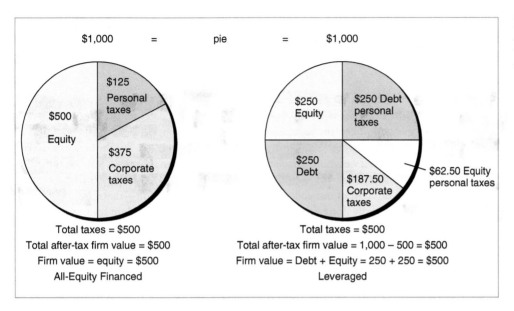

FIGURE 11-5
A "pie" representation of
the personal tax view of
capital structure.

personal taxes. Let T_d, T_e, and T represent the tax rates for debtholders, equityholders, and the corporation, respectively. The difference in equity and debt personal taxes exactly cancels out the corporate tax asymmetry *only* when

(11.7)
$$(1 - T_d) = (1 - T_e)(1 - T)$$

When this condition holds, the effective tax rates are the same and the after-corporate-and-personal-taxes portion of the firm's cash flow that "reaches" an investor is the same, whether the investor has an equity or debt claim. That is, a before-tax dollar singly taxed at T_d provides the same net amount to an investor as a before-tax dollar taxed at T and then taxed again at T_e.

EXAMPLE Neutral Tax Rates

If T_e = 10%, T = 30%, and T_d = 37%, then Equation (11.7) is satisfied:

$$(1 - 0.37) = (1 - 0.1)(1 - 0.3) = 0.63$$

Figure 11-6 illustrates the tax process using these tax rates. Note once again how the cash flows to the shareholders are taxed twice, whereas those going to the debtholders are taxed only once, but at a higher rate.

		Before-tax firm income	minus	Corporate taxes	minus	Personal taxes	equals	After-tax investor income	Recipient
$2.00 Before-tax income	FIRM	$1.00		−0.30		−0.07		$0.63	Shareholder
		$1.00		−0.00		−0.37		$0.63	Debtholder

FIGURE 11-6   An example of corporate and personal taxation of cash flows going to shareholders and debtholders.

It is important to understand that the personal tax view that capital structure is irrelevant depends on having tax rates that satisfy Equation (11.7).

Combined Effect of Corporate and Personal Income Taxes

Suppose tax rates are such that (1) personal taxes do not *exactly* cancel out the corporate tax asymmetry and (2) the single tax rate on debt income is smaller than the combined tax rate on corporate income and equity returns. Then the conclusion of the corporate tax view of capital structure still holds—more leverage increases firm value by reducing the net loss to taxes. But the benefit to leverage is significantly less than if we ignore personal taxes. Therefore, even if personal taxes do not eliminate the corporate tax asymmetry, they significantly reduce it, along with the net benefit to leverage.

We believe—as do most of our colleagues in the finance profession—that there is a net tax benefit to leverage. If so, why don't firms employ 100% leverage? We explore reasons for this in the next three sections of the chapter.

> ### REVIEW
>
> 1. What is the personal tax view of capital structure?
> 2. How can the personal tax view reach the same conclusion as the perfect market view concerning the irrelevance of capital structure?

11.3 THE ROLE OF AGENCY COSTS AND FINANCIAL DISTRESS COSTS

Certain conflicts of interest among the debtholders, shareholders, and managers that are caused by the problem of asymmetric information create agency costs (see Chapter 14). These conflicts give rise to the **agency cost view of capital structure**. In this view, capital market imperfections resulting from agency costs create a complex environment in which capital structure affects a firm's value. This view also concludes that a firm's value is maximized by a mixture of debt and equity.

Agency Costs of Debt

A major conflict that arises from the use of debt financing is the possibility that shareholders will expropriate wealth from the debtholders through *asset substitution*. Suppose that debtholders loan money to the firm assuming that the firm will invest in a low-risk project; therefore, they agree to a low interest rate on the loan. If the firm then invests in a (substitute) high-risk project, the risk of the loan will increase. This increases the required return on the loan and lowers the present value of the loan.

As a second example, consider the problem of *claim dilution*. Assume the firm has existing debt and the firm's managers do a leveraged buyout. That is, they take over ownership of the firm with a very small amount of equity financing and a tremendous amount of debt. What happens to the value of the original debt? Because of the higher risk, the present value of the original debt decreases, and the decrease is lost by those debtholders, but gained by the shareholders.[3]

However, the asset-substitution and claim-dilution agency costs may not be significant for low levels of leverage. Furthermore, the use of leverage may provide some benefits to shareholders. The bondholders will provide some monitoring of management activities that may benefit shareholders. The bond restrictive covenants in bond contracts may also protect shareholders from managerial abuse in addition to protecting bondholders. Small amounts of debt may

---

[3]Other debtholder–stockholder conflicts that are relevant to a firm's capital structure include the underinvestment problem and the effect of asset uniqueness.

actually benefit the corporation. Of course, at higher debt levels, the effects of asset substitution and claim dilution could more than offset the agency benefits of debt financing.

Agency conflicts among the firm's various claimants must be resolved in some way. When possible, contracts that eliminate these conflicts are created. For example, restrictive covenants, such as a restriction on leverage, are used to limit potential conflicts. The agency costs of debt tend to increase with leverage. These costs limit how much leverage is beneficial to shareholders.

The trade-off among the agency costs of all the firm's various claimants (stakeholders) leads to the agency cost view. This view holds that the optimal capital structure is a mix of multiple types of securities, rather than simply all debt or all equity. A financing mix reduces the firm's *total* agency costs.

There is also an aspect of debt financing that reduces the firm's agency costs: the benefits of the debtholders monitoring the shareholders, and of the shareholders monitoring the managers. Whenever the firm issues new debt, prospective debtholders will analyze the firm very carefully to determine a fair price to offer for the debt. Each time new debt is issued, then, existing debtholders and shareholders are provided with a free outside "audit" of the firm. This outside audit reduces the cost of monitoring to ensure that agents (managers) are acting responsibly.

Debt can also reduce problems of asymmetric information. For example, a sinking fund provides monitoring. With a sinking fund, the firm must be able to meet the periodic required payments in addition to the interest payments. Difficulty in doing so can provide a relatively early warning that the firm is in trouble. Inability to make the required sinking fund payments can trigger default. Obviously, this monitoring function is beneficial for debtholders, but it also provides further monitoring of the managers for the benefit of the shareholders.

Securing debt by using specific tangible assets as collateral can play a role in reducing the agency costs of debt. Secured debt limits the potential for debtholder loss in case of bankruptcy, thereby limiting the amount of wealth shareholders can expropriate from the debtholders. Assets securing a debt instrument cannot be sold without the permission of the debtholders or the bankruptcy court.

REVIEW

1. What is the agency cost view of capital structure?
2. How does increased leverage provide incentives for asset substitution?

Financial Distress and Bankruptcy Costs

With debt in its capital structure, a firm has an expected cost of bankruptcy. This gives rise to the **bankruptcy cost view of capital structure**. In this view, capital market imperfections associated with financial distress and bankruptcy offset the net benefits from leverage due to taxes and agency costs.

IT IS AN EXPECTED COST   Financial distress or bankruptcy costs occur only if financial distress or bankruptcy actually occurs. Therefore, it is important to note that with an ongoing firm that is not in financial distress, the cost is a mathematical expectation. This expected value is considerably less than the actual cost when there is only a small chance of bankruptcy.

The expected cost of financial distress and bankruptcy includes *indirect costs* and *direct costs*, such as notification costs, court costs, and legal fees. Somewhat surprisingly, the direct costs are relatively small when compared with the firm's value or the indirect costs of bankruptcy.

The indirect costs of financial distress and bankruptcy can involve virtually every aspect of the firm. It can be very costly to have management's attention diverted from the day-to-day operation of the business in order to deal with the financial distress and bankruptcy process. After filing for bankruptcy, every major decision a firm makes may require approval by the bankruptcy court. When financial distress occurs, suppliers may refuse to ship goods other than on a COD basis, or even refuse to ship altogether. For example, at one point, K-Mart experienced financial difficulties that led many suppliers to halt shipments of goods.

A firm may lose tax shields during periods of financial distress. This is another tax asymmetry that can affect a firm's value.[4] Loss carryforwards and loss carrybacks are sometimes limited. As a result, some of the corporate tax shields due to leverage may be lost during a period of financial distress. Even if all current losses can be fully carried forward and eventually deducted from future income, the firm still loses the time value of money on the tax shields. So the possibility of lost tax-shield value limits the net tax benefits of leverage and makes "too much" leverage undesirable.

The most significant potential cost of financial distress and bankruptcy is an indirect cost that can be difficult to measure but should not be underestimated. It arises because of the possibility that the firm will not continue as a going concern. This likelihood is important, because it can dramatically affect the value of the firm's products. Consider the case when consumers believe the firm may not be able to honor warranties, provide service, or even supply replacement parts in the future. Such a belief can dramatically hurt sales, as it once did for a U.S. car manufacturer in financial distress.[5]

When potential customers fear product discontinuation, they will force the firm to sell its product for a lower price than what it would otherwise be worth. The lower price reduces and can easily eliminate the manufacturer's profit margin on the product. This forgone profit can be very substantial. In fact, even though it is an opportunity cost that is difficult to measure, *this loss is the largest of the financial distress and bankruptcy costs by a wide margin.*

EFFECT OF LEVERAGE   The expected costs of financial distress and bankruptcy depend in part on the uniqueness, or degree of specialization, of the firm's assets. The higher the degree of specialization, the lower the degree of liquidity and the greater the sales transaction costs. In the extreme case, a specially designed piece of equipment that is unique to just one firm's production process might be worth only its scrap value if the firm goes bankrupt.

An argument similar to the argument concerning specialized assets also applies to a firm's type of assets: A firm with primarily tangible assets can borrow more than an otherwise comparable firm with primarily intangible assets (such as patents and trademarks). Intangible assets are less liquid and have higher sales transaction costs than tangible assets, and their value may be more firm specific. The values of patents and trademarks depend on how they are used and on past conditions. Another firm may not be able to realize as much value from them. For example, the good-service reputation of a trademark product may be damaged or even destroyed by bad service resulting from otherwise-unrelated financial distress problems. As a consequence, firms with more intangible assets have greater expected bankruptcy costs.

The effect on capital structure of possible financial distress and bankruptcy costs is as follows. Suppose all other factors—such as personal and corporate taxes, agency costs, and other transaction costs—combined create a net value benefit to leverage, thereby making leverage desirable. But leverage will be desirable only up to a certain point because, as the firm increases its debt financing, expected bankruptcy costs also increase and offset that benefit. So bankruptcy costs

---

[4]This loss includes lost tax deductions and lost tax credits. Tax credits are the more valuable of the two. Tax credits offset taxes owed dollar for dollar. Tax deductions reduce taxable income; their value equals the tax rate times the reduction in the amount of taxable income.

[5]This possibility helped convince the U.S. Congress to provide loan guarantees for the Chrysler Corporation when it was in financial distress. The loan guarantees made Chrysler's warranties and promises of future service and parts availability believable.

reduce the net value benefit of leverage and make "too much" leverage undesirable. (Of course, if there were no net benefit to leverage from all the other factors combined, expected bankruptcy costs would make it so that even the first dollar of leverage would reduce a firm's value and therefore be undesirable.)

The bankruptcy effect produces an "optimal" capital structure that balances the expected bankruptcy cost against the other benefits. This is similar to the net effect of the various agency costs. Also like agency costs, a solution is hard to quantify. The bankruptcy view, however, is more realistic than the corporate tax view, because it does not call for the extreme of 100% debt financing.

REVIEW

1. What is the bankruptcy cost view of capital structure?
2. Describe the difference between the direct and indirect costs of financial distress and bankruptcy. Which is more significant?
3. Explain why "too much" leverage is undesirable if the firm may lose tax shields.
4. Why do tangible assets support higher leverage than intangible assets?

11.4 EXTERNAL FINANCING TRANSACTION COSTS

The transaction costs associated with obtaining new external financing can play an important role in a firm's capital structure decisions. As in the case of bankruptcy, there are both direct and indirect costs. These costs lead to the **pecking order view of capital structure**. In the pecking order view, firms use internally generated funds as much as possible for financing new projects. New debt is less preferred than internal funds, but more preferable than other sources of financing. Debt–equity combinations, such as convertible debt, are third in the pecking order, with securities that have smaller proportions of equity being preferred to those with larger proportions of equity. Last in the pecking order is new external equity.

The cost of obtaining new financing affects the firm's management of its capital structure. These costs affect the firm's capital structure decisions over time in a dynamic way.

The transaction costs associated with obtaining new external financing make it much more costly for a firm to sell a series of small issues compared with issuing a single large amount when it needs to obtain additional external funds. So the firm should sell larger issues, less often, to reduce the net transaction costs of new external financing.

The idea of issuing a relatively large amount of a security when the firm obtains new external financing does not imply a preference for any particular method of financing. However, it does imply that the dynamic management of the firm's capital structure is important to the value of the firm. A firm can waste resources on issuance expenses if it does not manage its capital structure carefully.

Concerning particular methods, the total cost of new debt (negotiating private debt or the combination of the underwriting spread and direct issuance expenses connected with public debt) is typically lower than the total cost of obtaining other new external financing. Therefore, whether or not other factors create a net value benefit to leverage, debt is generally attractive *relative* to equity when a firm has already decided that it is going to obtain additional outside financing.

Signaling and the Choice of Financing Method

A firm's decision about how to finance a project reflects its choice of capital structure. It may also convey information about the project and about how the firm's managers view its current market value.

Consider two examples. The first illustrates how the choice between internal (equity) and external financing can convey information about project value. The second illustrates how the debt–equity choice can convey information about any perceived under- or overvaluation of the firm's shares.

EXAMPLE Internal Financing Versus Issuing Securities

Two firms, G and N, are identical except for new projects they are about to undertake. G has a good project that has a large positive NPV, whereas N has a neutral project that has a zero NPV. The owners of G are eager to provide the financing for the new project themselves, using personal funds so that they alone will earn the large expected NPV. In contrast, the owners of N are indifferent to allowing outside investors to invest in the new project because it has a zero NPV. Generalizing the argument, then, the percentage of owner financing may provide a signal of the owners' opinion of investment opportunities.

EXAMPLE Debt Versus Equity Financing

Suppose the shareholders know the firm is currently overvalued. They would like to have partners to share in the decline in market value that will take place in the future when others realize the firm is overvalued. Suppose instead they know the firm is currently undervalued. Then they would not want to have new partners who will get a share of the increase in market value that will take place in the future when others realize the firm is undervalued. Shareholders of properly valued firms would be indifferent to having new partners.

This leads to the idea that if additional financing is needed, the firm will choose debt or equity depending on whether or not they want new partners. That is, undervalued firms will issue new debt, whereas overvalued firms will issue new equity. Of course, in this simple world we have just described, shareholders of overvalued firms may not want to be identified as such. Therefore, they may try to imitate undervalued firms by issuing debt instead of equity. Situations such as this will require other information to allow investors to interpret the firm's actions.

Sometimes firms with existing publicly traded stock issue additional new shares. Apparently, therefore, there are cases when managers believe a new project is sufficiently good to justify the potential loss connected with issuing new equity.

One way in which firms may try to overcome the negative impression of issuing additional new shares is to use underwriters, rather than selling securities themselves. This can be especially useful if there is a need to protect trade secrets. The underwriter may be able to "certify" the value of the firm and its new projects by standing ready to purchase all the new shares without revealing (and therefore destroying the value of) certain types of private information.

Changes in Capital Structure

Evidence indicates that the stock market reacts favorably to increases in leverage and negatively to decreases in leverage. Investors apparently interpret an increase in leverage as a signal that the firm's prospects have improved. Its future cash flow will support greater leverage. A decrease in leverage signals the opposite. Weaker prospects reduce the firm's ability to service debt.

REVIEW

1. Based on the transaction costs of obtaining funds, what is the pecking order among internally generated funds, external debt financing, external debt–equity financing (such as convertible debt), and external equity?
2. Why is internal financing often a more positive signal about the firm than external financing?
3. Why is debt financing often a more positive signal about the firm than equity financing?

11.5   FINANCIAL LEVERAGE CLIENTELES

Both personal tax and corporate tax considerations affect the desirability of a particular capital structure. Investors will take their own tax situations into account in deciding whether to invest in a particular firm. The idea that investors "sort" themselves into groups, where each group prefers the firms it invests in to follow a certain type of policy, is called the **clientele effect**.

How the Clientele Effect Works

When applied to financial leverage, the clientele effect refers to those investors who prefer a particular type of security or capital structure. A similar concept in marketing is called *market segmentation*. A market segment is an identifiable group of consumers who purchase a product with particular attributes distinct from the attributes of alternative products. An example would be a market segment that buys luxury cars versus one that buys economy cars.

The existence of various leverage clienteles mitigates some, but not all, of the arguments in favor of capital structure relevance. With respect to taxes, some securities may be more or less attractive for certain investors. For example, investors with a high marginal income tax rate may find debt securities less attractive, whereas tax-exempt investors may find debt securities relatively more attractive. Similarly, investors with a low marginal income tax rate may prefer firm leverage to personal leverage because of the higher corporate tax rate. The interest expenses generate more tax savings for the corporation than they would for an individual if the corporation has the higher tax rate. Investors can increase their risk and lower combined corporate and personal taxes (and avoid transaction costs of personal leverage) by simply investing in a firm that already has their preferred amount of leverage.

Taxes and transaction costs reduce the return to shareholders. Therefore, investors should, and do, invest in securities that minimize their aggregate taxes and transaction costs for any particular combination of risk and return. The result of taking taxes and transaction costs into account is that a particular clientele group may pay a premium for a certain type of security. (Note that the premium is measured relative to the prices of securities that are equivalent.) Such a premium gives firms an incentive to follow particular policies that appeal to various clientele groups. Of course, this is simply another application of the Principle of Valuable Ideas: Being the first to have the idea has the potential to create value.

The result is that it may be possible to earn a premium for supplying a security or capital structure policy that is in short supply. (Note that this gain must be weighed against the transaction costs of investors' rearranging their security holdings.) Whenever a law is changed that affects the taxes and transaction costs for a particular financial leverage clientele, opportunities may arise for a firm to earn a positive NPV by changing its capital structure.

Practical Limitations

Opportunities to profit from capital structure changes have natural limitations. First, direct transaction costs to the firm reduce the potential benefit from a change in capital structure. Second, shareholder transaction costs make it expensive for investors to buy and sell shares. This can affect the market price of the firm's stock.

These factors make sudden or frequent shifts in a firm's capital structure generally undesirable. A sudden shift may be disruptive to the firm's stock price in the near term, and frequent major shifts may be disruptive over the longer term.

In practice, most firms maintain a stable capital structure. It appears, then, that firms depart from a stable capital structure only when the managers believe there are valid reasons to do so. These reasons include significant changes in the firm's investment opportunities, its earnings, or its own or its shareholders' tax position.

> ### REVIEW
>
> 1. Explain what is meant by the clientele effect.
> 2. According to the clientele effect, investors with low marginal income tax rates should prefer to invest in firms with high leverage. Do you agree? Explain.
> 3. How might a firm profit when a change in tax law causes a particular financial leverage clientele to change its investment preferences?

11.6 THE CAPITAL MARKET IMPERFECTIONS VIEW OF CAPITAL STRUCTURE

Taken in total, the view that emerges from the various factors we have discussed can be characterized as a dynamic process that involves various trade-offs and results in a general preference order among a firm's financing alternatives. We call this the **capital market imperfections view of capital structure**. In this view, debt is generally valuable.

With a low amount of leverage, there is little chance of incurring financial distress, so the *expected* value of the costs of financial distress is low. Therefore, an increase in leverage at lower levels offers benefits from taxes and agency considerations (monitoring and reducing asymmetric information problems). At lower levels of leverage, these benefits dominate the combination of agency costs (misbehavior) and expected costs of financial distress. At some point, the set of costs overcomes the set of benefits. Along the way, dynamic considerations involving transaction costs, asymmetric information considerations, and monitoring benefits also affect the attractiveness of the various alternative types of financing at particular points in time.

The firm's choice of capital structure, then, is a dynamic process that involves all these various considerations in conjunction with its investment opportunities and the amount of internal funds it is able to generate. The firm "factors them all in" when deciding on the type, amount, and timing of new external financing.

Total Market Value and Market Imperfections

The optimal capital structure is the one that maximizes the firm's total value. Figure 11-7 is a conceptual picture of the effect on firm value of all the various factors we have examined. It is not as complicated as it looks. Let's walk through it. In the figure, V_T is the value of the unleveraged firm plus the net tax benefits. V_A is the agency cost of debt. V_A is initially positive, because of the benefits from monitoring and reducing problems of asymmetric information. Leverage is initially beneficial to the firm. At higher amounts of leverage, this benefit begins declining and becomes negative because of conflicts of interest. V_B is the expected financial distress and bankruptcy costs. They are zero for low amounts of leverage but become ever-increasingly negative for the firm when leverage increases. Finally, V_L is the total value of the leveraged firm, including the effects of taxes, agency costs, and financial distress costs.

Let's summarize. For low amounts of leverage, the tax benefit and the agency considerations lead to increases in the total value of the firm. Eventually, however, the negative effects

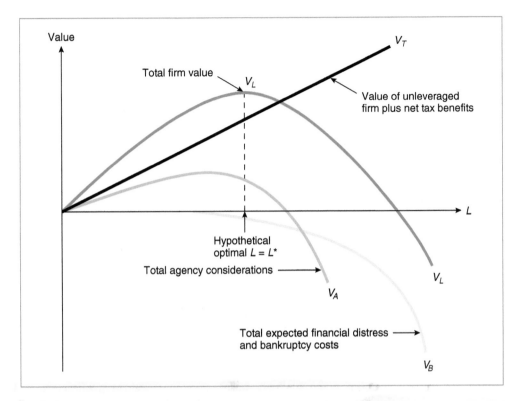

FIGURE 11-7
The capital market
imperfections view of
capital structure.

consisting of the expected costs of financial distress, bankruptcy, and agency considerations offset the benefits, resulting in an optimal capital structure at the point in the figure where the total value of the firm is at its maximum.

It is important to understand that Figure 11-7 is only a "snapshot"; it cannot include the dynamic considerations that transaction costs, asymmetric information considerations, and monitoring benefits connected with external financing introduce into the picture. These managerial considerations mean that the "optimal" capital structure is not a simple fixed proportion of debt financing.

The Cost of Capital and Market Imperfections

Figure 11-7 illustrates the capital market imperfections view in terms of a firm's total value. Once again, the view can be represented in a corresponding way in terms of the firm's WACC, its weighted average cost of capital. The optimal capital structure is the point where firm value reaches its maximum by minimizing the firm's WACC.

Figure 11-8 illustrates the capital market imperfections view of capital structure that takes into account all of the factors we have discussed. In Figure 11-8, WACC is expressed in terms of hypothetical functions of r_d and r_e.

Figure 11-8 is a "snapshot" like Figure 11-7. So choosing the firm's optimal capital structure is in truth more complex than these figures indicate. Although Figure 11-8 provides a visual aid to understanding the impact of capital structure on the WACC, we need an equation for WACC to determine more-precise values.

The Net Benefit to Leverage

To capture the impact of *all* the relevant dimensions connected with debt financing, define T^* as the **net-benefit-to-leverage factor**. T^* is assumed to be derived from a linear approximation to the actual net-benefit-to-leverage relationship over some relevant range of values for the leverage

FIGURE 11-8
WACC (weighted aver-
age cost of capital), r_e
(required return for
equity), and r_d (required
return for debt) as hypo-
thetical functions of L
(the leverage ratio) under
the capital market
imperfections view of
capital structure.

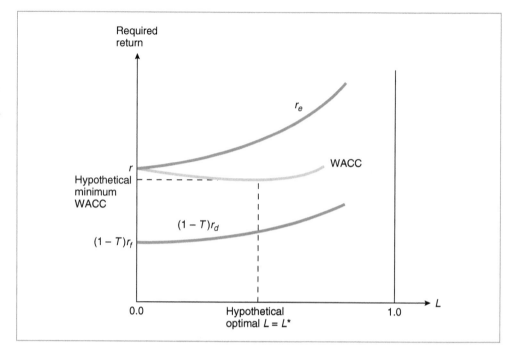

ratio L. T^* allows us to operationalize the total impact of leverage on firm value in the capital market imperfections view. We can use the same sort of mathematics we used with the corporate tax view to adjust the WACC for all of the relevant factors. In this more-general case, we can express the value of the leveraged firm as

$$(11.8) \qquad V_L = V_U + T^*D = \frac{\overline{I}(1-T)}{r} + \frac{T^* r_d D}{r_d}$$

which is a generalization of Equation (11.5).

Once again, V_L can be viewed as being made up of two components. The first component is the basic value of the firm if it is unleveraged, V_U. The second component is the net benefit to leverage. Each component represents the present value of a stream of expected future cash flows. The first stream is $\overline{I}(1-T)$, the firm's after-tax income each period, its CFAT. The second stream is the net benefit from maintaining an amount D of debt. This net benefit can be expressed as T^* times the interest payment each period, or $T^* r_d D$.

For the perpetuity case, the present value is simply these cash flow streams divided by their required returns. The required return for the firm's (unleveraged) after-tax income stream, its CFAT, is r. Because of lower risk, the required return for the net-benefit-to-leverage stream is r_d, which is lower than r.

Finally, the parallel is completed by expressing the impact on firm value in terms of the firm's WACC (its required return). As before, we will not prove it, but the result is

$$(11.9) \qquad \text{WACC} = r(1 - T^*L)$$

The usefulness of Equation (11.9) is based on how easily it fits into our framework for making capital budgeting decisions. It is simply an adjustment made to the project's cost of capital, which accounts for the effect of leverage on project value. The adjusted rate is then used to compute the present value of the project's CFATs, its NPV.

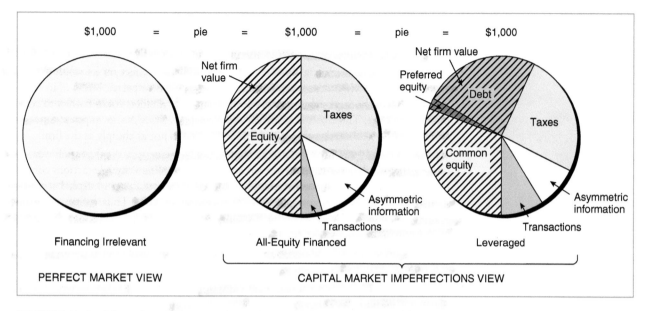

FIGURE 11-9   These three "pie" views of capital structure illustrate the loss of firm value from all the various capital market imperfections and the minimization of that loss through the choice of capital structure.

Total Firm Value and Capital Market Imperfections

There is one final point we want to make. All of the views of capital structure, beyond that of a perfect capital market, are based on minimizing the value lost to one or more imperfections. Therefore, even though we talk about using leverage to increase firm value, in fact we are actually describing ways to use leverage to *reduce the loss* connected with various imperfections. What this means is that the total value of the firm is never more than what it would be in a perfect capital market. We illustrate this point in Figure 11-9 by using three "pie" views of a $1,000 firm.

In Figure 11-9 the far-left "pie" shows the perfect market view. In it, there is no loss in value from imperfections. A firm's value does not depend on its capital structure. The other two pies reflect the capital market imperfections view of capital structure. In them, a dynamic optimal capital structure minimizes the total loss from all the various imperfections. In the middle pie, the firm is all-equity financed. In the far-right pie, the firm has multiple types and amounts of financing that might typically be found in the practice of financial management.

The net benefit to leverage can be seen in Figure 11-9. It is the difference between the value of the firm on the far right (the combined values of common equity, preferred equity, and debt) and the value of the firm in the middle pie (the equity value). However, despite this positive net benefit to leverage, the total value of the firm on the far right is substantially less than what the firm value would be in a perfect capital market. This is because of losses to capital market imperfections.

REVIEW

1. What is the capital market imperfections view of capital structure?
2. What is the shape of the WACC curve according to the capital market imperfections view?
3. What is the net-benefit-to-leverage factor?

SUMMARY

- The critical issue concerning capital structure is whether it affects the value of the firm.
- In a perfect capital market, a firm's capital structure has no effect on its value. A firm's value is based entirely on the profitability of its assets and the expected NPVs of its future projects. Even if leverage enhanced investment value, shareholders could borrow to create personal leverage. Therefore, in a perfect capital market, firms cannot capture any value due to leverage because shareholders can do it themselves just as cheaply as the firm.
- But our financial system contains some important persistent imperfections. Information is not costless and freely available to everyone, so the Signaling Principle (actions contain information) is a very important consideration. Capital structure and capital structure changes may provide information about the firm to the public. Thus, a firm should be careful to choose the best method of financing, taking all costs into account—including the information investors will infer from the firm's financing transactions.
- There are other market imperfections. The system of corporate income taxation imposes a bias in favor of debt over equity, as do issuance costs.
- However, the system of individual income taxation, as well as direct and indirect financial distress/bankruptcy costs, have an opposite bias.
- Aggregate agency costs and tax-timing options both favor a mix of debt and equity rather than using one or the other exclusively. Taken together, these market imperfections lead to a view that there is some dynamic optimal capital structure that maximizes the value of a firm.
- The clientele effect, when individuals make investments in firms that have capital structures that are best for the individuals, may mitigate some of these considerations. Changes in laws, particularly the tax code, sometimes create a demand for new types of securities or alter the demand for existing ones. Such changes in demand may in turn create profitable opportunities for a firm to supply a particular type of security to satisfy this new demand.
- Firms manage their capital structures carefully. Choosing an appropriate capital structure balances the net tax advantage against the (1) agency costs, (2) larger expected cost of financial distress, and (3) cost of reduced financial flexibility from additional debt. Simultaneously, transaction costs and information effects must also be considered. Unfortunately, these costs cannot be measured precisely. As a result, the "best" capital structure cannot be precisely determined.

EQUATION SUMMARY

(11.1)
$$\text{WACC} = (1 - L)r_e + L(1 - T)r_d$$

(11.2)
$$V_U = \frac{\overline{I}(1-T)}{r}$$

(11.3)
$$V_L = \frac{\overline{I}(1-T)}{\text{WACC}}$$

(11.4)
$$V_L = \frac{\overline{I}(1-T)}{r} + \frac{Tr_d D}{r_d} = \frac{\overline{I}(1-T)}{r} + TD$$

(11.5)
$$V_L = V_U + TD$$

(11.6)
$$\text{WACC} = r(1 - TL)$$

(11.7) $$(1 - T_d) = (1 - T_e)(1 - T)$$

(11.8) $$V_L = V_U + T^*D = \frac{\overline{I}(1-T)}{r} + \frac{T^*r_d D}{r_d}$$

(11.9) $$\text{WACC} = r(1 - T^*L)$$

QUESTIONS

1. Briefly explain the corporate tax view of capital structure.
2. Give an example of a tax-timing option and explain why it is valuable.
3. Cite an example of how transaction costs might affect a firm's choice of financing.
4. Define the term *leverage clientele.*
5. Briefly explain in your own words why taxes would not be asymmetric if Equation (11.7) holds.
6. What is the shape of the WACC curve according to the perfect market view?
7. What is the shape of the WACC curve according to the capital market imperfections view?
8. Briefly explain how the personal tax view of capital structure mitigates the corporate tax view.
9. True or false: The *direct* costs connected with financial distress and bankruptcy are large as a proportion of the value of the firm.
10. True or false: The *direct* costs connected with financial distress and bankruptcy are much larger than the indirect, implicit opportunity costs such as lost sales, depressed product price, and lost tax credits.
11. Why might potential new equity investors in a firm be leery of buying newly issued stock in a firm?
12. Why should a firm's ability to use tax credits affect its capital structure?
13. Describe the capital market imperfections view of capital structure.

CHALLENGING QUESTIONS

14. Explain how financial distress can affect the value of the firm through its tax credits, even when a firm is able to use completely all tax credits via loss carryforwards.
15. Suppose that a firm is operating with neutral corporate and personal taxes in an otherwise perfect capital market and Equation (11.7) currently holds. In such a world, a firm would never take on any risky debt. Why not? (*Hint:* Consider what would happen in financial distress.)
16. Leverage increases the risk (and therefore the required return) of equityholders. Above some point, an increase in leverage also increases the risk (and required return) of debtholders. How is it possible, then, that in a perfect capital market environment, the weighted average of the two is constant because both required returns are increasing?
17. How can restrictive debt covenants reduce agency costs?
18. Why might a firm that manufactures a unique product using specialized employee expertise tend to finance with less debt than an otherwise identical firm that manufactures a generic product?
19. What is the basis for the view that a firm's total market value is invariant to its choice of capital structure? Cite three broad types of capital market imperfections that can cause the

capital structure of a firm to have an effect on the value of that firm. Give three examples (one for each type) when such an imperfection would cause a firm's capital structure to have an effect on the value of that firm. Explain *how* each of the three examples you gave would cause a firm's capital structure to have an effect on the value of that firm.

20. A journalist once commented that the trouble with U.S. corporations was obvious from reading their balance sheets: They owed more money than they had! His conclusion was based on the firm's debt being larger than its equity. How would you respond to such a comment? (Think about it before responding.)

21. The good fairy has decided to smile upon you and has offered you a choice between two "great" outcomes. The alternatives concern an investment that has the same risk as the market portfolio and requires an initial investment of $10 million. The alternatives are: (1) The cost of financing for the investment will be three standard deviations less than the current average market required return for financing such investments, but the investment will have an otherwise zero NPV, or (2) the expected future cash inflows from the investment will be three standard deviations larger than those that would make the investment have a zero NPV, but the cost of financing for the investment will be at the current average market required return for financing such investments. Therefore, either alternative will provide you with a positive-NPV investment. Alternative 1 does so by virtue of "great" financing, whereas alternative 2 does so by virtue of "great" investing. Which alternative should you choose, and why?

PROBLEMS

LEVEL A (BASIC)

A1. (Calculating a leverage ratio) William Bates is contemplating starting a new firm that will provide background music for elevators, dentist offices, and the like. He estimates a positive NPV of $270,000 for the investment. Mr. Bates plans to call the firm Tarry-Tune, Unlimited. He estimates that the initial investment needed to start Tarry-Tune is $325,000. He plans to borrow $200,000 of the initial investment. What is the expected leverage ratio, L, for Tarry-Tune?

A2. (Taxes, leverage, and WACC) Suppose a firm is unleveraged and has an unleveraged required return, $r = 15\%$. The firm borrows 30% of the value of the firm at $r_d = 8\%$. Because of the financial leverage, r_e becomes 18%. What is the firm's WACC:

a. Assuming the firm is operating in a perfect capital market (including no taxes)?

b. Assuming there are only corporate taxes at a rate of 35% in an otherwise perfect capital market?

A3. (Value of firm and WACC) Suppose a firm currently has an unleveraged required return of 13% and perpetual unleveraged after-tax income of $100,000 per year. The firm has come up with an investment opportunity that would alter the firm's asset makeup so that it would increase its perpetual unleveraged after-tax income to $120,000 per year. Because the new asset mix is riskier, the firm's unleveraged required return would also increase to 15%. Should the firm undertake this investment opportunity?

A4. (Corporate taxes and firm value) Jahera Mines issues $50,000,000 of perpetual new debt paying 9% interest. Jahera is in the 40% marginal income tax bracket. Assume no market imperfections except corporate taxes.

a. What are the annual tax savings that result from the debt financing?

b. What is the increase in the value of Jahera Mines that results from this debt issue?

A5. (Corporate taxes and leverage) Caples Communications is evaluating how to finance the firm. Caples expects to have a perpetual operating cash flow of $1,000 and a marginal tax rate of 40%. As an unleveraged firm, Caples will have a cost of capital of 12%. As a leveraged firm, Caples will issue $3,000 of perpetual debt paying 8% interest.

a. Assume that Caples chooses to be an all-equity (unleveraged) firm. What is the after-tax cash flow to stockholders? What is the value of Caples as an unleveraged firm?

b. Assume that Caples chooses the leveraged capital structure. What is the after-tax cash flow to stockholders and bondholders of the leveraged firm? What is the value of the unleveraged firm? What is the leveraged firm's cost of capital?

c. What accounts for the difference in the value of the two firms?

A6. (Corporate taxes and leverage) An unleveraged firm has a perpetual operating cash flow of $100, a marginal tax rate of 40%, and an unleveraged cost of capital of 10%. An otherwise-identical firm is leveraged with $400 of perpetual debt paying 8% interest.

a. What is the after-tax cash flow to stockholders of the unleveraged firm? What is the value of the unleveraged firm?

b. What is the after-tax cash flow to stockholders and bondholders of the leveraged firm? What is the value of the unleveraged firm? What is the leveraged firm's cost of capital?

c. What accounts for the difference in the value of the two firms?

A7. (Corporate and personal taxes) Sarin Software Corporation has a corporate tax rate of 30%, its bondholders have a personal tax rate of 30%, and the effective tax rate that its stockholders pay is 20%.

a. Sarin has $100 of before-tax cash flows, which it pays as interest to its bondholders. What is the total corporate and personal tax on this cash flow? What is after-tax bondholder income?

b. Sarin has $100 of before-tax cash flows. After corporate taxes, it is distributing the balance to stockholders. What is the total corporate and personal tax on this cash flow? What is after-tax stockholder income?

c. Are these tax rates neutral? Which form of financing is favored, debt or equity financing?

A8. (Corporate and personal taxes) LaPlante Corporation has a corporate tax rate of 30%, its bondholders have a personal tax rate of 44%, and the effective tax rate that its stockholders pay is 20%.

a. LaPlante has $100 of before-tax cash flows, which it pays as interest to its bondholders. What is the total corporate and personal tax on this cash flow? What is after-tax bondholder income?

b. LaPlante has $100 of before-tax cash flows. After corporate taxes, it distributes the balance to stockholders. What is the total corporate and personal tax on this cash flow? What is after-tax stockholder income?

c. Are these tax rates neutral? Which form of financing is favored, debt or equity financing?

A9. (Excel: WACC) The managers of Dadalt Company expect the before-tax costs of debt and equity as a function of the firm's capital structure that are shown here. Dadalt's tax rate is 25%.

a. Calculate the WACC for each amount of leverage.

b. Plot the after-tax costs of debt and equity and the WACC as a function of L.

c. What is Dadalt's optimal capital strucure?

DEBT (L)	0.0	0.1	0.2	0.3	0.4	0.5	0.6	0.7	0.8
r_d (%)	—	8.0	8.1	8.3	8.5	8.8	9.1	9.5	10.0
r_e (%)	12.0	12.1	12.2	12.5	13.0	13.5	14.2	15.6	17.0

LEVEL B

B1. (Leveraged and unleveraged returns) You invest $12,000 in Joe's Garage, Inc., borrowing $5,000 of the money at 10%. If you expect to earn 24% on your investment under this arrangement, what would you expect to earn if you put up the entire $12,000 from your own money? Ignore taxes.

B2. (Leveraged and unleveraged returns) You invest $50,000 in George's House Painting Inc., borrowing $30,000 of the money at 9%. If you expect to earn 20% on your investment under this arrangement, what would you expect to earn if you put up the entire $50,000 from your own money? Ignore taxes.

B3. (Capital structure arbitrage) Consider two firms operating in a perfect capital market environment. Each will generate $10 million of operating income, and they are identical in every other respect, except that firm L has debt in its capital structure and firm U has an all-equity capital structure. Suppose that investors currently value L as indicated in Table 11-1, but the market value of the equity in U is $65 million. According to the perfect market view, this situation cannot persist. Suppose an investor owns 1% of the shares of U. Show how this owner can profit from arbitrage.

B4. (Capital structure arbitrage) Miles's Manor, an unassuming resort in midstate Pennsylvania, currently has an all-equity capital structure. Miles's Manor has an expected income of $10,000 per year forever and a required return to equity of 16%. There are no personal taxes, but Miles's pays corporate taxes at the rate of 35%. All transactions take place in an otherwise-perfect capital market.

   a. What is Miles's Manor worth?

   b. How much will the value of the firm increase if Miles's Manor leverages the firm by borrowing half the value of the unleveraged firm at an interest rate of 10% and the leverage causes the required return on equity to increase to 18.89%?

B5. (Corporate and personal taxes) Dick's Pet-Way Corporation (DPC) is a chain of pet stores that has an expected cash inflow of $1,000 each year forever. DPC's required return is 20% per year. Assume all of DPC's income is paid out to the firm's investors.

   a. If DPC is all-equity financed and there are no taxes, what would DPC be worth in a perfect capital market?

      Now suppose DPC's corporate tax rate is 30%.

   b. If DPC is all-equity financed and there are no personal taxes, what would DPC be worth in an otherwise-perfect capital market?

      In addition to corporate taxes, suppose DPC borrows $1,400 at a required return on the debt of 10%. (Note: Because of risk, the required return on equity increases to 23.89%.)

   c. If there are no personal taxes, what would DPC be worth in an otherwise-perfect capital market? What would be DPC's leverage ratio, L?

   d. If there are personal taxes on debt income at a rate of 37%, and personal taxes on equity income at a rate of 10%, what would DPC be worth in an otherwise-perfect capital market?

   e. If there are personal taxes on debt income at a rate of 25%, and personal taxes on equity income at a rate of 10%, what would DPC be worth in an otherwise-perfect capital market?

   f. Finally, compute the value of DPC as a 35.7%-leveraged firm, with a 10% interest rate on the debt when there are no taxes at all in a perfect capital market.

B6. (Cost of capital) The Query Company has identified two alternative capital structures. If the firm borrows 15% of the value of the firm, it can borrow the money at $r_d = 10\%$, and the shareholders will have a required return of $r_e = 18\%$. If the firm borrows 45% of the value of the firm, it can borrow the money at $r_d = 12\%$, and the shareholders will have a required return of $r_e = 23.21\%$. Query pays corporate taxes at the rate of 35%. Which capital structure should Query adopt? If Query is operating in an essentially perfect capital market except for taxes, are the taxes approximately symmetric, or are they asymmetric?

B7. (Cost of capital) ACE Corp. has identified two alternative capital structures. If the firm borrows 25% of the value of the firm, it can borrow the money at $r_d = 9\%$, and the shareholders will have a required return of $r_e = 17\%$. If the firm borrows 50% of the value of the firm, it can borrow the money at $r_d = 11\%$, and the shareholders will have a required return of $r_e = 20.82\%$. ACE pays corporate taxes at the rate of 40%. Which capital structure should ACE adopt? If ACE is operating in an essentially perfect capital market except for taxes, are the taxes approximately symmetric, or are they asymmetric?

B8. (Excel: Leverage, taxes, and WACC) The RTE Corporation expects to pay a dividend next year of $2.22. It expects its cash dividends to grow 5% per year forever. RTE has a debt ratio of $L = 35\%$. Its borrowing rate is $r_d = 9\%$. RTE pays corporate taxes at the rate of 30%. If $r_f = 6\%$, $r_M = 12\%$, and RTE's common stock is currently selling for $20 per share:

a. What is the current (leveraged) required return, r_e, on RTE's common stock?

b. What is RTE's WACC?

c. What is RTE's unleveraged required return, r?

d. What unleveraged beta is implied by r?

B9. (Excel: Leverage, taxes, and WACC) The LPE Corporation expects to pay a dividend next year of $1.50. It expects its cash dividends to grow 6% per year forever. LPE has a debt ratio of $L = 20\%$. Its borrowing rate is $r_d = 6\%$. LPE pays corporate taxes at the rate of 25%. If $r_f = 4\%$, $r_M = 10\%$, and LPE's common stock is currently selling for $17 per share:

a. What is the current (leveraged) required return, r_e, on LPE's common stock?

b. What is LPE's WACC?

c. What is LPE's unleveraged required return, r?

d. What unleveraged beta is implied by r?

LEVEL C (ADVANCED)

C1. (Capital structure arbitrage) Firms A and B are identical except for their capital structures. A has a debt ratio of 25%. B has a debt ratio of 33.33%. Suppose that the interest rate on both firms' debt is 10% and that investors can also borrow at a 10% interest rate.

a. An investor owns 5% of the common stock of firm A, half of which is financed through borrowings. What investment–loan package involving B will produce identical returns?

b. An investor owns 10% of the common stock of B, none of which is financed through borrowings. What investment–loan combination involving A will produce identical returns?

C2. (WACC and net benefit to leverage) Both the common stock and long-term bonds of Crib-Tick, Inc., makers of baby furniture, are traded publicly on the NYSE. Currently, the market value of Crib-Tick common stock is $14 per share, and there are 4 million shares outstanding. Crib-Tick's latest earnings were $2.09 per share, and next year's dividend is expected to be $1.02 per share. Five years ago, Crib-Tick paid a dividend of $0.72 per share. Crib-Tick has long-term bonds with a total market value of $30 million. The bonds mature in 11 years and have an 8% coupon. They are currently selling for $880. (Assume the bonds have 22 more coupon payments until maturity.) In addition to long-term bonds, Crib-Tick has $5 million in notes payable and $10 million in other current liabilities. Current market conditions are $r_f = 6\%$ and $r_M = 13.75\%$. Crib-Tick has a beta of 1.1, and it pays corporate taxes at a rate of 30%. It has estimated $T^* = 0.18$. Estimate Crib-Tick's WACC.

C3. (Financing-investment puzzle) The Ida Rather Knot Corporation, a modest rope manufacturing firm in the northeast corner of the Yukon, has been contacted by Wile E. Coyote and offered an investment opportunity that will pay her $2,500 per month for 60 months. Ida must invest $10,000 now and borrow $90,000 from Wile E. at 16% APR, for a total initial investment of $100,000. The entire loan must be paid back at the end of the 60 months (principal and interest will total $199,242.62). There are no taxes. Assume that this investment is riskless, as Wile E. Coyote has claimed. Under what conditions would you recommend that Ida undertake this investment?

C4. (Financing-investment puzzle) Suppose you have been offered an investment opportunity that will pay you $2,200 per month for 60 months. However, you must invest $10,000 now and borrow $90,000 from a specified institution at 16% APR, for a total initial investment of $100,000. The entire loan must be paid back at the end of the 60 months (principal and interest will total $199,242.62). There are no taxes. Assume this investment is riskless. Under what conditions would you want to undertake this investment?

MINICASE   PEPSICO'S CAPITAL STRUCTURE CHOICE

PepsiCo, the soft drink and snacks company, has established a long-term target range of 20% to 25% for what it calls its "net debt ratio." PepsiCo measures its net debt ratio on a market-value basis. Net debt equals total debt, including the present value of its operating lease commitments, minus the cash and marketable securities it holds outside the United States (it does so mainly for tax reasons). The net debt ratio is defined as

$$L^* = \frac{D + PVOL - CMS}{(N)(P) + D + PVOL - CMS}$$

where D is the total market value of debt, PVOL is the present value of operating lease commitments, CMS is cash and marketable securities (net of the cost of remitting these funds to the United States), N is the number of common shares, and P is the common stock price. PepsiCo's annual report shows that the firm had 788 million shares of common stock outstanding, and the stock price closed at $55.875.

This table provides information regarding comparable firms.

FIRM	DEBT RATINGS (MOODY'S/ S&P)	ANNUAL EBIT	ANNUAL RENTAL EXPENSE	ANNUAL INTEREST	CASH AND MARKETABLE SECURITIES	MARKET VALUE OF LONG-TERM DEBT	MARKET VALUE OF TOTAL DEBT	ANNUAL CASH FLOW	NUMBER OF SHARES (MILLIONS)	YEAR-END SHARE PRICE
PepsiCo	A1/A	$3,114	$479	$682	$1,498	$8,747	$9,453	$3,742	788.00	55.88
Cadbury Schweppes	A2/A	661	25	135	129	864	1,490	492	247.75	35.13
Coca-Cola	Aa3/AA	4,600	—	272	1315	1,141	1,693	3,115	2,504.60	40.25
Coca-Cola Enterprises	A3/AA–	471	31	326	8	4,138	4,201	644	385.65	10.00
McDonald's	Aa2/AA	2,509	498	340	335	4,258	4,836	2,296	699.70	48.00

QUESTIONS

1. Calculate PepsiCo's net debt ratio, assuming the present value of operating leases is five times the annual rental expense and that remitting the cash and marketable securities to the United States reduces them by 25% due to taxes and transaction costs.

2. For each firm in the table, calculate the interest coverage ratio, the fixed-charge coverage ratio, the long-term debt ratio, the total debt to adjusted total capitalization (recall that adjusted capitalization includes short-term debt), the ratio of cash flow to long-term debt, and the ratio of cash flow to total debt.

3. (Supplemental question based on Chapter 12) Suppose PepsiCo's real objective is to maintain a single-A senior debt rating. Does its net debt ratio target seem reasonable, or would you recommend a different target?

MANAGING CAPITAL STRUCTURE

12

C orporations manage their capital structure carefully. As we described in the preceding chapter, the factors involved with choosing a capital structure are complex, and the impact of each factor on the value of the firm is not clear-cut. In principle, a firm should balance the incremental advantage of more financial leverage against the incremental costs. Unfortunately, we do not have methods to precisely measure such things as the expected costs of financial distress, agency costs, and the cost of reduced financing flexibility.

A number of methods exist for analyzing the impact of alternative capital structures but, in the end, the choice of capital structure requires expert judgment. The analytical models give us a range of reasonable capital structures, rather than pinpointing the absolute best.

In this chapter, we describe how a firm can take into account the various relevant factors to select an appropriate capital structure. We then show how to incorporate the effect of that capital structure choice on the cost of capital for a firm or one of its capital budgeting projects. The method is very practical because it simply adjusts the WACC (weighted average cost of capital), which is then used in a "standard" NPV calculation without any other changes.

FOCUS ON PRINCIPLES

- *Behavioral:* Look to the information contained in the capital structure decisions and financing transactions of other firms for guidance in choosing a capital structure.
- *Risk-Return Trade-Off:* Recognize that capital structure changes made at fair-market security prices are simply a risk-return trade-off. Such transactions do not affect firm value (except for possible signaling effects), although they change equity–debt risk sharing.
- *Incremental Benefits:* Consider the possible ways to minimize the value lost to capital market imperfections, such as asymmetric taxes, asymmetric information, and transaction costs. At the same time, be sure to include all of the transaction costs of making potentially beneficial financing transactions, because they reduce the *net* benefit from such transactions.
- *Valuable Ideas:* Look for opportunities to create value by issuing securities that are in short supply, perhaps resulting from changes in tax law.
- *Signaling:* Consider any possible change in capital structure carefully, because financing transactions and capital structure changes convey information to outsiders and can be misunderstood.
- *Time Value of Money:* Include any time-value-of-money tax benefits from capital structure choices.
- *Capital Market Efficiency:* Recognize that the potential to increase firm value through capital structure is smaller than the potential to increase firm value through the introduction of *valuable new ideas* and wise use of the firm's *comparative advantages.*

12.1 INDUSTRY EFFECTS

We have a pretty good understanding of the main factors that affect a firm's choice of capital structure. But financial theory does not tell us *precisely* how they determine a firm's *optimal* capital structure. In practice, firms usually apply the Behavioral Principle to select an *appropriate* capital structure. They look to the capital structure choices of comparable firms for guidance about their choice of capital structure.

Studies show systematic differences in capital structures across industries. These are due mostly to differences in:

1. The degree of operating risk
2. Availability of tax shelters provided by things other than debt, such as accelerated depreciation, investment tax credits, and operating tax loss carryforwards
3. The ability of assets to support borrowing
4. Management's attitude toward the risk created by financial leverage

Debt Ratings

Differences among average industry capital structures, however, are only part of the story. A firm cannot simply adopt the industry average debt ratio because differences exist among firms in any particular industry with respect to tax position, size, competitive position, operating risk, business prospects, and other factors. Firms also differ in their willingness to bear financial risk and in their desire to maintain access to the capital markets.

In practice, a firm's bond rating has important implications concerning the choice of capital structure. Table 12-1 shows the debt rating definitions of two major rating agencies, Moody's Investors Service and Standard & Poor's. The highest four rating categories are known as **investment-grade ratings**. For Moody's, the investment-grade ratings are Aaa, Aa, A, and Baa. For Standard & Poor's, investment-grade ratings are AAA, AA, A, and BBB. Ratings lower than investment grade are called **speculative-grade ratings**.

Each agency distinguishes different levels of credit quality within each rating category below triple A. Moody's attaches the numbers 1 (high), 2 (medium), and 3 (low). Standard & Poor's attaches a plus sign for the highest and a minus sign for the lowest. For example, a medium-grade single-A credit would be rated A2 by Moody's and A by Standard & Poor's. It would be somewhat higher in quality than one rated A3 by Moody's or A– by Standard & Poor's.

TABLE 12-1   Bond rating definitions.

MOODY'S INVESTORS SERVICE[a]	STANDARD & POOR'S[b]
Investment-Grade Ratings	
Aaa	**AAA**
Bonds and preferred stock which are rated Aaa are judged to be of the best quality. They carry the smallest degree of investment risk and are generally referred to as "gilt-edged." Interest payments are protected by a large or by an exceptionally stable margin, and principal is secure. While the various protective elements are likely to change, such changes as can be visualized are most unlikely to impair the fundamentally strong position of such issues.	Debt rated AAA has the highest rating assigned by Standard & Poor's. Capacity to pay interest and repay principal is extremely strong.
Aa	**AA**
Bonds and preferred stock which are rated Aa are judged to be of high quality by all standards. Together with the Aaa group, they comprise what are generally known as high-grade bonds. They are rated lower than the best bonds because margins of protection may not be as large as in Aaa securities, fluctuation of protective elements may be of greater amplitude, or there may be other elements present that make the long-term risk appear somewhat larger than the Aaa securities.	Debt rated AA has a very strong capacity to pay interest and repay principal and differs from the higher-rated issues only in small degree.
A	**A**
Bonds and preferred stock which are rated A possess many favorable investment attributes and are to be considered as upper-medium-grade obligations. Factors giving security to principal and interest are considered adequate, but elements may be present that suggest a susceptibility to impairment some time in the future.	Debt rated A has a strong capacity to pay interest and repay principal, although it is somewhat more susceptible to the adverse effects of changes in circumstances and economic conditions than debt in higher-rated categories.
Baa	**BBB**
Bonds and preferred stock which are rated Baa are considered medium-grade obligations (they are neither highly protected nor poorly secured). Interest payments and principal security appear adequate for the present, but certain protective elements may be lacking or may be characteristically unreliable over any great length of time. Such bonds lack outstanding investment characteristics and in fact have speculative characteristics as well.	Debt rated BBB is regarded as having an adequate capacity to pay interest and repay principal. Whereas it normally exhibits adequate protection parameters, adverse economic conditions or changing circumstances are more likely to lead to a weakened capacity to pay interest and repay principal for debt in this category than in higher-rated categories.

TABLE 12-1 *Continued*

MOODY'S INVESTORS SERVICE[a]	STANDARD & POOR'S[b]

Speculative-Grade Ratings

Ba

Bonds and preferred stock which are rated Ba are judged to have speculative elements; their future cannot be considered as well-assured. Often the protection of interest and principal payments may be very moderate, and thereby not well safeguarded during both good and bad times over the future. Uncertainty of position characterizes bonds in this class.

B

Bonds and preferred stock which are rated B generally lack characteristics of the desirable investment. Assurance of interest and principal payments or of maintenance of other terms of the contract over any long period of time may be small.

Caa

Bonds and preferred stock which are rated Caa are of poor standing. Such issues may be in default, or there may be present elements of danger with respect to principal or interest.

Ca

Bonds and preferred stock which are rated Ca represent obligations that are speculative in a high degree. Such issues are often in default or have other marked shortcomings.

C

Bonds and preferred stock which are rated C are the lowest-rated class of bonds, and issues so rated can be regarded as having extremely poor prospects of ever attaining any real investment standing.

BB

Debt rated BB has less near-term vulnerability to default than other speculative issues. However, it faces major ongoing uncertainties or exposure to adverse business, financial, or economic conditions that could lead to inadequate capacity to meet timely interest and principal payments. The BB rating category is also used for debt subordinated to senior debt that is assigned an actual or implied BBB− rating.

B

Debt rated B has a greater vulnerability to default but currently has the capacity to meet interest payments and principal repayments. Adverse business, financial, or economic conditions will likely impair capacity or willingness to pay interest and repay principal. The B rating category is also used for debt subordinated to senior debt that is assigned an actual or implied BB or BB− rating.

CCC

Debt rated CCC has a currently identifiable vulnerability to default and is dependent upon favorable business, financial, and economic conditions to meet the requirements of timely payment of interest and repayment of principal. In the event of adverse business, financial, or economic conditions, it is not likely to have the capacity to pay interest and repay principal. The CCC rating category is also used for debt subordinated to senior debt that is assigned an actual or implied B or B− rating.

CC

The rating CC is typically applied to debt subordinated to senior debt that is assigned an actual or implied CCC rating.

C

The rating C is typically applied to debt subordinated to senior debt that is assigned an actual or implied CCC− rating. The C rating may be used to cover a situation where a bankruptcy petition has been filed but debt-service payments are continued.

CI

The rating CI is reserved for income bonds on which no interest is being paid.

D

Debt rated D is in payment default. The D rating category is used when interest payments or principal payments are not made on the date due even if the applicable grace period has not expired, unless S&P believes that such payments will be made during such grace period. The D rating also is used upon the filing of a bankruptcy petition if debt-service payments are jeopardized.

---

[a]Moody's applies numerical modifiers 1, 2, and 3 in each generic rating classification from Aa through Caa. The modifier 1 indicates that the obligation ranks in the higher end of its generic rating category; the modifier 2 indicates a mid-range ranking; and the modifier 3 indicates a ranking in the lower end of that generic rating category.
[b]The ratings from "AA" to "CCC" may be modified by the addition of a plus or minus sign to show relative standing within the major rating categories.
Sources: Reprinted by permission of Moody's Investors Service and of Standard & Poor's.

As you can see by reading Table 12-1, the ratings are indicators of the likelihood of financial distress, as judged by the rating agencies. Bonds in the top three investment-grade categories are judged from "favorable" to "gilt-edged" (edged with gold). They have a capacity to pay interest that ranges from "strong" to "extremely strong." Bonds rated in the lowest category (Baa or BBB) offer investors less protection than higher-rated bonds. The risk of financial distress is greater for lower-rated bonds.

The distinction between investment-grade and speculative-grade ratings is important because of institutional investment restrictions. To qualify as *legal investments* for commercial banks, bonds must usually be investment-grade. In addition, various state laws impose minimum rating standards and other restrictions for bonds to qualify as legal investments for savings banks, trust companies, public pension funds, and insurance companies. Bonds rated speculative-grade fail to qualify as legal investments for many financial institutions. Consequently, a firm's bond rating is very important for maintaining access to capital markets on acceptable terms.

The National Association of Insurance Commissioners (NAIC) has established six bond rating categories. The amount of reserves an insurance company must maintain for each bond investment depends on the bond's rating. Bonds rated NAIC-3 or below are speculative-grade. They require significantly more capital.[1] With the introduction of this new rating system and capital-maintenance standards, speculative-grade bonds have become much less attractive to insurance companies. And of course, the yields that insurance companies require from speculative-grade bonds are significantly higher to compensate for the greater amount of capital they must maintain.

Choosing a Bond Rating Objective

A firm can choose a bond rating objective. Such a choice involves a decision about (1) the chance of future financial distress and (2) the desire to maintain access to the capital markets. When it looks like a firm could gain value from raising its proportion of debt financing but it chooses not to (because it has a higher bond rating objective), the value that is missed can be viewed as a "margin of safety." The desired margin of safety is determined by how much risk of future financial distress, or restricted market access, the firm is willing to bear. A single-A rating would seem to be a reasonable rating target, but some firms are more or less risk averse than this standard implies.

Bond Ratings and Financial Ratios

Once a firm has chosen its rating target, what financial steps should it take to hit the target? The rating agencies use many criteria to rate a bond. For example, in the case of industrial firms, Standard & Poor's evaluates (1) operating risk, (2) competitive position, (3) size and diversification, (4) margins and other measures of profitability, (5) management quality, (6) conservatism of accounting policies, (7) fixed charge coverage, (8) financial policies, (9) leverage (including off-balance-sheet debt) compared with the liquidation value of assets, (10) adequacy of cash flow to meet future debt service obligations, (11) need for outside capital, and (12) future financial flexibility in light of future debt service obligations and planned capital expenditure requirements.

Each factor bears on the risk of future financial distress. When the rating agencies weigh the relevant factors in order to assign a bond rating, there is no all-purpose formula. In fact, several factors are difficult to quantify. Nevertheless, certain key credit statistics for comparable firms whose debt carries the target rating offer useful guidance.

---

[1]NAIC-2 corresponds to Moody's Baa (and to Standard & Poor's BBB). NAIC-3 corresponds to Moody's Ba (and to Standard & Poor's BB). Life insurance companies' reserve requirements for NAIC-3 bonds are more than three times as high as for NAIC-2 bonds. Property and casualty insurance companies can account for bonds rated NAIC-3 or higher based on their historical cost but must account for bonds rated NAIC-4 or lower based on their current market value.

Table 12-2 shows how the values of seven key credit statistics vary across the seven highest rating categories assigned by Standard & Poor's. Note how all the ratios are progressively better, the higher the firm's senior debt rating. Taken together, they go a long way toward distinguishing a stronger credit rating from a weaker one.

Having selected a rating target, a firm can use the values of the key credit statistics of comparable firms with that target rating as a rough guide to the ratio targets it should set for

TABLE 12-2
Senior debt ratings as indicators of credit quality.

Three-year (2002 to 2004) Medians

	AAA	AA	A	BBB	BB	B	CCC
EBIT interest coverage (x)	23.8	19.5	8.0	4.7	2.5	1.2	0.4
EBITDA interest coverage (x)	25.5	24.6	10.2	6.5	3.5	1.9	0.9
FFO/total debt (%)	203.3	79.9	48.0	35.9	22.4	11.5	5.0
Free operating cash flow/total debt (%)	127.6	44.5	25.0	17.3	8.3	2.8	(2.1)
Total debt/EBITDA (x)	0.4	0.9	1.6	2.2	3.5	5.3	7.9
Return on capital (%)	27.6	27.0	17.5	13.4	11.3	8.7	3.2
Total debt/(total debt + equity) (%)	12.4	28.3	37.5	42.5	53.7	75.9	113.5

Formulas

1. EBIT interest coverage	Earnings from continuing operations[a] before interest and taxes/gross interest incurred before subtracting capitalized interest and interest income
2. EBITDA interest coverage	Adjusted earnings from continuing operations[b] before interest, taxes, depreciation, and amortization/gross interest incurred before subtracting capitalized interest and interest income
3. Funds from operations (FFO)/total debt	Net income from continuing operations, depreciation and amortization, deferred income taxes, and other noncash items/long-term debt[c] + current maturities + commercial paper, and other short-term borrowings
4. Free operating cash flow/total debt	(FFO − capital expenditures − (+) increase (decrease) in working capital (excluding changes in cash, marketable securities, and short-term debt)/(long-term debt[c] + current maturities, commercial paper, and other short-term borrowings)
5. Total debt/EBITDA	(Long-term debt[c] + current maturities, commercial paper, and other short-term borrowings)/adjusted earnings from continuing operations before interest, taxes, and D&A
6. Return on capital	EBIT/average of beginning-of-year and end-of-year capital, including short-term debt, current maturities, long-term debt,[c] noncurrent deferred taxes, minority interest, and equity (common and preferred stock)
7. Total debt/(total debt + equity)	(Long-term debt[c] + current maturities, commercial paper, and other short-term borrowings)/(long-term debt[c] + current maturities, commercial paper, and other short-term borrowings + shareholders' equity) (including preferred stock) + minority interest

[a]Including interest income and equity earnings; excluding nonrecurring items.
[b]Excludes interest income, equity earnings, and nonrecurring items; also excludes rental expense that exceeds the interest component of capitalized operating leases.
[c]Including amounts for operating-lease debt equivalent and debt associated with accounts receivable sales/securitization programs.
Source: Standard & Poor's, *Corporate Ratings Criteria 2006.*

itself. We show how to do this later in the chapter. For now, four points of caution should be emphasized:

1. Quantitative factors are not the entire story. A deteriorating market position, or perceived weaknesses in management, will negatively affect the credit rating.
2. Achieving an improved credit rating requires a proven track record. Simply improving credit statistics will not guarantee a higher credit rating unless the firm demonstrates that it can maintain the statistics.
3. The averages may change over time.
4. Cyclical industries, such as mining and chemicals, exhibit substantial swings in credit statistics over the industry cycle. This makes it very important to compare firms in the same industry.

REVIEW

1. What four factors might explain the systematic differences in capital structures across industries?
2. What are investment-grade ratings, and what are speculative-grade ratings? Why is this distinction important?
3. Cite three factors Standard & Poor's evaluates to determine a bond rating for an industrial firm.

12.2 FACTORS AFFECTING A FIRM'S CHOICE OF CAPITAL STRUCTURE

There are five basic considerations involved in a firm's choice of capital structure: (1) Ability to service debt; (2) ability to use interest tax shields fully; (3) ability of assets to support debt (protection against illiquidity); (4) desired degree of access to capital markets; and (5) dynamic factors and debt management over time. Let us look at each of these factors in turn.

Ability to Service Debt

A careful financial manager will not recommend that a firm take on more debt unless she is confident the firm will be able to service the debt, that is, be able to make the contractually required payments on time, even under adverse conditions. Many firms appear to maintain a margin of safety, or unused debt capacity, to control the risk of financial distress and maintain access to the capital markets.

There are various measures of debt-servicing capacity. One is the **interest coverage ratio**:

$$(12.1) \qquad \text{Interest coverage ratio} = \frac{\text{EBIT}}{\text{Interest expense}}$$

where EBIT denotes earnings before interest and income taxes. Rental (including lease) payments include an interest component. Fixed charges, which include interest expense and one-third of rental expense, represent a better indicator of true interest expense. To take these factors into account, we can calculate a **fixed charge coverage ratio:**[2]

$$(12.2) \qquad \text{Fixed charge coverage ratio} = \frac{\text{EBIT} + 1/3 \text{ Rentals}}{\text{Interest expense} + 1/3 \text{ Rentals}}$$

[2]The fixed charge coverage ratio in Equation (12.2) is the one specified by the Securities and Exchange Commission. However, some analysts prefer to use total rentals rather than one-third of this amount.

The one-third rentals is an attempt to approximate the interest component of rental expense.

To avoid default, a firm must meet its principal repayment obligations as well as its interest obligations on schedule. A more comprehensive measure of a firm's ability to service its debt obligations is its **debt service coverage ratio:**

$$(12.3) \quad \text{Debt service coverage ratio} = \frac{\text{EBIT} + 1/3 \text{ Rentals}}{\text{Interest expense} + 1/3 \text{ Rentals} + \dfrac{\text{Principal repayments}}{1 - \text{Tax rate}}}$$

The amount of principal repayments is divided by 1 minus the tax rate because principal repayments are not tax deductible. They are paid with after-tax dollars, whereas interest expense and rental expense are tax deductible.

The coverage ratios can be used in pro forma analysis to gauge the impact of a new issue.

EXAMPLE Pro Forma Credit Analysis

A firm has EBIT of $25 million and interest expense of $10 million. It is considering issuing $50 million of 10% debt. Calculate its pro forma interest coverage ratio assuming the entire proceeds are invested in a plant under construction. Recalculate it assuming the investment produces additional EBIT of $10 million per year.

In the first case,

$$\text{Interest coverage ratio} = \frac{25}{10 + (50)(0.1)} = 1.67x$$

In the second case,

$$\text{Interest coverage ratio} = \frac{25 + 10}{10 + 5} = 2.33x$$

A firm can evaluate the impact of alternative capital structures using *sensitivity analysis.* The firm calculates the interest coverage ratio, fixed charge coverage ratio, and debt service coverage ratio for each capital structure under a variety of projected business scenarios. Then the calculated values are compared to benchmarks that reflect the firm's desired credit rating. Table 12-2 suggests the following rough benchmarks. If a firm's industry has average operating risk, and the firm wishes to meet minimum investment-grade standards (a BBB rating), it should strive for an annual interest coverage ratio of at least 4.7 under reasonably conservative "expected case" assumptions. It should strive for a debt service coverage ratio of at least 1.00 under pessimistic assumptions.[3]

A firm in a highly cyclical industry should set higher interest coverage and fixed charge coverage ratio standards to compensate for the greater operating risk, whereas a firm in a noncyclical industry can safely set lower standards. For example, an electric utility can set lower coverage ratio standards than a manufacturer of rollerblades.

A firm that wishes to maintain single-A-type ratios would aim toward an interest coverage ratio of at least 8.0 if it is in an industry of average operating risk. Higher (or lower) standards would be appropriate for firms in industries that have more (or less) operating risk. You could obtain more precise benchmarks by calculating ratios for firms in the same industry that have the target rating.

---

[3]The particular minimum chosen for the debt service coverage ratio depends, to a certain extent, on the firm's confidence in its ability to refinance its debt.

Ability to Use Interest Tax Shields Fully

Firms using debt financing must generate sufficient income from operations to claim the interest deductions. A firm that does not pay income taxes and does not expect to become a taxpayer has less incentive to incur additional debt. The tax shields would go unused. That would raise the after-tax cost of debt, and the additional debt would also increase the risk of financial distress. A firm can carry tax losses forward. The added debt will be beneficial only if the expected present value of the tax shields exceeds the expected present value of the costs of financial distress plus the expected present value of the increase in agency costs.

A firm's capital structure should probably contain no more debt than its future tax position will let it use. For example, firms in industries with other substantial tax shelter opportunities, such as oil and gas companies (with their depletion allowances) and steel makers (with their depreciation and loss carryforwards), should have lower leverage ratios than firms in other industries.

As we have said before, there are frequent changes to the tax code. These changes complicate this analysis and can cause the firm's target capital structure to change over time.

Ability of Assets to Support Debt

A firm should not incur additional debt if doing so would involve a significant chance of insolvency. The risk of insolvency depends not only on the projected debt service coverage, but also on the firm's ability to generate cash through additional borrowing, the sale of equity securities, or the sale of assets.

Assets vary in their ability to support debt. Lower-risk assets with more-stable market values provide better collateral for debt. This allows a firm to borrow a larger proportion of such assets' market values. For example, a real estate firm or a credit company can generally support a relatively large amount of leverage.

> **EXAMPLE Leverage and Discovering Oil**
>
> Imagine you bought 200 acres of land in order to create a catfish ranch. You paid $100,000 for the land and have an $80,000 mortgage on it. You plan to use an additional $60,000 of your own money to develop the ranch. You figure the project has an NPV of $40,000, so the total value of the project is $200,000 (= 100 + 60 + 40) at a cost of $160,000. Therefore, your ranch project has a 40% leverage ratio (its proportion of debt financing is $L = 80/200$).
>
> In the process of digging a pond for the catfish, you discover oil on your land. An analysis of the discovery puts the new value of your land at $15.25 million. Now your project is only about $L = 0.5\%$ debt financed! But not to worry. You can, of course, increase your leverage by borrowing against the increased market value of your land.

Desired Degree of Access to Capital Markets

A firm planning a substantial capital expenditure program will want to maintain access to the capital markets on acceptable terms. This requires adequate credit strength. Historically, a firm large enough to sell debt publicly could be reasonably confident of maintaining such access if it had a senior debt rating of single-A or better. In 1983, the "junk bond" market expanded rapidly and appeared to lessen the need to have such a high credit standing for maintaining market access. In 1990, however, the junk bond market all but collapsed, emphasizing the risk inherent in increasing leverage to such an extent that a firm's debt rating falls below investment-grade.

Dynamic Factors and Debt Management over Time

The four factors just discussed all affect a firm's capital structure target. The capital market imperfections view of capital structure also plays a role. A firm might appear to deviate from the normal financing preference order. This could be, for example, because one large issue has proportionally lower transaction costs than two or more smaller issues. Similarly, a firm that needs only a relatively small amount of external funds would tend to use bank lines of credit rather than issue securities, even if issuing securities would appear to be better.

The dynamic process can even make it appear that a firm has *no* target capital structure. For example, if a firm takes advantage of an attractive but temporary financing opportunity (say, the opportunity to issue tax-exempt securities prior to the date the authority to issue such securities expires), its capital structure may move away from its "target." Such apparent deviations in a firm's capital structure policy can simply reflect the dynamic nature of an optimal capital structure.

REVIEW

1. What are the five basic considerations involved in a firm's choice of capital structure?
2. What are coverage ratios? What do they measure? Why should a firm and its investors be concerned with the values of the firm's coverage ratios?
3. Explain why some assets provide better collateral value than others.

12.3 CHOOSING AN APPROPRIATE CAPITAL STRUCTURE

In this section we will tie together the considerations just discussed into a single framework for determining an appropriate capital structure. To do this, we will use comparative credit analysis and pro forma capital structure analysis. A *comparative credit analysis* suggests a range of target capital structures that might be appropriate. A *pro forma capital structure analysis* shows the impact of the alternatives within the target range on the firm's credit statistics and reported financial results, and indicates whether the firm will be able to fully use tax shield benefits. This enables the firm to select a specific target capital structure.

Comparative Credit Analysis

In practice, a comparative credit analysis is the most widely used technique for selecting an appropriate capital structure. This approach is an application of the Behavioral Principle. It involves the following steps:

1. Select the desired rating objective.
2. Identify a set of comparable firms that also have the target senior debt rating.
3. Perform a comparative credit analysis of these firms to define the capital structure (or range of capital structures) most consistent with this rating objective.

Earlier, we discussed five considerations that enter into the capital structure decision. Choosing a target debt rating actually encompasses three of the five. The only two not covered are the ability to use tax benefits and debt management considerations (such as issuance expenses) that affect the immediate preference order of the various sources of funds. We must evaluate these two factors separately.

As we said earlier, a single-A rating provides a compromise between maintaining capital market access and getting more tax savings from additional leverage. However, more conservative firms, and firms with very heavy future financing programs, might strive for a higher rating. Other firms that are willing to bear greater financial risk might set a lower rating target.

EXAMPLE **Comparative Credit Analysis**

Table 12-3 illustrates a comparative credit analysis of specialty chemicals firms that are comparable to the firm being analyzed, Washington Chemical Corporation. There are six specialty chemicals firms with rated debt. The senior debt ratings (Moody's/Standard & Poor's) range from a low of Ba1/BB to a high of A2/A.

Washington Chemical has decided on a target senior debt rating "comfortably within" the single-A range. Three of the firms in Table 12-3 have at least one senior debt rating in the single-A category, and Johnson Chemical and Wilson Chemical are rated in the middle of the single-A category by both agencies.

Washington Chemical is significantly more profitable than one of the A2/A issuers and only slightly less profitable than the other. Washington Chemical's debt-to-capitalization, funds-from-operations-to-debt, and fixed charge coverage ratios fall between the higher and lower of the two values for each ratio exhibited by the two A2/A specialty chemicals firms. Washington Chemical's ratios are substantially better than those of Myers Chemicals, which is a borderline triple-B/single-A. Washington Chemical concluded from this analysis that its financial condition is of medium-grade single-A quality.

We need to clarify one point regarding this example. We have emphasized the importance of basing financial decisions on market values, but the financial ratios in Table 12-3 contain some book value items. This is because it is simply not practical to include current market values in every case. The rating agencies consider the market value of a firm's assets in assessing its leverage. But they value these assets conservatively, assuming they could be sold in fair-market-value transactions.

The actual debt-to-capitalization ratio should value the common equity component on the basis of the liquidation value of the assets rather than on the basis of the firm's prevailing share price (which reflects the value of the firm on a going-concern basis). Assets such as proven oil and gas reserves, which are relatively liquid, will support a higher degree of leverage than less liquid assets. New plant and equipment will tend to support greater leverage than an equal book value amount of old plant and equipment. But determining these liquidating values is necessarily subjective, because there are no liquid markets for fixed assets, and appraisals generally are not available. Still, the quality of assets will vary systematically from one industry to another. Thus, for a particular rating category, the debt-to-capitalization ratios for firms in one industry, when compared with the debt-to-capitalization ratios for firms in another industry whose debt bears the same rating, will reflect interindustry differences in liquidating-asset value.

An analysis like the one in Table 12-3 is necessarily imperfect. But if comparable firms are chosen carefully and if differences between the comparable firms and the firm being analyzed are carefully weighed, the comparative credit analysis can produce useful guidelines.

EXAMPLE **Comparative Credit Analysis (continued)**

As we said, in the final analysis the choice of capital structure requires judgment. Before reaching a decision, Washington Chemical evaluated its expected profitability. Washington Chemical believed that its profitability would exceed that of its single-A competitors. Based on its careful consideration of all these factors, Washington Chemical decided to try to stay within the following ranges:

Annual fixed charge coverage ratio: $3.50x$ to $4.00x$

Annual funds-from-operations-to-total-debt ratio: 40% to 50%

Long-term debt ratio: 30% to 35%

TABLE 12-3 A comparative credit analysis of specialty chemicals firms.

	WASHINGTON CHEMICAL CORP.	MYERS CHEMICAL CORP.	NORTHWEST CHEMICALS INC.	DELAWARE CHEMICALS CORP.	WESTERN INDUSTRIES	JOHNSON CHEMICAL INC.	WILSON CHEMICAL CORP.
Senior debt rating (Moody's/Standard & Poor's)	—	A3/BBB+	Ba1/BBB–	Baa2/BBB–	Ba1/BB	A2/A	A2/A
Profitability							
Operating profit margin	7.4%	5.9%	1.9%	4.5%	8.9%	4.1%	9.2%
Net profit margin	3.9	2.6	1.0	2.3	2.2	2.3	4.1
Return on assets	4.8	3.2	2.2	4.9	2.8	4.3	4.9
Return on common equity	10.3	9.2	5.0	13.9	8.8	10.8	10.0
Capitalization							
Short-term debt	$ 16	$ 60	$ 10	$ 10	$ 16	$ 8	$ 36
Senior long-term debt	$158	$144	$ 49	$163	$110	$140	$245
Capitalized lease obligations	—	22	10	20	—	—	1
Subordinated long-term debt	—	—	—	13	80	8	—
Total long-term debt	158	166	59	196	190	148	246
Minority interest	—	—	3	2	—	—	—
Preferred equity	—	2	35	5	—	—	—
Common equity	321	253	165	334	162	278	659
Total capitalization	$479	$421	$262	$537	$352	$426	$905
Long-term debt ratio	33%	39%	23%	36%	54%	35%	27%
Total-debt-to-adjusted-capitalization ratio	35	47	25	38	56	36	30
Funds-from-operations-to-long-term-debt ratio	60	42	45	35	27	51	63
Funds-from-operations-to-total-debt ratio	55	31	39	33	25	49	55
Liquidity							
Current ratio	2.4x	1.9x	2.7x	2.1x	1.9x	2.2x	2.6x
Fixed Charge Coverage Ratio							
Last 12 months	3.5x	2.3x	2.4x	3.3x	2.0x	3.3x	3.7x
Latest fiscal year	4.3	4.0	3.8	2.9	2.3	4.4	4.2
One year prior	5.6	3.0	3.2	2.7	2.8	5.4	5.7
Two years prior	6.3	4.0	2.8	2.2	3.8	7.9	4.9

TABLE 12-4   A pro forma capital structure analysis (table continues).

	INITIAL	PROJECTED AHEAD				
		1 YEAR	2 YEARS	3 YEARS	4 YEARS	5 YEARS
Case 1: Leverage at upper end of range/expected case operating results						
Pre-interest taxable income[a]	$ 61	$ 67	$ 74	$ 81	$ 89	$ 98
Interest	18	20	22	24	26	28
Surplus (Deficit)[b]	$ 43	$ 47	$ 52	$ 57	$ 63	$ 70
Earnings before fixed charges and income taxes[c]	$ 70	$ 77	$ 85	$ 93	$102	$113
Fixed charges[d]	20	22	24	26	28	30
Fixed charge coverage	3.5x	3.5x	3.5x	3.6x	3.6x	3.8x
Net income	$ 30	$ 33	$ 36	$ 42	$ 45	$ 51
Noncash expenses	65	72	79	84	94	102
Funds from operations[c]	95	105	115	126	139	153
Dividends	(10)	(11)	(12)	(14)	(15)	(17)
Internal cash generation	85	94	103	112	124	136
Capital expenditures	(125)	(125)	(125)	(135)	(150)	(160)
Cash required	$ 40	$ 31	$ 22	$ 23	$ 26	$ 24
External debt requirement[e]	$ 20	$ 17	$ 14	$ 15	$ 17	$ 17
External equity requirement[e]	$ 20	$ 14	$ 8	$ 8	$ 9	$ 7
Funds from operations to total debt[f]	55%	55%	56%	57%	59%	60%
Case 2: Leverage at lower end of range/expected case operating results						
Pre-interest taxable income[a]	$ 61	$ 67	$ 74	$ 81	$ 89	$ 98
Interest	18	19	21	23	25	26
Surplus (Deficit)[b]	$ 43	$ 48	$ 53	$ 58	$ 64	$ 72
Earnings before fixed charges and income taxes[c]	$ 70	$ 77	$ 85	$ 93	$102	$113
Fixed charges[d]	20	21	23	25	27	28
Fixed charge coverage	3.5x	3.7x	3.7x	3.7x	3.8x	4.0x
Net income	$ 30	$ 33	$ 36	$ 42	$ 45	$ 51
Noncash expenses	65	72	79	84	94	102
Funds from operations[c]	95	105	115	126	139	153
Dividends	(10)	(11)	(12)	(14)	(15)	(17)
Internal cash generation	85	94	103	112	124	136
Capital expenditures	(125)	(125)	(125)	(135)	(150)	(160)
Cash required	$ 40	$ 31	$ 22	$ 23	$ 26	$ 24
External debt requirement[g]	$ 17	$ 15	$ 12	$ 13	$ 15	$ 15
External equity requirement[g]	$ 23	$ 16	$ 10	$ 10	$ 11	$ 9
Funds from operations to total debt[f]	55%	56%	57%	59%	61%	63%

Before deciding where to aim within each of these ranges, Washington Chemical decided to (1) confirm its ability to fully use the estimated tax shield benefits, particularly under somewhat-adverse conditions, and (2) assess the impact of these obligations on its future financing requirements. Table 12-4 contains a pro forma capital structure analysis.

In its evaluation, Washington Chemical realized the importance of considering a reasonably pessimistic case as well as its expected case. Consequently, there are four cases considered in Table 12-4. They correspond to two degrees of leverage (long-term debt ratio of 30% and 35%) and two operating scenarios (10% growth and 5% growth).

It is evident from cases 1 and 2 that Washington Chemical could justify a 35% long-term debt ratio in the expected case. Both the fixed charge coverage and funds-from-operations-to-total-debt

TABLE 12-4   *Continued*

			PROJECTED AHEAD			
	INITIAL	1 YEAR	2 YEARS	3 YEARS	4 YEARS	5 YEARS
Case 3: Leverage at upper end of range/pessimistic case operating results						
Pre-interest taxable income[a]	$ 61	$ 64	$ 67	$ 71	$ 74	$ 78
Interest	18	20	22	24	27	30
Surplus (Deficit)[b]	$ 43	$ 44	$ 45	$ 47	$ 47	$ 48
Earnings before fixed charges and income taxes[c]	$ 70	$ 74	$ 78	$ 82	$ 86	$ 90
Fixed charges[d]	20	22	24	26	29	32
Fixed charge coverage	3.5x	3.4x	3.3x	3.2x	3.0x	2.8x
Net income	$ 30	$ 30	$ 33	$ 33	$ 33	$ 33
Noncash expenses	65	70	72	77	82	88
Funds from operations[c]	95	100	105	110	115	121
Dividends	(10)	(10)	(11)	(11)	(11)	(11)
Internal cash generation	85	90	94	99	104	110
Capital expenditures	(125)	(125)	(125)	(135)	(150)	(160)
Cash required	$ 40	$ 35	$ 31	$ 36	$ 46	$ 50
External debt requirement[e]	$ 20	$ 18	$ 17	$ 19	$ 23	$ 25
External equity requirement[e]	$ 20	$ 17	$ 14	$ 17	$ 23	$ 25
Funds from operations to total debt[f]	55%	52%	50%	48%	46%	44%
Case 4: Leverage at lower end of range/pessimistic case operating results						
Pre-interest taxable income[a]	$ 61	$ 64	$ 67	$ 71	$ 74	$ 78
Interest	18	19	21	23	26	28
Surplus (Deficit)[b]	$ 43	$ 45	$ 46	$ 48	$ 48	$ 50
Earnings before fixed charges and income taxes[c]	$ 70	$ 74	$ 78	$ 82	$ 86	$ 90
Fixed charges[d]	20	21	23	25	28	30
Fixed charge coverage	3.5x	3.5x	3.4x	3.3x	3.1x	3.0x
Net income	$ 30	$ 30	$ 33	$ 33	$ 33	$ 33
Noncash expenses	65	70	72	77	82	88
Funds from operations[c]	95	100	105	110	115	121
Dividends	(10)	(10)	(11)	(11)	(11)	(11)
Internal cash generation	85	90	94	99	104	110
Capital expenditures	(125)	(125)	(125)	(135)	(150)	(160)
Cash required	$40	$ 35	$ 31	$ 36	$ 46	$ 50
External debt requirement[g]	$ 17	$ 16	$ 15	$ 17	$ 20	$ 22
External equity requirement[g]	$ 23	$ 19	$ 16	$ 19	$ 26	$ 28
Funds from operations to total debt[f]	55%	53%	51%	50%	48%	46%

[a]As computed for federal income tax purposes. Estimated to grow at 10% per annum in the "expected case" and 5% per annum in the "pessimistic case."
[b]Calculated as pre-interest taxable income minus interest.
[c]Estimated to grow at 10% per annum in the "expected case" and 5% per annum in the "pessimistic case."
[d]Assumes rental expense of $6 million per year. Under the SEC method, one-third of this amount is included in fixed charges.
[e]Calculated to preserve a ratio of 35% long-term debt financing to 65% additional common equity.
[f]The amount of total debt at the end of the initial year is $174 (= 16 + 158 from Table 12-3). The debt level for any single year projected ahead is the initial amount plus the sum of the annual external debt requirements up to the year in question. The debt level projected ahead 2 years is $205 (= $174 + 17 + 14) so that funds from operations to total debt equals 56% (= 115/205) in Case 1. Similar calculations apply in the other three cases.
[g]Calculated to preserve a ratio of 30% long-term debt financing to 70% additional common equity.

ratios increase steadily and remain comfortably within their target ranges. Moreover, Washington Chemical could fully use the tax benefits of ownership and fully claim all interest deductions.

Under a more pessimistic scenario, cases 3 and 4 show that Washington Chemical's fixed charge coverage and funds-from-operations-to-total-debt ratios would eventually fall below their target ranges. The deterioration is less severe in case 4, because the long-term debt ratio is only 30%. However, the external equity financing requirement is greater. Washington Chemical decided to finance itself with a leverage ratio of 1/3.

Other Aspects of the Capital Structure Decision

Washington Chemical's target capital structure contains only long-term debt and common equity. Firms often adopt more complex capital structures that include one or more layers of subordinated debt, convertible debt, capitalized lease obligations, or preferred equity. Let us take a quick look at each of these.

SUBORDINATED DEBT   Subordinated debt ranks below senior debt in case of default. If strict priority was preserved in bankruptcy, a layer of subordinated debt would be just as beneficial to senior debtholders as more equity. In addition, the interest payments to subordinated debtholders are tax deductible, whereas payments to shareholders are not, which benefits the issuer. However, interest payments and principal repayments must be made in a timely fashion on subordinated debt as well as on senior debt for the issuer to avoid default.

In view of the greater exposure to default risk, the rating agencies usually rate subordinated debt one step below senior debt if the senior debt is rated investment-grade, and two steps below if the senior debt is rated speculative-grade.[4] The rating differential increases the cost of a new debt issue (consistent with the Principle of Risk-Return Trade-Off). Moreover, because strict priority is not always preserved in bankruptcy, the rating agencies will generally add nonconvertible subordinated debt to senior debt for purposes of their ratio calculations. In view of the higher interest cost, $1 of subordinated debt has a more severe impact than $1 of senior debt on a firm's coverage and funds-from-operations-to-debt ratios. Consequently, investment-grade manufacturing firms seldom find it attractive to issue nonconvertible subordinated debt.

Finance firms, on the other hand, often do issue subordinated debt. Because of the comparatively close matching of the maturity structures of their assets and their liabilities, credit firms can support a high degree of leverage. The bulk of their business consists of lending funds at a favorable spread over their funding costs. So a well-run finance firm will have the capacity to fully use the interest tax shields, even when it is very highly leveraged. The subordinated debt, like equity, will provide comfort to senior lenders and tax deductions to the issuer, which equity would not provide.

CONVERTIBLE DEBT   Firms usually issue convertible debt on a subordinated basis. Both issuers and investors expect the issue to be converted into common equity within a few years. It is thus appropriate that convertible debt be junior to nonconvertible debt with respect to bankruptcy priority.

---

[4]For example, a senior debt rating of A2/A would imply a subordinated debt rating of A3/A−. Conversely, a senior debt rating can be inferred from a subordinated debt rating when a firm has only rated subordinated debt outstanding. For example, Western Industries has convertible subordinated debt outstanding, which is rated Ba3/B+. This implies the senior debt rating of Ba1/BB (i.e., up two notches because it is speculative-grade), as indicated in Table 12-3.

CAPITALIZED LEASE OBLIGATIONS   Firms that cannot fully use the tax benefits of ownership often find it attractive to lease assets from entities that can claim these tax deductions and are willing to pass on part of the tax benefits in the form of reduced lease payments. But failure to make a timely lease payment places a firm in default under the lease agreement. Consequently, leases are really a form of secured debt. Rating agencies customarily include capitalized leases, which are reported on the face of the balance sheet, in long-term debt. The decision whether to take on capitalized leases or conventional debt thus hinges principally on tax considerations.

PREFERRED EQUITY   Preferred stock is a hybrid security. It incorporates certain debt features and certain equity features. Failure to make a timely preferred dividend or preferred sinking fund payment will not put the issuer into default. Consequently, substituting preferred stock for a portion of a firm's debt will enhance the position of debtholders in case of default. However, firms normally treat their preferred stock payment obligations as though they were fixed. If a firm issues a significant amount of preferred stock, particularly if it contains a sinking fund, these payment obligations can impair the credit standing of the firm's debt securities.

The rating agencies give greater equity weight to preferred stock the longer its remaining maturity. Mandatory convertibles (into common stock) are given more equity weight than standard convertibles, which are given more weight than nonconvertible preferred.

Making a Capital Structure Change

When a firm finds that its desired capital structure differs significantly from its current capital structure, what should it do? There are two basic choices: change its capital structure slowly, or change it quickly. A firm can alter its capital structure slowly by adjusting its future financing mix appropriately.

For example, suppose a firm's target capital structure consists of 35% long-term debt and 65% common equity, and its current capital structure contains 25% long-term debt and 75% common equity. The firm could cure this underleveraged condition by using long-term debt for all new external financing until the long-term debt ratio reaches 35%. However, this means that the firm's capital structure would continue to be "suboptimal" while the firm changes it over time.

Alternatively, the firm could change its capital structure quickly through an exchange offer, recapitalization offer, debt or share repurchase, or stock-for-debt swap. This would enable the firm to begin immediately employing a mix of financing that conforms to its desired capital structure. Of course, this approach is not without cost either. The firm will incur transaction costs. Also, there will be signaling effects associated with the capital structure change.

If the distance of a firm's capital structure from its target corresponds to one full rating category or more, some type of one-time transaction to make an immediate change in capital structure is probably warranted. A leverage increase for a significantly underleveraged firm is likely to increase the firm's share price. If the firm is less than one full category away from its rating objective (for example, it is a weak single-A and wants to become a strong single-A), altering its retention ratio and its external financing mix is probably more cost-effective.

REVIEW

1. What are the three steps in a comparative credit analysis?

2. How can a firm select an appropriate rating objective?

3. Why is it useful to consider different economic scenarios when conducting a pro forma capital structure analysis?

4. What is subordinated debt? Why do firms usually issue convertible bonds in that form rather than as senior debt?

5. Suppose a firm's capital structure is different from its target capital structure. Explain how it could bring its capital structure back into line with the target. How might it do so quickly?

12.4 ADJUSTING PRESENT VALUE AND REQUIRED RETURNS FOR CAPITAL STRUCTURE EFFECTS

We described a basic method of estimating a cost of capital. We treated the investment and financing decisions independently of one another. But in Chapter 11, we saw that capital structure can affect a firm's value and, therefore, the value of an investment it undertakes. Because of this interaction, the investment and financing decisions cannot be completely separated. In the balance of this chapter, we will show you how to account for the valuation impact of capital structure.

In practice, the cost of capital, WACC, is simply adjusted to reflect the capital structure impact on firm value. In many cases, the adjustment is only an estimate of a complex process. Yet this method is particularly useful. After adjusting WACC, we can use it directly in our valuation procedure without any other changes. The only difference is that the (adjusted) WACC reflects the firm's capital structure *in addition* to the project's risk.

A Capital Budgeting Project's Cost of Capital

Before going any further, we will review a few things. First, recall that the required return is an *opportunity cost of capital*. It is not a historical cost of funds. The required return is the rate at which investors would provide financing for the project under consideration *today*. Theoretically, each project has its own cost of capital. Second, remember that value is a function of both expected future cash flows and the required return. Value can remain unchanged even though both the expected future cash flows and the required return change, if the changes exactly offset each other. Third, because of the risk-return trade-off, there is a single return for each level of risk in an efficient capital market.

Recall that a firm's weighted average cost of capital, WACC, can always be described in terms of financing rates. This also holds for a capital budgeting project's cost of capital. We can think of the project as a "mini" firm. Therefore, a project's WACC can also always be represented as the weighted average of the market value proportions of any debt and equity financing package that will allow the project to be undertaken:

$$(12.4) \qquad \text{WACC} = (1 - L)r_e + L(1 - T)r_d$$

where L is the market value proportion of debt financing, T is the relevant corporate tax rate, r_d is the required return on debt, and r_e is the required return on equity. Both r_d and r_e are specific to the project. You may recognize that Equation (12.4) is identical to Equation (11.1).

As we have said, this equation is always correct. However, it can be difficult to apply in some situations. As we saw in Chapter 11, r_e and r_d depend upon tax laws, asymmetric information considerations, and transaction costs associated with a given capital structure. If accurate functions for r_e and r_d did exist, they could simply be substituted into Equation (12.4), and our job would be done. Unfortunately, we cannot do this without making assumptions that only approximate the circumstances of the firm and the world in which it operates.

The Basis for Adjusting for Capital Structure Effects

The effect of capital structure on value is based on the entire firm's financing. Therefore, the project's cost of capital must be adjusted on the same basis. This means that adjusting the project's cost of capital is fundamentally different from the adjustment for risk. In a sense, a project undertaken by an ongoing firm has no financial risk. Still, the firm itself does have financial risk. Financial risk is created by issuing financial obligations, such as long-term debt. The shareholders' obligation is not limited by the results of one investment. Rather, the financial obligation extends to the results of the whole firm. When one investment does poorly, the firm must still pay whatever debts come due from the proceeds of all its other investments. Thus, financing considerations cannot be accounted for on a project-by-project basis. Instead, the impact of financing on the project's cost of capital is determined by the capital structure of the whole firm.

In the event that a firm finances an investment through a separate corporate subsidiary, the parent firm has no direct liability for any of the subsidiary's financial obligations. The parent is a shareholder. The corporate firm thus limits its liability to what it has invested in the subsidiary. In that case, the subsidiary's capital structure is the relevant one on which to base the project's cost of capital.

When Capital Structure Effects Are Important

There are two situations in which it is particularly important to adjust explicitly for capital structure effects. The first is when the repayment of a loan is tied to one or more specific assets. Leverage will change as the loan is repaid and as the asset is used up and its value declines.[5] This planned reduction in leverage makes it *both* inappropriate to assume a constant debt ratio (as the procedure developed in Chapter 8 assumes) and impractical to assume some sort of time-weighted average debt ratio. The *adjusted-present-value (APV)* approach discussed in this chapter can handle this situation.

The second case occurs in practice when firms adjust their capital structures to coincide with their target capital structures. A firm's total amount of debt (as distinguished from the proportion, L) at any point in time therefore depends on the firm's profitability. More profitable firms accumulate retained earnings more quickly and can add debt faster. The reverse is true for less profitable firms. Capital structure rebalancing thus adds an element of risk to the firm's financial situation, which affects its cost of capital. Later in the chapter we will explain how to incorporate this factor into a firm's cost of capital calculation.

REVIEW

1. Explain why each capital investment project has its own cost of capital.
2. Describe two situations when it is important to adjust the cost of capital for capital structure effects.

12.5 ADJUSTED PRESENT VALUE

The value of a leveraged firm, or any investment, was given by Equation (11.8):

(11.8)
$$V_L = V_U + T^*D = \frac{\overline{I}(1-T)}{r} + \frac{T^*r_d D}{r_d}$$

The right-hand side expresses the total present value as the present value of two perpetuities (the cash flow divided by the discount rate). The first is the present value of the firm's operating cash flow stream, calculated as though the firm had no debt. The second is the present value of the stream of interest tax shields. Equation (11.8) implies the required return given by Equation (11.9):

(11.9)
$$\text{WACC} = r(1 - T^*L)$$

---

[5]An example is a leveraged buyout. It involves an asset-specific capital structure. By design, the leverage will decrease over time. Cash flows from asset sales and operations are dedicated to repay debt. The owners of the firm intend to restore its capital structure to one that is more "normal," typically within five to seven years.

which is appropriate for investments that are level perpetuities.[6] But most investments are not level perpetuities. We could still use Equation (11.9) as a less accurate estimate, but more accurate ones are available.

Suppose a firm's loan is tied to one or more specific assets by an agreement such as a mortgage or lease. In such cases, the interest and principal payments are prespecified to occur within the asset's life. Over that payment period, the value of the asset declines with its use because the project (asset) has a finite life. Finite-life projects with contractually specified debt payment schedules are fundamentally different from perpetual investments. In these cases, we know at the start of the project what the exact pattern of the "capital structure" will be (the remaining debt at any point) because of the repayment contract. Such a project's cost of capital can then be adjusted for the effects of this capital structure over the project's life. **Adjusted present value (APV)** is a method that can account for such patterns.

Equation (11.8) expresses the firm's value as the sum of two components. We can rewrite this equation to approximate a project's value as the sum of two components, each of which is the present value of a *finite* cash flow stream. The first is the "basic" project income, its CFATs, and the other is the net benefits from debt financing. So the value of the project, its APV, is

$$(12.5) \qquad APV_0 = \sum_{t=1}^{n} \frac{CFAT_t}{(1+r)^t} + \sum_{t=1}^{n} \frac{T^*INT_t}{(1+r_d)^t}$$

where n is the number of periods in the life of the project and INT_t is the interest payment in period t. Each sum is the present value of a finite stream, which corresponds to the present value of a perpetuity in Equation (11.8).

EXAMPLE Calculating an APV at Borden

Borden is evaluating an investment in a new type of soybean processing plant. The investment would be set up as a wholly owned subsidiary, called SBP. SBP would be financed with $2.5 million of debt and $1.5 million of cash, provided by Borden as equity. The (unleveraged) after-tax cash flows, the CFATs, expected to result from SBP are $1 million per year for six years. After that time, the project is expected to be sold off for a net after-tax $2 million in cash. SBP will have six-year debt at an interest rate of 13.2% per year. Principal repayments will be $200,000 per year for five years, and $1.5 million at the end of year 6. Suppose the net-benefit-to-leverage factor, T^*, for this investment is 0.25 and the (unleveraged) required return for the project, r, is 20%. What is the value of the project to Borden? In other words, what is the project's *net* APV?

Table 12-5 gives an amortization schedule for SBP's loan. It identifies the interest payments that SBP must make over the life of the loan. From Equation (12-5), we have

$$APV_0 = \sum_{t=1}^{6} \frac{1.0}{(1.2)^t} + \frac{2.0}{(1.2)^6} +$$

$$\left[\frac{0.3300}{1.132} + \frac{0.3036}{(1.132)^2} + \frac{0.2772}{(1.132)^3} + \frac{0.2508}{(1.132)^4} + \frac{0.2244}{(1.132)^5} + \frac{0.1980}{(1.132)^6} \right][0.25]$$

$$APV_0 = 3.325510 + 0.941571 = \$4.267 \text{ million}$$

The net APV (APV_0 minus the initial cost) is then $0.267 million (= 4.267 − 4.0).

---

[6]We say *level* perpetuity to emphasize that the cash flow is constant, and to distinguish it from a *growing* perpetuity.

YEAR	0	1	2	3	4	5	6
(a) Loan balance at start of period	0	2.5000	2.3000	2.1000	1.9000	1.7000	1.5000
(b) Interest for the period (13.2% of loan balance)	0	0.3300	0.3036	0.2772	0.2508	0.2244	0.1980
(c) Principal repayment	0	0.2000	0.2000	0.2000	0.2000	0.2000	1.5000
(d) Loan balance at end of period, (a)–(c)	2.5000	2.3000	2.1000	1.9000	1.7000	1.5000	0

TABLE 12-5
Loan amortization schedule for SBP (dollar amounts in millions).

REVIEW

1. What are the two components of the adjusted present value of a project?
2. Explain why Equation (12.5) for a particular project is analogous to Equation (11.8) for the whole firm.

12.6 MANAGING CAPITAL STRUCTURE AND ITS IMPACT ON FIRM VALUE

APV is very useful in situations when the financing and investment are tied together, such as leases and leveraged buyouts. However, capital budgeting decisions usually do not involve financing that is tied to the project. Nevertheless, even if the firm's financing decisions are separate from its capital budgeting decisions, if T^* is positive, capital structure affects the value of the firm's investments. To include that value effect, we must know the *pattern* of debt payments.

Leverage Rebalancing

A firm generally establishes a capital structure policy that involves a target debt ratio, L^*. The firm's actual debt ratio, L, might be above or below L^* at any point in time. Although the firm does not maintain $L = L^*$ at all times, periodically the firm adjusts its capital structure back to $L = L^*$. Such adjustments are especially common when a firm has additional reasons for making a major financial transaction, such as issuing new bonds or paying off old ones. When a firm adjusts its capital structure back to L^*, it is referred to as **leverage rebalancing.**

Unintended changes in a firm's capital structure may necessitate leverage rebalancing. These unintended changes can occur for a number of reasons. Most often such changes occur because new information arrives. For example, an innovation in technology can cause an increase or decrease in the value of a firm. Because L is the ratio of debt to the *total market value* of the firm, a change in the firm's value causes L to change.

A General Pattern for Debt Payments

Suppose a firm has a target leverage ratio, and it periodically rebalances its leverage to that target. In particular, suppose leverage is rebalanced each period on the basis of the project's realized market value. This sounds much more complex than it turns out. Under such a policy, there is a simple adjustment to the unleveraged required return, r, to get the cost of capital for correctly computing the value of an investment. And this works even when the project's CFAT stream is not a level perpetuity.

When leverage is rebalanced each period on the basis of the realized market value, the net benefit to leverage in future periods will vary with the value of the project. So the net benefit to leverage in future periods is riskier with leverage rebalancing than it is with a fixed debt payment schedule. In fact, the actual debt pattern will vary in the same way project value varies.

With leverage rebalancing, the present value of the net benefits to leverage is not determined by r_d. Only the net benefit from the first period is discounted at r_d, because only the first period's debt is known at the start ($t = 0$). The net benefit to leverage in later periods must be discounted at r, the project's unleveraged required return, because this net benefit will vary as the project value varies in future periods.

Adjusting WACC for Capital Structure Valuation Effects

We will derive the adjustment to r that gives the project's correct cost of capital assuming income that is a level perpetuity, because it is easier to understand. However, the answer also applies to projects that have finite lives.

With level perpetual income, there is a "basic" expected after-tax cash flow, CFAT, of $\overline{I}(1-T)$ each period. There is also an expected (mathematical expectation) net benefit to leverage each period of $T^*Lr_dE[V_L]$, where $E[V_L]$ is the expected value of the project. Note that the actual value of the project at each future time is a *realization*. It will almost surely differ from the expectation, just as the realized return differs from the expected return.

According to Equation (11.8), the total value of the investment is the sum of the two present values. However, to compute these present values, we need to know the required return for each income stream. The required return for the first stream is straightforward. It is the unleveraged required return, r. Thus, the present value, V_U, is:

$$(11.2) \qquad V_U = \frac{\overline{I}(1-T)}{r}$$

Determining the required return for the second stream is more complex. V_L is the value of the project at $t = 0$. The net benefit to leverage in the first period is $T^*Lr_dV_L$, because the debt level is LV_L. This amount has the same risk as the debt. However, the net benefits to leverage in later periods are based on the expected value, $E(V_L)$. They are therefore riskier. The amount of debt in each future period depends on what the project's value turns out to be at that time. The risk of those tax benefits is therefore comparable to the risk of the unleveraged cash flows.

Let the net benefit to leverage in the first period be $\Delta = T^*Lr_dV_L$. Let the expected net benefit to leverage in all periods after the first be $h = T^*Lr_dE(V_L)$. The stream of net benefits to leverage and the present value calculation for them are illustrated in Figure 12-1.

At time $t = 1$, the stream of future net benefits to leverage is a level perpetuity with an expected value of h each period. So the value, at $t = 1$, of future benefits in periods 2, 3, 4, . . . is simply h/r—the present value of a perpetuity. The total value attributable to leverage, at $t = 1$,

FIGURE 12-1

Present value calculation for the net benefit to leverage.

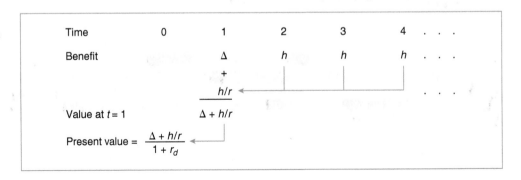

equals $\Delta + h/r$. To get the total value at $t = 0$, we must discount the value at $t = 1$ back one period. We discount it at r_d because it belongs to the same risk class as the debt itself. The present value of all the net benefits to leverage over the life of the project is then

$$(12.6) \qquad \text{PV(net benefit to leverage)} = \frac{\Delta + h/r}{1 + r_d}$$

The total value of the leveraged investment, V_L, equals the sum of V_U and the PV (net benefit to leverage):

$$(12.7) \qquad V_L = \frac{\overline{I}(1-T)}{r} + \frac{\Delta + h/r}{1 + r_d}$$

$\overline{I}$ is a level expected perpetuity. Its expected value at any future point in time is the same as its current expected value. Therefore $E(V_L) = V_L$ and $h = \Delta$. Thus, we can substitute $T*Lr_dV_L$ for both Δ and h in Equation (12.7). Making these substitutions and rearranging terms (which we will not drag out here) gives the following expression for the total value of the leveraged investment:

$$(12.8) \qquad V_L = \frac{\overline{I}(1-T)}{r - T*Lr_d\left[\dfrac{1+r}{1+r_d}\right]}$$

Equation (12.8) expresses V_L as the present value of a perpetuity consisting of CFAT = $\overline{I}(1-T)$. Therefore, the denominator must be the required return for this perpetuity. Therefore

$$(12.9) \qquad \text{WACC} = r - T*Lr_d\left[\frac{1+r}{1+r_d}\right]$$

Equation (12.9) shows a firm's or project's (weighted average) cost of capital, assuming the firm follows a policy of leverage rebalancing each period based on the investment's realized market value.

EXAMPLE Calculating Bausch & Lomb's WACC

Let us say the unleveraged required return, r, for Bausch & Lomb's entire portfolio of assets is 18%. Suppose $T* = 0.25$ and Bausch & Lomb rebalances its capital structure each year to a target of $L = 0.35$. Bausch & Lomb can borrow currently at a rate of $r_d = 11.5\%$. What is Bausch & Lomb's WACC?
From Equation (12.9) we have

$$\text{WACC} = 0.18 - 0.25(0.35)(0.115)\left[\frac{1.18}{1.115}\right] = 0.1694, \text{ or } 16.94\%$$

Estimating the Unleveraged Required Return

Equation (12.9) shows the WACC for a firm or project based on the unleveraged required return, r. Often we need to reverse this process and estimate r based on the WACC.
We know that Equation (12.4) is always correct. And we have said that the debt management pattern assumed in Equation (12.9) represents typical corporate policy quite well.

Therefore, we can use Equation (12.4) to estimate the WACC and use that value to calculate r. To simplify the notation (if you can imagine it), we will use a variable, H:

(12.10)
$$H = \frac{T^* L r_d}{1 + r_d}$$

Then, expressing Equation (12.9) in terms of H and solving for r gives the following expression for the unleveraged required return:[8]

(12.11)
$$r = \frac{\text{WACC} + H}{1 - H}$$

EXAMPLE Estimating Conoco's Unleveraged Required Return

Suppose Conoco wants to estimate the unleveraged required return for a project it is considering. Conoco's finance staff has identified Prairie Oil and Gas, a publicly traded firm in the same business as the Conoco project. Prairie's operating risk profile should therefore be similar to that of the project. Prairie's leverage ratio is $L = 0.40$. They estimate that Prairie's new issue debt rate is $r_d = 12\%$ and calculate Prairie's WACC = 15%. They also estimate $T^* = 0.25$. What is the project's unleveraged required return?

Substituting into Equation (12.10),

$$H = \frac{(0.25)(0.40)(0.12)}{1.12} = 0.01071$$

Substituting into Equation (12.11),

$$r = \frac{0.15 + 0.01071}{1 - 0.01071} = 0.1625$$

So the unleveraged required return for the Conoco project is estimated to be 16.25%.

REVIEW

1. What does it mean to say that a firm follows a capital structure policy of periodically rebalancing its debt level?
2. Explain why r, and not r_d, is the appropriate discount rate for calculating the present value of the future interest tax shields when the firm regularly rebalances its debt level.
3. As long as T^* can never be negative, explain why the WACC can never exceed the unleveraged required return, r.

ESTIMATING THE WACC FOR A CAPITAL
12.7 BUDGETING PROJECT

Now let us see how to calculate the WACC for a project when the firm regularly rebalances its capital structure. We will combine the procedure outlined in the previous section with the other basic steps discussed previously. That will give you the complete set of steps you need to follow.

---

[8]Equation (12.9) becomes WACC = $r - (1 + r)H$. Then solving for r we get Equation (12.11).

The process for estimating a WACC can be outlined as follows:

1. Choose one or more comparable firms (with publicly traded securities) that have similar risk and industry characteristics as that of the project.

2. For each comparable firm:
   a. Estimate L. L is the market value of all the firm's debt (total liabilities) divided by the sum of the total market values of the firm's debt and equity. Sometimes the book value of debt approximates the market value of debt pretty well.
   b. Estimate r_d. r_d can be estimated as the yield to maturity on the firm's outstanding debt.
   c. Estimate r_e. Estimating r_e is more difficult and requires professional judgement. The dividend growth model or the capital-asset-pricing model[9] can be used to estimate r_e.
   d. Estimate the firm's marginal tax rate, T, using publicly reported data.
   e. Estimate the net-benefit-to-leverage factor for the firm, T^*. T^* is the most difficult parameter to estimate. Estimating T^* involves considering the firm's marginal tax rate, the uniqueness of its products, and the amount of nondebt tax shields, among other factors discussed in Chapter 16. The estimate of T^* is ultimately based on subjective professional judgment. Based on empirical research, we would expect most estimates for a healthy firm to fall somewhere between 0.10 and 0.20.

3. For each comparable firm, use the parameter estimates from point 2 above to estimate H using Equation (12.10) and the WACC using Equation (12.4). Then use Equation (12.11) to estimate r.

4. Based on the set of one or more estimates of r from comparable firms, make a single estimate of r. Usually an average can be used. However, judgment is necessary when the variation in the estimates is large or some of the estimates are very different from each other. r must reflect the project's business risk.

5. The estimate of the project's WACC (which includes both business risk and the effects of capital structure) can now be computed using Equation (12.9), the single estimate of r derived above, and estimates for the firm considering the investment:
   a. the firm's target capital structure, L^*, which the firm plans to maintain;
   b. the firm's current r_d based on L^*; and
   c. the firm's net-benefit-to-leverage factor, T^*.

EXAMPLE **Estimating a Project's WACC for PepsiCo**

Suppose PepsiCo is considering an investment opportunity in laser printers, an area in which it has no previous experience. PepsiCo has identified several firms that are primarily in this business. One of these firms is H-P, whose common stock and bonds are traded publicly on the NYSE. Suppose the market value of H-P common stock is $27 per share. H-P has 10 million shares outstanding. H-P's latest earnings were $3.40 per share. Next year's dividend is expected to be $1.60 per share. Five years ago, H-P paid a dividend of $0.73 per share. H-P has long-term bonds with a total market value of $120 million. Its 9% coupon bonds maturing in 18 years are currently selling for $860. In addition to long-term bonds, H-P has $20 million in notes payable and $40 million in other current liabilities.

   H-P has total liabilities of $180 million consisting of long-term bonds and current liabilities (= 120 + 20 + 40). Current liabilities mature soon enough that the book and market

---

[9]If you do not have enough information to use one of these analytical methods, Emery's rule says that r_e is normally about 1.5 times r_d.

CALCULATOR SOLUTION

Data Input	Function Key
36	N
−860	PV
45 (=90/2)	PMT
1,000	FV
5.39%	I

values are sufficiently close to ignore the difference and simply use the book value in our calculations. Total equity is $270 million [=(27)10 million]. The total market value of H-P is $450 million (= 120 + 60 + 270), and $L = 0.40$ (= 180/450). H-P's 9% coupon bonds have a 10.78% yield to maturity, and an 11.07% APY.

Because the bonds are selling at a discount and will incur lower taxes due to capital gains tax deferral, we estimate that new debt for H-P has a required return that is slightly higher than the 11.07% APY. We estimate r_d to be 11.25% APY.

Lasser Financial Services estimates that H-P's beta is 1.25. Short-term U.S. government securities are currently earning 7%, so we estimate the riskless rate, r_f, to be 7%. The required return on the market portfolio, r_M, is estimated to be 15%. The CAPM estimate of H-P's required return on equity is $r_e = 0.07 + 1.25(0.15 - 0.07) = 0.17$, or 17%. During the six-year period from five years ago until next year, H-P's cash dividend grew from $0.73 to $1.60, which represents an annual growth rate of $g = 14\%$. The current market value is $P_0 = \$27$, and next year's expected dividend is $D_1 = \$1.60$. The dividend growth model estimate of the required return for equity is $r_e = (1.6/27) + 0.14 = 0.20$, or 20%.

The estimate obtained from the dividend growth model is based on a growth rate that is almost as large as the return to the market portfolio and is considerably larger than the return on the riskless asset. It is unlikely that growth of this magnitude could be maintained indefinitely. Thus, the dividend growth model estimate of r_e is probably too large. However, it is plausibly close to the CAPM estimate. Therefore, the two estimates do not appear to significantly contradict one another. Because the CAPM estimate is more reliable, we will use it as our estimate of H-P's required return on equity.

PepsiCo's financial staff estimates that H-P's net-benefit-to-leverage factor is $T^* = 0.2$. Applying Equation (12.10), with $T^* = 0.20$, $L = 0.40$, and $r_d = 11.25\%$,

$$H = \frac{T^* L r_d}{1 + r_d} = \frac{(0.2)(0.4)(0.1125)}{1.1125} = 0.00809$$

The relevant marginal tax rate is estimated as $T = 35\%$. Therefore, with $r_e = 17\%$, applying Equation (12.4) we get

$$\text{WACC} = (1 - L)r_e + L(1 - T)r_d = 0.6(0.17) + 0.4(0.65)(0.1125) = 0.13125$$

Finally, putting $H = 0.00809$ and WACC = 13.125% into Equation (12.11), we have

$$r = \frac{\text{WACC} + H}{1 - H} = \frac{(0.13125 + 0.00809)}{(1 - 0.00809)} = 0.1405$$

Assume that the above procedure was followed for other comparable firms in addition to H-P and the single estimate of r based on the set of comparable firms is 14%. We can now estimate WACC for the project based on this "best" estimate of r and the following estimates of PepsiCo's financial parameters: $r_d = 11\%$, $L^* = 0.3$, and (because of its unique tax situation) $T^* = 0.15$. From Equation (12.9),

$$\text{WACC} = r - T^* L r_d \left[\frac{1 + r}{1 + r_d} \right] = 0.14 - (0.15)(0.3)(0.11) \left[\frac{1.14}{1.11} \right] = 0.135, \text{ or } 13.5\%$$

Thus, PepsiCo should use a 13.5% WACC to compute the NPV of its proposed investment in laser printers.

REVIEW

1. List the steps in the five-step process for estimating the WACC for a capital budgeting project.
2. Explain why the estimate of r calculated at step 4 reflects the operating risk of the project under consideration *and does not* reflect any financial risk.
3. Explain how step 5 adjusts for financial risk based on the project sponsor's capital structure.

SUMMARY

The following procedure is useful for choosing and managing capital structure:

- Determine the *rating objective*. It reflects the desired margin of safety for the risk of financial distress and for maintaining access to the capital markets.
- Conduct a *comparative credit analysis* of comparable firms to determine the capital structure that is consistent with the chosen rating. It is particularly important to select firms with similar asset portfolios, because asset type affects the costs of financial distress and the amount of leverage for a particular rating. It is also important to select firms that are comparable in size, because other things being equal, the larger a firm, the greater the amount of debt the rating agencies will tolerate for a given rating.
- Determine the values of the *key financial ratios that characterize leverage*. Three such ratios that are particularly meaningful are annual fixed charge coverage ratio, annual funds-from-operations-to-total-debt ratio, and long-term debt ratio. However, three simple ratios usually do not tell the whole story. So many analysts use additional ratios to define the target capital structure.
- Conduct a *pro forma financial analysis* to test the firm's ability to use fully both the tax benefits of ownership under its planned capital expenditure program and the interest tax shields if it finances in accordance with its target capital structure. Also test the impact on financial ratios of different future operating scenarios to determine what adjustment to the target capital structure is appropriate in light of the firm's expected future operating environment.
- Determine the need for and desirability of a *share repurchase or other form of transaction* to adjust capital structure quickly.
- APV (adjusted present value) is a method for including the effect of capital structure on investment value, using the unleveraged value V_U and "adjusting" that basic value by adding the value obtained from leverage.
- With APV, the added value from leverage is the present value of a series of cash flow adjustments stemming from a fixed debt payment pattern, such as with leases or a leveraged buyout, or any unique debt pattern.
- A more general form of APV adjusts the WACC, using an approximation of leverage rebalancing on the basis of realized market value. Although the adjustment is only an estimate of a more complex process, this method is widely used in practice and is particularly useful because it simply modifies the rate used in an otherwise "standard NPV calculation."

EQUATION SUMMARY

$$(12.1) \qquad \text{Interest coverage ratio} = \frac{\text{EBIT}}{\text{Interest expense}}$$

$$(12.2) \qquad \text{Fixed charge coverage ratio} = \frac{\text{EBIT} + 1/3 \ \text{Rentals}}{\text{Interest expense} + 1/3 \ \text{Rentals}}$$

$$(12.3) \qquad \text{Debt service coverage ratio} = \frac{\text{EBIT} + 1/3 \ \text{Rentals}}{\text{Interest expense} + 1/3 \ \text{Rentals} + \dfrac{\text{Principal repayments}}{1 - \text{Tax rate}}}$$

$$(12.4) \qquad \text{WACC} = (1 - L)r_e + L(1 - T)r_d$$

$$(12.5) \qquad \text{APV}_0 = \sum_{t=1}^{n} \frac{\text{CFAT}_t}{(1+r)^t} + \sum_{t=1}^{n} \frac{T*\text{INT}_t}{(1+r_d)^t}$$

$$(12.6) \qquad \text{PV (net benefit to leverage)} = \frac{\Delta + h/r}{1 + r_d}$$

$$(12.7) \qquad V_L = \frac{\bar{I}(1-T)}{r} + \frac{\Delta + h/r}{1 + r_d}$$

$$(12.8) \qquad V_L = \frac{\bar{I}(1-T)}{r - T*Lr_d \left[\dfrac{1+r}{1+r_d} \right]}$$

$$(12.9) \qquad \text{WACC} = r - T*Lr_d \left[\frac{1+r}{1+r_d} \right]$$

$$(12.10) \qquad H = \frac{T*Lr_d}{1 + r_d}$$

$$(12.11) \qquad r = \frac{\text{WACC} + H}{1 - H}$$

QUESTIONS

1. Why is a pro forma analysis an important prerequisite to choosing a capital structure?
2. What is the major reason that subordinated debt is typically rated lower than senior debt?
3. Explain why selecting a target senior debt rating is a reasonable approach to choosing a capital structure. Explain why a target senior debt rating of single-A is a prudent objective when there is only a very limited new issue market for non-investment-grade debt, and when investor willingness to purchase triple-B-rated debt is likely to be highly sensitive to the state of the economy.
4. A firm's capital structure consists solely of debt and common equity. What form would an exchange offer take if the firm believes it is (a) overleveraged? (b) underleveraged?

5. Because the weighted average given in Equation (12.4) is always a correct measure of a required return, why do firms not create securities to finance each project and offer them in the capital market in order to accurately determine the required return for the project?

6. Why should a firm's ability to use tax credits affect its capital structure?

7. How does a firm's size (as measured by total assets or total sales, for example) affect its choice of capital structure under the comparable-firms approach?

8. Why would lenders be willing to lend a larger proportion of the market value of tangible assets such as plant and equipment than of the market value of intangible assets such as "special" formulas and goodwill?

9. Suppose that a firm wishes to maintain a capital structure that is consistent with an A senior debt rating. Under what circumstances would the firm maintain a lower degree of leverage than a cross section of single-A-rated firms?

CHALLENGING QUESTIONS

10. Which factor is most difficult to estimate, r, T^*, L, or r_d? Why?

11. Why is it so important to note that the required return is not a historical cost of funds? Cite two factors that can render the use of a firm's historical cost of funds (to evaluate a new investment) to be potentially damaging to the firm.

12. In what sense is subordinated debt advantageous to senior debtholders, and in what sense is it disadvantageous to them?

13. Explain in your own words why you might expect to observe a negative correlation between financial leverage and operating leverage.

14. Using agency theory concepts, explain how restrictive covenants that forbid leases and liens on a firm's assets might cause the firm to achieve a higher rating on its bonds than would be possible without such covenants.

15. The development of the new issue junk bond market had important implications for capital structure choice. The existence of a viable junk bond market means that firms can comfortably maintain higher degrees of leverage than they could prior to the development of this market. Do you agree or disagree? Justify your answer.

16. A balance sheet sometimes has something called minority interest, which appears below long-term debt and above preferred stock. Discuss whether minority interest should be treated as debt or equity, assuming

   a. It consists of outstanding common stock of a subsidiary, and the parent firm has no intention of repurchasing or otherwise retiring that common stock.

   b. It consists of redeemable preferred stock of a subsidiary, which the firm is obligated to redeem in equal annual amounts over the next five years.

   c. What is your conclusion regarding whether minority interest is really debt or equity?

PROBLEMS

■ LEVEL A (BASIC)

A1. (Coverage ratio) A firm's latest 12 months' EBIT is $30 million, and its interest expense for the same period is $10 million. Calculate the interest coverage ratio.

A2. (Coverage ratio) The firm in the preceding problem also had $15 million of rental expense during the latest 12 months. Calculate the firm's fixed charge coverage ratio.

A3. (Coverage ratio) The firm in the two preceding problems also had $6 million of principal repayments during the latest 12 months. Its marginal tax rate is 40%. Calculate the debt service coverage ratio.

A4. (WACC with rebalancing) Nathan's Catering is a gourmet catering service located in Southampton, New York. It has an unleveraged required return of $r = 43\%$. Nathan's rebalances its capital structure each year to a target of $L = 0.52$. $T^* = 0.20$. Nathan's can borrow currently at a rate of $r_d = 26\%$. What is Nathan's WACC?

A5. (Unleveraging the cost of equity) Maxicomputer Corporation is considering building a new manufacturing facility in Taiwan. Maxicomputer's debt ratio is $L = 0.5$. Maxicomputer's cost of debt is $r_d = 10\%$. Maxicomputer estimates that the leveraged cost of equity capital for the project is $r_e = 16\%$. $T^* = 0.25$. Maxicomputer's marginal ordinary income tax rate is 40%. Calculate the project's unleveraged required return, r.

A6. (Estimating a project's WACC) Reconsider the PepsiCo example. PepsiCo has identified a second firm that is closely comparable to H-P. Epson has a debt ratio of $L = 0.60$, a cost of debt of $r_d = 12\%$, a leveraged required return to equity of $r_e = 20\%$, a 40% marginal tax rate, and a net-benefit-to-leverage factor of $T^* = 0.20$.

a. Calculate Epson's unleveraged required return, r.

b. Recalculate the estimate of r for PepsiCo to use by averaging H-P's and Epson's unleveraged required returns.

c. What is the required return that PepsiCo should use to compute the (adjusted) NPV of the capital budgeting project?

A7. (NPV of a risky project) Suppose a firm currently has an unleveraged required return of 10% and perpetual unleveraged after-tax income of $140,301 per year. The firm has come up with an investment opportunity that would alter the firm's asset makeup so that it would increase its perpetual unleveraged after-tax income to $170,650 per year. Because the new asset mix is riskier, the firm's unleveraged required return would also increase to 12.165%. Should the firm undertake this investment opportunity?

▪ LEVEL B

B1. (Choosing financial targets) Bixton Company's new chief financial officer is evaluating Bixton's capital structure. She is concerned that the firm might be underleveraged, even though the firm has larger-than-average research and development and foreign tax credits when compared to other firms in its industry. Her staff prepared the industry comparison shown here.

a. Bixton's objective is to achieve a credit standing that falls, in the words of the chief financial officer, "comfortably within the 'A' range." What target range would you recommend for each of the three credit measures?

b. Before settling on these target ranges, what other factors should Bixton's chief financial officer consider?

c. Before deciding whether the target ranges are really appropriate for Bixton in its current financial situation, what key issues specific to Bixton must the chief financial officer resolve?

RATING CATEGORY	FIXED CHARGE COVERAGE	FUNDS FROM OPERATIONS/ TOTAL DEBT	LONG-TERM DEBT/ CAPITALIZATION
Aa	4.00–5.25x	60–80%	17–23%
A	3.00–4.30	45–65	22–32
Baa	1.95–3.40	35–55	30–41

B2. (Choosing financial targets) Sanderson Manufacturing Company would like to achieve a capital structure consistent with a Baa2/BBB senior debt rating. Sanderson has identified six comparable firms and calculated the credit statistics shown here.

   a. Sanderson's return on assets is 5.3%. It has a total capitalization of $600 million. What are reasonable targets for long-term debt/cap, funds from operations/LT debt, and fixed charge coverage?

   b. Are there any firms among the six who are particularly good or bad comparables? Explain.

   c. Suppose Sanderson's current ratio of long-term debt to total cap is 60% but its fixed charge coverage is 3.00. What would you recommend?

FIRM	A	B	C	D	E	F
Senior debt rating	Baa2/BBB	Baa3/BBB–	Baa2/BBB	Baa1/A–	Baa1/BBB–	Baa2/BBB+
Return on assets	5.2%	5.0%	5.4%	5.7%	5.2%	5.3%
Long-term debt/cap	38%	41%	45%	40%	25%	43%
Total cap ($MM)	425	575	525	650	210	375
Funds from						
operations/LT debt	39%	43%	28%	46%	57%	43%
Fixed charge cov	2.57	2.83	2.75	2.38	3.59	2.15

B3. (Coverage ratios) Show that of the interest coverage ratio, fixed charge coverage ratio, and debt service coverage ratio, (1) the interest coverage ratio will always have the greatest value and (2) the debt service coverage ratio will always have the smallest value, as long as interest coverage exceeds 1. Under what circumstances will all three ratios have the same value?

B4. (Coverage ratios) Mi Furst, Inc., has $100 million of earnings before interest and taxes and $40 million of interest expense.

   a. Calculate Mi Furst's interest coverage ratio.

   b. Calculate the pro forma interest coverage ratio assuming the issuance of $100 million of 10% debt with the issue proceeds to be invested fully in a plant under construction.

   c. Calculate the pro forma interest coverage ratio assuming the issuance of $100 million of 10% debt with the proceeds to be invested temporarily in commercial paper that yields 8%.

B5. (APV) Suppose a firm is evaluating a potential new investment. The investment will be financed with $100,000 of debt and $100,000 of equity. The (unleveraged) after-tax cash flows, the CFATs, expected to result from the investment are $150,000 per year for four years. At that time the firm expects to be able to sell the project for a net after-tax $100,000 in cash. The debt financing will be four-year debt with interest payments of 14% per year on the remaining balance. Principal payments will be zero in year 1, $20,000 in year 2, $30,000 in year 3, and a final principal payment of $50,000 at the end of year 4. The net-benefit-to-leverage factor, T^*, is 0.20. The (unleveraged) required return for the project is 20%. What is the project's net APV?

B6. (WACC, leverage, beta) Rusty-Sell, Inc., a midstate Pennsylvania recycling facility, is $L = 27\%$ debt financed. It pays corporate taxes at the rate of 35%. The firm's (leveraged) beta is 1.45. $T^* = 0.21$, $r_d = 12\%$, $r_f = 8\%$, and $r_M = 15\%$. Assume annual capital structure rebalancing.

   a. What is Rusty-Sell's required return to (leveraged) equity, r_e?

   b. What is Rusty-Sell's WACC?

   c. What is Rusty-Sell's unleveraged required return, r?

   d. What unleveraged beta is implied by r?

B7. (Cost of capital estimation) Managers of the Stan Lee Martin Corporation are considering a capital budgeting project that is unrelated to their current investments. The proposed project will be 40% debt financed at $r_d = 11.25\%$. They have identified three firms that they believe are basically comparable to the capital budgeting project under consideration, and they have collected the information about those comparable firms as shown below. Assume the following hold for all firms: (1) $r_M = 15\%$, (2) $r_f = 7\%$, (3) $T = 0.35$, (4) $T^* = 0.2$, and (5) the total debt is the number of bonds indicated, each with a par value of $1,000 and 10 years to maturity. What cost of capital would you recommend the managers of Stan Lee Martin Corporation use to evaluate the proposed capital budgeting project?

FIRM	STOCK BETA	STOCK PRICE	# SHARES	BOND PRICE	COUPON	# BONDS
A	1.10	$25	1 million	$1,100	12%	10,700
B	1.20	$30	2 million	$900	10%	67,000
C	1.15	$22	5 million	$850	8%	32,350

B8. (Review, CAPM) The riskless return is 8%. The expected return on the market portfolio is 16%. A stock's beta is 1.5. Calculate the cost of equity capital.

B9. (Review, dividend growth model) A stock's current market price is $25. The expected annual cash dividend is $1 per share. In addition, investors expect the firm to pay a 4% dividend in common stock. The expected growth rate of the cash dividend is 10% per year.

a. Calculate the cost of retained earnings.

b. If a new share issue would require 5% flotation costs, what is the cost of the new issue?

B10. (Review, CAPM) The riskless return is 6%. The expected excess return on the market portfolio is 8%. A stock's beta is 1.35. Calculate the cost of equity capital.

B11. A stock's unleveraged beta is 0.8. The firm's debt ratio is $L = 0.4$. The riskless return is 5%, the tax rate is 30%, and the expected return on the market portfolio is 15%. What is the firm's cost of equity capital?

B12. A perpetual preferred stock issue can be sold for $25 per share. It would require a quarterly dividend rate of $0.50 per share. The underwriting fees and out-of-pocket expenses amount to 1.75% of the public offering price. What is the cost of preferred stock?

B13. (Excel: APV and WACC) Cans-R-Us, Inc. (CRU) is a recycling firm located in the suburbs of Missouri City, Kansas. CRU is currently evaluating a potential new investment. The investment will be financed with $700,000 of debt and $1,200,000 of equity. The (unleveraged) after-tax cash flows, the CFATs, expected to result from the investment are $1 million per year for three years, after which time the project is expected to be sold off for a net after-tax $1 million in cash. The debt financing will take the form of three-year debt with interest payments of 15% per year on the remaining balance. Principal payments will be $100,000 in year 1, $200,000 in year 2, and $400,000 at the end of year 3. The net-benefit-to-leverage factor, T^*, is 0.25 for this investment. The (unleveraged) required return for the project is 25%. The corporate tax rate is 30%.

a. What is the project's net APV?

b. Based on the net APV computed in part a, what is L for this project?

c. Also based on the net APV computed in part a, what is the project's WACC? (*Hint:* You will need to use trial and error to solve for WACC.)

d. Based on the WACC computed in part c, what is the unleveraged required return, r, for this project?

■ LEVEL C (ADVANCED)

C1. (Excel: APV and WACC) Alpha Manufacturing is considering building a new distribution center that would cost $1 million. Alpha would finance the investment with $250,000 of equity and $750,000 of debt. The (unleveraged) after-tax cash flows, the CFATs, expected to result from the investment are $400,000 per year for 10 years, after which the distribution center will be sold off for a net after-tax amount of $200,000 cash. The loan will bear interest at a rate of 12% payable annually. It will be repaid in equal annual installments of $75,000, beginning at the end of year 1. The corporate tax rate is 35%, $T^* = 0.30$, and the unleveraged cost of equity for the project is 17%.

  a. Calculate the project's net APV.

  b. Calculate the WACC and the leveraged required return to equity, r_e, for the project.

  c. Calculate the (adjusted) NPV of the project.

  d. Reconcile your answers to parts a and c.

MINICASE   DEBT-FOR-EQUITY EXCHANGE AT AMERICAN AIRLINES

AMR Corporation (AMR), the parent firm of American Airlines, found that its profitability had improved a few years ago. Several years prior, AMR had issued privately about $1.1 billion of convertible preferred stock. As you know, interest is tax deductible whereas dividends are not. AMR decided to offer the preferred stockholders the chance to exchange their shares for a new issue of convertible Quarterly Income Capital Securities ("QUICS"). AMR offered to exchange $1,000 face amount of 6.125% convertible QUICS for $1,000 face amount of 6% convertible preferred stock. All $1.1 billion of preferred stock could be exchanged at the holder's option.

The QUICS would carry a slightly higher yield and would rank senior to the preferred stock. But QUICS include an interest-deferral feature: AMR can defer interest payments from time to time for up to 20 consecutive quarters. It was reported that because of this feature, the rating agencies view QUICS as "virtually identical to the preferred."

AMR's main purpose in offering to exchange convertible QUICS for convertible preferred was to improve the firm's after-tax cash flow because of the tax deductibility of interest. The table below compares the QUICS and the preferred stock.

Just prior to the exchange offer, AMR's capitalization was (dollar amounts in millions):

Long-term debt:	
Current maturities	$ 189
Long-term debt, less current maturities	7,710
QUICS	0
Total long-term debt	7,899
Convertible preferred stock	1,081
Common stock	3,318
Total stockholders' equity	4,399
Total capitalization	$12,298

	QUICS	PREFERRED
Interest/Dividend Rate	6⅛ APR; payable quarterly; interest payments can be deferred for up to 20 calendar quarters; at the end of the deferral period, all accrued and unpaid interest must be repaid, together with interest on the unpaid amount compounded quarterly at the 6⅛ APR.	6% APR; payable quarterly out of funds legally available therefore.
Conversion	At $79.00 per common share.	At $78.75 per common share.
Subordination	Subordinated to all existing and future senior debt of AMR and its subsidiaries but senior to AMR's preferred stock.	Subordinated to all debt of AMR.
Market	Registered for public trading; listed on the New York Stock Exchange.	Privately placed; not registered for public trading.

QUESTIONS

1. Describe the QUICS. Are they debt, or are they equity? How do they differ from the convertible preferred stock?

2. Recalculate AMR's capitalization if holders of (i) 50% and (ii) 100% of the convertible preferred stock exchange them for QUICS.

3. Calculate the increase in net income available for common stock that would result from (i) 50% and (ii) 100% of the convertible preferred stock being exchanged for QUICS.

4. Why does this debt-for-equity exchange increase the risk of the common stock? How does the interest-deferral feature affect your interpretation of the QUICS? The risk of the common stock?

5. What trade-off did AMR have to evaluate as it considered whether to proceed with the exchange offer?

GLOSSARY

Abandonment option The option of terminating an investment earlier than originally planned.

ABC system of inventory control An inventory management system that categorizes inventory into one of three groups—A, B, or C—on the basis of critical need.

Absolute priority doctrine The requirement that any distribution of a debtor's assets should be strictly according to claim priority.

Accounting exposur Another name for translation exposure. *See* Translation exposure.

Acid test ratio The difference between current assets and inventories divided by current liabilities.

Ad valorem duty A customs duty levied as a percentage of the assessed value of goods entering a country.

ADB Asian Development Bank.

Adjusted present value (APV) A method that determines total value by adding the "basic" present value of unleveraged cash flows to the present value of net benefits to leverage.

ADR *See* American Depositary Receipt.

AfDB African Development Bank.

Affiliate A foreign enterprise in which the parent company owns a minority interest.

Agency cost view (of capital structure) The argument that the various agency costs create a complex environment in which total agency costs are at a minimum with some, but less than 100%, debt financing.

Agency costs The incremental costs of having an agent make decisions for a principal.

Agency for International Development (AID) A unit of the U.S. government dealing with foreign aid.

Agency problem A potential conflict of interest in a principal-agent relationship.

Agency theory The analysis of principal-agent relationships, wherein one person, an *agent,* acts on behalf of another person, a *principal.*

Agent The decision maker in a principal-agent relationship.

Aging schedule A table of accounts receivable broken down into age categories (such as 0–30 days, 30–60 days, and 60–90 days), which is used to see whether customer payments are keeping close to schedule.

All-equity discount rate A discount rate in capital budgeting that would be appropriate for discounting operating cash flows if the project were financed entirely with owners' equity.

American Depositary Receipt (ADR) A certificate of ownership, issued by a U.S. bank, representing a claim on underlying foreign securities. ADRs may be traded in lieu of trading in the actual underlying shares.

American option An option that can be exercised at any time during its life.

American option An option that can be exercised at any time up to and including the expiration date.

American selling price (ASP) For customs purposes, the use of the domestic price of competing merchandise in the United States as a tax base for determining import duties. The ASP is generally higher than the actual foreign price, so its use is a protectionist technique.

American terms Foreign exchange quotations for the U.S. dollar, expressed as the number of U.S. dollars per unit of non-U.S. currency.

A/P In international trade documentation, abbreviation for authority to purchase or authority to pay. In accounting, abbreviation for accounts payable.

Annual percentage rate (APR) The periodic rate times the number of periods in a year. For example, 2% per quarter is an 8% APR.

Annual percentage yield (APY) The effective (true) annual rate of return. The APY is the rate you actually earn or pay in one year, taking into account the effect of compounding. For example, as shown in Table 4-3, 1% per month is a 12.68% APY.

Annual report A report issued annually by a firm. It includes, at a minimum, an income statement, a balance sheet, a statement of cash flows, and accompanying notes.

Annuity due An *annuity* with n payments, wherein the first payment is made at time $t = 0$ and the last payment is made at time $t = n - 1$.

Annuity A series of identical cash flows each period for n periods.

Appreciation In the context of exchange rate changes, a rise in the foreign exchange value of a currency that is pegged to other currencies or to gold. Also called revaluation.

APR See *Annual percentage rate.*

APT See *Arbitrage pricing theory.*

APV See *Adjusted present value.*

APY See *Annual percentage yield.*

Arbitrage pricing theory (APT) A theory of asset pricing in which the risk premium is based on a specified set of risk factors in addition to (or other than) the correlation with the expected excess return on the market portfolio.

Arbitrage The act of buying and selling an asset simultaneously, where the sale price is larger than the purchase price, so that the difference provides a riskless profit.

Arbitragers Persons who search for and exploit arbitrage opportunities. Also spelled *arbitrageurs.*

Arbitrageur An individual or company that practices arbitrage.

Arithmetic return The mean is simply the average of the annual percentage changes in capital appreciation plus dividend distributions.

Arm's-length price The price at which a willing buyer and a willing unrelated seller freely agree to carry out a transaction. In effect, a free market price. Applied by tax authorities in judging the appropriateness of transfer prices between related companies.

Asian currency unit A trading department within a Singaporean bank that deals in foreign (non-Singaporean) currency deposits and loans.

Ask price The price at which a dealer is willing to sell foreign exchange, securities or commodities. Also called offer price.

Asset activity ratios Ratios that measure how effectively the firm is managing its assets.

Asset market approach Whether foreigners are willing to hold claims in monetary form depends on an extensive set of investment considerations or drivers.

Asset substitution A firm's investing in assets that are riskier than those that the debtholders expected.

Asset-based financing Methods of financing in which lenders and equity investors look principally to the cash flow from a particular asset or set of assets for a return on, and the return of, their investment.

Asymmetric information Information that is known to some people but not to others.

Asymmetric Lacking equivalence, such as the unequal tax treatment of interest expense and dividend payments.

At-the-money An option whose exercise price is the same as the spot price of the underlying currency.

Average age of accounts receivable The weighted average age of all the firm's outstanding invoices.

Average collection period The approximate number of days required to collect a firm's accounts receivable. Also called *days' sales outstanding.*

Average life The effective maturity of a debt issue, taking into account the effect of sinking fund payments.

Average tax rate Taxes as a fraction of income; total taxes divided by total taxable income.

Back-to-back loan A loan in which two companies in separate countries borrow each other's currency for a specific period of time and repay the other's currency at an agreed maturity. Sometimes the two loans are channeled through an intermediate bank. Back-to-back financing is also called link financing.

Balance of payments A financial statement summarizing the flow of goods, services, and investment funds between residents of a given country and residents of the rest of the world.

Balance of trade An entry in the balance of payments measuring the difference between the monetary value of merchandise exports and merchandise imports.

Balance sheet hedge Requires an equal amount of exposed foreign currency assets and liabilities on a firm's consolidated balance sheet.

Balance sheet identity Total Assets = Liabilities + Stockholders' Equity.

Balance sheet A statement of a firm's financial position at one point in time, including its assets and the claims on those assets by creditors (liabilities) and owners (stockholders' equity).

Balloon payment A debt payment that is larger than the loan's other payments. It is typically the final payment that repays the outstanding balance of the loan.

Bank for International Settlements (BIS) A bank in Basle, Switzerland, that functions as a bank for European central banks.

Bank rate The interest rate at which central banks for various countries lend to their own monetary institutions.

Bankers' acceptance An unconditional promise of a bank to make payment on a draft when it matures. The acceptance is in the form of the bank's endorsement (acceptance) of a draft drawn against that bank in accordance with the terms of a letter of credit issued by the bank.

Bankruptcy cost view (of capital structure) The argument that expected indirect and direct bankruptcy costs offset the other benefits from leverage so that the optimal amount of leverage is less than 100% debt financing.

Bankruptcy A formal legal process under which a firm experiencing financial difficulty is protected from its creditors while it works out a plan to settle its debt obligations under the supervision of the bankruptcy court.

Barter International trade conducted by the direct exchange of physical goods, rather than by separate purchases and sales at prices and exchange rates set by a free market.

Basic Balance In a country's balance of payments, the net of exports and imports of goods and services, unilateral transfers, and long-term capital flows.

Basis point One one-hundredth of one percentage point, often used in quotations of spreads between interest rates or to describe changes in yields in securities.

Basis risk That type of interest rate risk in which the interest rate base is mismatched.

Bearer bond Corporate or governmental debt in bond form that is not registered to any owner. Possession of the bond implies ownership, and interest is obtained by clipping a coupon attached to the bond. The advantage of the bearer form is easy transfer at the time of a sale, easy use as collateral for a debt, and what some cynics call taxpayer anonymity, meaning that governments find it hard to trace interest payments in order to collect income taxes. Bearer bonds are common in Europe, but are seldom issued any more in the United States. The alternate form to a bearer bond is a registered bond.

Benefit-cost ratio The present value of the future cash flows divided by the initial investment. Also called the *profitability index.*

Beta A linear measure of how much an individual asset contributes to the standard deviation of the market portfolio; calculated as the covariance between the return on the asset and the return on the market portfolio, divided by the variance of the return on the market portfolio.

Bid The price which a dealer is willing to pay for (i.e., buy) foreign exchange or a security.

Bid-ask spread The difference between a bid and an ask quotation.

Big Bang The October 1986 liberalization of the London capital markets.

Bill of exchange (B/E) A written order requesting one party (such as an importer) to pay a specified amount of money at a specified time to the order of the writer of the bill of exchange. Also called a draft. *See* Sight draft.

Bill of lading (B/L) A contract between a common carrier and a shipper to transport goods to a named destination. The bill of lading is also a receipt for the goods. Bills of lading are usually negotiable, meaning they are made to the order of a particular party and can be endorsed to transfer title to another party.

Black market An illegal foreign exchange market.

Blocked funds Funds in one country's currency that may not be exchanged freely for foreign currencies because of exchange controls.

Bond covenant A contractual provision in a bond indenture. A positive covenant requires certain actions. A negative covenant limits certain actions.

Bond indenture The explicit legal contract for a bond.

Bond refunding Replacing an outstanding bond before its maturity with a new bond.

Bond A long-term obligation for borrowed money; that is, a long-term *debt security.*

Book value The net amount (net book value) for something shown in accounting statements.

Border tax adjustments The fiscal practice, under the General Agreement on Tariffs and Trade, by which imported goods are subject to some or all of the tax charged in the importing country and re-exported goods are exempt from some or all of the tax charged in the exporting country.

Branch A foreign operation not incorporated in the host country, in contradistinction to a subsidiary.

Break-even point An accounting term defined as the point at which the total contribution margin equals the total fixed costs of producing a product or service.

Bretton Woods Conference An international conference in 1944 that established the international monetary system in effect from 1945 to 1971. The conference was held in Bretton Woods, New Hampshire, USA.

Bridge financing Short-term financing from a bank, used while a borrower obtains medium- or long-term fixed-rate financing from capital markets.

Budget A detailed schedule of a financial activity, such as an advertising budget, a sales budget, or a capital budget.

Bulldogs British pound-denominated bonds issued within the United Kingdom by a foreign borrower.

Bullet maturity Refers to debt that requires repayment of the entire principal at maturity.

Business risk The inherent or fundamental risk of a business, without regard to financial risk. Also called *operating risk.*

Cable The U.S. dollar per British pound cross rate.

CAD Cash against documents. International trade term.

Call option The right to *buy* something at a given price during the life of the option.

Call provision A provision that gives the firm the right to repay the bonds before the maturity date.

Capital account A section of the balance of payments accounts. Under the revised format of the International Monetary Fund, the capital account measures capital transfers and the acquisition and disposal of nonproduced, nonfinancial assets. Under traditional definitions, still used by many countries, the capital account measures public and private international lending and investment. Most of the traditional definition of the capital account is now incorporated in IMF statements as the financial account.

Capital Asset Pricing Model (CAPM) A theoretical model that relates the return on an asset to its risk, where risk is the contribution of the asset to the volatility of a portfolio. Risk and return are presumed determined in competitive and efficient financial markets.

Capital budget A firm's set of planned capital expenditures.

Capital budgeting The process of choosing the firm's long-term capital investments.

Capital flight Movement of funds out of a country because of political risk.

Capital gain The difference between what an asset is sold for and its book value, typically referring to an asset that has been owned for a sufficiently long time, such as a year or more.

Capital gains yield The price change portion of a stock's return.

Capital lease A lease obligation that has to be capitalized on the face of the balance sheet.

Capital market efficiency Reflects the relative amount of wealth wasted in making transactions. An efficient capital market allows the transfer of assets with little wealth loss.

Capital market imperfections view (of capital structure) The view that issuing debt is generally valuable but that the firm's optimal choice of capital structure is a dynamic process that involves the other views of capital structure (net corporate/personal tax, agency cost, bankruptcy cost, and pecking order), which result from considerations of asymmetric taxes, asymmetric information, and transaction costs.

Capital market line (CML) The line of investment possibilities extending outward from the *riskless rate, r_f,* and passing through the expected return on the *market portfolio.*

Capital market A market in which securities are bought and sold.

Capital markets The financial markets in various countries in which various types of long-term debt and/or ownership securities, or claims on those securities, are purchased and sold.

Capital mobility The degree to which private capital moves freely from country to country seeking the most promising investment opportunities.

Capital rationing Placing one or more limits on (rationing) the amount of new investment undertaken by a firm, either by using a higher cost of capital or by setting a maximum on parts of, and/or the entirety of, the capital budget.

Capital structure The makeup of the liabilities and stockholders' equity side of the balance sheet, especially the ratio of debt to equity and the mixture of short and long maturities.

Capital-asset-pricing model (CAPM) A model for determining the *required return* on an asset, taking into account the risk of the asset. A model for specifying the risk-return trade-off in the capital markets.

Capitalization rate A stock's *required return.*

CAPM See *Capital-asset-pricing model.*

Cash budget A forecasted summary of a firm's expected cash inflows and cash outflows as well as its expected cash and loan balances.

Cash budgeting The process of preparing the *cash budget.*

Cash conversion cycle The length of time between a firm's purchase inventory and the receipt of cash from its accounts receivable.

Cash discount An incentive offered to purchasers of a firm's product for payment within a specified time period, such as 10 days.

Cash flow after tax The *net operating cash flow.*

Cash flow coverage ratio The number of times that financial obligations (for interest, principal payments, preferred stock dividends, and rental payments) are covered by earnings before interest, taxes, rental payments, and depreciation.

Cash flow return on investment (CFROI) A measure of corporate performance in which the numerator is profit from continuing operations less cash taxes and depreciation. This is divided by cash investment which is taken to mean the replacement cost of capital employed.

Cash ratio The proportion of a firm's assets held as cash.

Cash-flow break-even point The point below which the firm will need either to obtain additional financing or to liquidate some of its assets to meet its fixed costs (for example, salaries and administrative costs, interest and principal payments, and planned cash dividends).

Certificate of Deposit (CD) A negotiable receipt issued by a bank for funds deposited for a certain period of time. CDs can be purchased or sold prior to their maturity in a secondary market, making them an interest-earning marketable security.

Characteristic line The plot of the periodic excess return on a stock (the difference between the return on the stock and the riskless return) and the excess return on the market portfolio.

CIF *See* Cost, insurance, and freight.

CKD Completely knocked down. International trade term for components shipped into a country for assembly there. Often used in the automobile industry.

Clearing house An institution through which financial obligations are cleared by the process of netting obligations of various members.

Clearinghouse Interbank Payments System (CHIPS) A New York-based computerized clearing system used by banks to settle interbank foreign exchange obligations (mostly U.S. dollars) between members.

Clientele effect The grouping of investors who have a preference that the firm follow a particular financing policy, such as the amount of leverage it uses.

Closing price The price of a financial security in the last trade before the market closed.

Collar option The simultaneous purchase of a put option and sale of a call option, or vice versa. Thus a form of hybrid option.

Collateral Assets that can be repossessed if the borrower defaults.

Collection float The negative float that is created between the time when you deposit a check in your account and the time when funds are made available.

Collection fractions The percentage of a given month's sales collected during the month of sale and each month following the sale.

Collective wisdom The combination (net result) of all of the individual opinions about a stock's value.

COMECON Acronym for Council for Mutual Economic Assistance. An association of the former Soviet Union and Eastern European governments formed to facilitate international trade among European Communist countries. COMECON ceased to exist after the breakup of the Soviet Union.

Commercial paper A promissory note sold by a large, creditworthy corporation in large denominations with maturities of 1 day to 270 days.

Commercial risk In banking, the likelihood that a foreign debtor will be unable to repay its debts because of business (as distinct from political) events.

Common market An association through treaty of two or more countries that agree to remove all trade barriers between themselves. The best known is the European Common Market, now called the European Union.

Common stock A proportional equity ownership interest—that is, a proportionate residual ownership interest—in a corporation. Common stock is the most junior security a corporation can issue.

Common-base-year analysis The representing of accounting information over multiple years as percentages of amounts in an initial year.

Common-size analysis The representing of balance sheet items as percentages of assets and of income statement items as percentages of sales.

Comparative advantage A theory that everyone gains if each nation specializes in the production of those goods that it produces relatively most efficiently and imports those goods that other countries produce relatively most efficiently. The theory supports free trade arguments.

Compensating balance An excess balance that is left at a bank to provide indirect compensation for loans extended or other bank services.

Competitive bidding A securities offering process in which securities firms submit competing bids to the issuer for the securities the issuer wishes to sell.

Competitive exposure *See* Operating exposure.

Compound interest Interest paid on previously earned interest as well as on the principal.

Compounding frequency The number of compounding periods in a year. For example, quarterly compounding has a compounding frequency of 4.

Concession agreement An understanding or contract between a foreign corporation and a host government defining the rules under which the corporation may operate in that country.

Conglomerate merger A merger involving two or more firms that are in unrelated businesses.

Consolidated financial statement A corporate financial statement in which accounts of subsidiaries and the parent are added together to produce a statement which reports the status of the worldwide enterprise as if it were a single corporation. Internal obligations are eliminated in consolidated statements.

Consolidation The combining of two or more firms to form an entirely new entity.

Consumer credit Credit granted by a firm to consumers for the purchase of goods or services. Also called *retail credit*.

Contagion The spread of a crisis in one country to its neighboring countries and other countries that have similar characteristics—at least in the eyes of cross-border investors.

Contingent claim A claim that can be made only if one or more specified outcomes occur—that is, a claim that is contingent on the value of some other asset or on a particular occurrence.

Controlled foreign corporation (CFC) A foreign corporation in which U.S. shareholders own more than 50% of the combined voting power or total value. Under U.S. tax law, U.S. shareholders may be liable for taxes on undistributed earnings of the controlled foreign corporation.

Conventional project A project with a negative initial cash flow (an outflow), which is expected to be followed by one or more future positive cash flows (cash inflows).

Convertible bond A bond that, at the option of its owner, can be exchanged for a contractually specified number of shares of the firm's common stock.

Convertible bond A bond or other fixed-income security that may be exchanged for a number of shares of common stock.

Convertible currency A currency that can be exchanged freely for any other currency without government restrictions.

Corporate financial management The application of financial principles within a corporation to create and maintain value through decision making and proper resource management.

Corporate governance The relationship among stakeholders used to determine and control the strategic direction and performance of an organization.

Corporate tax view (of capital structure) The argument that double (corporate and individual) taxation of equity returns makes debt a cheaper financing method.

Corporate wealth maximization The corporate goal of maximizing the total wealth of the corporation itself rather than just the shareholders' wealth. Wealth is defined to include not just financial wealth but also the technical, marketing and human resources of the corporation.

Corporation A legal "person" that is separate and distinct from its owners. A corporation is allowed to own assets, incur liabilities, and sell securities, among other things.

Correlation coefficient The covariance between two random variables divided by the product of the standard deviations of those random variables.

Correspondent bank A bank that holds deposits for and provides services to another bank, located in another geographic area, on a reciprocal basis.

Cost and freight (C&F) Price, quoted by an exporter, that includes the cost of transportation to the named port of destination.

Cost of capital The required return for a capital budgeting project.

Cost of limited partner capital The discount rate that equates the after-tax inflows with outflows for capital raised from limited partners.

Cost, insurance, and freight (CIF) Exporter's quoted price including the cost of packaging, freight or carriage, insurance premium, and other charges paid in respect of the goods from the time of loading in the country of export to their arrival at the named port of destination or place of transshipment.

Counterparty risk The potential exposure any individual firm bears that the second party to any financial contract is unable to fulfill its obligations under the contract's specifications.

Counterparty The opposite party to a double transaction; that is, to a transaction involving an exchange of financial instruments or obligations now and a reversal of that same transaction at some agreed-upon later date.

Countertrade A type of international trade in which parties exchange goods directly rather than for money. Hence a type of barter.

Countervailing duty An import duty charged to offset an export subsidy by another country.

Country risk In banking, the likelihood that unexpected events within a host country will influence a client's or a government's ability to repay a loan. Country risk is often divided into sovereign (political) risk and foreign exchange (currency) risk.

Country-specific risk Political risks that affect the MNE at the country level, such as transfer risk (blocked funds) and cultural and institutional risks.

Coupon payments A bond's interest payments.

Coupon rate A bond's annual percentage rate.

Covariance The mathematical expectation of the product of two random variables' deviations from their means.

Covenants Provisions in a *bond indenture* (or *preferred stock agreement*) that require the bond (or preferred stock) issuer to take certain specified actions (*affirmative covenants*) or to refrain from taking certain specified actions (*negative covenants*).

Coverage ratios Ratios that show the amount of funds available to "cover" a particular financial obligation compared to the size of that obligation.

Covered interest arbitrage The process whereby an investor earns a risk-free profit by (1) borrowing funds in one currency, (2) exchanging those funds in the spot market for a foreign currency, (3) investing the foreign currency at interest rates in a foreign country, (4) selling forward, at the time of original investment, the investment proceeds to be received at maturity, (5) using the proceeds of the forward sale to repay the original loan, and (6) having a remaining profit balance.

Covering A transaction in the forward foreign exchange market or money market that protects the value of future cash flows. Covering is another term for hedging. *See* Hedge.

Cramdown The ability of the bankruptcy court to confirm a *plan of reorganization* over the objections of some classes of creditors.

Crawling peg A foreign exchange rate system in which the exchange rate is adjusted very frequently to reflect prevailing rate of inflation.

Credit default swap An agreement to swap a series of cash payments in exchange for a promise to make a specific payment if a specified debt issuer defaults.

Credit derivative A derivative whose value is based on a promise to make a default payment.

Credit period The length of time for which the customer is granted credit.

Credit risk The possibility that a borrower's credit worth, at the time of renewing a credit, is reclassified by the lender.

Credit scoring A statistical technique wherein several financial characteristics are combined to form a single score to represent a customer's creditworthiness.

Crisis planning Educating management and other employees about how to react to various scenarios of violence.

Cross rate An exchange rate between two currencies derived by dividing each currency's exchange rate with a third currency. For example, if ¥/$ is 108 and DKr/$ is 6.80, the cross rate between ¥ and DKr is ¥108 ÷ DKr 6.80 = ¥15.88/DKr.

Cross-border acquisition A firm acquires through purchase another firm located in another country.

Cross-currency swap *See* Currency swap.

Cross-listing The listing of shares of common stock on two or more stock exchanges.

Crossover point A cost of capital at which two projects have equal NPV.

Cumulative translation adjustment (CTA) account An entry in a translated balance sheet in which gains and/or losses from translation have been accumulated over a period of years.

Currency basket The value of a portfolio of specific amounts of individual currencies, used as the basis for setting the market value of another currency. Also called currency cocktail.

Currency Board A currency board exists when a country's central bank commits to back its money supply entirely with foreign reserves at all times.

Currency future A *financial future* contract for the delivery of a stated amount of a specified foreign currency.

Currency option An *option* to buy or sell foreign currency.

Currency swap An agreement to swap a series of specified payment obligations denominated in one currency for a series of specified payment obligations denominated in a different currency.

Current account In the balance of payments, the net flow of goods, services, and unilateral transfers (such as gifts) between a country and all foreign countries.

Current assets Assets that are expected to become cash within one year.

Current liabilities Liabilities that mature, or are expected to be paid off, within one year.

Current rate method A method of translating the financial statements of foreign subsidiaries into the parent's reporting currency. All assets and liabilities are translated at the current exchange rate.

Current ratio A liquidity ratio that measures the number of times a firm's current assets cover its current liabilities.

Current yield The annual coupon payment divided by the closing price.

Current/noncurrent method A method of translating the financial statements of foreign subsidiaries into the parent's reporting currency. All current assets and current liabilities are translated at the current rate, and all noncurrent accounts at their historical rates.

D/A Documents against acceptance. International trade term.

D/P Documents against payment. International trade term.

D/S Days after sight. International trade term.

Days' sales in inventory ratio The average number of days' worth of sales that is held in inventory.

Days' sales outstanding (DSO) The approximate number of days required to collect a firm's accounts receivable. Also called *average collection period*.

Debenture Long-term bonds (typically of longer than 10-year maturity) not secured by specific assets.

Debt ratio Total debt divided by total assets; the fraction of the assets of the firm that are financed by debt.

Debt service coverage ratio Earnings before interest and income taxes plus one-third of rental charges, divided by interest expense plus one-third of rental charges plus the quantity principal repayments divided by one minus the tax rate.

Debt/equity ratio Total debt divided by total common stockholders' equity; the amount of debt per dollar of equity.

Debtor in possession A firm that is continuing to operate its business under Chapter 11 bankruptcy protection.

Deductive reasoning The use of a general fact to provide accurate information about a specific situation.

Deemed-paid tax That portion of taxes paid to a foreign government that is allowed as a credit (reduction) in taxes due to a home government.

Deferred annuity An annuity where the first payment is more than one period in the future.

Delta The change in an option's price divided by the change in the price of the underlying instrument. Hedging strategies are based on delta ratios.

Demand deposit A bank deposit that can be withdrawn or transferred at any time without notice, in contradistinction to a time deposit where (theoretically) the bank may require a waiting period before the deposit can be withdrawn. Demand deposits may or may not earn interest. A time deposit is the opposite of a demand deposit.

Depositary receipts *See* American depositary receipts.

Depreciate In the context of foreign exchange rates, a drop in the spot foreign exchange value of a floating currency; i.e., a currency the value of which is determined by open market transactions. *See* Devaluation. In the context of accounting, a periodic charge (expense) that represents the allocation of the cost of a fixed asset to various time periods.

Derivatives Securities that derive their value from another asset.

Devaluation A drop in the spot foreign exchange value of a currency that is pegged to other currencies or to gold. *See* Depreciate.

Dilution Reduction in earnings per common share resulting from a financial transaction.

Direct quote The price of a unit of foreign exchange expressed in the home country's currency. The term has meaning only when the home country is specified.

Directed public share issue An issue that is targeted at investors in a single country and underwritten in whole or in part by investment institutions from that country.

Dirty float A system of floating (i.e., market-determined) exchange rates in which the government intervenes from time to time to influence the foreign exchange value of its currency.

Disbursement float The positive float that is created between the time when a check is written and the time when it is finally cleared out of the checking account.

Discount (in foreign exchange market) The amount by which a currency is cheaper for future delivery than for spot (immediate) delivery. The opposite of discount is premium.

Discount bond A bond that is selling for less than its par value.

Discount loans Loans which require the borrower to pay the interest in advance.

Discount period The period during which a customer can deduct the *discount* from the net amount of the bill when making payment.

Discount rate A generic term for a rate of return that measures the time value of money.

Discount The percent a customer can deduct from the net amount of the bill if payment is made before the end of the *discount period.*

Discounted basis Selling something on a discounted basis is selling it below what its value will be at maturity, so that the difference makes up all or part of the interest.

Discounted payback The length of time it takes for an investment's *discounted* future cash flows to equal the investment's initial cost.

Discounted-cash-flow (DCF) analysis The process of valuing capital budgeting projects by discounting their future expected cash flows.

Discounted-cash-flow (DCF) framework The valuing of an asset by discounting its expected future cash flows at some discount rate.

Dividend policy An established guide for the firm to determine the amount of money it will pay out as dividends.

Dividend reinvestment plan A firm-sponsored program that enables common stockholders to pool their dividends (and, in many cases, supplementary cash) for reinvestment in shares of the firm's common stock.

Dividend yield The dividend income portion of a stock's return; more specifically, the dividend per share divided by the share price.

Dollarization Dollarization is the use of the U.S. dollar as the official currency of the country.

Domestic International Sales Corporation (DISC) Under the U.S.

tax code, a type of subsidiary formed to reduce taxes on exported U.S.-produced goods. It has been ruled illegal by the World Trade Organization.

Draft   An unconditional written order requesting one party (such as an importer) to pay a specified amount of money at a specified time to the order of the writer of the draft. Also called a bill of exchange. Personal checks are one type of draft.

Dragon bond   A U.S. dollar denominated bond sold in the so-called Dragon economies of Asia, such as Hong Kong, Taiwan, and Singapore.

Dumping   The practice of offering goods for sale in a foreign market at a price that is lower than that of the same product in the home market or a third country. As used in GATT, a special case of differential pricing.

Duration   The time until the "average" dollar of present value is received from an asset.

Dutch auction tender offer   A "reverse" tender process, wherein shareholders can offer to sell shares at prices within a specified range.

EAA   See *Equivalent annual annuity.*

EAC   See *Equivalent annual cost.*

Earning power   Earnings before interest and taxes (EBIT) divided by total assets.

Earnings before interest and taxes (EBIT)   Operating profit plus nonoperating profit, such as investment income, calculated before the deduction of interest and income taxes.

Earnings yield   The earnings per share divided by the market price per share; equals the reciprocal of the price/earnings ratio.

Economic exposure   Another name for operating exposure. *See* Operating exposure.

Economic order quantity (EOQ)   The order quantity that minimizes total inventory costs.

Economic Value Added (EVA)   A widely used measure of corporate financial performance. It is calculated as the difference between net operating profits after-tax of the business less the cost of capital invested (both debt and equity). EVA is a registered trademark of Stern Stewart & Company.

Edge Act and Agreement Corporation Subsidiary of a U.S. bank incorporated under federal law to engage in various international banking and financing operations, including equity participations that are not allowed to regular domestic banks. The Edge Act subsidiary may be located in a state other than that of the parent bank.

Effective exchange rate   An index measuring the change in value of a foreign currency determined by calculating a weighted average of bilateral exchange rates. The weighting reflects the importance of each foreign country's trade with the home country.

Efficiency   Reflects the amount of wasted energy.

Efficient frontier   The combinations of securities portfolios that maximize expected return for any given level of risk or, equivalently, minimize risk for any given level of expected return.

Efficient market   A market in which all relevant information is already reflected in market prices. The term is most frequently applied to foreign exchange markets and securities markets.

Efficient portfolio   A portfolio that provides the highest expected return for a given amount of risk and the lowest risk for a given expected return.

Electronic data interchange (EDI) The exchange of information electronically, directly from one firm's computer to another's, in a structured format.

Enhancement   An innovation that has a positive impact on one or more of a firm's existing products.

EOM   End of month. International trade term.

EOQ   See *Economic order quantity.*

Equity multiplier   Total assets divided by total common stockholders' equity; the amount of total assets per dollar of equity.

Equity risk premium   The average annual return of the market expected by investors over and above riskless debt.

Equity   An ownership interest in a firm.

Equityholders   Those holding some shares of the firm's equity. Also called *stockholders* and *shareholders.*

Equivalent annual annuity (EAA) The equivalent amount per year for some number of years that has a present value equal to a given amount.

Equivalent annual cost (EAC)   The equivalent cost per year of owning an asset over its entire life.

Euro equity public issue   A new equity issue that is underwritten and distributed in multiple foreign equity markets, sometimes simultaneously with distribution in the domestic market.

Euro   A new currency unit that replaced the individual currencies of 12 European countries that belong to the European Union.

Eurobank   A bank, or bank department, which bids for time deposits and makes loans in currencies other than that of the country where the bank is located.

Eurobond   A bond that is sold outside the country in whose currency the bond is denominated.

Euro-Commercial Paper   Short-term notes (30, 60, 90, 120, 180, 270, and 360 days) sold in international money markets.

Eurocredit   Bank loans to MNEs, sovereign governments, international institutions, and banks denominated in Eurocurrencies and extended by banks in countries other than the country in whose currency the loan is denominated.

Eurocurrency   A currency deposited in a bank located in a country other than the country issuing the currency.

Eurodollar bond market   The market for U.S. dollar-denominated bonds outside the United States.

Eurodollar   A U.S. dollar deposited in a bank outside the United States. A Eurodollar is one type of Eurocurrency.

Euronote   Short- to medium-term debt instruments sold in the Eurocurrency market.

European Central Bank (ECB) Conducts monetary policy of the European Monetary Union. Its goal is to safeguard the stability of the euro and minimize inflation.

European Currency Unit (ECU) Composite currency created by the European Monetary System prior to the euro to function as a reserve currency numeraire. The ECU was used as the numeraire for denominating a number of financial instruments and obligations.

European Economic Community (EEC)   The European common market composed of Austria, Belgium, Denmark, Finland, France, Germany, Greece, Ireland, Italy, Luxembourg, the Netherlands, Portugal, Spain, and the United Kingdom. Officially renamed the European Union (EU) January 1, 1994.

European Free Trade Association (EFTA)   European countries not part of the European Union but having no internal tariffs.

European Monetary System (EMS) A monetary alliance of fifteen European countries (same members as the European Union).

European option An option that can be exercised only at its expiration.

European terms Foreign exchange quotations for the U.S. dollar, expressed as the number of non-U.S. currency units per U.S. dollar.

European Union (EU) The official name of the former European Economic Community (EEC) as of January 1, 1994.

Event study A statistical analysis that examines average returns for stocks in reaction to an event. Examples of "events" include announcements of mergers, new issues of securities, repurchasing securities, exercising call options, dividends, and earnings, among many others.

Events of default Contractually specified events that allow lenders to demand immediate repayment of a debt.

Ex dock Followed by the name of a port of import. International trade term in which seller agrees to pay for the costs (shipping, insurance, customs duties, etc.) of placing the goods on the dock at the named port.

Exchange offer An offer by the firm to give one security, such as a bond or preferred stock, in exchange for another security, such as shares of common stock.

Exchange Rate Mechanism (ERM) The means by which members of the EMS formerly maintained their currency exchange rates within an agreed upon range with respect to the other member currencies.

Exchange rate pass-through The degree to which the prices of imported and exported goods change as a result of exchange rate changes.

Exchange rate The price of one country's currency expressed in terms of another country's currency.

Ex-dividend date The date beginning on which a dividend is not paid to a new owner of a share of the stock.

Exercise value The amount of advantage over a current market transaction provided by an in-the-money option.

Exercise To make the exchange specified in the option contract.

Expected return The return one would expect to earn on an asset if it were purchased.

Expiration The time when the option contract ceases to exist (expires).

Export credit insurance Provides assurance to the exporter or the exporter's bank that, should the foreign customer default on payment, the insurance company will pay for a major portion of the loss. *See also* Foreign Credit Insurance Association (FCIA).

Export-Import Bank (Eximbank) A U.S. government agency created to finance and otherwise facilitate imports and exports.

Expropriation Official government seizure of private property, recognized by international law as the right of any sovereign state provided expropriated owners are given prompt compensation and fair market value in convertible currencies.

Extra or special dividends A dividend that is paid in addition to a firm's "regular" quarterly dividend, either at the same time as one of the quarterly dividends or at some other time.

Face value The amount of money to be repaid at the end of the bond's life. Also called *par value.*

Factoring Specialized firms, known as factors, purchase receivables at a discount on either a non-recourse or recourse basis.

FAF Fly away free. International trade term.

Fair price A price that does not favor either the buyers' or the sellers' side of the transaction—that is, a zero-NPV investment.

FAQ Free at quay. International trade term.

FASB 52 A regulation of the Financial Accounting Standards Board requiring U.S. companies to translate foreign subsidiary financial statements by the current rate (closing rate) method. FASB 52 became effective in 1981.

FASB 8 A regulation of the Financial Accounting Standards Board requiring U.S. companies to translate foreign affiliate financial statements by the temporal method. FASB 8 was in effect from 1976 to 1981. It is still used under specific circumstances.

FI Free in. International trade term meaning that all expenses for loading into the hold of a vessel are for the account of the consignee.

FIFO First in, first out. An inventory valuation approach in which the cost of the earliest inventory purchases is charged against current sales. The opposite is LIFO, or last in, first out.

Financial account A section of the balance of payments accounts. Under the revised format of the International Monetary Fund, the financial account measures long-term financial flows including direct foreign investment, portfolio investments, and other long-term movements. Under the traditional definition, still used by many countries, items in the financial account were included in the capital account.

Financial derivative A financial instrument, such as a futures contract or option, whose value is derived from an underlying asset like a stock or currency.

Financial distress When a firm is having significant trouble paying its debts as they come due.

Financial engineering Those basic building blocks, such as spot positions, forwards, and options, used to construct positions that provide the user with desired risk and return characteristics.

Financial intermediary A firm that purchases financial securities and pays for them by issuing claims against itself (its own financial securities).

Financial lease See *Capital lease.*

Financial leverage The degree to which a firm's assets are financed by debt as opposed to equity.

Financial planning The process of evaluating the investing and financing options available to the firm. It includes attempting to make optimal decisions, projecting the consequences of these decisions for the firm in the form of a financial plan, and then comparing future performance against that plan.

Financial ratio The result of dividing one financial statement item by another. Ratios help analysts interpret financial statements by focusing on specific relationships.

Financial risk Risk that is created by financial leverage, which is the financial makeup, or *capital structure,* of the firm.

Financial security A standardized financial asset, such as common stock, preferred stock, bond, convertible bond, or financial future; a contract that provides for the exchange of money at various times.

Financing decisions Decisions concerning the liabilities and stockholders' equity (right) side of the firm's balance sheet, such as the decision to issue bonds.

Firm-specific risks Political risks that affect the MNE at the project or corporate level. Governance risk due to goal conflict between an MNE and its host government is the main political firm-specific risk.

Fisher Effect A theory that nominal interest rates in two or more countries should be equal to the required real rate of return to investors plus compensation for the expected amount of inflation in each country.

Fixed asset turnover ratio The ratio of sales to fixed assets.

Fixed charge coverage ratio Generally, the number of times that interest charges and rental payments are covered by earnings before interest, taxes, and rental payments. More specifically, earnings before interest and income taxes plus one-third of rental charges, divided by interest expense plus one-third of rental charges.

Fixed exchange rates Foreign exchange rates tied to the currency of a major country (such as the United States), to gold, or to a basket of currencies such as Special Drawing Rights.

Fixed-price tender offer A one-time offer to purchase a stated number of shares at a stated fixed price above the current market price.

Flexible exchange rates The opposite of fixed exchange rates. The foreign exchange rate is adjusted periodically by the country's monetary authorities in accordance with their judgment and/or an external set of economic indicators.

Float The difference between the firm's available or collected balance at its bank and the firm's book or ledger balance.

Floating exchange rates Foreign exchange rates determined by demand and supply in an open market that is presumably free of government interference.

Floating rate note (FRN) Medium-term securities with interest rates pegged to LIBOR and adjusted quarterly or semiannually.

FOB Free on board. International trade term in which exporter's quoted price includes the cost of loading goods into transport vessels at a named point.

Foreign affiliate A foreign business unit that is less than 50% owned by the parent company.

Foreign bond A bond issued by a foreign corporation or government for sale in the domestic capital market of another country, and denominated in the currency of that country.

Foreign Corrupt Practices Act of 1977 A U.S. law that punishes companies and their executives if they pay bribes or make other improper payments to foreigners.

Foreign Credit Insurance Association (FCIA) An unincorporated association of private commercial insurances companies, in cooperation with the Export-Import Bank of the United States, that provides export credit insurance to U.S. firms.

Foreign currency risk The risk that the value of one currency expressed in terms of another currency—the foreign exchange rate—may fluctuate over time.

Foreign currency translation The process of restating foreign currency accounts of subsidiaries into the reporting currency of the parent company in order to prepare a consolidated financial statement.

Foreign direct investment (FDI) Purchase of physical assets, such as plant and equipment, in a foreign country, to be managed by the parent corporation. FDI is in contradistinction to foreign portfolio investment.

Foreign exchange broker An individual or firm which arranges foreign exchange transactions between two parties, but is not itself a principal in the trade. Foreign exchange brokers earn a commission for their efforts.

Foreign exchange dealer (or trader) An individual or firm that buys foreign exchange from one party (at a bid price), and then sells it (at an ask price) to another party. The dealer is a principal in two transactions and makes a profit on the spread between its buying and selling prices.

Foreign exchange market The market within which one country's currency is traded for another country's currency.

Foreign exchange rate The price of one country's currency in terms of another currency, or in terms of a commodity such as gold or silver. *See also* Exchange rates and Foreign exchange.

Foreign exchange risk See *Foreign currency risk.*

Foreign sales corporation (FSC) Under U.S. tax code, a type of foreign corporation that provides tax-exempt or tax-deferred income for U.S. persons or corporations having export-oriented activities.

Foreign tax credit The amount by which a domestic firm may reduce (credit) domestic income taxes for income tax payments to a foreign government.

Forfaiting A technique for arranging nonrecourse medium-term export financing, used most frequently to finance imports into Eastern Europe. A third party, usually a specialized financial institution, guarantees the financing.

Forward contract A contract to exchange a stated amount of a specified asset for cash at a specific future date.

Forward differential The difference between spot and forward rates, expressed as an annual percentage.

Forward discount or premium The same as forward differential.

Forward rate agreement An interbank-traded contract to buy or sell interest rate payments on a notional principal.

Forward rate An exchange rate quoted today for settlement at some future date. The rate used in a forward transaction.

Forward transaction A foreign exchange transaction agreed upon today but to be settled at some specified future date, often one, two, or three months after the transaction date.

Free alongside (FAS) An international trade term in which the seller's quoted price for goods includes all costs of delivery of the goods alongside a vessel at the port of embarkation.

Free rider A follower who avoids the cost and expense of finding the best course of action by simply mimicking the behavior of a leader who, for example, makes investments.

Free trade zone An area within a country into which foreign goods may be brought duty free, often for purposes of additional manufacture, inventory storage, or packaging. Such goods are subject to duty only when they leave the duty-free zone to enter other parts of the country.

Freely floating exchange rates Exchange rates determined in a free market without government interference, in contradistinction to dirty float.

Frictions The "stickiness" in making transactions; the total "hassle," including the time, effort, money, and associated tax effects of gathering information and making a transaction such as buying stock or borrowing money.

Fronting loan A parent-to-subsidiary loan channeled through a financial intermediary such as a large international bank in order to reduce political risk. Presumably government authorities are less likely to prevent a foreign subsidiary repaying an established bank than repaying the subsidiary's corporate parent.

Functional currency In the context of translating financial statements, the currency of the primary economic environment in which a foreign subsidiary operates and in which it generates cash flows.

Future investment opportunities The options to identify additional, more valuable investment opportunities in the future that result from a current opportunity or operation.

Futures contract A standardized forward contract that is traded in a futures market.

Futures, or futures contracts Exchange-traded agreements calling for future delivery of a standard amount of any good, e.g., foreign exchange, at a fixed time, place, and price.

Future-value annuity factor Equation (4.5) without PMT.

Future-value factor Equation (4.3) without PV.

Future-value formula Equation (4.3).

Gamma A measure of the sensitivity of an option's delta ratio to small unit changes in the price of the underlying security.

Gap risk That type of interest rate risk in which the timing of maturities is mismatched.

General Agreement on Tariffs and Trade (GATT) A framework of rules for nations to manage their trade policies, negotiate lower international tariff barriers, and settle trade disputes.

General cash offer A *public offering* made to investors at large.

Generally accepted accounting principles (GAAP) A technical accounting term that encompasses the conventions, rules, and procedures necessary to define accepted accounting practice at a particular time.

Geometric return The mean uses the beginning and ending returns to calculate the annual average rate of compounded growth, similar to an internal rate of return.

Global registered shares Similar to ordinary shares, global registered shares have the added benefit of being able to be traded on equity exchanges around the globe in a variety of currencies.

Global-specific risks Political risks that originate at the global level, such as terrorism, the anti-globalization movement, environmental concerns, poverty, and cyber attacks.

Gold standard A monetary system in which currencies are defined in terms of their gold content, and payment imbalances between countries are settled in gold.

Greenfield investment An initial investment in a new foreign subsidiary being created from a brand new start with no predecessor operation in that location. This is in contrast to a new subsidiary created by the purchase of an already existing operation. Thus, a Greenfield investment is one that starts, conceptually if not literally, with the bare ground (presumably covered in green grass) and builds from that point forward.

Greenmail A firm's paying a takeover raider a premium to repurchase shares from the raider.

Gross profit margin Gross profit divided by sales, which is the amount of each sales dollar left over after paying the cost of goods sold.

Gross spread The fraction of the (gross) proceeds of an underwritten securities offering that is paid as compensation to the underwriters of the offering.

Gross underwriting spread See *Gross spread*.

Gross up *See* Deemed-paid tax.

Hard currency A freely convertible currency that is not expected to depreciate in value in the foreseeable future.

Hard" capital rationing Capital rationing that under no circumstances can be violated.

Hedge accounting An accounting procedure specifying that gains and losses on hedging instruments be recognized in earnings at the same time as the effects of changes in the value of the items being hedged are recognized.

Hedge The purchase of a contract (including forward foreign exchange) or tangible good that will rise in value and offset a drop in value of another contract or tangible good. Hedges are undertaken to reduce risk by protecting an owner from loss.

Hedging Reducing the risk of an investment through the use of financial security transactions.

Historical exchange rate In accounting, the exchange rate in effect when an asset or liability was acquired.

Holding period The amount of time money is invested in a particular asset.

Homemade dividend Sale of some shares of stock to get cash that would be similar to getting a cash dividend.

Horizontal merger A merger involving two or more firms in the same industry that are both at the same stage in the production cycle-that is, two or more competitors.

Hot money Money which moves internationally from one currency and/or country to another in response to interest rate differences, and moves away immediately when the interest advantage disappears.

Human capital The unique capabilities and expertise of individuals.

Hybrid foreign currency options Purchase of a put option and the simultaneous sale of a call (or vice versa) so that the overall cost is less than the cost of a straight option.

Hyperinflation countries Countries with a very high rate of inflation. Under United States FASB 52, these are defined as countries where the cumulative three-year inflation amounts to 100% or more.

IMM International Monetary Market. A division of the Chicago Mercantile Exchange.

Impossible Trinity An ideal currency would have exchange rate stability, full financial integration, and monetary independence.

Income statement A financial statement that reports the income, expenses, and profit (or loss) for a specific interval of time, usually a year or a quarter of a year.

Independent project A project that can be chosen without requiring or precluding any other investment.

Indirect quote The price of a unit of a home country's currency expressed in terms of a foreign country's currency.

Inductive reasoning The attempt to use information about a specific situation to draw a general conclusion.

Informational efficiency The speed and accuracy with which prices reflect new information.

In-house bank If an MNE's needs are either too large or too sophisticated for local banks, it can establish an in-house or internal bank within this firm. The in-house bank is not a separate corporation but is performing a set of functions by the existing treasury department. Acting as an independent entity, the in-house bank transacts with the various internal business units of the firm on an arm's length basis.

Initial public offering (IPO) A first-time public issuing of stock in a corporation.

Integrated foreign entity One that operates as an extension of the parent company, with cash flows and general business lines that are highly interrelated with those of the parent.

Intellectual property rights Grant the exclusive use of patented technology and copyrighted creative materials. A worldwide treaty to protect intellectual property rights has been ratified by most major countries, including most recently by China.

Interest coverage ratio Earnings before interest and income taxes divided by interest expense.

Interest rate futures *See* Futures, or futures contracts.

Interest rate parity A theory of relative exchange rates that states that the difference in interest rates in two currencies for a stated period should just offset the difference between the spot foreign exchange rate and the forward exchange rate corresponding to that period.

Interest rate swap An agreement to swap interest payment obligations.

Interest rate swaps Contractual agreements to exchange or swap a series of interest cash flows.

Interest-rate risk The risk of a change in the value of a bond because of a change in the interest rate.

Internal rate of return (IRR) The expected return of a capital budgeting project.

Internalization A theory that the key ingredient for maintaining a firm-specific competitive advantage in international competition is the possession of proprietary information and control of human capital that can generate new information through expertise in research, management, marketing, or technology.

International Bank for Reconstruction and Development (IBRD, or World Bank) International development bank owned by member nations that makes development loans to member countries.

International Banking Facility (IBF) A department within a U.S. bank that may accept foreign deposits and make loans to foreign borrowers as if it were a foreign subsidiary. IBFs are free of U.S. reserve requirements, deposit insurance, and interest rate regulations.

International Capital Asset Pricing Model The primary distinction in the estimation of the cost of equity for an individual firm using an international-ized version of the domestic capital asset pricing model is the definition of the "market" and a recalculation of the firm's beta for that market.

International Fisher effect A theory that holds that the difference between the interest rates in two currencies should just offset the difference between the expected inflation rates in the two countries that issued the currencies.

International Monetary Fund (IMF) An international organization created in 1944 to promote exchange rate stability and provide temporary financing for countries experiencing balance of payments difficulties.

International Monetary Market (IMM) A branch of the Chicago Mercantile Exchange which specializes in trading currency and financial futures contracts.

International monetary system The structure within which foreign exchange rates are determined, international trade and capital flows are accommodated, and balance of payments adjustments made.

In-the-money Said of an option that currently would provide an advantage, if exercised.

Intrinsic value The financial gain if an option is exercised immediately.

Inventory turnover ratio An asset turnover ratio that shows how many times inventory turns over in a year.

Investment agreement Spells out specific rights and responsibilities of both the investing foreign firm and the host government.

Investment banker A *financial intermediary* that specializes in marketing new securities issues and assisting with *mergers*.

Investment decisions Decisions concerning the asset (left) side of the firm's balance sheet, such as the decision to offer a new product.

Investment tax credit A provision of the tax code that permits a firm that makes qualifying capital expenditures to credit a specified percentage of those expenditures against its income tax liability for the period in which the qualifying expenditures are made. The Tax Reform Act of 1986 eliminated the investment tax credit, but the credit has been eliminated and restored several times during the postwar period.

Investment-grade ratings A long-term debt rating in one of the four highest rating categories.

Investments As a discipline, the study of financial securities, such as stocks and bonds, from the investor's viewpoint. This area deals with the firm's financing decision, but from the other side of the transaction.

Invoice date Usually the date when goods are shipped. Payment dates are set relative to the invoice date.

January effect A stock price pattern that has been observed over many years wherein stocks, on average, have abnormally good returns in January.

Joint venture A business venture that is owned by two or more other business ventures. Often the several business owners are from different countries.

Jumbo loans Loans of $1 billion or more.

Just-in-time (JIT) inventory systems Systems that schedule materials to arrive exactly as they are needed in the production process.

Kangaroo bonds Australian dollar-denominated bonds issued within Australia by a foreign borrower.

Lag In the context of leads and lags, payment of a financial obligation later than is expected or required.

Lambda A measure of the sensitivity of an option premium to a unit change in volatility.

Law of one price If the identical product or service can be sold in two different markets, and no restrictions exist on the sale or transportation costs of moving the product between markets, the product's price should be the same in both markets.

Lead In the context of leads and lags, payment of a financial obligation earlier than is expected or required.

Lease A long-term rental agreement; a form of secured long-term debt.

Lessee An entity that leases an asset from another entity.

Lessor An entity that leases an asset to another entity.

Letter of credit A form of guarantee of payment issued by a bank; used to guarantee the payment of interest and repayment of principal on bond issues.

Leverage ratios Generally, measures of the relative contribution of stockholders and creditors, and of the firm's ability to pay financing charges. More specifically, the ratio of the value of the firm's debt to the total value of the firm.

Leverage rebalancing Making transactions to adjust (rebalance) a firm's leverage ratio back to its target.

Leverage The use of debt financing.

Leveraged buyout The purchase of a firm that is financed with a very high proportion of debt.

Leveraged lease A lease arrangement under which the lessor borrows a large proportion of the funds needed to purchase the asset and grants the lenders a lien on the asset and a pledge of the lease payments to secure the borrowing.

Liability A debt claim against the firm's assets.

LIFO Last in, first out. An inventory valuation approach in which the cost of the latest inventory purchases is charged against current sales. The opposite is FIFO, or first in, first out.

Limited liability company A company which offers limited liability, like a corporation, but is normally taxed like a partnership.

Limited liability Limitation of possible loss to what has already been invested.

Limited partnership A partnership that includes one or more partners who have *limited liability*.

Line of credit An *informal* arrangement between a bank and a customer establishing a maximum loan balance that the bank will permit the borrower to maintain.

Link financing *See* Back-to-back loan or Fronting loan.

Liquidation When a firm's business is terminated, all its assets are sold and the proceeds are used to pay its creditors, and any leftover proceeds are distributed to its shareholders.

Liquidity ratios Ratios that measure a firm's ability to meet its short-term financial obligations on time.

Liquidity The extent to which something can be sold quickly and easily without loss of value.

Location-specific advantage Market imperfections or genuine comparative advantages that attract foreign direct investment to particular locations.

London Interbank Offered Rate (LIBOR) The deposit rate applicable to interbank loans in London. LIBOR is used as the reference rate for many international interest rate transactions.

Long position A position in which foreign currency assets exceed foreign currency liabilities. The opposite of a long position is a short position.

Long-term In accounting information, one year or more.

Maastricht Treaty A treaty among the 12 European Union countries that specified a plan and timetable for the introduction of a single European currency, to be called the euro.

Macro risk *See* country-specific risks.

Macroeconomic uncertainty Operating exposure's sensitivity to key macroeconomic variables, such as exchange rates, interest rates, and inflation rates.

Managed float A country allows its currency to trade within a given band of exchange rates.

Management's discussion A report from management to the stockholders that accompanies the firm's financial statements in the annual report. This report explains the period's financial results and enables management to discuss other ideas that may not be apparent in the financial statements in the annual report.

Managerial decisions Decisions concerning the operation of the firm, such as the choice of firm size, firm growth, and employee compensation.

Margin A deposit made as security for a financial transaction otherwise financed on credit.

Marginal tax rate The tax rate applied to the last, or marginal, dollar of income.

Marked to market The value of a futures contract is marked to market daily, and all changes in value are paid in cash daily. The value of the contract is revalued using the closing price for the day. The amount to be paid is called the variation margin.

Market cap A firm's market capitalization.

Market capitalization A firm's current stock value times its number of outstanding shares.

Market liquidity The degree to which a firm can issue a new security without depressing the existing market price, as well as the degree to which a change in price of its securities elicits a substantial order flow.

Market portfolio A value-weighted portfolio of every asset in a market.

Market risk premium The difference between the expected return on the market portfolio and the riskless return.

Market segmentation If all capital markets are fully integrated, securities of comparable expected return and risk should have the same required rate of return in each national market after adjusting for foreign exchange risk and

political risk. If the required rates of return diverge from full integration, that market is segmented.

Market value ratios Ratios that relate the market price of the firm's common stock to selected financial statement items.

Market value The price for which something could be bought or sold in a reasonable length of time, where "reasonable length of time" is defined in terms of the item's liquidity.

Market-to-book ratio The ratio of the market price per share to the book value per share.

Matching currency cash flows One way to offset an anticipated continuous long exposure to a particular currency is to acquire debt denominated in that currency.

Materials requirement planning (MRP) systems Computer-based systems that plan backward from the production schedule to make purchases and manage inventory levels.

Maturity date The date a bond's life ends; the date by which it must be fully repaid.

Maturity value The amount of money that must be repaid at the end of a bond's life. The maturity value is also called the *par value* or *face value*.

Maturity The end of a bond's life.

Max function A mathematical function that selects the item of greatest value from a list.

Mean The *expected value* of a *random variable*.

Merchant bank A bank that specializes in helping corporations and governments finance by any of a variety of market and/or traditional techniques. European merchant banks are sometimes differentiated from clearing banks, which tend to focus on bank deposits and clearing balances for the majority of the population.

Merger A combination of two firms in which the *acquiror* absorbs all the assets and liabilities of the *acquiree* and assumes the acquiree's business.

Micro risk *See* firm-specific risks.

Momentum The tendency for a stock's price to continue to move in the same direction, for example, to continue increasing after it has been increasing.

Monetary assets or liabilities Assets in the form of cash or claims to cash (such as accounts receivable), or liabilities payable in cash. Monetary assets minus monetary liabilities are called net monetary assets.

Monetary/nonmonetary method A method of translating the financial statements of foreign subsidiaries into the parent's reporting currency. All monetary accounts are translated at the current rate, and all nonmonetary accounts are translated at their historical rates. Sometimes called temporal method in the United States.

Money market hedge Use of foreign currency borrowing to reduce transaction or accounting foreign exchange exposure.

Money Markets The financial markets in various countries in which various types of short-term debt instruments, including bank loans, are purchased and sold.

Monitor To seek information about an agent's behavior; a device that provides such information.

Moral hazard A situation wherein an agent can take unseen actions for personal benefit when such actions are costly to the principal.

Mortgage bond A bond that is secured by a lien on one or more specific assets.

Most-favored-nation (MFN) treatment Application by a country of import duties on the same, or most favored, basis to all countries accorded such treatment. Any tariff reduction granted in a bilateral negotiation will be extended to all other nations that have been granted most-favored-nation status. Hence in fact most-favored-nation status means normal treatment rather than being discriminated against.

Multinational enterprise (MNE) A firm that has operating subsidiaries, branches, or affiliates located in foreign countries.

Multinational firms Firms that operate in more than one country.

Mutually exclusive Two projects that cannot both be undertaken; that is, choosing one precludes choosing the other.

nsf Not sufficient funds. Term used by a bank when a draft or check is drawn on an account not having sufficient credit balance.

Negative covenant (of a bond) A *bond covenant* that limits or prohibits altogether certain actions unless the bondholders agree.

Negotiable instrument A draft or promissory note that is in writing, signed by the maker or drawer, contains an unconditional promise or order to pay a definite sum of money on demand or at a determinable future date, and is payable to order or to bearer. A holder in due course of a negotiable instrument is entitled to payment despite any personal disagreements between drawee and maker.

Negotiated offering An offering of securities for which the terms, including underwriters' compensation, have been negotiated between the issuer and the underwriters.

Nepotism The practice of showing favor to relatives in preference to other qualified persons in conferring such benefits as the awarding of contracts, granting of special prices, promotions to various ranks, etc.

Net acquisition cost (NAC) The cost of purchasing the target's equity plus transaction costs plus the cost of assuming the target's debt minus the target's excess assets.

Net advantage to leasing The net present value of entering into a lease financing arrangement rather than borrowing the necessary funds and buying the asset.

Net advantage to merging The difference in total post- and pre-merger market value minus the cost of the merger.

Net book value The current book value of an asset or liability; that is, its original book value net of any accounting adjustments such as depreciation.

Net operating cash flow The change in periodic revenue minus the change in periodic cash operating expense connected with undertaking the project minus also the tax liability on revenue net of cash operating expenses.

Net present value (NPV) The present value of the expected future cash flows minus the cost.

Net present value A capital budgeting approach in which the present value of expected future cash inflows is subtracted from the present value of outflows to determine the net present value.

Net profit margin Net income divided by sales; the amount of each sales dollar left over after all expenses have been paid.

Net salvage value The after-tax net cash flow for terminating the project.

Netting The mutual offsetting of sums due between two or more business entities.

Nominal exchange rate The actual foreign exchange quotation, in contradistinction to real exchange rate, which is adjusted for changes in purchasing power.

Nonconventional project A project in which the cash flow pattern is different in some way from conventional projects.

Nondiversifiability of human capital The difficulty of diversifying one's *human capital* (the unique capabilities and expertise of individuals) and employment effort.

Nonoperating cash flows Cash flows not associated with operations.

Nontariff barrier Trade restrictive practices other than custom tariffs. Examples are import quotas, voluntary restrictions, variable levies, and special health regulations.

North American Free Trade Agreement (NAFTA) A treaty allowing free trade and investment between Canada, the United States, and Mexico.

Note issuance facility (NIF) An agreement by which a syndicate of banks indicates a willingness to accept short-term notes from borrowers and resell those notes in the Eurocurrency markets. The discount rate is often tied to LIBOR.

Note A debt obligation with an initial maturity between one and ten years.

Notes to the financial statements A detailed set of notes immediately following the financial statements that explain and expand on the information in the financial statements.

Notional principal The size of a derivative contract, in total currency value, as used in futures contracts, forward contracts, option contracts, or swap agreements..

NPV profile A graph of NPV as a function of the discount rate.

NPV See *Net present value.*

O/A Open account. Arrangement in which the importer (or other buyer) pays for the goods only after the goods are received and inspected. The importer is billed directly after shipment, and payment is not tied to any promissory notes or similar documents.

Offer The price at which a trader is willing to sell foreign exchange, securities, or commodities. Also called ask.

Official Reserves Account Total reserves held by official monetary authorities within the country, such as gold, SDRs, and major currencies.

Offshore finance subsidiary A foreign financial subsidiary owned by a corporation in another country. Offshore finance subsidiaries are usually located in tax-free or low-tax jurisdictions to enable the parent multinational firm to finance international operations without being subject to home country taxes or regulations.

OLI paradigm An attempt to create an overall framework to explain why MNEs choose foreign direct investment rather than serve foreign markets through alternative modes such as licensing, joint ventures, strategic alliances, management contracts, and exporting.

Open account A credit account where the customer makes purchases and the signed invoices are evidence of indebtedness.

Operating exposure The potential for a change in expected cash flows, and thus in value, of a foreign subsidiary as a result of an unexpected change in exchange rates. Also called economic exposure.

Operating lease A lease obligation that does not have to be capitalized on the face of the balance sheet.

Operating risk The inherent or fundamental risk of a firm, without regard to *financial risk*. The risk that is created by *operating leverage*. Also called *business risk*.

Opportunity cost The difference between the value of a course of action and the value of the next best alternative.

Optimal contract The contract that balances the three types of agency costs (contracting, monitoring, and misbehavior) against one another to minimize the total cost.

Option A right to do something without an obligation to do it.

Order bill of lading A shipping document through which possession and title to the shipment reside with the owner of the order bill of lading.

Ordinary annuity A kind of annuity where the payments occur at the end of each period.

Organization of Petroleum Exporting Countries (OPEC) An alliance of most major crude oil producing countries, formed for the purpose of allocating and controlling production quotas so as to influence the price of crude oil in world markets.

Original maturity The length of a bond's life when it is issued.

Out-of-the-money Said of an option that currently would provide a disadvantage, if exercised.

Out-of-the-money An option that would not be profitable, excluding the cost of the premium, if exercised immediately.

Outright quotation The full price, in one currency, of a unit of another currency. *See* Points quotation.

Outsourcing *See* Supply chain management.

Overseas Private Investment Corporation (OPIC) A U.S. government-owned insurance company that insures U.S. corporations against various political risks.

Over-the-counter market A market for share of stock, options (including foreign currency options), or other financial contracts conducted via electronic connections between dealers. The over-the-counter market has no physical location or address, and is thus differentiated from organized exchanges which have a physical location where trading takes place.

Overvalued currency A currency with a current foreign exchange value (i.e., current price in the foreign exchange market) greater than the worth of that currency. Because "worth" is a subjective concept, overvaluation is a matter of opinion. If the euro has a current market value of $1.20 (i.e., the current exchange rate is $1.20/) at a time when its "true" value as derived from purchasing power parity or some other method is deemed to be $1.10, the euro is overvalued. The opposite of overvalued is undervalued.

Owner-specific advantage A firm must have competitive advantages in its home market. These must be firm-specific, not easily copied, and in a form that allows them to be transferred to foreign subsidiaries.

Par value The amount of money to be repaid for a bond at the end of its life. The par value is also called the *face value*.

Parallel loan Another name for a back-to-back loan, in which two companies in separate countries borrow each other's currency for a specific period of time, and repay the other's currency at an agreed maturity.

Parallel market An unofficial foreign exchange market tolerated by a government but not officially sanctioned. The exact boundary between a parallel market and a black market is not very clear, but official tolerance of what would otherwise be a black market leads to use of the term parallel market.

Parity conditions In the context of international finance, a set of basic economic relationships that provide for equilibrium between spot and forward foreign exchange rates, interest rates, and inflation rates.

Participating forward A complex option position which combines a bought put and a sold call option at the same strike price to create a net zero position. Also called zero-cost option and forward participation agreement.

Partnership Shared ownership among two or more individuals, some of whom may, but do not necessarily, have limited liability. See *Limited partnership*.

Payback The length of time it takes to recover the initial cost of a project, without regard to the time value of money.

Payment date The date on which each *shareholder of record* will be sent a check for the declared dividend.

Payout ratio Generally, the proportion of earnings paid out to common stockholders as cash dividends. More specifically, the firm's cash dividend divided by the firm's earnings in the same period.

Pecking-order view (of capital structure) The argument that external financing transaction costs, especially those associated with the problem of adverse selection, create a dynamic environment in which firms have a preference, or pecking, order of preferred sources of financing, when all else is equal. Internally generated funds are the most preferred, new debt is next, debt-equity combinations are next, and new external equity is the least preferred source.

Perfect market view (of capital structure) Analysis of a decision (capital structure), in a perfect capital market environment, that shows the irrelevance of capital structure in a perfect capital market.

Perpetuity An infinite annuity. A series of identical cash flows each period forever.

Perquisites Personal benefits, including direct benefits, such as the use of a firm car or expense account for personal business, and indirect benefits, such as an up-to-date office decor.

Personal tax view (of capital structure) The argument that the difference in personal tax rates between income from debt and income from equity eliminates the disadvantage from the double taxation (corporate and personal) of income from equity.

Phi The expected change in an option premium caused by a small change in the foreign interest rate (interest rate for the foreign currency).

Planning horizon The length of time a model projects into the future.

Points quotation A forward quotation expressed only as the number of decimal points (usually four decimal points) by which it differs from the spot quotation.

Points A point is the smallest unit of price change quoted, given a conventional number of digits in which a quotation is stated.

Political risk The possibility that political events in a particular country will have an influence on the economic well-being of firms in that country. *Also see* Sovereign risk.

Portfolio investment Purchase of foreign stocks and bonds, in contradistinction to foreign direct investment.

Portfolio (1) The collection of securities that an investor owns. (2) The collection of real and financial assets that a firm owns.

Positive covenant (of a bond) A *bond covenant* that specifies certain actions the firm must take. Also called an *affirmative covenant*.

Possessions Corporation A U.S. corporation, the subsidiary of another U.S. corporation located in a U.S. possession such as Puerto Rico, which for tax purposes is treated as if it were a foreign corporation.

Postaudit A set of procedures for evaluating a capital budgeting decision after the fact.

Postponement option The option of postponing a project without eliminating the possibility of undertaking it.

Precautionary demand (for money) The need to meet unexpected or extraordinary contingencies with a buffer stock of cash.

Premium (in foreign exchange market) The amount by which a currency is more expensive for future delivery than for spot (immediate) delivery. The opposite of premium is discount.

Premium bond A bond that is selling for more than its par value.

Prepackaged bankruptcy A *bankruptcy* in which a debtor and its creditors pre-negotiate a *plan of reorganization* and then file it along with the bankruptcy petition.

Present-value annuity factor Equation (4.6) without PMT.

Present-value factor Equation (4.4) without FV.

Present-value formula Equation (4.4).

Price-earnings ratio, or P/E A stock's market price per share divided by the firm's annual earnings per share.

Primary market A market consisting of newly created securities.

Primary offering A firm selling some of its own newly issued shares to investors.

Prime rate The benchmark interest rate that banks charge large, creditworthy firms.

Principal (1) The total amount of money being borrowed. (2) The party affected by agent decisions in a principal-agent relationship.

Principal-agent relationship A situation that can be modeled as one person, an *agent*, who acts on behalf of another person, a *principal*.

Private placement The sale of securities directly to investors (often institutions) without a *public offering*.

Private placement The sale of a security issue to a small set of qualified institutional buyers.

Pro forma statement A financial statement showing the forecast (or projected) operating results or impact of a particular transaction, as in pro forma income statements in the *long-term financial plan* or the pro forma *balance sheet* for a share repurchase.

Profitability index (PI) The present value of the future cash flows divided by the initial investment. Also called the *benefit-cost ratio*.

Profitability ratios Ratios that focus on the profitability of the firm. *Profit margins* measure performance in relation to sales, and *rate of return ratios* measure performance relative to some measure of the size of the investment.

Progressive tax system A tax system wherein the average tax rate increases for some increases in income but never decreases with an increase in income.

Project finance Arrangement of financing for long- term capital projects, large in scale, long in life, and generally high in risk.

Project financing A form of asset-based financing in which a firm finances a discrete set of assets (project) on a stand-alone basis.

Prospectus A legal disclosure document that must be distributed both to purchasers and to persons whose purchase interest is solicited in connection with a public offering of securities.

Protectionism A political attitude or policy intended to inhibit or prohibit the import of foreign goods and services. The opposite of free trade policies.

Proxy contest A battle for the control of a firm in which the dissident group seeks, from the firm's other shareholders, the right to vote those shareholders' shares in favor of the dissident group's slate of directors.

Psychic distance Firms tend to invest first in countries with a similar cultural, legal, and institutional environment.

Purchase method A method of accounting for a *merger* or *consolidation* in which one of the firms is identified as the acquiror.

Purchasing power parity A theory of relative exchange rates that states that the expected difference in inflation rates for two countries over some period must equal the differential between the spot exchange rate currently prevailing and the spot exchange rate expected at the end of the period.

Pure-discount bond A bond that will make only one payment of principal and interest. Also called a *zero-coupon bond*.

Put an option To *exercise* a put option.

Put option The right to *sell* something at a given price during the life of the option.

Put An option to sell foreign exchange or financial contracts. *See* Option.

Put-call parity The relationship between the value of a put option and the value of a call option.

Pyramid scheme An illegal, fraudulent scheme in which a con artist convinces victims to invest by promising an extraordinary return but simply uses newly invested funds to pay off any investors who insist on terminating their investment.

Qualified institutional buyer An entity (except a bank or a savings and loan) that owns and invests on a discretionary basis $100 million in securities of nonaffiliates.

Quick (acid test) ratio A liquidity ratio that measures the number of times a firm can cover its current liabilities using its current assets (but not including its inventories, which are less liquid).

Quota A limit, mandatory or voluntary, set on the import of a product.

Quotation In foreign exchange trading, the pair of prices (bid and ask) at which a dealer is willing to buy or sell foreign exchange.

Range forward A complex option position that combines the purchase of a put option and the sale of a call option with strike prices equidistant from the forward rate. Also called flexible forward, cylinder option, option fence, mini-max, and zero-cost tunnel.

Real exchange rate An index of foreign exchange adjusted for relative price level changes since a base period. Sometimes referred to as real effective exchange rate, it is used to measure purchasing-power-adjusted changes in exchange rates.

Real option analysis The application of option theory to capital budgeting decisions.

Real options Options connected with real assets (capital budgeting projects). Often such options can be what are often called "hidden" options, such as the option to expand, postpone, or abandon.

Realized return The return that is actually gotten over a given time period.

Receivables balance fractions The percentage of a month's sales that remain uncollected (and part of accounts receivable) at the end of the month of sale and at the end of succeeding months.

Receivables turnover ratio The number of times receivables turn over in a year, measured as the total annual credit sales divided by the current accounts receivable balance.

Record date A date established to determine who will actually get the dividend check for a share of stock, in case the share is sold between when the dividend is declared and when it is paid.

Reference rate The rate of interest used in a standardized quotation, loan agreement, or financial derivative valuation.

Registered bond Corporate or governmental debt in a bond form in which the owner's name appears on the bond and in the issuer's records, and interest payments are made to the owner.

Registration statement A legal document that is filed with the Securities and Exchange Commission to register securities for public offering.

Reinvestment rate assumption The return that the cash flows from a capital budgeting project are expected (assumed) to earn from being reinvested.

Reinvoicing center A central financial subsidiary used by a multinational firm to reduce transaction exposure by having all home country exports billed in the home currency and then reinvoiced to each operating subsidiary in that subsidiary's local currency.

Relative purchasing power parity If the spot exchange rate between two countries starts in equilibrium, any change in the differential rate of inflation between them tends to be offset over the long run by an equal but opposite change in the spot exchange rate.

Remaining maturity The length of time remaining until a bond's maturity.

Reorganization Creating a plan to restructure a debtor's business and restore its financial health.

Replacement cycle The frequency with which an asset is replaced by an equivalent asset.

Reporting currency In the context of translating financial statements, the currency in which a parent firm prepares its own financial statements. Usually this is the parent's home currency.

Repositioning funds An MNE faces a variety of political, tax, foreign exchange, and liquidity constraints that limit its ability to move funds easily and without cost from one currency or country to another.

Representative office A bank establishes a representative office in a foreign country to help bank clients doing business in that country. It also functions as a geographically convenient location from which to visit correspondent banks in its region rather than sending bankers from the parent bank at greater financial and physical cost.

Repricing risk The risk of changes in interest rates charged or earned at the time a financial contract's rate is reset.

Required return The minimum *expected return* you would require to be willing to purchase the asset (that is, to make the investment).

Return on assets (ROA) Net income divided by total assets.

Return on equity (ROE) Net income available to common stockholders divided by common stockholders' equity.

Revaluation A rise in the foreign exchange value of a currency that is pegged to other currencies or to gold. Also called appreciation.

Revolving credit agreement A *legal* commitment wherein a bank promises to lend a customer up to a specified maximum amount during a specified period.

Rho The expected change in an option premium caused by a small change in the domestic interest rate (interest rate for the home currency).

Rights issue The process of offering common stock to existing shareholders by issuing *rights*.

Risk class A group of capital budgeting projects that all have approximately the same amount of risk.

Risk The likelihood that an actual outcome will differ from an expected outcome. The actual outcome could be better or worse than expected (two-sided risk), although in common practice risk is more often used only in the context of an adverse outcome (one-sided risk). Risk can exist for any number of uncertain future situations, including future spot rates or the results of political events.

Risk-averse Choosing lower risk when alternative returns are equal, or choosing higher returns when alternative risks are equal.

Risk-sharing agreement A contractual arrangement in which the buyer and seller agree to share or split currency movement impacts on payments between them.

Risky debt Debt that has some possibility of not being fully repaid on time.

Rule 144A private placement The sale of unregistered securities to one or more investment banks, which then resell them to qualified institutional buyers (QIBs), or the direct sale to QIBs.

Rules of the Game The basis of exchange rate determination under the international gold standard during most of the 19th and early 20th centuries. All countries agreed informally to follow the rule of buying and selling their currency at a fixed and predetermined price against gold.

Runs test A test of the time-series independence of stock returns, which tests whether the pattern (runs) of positive and negative returns over time is random.

Safety stock Inventory buffer stock that a firm holds to hedge uncertainties in delivery times, usage, or sales.

Sale-and-lease-back An agreement to sell an asset and lease it back from the purchaser.

Salvage value The before-tax difference between the sale price of the assets and the clean-up and removal expenses.

Samurai bonds Yen-denominated bonds issued within Japan by a foreign borrower.

Sarbanes-Oxley Act An act passed in 2002 to regulate corporate governance in the United States.

Seasoned offering A public issuing of shares by a corporation that already has shares that are trading in the capital markets.

SEC Rule 144A Permits qualified institutional buyers to trade privately-placed securities without requiring SEC registration.

Secondary market A market where securities that are already outstanding are traded.

Secondary offering Shareholders (usually insiders or large institutions) selling previously issued shares they own to investors at large in an offering that has been registered with the *SEC*.

Section 482 The set of U.S. Treasury regulations governing transfer prices.

Securitization The replacement of nonmarketable loans (such as direct bank loans) with negotiable securities (such as publicly traded marketable notes and bonds), so that the risk can be spread widely among many investors, each of whom can add or subtract the amount of risk carried by buying or selling the marketable security.

Security market line (SML) The linear relationship between required return and beta.

Self-sustaining foreign entity One that operates in the local economic environment independent of the parent company.

Semi-strong form of capital market efficiency Prices reflect all *publicly available* information about an asset's value.

Sensitivity analysis Varying key parameters of a process to determine the sensitivity of outcomes to that variation.

Serial correlation test A test of the time-series independence of stock returns, which tests whether a stock's returns are correlated with its returns in earlier time periods, for example, whether daily returns are correlated with returns one or more days earlier.

Set-of-contracts model A model that describes the firm as a collection of implicit and explicit contracts among the *stakeholders.*

Share repurchase A firm's purchase of its own shares of stock.

Shared services A charge to compensate the parent for costs incurred in the general management of international operations and for other corporate services provided to foreign subsidiaries that must be recovered by the parent firm.

Shareholder wealth maximization Maximizing the value of the firm to its owners. For a publicly traded firm, the value of the firm to its owners is the market value of the shares owned.

Shareholders Those holding some shares of the firm's equity. Also called *stockholders* and *equityholders*.

Sharpe measure Calculates the average return over and above the risk free rate of return per unit of portfolio risk. It uses the standard deviation of a portfolio's total return as the measure of risk.

Shelf registration The process of registering a two-year inventory of securities by filing a single registration statement.

Shirking An agent's putting forth less than "full effort."

Shogun bonds Foreign currency-denominated bonds issued within Japan by Japanese corporations.

Short position *See* Long position.

Short-term Typically, less than a year.

SIBOR Singapore interbank offered rate.

Sight draft A bill of exchange (B/E) that is due on demand; i.e., when presented to the bank. *Also see* Bill of exchange.

SIMEX Singapore International Monetary Exchange.

Simple interest Interest that is received on the initial principal amount only, rather than compounded.

Simulation The use of a mathematical model to imitate a situation many times in order to estimate the likelihood of various possible outcomes.

Sinking fund A bond provision specifying principal repayments prior to the maturity date.

Society for Worldwide Interbank Financial Telecommunications (SWIFT) A dedicated computer network providing funds transfer messages between member banks around the world.

Soft currency A currency expected to drop in value relative to other currencies. Free trading in a currency deemed soft is often restricted by the monetary authorities of the issuing country.

"Soft" capital rationing Capital rationing that under certain circumstances can be violated or even viewed as made up of targets rather than absolute constraints.

Sole proprietorship A firm wherein a single individual owns all the firm's assets directly and is responsible for all its liabilities.

Sovereign risk The risk that a host government may unilaterally repudiate its foreign obligations or may prevent local firms from honoring their foreign obligations. Sovereign risk is often regarded as a subset of political risk.

Special Drawing Right (SDR) An international reserve asset, defined by the International Monetary Fund as the value of a weighted basket of five currencies.

Specific risk The standard deviation of an investment's return.

Speculation An attempt to make a profit by trading on expectations about future prices.

Speculative demand (for money) The need for cash to take advantage of investment opportunities that may arise.

Speculative-grade rating A long-term debt rating other than an *investment-grade rating.*

Spot market A market to trade today an asset that is also traded on a futures market.

Spot rate The price at which foreign exchange can be purchased (its bid) or sold (its ask) in a spot transaction. *See* Spot transaction.

Spot trade The purchase or sale of a foreign currency, commodity, or other item for "immediate" delivery.

Spot transaction A foreign exchange transaction to be settled (paid for) on the second following business day.

Spread The difference between the bid (buying) quote and the ask (selling) quote.

Stakeholder capitalism Another name for corporate wealth maximization.

Stakeholder Anyone with a legitimate claim of any sort on the firm, such as stockholders, bondholders, creditors, employees, customers, the community, and the government.

Standard deviation The square root of the *variance.*

Stock and bond guide A document that contains detailed information about stocks and bonds.

Stock dividends A bookkeeping reapportioning of the claim size of a share of stock so that there are more shares and each share has a proportionately smaller ownership interest. For example, if a firm declares a 5% stock dividend, a shareholder will receive 5 new shares for every 100 shares owned. Money from the retained earnings account is transferred to the "Paid-in Capital" and "Capital Con-tributed in Excess of Par Value" accounts.

Stock split A bookkeeping reapportioning of the claim size of a share of stock so that there are more shares and each share has a proportionately smaller ownership interest. For example, if a firm declares a 2-for-1 stock split, then each shareholder owns twice as many shares, but each new share has half the claim size of each old share. The stock's par value per share is adjusted to reflect the change, but no money is transferred among balance sheet accounts.

Stockholders Those holding some shares of the firm's equity. Also called *shareholders* and *equityholders*.

Stockholders' equity Residual ownership claims against the firm's assets.

Strategic alliance A formal relationship, short of a merger or acquisition, between two companies, formed for the purpose of gaining synergies because in some aspect the two companies complement each other.

Strike price The price specified in the option contract for buying or selling the underlying asset. That is, the asset is exchanged for the strike price.

Stripped bonds Bonds issued by investment bankers against coupons or the maturity (corpus) portion of original bearer bonds, where the original bonds are held in trust by the investment banker. Whereas the original bonds will have coupons promising interest at each interest date (say June and December for each of the next twenty years), a given stripped bond will represent a claim against all interest payments from the entire original issue due on a particular interest date. A stripped bond is in effect a zero coupon bond manufactured by the investment banker.

Strong form of capital market efficiency Prices reflect *all* information that exists about an asset's value.

Subpart F A type of foreign income, as defined in the U.S. tax code, which under certain conditions is taxed immediately in the United States even though it has not been repatriated to the United States. It is income of a type that is otherwise easily shifted offshore to avoid current taxation.

Subsidiary A foreign operation incorporated in the host country and owned 50% or more by a parent corporation. Foreign operations that are not incorporated are called branches.

Sunk cost A cost that has already been incurred and cannot be altered by subsequent decisions. Previously incurred sunk costs can be ignored when making most decisions.

Supply chain management Focuses on cost reduction through imports from less costly (lower wages) foreign locations.

Sushi bonds Eurodollar or other non-yen denominated bonds issued by a Japanese corporation for sale to Japanese investors.

Swap An agreement to exchange specified payment obligations, such as an *interest rate swap*.

SWIFT *See* Society for Worldwide Interbank Financial Telecommunications.

Syndicate A group of securities firms formed to share the underwriting risk in connection with an *underwritten offering* of securities.

Syndicated loan A large loan made by a group of banks to a large multinational firm or government. Syndicated loans allow the participating banks to maintain diversification by not lending too much to a single borrower.

Synthetic forward A complex option position which combines the purchase of a put option and the sale of a call option, or vice versa, both at the forward rate.

Systematic risk In portfolio theory, the risk of the market itself, i.e., risk that cannot be diversified away.

T/A Trade acceptance. International trade term.

Target payout ratio A *payout ratio* objective that a firm sets to guide its dividend policy.

Tariff A duty or tax on imports that can be levied as a percentage of cost or as a specific amount per unit of import.

Tax asymmetry A situation in which two parties to a transaction are taxed at different rates and can structure the transaction (or their relationship) to reduce their collective tax bill.

Tax deferral Foreign subsidiaries of MNEs pay host country corporate income taxes, but many parent countries, including the United States, defer claiming additional taxes on that foreign source income until it is remitted to the parent firm.

Tax exposure The potential for tax liability on a given income stream or on the value of an asset. "Tax exposure" is usually used in the context of a multinational firm being able to minimize its tax liabilities by locating some portion of operations in a country where the tax liability is minimized.

Tax haven A country with either no or very low tax rates that uses its tax structure to attract foreign investment or international financial dealings.

Tax morality The MNE must decide whether to follow a practice of full disclosure to local tax authorities or adopt the philosophy, "When in Rome, do as the Romans do."

Tax neutrality *Domestic tax neutrality* requires that the burden of taxation on earnings in home country operations by an MNE be equal to the burden of taxation on each currency equivalent of profit earned by the same firm in its foreign operations. *Foreign tax neutrality* requires that the tax burden on each foreign subsidiary of the firm be equal to the tax burden on its competitors in the same country.

Tax treaties A network of bilateral tax treaties provides a means of reducing double taxation.

Taxable acquisition A *merger* or *consolidation* that is not a *tax-free acquisition*. The selling shareholders are treated as having sold their shares.

Tax-free acquisition A *merger* or *consolidation* in which (1) the acquiror's tax basis in each asset whose ownership is transferred in the transaction is generally the same as the acquiree's and (2) each seller who receives only stock does not have to pay any tax on the gain he realizes until the shares are sold.

Tax-timing option The option to sell an asset and claim a loss for tax purposes or not to sell the asset and defer a capital gain tax.

Technical analysis Technical analysts focus on price and volume data to determine past trends that are expected to continue into the future. They believe that future exchange rates are based on the current exchange rate.

Temporal method In the United States, term for a codification of a translation method essentially similar to the monetary/nonmonetary method.

Tender offer premium The premium offered above the current market price in a tender offer.

Tender offer A general offer to purchase securities that is made publicly and directly to all holders of the desired securities.

Tequila effect Term used to describe how the Mexican peso crisis of December 1994 quickly spread to other Latin American currency and equity markets through the contagion effect.

Term loan A bank loan, typically with a floating interest rate, for a specified amount that matures in between one and ten years and requires a specified repayment schedule.

Term structure (1) The yield curve for zero-coupon U.S. Treasury securities. (2) The general relationship between debt maturity and interest rates.

Terms of trade The weighted average exchange ratio between a nation's export prices and its import prices, used to measure gains from trade. Gains from trade refers to increases in total consumption resulting from production specialization and international trade.

Territorial approach to taxes Taxes income earned by firms within the legal jurisdiction of the host country, not on the country of the firm's incorporation.

Theta The expected change in an option premium caused by a small change in the time to expiration.

Time draft Allows a delay in payment. It is presented to the drawee, who accepts it by writing a notice of acceptance on its face. Once accepted, the time draft becomes a promise to pay by the accepting party. *See also* Bankers' acceptance.

Time premium of an option The value of an option beyond its current exercise value representing the optionholder's control until expiration, the risk of the underlying asset, and the riskless return.

Times-interest-earned ratio The ratio of EBIT to interest expense, also called the *interest coverage ratio.*

Total asset turnover ratio The ratio of sales to total assets.

Total Shareholder Return (TSR) A measure of corporate performance based on the sum of share price appreciation and current dividends.

Trade credit Credit granted by a firm to another firm for the purchase of goods or services.

Traders Persons engaged in short-term speculation.

Trading rule A trading process that makes trades on the basis of a set of predetermined criteria an investor follows to try to "beat" the market. For example: buy a stock when it has decreased 8% in value and then sell it when it has increased 20% in value.

Trading Buying and selling securities.

Tranche An allocation of shares, typically to underwriters that are expected to sell to investors in their designated geographic markets.

Transaction costs The time, effort, and money necessary to make a transaction, including such things as commission fees and the cost of physically moving the asset from seller to buyer.

Transaction exposure The potential for a change in the value of outstanding financial obligations entered into prior to a change in exchange rates but not due to be settled until after the exchange rates change.

Transaction loan A loan extended by a bank for a specific purpose. In contrast, lines of credit and revolving credit agreements involve loans that can be used for various purposes.

Transactions demand (for money) The need to accommodate a firm's expected cash transactions.

Transfer pricing The setting of prices to be charged by one unit (such as a foreign subsidiary) of a multiunit corporation to another unit (such as the parent corporation) for goods or services sold between such related units.

Transferable put right An option issued by the firm to its shareholders to sell the firm one share of its common stock at a fixed price (the strike price) within a stated period (the time to maturity). The put right is "transferable" because it can be traded in the capital markets.

Translation exposure The potential for an accounting-derived change in owners' equity resulting from exchange rate changes and the need to restate financial statements of foreign subsidiaries in the single currency of the parent corporation. Also called Accounting exposure.

Transnational firm One that is owned by a coalition of investors located in different countries.

Transparency Describes the degree to which an investor can discern the true activities and value drivers of a company from the disclosures and financial results reported.

Treynor measure Calculates the average return over and above the risk free rate of return per unit of portfolio risk. It uses the portfolio's beta as the measure of risk.

Unbiased predictor A theory that spot prices at some future date will be equal to today's forward rates.

Unbundling Dividing cash flows from a subsidiary to a parent into their many separate components, such as royalties, lease payments, dividends, etc., so as to increase the likelihood that some fund flows will be allowed during economically difficult times.

Uncovered interest arbitrage Investors borrow in countries and currencies exhibiting relatively low interest rates and convert the proceeds into currencies that offer much higher interest rates. The transaction is "uncovered" because the investor does not sell the higher yielding currency proceeds forward.

Underinvestment The mirror image of the *asset substitution problem,* wherein stockholders refuse to invest in low-risk assets to avoid shifting wealth from themselves to the debtholders.

Underlying asset The asset that an option gives the optionholder the right to buy or to sell.

Undervalued A currency with a current foreign exchange value (i.e., current price in the foreign exchange market) below the worth of that currency. Because "worth" is a subjective concept, undervaluation is a matter of opinion. If the euro has a current market value of $1.20 (i.e., the current exchange rate is $1.20/) at a time when its "true" value as derived from purchasing power parity or some other method is deemed to be $1.30, the euro is undervalued. The opposite of undervalued is overvalued.

Underwrite To guarantee, as to guarantee the issuer of securities a specified price by entering into a purchase and sale agreement.

Underwriter A party that guarantees the proceeds to the firm from a security sale, thereby in effect taking ownership of the securities.

Unsystematic risk In a portfolio, the amount of risk that can be eliminated by diversification.

Urgency A dangerous but widely used method of allocating resources in which a firm puts off making a capital budgeting decision until it is left with no choice but to make the investment.

Value additivity Prevails when the value of the whole (a group of assets) exactly equals the sum of the values of the parts (the individual assets).

Value date The date when value is given (i.e., funds are deposited) for foreign exchange transactions between banks.

Value today A spot foreign exchange transaction in which delivery and payment are made on the same day as the contract. Normal delivery is two business days after the contract.

Value tomorrow A spot foreign exchange transaction in which delivery and payment are made on the next business day after the contract. Normal delivery is two business days after the contract.

Value-added tax A type of national sales tax collected at each stage of production or sale of consumption goods, and levied in proportion to the value added during that stage.

Variance The mathematical expectation of the squared deviations from the mean.

Vertical merger A merger in which one firm acquires another that is in the same industry but at another stage in the production cycle—for example, the acquiree serves as a supplier to the acquiror or purchases the acquiror's goods or services.

Volatility In connection with options, the standard deviation of daily spot price movement.

WACC See *Weighted average cost of capital.*

Warrant A long-term call option issued by a firm on its own stock.

Weak form of capital market efficiency Prices reflect information about an asset's value that is *contained in past asset market prices.*

Weighted average cost of capital (WACC) The weighted average of financing costs for a financing package that would allow a project to be undertaken.

Weighted average cost of capital (WACC) The sum of the proportionally weighted costs of different sources of capital, used as the minimum acceptable target return on new investments.

Working capital management The management of current assets and current liabilities.

Working capital ratio Net working capital expressed as a proportion of sales.

Working capital Current assets minus current liabilities.

World Bank *See* International Bank for Reconstruction and Development.

World market portfolio A portfolio that includes all the capital assets in the world.

Worldwide approach to taxes Levies taxes on the income earned by firms that are incorporated in the host country, regardless of where the income was earned.

Yankee bonds Dollar-denominated bonds issued within the United States by a foreign borrower.

Yield to call (YTC) The annual percentage rate of a bond, assuming it will be paid off at a particular call date.

Yield to maturity (YTM) The annual percentage rate that equates a bond's market price to the present value of its promised future cash flows.

Zero-coupon bond A bond that will make only one payment of principal and interest. Also called a *pure-discount bond.*

Zero-sum game A type of game wherein one player can gain only at the expense of another player.

AUTHOR INDEX

INDEX